The Life and Work of

FRANCIS WILLEY KELSEY

Portrait of Francis W. Kelsey toward the end of his life. Bentley Historical Library, University of Michigan HS 5944. Photo: Enoch Peterson.

The Life and Work of

FRANCIS WILLEY KELSEY

Archaeology, Antiquity, and the Arts

John Griffiths Pedley

The University of Michigan Press · *Ann Arbor*

Published in the United States of America by
The University of Michigan Press
Manufactured in the United States of America
♾ Printed on acid-free paper

2015   2014   2013   2012   4   3   2   1

A CIP catalog record for this book is available from the British Library.

Library of Congress Cataloging-in-Publication Data

Pedley, John Griffiths.
    The life and work of Francis Willey Kelsey : archaeology,
antiquity, and the arts / John Griffiths Pedley.
        p. cm.
    Includes bibliographical references and index.
    ISBN 978-0-472-11802-1 (cloth : alk. paper) — ISBN 978-0-472-
02805-4 (e-book)
    1. Kelsey, Francis W. (Francis Willey), 1858–1927.
2. Classicists—United States—Biography.   3. Archaeologists—United
States—Biography.   4. College teachers—Michigan—Biography.
5. Classical philology—Study and teaching—United States.   6. University
of Michigan—Biography.   I. Title.
PA85.K45P44   2012
880.092—dc23
    [B]   2011028329

For Mary

Acknowledgments

᠀

FIRST AND FOREMOST, I wish to thank my wife, Mary, who helped in myriads of ways and without whose limitless patience and good cheer this book might never have been finished. Prominent among friends and colleagues whose assistance has been invaluable are Easton Kelsey Jr. of Rochester, New York, who kindly allowed me perusal of family papers in his possession; Carol Finerman of Ann Arbor, Michigan, whose organization of the Francis Kelsey material in the Kelsey Museum of Archaeology at the University of Michigan into a useful archive some thirty years ago has been an indispensable aid; and Michael Gnat of Brooklyn, New York, whose editorial skills improved the text and notes beyond measure and whose control of the Internet world and sharp turn of phrase were a constant source of support and amazement.

Curators and librarians in charge of archives to whom I offer warm thanks include Carol F. Coburn, Ogden/Spencerport historian; Nancy Martin, university archivist and Rochester Collections librarian at Rush Rhees Library, University of Rochester, New York; Arthur H. Miller, archivist and librarian for special collections at Lake Forest College, Illinois; Rachel Stockdale, head of manuscripts cataloging and collection management at the British Library, London; and Elizabeth Gilgan, director of programs and services at the Archaeological Institute of America, Boston, Massachusetts. In particular, I thank Karen Jania, Malgosia Myc, and Marilyn McNitt, archivists at the Bentley Historical Library at the University of Michigan, and their assistants, whose friendliness, cooperation, advice, and dedication enabled the work to go forward steadily.

Elsewhere at the University of Michigan, Peggy Daub, head of Rare Books and Special Collections at the University Library, pointed me toward relevant documents. At the Kelsey Museum of Archaeology, Todd Gerring provided important logistical help, and Terry Wilfong taught me about Islamic manuscripts and Egyptian topography. At the Department of Classical Studies, Laurie Talalay and Artemis Leontis gave me access to their research into some of Kelsey's adventures in Constantinople, Traianos Gagos has been a source of sage advice about papyri, Don Cameron was constantly supportive, and Richard Janko was always ready with words of encouragement. Michelle Biggs and Pam Levitt took care of administrative problems. Former president of the university Jim Duderstadt and his wife, Anne, generously shared some of their photographs with me, and the offices of the provost of the university and the dean of the College of Literature, Science, and the Arts provided much needed help by their endorsement of the project and with funds.

I am much indebted to John P. Keusch of the law firm of Keusch, Flintoft, and Conlin of Chelsea, Michigan, for help with details of Kelsey's properties at Lake Cavanaugh and to Tom Diab of Chelsea for photographs. For information about mining and logging companies and their activities in the Southwest and Mexico, I thank Professor Sam Truett of the University of New Mexico. Help with the provision of photographs and permissions was kindly provided by Karen Jania, head of Reference Services, and Malgosia Myc, archivist, at the Bentley Historical Library; by Sebastian Encina, museum collections manager, and Michelle Fontenot, registrar, at the Kelsey Museum; by Joseph A. Greene at the Semitic Museum, Harvard University; by Wendi Goen, archivist of the photographic collections at the Arizona State Library; and by Mary Pedley. The maps were drawn by Lorene Sterner, graphic artist at the Kelsey Museum, with her customary care and skill. I'd also like to thank Michael Gnat for his prompt and cheerful preparation of the index and Jill Butler Wilson, whose copy editing skills made short work of several problems in the text.

Finally, for their encouragement, good cheer, hard work, and patience, I thank Ellen Bauerle, manager of the Acquisitions Department; Alexa Ducsay; Christina Milton; and their colleagues at the University of Michigan Press.

Contents

꽃

Abbreviations

{❦}

AIA	Archaeological Institute of America
AJA	*American Journal of Archaeology*
EOP	*Excavating Our Past,* ed. Susan Heuck Allen
FWK Papers	Francis Willey Kelsey Papers, 1894–1928, Bentley Historical Library, University of Michigan
KMA Papers	Papers of Francis Willey Kelsey, Kelsey Museum of Archaeology, University of Michigan
LFUR	*Lake Forest University Review*
PTSJ	Papers of Thomas Spencer Jerome, Bentley Historical Library, University of Michigan
"RNMF"	"Random Notes on Memories of Father," by Charlotte Badger Kelsey
TAPA	*Transactions of the American Philological Association*

Introduction

ᶓ

FRANCIS KELSEY WAS PROFESSOR OF LATIN at the University of Michigan from 1889 to 1927 and chair of the Department of Latin from 1890 until his death. He served as president of both the American Philological Association (1906–7) and the Archaeological Institute of America (1907–12). He was a member of the American Association for the Advancement of Science, the American Historical Association, the Classical Association of Great Britain, the Deutsches Archäologisches Institut, and the Académie des Inscriptions et Belles-Lettres. In these offices and memberships, he was not unlike many of his contemporaries. But he possessed a character and an imagination that put him at the center of developments in American education and of the University of Michigan's growth and change in the early twentieth century.

He ardently supported the importance of the research university at a time when the debate about the future of higher education in America was at its fiercest. At the same time, he strove for the highest standards of undergraduate teaching and for a close rapport between teachers in colleges and those in high schools. His inspiring advocacy of a liberal arts education and particularly of the classics found expression in lectures, conferences, and publications, most notably in a volume of papers he edited, three chapters of which he wrote himself: *Latin and Greek in American Education, with Symposia on the Value of Humanistic Studies* (New York: Macmillan, 1911). He wrote constantly—innumerable articles, memorandums, letters, and diaries. The vast majority of this voluminous correspondence all supported his vision of the centrality of the ancient past to the human condition.

A firm believer in education as a means of self-improvement and in the human instinct for learning, he was an early exponent of outreach programs. He vigorously promoted the construction and expansion of libraries. In the interests of the general public as much as those of scholars, he placed a high priority on the conservation of archaeological sites and historical monuments and on the expansion of the activities of the Archaeological Institute of America into the West and Southwest and into Canada.

A wide-ranging scholar and careful editor, his editions of Caesar, Cicero, Ovid, Lucretius, and Xenophon became the standard teaching texts of the time; in their emphasis on archaeological and historical contexts and in their extensive use of lithography, line drawings, and photographs, they broke new ground. He is perhaps best known, however, for his authoritative translation and edition of August Mau's *Pompeii: Its Life and Art*. To support his belief in the research university and the publication of new knowledge, he inaugurated the publication of the Humanistic Series at Michigan, the precursor of the University of Michigan Press. This work—the editing, printing, and publishing of numerous books—throws a clear light on his exceptional scholarly, administrative, and organizational abilities.

He was in the forefront in the development of archaeology in Mediterranean lands, emphasizing the importance of international cooperation and innovation. In 1924 he organized an expedition to Pisidian Antioch (in Turkey) in collaboration with Sir William Ramsay, and in 1924–25 he directed the Franco-American work at Carthage. In 1925 he began excavations at Karanis in Egypt. His fieldwork expanded beyond the examination of public monuments (at Antioch) and sanctuary studies (at Carthage) to the investigation of domestic contexts (at Karanis), where the advantages of studying archaeology and papyrology together were first realized. His investigations into aerial photography and underwater archaeology were ahead of their time.

His enthusiastic approach to antiquity did not stop at publications and fieldwork. He began acquiring antiquities for the teaching programs of the university in the 1890s; and in 1920, in the interests of the University Library and scholarly research, he turned his attention to papyri and manuscripts. With inexhaustible energy and determination, he put together in Michigan what may still be regarded as the best collection in America. He arranged much of the funding for these programs of fieldwork and acquisition himself, through the generosity of donors in Detroit, of whom Horace H. Rackham (who contributed in excess of $240,000) was only one. Kelsey was as masterful at raising money as he was in organizing expeditions.

He was a man of great human sympathy and wide cultural interests. He was awarded a medal by the king of Belgium for his work on behalf of Belgian refugee children in World War I and actively participated in the work of the American Committee for Relief in the Near East in the years after that war. He was a keen musician and devotee of the opera, and as president of the University Musical Society and the Ann Arbor School of Music for many years, he strove continually for the incorporation of the School of Music into the university. Given his cultural contacts in New York, he was instrumental in bringing many distinguished artists, including both Caruso and Paderewski, to Ann Arbor. As a member of the campus planning committee, he envisioned—and argued for—the construction of a nucleus of buildings on the north side of the campus to draw attention to the arts and humanities: a museum of art, a college of fine arts (to include a school of music), a hall of the humanities, and an auditorium. Of these projects, he was to see only one, Hill Auditorium, completed in his life time.

His vision and creative imagination mirrored the climate of the times. Brought up in modest circumstances far from the cushioned extravagance of some of his interlocutors, Kelsey came to maturity in a period of technological change in Europe and America, a golden age for those who shared Teddy Roosevelt's penchant for brisk action and affection for the natural world. In 1889, his first year in Michigan, the French government mounted the Exposition Universelle in Paris, which celebrated French technology—the hallmark of which was Gustave Eiffel's "iron tower"—rationalism, and colonial power; it marked a critical moment in the growth of European modernity. Four years later, Chicago followed suit, staging the World's Columbian Exposition, at which examples of technological know-how were again key features; as in Paris, the phonograph, electric light, and motion pictures were prominent. As with the exposition in Paris, the Chicago exposition both highlighted scientific and engineering innovations and was a harbinger of changes to come.

The half century after the Civil War, overlapping with the first fifty years of Kelsey's life, traced the making of modern America. Innovations in communications, transportation, and manufacture could be seen across the continent. It was the era of the vanishing frontier, railroad expansion, the automobile, the dictaphone, more and more roads, and improvements in telephone services and photography, all driven by new technology. In the home, the discovery of electricity and the invention of steam heating systems, the vacuum cleaner, the electric washing machine, and the refrigerator released women from the tyranny of candle grease, soot, dust, dirt, and moldy food. Kelsey was neither unmoved nor deterred by these advances in technology; rather, he embraced them.

He believed in growth and in seizing opportunities. He invested in mining and milling companies in Mexico and the West and was persuasive enough at shareholders' meetings in Washington and New York for company officers to welcome him to directors' meetings. His industry, determination, persistence, geniality, and can-do approach made him attractive to the burgeoning industrialists and men of affairs in Detroit. Hence, they opened their pocketbooks, allowing him to drive Michigan and education in America forward. To describe him as visionary is to underestimate his contributions and his powers.

A substantial part of this book draws on diaries written by Kelsey between 1901 and 1927, now housed among the Francis Willey Kelsey Papers in the Bentley Historical Library at the University of Michigan. The diaries begin abruptly in the middle of a year spent in Rome (1900–1901), suggesting that there were other diaries, now lost, describing earlier years of his life. Even the extant diaries have gaps, some of a few days, some of a few weeks; these remain unexplained, but other sources shed some light on events in these periods. Unedited and never intended for publication, the diaries contain Kelsey's spontaneous record of events and sometimes his reactions to them. Their validity resides in the first-person immediacy that colors a rich and continuous narrative of his life—all the better for being corrected or endorsed here and there by correspondence, university memorandums, local histories, family records, and other archival material.

More important, because they record so many aspects of Kelsey's life, the diaries provided the clues that revealed the wide range of his activities. Without them, his mining adventures in the Southwest, the full range of his fundraising connections in the Detroit community, and the complexity of the establishment of the Humanistic Series, for example, would remain little known. For the period they cover, there is no other source of comparable authority. The richness and thickness of detail of so many facets of his life argued for the chronological, rather than thematic or episodic, approach adopted in this book. Reflecting the pace, complexity, and energy of his life, the diary-driven narrative of much of the book hopes to communicate to the reader the man's character and the energy with which he conducted his life.

The bias of the diarist, the constructed slant on situations and personalities, may be taken for granted. Yet in the instance of Kelsey's diaries, it offers, by its very authenticity, notes of spontaneity, especially in matters relating to his family and in his personal assessment of his own efforts, as found in the revelatory and heartfelt sentences at the end of the diaries for 1906 and 1909. These accounts of events and emotions were written in the moment, with an immediacy that is transparent. We read them in the full knowledge that they are as conditioned by circumstances and predispositions as are our reactions to them. But their great value lies in the voice of Kelsey himself.

His unflagging capacity for work, intensity of interest, firmness of purpose, restless energy, and plain speaking led to professional achievements beyond the range of most scholars. His life, enlarged immeasurably by his family—seriously minded in public life, he exuded plenty of twinkle at home—and by his love of nature and his interest in music, was a source of inspiration and insight to others, as were the pace and scale of his endeavors. In a tribute penned after his death, Esther Van Deman, a former student and expert Roman archaeologist, perhaps best encapsulates the effect he had on others: "I think few men touched so many lines of life, and few had more lives so tangled in the thread of their own that they felt a personal wrench at his going."[1] This biography attempts to untangle the thread of Kelsey's great circle of acquaintance and to highlight once again the effect he had on so many.

---

1. Carol Finerman, "Visions of Excellence: The Career of Francis W. Kelsey," *University of Michigan LSA Magazine* 10 (1987): 15.

CHAPTER 1

Setting the Stage

੶੶

THE FREEZING WINTER OF 1858 in New York State had given way to early summer by the time Olive Trowbridge Kelsey, wife of Henry Kelsey, gave birth to her fourth child. He joined three other children, two boys and a girl. So the newcomer, who was to become a professor at the University of Michigan, head of the Department of Latin, president of the American Philological Association, and president of the Archaeological Institute of America, was the baby of the family, born when his mother was already thirty-eight years of age. He was given the names Francis Willey (after his maternal grandmother).

The family traced its roots back to seventeenth-century England (Essex) and to an ancestor, William Kelsey, who crossed the Atlantic with Thomas Hooker and settled in Cambridge in 1632.[1] Some two centuries later, William's descendants in New York were well aware that it was Francis's grandfather, Benjamin Kelsey, who had come west to New York in 1815 (or thereabouts) in search of land to farm. He staked a claim in Ogden, a settlement some fifty miles west of Rochester, and returned to Vermont for his wife, Hepsibah, and two young children, Henry and Salome. Their new home was a small log cabin with a single fireplace and windows that were little more than gaps in the walls to let in the light—windows that were covered only by the greased brown paper they had brought from Vermont. Over time, five more children joined Henry and Salome: Elmira, Absalom, Seneca, Elihu, and Benjamin.

---

1. H. N. Kelsey et al., *A Genealogy of the Descendants of William Kelsey*, vols. 1–4 (Bridgeport, CT: Marsh, 1975).

Francis's grandparents had been brought up in a world of austerity, industry, and godliness, and they applied the same rules of conduct to their own children. When Henry, a boy still in school, brought home a violin, bought with money he had earned himself, his parents did not approve. His mother lamented what she called the devil's work, and his father smashed the instrument to bits.

IMMEDIATE FAMILY

Henry, Francis's father, attended school in a single-room log cabin, warmed in winter by a fireplace at either end of the building. The curriculum focused on reading and writing. A preliminary spelling book with the alphabet, short sentences, and easy paragraphs was followed by an English reader from which children learned prose passages in high-flown, Victorian style and verse excerpts from poets like Milton and Dryden. This was ambitious fare for young minds, intended not only to broaden vocabularies and knowledge of grammar and syntax but also to reinforce the current moral attitudes.

At first, Henry set his sights on a career in medicine rather than farming. To pay for his medical training, he taught school for ten years and supplemented his income by riding far and wide across the county to give singing lessons in the evenings. By age twenty-eight, he had saved enough to join a doctor's office in Rochester as a student, but he quickly discovered that his lack of Greek and Latin, still in widespread use in medical books, would make his training longer than he had thought. Discouraged, he gave up and used his medical savings to buy a small farm at Stony Point, not far from his parents' place.[2]

In 1842 he married Olive Cornelia Trowbridge, daughter of Windsor Trowbridge and Rebecca Willey. Olive's brother was John Townsend Trowbridge, the famous author of adventure and antislavery stories and friend of Mark Twain,[3] whose talents and interests no doubt influenced his young and academically minded nephew. Years later, John Townsend Trowbridge and his

---

2. Harriet Kelsey Fay, "The Kelsey Family," in *Ogden Centennial Pioneer Reminiscences, 1802–1902*, comp. Augusta E. N. Rich, with Sarah Flagg Smith and H. H. Goff (Rochester, NY: John C. Moore, 1902), 58–59.

3. John Townsend Trowbridge, too, was born and brought up in Ogden. As a young man, he moved to New York City and then Boston, where he found work as a journalist, editor, and writer of many novels and magazine articles. He published numerous boys' stories, of which the Jack Hazard tales became famous. Perhaps the best known of his novels is *Neighbor Jackwood*, in which the author's antislavery views are easily recognizable. He was one of the contributors to the first issue of the *Atlantic Monthly*.

second wife, Ada, lived in Arlington, Massachusetts; Francis, often in Boston to talk with his publishers or on the business of the Archaeological Institute of America, visited them there whenever possible.

Henry and Olive's first child was born in 1845, a boy named after his father. Little is known about the younger Henry except that he became a farmer in Missouri, married, and had three children—two girls and a boy. A daughter, Harriet Rebecca, with whom Francis was to enjoy a warm friendship all his life, was born three years later, in 1848. In 1850 another boy was born, Frederick Wallace, later a successful businessman in New York City and first vice president of the Essex County Parks Commission in New Jersey.[4] It was not, however, until a couple of years before Abraham Lincoln's election to the presidency, in the troubled years leading to the Civil War, that Francis Willey Kelsey made his appearance—on May 23, 1858.

OGDEN AND BEYOND: EDUCATING FRANCIS

Francis's infancy was spent on the hardscrabble farm at Stony Point. It was unpromising land, mostly clay and, as its name implies, rock. A stream meandered through the property, which might have been useful for milling if only it had flowed more strongly. Instead, its slow current only added weight to the earth and soaked the fields, which begrudgingly yielded mainly vegetables and fruit. The family's few cows provided milk and cream. The 1858 plat book of the town of Ogden shows a farm of fifty-six acres, and tax records valued it at $953.[5] The family grew up here until Francis turned two, when Henry and Olive moved to the larger family farm at Churchville,[6] only a few miles away from their smallholding at Stony Point.

The nearby school was maintained by additional taxes paid by parents, who also supplied firewood in winter. Two of Francis's schoolbooks have survived.[7] He inscribed his school reader with his name and the year: "Francis W.

---

4. He was also the author of *The First County Park System: A Complete History of the Inception and Development of the Essex County Parks of New Jersey* (New York: J. S. Ogilvie, 1905).

5. "Ogden," map (plat book) after *Gillette's Map of Monroe Co.: From Actual Surveys by P. J. Browne* (Philadelphia: John E. Gillette, 1858), lot no. 208, H. Kelsey.

6. "Town of Riga," map in *Atlas of Monroe County, New York,* by F. W. Beers et al. (New York: F. W. Beers, 1872), lot nos. 19 and 31, B. Kelsey. Churchville, a small village within the area known as Ogden, grew up around a crossroads. By 1872 it enjoyed the benefits of a post office and railroad station.

7. These books are in the care of Carol F. Coburn, Ogden/Spencerport Historian, Ogden Town Hall, Spencerport, NY. I am most grateful to her for drawing my attention to these books and for assistance in locating the Kelsey properties on the plat books.

1. Page from Francis Kelsey's schoolbook, Town Pump School District, Ogden, 1871. Ogden/Spencerport Historian's Office, Town of Ogden, County of Monroe, State of New York. Photo: John Pedley.

Kelsey, 1866." His grammar was even more freely inscribed: one page has the names of all the Kelsey children, though the similar handwriting suggests that Francis wrote them all. He wrote his own name, "F. W. Kelsey," boldly and added "twelve years old" in different ink and his sister's name, "H. R. Kellsey [*sic*]," followed by "Ogden, Monroe County, NY." Harriet appears on another page as "Hattie R. Kelsey" (not to be confused with a cousin Hattie, whose middle name was Olive). Another page (fig. 1) reveals a boyish experiment with another name and address: "Frank W. Kelsey, Ogden, Monroe Co, NY. Town Pump School Dist. Formerly of Stony Point, March 1871"; "H. Kelsey, tutor" appears in parentheses—his sister was helping him in his work. Randomly, nearby, the name and initials are repeated, the initials as a ligature, Francis displaying every boy's interest in the task-avoiding doodle.

His grammar book[8] included style and usage information under such titles as "Of the Exclamation Point" and "Of the Parenthesis." Students were asked to correct and expand simple sentences. The twelve-year-old brain was expected to grapple with such sentences as "The interrogation and exclamation points are indeterminate as to their quantity and time, and may be equivalent, in that respect, to a semicolon, a colon, or a period, as the case

8. Roswell Chamberlain Smith, *Intellectual and Practical Grammar, in a Series of Inductive Questions, Connected with Exercises in Composition* (Boston: Perkins & Marvin, 1831).

may require. They mark an elevation of the voice." The pupils were expected to read and use English with precision and to think clearly. To these skills were added literary compositions, arithmetic, weights and measures, and geography.

The neighborhood of Ogden and Churchville did not support a secondary school, for which the Kelseys had to look to Lockport, some sixty miles west of Monroe County. By act of the New York State Legislature, the Lockport Union School had been opened in 1848 as a public high school to serve the consolidated school districts of Lockport.[9] Funded, after long and noisy debate, by a progressive property tax, this school was an American pioneer in offering schooling beyond the elementary level for free[10]—well, almost free: a small tuition fee was levied of $2 (juniors) or $3 (seniors) a semester for residents, $3 or $4 for nonresidents. Some subjects, however, did require additional payments: for example, $1.30 for Latin and Greek; $1.50 for German, French, Spanish, or Italian; 50¢ for bookkeeping.[11] But the basic $2 tuition fee covered the subjects of English (reading, spelling, writing, and grammar), mathematics, commercial business, natural science (including intellectual and moral philosophy), and teacher training.

In establishing the Lockport school, the Union School Act of 1847 was following an education trend promulgated widely in New England in the 1830s, where district school reform and the establishment of a public school system had found a tireless advocate in Horace Mann, the secretary of the Massachusetts Board of Education. The extension of public education from the elementary to the secondary level was a key component in his program. Mann's ideas spread rapidly westward, finding fertile ground in communities committed to the Protestant ethic of hard work, growth, reliability, and a fair deal.

The Lockport Union School was fully supplied with the most up-to-date equipment, causing the *Niagara Democrat* of June 29, 1848, to exclaim proudly,

> For the use of students and to aid them in their pursuit of scientific knowledge, the Board has procured very extensive and valuable apparatus, Pneumatic, Mechanical, Electrical, Hydrostatic, Acoustic, Optical, Magnetic, Electro-Magnetic, and Chemical. They have procured a Transit Instrument for the purpose of Surveying, Leveling, Calculating heights and distances, which is one of the best pieces of Mathematical ap-

---

9. *Union School Bulletin* (Lockport, NY) 1.1 (December 1894): 1.

10. Ralph L. Shattuck, ed., *100 Years of Education, 1847–1947* (Lockport, NY: Board of Education, [1948?]), 23, 24, 29.

11. Ibid., 90. The availability of foreign-language learning is worth noting.

paratus ever manufactured in this country. The apparatus has been selected from the best shops in New York, Boston, Albany and Troy. The library attached to the Institution is large and will be increased yearly. It already numbers 2000 volumes. They have also a Cabinet of Minerals for
the use of students.

The structure and curriculum of the school addressed the needs of elementary, preparatory, and college education.

> The Union School is divided into two Departments, Junior and Senior,
> and connected with the Union School are two other Departments, Pri-
> mary and Secondary. Suitable buildings for the latter are erected in the
> several districts. A regular course of study is prescribed for each Depart-
> ment, commencing with the simple elementary branches in the Primary
> and advancing higher in other Departments. In the Senior Department
> not only is the most thorough instruction given in all the branches for the
> first and second years in College, but particular attention is paid to those
> branches of natural Science, commerce and Agriculture, Chemistry, Nat-
> ural Intellectual and Moral Philosophy, Surveying, Trigonometry, and all
> the Mathematics and higher English branches, so useful and necessary to
> every citizen whatever be his occupation.[12]

To pursue this "useful and necessary" instruction, Francis Kelsey entered the
school at the age of fifteen. Far from home, he probably became a "boarder,"
living at Lockport on the third floor of the main school building with other
nonresident students. Most students came from the neighborhood, but in the
school's early years, several came from other states, some from Canada, and
one even from Japan.[13] Francis would have been exposed to a varied and rigorous curriculum, including English literature, rhetoric, antiquities, and pen-
manship, as well as Latin and Greek and other languages, fine arts, music, and
history. Science classes, which included chemistry, botany, geography, government, and philosophy, were well equipped with apparatuses, specimens,
and maps; math classes included trigonometry and surveying.[14] Athletics or
other social activities found no place at Lockport. Muscular Christianity, the
credo of many boarding schools in England at the time (*Mens sana in corpore
sano*), had not crossed the Atlantic to Horace Mann's program. Observe,
think, study, and work were the prevailing admonitions.[15]

Having exhausted the resources of Lockport, Kelsey was ready in the fall

12. Ibid., 27.
13. Ibid., 30.
14. Ibid., 90, 96, 110.
15. Ibid., 116.

of 1876, at the age of eighteen, to enter the University of Rochester. He took rooms at 60 Tappan Street. His expenses were now much larger: the fee for tuition was $25 per term, while the charge for boardinghouse rooms varied between $3.50 and $5.00 per week, costs that we can only assume were met by his father.

The university's annual catalogs reveal that he followed the Classical Course, surprisingly a much broader range of studies than its name might suggest. For his first two years, Francis concentrated on languages, both ancient and modern: Latin, Greek, English, German, and French. In his junior and senior years, the curriculum broadened into a rich program.[16] The junior year included the following courses:

Term 1: Logic, Chemistry, Physics, Greek Tragedy

Term 2: Rhetoric, Physics, Chemistry, Comparative Philology

Term 3: Cicero, Astronomy, Philosophy, Longinus, Greek Literature, French & German Literature

In the senior year, the range is even more remarkable:

Term 1: Philosophy, Justinian, Roman Law, Zoology, Art History

Term 2: Constitutional Law, Plato & Aristotle, Greek Philosophy, European Civilization, Art History

Term 3: Geology, Advanced German or Recent English Literature, Moral Philosophy, Physical Geography

He would enjoy small classes, in which every student recited to the heads of departments: these included such distinguished scholars as J. H. Gilmore (English) and William C. Morey (Latin). Francis would also have studied with two of the most influential faculty members—Asahel Kendrick (Greek)[17] and Martin B. Anderson (the president of the university).[18] He was an exceptional student, almost from the start. He won a sophomore prize in Latin and a junior prize in Greek. He did special work in Sanskrit and comparative philology with Professor Henry F. Burton. He won the Sherman

---

16. Annual catalogs of the University of Rochester, 1876–80. I am most grateful for the help of Nancy Martin, university archivist and Rochester Collections librarian, for guidance toward these and other materials.

17. Florence Hopkins Kendrick Cooper, *American Scholar: A Tribute to Asahel Clark Kendrick, 1809–1895* (New York: n.p., 1913).

18. Asahel C. Kendrick, with Florence Kendrick Cooper, *Martin B. Anderson LL.D.: A Biography* (Philadelphia: American Baptist Publication Society, 1895).

Scholarship for history and political science in competitive examination. Holding the highest average of marks in his class for the classroom work of the entire course, he was elected valedictorian.

The doodling lad from Ogden did not work all the time: he enjoyed a prank. Since classes were held only in the mornings, there was plenty of time for the library and work at home. So Francis built a chemistry lab for home experiments in a small room at the head of the stairs in his boardinghouse. Having taken exception to the noisy visits paid by suitors to the landlady's daughter, he concocted stink bombs; these produced such appalling smells in the parlors where the assignations took place that the visits came to an end. Francis thought this a huge joke.[19]

He was diligent, thoughtful, and alert. He kept his eyes open, and he loved his work. It seems that the faculty at Rochester had earmarked him as a future scholar and that word about him was going around. After graduation in the summer of 1880, he was appointed immediately to the faculty at Lake Forest University. His later professional success did not escape the notice of his alma mater, which awarded him his A.M. in 1883, his Ph.D. in 1888, and an Honorary LL.D. degree in 1910.

From this improbable but sturdy background—a childhood on a hardscrabble farm supported by a firm parental belief in education, perhaps spurred by his father's thwarted aspirations to a medical career—emerged the mix of character and conduct that was to propel Francis to the top of his profession. Yet aspects of the background unveil clues to behavioral traits that stamped his life. His father's musical aspirations foreshadowed his own delight in music and commitment to its promulgation in Ann Arbor. His Uncle John Trowbridge's life and work showed the way to a sense of literature and pleasure in writing—not to mention an awareness of social inequities. His pleasure in physical exertion was rooted in his life on the farm. His appetite for mental work appeared first at Lockport, where work, work, and more work were the guiding principles for students; it is not hard to see where his lifelong relish for books and the routines of daily work took shape. At the University of Rochester, his intellectual prowess and capacity for leadership were widely recognized and blossomed. The ancient Greek and Latin authors faced him

---

19. Ruth Kelsey Diel, "Francis W. Kelsey in Lighter Vein," 1952, typescript, private collection of Easton Kelsey Jr., Rochester, NY. This reminiscence was written by Francis's daughter Ruth, who also says that when Isabelle, Kelsey's wife, heard about it, she was not amused.

with the great moral and philosophical dilemmas; the New Testament in Greek steered him more firmly to Christianity—though what in particular drew him to the Presbyterian Church in Rochester remains unclear. Unlikely as it might appear, by the summer of 1880, this accomplished graduate from Rochester was ready for the challenges of a professor's life, unimaginable from the barren childhood fields of Ogden.

CHAPTER 2

Apprenticeship

Lake Forest University

ॐ

AT THE TIME OF KELSEY'S GRADUATION from the University of Rochester, the United States was experiencing a period of unprecedented innovation and growth. Developments in technology, engineering, and science were having profound effects on society, every invention designed to capture time and productivity. Technology saw the appearance of the camera, the typewriter, the telegraph, and the telephone, while other applications of electricity revolutionized the workplace and the home. Railroads and steam engines, already in use, multiplied across the country; more locally, electric trolleys and streetcars were soon to offer speed and comfort to the pedestrian. Even before the first automobile appeared on the scene—and at the time of Kelsey's arrival in Michigan—Detroit was already a hive of capitalists and workers, its factories churning out iron and copper, drugs, beer, rolling stock, freight and passenger cars for the railroads, and ships.

Such was the availability of natural resources—timber, metals, manpower—and so abundant the ready capital that many made large fortunes rapidly. So brazen was the use of wealth to build ornate mansions overstuffed with furnishings and paraphernalia that the period is sometimes known as the American Gilded Age—an era characterized by a spirit of energetic enterprise and also by vulgarity of taste. Yet the crescendo of materialism went hand in hand with belief in religion—not least that intensely Protestant view that worldly success evidenced personal salvation—and a belief in philanthropy, which flourished. Rich citizens used their wealth to build libraries for the public good, to support the establishment of museums and orchestras, and to found universities to which they gave their names.

Education in particular experienced growth at every level. Thanks to the American belief (enshrined in the Northwest Ordinance of 1783) that education should be offered to every child, school systems—in the cities at any rate—were well supported and growing to serve the increasing population. In 1870 there were a mere 160 public high schools in the country; by 1900 there were more than 6,000. At the college level, new institutions were cropping up everywhere, many heavily influenced by Americans who had studied in Germany and wished to adopt the German university model, giving as much emphasis to research and graduate education as to undergraduate studies. In addition, growing interest in professional training encouraged the establishment of graduate schools.

Lake Forest University was founded in the midst of much of this ferment. In its mission, it exemplifies the dilemma of American higher education at the time, which included questions about the purpose of the liberal arts for the undergraduate, what methods of teaching should be employed, and whether undergraduate education was an end in itself or merely a stepping stone to further training. Francis Kelsey quickly found his feet in these educational shallows. His positive attitude toward innovation was fostered by the attitudes of the society around him, hence his love of hard work and novelty, his determination never to lose a moment, his energy, and, more practically, his interest in railroads, the telegraph, the stereopticon, and photography. Added to his energy and productivity were his innate talent for languages and his intense belief in the discipline and order that study of the classical world could bring.

He had barely seen the ink dry on his B.A. diploma from Rochester when he joined the university. Appointed instructor in classics, he also had teaching duties in the university's two preparatory schools, Lake Forest Academy for boys and Ferry Hall for girls. His nine years on the faculty would allow him to test his aptitude for teaching, develop ideas for improving Greek and Latin instruction, and put some of these ideas to work in new textbooks. Service and tenure would encourage him to contribute to the debate on the place of research in the American university and decide its significance in his own life. A summer in Italy would introduce him to European methods of archaeological research—more specifically to the wonders of Rome and Pompeii. A year's leave in Europe would acquaint him with the German system of higher education and, more important, would invite him to explore the whole of the ancient world in situ, not just via the text. These years would see the indigent farm boy become a world traveler and educational philosopher.

LAKE FOREST

Lake Forest was the brainchild of a group of Chicago Presbyterians who came together in the middle of the nineteenth century to found a community—a town and a university together—that would embody their Puritan ideals of education and the virtuous life. From the start, they foresaw a town endowed with a comprehensive educational system leading from preparatory school through undergraduate work to professional university training. This system would be supported financially and morally by the families that lived in the town. Academic learning and exemplary living were to go hand in hand, with the church as the spiritual center, a Utopia of like-minded folk. Fueled by the industry and savvy of businessmen in the big city, Lake Forest would promulgate Puritan and Presbyterian values, by linking bustling city with tranquil country, good thinking with good business, godliness with commercial success.[1]

The First Presbyterian Church in Chicago, a city seeing very rapid growth in this period, had already helped found Knox College at Galesburg, Illinois. The Second Presbyterian Church, however, did not share the more liberal views of the First Presbyterian Church and thought a more conservative Presbyterian college was called for. Five members of the congregation of the Second Presbyterian Church—four clergymen and a layman—were therefore charged with locating a suitable site near Chicago for such a college. In 1855 they found it, on a promontory overlooking Lake Michigan. With the forest on one side of the cliff and the lake on the other, the search committee unhesitatingly called the place Lake Forest.[2]

At a meeting in the Second Presbyterian Church in the winter of 1856, the Lake Forest Association was organized to arrange the purchase of the land; and early in the following year, the state legislature approved a charter for the university. In short order, twenty-three hundred acres of land on either side of

---

1. This chapter draws heavily on Franz Schulze, Rosemary Cowler, and Arthur H. Miller, *Thirty Miles North: A History of Lake Forest College, Its Town, and Its City of Chicago* (Lake Forest, IL: Lake Forest College, 2000), chaps. 1 and 2. I owe this reference to Arthur Miller, archivist and librarian for special collections at Lake Forest College, and am most grateful for his help in this and other matters.
2. Ibid., 11.

the Chicago-Waukegan railroad line were acquired. The first building to go up was the Lake Forest Hotel, finished in 1858, made popular by Chicagoans escaping the city in the summer heat, and also used by the Lake Forest Academy, the preparatory school for boys. Other educational buildings appeared in 1859: a private preparatory school for girls and a public school for the children of servants and local workers. So, on the eve of the nomination in Chicago of Abraham Lincoln as the Republican candidate for the presidency of the United States, the community at Lake Forest seemed well launched.

The first freshman class began studies in the fall of 1861. There were just six students. They followed a curriculum standard for colleges at the time: classical authors (Cicero, Xenophon, and Homer), geometry, declamation, and English composition. They played an active part in the life of the village, helping clear streets of trees and bushes and roofing the church, as well as taking part in religious and social events. Town and gown worked together. But as soon as the Civil War got under way, the students drifted away to enlist; with half of the freshman class joining the army, the college became a casualty of the war, and in 1863 it closed its doors.[3]

The resuscitation of the university, its name changed in 1865 from the original Lind University to Lake Forest University, was due largely to the generosity of two brothers, Charles and John Farwell. Owning the largest dry goods warehouse in Chicago, they each made massive fortunes, to which the Civil War—thanks to the increased movement of supplies on the rail network (Chicago was a major hub)—contributed substantially. Both moved their households to Lake Forest in the late 1860s and built extravagant stately homes within a stone's throw of one another.

Two other important buildings went up at about the same time. In 1869 a new girls' school, called Ferry Hall after the Reverend William Ferry, a Michigan man who left money in his will to build it, replaced the earlier institution.[4] A new Lake Forest Hotel, known locally as the New Hotel and more comfortably appointed than the first Lake Forest Hotel, opened in 1871. Things in Lake Forest were looking up. But there were more troubles ahead.

The repercussions of the Great Chicago Fire of 1871 were extreme. Practically the whole of the city was destroyed, and its population, now some three hundred thousand souls, was left homeless. On top of the fire came the sharp economic recession of 1873, which left no one unscathed, and the luxurious new

---

3. Ibid., 20.
4. The public school founded at the same time as the private school for girls continued to function through these difficult days and exists to this day.

Lake Forest Hotel succumbed after operating for only two years. When bankruptcy was declared, the hotel and its grounds were returned to the Lake Forest Association, which used the empty hotel as the cornerstone of a refounded university. The money for this step was provided by Charles Farwell, but the guiding light of the enterprise was his wife, Mary Eveline Smith Farwell.

Mary Eveline Smith was a New Englander whose private education and steady home life had instilled in her a firm belief in a liberal education for all, men and women alike. In 1875 her and Charles's eldest daughter, Anna, was ready to go to college. Since her parents wanted Anna to pursue her education nearby and to continue to move in social circles acceptable to them, a revitalized Lake Forest University seemed the obvious answer. Anna's eagerness to pursue her education, the availability of Charles's money, Mary's commitment to the cause of women's education, and both parents' desire that Anna's social arrangements should be suitable were the prime motivating factors in their reestablishment of the university. In this reanimated institution, the education of women was to have a secure place.

The university reopened in the fall of 1876, using dormitories and classrooms newly installed in the Lake Forest Hotel. There were three faculty members and twelve students, of whom Anna Farwell was one, each of them supported by a Farwell Fellowship. The Reverend Robert Patterson, who, as minister of the Second Presbyterian Church, had been one of the five explorers who identified the site for the Lake Forest enterprise in 1855, became the first president. But the university's teething troubles were not yet over. When a fire destroyed the hotel almost completely, Charles and Mary Farwell intervened again to fund the construction of a large multipurpose academic building, University Hall, completed in 1878.

A new president, the Reverend Daniel Gregory, took office in June 1878 and instantly began the search for promising new faculty. It was his decision to appoint the young Francis Kelsey, aged only twenty-two, and, following the departure of John Hewitt to Williams College in 1882, to promote him to professor of Latin. What was it that Gregory saw in Kelsey to induce him to make such a young appointment? His exceptional academic record at the University of Rochester (the recommendation of whose president, the influential Martin Anderson, will have carried great weight) and his enthusiasm for Presbyterianism were strong factors. But more than that, the faltering beginnings of Lake Forest echoed the hard row that Kelsey had had to hoe, and his prodigious work ethic paralleled the hard work that had gone into the birth and rebirth of Lake Forest University. Furthermore, both university and man had at their core a transparent and passionate belief in education.

FIRST IMPRESSIONS

In January 1880, a university publication, the *Lake Forest University Review,* appeared.[5] Planned as a news and literary periodical to which students, faculty, and alumni could contribute short articles of historical, scientific, or literary interest, it aimed at a wide audience. The range of authors meant that the quality of the writing varied considerably. Its first editor was the young Anna Farwell. This venture launched her lifelong career as editor, supporter of literary projects (the *Review* was funded by her family), author, and prominent American literary figure.[6] President Gregory himself, writing a blatantly commercial piece on the last page of each issue, trumpeted the school's claims as the epitome of "Christian Collegiate education," listed the qualifications of the ten professors on the faculty, and pointed to the ideal location and the absence of alcohol as further attractive features.[7]

University affairs were prospering in the fall of 1880. The December issue of the *Review* introduced a new faculty member: "F. W. Kelsey, University of Rochester, is instructor in special English and Philology in the College and has some work in Ferry Hall and the Academy."[8] Kelsey was not slow to reveal his early educational philosophy, which he did in two articles in the *Review* in 1881. In the April issue, he vigorously argued for the value of the study of Latin. Since Latin is a logical system with underlying laws of form and syntax, it teaches concentration of thought, trains the memory, and develops judgment: it promotes right thinking. Since Latin is also a historical organism, it invites comparison with other languages in terms of growth, linguistic influence, effect, and power as an instrument of thought. Moreover, since language represents thought, Latin paves the way to the study of the workings of the Roman mind and the fundamental ideas of Roman life—its literature, art, law, philosophy, and civilization. Kelsey closed by addressing the question

---

5. Launched in January 1880, the short-lived *Lake Forest University Review* (hereinafter *LFUR*) folded in June 1883.

6. Anna Farwell edited the first six numbers of the *LFUR,* through June 1880. She left Lake Forest in 1890 to live in Washington, New York, and Europe. At some point during the 1880s, she met and married Reginald de Koven, at that time a stockbroker in Chicago but later an assiduous composer of popular songs and operettas. As well as contributing financially to literary publications, she herself wrote many articles and books, notable among which are *A Sawdust Doll* (1895) and *A Cloud of Witnesses* (1920). She also produced a valuable edition, in two volumes, of *The Life and Letters of John Paul Jones* (1913).

7. Schulze, Cowler, and Miller, *Thirty Miles North,* 36.

8. *LFUR* 2.1 (December 1880): 6. The "College" was the undergraduate department (or division) of the university; Ferry Hall (for girls) and the "Academy" (for boys) were the preparatory schools.

of relevancy: what useful lessons for today are to be drawn from the study of the past? In this regard, the study of Roman history as the development of social and political organizations is of special interest.[9]

This article outlines ideas about the importance of the study of broader contexts that Kelsey would later implement. In showing his willingness to contribute to the *Review* and thus engage a wider audience, it reveals him as an eager advocate for classical education as a guide to the rational and balanced life, as an early proponent of university outreach. It also foreshadows a much later article in which he compares the logic of language to the logic of the hard sciences.[10]

In the September issue of the *Review,* he wrote an article on Julius Caesar, one that describes Caesar's family background, support for the popular party, shrewd political alliances, campaigns in Gaul, and relationships with Pompey, as well as the civil war that broke out in 49 BC and culminated in Pompey's death. He places Caesar's life in the context of the growth of the state from a small municipality into a great republic, with tensions between localizing and centralizing tendencies. Constitutional paralysis followed struggles between the elite and the plebs, to the point that the continuing existence of Rome appeared to demand a monarchy. By 44 BC, it seemed, to the fury of conservative diehards, that there already was one. The assassination of Caesar followed. One scholarly view, Kelsey said, held that Caesar was virtually a criminal who put personal ambition ahead of the freedom of Rome; another held that he was a great statesman who, as dictator, brought law and order in chaotic times. Kelsey argued that the first view placed too much emphasis on the negative side of his character, whereas the second relied too heavily on projections onto Caesar of centuries of scholarship. He suggested that the principle of imperialism had been flexing its muscles in Rome since the second century and that Caesar's career was merely a culmination of this tendency. Thus, Kelsey followed the rehearsal of familiar interpretations by embarking on a new angle.[11] This article reveals a major academic interest of Kelsey's (Julius Caesar as general, politician, and statesman and the slow unraveling of republicanism at Rome) and points forward to his edition of Cae-

---

9. Francis W. Kelsey, "The Study of Latin in Collegiate Education," *LFUR* 2.6 (April 1881): 54–56. It is worth quoting the first sentence of the prospectus of the Latin Department in the university catalog for 1888–89: "The Latin Department aims not only to train the student to a practical mastery of the language, but also, through the study of texts and monuments, to give him a comprehensive view of the Roman civilization in its various aspects."

10. Francis W. Kelsey, "Is There a Science of Classical Philology?" *Classical Philology* 3.4 (October 1908): 369–85.

11. Francis W. Kelsey, "The Political Character and Aims of Julius Caesar," *LFUR* 2.9 (September 1881): 95–96.

sar's *Gallic War*, which Kelsey was to publish in 1886.[12] In that edition, Kelsey placed Caesar in the context of the times and emphasized the incorporation of such contextual material in a textbook, continuing the pattern he had initiated in his earliest texts. The approach taken was so successful that the book was already in its tenth edition by the end of the century, elaborated with half a dozen colored plates and fourteen plans of battles, sieges, and expedition routes. Its association with Kelsey was so strong that he was even introduced, on one occasion, as "the author of Caesar's *Gallic War*."

The *Review* was edited by President Gregory in 1881, but Kelsey became the new editor in the following year. With his very first issue, the tone changed. In his opening remarks, Kelsey claimed that the *Review* was to be much more than a college journal. It was to publish discussion of "educational questions of vital interest throughout the west and especially to the Presbyterian church." "There has too long been," he went on, "an apathy, an indifference in regard to Christian higher education." He took the view that those who desired "the good of both Church and Nation" should help in every way the work "not merely of higher, but of Christian higher education." Another side of Kelsey's character was becoming clear: he was a serious churchman. Further witness to his beliefs is found in his 1883 return to his church in Rochester, the Memorial Presbyterian Church, to preach. The sermon he delivered, taking as his text a passage from the Gospel of St. John ("I am the Light of the World"), was described in the local press as eloquent, impressive, and gratifying. In subsequent editorials of the *Review*, Kelsey continued his advocacy of religious instruction—not least the tenets of the Presbyterian Church—in higher education. But he also included other topics of interest to students, among which were new acquisitions to the library and the question of aid to students.[13] The *Review* lacked serious institutional support, however, and ceased publication before the end of the year. Despite the undoubted commitment of the Board of Trustees, Kelsey had lost this vehicle for the promulgation of his Presbyterian views.

Although his command of ancient texts was firm and his enthusiasm for the languages contagious, Kelsey was aware that he had no direct knowledge of the landscapes of Italy and Greece and that his appreciation of Greek and Roman archaeology was not what he would have liked it to be. Moreover, to improve his philological skills to the degree he himself advocated, he

---

12. Francis W. Kelsey, ed., *Caesar's "Gallic War," with an Introduction, Notes, and Vocabulary* (Boston: John Allyn, 1886).

13. Francis W. Kelsey, editorial, *LFUR* 4.1 (September and October 1882): 36; 4.2 (November and December 1882): 69; 4.4 (March and April 1883) 134.

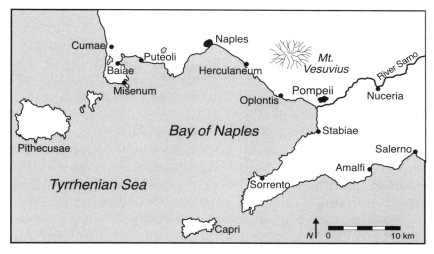

2. Map of Italy's Bay of Naples showing Pompeii, Herculaneum, Capri, Vesuvius, and environs. Drawing: Lorene Sterner.

thought he could benefit from the German university curriculum. His eyes turned inevitably to Europe. So, at the end of the university year in 1883, he set out; the experiences he enjoyed that summer would mark the whole of his career. We do not have the details of his itinerary, but he certainly visited Italy and, traveling through the Po Valley, saw Rome, Naples, Pompeii (see fig. 2), and Sicily.[14]

It seems likely that this was when he met the great German scholar August Mau. Mau had worked in Italy since 1872 as a member of the Deutsches Archäeologisches Institut, publishing the inscriptions from Pompeii, excavating with the Italians, and studying the site. Mau knew as much about Pompeii as any other scholar at the time and seems always to have been willing to share the latest information from new excavations with visiting scholars. Kelsey benefited from Mau's generosity; perhaps this was the time he was first invited to go round the site with Mau, examining buildings, discussing problems, and absorbing the older scholar's insights. Kelsey's contact with Mau continued over the years as his interest in Pompeii intensified, and it is hard to overemphasize the influence that the experienced German scholar had on him. A firm friendship developed, reflected in their extended correspon-

---

14. In 1920, for example, his diary (March 20, July 7) mentions having seen the Po Valley and Mount Etna in 1883.

dence, which led to collaboration between the two: Kelsey's translation and edition of Mau's *Pompeji in Leben und Kunst*.[15]

Meeting Mau must have confirmed Kelsey in his view of the advantages of more study in Europe. Many of his contemporaries who held appointments in classics in major American universities had studied at some point in German universities, and many had taken degrees there. Accordingly, having taken leave for 1884–85 to try the German system, he matriculated in the fall of 1884 at the University of Leipzig. But he was soon disillusioned. He withdrew early from courses taught by eminent classical scholars, commenting at a later date that he thought they concentrated too much on what he called a mechanical point of view. Literary works, he thought, were treated with too little sensitivity to artistic form or literary content.[16] He preferred to spend his time in southern Europe, familiarizing himself with ancient sites and topographies. He visited Italy again; and in 1885, probably with Catullus in mind,[17] he traveled to Asia Minor, where he visited the German excavations at Pergamon (begun in 1878) and was seen exploring Smyrna and Ephesos. In the same year, in Greece, he climbed Mount Parnassos and was thrilled to glimpse Mount Olympos in the distance. He was both getting a firsthand view of the results of archaeological fieldwork and scrutinizing the places and spaces that had inspired the great literature he loved. Dissatisfied by some of the German approaches to the classics but enthused by what he had seen in Italy and Greece, Kelsey was determined to make changes in the way the classics were taught in America.

The decades after the American Civil War had seen the continuation of profound social tensions in the United States. The claims of industrialization were at loggerheads with those of agriculture and the land: more and more citizens saw futures for their families in a mechanized world rather than on the farm or frontier. The influx of immigrants pitted residents against newcomers. For some, church and commerce went hand in hand; for others, materialism did not chime well with the Christian life. Philanthropy thrived, but so did greed. Restraint and altruism were to be found, but graft and corrup-

---

15. August Mau, *Pompeji in Leben und Kunst* (Leipzig: W. Engelmann, 1900), ed. and trans. Francis W. Kelsey as *Pompeii: Its Life and Art* (New York: Macmillan, 1899). For more on Mau and Kelsey, see chapter 3.

16. T. Hawley Tapping, ed., "Great Michigan Scholar Honored in German Publication," *Michigan Alumnus* 41 (1935): 269.

17. Catullus 46.6: "Ad claras Asiae volemus urbes" (Let us fly away to the glorious cities of Asia). Asia, of course, is the Roman province of Asia (Asia Minor), of which Ephesos was the capital.

tion were also evident in many walks of life. The definition of the good life was under constant debate.

Similar dilemmas swirled around academe, and a lively debate about the future of higher education engaged many scholars. Were colleges to be geared to the education of individuals to prepare them to take their place, as good citizens, in society? Or were they to be more narrowly focused on learning and research? Were they to become academic centers where advanced degrees could be pursued and scholars trained to generate new knowledge? Were the classical components of the curriculum to be set aside in favor of the sciences?

Since many American professors had received training in Germany, the influence of the German universities permeated all discussions. Throughout the 1880s and 1890s, argument raged, centering on the systems and purposes of higher education and on the efficacy of German methods. Some took the view that colleges should be for undergraduates alone, teaching the standard humanistic curriculum, training the mind, molding the character, and advocating the moral life. Others thought that colleges should have graduate programs for "professional training" (i.e., law, medicine, theology); yet others claimed that there should also be research programs in all literary and scientific subjects, in the interests of new knowledge. When it came to methods and the curriculum, a strong case was repeatedly made for the introduction of the seminar and tutorial system and more courses in the sciences, on the European model. Some new institutions—Johns Hopkins University in Baltimore, for example—wholeheartedly embraced German ideas.

Martin Anderson, the president of the University of Rochester, took a different view, however. Deeply involved in these matters, he brought to the discussions his characteristically fair-minded, balanced, and positive views. On one occasion, taking the American college as his topic, he declared,

> It should always be borne in mind that a discrimination should be made between institutions—like the German gymnasia and the typical American college—which contemplate giving a certain degree of culture preparatory to professional study, and institutions—like the University of Berlin—which are a mere aggregation of professional schools, presupposing an elementary liberal training on the part of all those who are admitted to their lectures.
>
> Our American college is an indigenous growth, adapted to our population and wants, which cannot be replaced by any exotic system unadapted to our intellectual soil and climate. Its best results are secured with a comparatively small number of pupils under a discipline that is personal and paternal. It may be questioned whether some of our older

and larger institutions are not, by their very size, outgrowing the training functions proper to the American college; and whether, in their efforts to compass the results and imitate the processes of the great continental universities, they are not losing sight of the most important duties which, from the nature of our educational system, necessarily devolve upon them.[18]

At Lake Forest, the founders' vision of an educational system including preparatory, undergraduate, and graduate phases was very much alive. The new president, Rev. William Roberts, who took office in 1886, believed firmly in the place of research and graduate study in a university context and moved things forward. Professional schools in law, medicine, and dentistry were established in Chicago, and a Ph.D. program in philosophy was instituted at Lake Forest itself. Among the faculty, there was widespread admiration for the intellectual achievements of the German universities and a desire to follow the outlines of the German systems.[19]

This was not, however, the view of the staunchly Presbyterian trustees. Their thinking was heavily influenced by social and religious factors in Chicago, not least by the conduct of the labor force. The workers were protesting their conditions of work and claimed the right to an eight-hour day, a claim vigorously resisted by the bosses. An organized demonstration in 1886 turned nasty and resulted in rioting and deaths in Haymarket Square.[20] These riots, instigated by German anarchists among the workers and directed at the McCormick Reaper Works, turned the Scots and English Protestant elite decisively against the workers. This animosity carried over, however illogically, into a dislike of all things German, including German educational methods, with the result that strain developed between the German-trained professors at Lake Forest and the businessmen trustees in Chicago.[21] There was disagreement about the future of the university: should it continue to grow into a fully fledged university or retrench as a college; should it follow German models? There was disagreement about faculty responsibilities:

---

18. Remarks made at the University Convocation of the State of New York (July 14, 1876); Martin Anderson, "Voluntaryism in Higher Education," in *Documents of the Senate of the State of New York, One Hundredth Session—1887*, vol. 4, nos. 53–59, pp. 627–37. Cf. Asahel C. Kendrick, with Florence Kendrick Cooper, *Martin B. Anderson, LL.D.: A Biography* (Philadelphia: American Baptist Publication Society, 1895), 170–73.

19. Schulze, Cowler, and Miller, *Thirty Miles North*, 39.

20. Ibid., 38.

21. Cyrus McCormick Sr. was a trustee of the university from 1869 until 1884, when his son, Cyrus Jr., took his place on the board.

should faculty concentrate on research, identified by some trustees as too professional (and hence, by implication, German), or on teaching?

Francis Kelsey's views on these topics did not fall entirely into one camp. He was a firm believer in research as a means both to expand knowledge and to improve teaching. But he did not like all the German methods of teaching the ancient authors and was therefore only partially supportive of the German university system. He saw the need for more courses in the sciences, but he feared their impact on the traditional curriculum, particularly on courses in Greek and Latin. He believed in expanding the classical curriculum, that while the languages themselves were unsurpassed in imparting powers of concentration and logic and in training the memory and could therefore be critical to the practice and enjoyment of the good life in the here and now, knowledge of the contexts—historical, archaeological, artistic, and philosophical—in which the ancient authors worked was essential to the understanding of ancient life. The only solution he saw was to try to broaden the existing curriculum as far as possible while ensuring that the classics were supremely well taught at all levels. He did not wish to oppose the trustees openly; after all, as a good Presbyterian, he believed that prosperity in commerce was a mark of divine favor, and he consequently admired their success and their philanthropy. So he sat on the fence: he favored the trustees' enthusiasm for undergraduate teaching while opposing their disregard for research.

Matters came to a head between faculty and trustees in 1887, when President Roberts agreed to allow a reduced teaching load (fifteen contact hours a week was normal) to Professor James Mark Baldwin, newly appointed to head the philosophy programs, to enable Baldwin to pursue his research. The trustees did not like this. Baldwin was a distinguished research scholar already, a Princeton man with experience of German educational models, and one of the new breed of specialists. Most trustees were more comfortable with generalist gentlemen scholars who taught. There was also the fact that Baldwin was paid, as one trustee pointed out, 25 percent more than "one of my clerks." "Let him go," he went on, "we'll save money." Baldwin defended himself brightly before the board, refused their suggestions, and offered his resignation. The situation was saved only by the intervention of President Roberts, whose plans for more graduate work depended on the appointment of people like Baldwin. Yet Baldwin saw difficult times ahead and left for the University of Toronto after two years.[22]

---

22. Schulze, Cowler, and Miller, *Thirty Miles North,* 40, 74.

PUTTING IDEAS TO PRACTICE: THE TEXTBOOKS

Intrigued as he was by the debates over the future of higher education and of Lake Forest, Kelsey continued also to concentrate on the improvement of classical pedagogy. His firm views on the value of antiquity and the importance of a broad context found their natural stage in the textbooks he was busily preparing. In 1882 the February issue of the *Review* published a list of "Lake Forest University Text-Books." At the foot of the list of seven books appears the first of the spate of texts that Francis Kelsey was to introduce over the next decade and to update periodically over the length of his career:

M. TULLI CICERONIS
Cato Maior de Senectute, Laelius de Amicitia
With Introduction by James S. Reid M.A., Fellow of Gonville & Caius College, Cambridge, Examiner in Classics to the University of London. American Edition, Revised by Francis W. Kelsey, Professor of Latin in Lake Forest University. John Allyn, Publisher, Boston. (Ready in May).[23]

It was customary for young classicists to begin their scholarly careers by publishing texts of authors, paying particular attention to the text itself and little to interpretation. In revising Reid's Cicero for an American audience, Kelsey followed the professional convention of the time. But his interest in contributing to the effectiveness of Latin teaching across the country led him to expand the conventional textual (grammatical and syntactical) commentaries to include considerations of literary form and content and to involve the broader contexts offered by history, topography, and archaeology.[24]

Before his return to the United States from Europe in 1885, the second of his Latin textbooks had appeared. This was the *De Rerum Natura* of Lucretius.[25] He wrote commentaries not on all six books but only on books I, III, and V. Kelsey gave two reasons for doing so: first, since the *De Rerum Natura* was a poem, a work of art, it should be printed as a whole; second,

---

23. *LFUR* 3.2 (February 1882): 23.

24. By 1892 this book was in its fifth edition. Some idea of the freshness and usefulness of the books produced by Kelsey may be gleaned from a comparison of pages allotted to text, introduction, and notes for, for example, the *Cato Maior* (thirty-five, twenty-six, and eighty-one pages, respectively) and the *Laelius* (thirty-eight, eleven, and seventy-two). In explaining the differences between the English and American editions, Kelsey said that the introductions were reshaped and expanded, the analyses of topics were recast, and some notes were reduced while others were enlarged. A comparison of the cost of Kelsey's textbooks to the student in 1892 may be of interest: his Caesar could be obtained for $1.25, his Cicero for $1.20, his Lucretius for $1.75, and his Ovid for $1.25.

25. Francis W. Kelsey, ed., *Lucretius, "De Rerum Natura," with an Introduction and Notes to Books I, III, and V* (Boston: John Allyn, 1884).

books I, III, and V contained the pith of the argument and the finest poetry. He added a substantial introduction (fifty pages) in which he discussed three aspects of Lucretius: the man, the poet, and the philosopher. He addressed topics such as Epicureanism before Lucretius, Lucretius's Epicureanism (theories of knowledge, the universe, organic life, and man), Lucretius's impact on history, and the literary characteristics of the *De Rerum Natura*. He was attempting to expand the teaching of Lucretius to include exploration of the philosopher's life and the cultural context of his work. He was not content for users of his book, students and teachers alike, to trudge mechanically through the text, examining grammar and syntax and discussing textual criticism. There were 168 pages of notes ranging over many topics—art, philosophy, geography, nature, myth, history, and archaeology as well as grammar and syntax. As an example, one short note indicates such interests: "V.1387 '*otia dia*' i.e. an absolute and unruffled calm, like the peace of the gods. The places in the poet's mind are probably the high mountain lands, with their infrequent flocks and shepherds."

The year of the Haymarket riots, 1886, saw the publication of the first edition of Kelsey's *Caesar's "Gallic War."* Following his experiences in Germany, he had written to his publisher, John Allyn in Boston, to stress again the need for new textbooks that would make it easier for teachers and students to appreciate the literary and historical significance of the Greek and Latin they were reading. He had also taken the liberty of sending Allyn an outline for an edition of Caesar's *Gallic War* to be written in such a way, suggesting that Allyn ask an experienced teacher to write it. Mr. Allyn's response was to engage Kelsey himself to do the work. Three years later, *Caesar's "Gallic War"* was already in its fourth edition. It was described in promotional literature as exceptional for "the accuracy and consistency of the text and vocabulary, the aptness of the notes, the fulness of the Introduction and the beauty of the illustrations." A high school principal in Albany, O. D. Robinson, wrote, "the Introduction and colored plates are invaluable as aids to a clear understanding of the text and are superior. . . . The maps, notes, vocabulary and table of idioms are unsurpassed in any text book of Caesar now in use." The price of a copy was $1.25.

The seventh, expanded and revised edition (1895) demonstrates Kelsey's typical approach to a text.[26] The introduction dealt with Caesar's life as general, politician, and man of letters; the army (weapons, standards, musical in-

---

26. Francis W. Kelsey, ed., *Caesar's "Gallic War," with an Introduction, Notes, and Vocabulary,* 7th ed. (Boston: Allyn & Bacon, 1895), 499, numerous illustrations. George Bacon joined John Allyn as a partner in the firm in 1888.

struments, pay, on the march, in camp, in battle array, against fortified positions, warships); the theaters of war (Gaul, Germany, Britain); and dates. The
text (49–211), notes (215–380), a table of idioms and phrases (381–90), and a
vocabulary of 109 pages followed. There were one map, fourteen color plates,
fourteen partially colored plans, and two monochrome illustrations. The
notes were designed to intensify the interest of the student both by explaining
the grammar, syntax, and translation and by opening wider contexts, as in the
examples that follow:

> [Book I, Chapter X.8] *trans Rhodanum.* Caesar crossed to the west of the
> Rhone, and went outside the province in order to intercept or overtake the
> Helvetii who with their vast throng of women and children and loaded
> carts had gone only about 100 miles in the time that he had taken (doubt-
> less 40–50 days) to bring the five legions from Cisalpine Gaul. The Segusi-
> avi were clients of the Aedui, hence on good terms with the Romans.

> [Book I, Chapter VI.33] *singuli;* "one by one" here = "in single file." The
> narrowest point of the defile is at Pas de l'Ecluse, 19 Roman miles (nearly
> 18 English miles) below Geneva. See Plan I. This route is now traversed by
> the railway from Paris by way of Macon to Geneva.

Sometimes the notes challenge, as in the following example:

> [Book II, Chapter XIV.18] *"civitati:* why dative?"

You can almost see Kelsey's smile. It is no wonder this book, with its extraordinary range of material, ran to twenty-one editions in Kelsey's lifetime and
is still available.[27] The widespread interest in the book was remarked by Lake
Forest's student newspaper, the *Stentor,* in its initial, June 1887 issue, when it
mentioned Kelsey in a well-meaning humorous vein. Repeated inquiries were
arriving from out of town asking where translations ("ponies," "cogs") of his
Caesar could be found.[28]

Kelsey's quick decision to prepare the *Caesar* and the rapidity with which
he put it together are fine examples of his habit throughout his life of seeing
what was needed and doing it; he seldom acted purely for personal reasons.
Another example of this trait is his agreement, toward the end of his life, to
take on responsibility for a new translation of the rare 1646 edition of Hugo

---

27. Reprint edition, Eugene, OR: Wipf & Stock, 2007.
28. *Stentor* 1.1 (June 1887): 17. A "pony" was an interlined copy of a textbook with a translation handwritten in above the Latin. A "cog" was any kind of translation. At a time when
students were denied access to libraries, a good pony was worth its weight in gold. See Caroline Winterer, *The Culture of Classicism: Ancient Greece and Rome in American Intellectual Life,
1780–1910* (Baltimore: Johns Hopkins University Press, 2002).

Grotius's treatise *De Jure Belli ac Pacis,* at the request of the Carnegie Endowment for International Peace in Washington.[29] This huge task did not fall readily into any of the research avenues Kelsey normally followed; it was a labor of love or, if not of love, of conscience.

The first edition of yet another textbook, written and edited in collaboration with a colleague on the Lake Forest faculty, Andreas C. Zenos, appeared in 1889. This time Kelsey switched from Latin to Greek: the author chosen was Xenophon; the book, the *Anabasis.* This edition, published by Allyn and Bacon, followed the pattern of the other books—introduction, text, notes, table of idioms, vocabulary, and illustrations—and was prepared in much the same spirit.[30] The *Stentor* was ecstatic: "a handsome book, with such clear print and good binding. It is one of those books one wishes to almost devour."[31]

Kelsey's commentaries add depth and immediacy. Sometimes they unfold the words, suggesting ambiguities and deepening meanings. Sometimes they check the progress of the text and set up a counterpoint between text and context, between the words themselves and the mind of the narrator-poet-philosopher or archaeological or historical or mythological circumstances. They point to implication and interpretation and draw in the reader.

PERSONAL AND SCHOOL LIFE, 1886–89

If one great event of 1886 with lasting repercussions was the publication of Kelsey's edition of *De Bello Gallico,* the other was his marriage. On December 22, in Niles, Michigan, he married Mary Isabelle Badger. The Badger family lived in Niles, and Isabelle's father, Edward Stephenson Badger, was a businessman with wide interests there.[32] Isabelle had entered Lake Forest Univer-

---

29. Francis W. Kelsey, ed. and trans., with Arthur E. R. Boak, Henry Sanders, Jesse S. Reeves, and Herbert F. Wright, *Hugo Grotius, "De Jure Belli ac Pacis," Libri Tres* [1646], vol. 2 (Oxford: Clarendon, 1925).

30. Francis W. Kelsey and Andreas C. Zenos, eds., *Xenophon's "Anabasis," Books I–IV, with an Introduction, Notes and Vocabulary,* 3rd ed. (Boston: Allyn & Bacon 1892), 564, twelve illustrations and plans. The printing of all four textbooks prepared by Kelsey and published first by John Allyn and then by Allyn and Bacon during the 1880s was entrusted to John Wilson and Son at Cambridge, Massachussetts.

31. *Stentor* 3.1 (October 1889): 2.

32. Edward Stephenson Badger appears in the 1880 U.S. census records for Berrien County, in southwestern Michigan, as a resident of the First Ward of Niles City, along with his wife, Emma; his daughter Isabelle (by Charlotte, his first wife, d.1865); and a servant, Jane Thayer. He was part owner of a sawmill and a flour mill at Dowagiac Creek and thus a merchant in lumber, flour, feed, and grain; he was also a director of the First National Bank of Niles and Eminent Commander of the Niles Commandery. See Franklin Ellis, Crisfield Johnson, et al., *History of Berrien and Van Buren Counties, Michigan* (Philadelphia: D. W. Ensign, 1880).

sity as a sophomore in the fall of 1881, just one year after Francis joined the faculty: she was nineteen years old.

Listed in the *Annual Register of Lake Forest University* as Belle Badger, she showed an interest in the world of antiquity immediately, in an article on Caesar and Pompey that she wrote for the *Lake Forest University Review*.[33] Since she was drawn to the study of Latin and ancient history, it was inevitable that she should attend courses offered by the twenty-three-year-old Francis. In the spring term, the sophomore class list for the course in Roman literature reveals that her designated author was Livy (she was to give her report on May 12), while in the freshman class list for the course in Roman civilization, her topic was Roman art. Evidently she covered the freshman and sophomore curriculum in a single year. In the spring, she contributed another article to the *Review*, a plea for justice for Chinese immigrants.[34] Though the *Annual Register* for 1882–83 continues to name her as Belle, her full name, Mary Isabelle Badger, is given in her senior year (1883–84).[35] Proximity and a shared appreciation of the Roman world brought her and Francis Kelsey together; and one thing led to another.

Kelsey family lore has it that Francis bought the diamond in Isabelle's engagement ring "at the Paris Exposition." The Exposition Universelle was held every eleven years, and the closest in date to 1886 are those that took place in 1878 (when Francis was still an undergraduate at Rochester) and in 1889. Accordingly, if the family story is to be entirely believed, the acquisition of this diamond took place three years after the marriage. Given that Francis's first known visits to Europe were in the summer of 1883 and then for the academic year 1884–85, it seems that these are the times at which the diamond was more likely to have been acquired.[36] There were to be three children: Ruth, born in 1894; Charlotte, named after her grandmother on her mother's side, Charlotte Augusta Colby,[37] in 1897; and a son, Easton, named after his great grandmother on his father's side, Tryphena Annette Easton, in 1904.

---

33. *The Annual Register of Lake Forest University for the Academical Year 1881–1882* (Lake Forest, 1882) 7; *LFUR* 3.2 (December 1881): 8–9.

34. "A Plea for the Chinaman," *LFUR* 3.3 (March 1882): 27, 33.

35. *The Annual Register of Lake Forest University for the Academical Year 1882–1883* (Chicago, 1883) 7; *Annual Register, 1883–84* (Chicago, 1884) 7. It is worth noting that in the commencement honors for 1883, she was awarded the second prize in oratory.

36. I owe the information about the diamond and the ring (the date of the setting of the diamond is unknown) to Francis's grandson, Easton Kelsey ("Kel"), to whom the ring was left by his mother "for the girl of my choice," and to his wife, Joanne, who has the ring to this day.

37. Charlotte Colby (1842–65) was sister to Horace Farnham Colby, another successful miller in Dowagiac, whose son Frederick Lee Colby moved to Detroit after his marriage to Frances Berry in 1899. Frederick and Isabelle were therefore first cousins. On the Colbys, see chapter 4 n. 28 and chapter 9 nn. 102, 191.

Marriage and textbooks did not prevent Kelsey from continued ruminations on the nature and prospects of American higher education. In two issues of the *Stentor,* Kelsey contributed an article entitled "The American University."[38] The titular phrase, he there notes, covers educational institutions from the level of a high school to that of a divinity school and from the level of small-scale business courses to that of courses for original research at universities like Johns Hopkins or the University of Michigan (is he already considering a move?). On the one hand, Harvard University comprises Harvard College; schools of divinity, law, veterinary medicine, dentistry, and science; the Graduate Department; the library; the botanic gardens and herbarium; the observatory; and the museums of comparative zoology and of American archaeology and ethnology. On the other hand, the University of Rochester is a college and does not seem to aspire "to extend its facilities." Some universities have preparatory, undergraduate, and graduate courses; others have just preparatory and college departments. The typical "American university" does not exist.

Some have recently begun, he continued, to bring in the organization and methods of the German university, while others retain the college, an American product developed to meet the needs of the American people (Kelsey here echoes his old mentor, President Martin Anderson of Rochester). In the future, a university, as distinct from a college, will be recognized by its advanced professional work. On the issue of support, no help should be sought at either federal or state level, since this would expose education to political influence and the complaints of taxed citizens who receive no benefits. It is best if American private wealth takes the place of the European royal foundations and government grants. On the issue of control, trustees might best be in charge; there is a need, too, for theological faculty to promote a Christian atmosphere in accordance with founders' wishes; and feedback from the public and alumni should be sought (Kelsey is sounding very much like a conscientious Presbyterian). An orderly organization might have a college, professional schools, and schools for research in any field. There might well be four faculties: arts, theology, law, and medicine, with further subdivisions. The arrangement would be comprehensive, simple, and symmetrical.

Such views were evidently met with pleasure: the March 1888 *Stentor* reported that Kelsey had been elected alderman by "discreet citizens," and the May issue noted his appointment to the Scholarship Committee.[39] Further afield, recognition came from another quarter: his work and ideas were

---

38. *Stentor* 1.1 (June 1887): 17; 1.5 (January 1888): 107–10.
39. *Stentor* 1.7 (March 1888): 166; 1.9 (May 1888): 212.

sufficiently appreciated by the University of Rochester for them to award him the Ph.D. He wrote gratefully to President Anderson on July 2 to thank him for "informing me that the conferring of the degree of 'Doctor of Philology' is at hand. I am specially pleased at this time because I have had much to do in laying out post graduate courses in classical philology."[40] His letter shows that while fully occupied in preparing editions for the preparatory and undergraduate level and deeply involved in defining the character and nature of American education, Kelsey also helped write a curriculum and course descriptions for a graduate program in classics.

Meanwhile, in addition to teaching fifteen hours a week, he was busy with other writing projects. During early 1889, he prepared a handbook, *An Outline of Greek and Roman Mythology,* for his Boston publishers. Though the prefatory note is dated November 15, 1889, at Ann Arbor, Michigan, the main text must have been completed while he was still at Lake Forest. He explained his reasons for putting this handbook together: "students who are otherwise well read in the classics find their ideas about mythology vague and scattered, having no comprehension of the subject as a whole, or of its full significance in relation to the religious and philosophical doctrines, literature, art, and life of the Greeks and Romans."[41]

The man who wrote the textbooks and handbooks was matched by the professor who used them. Kelsey's excellence as a teacher was remarked by the January 1889 issue of the *Stentor,* which singled out both him and Professor Halsey for excellence of teaching.[42] Further testimony comes from an alumnus, "now a lawyer in one of our larger cities," who was asked what line of study pursued in his college course he now thought of the most practical advantage.

> I cannot say that I was known as a very close student in my college days, my old professors might tell you, without misrepresentation, that I verged on block-headedness at times. I was like a stone. I rolled through the Latin department and adhered to considerable of the dust of old Rome; I got some knocks from that "hard-fisted Roman peasant" whom Prof. Kelsey

---

40. Francis W. Kelsey to President Martin B. Anderson, University of Rochester, NY, July 2, 1888, University of Rochester Archives, Rush Rhees Library.

41. Francis W. Kelsey, *An Outline of Greek and Roman Mythology* (Boston: Allyn & Bacon, 1889), 3.

42. *Stentor* 2.5 (January 1889): 121: "It would pay to study closely the teaching of Prof. Halsey and Prof. Kelsey." Professor John J. Halsey, LL.D., would serve as acting president of Lake Forest University during 1896–97 and author *A History of Lake County, Illinois.*

loved so much.[43] I cannot estimate on paper the good those Latin studies are doing me today. I trust I look on all questions with larger eyes, because I saw so much of those old Roman times. And I am not saying a word about the pure discipline I received.[44]

Kelsey endeavored in other ways, too, to nourish the students: the March 1889 issue of the *Stentor* included his report on the activities of the Scholarship Committee. Four new scholarships are announced, all the result of donations, two for freshmen from trustees and two from Mr. James Scott of the *Chicago Herald* for members of any class. The conditions are described, and Kelsey issues his usual exhortation to work: "Those who wish to compete for the Herald Scholarships for the ensuing year would do well to begin to prepare at once."[45] A photograph taken on the eve of his departure from Lake Forest (it is dated June 24, 1889, on the back) captures the seriousness of purpose and some sense of the powers of concentration of the young scholar (fig. 3).

A teacher with such gifts as Kelsey's is most appreciated when about to leave. When the editors of the *Stentor* learned of his resignation from the Lake Forest faculty, they published in their July issue, "with great regret," a remarkable notice that testified to his talents and the admiration in which he was held.

> He has been with the institution for about 8 years. During the whole period he has zealously striven to advance the position of the University. He has not confined his work to the Latin department, but has always rendered most valuable assistance whenever any interests of the school have been under consideration. His ability as an editor has become national. We feel that we are wholly unable to pay a proper tribute to the professor's ability as a teacher. All who have been familiar with his classroom work know how eminently successful he has been as an instructor. Professor Kelsey has endeared himself to the students, whose best wishes he most assuredly has, as he goes to his new field in Ann Arbor.[46]

Kelsey's departure linked him to James Mark Baldwin and others in leaving Lake Forest University for institutions more firmly committed to graduate education and research. In Kelsey's case, his belief in education for all and

---

43. If he had known about Kelsey's upbringing on the farm in upper New York, he would have understood more easily Kelsey's affection for those who work the land.

44. *Stentor* 3.2 (November 1889): 43.

45. *Stentor* 2.6 (March 1889): 171.

46. *Stentor* 2.10 (July 1889): 249.

3. Cabinet portrait of Francis Kelsey dated (on the back) June 24, 1889, the photograph taken on the eve of Kelsey's departure from Lake Forest. A cabinet portrait is a large photograph mounted on a firm card and suitable for display propped up on a cabinet. Lake Forest College Special Collections, Donnelley and Lee Library. Photo: E. P. Ford of Kalamazoo, Michigan.

open to all—a belief derived from his own experience—may well have played a part.

In the fall of 1888, the Department of Latin at the University of Michigan was in a state of flux. The death in August of Professor Elisha Jones had created a great gap, felt most acutely by the head of the department, Professor Henry Frieze, whose close friend he had been for many years. Moreover, Joseph Drake, who had just been appointed instructor in Latin, was to take a leave of absence for study abroad in the following year. President James Burrill Angell[47] moved decisively to fill the gap. Among those he consulted early in 1889 was Dr. George Bacon (of Allyn and Bacon), who did not hesitate to nominate Francis Kelsey for the job. Frieze, who was impressed by Kelsey's reputation as teacher and scholar, his views on the liberating power of classical culture and the future of American higher education, and his enthusiasm for music, fully supported him. On President Angell's recommendation to the Board of Regents, Kelsey was invited to join the Michigan faculty as professor of Latin in the fall, an invitation he was not slow to accept. His appointment at Michigan rewarded the young professor for his ceaseless application to the teaching of Latin and Greek in new ways and for his commitment to the world of antiquity in all its aspects. His new position would allow him to spread his wings and would launch him on a path to a leadership role in American education.

---

47. Angell was president of the University of Michigan from 1871 to 1909 and the famous father of a famous son, James Rowland Angell, president of Yale from 1921 to 1937.

CHAPTER 3

Quickening the Pace

The First Decade at Michigan,
1889–1900

࿎

IN 1889 THE UNIVERSITY OF MICHIGAN was in the midst of a period of great growth. Student enrollments had risen from 1,534 in 1880 to 2,153 in 1889, making Michigan the largest university in the nation. It comes as no surprise to find that the success of the university had attracted attention in Washington. President Grover Cleveland had appointed University of Michigan president James Burrill Angell a member of the Fishery Commission; Professor Thomas M. Cooley of the Law Department as chair of the Interstate Commerce Commission; and a Detroit alumnus, Don Dickinson, as postmaster general. During his second term, when a Michigan alumnus, Henry Thurber, was his private secretary, Cleveland appointed other Michigan men to positions of responsibility: J. S. Morton, secretary of agriculture; Edwin Uhls, assistant secretary of state; Lawrence Maxwell, solicitor general; and William Quimby, minister to the Netherlands.[1]

Although faculty numbers across the university had increased to a healthy ninety or so, the Department of Latin was experiencing difficulties. Professor Elisha Jones had died recently; Joseph Horace Drake, appointed instructor in

---

1. Howard H. Peckham, *The Making of the University of Michigan, 1817–1992,* ed. Margaret L. Steneck and Nicholas H. Steneck (Ann Arbor: University of Michigan, Bentley Historical Library, 1994), 94, 100.

1888, was on leave in Europe; and the head of the department, Henry Frieze, was gravely ill. This was the situation when Francis Kelsey arrived to take up his duties in the fall of 1889. These responsibilities increased beyond his imagination when Professor Frieze died on December 7. Kelsey was then appointed department head. He was only thirty-one.

HENRY SIMMONS FRIEZE

Henry Simmons Frieze was an impossible act to follow. He had served as head of the Department of Latin since 1854. A man of tremendous charm and dignity, he had acted decisively when serving as interim president during 1869–71. In that period, he had initiated the construction of University Hall[2] with an appropriation from the state of one hundred thousand dollars, and he had expanded the library. A large collection (approximately ten thousand items) of books, monographs, and journals was acquired from Germany, and the cataloging of the whole library collection of about forty thousand volumes was set in motion. More significantly, Frieze had calmly, over the objections of the Medical Department and other faculty, initiated the enrollment of women.

For more than a decade in Michigan, there had been strident opposition to coeducation but equally tenacious advocacy. Following a narrow vote at the January 1870 meeting of the Board of Regents, the way was finally cleared for the admission of women. Preceded by Oberlin and by several state universities further west, Michigan was not the first to adopt this policy; but it was one of the largest universities in the nation and, with the exception of the East Coast colleges, the most prestigious and influential. Numbers of women on campus increased rapidly. In 1875 over 100 women attended the university, a figure that had grown to 445, or almost 18 percent of total enrollments, by 1890. In 1882 President Angell, a firm supporter of coeducation, happily reported that a Michigan graduate, Alice Freeman (Palmer, after her marriage), was president of Wellesley College; that she was appointed at the age of twenty-six, the youngest college president in the United States; and that no fewer than five other Michigan alumnae were faculty members at Wellesley. No further justification for the role of women in higher education was necessary.

---

2. University Hall was an imposing building comprising an auditorium seating three thousand, administrative offices for the president and regents, offices for faculty and the steward, classrooms, and a chapel. See Anne Duderstadt, *The University of Michigan: A Photographic Saga* (Ann Arbor: University of Michigan, Bentley Historical Library, 2006), 35–37.

Faced with a public education system that operated mainly at the primary level and that therefore obliged colleges to set up their own schools to prepare students for college, Frieze had introduced a policy whereby the university accredited certain Michigan schools. Accredited schools were deemed capable of providing preparatory work for college, and students from these schools would therefore gain entry to the University of Michigan more easily. This released the university from the need to provide preparatory classes, offered a persuasive incentive for schools to extend their teaching to include preparatory-level work, and made such schools more attractive to students. Frieze was the first dean of the Literary Department, appointed in 1875. He was a keen musician and had been one of the founders of the University Musical Society in 1880. He had also served a second term as interim president during President James Burrill Angell's absence as American ambassador in China (1880–82) and again for a third time from October 1887 to February 1888.

Frieze was a careful scholar and an exceptional teacher. President Angell had been his student in a prep school in the East and spoke of his talents in the following terms:

> Contact with this inspiring teacher formed an epoch in my intellectual life. He represented the best type of the modern teacher, at once critical as a grammarian and stimulating with the finest appreciation. . . . [T]here was such a glow of enthusiasm in the instructor and in the class, there was such delight in the tension in which we were kept by the daily exercises, that no task seemed too great to be encountered . . . for we now felt how the increasing accuracy of our knowledge of the structure of the language enhanced our enjoyment of the Virgil and the Cicero, whose subtle and less obvious charms we were aided by our teacher to appreciate.[3]

As well as the classics, Henry Frieze also taught sculpture, architecture, and painting and can fairly be described as the first teacher of art history in the university. Commenting on the absence of materials for illustrating lectures in classical art and antiquities, he stated as early as 1879 that the collection that he himself had begun for the university—the embryonic Museum of Art and Antiquities—was inadequate and that a university that lacked "appara-

---

3. James Burrill Angell, *The Reminiscences of James Burrill Angell* (New York: Longmans, Green, 1912), 17–18. See also idem, "A Memorial Discourse on the Life and Services of Henry Simmons Frieze, LL.D., Professor of Latin Language and Literature in the University from 1854 to 1889," address delivered at University Hall, University of Michigan, Ann Arbor, March 16, 1890, in *Selected Addresses* (New York: Longmans, Green, 1912), 155–87.

tus" of this kind was imperfectly equipped. A man of wide humanist interests, Frieze typified the very best of American nineteenth-century scholar-teachers. He was universally admired by students and colleagues, and his death late in 1889 brought a great sense of loss to the campus.

He and Francis Kelsey had much in common. Both believed in the inextricability of secondary and college education and in the need to support secondary teaching and teachers with the utmost vigor. They shared a quickening and contagious interest in music. Their interest in the worlds of Greece and Rome knew no bounds. They firmly believed in teaching the ancient literatures in the contexts in which they were written, that is, together with ancient art and architecture and, in Kelsey's case, in the context of daily life: only this way, they thought, could a sense of the civilizations and cultures of Greece and Rome be communicated.

After Frieze's death, the provision of a memorial appropriate to the man involved university-wide discussions, ending in the decision to acquire the great organ from the World's Columbian Exposition in Chicago and move it to Ann Arbor.[4] This organ, built by the Farrand and Votey Organ Company of Detroit, would be available for purchase at the close of the exposition in 1893. Nothing could celebrate the life of Henry Frieze more fittingly than a memorial organ, but the problem was the money. The estimated cost of buying, transporting, and installing the organ was fifteen thousand dollars. Francis Kelsey, Frieze's successor as head of the Department of Latin and president of the University Musical Society,[5] and Albert Stanley, the university's professor of music, were the logical choices to lead the fund-raising campaign.

Francis turned to this task with characteristic vigor. He wrote hundreds of letters, many by hand (*mea manu,* as he used to say), to Frieze's former students, colleagues, and friends. He identified individuals across the nation to lead fund drives, and he kept after them persistently. Donations and pledges

---

4. The secretary of the Bureau of Music of the Columbian Exposition, George H. Wilson, decided that music should be represented on a par with architecture, sculpture, and painting and that an organ exemplifying the great progress of organ construction in the United States should be installed in the Festival Hall. The organ contract was signed on December 1, 1892, and the work was finished within seven months. No fewer than sixty-two recitals of organ music were given during the course of the exposition, by the most distinguished American and European organists.

5. See below, "The University Musical Society." For more on the organ and its capture, see James E. Tobin, "The Frieze Memorial Organ," in *Documenting the Arts at the Bentley Historical Library,* Bentley Historical Library Bulletin 57 (Ann Arbor: University of Michigan, Bentley Historical Library, 2010), 16–20.

varied from one to five hundred dollars, but the goal was large, and the funds were slow to come. Farrand and Votey, the company of the original builders, was chosen to do the job. Its representatives and specialist builders were patient and effective. Within five months, they had taken the organ apart, moved it to Ann Arbor, and installed it in University Hall. It was formally dedicated on December 14 as a gift of friends and alumni to the university and the state and as a memorial to Professor Henry Simmons Frieze. Amid a distinguished array of speakers, Francis Kelsey made the formal presentation, as president of the society. President Angell, accepting the great organ on behalf of the university, replied. It was a dignified and worthy occasion.

At the dedication, only $8,250 of the required $15,000 had been raised; $4,000 had come from Detroit alone, where Dexter M. Ferry[6] and James E. Scripps[7] were the leading benefactors. Souvenir programs of the dedication exercises were sold, and slowly the debt was worked off; yet one year later, the sum of $6,235 was still owing, and the arrears were not fully discharged even by December 1896. But a suitable memorial to Frieze was in place, due largely to Kelsey's energy and drive.

Kelsey's fund-raising talents were soon called on again by the class of 1867. At their reunion in 1897, they visited the site of Frieze's burial in Forest Hill Cemetery, where they were surprised to find no memorial monument and immediately decided to provide one. Nothing could be more fitting, they thought, than a replica of the model of the Roman sarcophagus of Scipio Barbatus that Frieze used to keep in his classroom.[8] A subscription list was run up by the leaders of the class, who thought that five hundred dollars would do it. In fact, with Kelsey's help, over twelve hundred dollars was raised in next to no time, with which they were able to provide the handsome stone sarcophagus, still standing today (fig. 4). It was unveiled on June 21, 1899.[9]

---

6. Dexter Mason Ferry was a successful businessman who was head of one of the largest seed companies in the United States and a director of several other corporations and banks. Active for many years in state politics, he was unsuccessful in his bid to become the governor of the state. The fifteen acres or so of land he purchased in 1902 to enable the university to expand its athletic activities still bears his name, as Ferry Field.

7. James Edmund Scripps was a farm boy who came to Detroit in 1859 and worked as a journalist. In 1873 he began his own newspaper (it became the *Detroit News*) and rapidly became wealthy. He took part in the founding of the Detroit Institute of Arts and contributed to it his own collection of old masters.

8. Lucius Cornelius Scipio Barbatus, consul in 298 BC, had also served as aedile and censor and won a famous victory over the Etruscans near Volaterrae. The sarcophagus, inscribed with his epitaph in Old Latin, is in the Vatican Museums.

9. There are two collections of the papers of Francis Willey Kelsey at the University of Michigan. One, the Francis Willey Kelsey Papers, 1894–1928, at the Bentley Historical Library,

4. Memorial monument for Henry Simmons Frieze, 1898 (a replica of the sarcophagus of Scipio Barbatus, consul in 298 BC), Forest Hill Cemetery, Ann Arbor, Michigan. The inscription in English reads, in part, "erected by alumni of the University in affectionate remembrance"; that in Latin reads, "candidiorem animam terra non tulit" (see Horace *Satires* 1.5). Photo: Mary Pedley.

THE DEPARTMENT OF LATIN

Though Kelsey could not have hoped to live up to the standards that Frieze had set, he did not hesitate to try. Already in his very first semester, he insisted that the library put books on reserve for his students and arranged for some 150 books to be kept near the loan desk. This was unprecedented. Objections raised by the librarians were overcome by Kelsey guaranteeing to replace at personal expense any books lost. Unbelievably (in retrospect), it was not until 1915 that the practice of putting books on reserve for undergraduate courses was accepted as helpful enough to warrant special provision in the li-

is abbreviated in this book as FWK Papers. The second, the Papers of Francis Willey Kelsey at the Kelsey Museum of Archaeology (though currently housed at the Bentley), is abbreviated in this book as KMA Papers. In this instance, the evidence is drawn from FWK Papers, box 1, folders 2–5.

brary.[10] But by the end of 1889, it was clear that there was a new professor on campus and that new initiatives were afoot.

One of his first courses at Michigan, in the fall of 1889, was a great success. The class of fifty-eight students met forty-one times during the semester (which ran until early February). Focusing on the Roman poet Horace, the class branched out from language and literary analysis to examine different aspects of Roman life. More precisely, not only studying the language, style, and thought of the author, the students also investigated the times in which he lived, through the history and archaeology of the period. Students therefore both studied the Latin and wrote papers on topics as widely different as the Roman house, Roman law, Roman agriculture, Roman dress, Roman luxury, and so on. A bibliography of 197 items was put together, and the course outline was published as a pamphlet by the Register Press in Ann Arbor.[11] To reinforce the importance of the physical context of the languages, a classical fellowship that included the study of archaeology was set up. This broader approach to teaching Latin was guided and inspired by a forceful leader.

Charged, then, in early 1890, with the leadership of the department, Kelsey brought to the task new vigor, enormous enthusiasm, and a bright intellect. He was familiar with the German model of the university and admired many of its aspects. He believed in the value of the new sciences and the adjustment of the classical curriculum to make room for them, but not in any arrangement that might lead to a diminution of the position of prominence and prestige that the classics enjoyed.

At once, he determined to continue the practice, so successfully begun in the Horace course in the fall, of assigning other than literary topics to each student, thus integrating the study of language and literature with the study of contemporaneous historical circumstances. Instructors were to require students to research and write papers about their chosen subjects. Where

---

10. Kelsey always worked to improve the library, not least by increasing the collection. A minute of the November 1896 meeting of the university's Board of Regents records a request from Kelsey for acknowledgment of a gift of books and of a graduate fellowship. Addressed to President Angell, it begins by framing a suggestion as a question: "Would it not be well to ask the Board of Regents to make formal acknowledgment of the following gifts to the University: . . . ." President Angell evidently appreciated the style of this approach. See University of Michigan, *Proceedings of the Board of Regents (1896–1901)*, "November Meeting, 1896" (November 18), 5.

11. "Outlines in Roman Archaeology and Life by Members of the Class in Horace, 1st Semester, 1889–1890" (Ann Arbor: Register Press, 1890). The general idea of teaching text and context together had been advanced before, as early as Professor Boise and his sophomore Greek class of 1853, but had never before been pursued with such energy and success.

classes were small enough, the German seminar method was embraced.[12] A distinct innovation in the department was weekly meetings of all instructors, assistants, and graduate students at which each reviewed a periodical previously assigned to them. In this way, the department kept abreast of the most recent developments in the field.

In 1891 the first Michigan Ph.D. in Latin and Greek was awarded, and the university's first graduate seminar in Roman archaeology was offered.[13] Other new courses at Michigan, introduced over the period 1890–91 and taught by Kelsey, included a course entitled "Seminary in Latin Philology," given in both semesters, and another entitled "Methods, Province, and Scope of Classical Philology." The year 1892 witnessed the award of the first Michigan Ph.D. in Latin alone. Kelsey was setting a rapid pace.

For such innovations and the demands of an accelerated pace, help was needed in an understaffed department. Joseph Drake returned from leave in Europe in 1890 and was promoted to assistant professor. That same year marked the arrival of John Carew Rolfe, who would go on to a distinguished career at the University of Pennsylvania in 1902. Other appointments followed. Henry Sanders, later to be Kelsey's stalwart colleague in the publication of the Michigan Humanistic Series, joined the faculty in 1893; so did Clarence Meader, who became the mainstay of the department's undergraduate teaching and principal liaison with the high schools across the state. Equally significant was the appointment of Walter Dennison—a native of Saline, Michigan, and himself a graduate of the department—as instructor in Latin in 1897.[14] More new courses were introduced, in Latin inscriptions (Rolfe), ancient history (Drake), the *Institutes* of Justinian (Meader), and Latin paleography (Dennison). By the end of the decade, six doctorates and twenty-three master's degrees had been awarded. Kelsey had gathered an impressive cohort of colleagues.

---

12. This method had been introduced at Michigan by the historian C. K. Adams in 1869: each student delivered a research paper to the others, seated in a circle, and then suffered a barrage of comments from the instructor and the other participants.

13. The seminar was titled "Topography and Architectural History of the City of Rome and Sculpture and Painting in the Roman Period."

14. Dennison had spent three years (1894–97) studying in Germany and Italy and was instrumental in the acquisition of inscriptions and other archaeological materials for the university. He served as instructor at Michigan in 1897–99 and as assistant professor at Oberlin during 1899–1902. He returned to Michigan as junior professor of Latin in 1902, but after another year in Rome as professor at the American School of Classical Studies (1908–9), he moved on in 1910 to become chair of the Department of Greek and Latin at Swarthmore College (1910–17).

Kelsey's determination in building the department may be seen in the tenacity with which he pursued Dennison's appointment in 1897, through a request lodged directly with Regent Levi Barbour.[15] Francis was not shy about communicating directly with President Angell or with the Board of Regents, whether about appointments in classics or in other fields where he saw the need. Such interest is amply reflected in the series of requests made by him and others in 1898 for the appointment of an assistant professor of fine arts.[16] The minutes of the regents' meetings are in fact peppered with Kelsey's determined requests, not all of which were for money or for appointments. Many were for acknowledgment from the regents of gifts to the university. For example, in November 1899, he asked the regents to acknowledge Henry Glover's gift of the de Criscio collection of Latin inscriptions; and in June 1900, he requested that a message of appreciation be sent to a long list of contributors to the fund for the plaster casts of the Arch of Trajan at Benevento. The total cost of the casts, shipment, and insurance was in excess of $1,780, of which $303 came from the class of 1896, $544 from the budget of the Latin Department, and the balance from contributors to the Detroit Archaeological Fund. Prominent contributors included such Detroit worthies as Theodore D. Buhl,[17] Dexter M. Ferry, Charles Lang Freer, Colonel Frank J. Hecker,[18] and James Scripps, all of them Kelsey's acquaintances.

Kelsey's output in publication continued to offer a model of industry to the others. He reworked the results of the course he had initiated in the fall of 1889 into a teaching and research aid in Roman antiquities. The preface was signed in September 1890, but the book was not available until the following year.[19] It included such topics as the Roman family, Roman musical instru-

---

15. Recorded in the minutes of the January 1897 meeting of the board.

16. Minutes of the regents' meetings for February, April, and December 1898; despite Kelsey's tenacity, a professor of fine arts was not appointed until 1910.

17. Buhl was a multimillionaire manufacturer and capitalist. Son of Detroit mayor Christian Buhl and nephew of Detroit mayor Frederick Buhl, he was president of numerous companies, including the Buhl Malleable Iron Works, the Buhl Stamping Company, the Buhl and Sons Hardware stores, the Detroit National Bank, and the pharmaceutical company Parke-Davis (now Pfizer).

18. Hecker and Freer, colleagues in early life in railroad management in Indiana, moved to Detroit in the late 1870s and founded the Peninsular Car Company. This company built railroad cars and merged with the Michigan Car Company in 1892 to become the most prosperous producer of railroad cars in the country. In later life, Freer became an avid art collector, and he left much of his collection to the Smithsonian Institution in Washington.

19. Francis W. Kelsey, *Fifty Topics in Roman Antiquities, with References* (Boston: Allyn & Bacon, 1891), 101 pages, prefatory note on 3–4.

ments, early Christian art in Rome, and the Roman art of war. Another aid on Latin literature, employing the same format of topics and bibliography, followed rapidly.[20] Hot on the heels of these two came another author textbook. Turning his attention to Ovid, Kelsey produced an edition that displayed many of the same traits as his others. In the following year (1892), Kelsey produced yet another illustrated and annotated text: selections of Cicero's letters and orations. He continued his successful format: a long introduction described Cicero's life and provided outlines of the speeches, the circumstances of their delivery, and the contexts of the letters. The speeches, Kelsey said, throw light on legal procedures, forms of government, and the whole environment of the orator, while the letters give glimpses of Cicero's private life, revealing more of Cicero the man than Cicero the politician.[21] In the space of ten years, Kelsey had published no fewer than six new textbooks, all of which enjoyed several new editions: by 1896 his edition of Cicero's *De Senectute* and *De Amicitia* was in its sixth edition; his Lucretius, its third; his Caesar, its seventh; his Ovid, its third; his edition of Cicero's letters and orations, its fourth; and his Xenophon, its fourth.

One of the busiest bees in Henry Frieze's bonnet had been the standard of teaching in the high schools. As interim president of the university during 1869–71, he had introduced the policy of granting high school accreditation. This entailed the university monitoring standards across the state so as to grant or withhold accreditation. Faculty committees had to agree to visit high schools, and high schools had to agree to let them come, so some diplomacy was involved. But graduates of accredited schools entered the university without examination, a desirable attribute for any public high school, and so standards of teaching rose. Frieze had signaled his interest in teaching skills some ten years earlier by publishing recommendations for a preparatory Latin course and, starting in 1859, a class in the ancient languages for those aspiring to teach in Union and high schools. This may have been the first course in the United States to be given on the subject, and this "Teachers' Class" was later (1884) renamed the "Teachers' Seminary." Pedagogy had arrived.

Kelsey took up Frieze's mantle eagerly. Although committed to the importance of research, he nevertheless was sure that the future of classical

---

20. Francis W. Kelsey, *Topical Outline of Latin Literature, with References* (Boston: Allyn & Bacon, 1891), 47 pages.

21. Francis W. Kelsey, ed., *Select Orations and Letters of Cicero, with an Introduction, Notes, and Vocabulary* (Boston: Allyn & Bacon, 1892), 513 pages (of which 142 were vocabulary).

studies as a steadying and satisfying force in American culture depended on the aptitudes, strength, and skills of the teachers in the secondary schools. Convinced that early exposure to the languages was beneficial, he became a keen proponent of introducing Latin in the seventh and eighth grades and of beginning Greek before college. He firmly believed that active cooperation among all those teaching Greek and Latin and the classical cultures, whether at high school or college, would yield the best results.

With this in mind, he helped launch the Michigan Classical Conference in 1895, as an additional activity of the Michigan Schoolmasters' Club. Founded in 1886, the Schoolmasters' Club met every spring.[22] Its membership already included both schoolteachers and professors, but its proceedings focused rather narrowly on teaching methods. The Michigan Classical Conference, which fully endorsed discussion of all problems encountered in the classroom, wished to add research topics to the discussions. So it offered opportunities for members to give papers on their research activities, and it anticipated that meritorious research papers would be published alongside other reports of the club in the *School Review*. As the years passed, many papers were published in various forms, including a volume of the more important scholarly papers and addresses.[23] From the very first meeting of the conference, distinguished scholars were invited from outside Michigan to address issues of both research and pedagogy.[24]

In 1916 the program of the Michigan Classical Conference expanded beyond the customary papers of twenty minutes' duration to include plays put on by the University of Michigan Classical Club. That year, Plautus's *Menaechmi* was performed in Latin, accompanied by a libretto with stage directions and an English translation on facing pages. In 1917 Euripides's *Iphigenia in Tauris* was performed in Greek.[25] The *Iphigenia* was a remarkably ambitious production accompanied by music written for the play by Professor Albert A. Stanley and choreographed by Professor Herbert A. Kenyon. Further expansion of the program came in 1917, when the idea of a short course (not more than four lectures) was introduced. The inaugural short course, on Roman private life, was given that year by Professor Ralph

---

22. John Dewey (1859–1952), the famous philosopher, psychologist, social critic, and political activist, who taught at Michigan during 1884–94, had been a founding member.

23. Francis W. Kelsey, ed., *Latin and Greek in American Education, with Symposia on the Value of Humanistic Studies* (New York: Macmillan, 1911; 2nd ed., 1927).

24. For example, the first meeting in 1895 was addressed by Professor Andrew F. West of Princeton and by Professor William Hale of the University of Chicago.

25. Herbert H. Yeames, "Iphigenia in Michigan," *Nation*, April 19, 1917, reprinted in *Classical Weekly* 10.26 (May 7, 1917).

Magoffin of Johns Hopkins University, followed the next year by Professor Gordon Laing of the University of Chicago, whose topic was Roman religion. Francis Kelsey had a hand in or personally attended the conference every year until his death, in 1927.

THE UNIVERSITY MUSICAL SOCIETY

In another sphere, too, Kelsey took over work that Henry Frieze had initiated. In 1880 Frieze had helped found the University Musical Society (UMS) and in the preceding year when four Ann Arbor church choirs, which came to be called the Choral Union, had linked up to sing excerpts from Handel's *Messiah,* Frieze had provided the accompanying music on the organ. Eager to promote musical interest in the university and Ann Arbor, Frieze thought that the UMS could capture both audiences. At first it consisted mainly of university professors and instructors, but it gradually grew to include more and more townspeople and indeed citizens of Detroit. A keen musician himself, Frieze played the organ and the piano and was a member of a chamber music trio; music in fact could be heard almost every evening in his house;[26] and now there was to be music for the students and the general public, too. Astonishing as it may seem, there was no School of Music formally incorporated in the university until 1929. Music had, however, appeared in the curriculum of the Literary Department in 1880, the very same year in which Frieze had helped found the UMS. It was taught by a newly appointed instructor, Calvin B. Cady, who sought permission to give music lessons to private pupils outside his university teaching commitments. When this was granted, the Ann Arbor School of Music opened its doors, as a department of the UMS, in 1881. However, this private school faltered during the 1880s for lack of funds, and the society's directors had to step in.

In 1891 the UMS established a new school, with a new name: the University School of Music. This school was much more securely funded (by subscription), but it, too, had problems: it lacked suitable rooms. So a group of Ann Arbor citizens put together a School of Music Building Association in 1893. This association issued shares of stock to some two hundred firms and individuals, raised twenty-five thousand dollars, bought a site at 325 Maynard

---

26. Music was such a large part of his life that when badgered by editors for his book on Virgil, the only way he could concentrate on his Latin was by moving the piano out of the house.

5. University School of Music, 325 Maynard Street, Ann Arbor, 1893, built, owned, and managed by the University Musical Society, wholly independent of the University of Michigan. Post card, courtesy Anne Duderstadt, Ann Arbor.

Street, and erected a brand-new building (fig. 5). It is easy to detect the hand of Francis Kelsey in this maneuver: as the president of the UMS, he was becoming familiar with the need for fund-raising. The school prospered and regularly held graduation exercises, which were reported in the press and at which Kelsey presided, but it remained outside the formal purview of the University of Michigan.[27] Kelsey strove, time and again, to get the Board of Regents to incorporate it in the university, but not until 1929—following the transfer of the property at 325 Maynard to the UMS in 1925—was the title handed over. Thereupon the School of Music finally became an accepted, integrated academic unit of the university.

A year before Kelsey arrived in Ann Arbor, Albert Stanley (b. 1851) had been appointed professor of music and director of the Choral Union. It was Stanley who envisioned a festival of music in Ann Arbor in May as a grand finale to the year's concerts. Enthusiastically endorsed by Kelsey and the board of the UMS, the first May Festival took place in 1894, with three con-

27. The University School of Music is listed in the 1899 Ann Arbor Directory immediately after the University of Michigan, even though it had no formal association with the university. The school mustered thirteen faculty members and offered instruction in piano, violin, cello, voice, organ, flute, mandolin, and guitar.

certs in two days. Special trains from Detroit were laid on, and accommodations were provided in Ann Arbor: they thought big in those days. The reaction was uniformly positive, and the enthusiasm for the music generated was so compelling and continuous that the program was later (in 1919) increased to six concerts in four days. This popular festival continued for many years, ceasing operations only in 1995.

ITALY

Having successfully established himself at the University of Michigan during his first three years heading the Department of Latin, Kelsey took leave in 1892–93. His appetite whetted by his previous trips to Europe, his first purpose was to pursue research in Italy (see fig. 6). A second incentive was the acquisition of more teaching and research materials for the university. To the acquisition of such materials, he applied the same zeal he had brought to the provision of books. Following once more in Frieze's footsteps, he set out to find objects of art, artifacts, and photographs to improve the university's teaching and research.[28]

In 1893 he visited Tunisia and acquired from the French authorities in Carthage and from dealers in Tunis a number of ancient lamps, pots, and building materials. These he augmented by visits to dealers in Sicily, Naples, and Rome from whom he purchased more materials illustrating Roman daily life and social history: pots, terra-cotta figurines, objects of glass, painted stucco, funerary markers, and a single inscription in Latin.[29] In all, he shipped more than a thousand objects back to Ann Arbor, and he thus greatly increased the collection of ancient Greek and Roman materials at Michigan. In the years immediately following his return to Ann Arbor, he was too busy to return to Europe himself. His university and other professional commitments—as well as the birth of his first child, Ruth Cornelia, on July 3, 1894, and another daughter, Charlotte Badger, on April 19, 1897—kept his hands full. Yet the acquisition of teaching and research materials did not falter.

Even though anchored in Ann Arbor, Kelsey was still able to act through

---

28. Between 1893 and 1903, Kelsey purchased thousands of photographs, patronizing especially Giorgio Sommer, a German photographer in Naples who specialized in images of material in the Naples Archaeological Museum and in views of archaeological monuments and sites, not least Pompeii.

29. The precise provenance of most objects acquired from dealers was unknown, but Kelsey carefully records that the first fragment of a brick stamp (an inscribed brick) to enter the Michigan collections was bought by him on the island of Capri, from an old woman on the road to the Villa Jovis.

6. Francis Kelsey in conversation with a friend at Pompeii, 1892–93. Kelsey Museum of Archaeology, University of Michigan, 128.

friends and colleagues. In 1898 Clarence Meader acquired more than three hundred artifacts in Rome, and in 1899 Duane R. Stuart, instructor in Latin, acquired thirty-four Roman lamps for the study collection. Particularly helpful was Walter Dennison, his former student at Michigan, who was in Europe during 1894–97. Following a year at the University of Bonn in Germany, Dennison spent two years in Rome as one of the first fellows of the recently founded American School of Classical Studies in Rome. Dennison visited Naples and Pompeii in 1897, where he learned that the parish priest of Puteoli, Canon Giuseppe de Criscio, was willing to part with his collection of antiquities. This varied collection included inscriptions on stone, which yielded information about the Roman fleet at Misenum and details of the local cursus honorum. There were also a few brick stamps (baked building bricks with an incised maker's stamp). All the de Criscio material came from neighboring districts to the immediate west of Naples: Puteoli, Misenum, Cumae, and Baiae. Thus, though the precise provenance of the objects was not recorded, it offered new light on the social history of a particular area.

Dennison immediately wrote to Kelsey, who in turn wrote to W. W. Bishop, another of the fellows at the American School of Classical Studies, asking him to send copies of the inscriptions to him. When he had seen the copies, Kelsey wrote that Dennison should declare the university's interest while Kelsey searched for a donor. The money was found,[30] and the results of Dennison's negotiations were that he himself was able to publish some of the inscriptions in 1898[31] and that over 250 of the inscriptions arrived in Ann Arbor in 1899.[32] Kelsey, surprised that the Italians allowed some of the more significant inscriptions to be exported, remarked in a message to Dennison that "the outcome of this aspect of the negotiations must be credited to Professor Mau."[33]

August Mau was a well-known nineteenth-century German archaeologist and librarian, whose important book *Pompeji in Leben und Kunst* Francis Kelsey translated, with some modifications. So rapid was Kelsey's work and so efficient the New York publisher that the book appeared in English in 1899, a year before the German edition (1900).[34] Mau had moved to Italy in 1872 for health reasons and became secretary of the Deutsches Archäologisches Institut in Rome. The Italian excavations at Pompeii were in full swing, and it fell to Mau to study, under the eagle eye of historian and archaeologist Theodor Mommsen, the flood of emerging inscriptions. This work required Mau's presence at Pompeii for a good part of the summers, where he familiarized himself with the site and its buildings; he spent the winters in Rome, working up the inscriptions in the institute's library, the catalog of which he helped publish.[35]

---

30. The benefactor was Henry P. Glover of Ypsilanti. See University of Michigan, *Proceedings of the Board of Regents (1896–1901)*, "November Meeting, 1899" (November 17), 458–59.

31. Walter Dennison, "Some New Inscriptions from Puteoli, Baiae, Misenum, and Cumae," *American Journal of Archaeology* (hereinafter *AJA*) 2 (1898): 373–98.

32. University of Michigan, *Proceedings of the Board of Regents (1896–1901)*, "November Meeting, 1899" (November 17), 459.

33. Wilfred B. Shaw, ed., *The University of Michigan, an Encyclopedic Survey*, vol. 4, part 8, *The Museums and Collections* (Ann Arbor: University of Michigan Press, 1942), 1474.

34. August Mau, *Pompeji in Leben und Kunst* (Leipzig: W. Engelmann, 1900), ed. and trans. Francis W. Kelsey as *Pompeii: Its Life and Art* (New York: Macmillan, 1899). For more on Mau and Kelsey, see chapter 2, "First Impressions."

35. August Mau, *Katalog der Bibliothek des Kaiserlich Deutschen Archäologischen Instituts in Rom*, 2 vols. (Rome: Löscher, 1902), rev. ed. by Eugen von Mercklin [and Friedrich Matz] (Rome: Löscher, 1913–14; reprint, Berlin: Walter de Gruyter, 1930–32). Mau's affection for Pompeii (and Kelsey's, for that matter) reflects Goethe's comment that not many disasters have given as much pleasure to posterity as the destructions caused by the eruption of Vesuvius: see Norman Douglas, *Old Calabria*, 6th ed. (New York: Harcourt Brace, 1956), 246.

While in Pompeii, Mau had met the director of the excavations, Giuseppe Fiorelli. It was a serendipitous moment when Fiorelli encouraged him to turn his attention to the wall paintings, the result of which was his magisterial study *Geschichte der decorativen Wandmalerei in Pompeji*.[36] His conclusions regarding the styles and changes of style over time in the paintings at Pompeii still provide a framework for the study of Roman wall painting. He was a voracious reader, a diligent scholar, and a careful publisher. Aside from his contributions to the study of Roman wall painting, he wrote many authoritative articles and reports in the *Römische Mitteilungen,* the official publication of the Deutsches Archäologisches Institut. In 1893 he published *Führer durch Pompeji,*[37] followed by the monumental *Pompeji in Leben und Kunst.*

In the preface to the first edition of *Pompeii: Its Life and Art,* Kelsey is careful to point out that the book is not a translation of a book already in print. It is a new work published first in English, a translation of a book written in German but yet to appear.[38] As well as text, the book includes Mau's interpretations of the excavated buildings in the form of drawings and restorations, which Kelsey insists "are not fanciful. They were made with the help of careful measurements and computations based on the existing remains."[39] Kelsey does, however, concede that the author occasionally resorts to the evidence of wall paintings and reliefs for help with the restoration of a building. With Mau's agreement, Kelsey deleted some passages and added others, and Kelsey concludes his preface by saying that "the preparation of the English form of the volume, undertaken for reasons of friendship, has been less a task than a pleasure."[40]

Both Mau and Kelsey signed the preface to the second edition in Pompeii on August 2, 1901. They point out that the book was "revised on the spot" and that the new edition includes discussions of buildings recently discovered, new restorations, and some new illustrations. They note those parts of the book, including the concluding chapter, that were written by Kelsey.[41] A letter from Kelsey to Thomas Spencer Jerome in 1913 indicates Kelsey's never-realized intention to prepare a third edition, as well as a sense of the collegiality

---

36. August Mau, *Geschichte der decorativen Wandmalerei in Pompeji* (Berlin: G. Reimer, 1882).

37. August Mau, *Führer durch Pompeji* (Naples: F. Furchheim, 1893).

38. Kelsey, *Pompeii: Its Life and Art,* v. In addition to the twenty-two pages of preliminary material, Kelsey's book has 509 pages, including 263 figures, twelve plates, and six plans.

39. Ibid., vii.

40. Ibid.

41. August Mau and Francis W. Kelsey, "Preface to the Second Edition," in Kelsey, *Pompeii: Its Life and Art,* 2nd ed. (New York: Macmillan, 1902), viii.

and affection that existed between Kelsey and Mau.[42] The book remains an important resource a century later and has recently (2007) been made available online in PDF form by individual chapters.[43] This book, a culmination of Mau's years of direct observation and dedicated scholarship, along with his work on the wall paintings, solidified Mau's reputation as one of the most distinguished Romanists of his generation. Mau died in March 1909. Sometime later, a group of his colleagues undertook to raise money for a memorial and contacted Kelsey, whose letter soliciting help appeared on May 12, 1910, in the *Nation*. Describing a bronze bust of Mau to be erected at Pompeii, he expressed hope that American sources would provide two hundred dollars toward the cost. Kelsey led the way in securing most of these funds.[44]

Pompeii: Its Life and Art marked Kelsey as the American scholar who understood Pompeii more profoundly than any other. This reputation conceivably led to his appointment to the professorship at the American School of Classical Studies in Rome for the academic year 1900–1901 and, more certainly, to numerous invitations to lecture throughout the United States after his return from Rome.

THE PRESBYTERIAN CHURCH

Kelsey's attention during his early years in Ann Arbor was not entirely focused on the ancient world. The present was very much with him in his grow-

---

42. " I must come to Italy to revise the Mau Pompeii.... The task will be saddened by the loss of that companionship which I count among the happiest of my own years of scholastic work" (Kelsey to Jerome, May 10, 1913, Bentley Historical Library, University of Michigan, Papers of Thomas Spencer Jerome [hereinafter PTSJ], box 1.1.34).

43. For the online version of the second edition, see http://academic.depauw.edu/~pfoss/Mau/maukelsey.html (accessed September 19, 2008).

44. Kelsey suggested that leading American universities contribute $10 each, with smaller institutions offering smaller amounts. He also hoped that students who had heard Mau lecture at the American School of Classical Studies in Rome (Mau had lectured there every year from the school's foundation until his death) would contribute $1 apiece. He got hold of a list of all students who had attended the school up to 1909 and wrote hundreds of letters. The money trickled in: $11 from Yale, $2 from Cornell, and many $1 gifts. Money also came from unexpected sources—his publishers: $5 from Paul Bacon at Allyn and Bacon in Boston and $10 from George Brett at Macmillan in New York. On February 5, 1912, he was able to write to the director of the school in Rome, saying that $176.75 of the $200 was in hand and expressing the hope that the balance could be found in Rome. In the *Classical Weekly* of October 11, 1913 (vol. 7, no. 2), Walter Dennison reported that a bronze bust of Mau, with a suitable inscription describing him, inter alia, as "indagatori sagacissimo," had been set up at Pompeii close to the entrance to the excavations (KMA Papers, Professional Organizations and Meetings Series, box 44, folder 1).

ing family (he had two daughters as of 1897)[45] and in his church. In the latter, he showed that he had not left Lake Forest far behind. The Lake Forest students' *Stentor*, quoting one of his letters, reported that "the professor's friends will be pleased to learn that he and Mrs. Kelsey find their new surroundings at Ann Arbor very congenial."[46] A further issue of the *Stentor* mentions that he had initiated a series of Sunday-afternoon talks at the First Presbyterian Church.[47] Kelsey's theme was the "rational basis of Christian belief," for which he had prepared a list of references on Christian evidences, which the students published, along with outlines of the talks, in pamphlet form.

Kelsey's affinity for the Presbyterian Church had been welcome to the leaders of the community in Lake Forest and well known. His advocacy of the role of the church in students' lives was clear in the pages of the *Stentor*. On occasion, when visiting his parents at Churchville, he had returned to preach at his church in Rochester, where his sermons were well received. Moreover, Cyrus McCormick Jr., one of the most generous supporters of the Lake Forest enterprise, was impressed enough by Kelsey's character to ensure, at a later date, that he was invited to join the board of directors of the McCormick Theological Seminary in Chicago, the leading Presbyterian seminary in the West.[48]

Kelsey was a man the Presbyterians could count on. He attended church regularly when in the United States and whenever he could when abroad. He participated wholeheartedly in its activities. He believed in the religious teachings of Presbyterianism, as guides to good habits and good conduct. He had expressed his views vigorously both in Rochester and at Lake Forest, and he continued to do so in Ann Arbor. Major concerns for him were the welfare of Michigan students from Presbyterian families and the relationship between the church and state universities—in particular, between the church and the University of Michigan.

On the face of it, the situation in Ann Arbor was healthy. In 1887 the Michigan Synod had reiterated its concern for the spiritual well-being of Presbyterian students and had endorsed the prospect of taking care of university students. It had approved the Tappan Presbyterian Hall Association in Ann Arbor, formed for the benefit of Presbyterian students at the university and named after Henry Philip Tappan, a Presbyterian minister and the university's first president. The association's purpose, as articulated by the 1887

---

45. See above, "Italy."
46. *Stentor* 3.3 (November 1889): 45.
47. *Stentor* 3.6 (March 1890): 145.
48. See also chapter 4, "Community Involvement."

synod, was "to bring the Presbyterian students of the University of Michigan into close acquaintance and more intimate communion with each other, to confirm the faith of students coming from Presbyterian families, to promote the spiritual welfare of members of the Association and increase their influence in advancing the cause of Christianity."[49]

Almost at once, the Tappan Association received two enormous gifts. Harriet Louise Doe Sackett gave the church her house and its large lot at the corner of Huron and State streets (a prominent and convenient location) "for the sole and only purpose, use and benefit" of the association, "as a permanent memorial to her dear, departed and only son, Walter A. Sackett."[50] Her son had died young, years earlier. Before Harriet died, in 1892, she was to learn of another remarkable gift. Adjacent and linked by a corridor to the Sackett house, now renamed Sackett Hall, a new big building was to go up, called McMillan Hall after the Honorable James McMillan, a U.S. senator from Michigan (1889–1902). Sackett Hall became a student residence and a place for student meetings and study, while the purpose-built McMillan Hall was equipped with a library, an auditorium, a bowling alley, and a gymnasium. This was a real innovation in a period when the university had no gymnasiums,[51] no dormitories (for men or women), and no unions where students could get together and socialize.

The Tappan Association sponsored courses and lectures in which Kelsey played his part. Attempting to link church and university more closely, he had given, as early as his first year in Ann Arbor, a course of lectures in the church for association students. In the very same year, he had conducted what a church elder, William Campbell, described in his diary as "a very large Bible class."[52] Kelsey continued to campaign for church and university collaboration in no uncertain terms: "[T]he responsibility of supplementing the resources of state universities on the religious side rests on God-fearing men

49. María E. Montoya and Roderick M. Hills Jr., *First Presbyterian Church and the Larger World* (Ann Arbor: First Presbyterian Church, 2005), 39. These sentiments chimed well with Francis's thoughts and were echoed by a trustee some years later (1937): "The Association was the pioneer organization among Presbyterian churches in America especially created to look after the religious and spiritual welfare of students in state universities" (Lila Miller, Robert M. Warner, and Carl R. Geider, eds., *The First Presbyterian Church of Ann Arbor, Michigan, 1826–1988, Incorporating "A Sesquicentennial History," 1976* [Ann Arbor: First Presbyterian Church, 1988], 12). The Tappan Presbyterian Hall Association is more frequently referred to as the Tappan Presbyterian Association, the Tappan Association, or the Association.

50. Miller, Warner and Geider, eds., *The First Presbyterian Church*, 12.

51. The Waterman Gymnasium was built in 1894, the Barbour Gymnasium in 1903.

52. Miller, Warner, and Geider, *First Presbyterian Church of Ann Arbor*, 69.

and women who appreciate the menace to American society that lurks in the dissociation of advanced learning from things of the spirit. No religious body has more at stake in this matter than the Presbyterian Church."[53] He was afraid that students, away from home and the influence of their home churches, would fall prey to the lures of the intellect and/or the flesh, and he felt bound to argue the case for church involvement. Such concerns cast him as a man of principle, strong willed and determined.

In 1895 he was invited to address the Michigan Synod of the Presbyterian Church at Adrian, his topic being the Presbyterian Church and the University of Michigan. His call to arms exhorted the church to pay more attention to the Presbyterian students in Ann Arbor. He deprecated the church's reasons for ignoring the state universities, refusing to accept the argument that state universities would not last, that they produced few ministers, or that the moral tone in these schools was low. He retorted that these universities were the logical continuation of the secondary system of public education, "the corner-stone of our civic life, and . . . fundamental to our civilization."[54] Yet he readily admitted that a new danger existed: the danger that the students' spiritual lives might wither in the face of devotion to the pursuit of knowledge.

Kelsey outlined, in remarkably prophetic terms, his vision of the future for state universities, what they would look like, and the opportunities they would present. "Our higher education is now in a process of differentiation and rapid development," he said. "According to present tendencies the university of the future will be an aggregation of schools for specialists, or professional schools, among which a philosophical faculty, *represented to-day by the so-called graduate school,* will hold a prominent place. After a time, a full undergraduate course will be reckoned equally essential as a preparation for all advanced studies."[55] He did not minimize the cost or the fact that public monies would be needed.

He described the situation of the Presbyterian students at Michigan, their numbers and organization. Membership in the Tappan Association had grown from 401 in 1894 to 475 in 1895: thus, at the time he was speaking, one in every six students at the university was a Presbyterian.[56] The association had received gifts amounting to forty-two thousand dollars, the major contributors being Mrs. Sackett (twelve thousand) and the Honorable James

53. Montoya and Hills, *First Presbyterian Church and the Larger World,* 37.

54. Francis W. Kelsey, "The Presbyterian Church and the University of Michigan," published as a supplement to the *Michigan Presbyterian,* August 13, 1896, 19.

55. Ibid., 16; italics mine.

56. Ibid., 7–8 and table I on 28.

McMillan (twenty-one thousand).[57] Surely, Kelsey argued, the Presbyterian Church in Michigan, blessed in material resources and ministered by educated and powerful men, could send a pastor to the university to teach Bible courses. There was a golden opportunity to nourish and guide the students.

He ended with a direct challenge. In the rhetoric of Presbyterian fire and brimstone, he lambasted his audience by declaring, "If Presbyterian students come to Ann Arbor . . . and . . . let the training of intellect choke out the spiritual life, . . . their blood will be required at your hands. . . . Confronted thus, will you have the shadow of an excuse to offer in justification of your indifference and neglect?"[58] Such forthrightness did not always work to Kelsey's advantage, but his admirers called it honest plain speaking and thought him all the more courageous for it.

For Kelsey, the relationship between the state universities and the churches was a recurring topic on the national scene. As he noted, Thomas Jefferson had written to a friend in 1822 regarding the University of Virginia, "In our University you know there is no professorship of divinity. A handle has been made of this to disseminate an idea that this is an institution, not merely of no religion, but against all religion."[59] In Kelsey's time, this notion of hostility to the church was evidently still in the air. To put these anxieties to rest, President Angell invited the presidents of other state universities to join him in the fall of 1896 in taking a religious census of students, and for comparative purposes, he asked the Presbyterian colleges (as the most numerous of the denominational colleges) to conduct a similar census. Statistics were collected from sixteen state universities and thirty-six Presbyterian colleges; but before all were gathered, in the summer of 1897, Angell accepted the invitation of President McKinley to serve as minister to Turkey and was called away.

Kelsey was entrusted with completing the task. A digest of the results was published in the December 1897 issue of the *Nation*. Far from being antagonistic to the churches, the state universities were entirely neutral. According to Kelsey, it was clear from the raw statistics that since enrollments in state universities were more numerous than in Presbyterian colleges, the majority of laymen who had the benefit of higher education and who managed the af-

---

57. Ibid., 18 n. 19, which notes that the library at McMillan Hall now boasted six thousand volumes.

58. Ibid., 27.

59. Francis W. Kelsey, ed., *The Religious Census of the State Universities and of the Presbyterian Colleges in the Collegiate Year 1896–97* (Ann Arbor: Wesleyan Guild of the Methodist Episcopal Church, 1897), 7.

7. Francis Kelsey in a classroom at the University of Michigan, ca. 1900.
Directly above him is a portrait of Henry Frieze, with adjacent Piranesi
prints of the Pantheon and the Arch of Constantine. Note the Roman
house plan clipped to the blackboard and rolls of maps and plans beneath
the table. Kelsey Museum of Archaeology, University of Michigan.

fairs of the churches would be graduates of the state universities.[60] He repeated President Angell's view that the influence of the state universities
would only grow: "The old questioning about their merits and their probable
duration has come to an end. . . . The work which these institutions have done
and are doing, so much larger and more varied than that of the ordinary incorporated colleges in the West, valuable as that is, has commended them to
the public, which could not now be persuaded to dispense with them."[61]

60. Ibid., 11. The statistics (ibid., 8–11), broken down in state universities according to de-
nomination, may be summarized briefly: a majority of all students in state universities were
members of churches; in state universities, 57.6 percent of students considered themselves
church members, and 88.8 percent considered themselves either church members or adherents; the proportion of church members was higher among women than among men. The
situation in the Presbyterian colleges was similar.

61. Ibid., 31.

Kelsey's impact on the university had been immediate and profound. He had stepped into Professor Frieze's very large shoes in 1889 and assumed the leadership of both the Department of Latin and the University Musical Society. He had transformed the teaching of classics by his own example, his textbooks, and his commitment to the ancient sites and archaeology as well as to literature (see fig. 7). His scholarship had found new venues in his collaborations with August Mau, and he had carried his ideas about education and the whole person into the community with his exhortations to his church.

In the fall of 1900, Kelsey was about to leave with his young family for a year in Rome. His appointment to the professorship at the American School of Classical Studies would allow him direct observation of the physical world in which ancient Romans had lived their daily lives and in which writers had created the literature that so deeply engaged him. It would also permit him to take a group of students to Greece in spring 1901, which would open his eyes to landscapes and monuments he had never fully experienced. By the time of his return to the United States, he was prepared and poised to assume even more and greater responsibilities: to launch the publication in Ann Arbor of the long-lived and mightily successful University of Michigan Humanistic Series and to answer the call to serve the Archaeological Institute of America in a nationwide leadership role. His work was before him.

CHAPTER 4

A Man of Many Parts,
1900–1906

❧

TURN OF THE CENTURY: 1900–1901

The University and the Curriculum

At the turn of the century, the University of Michigan was riding high. Enrollment in the university had soared to 3,303 students, 20 percent of whom were women, and the state legislature was sympathetic. President Angell, everywhere revered, had been chosen by President McKinley in 1897 as minister to Turkey. Michigan men were in such demand that President Cleveland, reelected in 1892, had in fact been heard to remark, "When I was in office and needed help, I usually turned to the University of Michigan."[1] Despite these evident signs of the university's growth and success, things were not quite so rosy in the Latin Department.

The central role that Greek and Latin had enjoyed in the educational curriculum of the United States in the years preceding the Civil War was under scrutiny again. Whether functioning as instruments for training the mind or as repositories of wisdom to guide the civic-minded, the languages and literatures of Greece and Rome had once been at the center of the educational stage. They were viewed as necessary for professional men, and it was thought

---

1. Howard H. Peckham, *The Making of the University of Michigan, 1817–1992*, ed. Margaret L. Steneck and Nicholas H. Steneck (Ann Arbor: University of Michigan, Bentley Historical Library, 1994), 100, 112.

that they provided guidelines to moral conduct for every citizen and helped counteract the secularizing influences of materialism.[2] But this view was changing.

At the University of Michigan, moves to "liberalize" the curriculum began early under its first president, Henry Tappan (1852–63). Tappan ambitiously planned to transform the tradition-bound institution in Ann Arbor into a modern university. With the German university as his model, he set out his objectives in his inaugural speech. He would initiate a new course leading to a bachelor of science degree, thus broadening the curriculum. He wanted not to minimize the importance of Greek and Latin, he claimed, but to open other areas of knowledge to inquiring minds. He would encourage study beyond the undergraduate level, pointing effectively toward the need for a graduate school. He would bring distinguished scholars to pursue their own research and teach both undergraduates and graduate students. To accommodate these aims, he would expand the library and the laboratory and begin an art collection. He saw Ann Arbor as a center of both teaching and research and expected faculty members to be active in both areas. A bachelor of science degree was indeed instituted, with the first degrees awarded in 1855; earned M.A. degrees followed in 1859.[3] More and various courses of study continued to be introduced, with the result that as many as six—classical, scientific, Latin and scientific, civil engineering, mining engineering, and pharmacy—were available for students by the end of the 1860s, leading to one of three different degrees: the bachelor of arts, the bachelor of science, and the bachelor of philosophy. The trend was well and truly set.[4]

Nevertheless, complaints that too much emphasis was given to the ancient languages persisted, even though by 1900 neither language was required for admission or for graduation. Despite strenuous objection by both the Department of Greek and the Department of Latin to any change that would diminish the prestige of the B.A. degree and their identification with it, the faculty took advantage of Professor Kelsey's absence on leave in Italy in early 1901 to alter the status of the bachelor of arts degree. Henceforth, all graduating seniors in the College of Literature, Science, and the Arts were to receive the B.A. degree, thus placing all courses on a par and effectively diluting the prestige and distinction of the classics departments.

---

2. See especially Caroline Winterer, *The Culture of Classicism: Ancient Greece and Rome in American Intellectual Life, 1780–1910* (Baltimore and London: Johns Hopkins University Press, 2002).

3. Up to this moment, only honorary M.A. degrees had been awarded.

4. Peckham, *Making of the University of Michigan*, 35–57, 65.

This introduction of a basically elective system of courses had a drastic impact on the Department of Latin. Enrollment in freshman Latin fell from seven sections in 1900–1901 to four in 1905–6, a loss of some 40 percent in the number of students. Some consolation was found in the higher percentage of students continuing into the junior and senior years, but other compensations were needed. Kelsey was not bowled over by these developments. On his return from Rome, he introduced new courses and courses in translation. His work with Mau fresh in his mind, he prepared a new course on antiquities of Pompeii and expanded his Roman archaeology course into two semesters. Thanks to his colleagues' energetic innovations in offering new and more general courses and to the continuing increase in the number of students attending the university, the hemorrhaging of enrollments abated. More undergraduates (many trained at Michigan) were encouraged to continue their education. Between 1900 and 1910, as many as fifty-seven M.A. degrees were awarded in Latin, and the Ph.D. degree was awarded to twelve students, eleven in Latin and one in Greek and Latin. Michigan's core Latin faculty had responded well to the challenge to the role of classics in the University's curriculum.

The American School of Classical Studies in Rome

Kelsey's energy for meeting such challenges may have derived in part from his time abroad. He was granted leave for the year 1900–1901 to take up his appointment as professor at the American School of Classical Studies in Rome. Much information about Kelsey's activities between 1901 and 1927 may be found in his leather-bound diaries, a powerful source of knowledge, introducing the reader (whose eyesight is up to it!) to aspects of Kelsey's life largely unrecorded elsewhere (his family life and his life as a businessman, for example), to important personalities on the national and international stage with whom he had dealings (e.g., Theodore Roosevelt or Colonel Emilio Kosterlitzky), and to the movers and shakers in Detroit at the time of the city's greatest prosperity (the Buhls, the Webbers, the Pendletons, the Ferrys, the Walkers).[5]

The diaries (of which those known to me that survive begin in January

5. The diaries are among the Francis Willey Kelsey Papers (abbreviated in this book to FWK Papers) kept at the Bentley Historical Library of the University of Michigan. Material in the present volume that is ascribed to Kelsey yet not to any particular publication may be assumed to derive from these diaries. Most, but not all, quotations from the diaries are cited by date.

1901) do not reveal when exactly Kelsey arrived in Italy for his year's leave or when his family joined him; but since his appointment at the school was for the whole academic year, which began in early October, he must have been in Rome by early fall of 1900. Given that he had taken in hand the revision of *Pompeii: Its Life and Art,* which we are told was revised "on the spot," it is logical to suppose that he would have made his way to Italy as soon as he could.

In the aftermath of the appearance of *Pompeii: Its Life and Art,* Kelsey's invitation to be a professor at the American School of Classical Studies in Rome was to be expected. It was nonetheless a great honor. The school had been founded in 1895, one year after the opening of the American School of Architecture, founded by American architects influenced by their training in the École des Beaux-Arts of Paris and their exposure to the architectures of ancient Rome and the Renaissance. These schools joined in 1912 to become the American Academy in Rome. In 1895 the American School of Classical Studies took rooms in the Villa Aurora and opened for business. Its first influential director was, tellingly, Richard Norton,[6] whose training in Greek archaeology and at the American School of Classical Studies at Athens (founded 1882) had equipped him well to teach Greek art, though he was less well versed in Roman art and archaeology. His courses, however, regularly included lectures on Roman sculpture and Roman versions of Greek statues, with which Rome's museums and collections, both papal and princely, abounded.

At the school, Professor Kelsey lectured on Roman archaeology, topography, history, and epigraphy and directed individual students' research. The courses taught by Norton and Kelsey were supplemented by lectures on Pompeii and Herculaneum given by August Mau. Other Italian scholars offered courses on Roman numismatics, Latin paleography, and the catacombs of Rome. The architecture and topography of Rome and Pompeii were Kelsey's special interests, and he naturally enlivened his talks by visits to the sites and monuments themselves: for example, Frascati, Tusculum, the catacombs at the Porta Salaria, and Hadrian's villa at Tivoli. He was also at pains to introduce the students to other scholars in Rome, allowing them to glimpse other methods and areas of specialization. They were privileged to visit Ostia with Rodolfo Lanciani, already well known for his publications of Roman archi-

---

6. Educated at Harvard College and in Germany, Norton was the son of the famous Harvard professor Charles Eliot Norton. He had studied in Germany with Adolf Furtwängler, one of the foremost experts of the time on Greek art, and in Greece with Charles Waldstein, under whose aegis he had excavated at the Argive Heraion.

tecture and topography and of the fragments of the Severan map of Rome, the Forma Urbis Romae.[7] They visited Palestrina in the company of Thomas Ashby, fresh from a brilliant degree at Oxford, where Roman antiquities had been the focus of his work. Ashby was writing regularly about the new archaeological work in the Roman Forum (initiated by Giacomo Boni in 1898) for British newspapers and contributed reports on the progress of the excavations to the *Classical Review* during 1899–1906. Already a force to be reckoned with, he became the first student of the British School at Rome in 1902, its assistant director during 1903–6, and director from 1906 to 1925.[8] Between school trips and lectures, other attractions of Rome diverted the whole Kelsey family. Kelsey's daughter Charlotte recalled being taken with her sister to see the Christmas Eve celebrations at St. Peter's—the long procession of cardinals in scarlet robes, the brilliantly mitered bishops, the Swiss Guard in their bright uniforms, and the pope himself.[9] Kelsey lifted her up on his shoulders to see it all, and Harry Gelston, one of the men at the school, did the same for Ruth.

Rome also had its health hazards. Early in the year, when both the children—Ruth was now six and Charlotte three—fell ill with scarlet fever, the whole family was put in quarantine for two weeks. Mercifully both children recovered, and the episode did not deter the parents from embarking on a trip to Greece with the school in March. Ruth and Charlotte were left in the charge of a Mrs. Cook at the Pensione Boos in the Palazzo Rospigliosi-Pallavicini, Francis Kelsey's home in Rome in the years ahead.

Given the historical connection between Greece and Rome in antiquity, the prominent role of classical Greece and particularly Athens in American intellectual life in the later nineteenth century, and the existence of numerous important Roman buildings and monuments in Greece, it was logical that a

---

7. Rodolfo Lanciani, *Ruins and Excavations of Ancient Rome: A Companion Book for Students and Travelers* (Boston: Houghton Mifflin, 1897); idem, *Forma Urbis Romae* issued in eight parts (Milan: U. Hoepli, 1893–1901); idem, *The Roman Forum: A Photographic Description of Its Monuments* (Rome: Frank, 1910). Lanciani was professor of Roman archaeology at the University of Rome.

8. Ashby became most famous for his topographical work: his *The Roman Campagna in Classical Times* (London: E. Benn; New York: Macmillan, 1927); his *The Aqueducts of Ancient Rome*, ed. I. A. Richmond (Oxford: Clarendon, 1935); and his completion and revision of Samuel B. Platner's *Topographical Dictionary of Ancient Rome* (London: Humphrey Milford; Oxford: Oxford University Press, 1929).

9. Charlotte Badger Kelsey, "Random Notes on Memories of Father," January 25, 1957, typescript, private collection of Easton Kelsey Jr., Rochester, NY (hereinafter "RNMF"). A copy of this typescript sent originally to her sister, Ruth, was made available to me through the kindness of Easton Trowbridge Kelsey Jr., Francis's grandson.

visit to Greece should be part of the curriculum of the American School of Classical Studies in Rome (see fig. 8). In the early spring of 1901, the school's party on the trip to Greece numbered twenty-two: there were six "seniors" (Professor and Mrs. Isabelle Kelsey, Professor and Mrs. Church, a Mrs. Burton-Brown, and her friend Miss Underwood), eleven "young ladies" (Misses Benson, Bishop, Kennan, Livingstone, May, Sabin, Van Valkenburg, Warren, Barnes, Malone, and Sedgwick), and five young men (Messrs. Beach, Crittenden, Gelston, Paxton, and Allen) in the party that left Italy.[10] From time to time while in Greece, the party was joined by others.

On March 14, Francis left Rome for Benevento to study the famous arch and the bridge on his own. After Isabelle and most of the party from the school arrived the next day, they studied the monuments together before traveling by train to Brindisi to board the boat for Greece. Here they were joined by the rest of the group. The steamer sailed the next day at 11:00 p.m., with the whole party on board. After stopping briefly at Corfu, they arrived at 5:00 a.m. on March 19 in Patras, where Herbert Fletcher De Cou boarded the steamer to greet them. De Cou, a Chicagoan, had graduated from the University of Michigan (B.A. 1888, M.A. 1890). A familiar figure at the American School of Classical Studies at Athens, he became an experienced excavator under the guidance of Charles Waldstein at the Sanctuary of Hera at Argos. He was a dab hand at inscriptions. He was indispensable to the success of the school's trip: he knew his way around Greece, he could speak enough Greek to haggle over prices, and he could help make local arrangements and even find medical men in remote places.

Kelsey seems to have conducted the trip in what may seem now a rather freewheeling way, allowing participants to help decide on the goals and purposes of each day's plan. Little seems to have been compulsory, so that numbers of participants fluctuated from excursion to excursion. In the face of emergencies or divergent preferences, plans were often impromptu. On arrival in Patras, Kelsey took a large room at the Hotel d'Angleterre, where the whole party sat down and thrashed out where they wanted to go. The majority were for a tour of the Peloponnese, starting with Olympia, whereas a few

---

10. The trip is described in great detail in Kelsey's diary. Notice the preponderance of women in the group, several of them Michigan students. On women students at Michigan and the university's vanguard role in women's education, see D. G. McGuigan, *A Dangerous Experiment: 100 Years of Women at the University of Michigan* (Center for Continuing Education for Women, The University of Michigan, Ann Arbor, 1970). Albert Robinson Crittenden was a Michigan graduate (A.B. 1894), who, after teaching at Olivet College, joined the Michigan faculty as instructor of Latin in 1908.

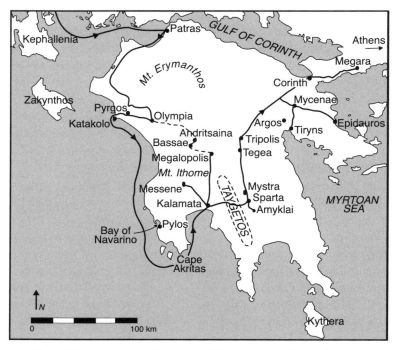

8. Map of Greece showing the route of the 1901 tour of the Peloponnese by members of the American School of Classical Studies in Rome. Drawing: Lorene Sterner.

voted to go on to Athens immediately after visiting Olympia. As all agreed on Olympia as the starting point, they celebrated with a splendid lunch at the hotel—which Francis thought very reasonably priced at 3.50 drachmas per person[11]—before taking the 4:00 p.m. train for Olympia. They spent an afternoon and the following morning at the site, with De Cou lecturing on the temples, treasuries, altars, rituals, and games, followed by an afternoon at the museum, where he talked at length about the sculptures, reliefs, bronzes, inscriptions, and other votive materials. On March 22, a few members of the party left for Athens by train, while the others planned to set off on horseback for Andritsaina and Megalopolis. But Professor Church was suffering from a nasty infection on his neck, which required medical attention (De Cou found

---

11. He had just changed money at the Ionian Bank at the rate of 42.60 drachmas to the British pound.

a doctor), and Kelsey thought it best to stay behind with him, hoping to catch up later. Undaunted, the rest of the party, including Isabelle Kelsey, set off. The weather was poor, and the slow progress forced them to make an overnight stop, delaying their arrival at Andritsaina until the next day, with the weather worsening. On the following day, the rain was turning to snow when some of the party climbed up the tough three-hour path to the Temple of Apollo at Bassae. Isabelle and other less adventurous souls stayed behind. From Andritsaina, they reached Megalopolis on the evening of March 25, after a testing few days.

Meanwhile, Professor Church recovered rapidly, but the horses Kelsey had hired did not arrive. Plans had to be changed. They traveled by carriage to Pyrgos near the coast, spent the night there, and got passage from Katakolo the next day on a coastal steamer, docking at Kalamata on March 25. Kelsey's notebook describes their inn there as primitive, so they were not sorry to leave the next morning by the 5:00 a.m. train for Megalopolis, where they found the others, saddle-sore but safe and sound. They spent the afternoon at ancient Megalopolis (De Cou lecturing again) before taking the late afternoon train back to Kalamata. There they enjoyed better lodgings at the Hôtel de l'Europe and good food at the restaurant Grande Bretagne, where Kelsey remarked on the quality of his steak. The next day, they were off to Mount Ithome and Messene.

They made an early start, first by train and then by mule. By 9:00 a.m., they were being entertained at a monastery en route by monks offering cheese, bread, and, rather to their surprise, raki. Messene sits on the flank of Mount Ithome and covers a very large area. After studying the walls, gates, and towers of the fortified circuit—arguably the best-preserved example of military architecture of the classical period—the party went on up the zigzag path to the flat summit of the mountain. From there, the views over the Messenian plains to the east and south and to Mount Erymanthos, the coast, and Zakynthos to the north and northwest were spectacular. Back in Kalamata, Kelsey could exclaim, as he frequently did, "A most successful day!"

They set out the next day on the sixty-kilometer ride to Sparta by mule over the Taygetos (the range of mountains separating Messenia from Laconia) through the Langhada Gorge. It was tough going (there was no road here until 1940), but they reached the top of the 4,250-foot pass by two o'clock, and after a pause for lunch, they began the long, slow descent. Some compensation for the arduous journey was found in glorious views over the Laconian plain and then, as night fell, in the moonlit ride through the fields to Sparta. The next week of the Peloponnesian tour followed a familiar pattern, with visits to sites and museums, lectures and discussions, and magnificent land-scapes and views. From Sparta, they went to the Sanctuary of Menelaos and Helen and, at Amyklai, the Sanctuary of Apollo; they trooped two miles through the fields to the remains of the beehive tomb at Vapheio; they climbed by mule to the top of Byzantine Mystra. Kelsey wrote in his diary that the view from there of the plain to the south seemed to his eye like nothing less than "a great garden." Moving north from Sparta, they stopped at Tegea, Tripoli, and Argos. Visits to more sites—Epidauros, Tiryns, the Argive Heraion, and Mycenae—followed, before they returned to Athens on April 6. They had been in Greece just nineteen days. De Cou, whose familiarity with the sites and knowledge of Greece was invaluable, had been with them the whole time.

Joined by the rest of the party, they spent the next ten days exploring Athens and Attica. They climbed the Acropolis more than once to examine the sanctuary, its plan, individual buildings, and dedications and to discuss its growth over time and the festivals and rituals performed there. They visited the Theseum (the Temple of Athena and Hephaistos), north of the Acropolis, overlooking the not-yet-excavated Agora, and to the east of the Acropolis, the Temple of Olympian Zeus. They went to the museum, where they saw De Cou studying the bronzes from the Argive Heraion; they went to look at Athens's harbors and the ancient ship sheds.[12] Twenty members of the group traveled to Eleusis in four carriages to the site of the Sanctuary of Demeter and Kore. On another day, many went, with the help of mules and donkeys for the last part of the way, to the quarries on Mount Pentelikon: it was hot in the sun, but there were splendid views of Euboea and the plain of Marathon. Only fourteen members chose to join the excursion, on another day, to Marathon itself. There they walked over the plain, had lunch by the tumulus, and heard De Cou remind them about Herodotos, the topography, ancient warfare, and the Persians.

For the tour to the north (see fig. 9), the party divided into two groups. The first,[13] which left Athens on April 17, was led by De Cou and Professor and Mrs. Church. Their route took them by carriage to Thebes and then to Orchomenos and Livadia, allowing them to study sites and monuments along the way. At Livadia, they switched to mules to carry them around Mount Parnassos to Delphi. The second group (five students) remained in

---

12. These sheds sheltered triremes when the sailing season was over. Hauled up out of the water, the ships were protected from bad weather and the risk of getting waterlogged.

13. Misses Barnes, Benson, Livingston, Malone, Sabin, Kennan, and Van Valkenburg; Messrs. Crittenden, Gelston, Freeman, and Beach.

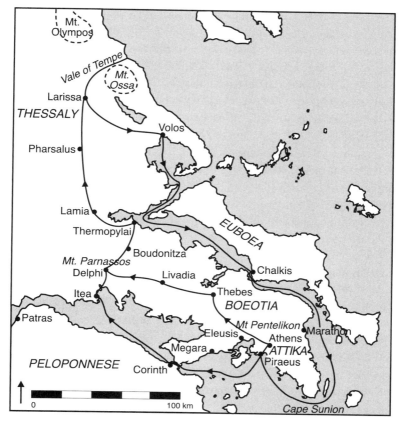

9. Map of Greece showing the route of the 1901 tour of part of Central and Northern Greece by members of the American School of Classical Studies in Rome. Drawing: Lorene Sterner.

Athens with Kelsey and his wife. Their next few days in Athens were enlivened by the arrival of Professor and Mrs. Percy Gardner. Gardner was professor of archaeology at Oxford and collaborator with Francis in editing the Macmillan Handbooks of Archaeology and Antiquities.[14] Together the two professors visited the Acropolis Museum one day; on another, they called on the director of the British School, R. C. Bosanquet; and on another, they joined their wives for lunch at the Grand Hotel.

14. Percy Gardner was the elder brother of Ernest Gardner, who was the first student, in 1886, at the newly founded British School at Athens; rapidly promoted to director in 1887, he became professor of archaeology at the University of London in 1895 and served as the founding editor of the *Journal of Hellenic Studies* for many years.

On April 20, the Kelseys and the five students[15] left for Piraeus to sail overnight through the Corinth Canal, opened only eight years earlier (1893), to Itea, the harbor town for Delphi. Five of the party drove up to Delphi in carriages, but Kelsey and Mr. Allen walked the stiff ten kilometers, mostly up-hill, to the village, where all seven of them joined the group that had arrived via Thebes and Livadia. For two days, they explored the site and the museum, and De Cou lectured. Some of the party then returned to Athens, while Francis and Isabelle, with De Cou and the others, set off northward by mule over the shoulder of Mount Parnassos, heading for the battlefields of Thermopylai and Pharsalus. They lodged one night in a "kind of khan" by the castle of Boudonitza (where the Pallavicini held court in the thirteenth and fourteenth centuries),[16] before continuing to Thermopylai. From there, they rode on to Lamia, casting occasional glances back at a "sublime view of the summit of Parnassos."

They stayed overnight in Lamia and left the next morning at 5:00 a.m. for Farsala (modern name), where some intended to catch the Athens train. They missed it; the only inn in town was closed, and Kelsey had to appeal to the mayor, who kindly found rooms for them. On the next day, the party investigated the site "where the battle may have been fought."[17] Then they journeyed on to Larisa and, later, further north to the Vale of Tempe. This cool and lux-uriant dale, with its green meadows, trees, and shrubs, sits in the midst of a spectacular ten-kilometer-long gorge, through which the river Peneios runs to the sea. It separates Mount Ossa from Mount Olympos and has often been described as the gate between northern and southern Greece. It looks like a strong defensive position, or so the Greeks thought when they tried to stop the Persian invasion here in 480 BC; but as at Thermopylai, there is another route through the mountains, and Xerxes found it.[18] On April 29, they took the train to Volos, where they boarded a steamer to Piraeus. The boat stopped

---

15. Francis and Isabelle Kelsey; Misses Bishop, May, and Warren; and Messrs. Allen and Martin.

16. The Pallavicini were a noble Italian family, one branch of which was established as feudal lords in northern Greece at the time of the Frankish conquest. Their special responsibility was the guardianship of the pass at Thermopylai. See William Miller, "The Marquisate of Boudonitza (1204–1414)," *Journal of Hellenic Studies* 28 (1908): 234–49.

17. This is the famous battle between Julius Caesar and Pompey in August of 48 BC, which pitted Roman legion against Roman legion and led to the assassination of Pompey in Egypt and the fateful encounter between Caesar and Cleopatra.

18. The Greeks also tried to stop the Romans here in 168 BC and the German army in 1941 but were equally unsuccessful.

at Chalkis, allowing time for a walk over the bridge to Boeotia and back before it left, crowded now with passengers and sheep.

The overnight boat ride took them along the east coast of Attica, around Cape Sunion, to reach Piraeus at 9:00 a.m. As on the coastal freighter that Francis had taken from Pyrgos (Katakolo) to Kalamata a month before, the sail from Volos was uncomfortable. The public cabins were jammed with passengers, the standing room on deck with sheep. Although three of the young ladies stumped up for a second-class cabin, Kelsey found them at dawn the next morning huddled together and bundled up against the cold among the sheep. They had not been able to sleep "because of the vermin and stench in the cabin." The ship's staff was not sympathetic: when De Cou complained to the steward about their cabin, the steward fell into a rage, "accusing the young ladies of stealing a blanket."

The first few days of May were spent in Athens, tying up loose ends as they prepared to return to Rome. On May 4, they went by train to Corinth, where they were shown around by Rufus B. Richardson.[19] On the following day, they arrived in Patras. As the boat for Italy was delayed, Kelsey spent a restful couple of days in reading, writing, shopping, and taking walks with Isabelle. They finally reached Brindisi on May 10. There was "the usual difficulty with the baggage men," but when some of the porters recognized the party (and they must have looked a motley group), "they were less troublesome than when we sailed." They took the train at once for Taranto, where they changed for Salerno, arriving late in the evening. The next day they went to Paestum[20] to see the Greek temples and then on to Pompeii.

Back on the Bay of Naples, Kelsey lost no time getting in touch with August Mau, who had kindly agreed to lecture on Pompeii to the American students on their return from Greece. The group was allowed a single day of rest (which fourteen of the students used to climb Vesuvius), before Mau began his talks on May 13. Thereafter, he gave nine more three-hour lectures, always

---

19. Richardson, who had been involved in the excavations at Corinth since the very beginning (1896), was an intermittent participant in the work of the American School of Classical Studies at Athens and author of *Vacation Days in Greece* (New York: Charles Scribner's Sons, 1903).

20. Their steps were followed eighty years later by another group from the University of Michigan, which, in collaboration with members of the University of Perugia and the Superintendency of Salerno, Benevento, and Avellino, excavated a sanctuary immediately outside the south wall of the city: see John G. Pedley and Mario Torelli, eds., *The Sanctuary of Santa Venera at Paestum,* vol. 1 (Rome: Giorgio Bretschneider, 1993); Rebecca Miller Ammerman, *The Sanctuary of Santa Venera at Paestum,* vol. 2, *The Votive Terracottas* (Ann Arbor: University of Michigan Press, 2002).

on site. He led the students around the buildings, discussing the architecture, topography, spaces, and decor—the sculptures, paintings, bronzes, and other finds. This comprehensive seminar conducted by a single person made the most strenuous demands on the stamina of all concerned and is hardly imaginable today. On May 24, the venue moved to the National Archaeological Museum in Naples, where Mau talked both morning and afternoon, on each occasion for three hours. There was not much to add when he had finished. In the evening, Kelsey called, with Mau, on the photographer Esposito, who "furnished me photographs of the latest finds." Such was the influence of Mau among the local researchers, and such was the recognition of Kelsey's contributions to Pompeii studies. On May 25, Francis and Isabelle at last reached Rome, as Kelsey noted in his diary, "having been separated from the children 10 weeks and 2 days, Isabelle 10 weeks and 1 day."

The whole experience says much about the stamina and good cheer of the participants. For the students, it was a chance to see, firsthand, the sites and landscapes of Greece and to get a direct sense of the civilization that was the great precursor of Rome. For Kelsey, it was a chance to visit sites he knew and others he did not know at all. It reinforces our sense of his organizational skill, his capacity for leadership, his enthusiasm for the study of antiquity, and his rapport with the students. Though De Cou did much of the lecturing and guiding, Kelsey bore the full brunt of responsibility for the morale and well-being of the party.

Kelsey spent June and the first part of July in Rome, taking students on trips to locations within easy reach—Hadrian's villa at Tivoli, Veii, and other Etruscan sites, for example—or working at his own studies in the Forum. A romance that had blossomed over the course of the year, between Mr. Crittenden and Miss Van Valkenburg,[21] came to a happy conclusion on June 20 with their wedding on the Capitoline, at which Francis and Isabelle were attentive guests. Later in the month, Francis's brother Fred, the New York businessman, and his wife, Ella, arrived at Naples to begin a European tour. Isabelle met them in Naples and showed them the sights around Vesuvius, the Bay of Naples, and the Sorrentine Peninsula. Among their excursions was a visit to Capri, where they called on Charles Lang Freer and Thomas Spencer Jerome, both successful and wealthy Detroit clubmen, acquaintances of the

---

21. Lisla Van Valkenburg was a member of the senior class of Ann Arbor High School in 1895, one year after Crittenden graduated from the university, so it is likely that their acquaintance began and perhaps flourished long before they were together at the American School of Classical Studies in Rome. Albert Robinson Crittenden would join the Department of Latin faculty in 1908.

Kelseys, who had recently acquired a villa on the island.[22] Kelsey joined Isabelle, Fred, and Ella later and returned with them to Rome, where he shepherded Fred and Ella around the city before they left for parts north. Francis then left for Pompeii, to continue work with Mau on the new edition of *Pompeii: Its Life and Art,* leaving Isabelle and the children in Rome with a new nanny. He and Mau worked busily in Pompeii until August 2, when they signed their preface together at the Albergo del Sole.[23] On the following day, Kelsey left for Rome.

He spent the next three weeks assembling his work on Pompeii and the Forum, preparing new editions of his Latin authors, and organizing the return to America. During his year abroad, he had kept his eye open, with some success, for antiquities that would be useful to the university in its teaching and research. He had acquired lamps, building materials, and painted terracottas and had shown a particular interest, natural enough for a language teacher, in inscribed objects. Lead water pipes with stamped inscriptions and examples of stamped Arretine pottery came his way, as well as 477 brick stamps, to be added to the handful already in the Michigan collection acquired from Canon de Criscio in 1899, plus the single stamp he had bought on Capri in 1893. These stamped bricks came both from dealers and workmen. As to provenance, Kelsey says only that "they are all from Rome." They provide good examples of the different types of stamped brick and a good range of consular dates, showing that the Roman brick industry lasted from the end of the republic until the sixth century AD. They thus demonstrate Kelsey's good sense in putting together a small group that is representative of the whole industry and thus ideal for teaching purposes.[24] On August 27, Francis shipped seventeen cases to Ann Arbor: four containing books and thirteen bearing the brick stamps, architectural fragments, and other antiquities. When these materials arrived in Ann Arbor three months later, they created quite a stir and, within a few days, were eagerly inspected by interested

---

22. Freer, who had made a large fortune in the railway and lumber businesses, was also an avid collector of art, antiquities, and manuscripts. (He had helped pay for the casts of the Arch of Trajan at Benevento; see chapter 3, "The Department of Latin.") Jerome, son of a governor of Michigan, a graduate of the University of Michigan, and a lawyer in Detroit, had a deep interest in the classical world. Both became important figures in Kelsey's life, and they share a section in chapter 7.

23. Regarding this edition, see chapter 3, "Italy."

24. John P. Bodel, *Roman Brick Stamps in the Kelsey Museum,* University of Michigan, Kelsey Museum of Archaeology, Studies 6 (Ann Arbor: University of Michigan Press, 1983), passim. So keen on brick stamps was Kelsey that he could not resist acquiring a couple in Greece (ibid., 6 n. 22).

colleagues and friends, including President Angell. On the evening of August 28, the family took the night train to Naples and was seen off at the station by De Cou and Charles Rufus Morey.[25] On the next day, they were joined by August Mau and his wife on board a ship in the harbor at Naples for a farewell meeting. It is not hard to imagine the heartfelt wishes with which they parted.

After the steamer passed Gibraltar, Francis Kelsey's diary is blank and does not resume for nearly three months. On the very same day that the cases carrying the antiquities arrived from Rome, he gave a lecture entitled "A Winter in Rome" to the Detroit Archaeological Society at the home of General Russell A. Alger, a former governor of the state.[26] The talk, on the latest archaeological developments in Italy, was published in the *Detroit Free Press* on December 1. On the day after the talk, Francis called, with a gift of books, on Mr. and Mrs. Dexter M. Ferry, whose generosity to the university was already well known and was to become famous.[27] Francis also visited Mr. and Mrs. Fred Colby[28] and Mr. Charles Freer (who Isabelle had introduced to Francis's brother Fred and his wife, Ella, on Capri). Since Francis enjoyed the company of others and saw that the university's future would depend substantially on the benevolence of the rich, he cultivated his acquaintanceships in Detroit with care.

His interest in reaching beyond the university for financial help had been clear enough in his fund-raising efforts for the Frieze memorials, the School of Music, and student fellowships. But he saw potential, too, for outreach in wider cultural terms, in the introduction of the general public to an appreciation of music and to archaeological news from Greece and Rome. So began his extensive career as a public speaker. In the middle of December, he fol-

---

25. Morey was a Michigan graduate (A.B., A.M.) and spent three years as a fellow of the American School of Classical Studies in Rome. He was appointed to the faculty of the Department of Classics at Princeton in 1903, transferred to the Department of Art and Archaeology in 1906, established himself as an authority in early Christian art, and chaired Princeton's Department of Art and Archaeology from 1924 to 1945.

26. From modest beginnings in Ohio, Alger (1836–1907) became a lawyer at twenty-three and, during the Civil War, a major general in the Union Army at twenty-seven. Later a lumber baron, railway man, and banker in Michigan (he expanded his interests in the timber business to Washington State, too), he was elected governor of Michigan for 1884–86, was appointed secretary of war in 1897 by President McKinley, and served finally in Washington as a Michigan senator.

27. Ferry had been a leading contributor to the fund for the Frieze Memorial Organ; see chapter 3, "Henry Simmons Frieze."

28. Frederick Lee Colby was first cousin to Isabelle Badger and therefore related to Kelsey. He and Frances Berry had married in 1899. Colby subsequently became president of Berry Brothers in Detroit (see chapter 9 nn. 102, 191).

lowed up his talk in Detroit with an exhausting lecture tour, speaking on four consecutive days in Cleveland, Oberlin, Chicago, and Columbia, Missouri, on the excavations at Pompeii. He traveled in all weathers, in all classes of rail travel, comfortable and uncomfortable, and at all hours.

THE YEARS 1902–6

The Professor

Following the reorganization of the curriculum in 1901, there was an initial dip in enrollments in the Latin Department. In a period, however, when the overall number of enrollments in the university was on the rise, Latin numbers gradually stabilized and even enjoyed a small increase, as did the number of faculty. The Board of Regents evidently approved of the department's work. In 1905 Clarence Meader was promoted to assistant professor, and in 1906 Kelsey's salary rose to three thousand dollars. In return, he was increasingly called on to represent the university: in 1904 he replied to the toast of the university at the New York State Club Banquet; in the following year, he represented the university at the inauguration of President Edmund J. James of the University of Illinois at Champaign. Moreover, Kelsey's interest, shared by the head of the Greek Department, Martin D'Ooge,[29] in promoting classical archaeology was endorsed by the regents when they authorized the appointment of a professor of Greek archaeology and Greek at a salary of twenty-five hundred dollars.[30] Arthur Fairbanks, professor at the University of Iowa, was appointed to the new position. A further notable addition to the faculty in the fall of 1906 was John Garrett Winter, a graduate of Hope Col-

---

29. Martin Luther D'Ooge was appointed assistant professor of Greek in 1867, later took leave to pursue studies in Europe, and was awarded his Ph.D. by the University of Leipzig in 1872. His experience in Germany led to the introduction at Michigan of new courses that, following the example set by Professor Boise in 1853, expanded the Greek curriculum from the teaching of author courses to broader themes and to courses in linguistics and archaeology. He taught courses in Homeric antiquities and in Greek inscriptions and was well enough regarded as a Hellenist to be appointed director for the year 1886–87 of the recently founded American School of Classical Studies at Athens, for which he became an enthusiastic advocate. When Dean Hutchins of the Law School was named acting president in President Angell's absence as minister to Turkey in 1897, D'Ooge, then dean of the Literary Department, was so disappointed that he resigned the deanship. His son, Benjamin D'Ooge, taught classical languages for over fifty years at Michigan State Normal College (subsequently Eastern Michigan University). See Peckham, *Making of the University of Michigan,* 101.

30. Kelsey's diary (April 24, 1906) records the vote: voting in favor were Regents Barbour, Knappen, Sawyer, and White; voting against were Regents Dean, Fletcher, and Hill.

lege and a Michigan Ph.D. Appointed instructor in Latin and Greek, he was to become, in 1928, Kelsey's successor as head of the department and an influential academic administrator.

Academic life followed its usual rhythms of teaching, examinations, department meetings, fellowship decisions, and visiting lecturers. Students were as boisterous as they are today: football was a major concern, and when Michigan defeated Chicago 22–12 on November 12, 1904, Kelsey noted "much drunkenness afterwards." Classes were frequently taught in instructors' homes. In 1904 Kelsey himself, for example, invited students to meet at his house early in the mornings (8:00 a.m.) or in the evenings. The Classical Club, too, would meet at his house, where, on December 20, 1904, for example, they heard talks by Professor D'Ooge on the Athenian Acropolis and by Professor Dennison on Platner's work on the topography of Rome.

Kelsey's energies extended beyond the classroom and the Classical Club's meetings. The Michigan Classical Conference and the Schoolmasters' Club met annually in Ann Arbor in the spring. The meetings were organized by the department and representatives of the schools, but the brunt fell on Francis. In 1902 he lectured to both groups, his diary claiming that as many as a thousand were in the audience at his evening talk to the schoolmasters in University Hall. He also took responsibility for entertaining—principals of schools at lunch, visiting professors at dinner, and, in the evening at home, members of the Michigan faculty and "out-of-town men." One evening, over fifty visitors were treated at his house to what he termed a "conversazione." This pattern of huge attendances, lectures, lunches, dinners, and soirees continued in 1906. Michigan was now recognized as a national center for classical studies; a link between colleges, universities, and high schools; a mediator of classroom activity, pedagogy, and research; and an active advocate in the reformulation of the claims of the classics.

Kelsey used his home to forge strong friendships with colleagues and potential donors, especially any who might contribute to support for students, and in particular with Theodore D. Buhl of Detroit, whose family he visited often. On some of these occasions, he managed to persuade President Angell to go with him.[31] Mr. Buhl began to contribute to a fellowship fund in the de-

---

31. His relationship with President Angell during these years seems to have been cordial. The president evidently did not hesitate when emergency required Kelsey to be away from campus. Summoned to Washington by an urgent telegram on February 25, 1905, Kelsey met Angell at the railroad station off the 9:25 p.m. train from Milwaukee and, getting the president's approval, took the 11:30 p.m. train two hours later for Buffalo and Washington. He was used to close connections on the railroads: returning from a business trip, he only just arrived

partment in 1901 and did so annually thereafter.[32] Following his death, his widow and son continued the support for forty years. More than fifty graduate students, among them Charles Rufus Morey,[33] benefited from the generosity of the Buhl family. The thriving industrial and manufacturing city of Detroit provided Kelsey an ever-widening circle of wealthy acquaintances, men like Colonel Hecker, Charles Freer, Dexter M. Ferry, Bethune Duffield, and Edward W. Pendleton.[34] Kelsey called on them whenever he could.

Over these years, he was in great demand as a lecturer. Mau and Kelsey's *Pompeii* book was out, and Kelsey knew more about Pompeii, a site that piqued everybody's interest, than any other American. The invitations came thick and fast. Appointed secretary of the Archaeological Institute of America (AIA) in 1902, he toured widely, drumming up interest in the institute and helping to organize new societies and lecturing. Local archaeological groups, schools, and colleges also wanted to know about Naples, Herculaneum, Pompeii, and Vesuvius, and Kelsey was happy to oblige.

In 1902, for example, he lectured in January, one day after another, to a local archaeological group in Duluth, Minnesota; to a university audience in Madison, Wisconsin; to a high school in Menominee, Wisconsin; and to a "normal school" (i.e., teachers' college) in Milwaukee. In March he spoke at Vassar; in Orange, New Jersey (where he stayed with his brother Fred); at Wellesley (where he dined with President Hazard and with Harriet Boyd Hawes);[35] and, the next day, both in Boston in the afternoon and at Harvard

---

in time for Mrs. Angell's funeral on December 19, 1903. Delayed by poor conditions, the overnight train from Kansas City to Milan had arrived too late for him to catch the Ann Arbor train. At the last minute, the dispatcher gave permission for Mr. James Wade (the secretary of the university, who was traveling with Kelsey) and two cousins of Mrs. Angell's to ride on a freight train from Milan to Ann Arbor.

32. Like Freer, Buhl had helped pay for the plaster casts of the Arch of Trajan at Benevento (see chapter 3, "The Department of Latin").

33. See n. 25 above and chapter 6, "The Morgan Manuscripts."

34. Duffield and Pendleton were both lawyers. Duffield, whose father, D. Bethune Duffield, had also been a respected Detroit lawyer, graduated from the University of Michigan in the class of 1883 with a B.A. (Classical Course). Edward Waldo Pendleton (1848–1923), a graduate of the University of Michigan (A. B. 1872, A. M. 1874) became a wealthy and influential lawyer in Detroit, with expertise in corporation law. Long interested in education (he spent one year as superintendent of schools in Owosso), he served as secretary of the Memorial Hall Building Committee at the University, as a trustee of the Detroit Museum of Art, and as president of the Board of Water Commissioners of the City of Detroit (1895–1905), as well as on the executive committee of the Archaeological Institute of America.

35. Harriet Boyd (Boyd Hawes after her marriage) was the pioneer excavator of the Bronze Age Cretan town of Gournia (1901–4). She was the first American to excavate in Crete (in 1900 at Kavousi) and the first woman of any nationality to direct an excavation and publish the results in an exemplary manner.

in the evening. Without seeming to tire, he visited his Uncle John[36] in Arlington, his publishers in Boston, and, the next day, Charles Eliot Norton in Cambridge, before going on to Yale. There he lectured to an audience of 550. More lectures followed, at the Sachs School in New York, in Philadelphia, and in Washington, D.C., where he helped establish the Washington Society of the AIA. A standing-room-only audience greeted him when he gave a talk at the Detroit Museum of Art on the evening of March 20, after which he was just in time to catch the 11:00 p.m. "motor"[37] to reach Ann Arbor at 1:00 a.m. The pace was less hectic the rest of the year, but he did not stop.

The Board of Regents, aware of Kelsey's popularity and the publicity he garnered for the university, granted him twenty-five days of leave to visit and lecture in the West, largely on behalf of the AIA. But a serious illness intervened,[38] and he could not undertake the task until 1903. For the early part of that year, he was still under the doctor's care, but he was able to begin the rescheduled trip in the fall. He went at it at a blistering pace, traveling by overnight train whenever possible.[39]

He left Ann Arbor on October 31 for Chicago, where he addressed an audience of Latin, Greek, and history teachers on the subject of the AIA. He spoke on November 2 in Madison, South Dakota, at the State Normal School; on the fourth in Des Moines to an audience of six hundred; on the fifth in St. Joseph, Missouri; and on the sixth in both Kansas City and Lawrence—everywhere to sizable audiences. In the middle of the month, he spoke in Pueblo, Colorado Springs, Boulder, and Denver. On November 18, at Salt Lake City, he called on Joseph Smith, head of the Mormon Church, and took the opportunity to describe the "high character and industry of Mormon students at the University of Michigan," before delivering a talk and moving on the next day to Reno. Arriving in California, he lectured at Berkeley and at Stanford on the days immediately before Thanksgiving Day and at the recently established San Francisco Society of the AIA on the day after Thanksgiving. Going on to Southern California, he lectured in Los Angeles, where he also helped organize a new society of the AIA, and in early December, he spoke in

36. On John Townsend Trowbridge, his mother's brother, see chapter 1, "Immediate Family."

37. The interurban trolleys with electric motors and transmissions were one element in the local public transport system: other elements were the horse-drawn trolleys, streetcars with overhead electric cables, and the railroad.

38. See below, "Pastimes and Hardships."

39. Whenever possible, he traveled in an upper berth with the window open. See diary, February 7, 1914.

Pasadena. At Claremont, the audience he addressed numbered about eight hundred. Whenever possible, he used the stereopticon to show the latest photographs of the landscape, the site, and the objects.

The talks he delivered were almost all variations on the topic of recent discoveries at Pompeii, sometimes a rapid survey of the work and the major finds, sometimes focusing on a single building and its decor,[40] sometimes making the historical context or the character of the eruption of Vesuvius the focal point. In his lecture at Berkeley on November 24, for example, Francis spoke about the destructive power of Vesuvius and traced the history of the excavations from their beginning up to the work of the past decade.[41] He described the most significant of the new discoveries: the richly decorated House of the Vettii, which came to light in 1894–95, and the Temple of Venus Pompeiana, discovered in 1897–98. Both were found during official archaeological excavation—unlike the villa of Fannius Synistor at Boscoreale, which, with its remarkable frescoes, its furniture still in situ, its eye-catching silverware, and its hoards of gold and silver coins, was excavated by what might generously be termed private enterprise.[42] Kelsey described the fate of the Boscoreale hoards.

> According to law the Italian government has first option on all valuable discoveries: but in this case the discoverer, being a long-headed chap, took his booty secretly to Paris where he sold the coins to two French numismatists. The silverware was purchased by Baron Rothschild and presented by him (except six pieces which he retained for his own collection) to the French government. The set, consisting of 102 pieces can now be seen in the Louvre.

His lecturing outside Ann Arbor continued through 1906, on a less demanding schedule but with the same variety of audiences. He lectured, for example, in 1904 in Kansas City at the Central High School; in March 1905 to

---

40. Titles of his talks included, for example, "The Pictures in the House of the Vettii" and "The Villa and Treasure of Boscoreale." Sometimes he spoke more directly in the interest of the AIA, as, for example, in a talk titled "The Work and Aims of the Archaeological Institute of America."

41. There had been four major phases of discovery at Pompeii: 1763–72, 1813–21, 1823–32, and 1893–1901.

42. In an early example of the privatization of public property, contracts had been issued to individuals to conduct excavations without official supervision. This led to the exploitation, if not rifling, of sites and their contents. Near Pompeii, the villa at Boscoreale offers a sad example of this kind of reckless "excavation." Such blatant scandals did, however, lead ultimately to the cancellation of the program of private contracts.

the Detroit Archaeological Society; and in 1906 at the Art Institute of Chicago, at the University of Kansas (Lawrence), and at Washburn University (Topeka). So successful had his lecturing become that President Seymour of the AIA wrote in a letter to Boston philanthropist and archaeology enthusiast Charles P. Bowditch in May 1906 that "no man from the faculties of Harvard, Yale or Columbia could draw such an audience as he in Kansas, Missouri or Utah."[43]

The Archaeological Institute of America and the International Commission of Archaeology and Ethnology

In 1902 Kelsey had accepted the invitation of Professor John Williams White, president of the AIA, to serve as the institute's secretary.[44] But when asked, in the next year, whether he would allow his name to be put forward as a candidate for the presidency, he declined, perhaps because of the pressure of work that had led him to seek help (an associate secretary of the AIA, Professor Mitchell Carroll of Columbian University, was appointed in 1903), perhaps because of his recent serious illness. The secretary's workload was challenging: inter alia, he was responsible for the organization of the publication and exploration programs and of the annual meeting for the reading and discussion of papers on archaeological topics; for relations with the foreign schools; and, above all, for the health of the local affiliated societies and the lecture program by which they were linked to the central office and shared in the latest archaeological news. Every year, he was part of the committee to appoint lecturers for the institute. In 1904 the committee met in St. Louis to coincide with the Congress of Arts and Science,[45] at which he was delighted to meet the celebrated German archaeologist Adolf Furtwängler. He also served on the managing committee of the American School of Classical Studies at Athens, and following his professorship at the American School in Rome, he served on the exec-

---

43. Seymour to Bowditch, May 26, 1906, as cited in C. M. Hinsley Jr., "Edgar Lee Hewett and the School of American Research in Santa Fe, 1906–1912" in *American Archaeology Past and Future: A Celebration of the Society for American Archaeology, 1935–1985*, ed. David J. Meltzer, Don D. Fowler, and Jeremy A. Sabloff (Washington, DC: Smithsonian Institution Press, 1986), 222. Thomas Day Seymour graduated from Western Reserve College in 1870 and, after a spell in Germany, was professor of Greek there from 1872 to 1880. He became professor of Greek at Yale in 1880, was chair of the managing committee of the American School of Classical Studies in Athens for many years, and served as president of the Archaeological Institute of America from 1903 to 1907. A midwesterner, he and Kelsey had much in common.

44. On the objectives and programs of the AIA and further details of Kelsey's involvement, see chapter 5.

45. Members of the committee that year were Thomas Day Seymour of Yale, George Moore of Harvard, and Martin D'Ooge and Kelsey of Michigan.

utive committee of that school, too. In 1903 the motion to reappoint Richard Norton as director of the latter school was moved by him.[46]

As one of the public faces of the AIA, Kelsey did not represent the world of ancient Europe alone. In introducing him at Berkeley, Professor William A. Merrill put his talk in the context of the establishment of new AIA societies at San Francisco and Los Angeles and stated clearly that these new societies were to be alive to the needs of New World archaeology as well as the archaeology of Greece and Rome. Kelsey pursued this theme himself throughout his term as secretary of the institute and again later as its president.

In the summer of 1903, he was appointed to the International Commission of Archaeology and Ethnology (founded with the intention of protecting ancient sites) and attended organizational meetings in Washington, D.C. In the face of unproductive argument, he joined others in calling on ex-senator J. B. Henderson to protest "against the action of the two representatives of the Smithsonian, Adler and Holmes, in endeavoring to block the way of the Commission." In the spring of the following year, he attended congressional hearings on the "archaeological hills" and advocated immediate protective legislation.[47] His diary reports (April 22, 1904) that the two committees of the House and the Senate "agreed to try to get the Rodenberg-Lodge Bill through by common consent" and that, on the next day, he discussed this bill, which was designed to provide a federal program of historic preservation, both with the secretary of state, John Milton Hay, and with President Roosevelt.[48] The

46. On the beginnings of and links between the AIA, the American School of Classical Studies at Athens, and the American School of Classical Studies in Rome, see Susan Heuck Allen, ed., *Excavating Our Past: Perspectives on the History of the Archaeological Institute of America,* AIA Colloquia and Conference Papers 5 (Boston: AIA, 2002) (hereinafter *EOP*), especially Caroline Winterer's contribution, "The American School of Classical Studies at Athens: Scholarship and High Culture in the Gilded Age" (93–104); Stephen L. Dyson, *Ancient Marbles to American Shores: Classical Archaeology in the United States* (Philadelphia: University of Pennsylvania Press, 1998); idem, *In Pursuit of Ancient Pasts: A History of Classical Archaeology in the 19th and 20th Centuries* (New Haven: Yale University Press, 2006).

47. *Hearing before the Subcommittee on the Committee on Public Lands of the United States Senate,* 58th Cong., 2nd sess., April 20, 1904, 3–8, 10, 12, 14, 22, 23, 27–30, etc. In his history of the Antiquities Act of 1906, Ronald F. Lee cites this hearing debating the Smithsonian Subcommittee Bill and the Lodge Bill, at which "objections to the Smithsonian Bill were offered in restrained but persuasive language by the Archeological Institute's secretary Kelsey, classicist and archeologist of the University of Michigan" (Ronald F. Lee, "The Antiquities Act, 1900–1906," chapter 6 in *NPS Archaeology Program, The Antiquities Act* [electronic version 2001]).

48. Vice President Theodore Roosevelt became president at the age of forty-two on the assassination of President McKinley in 1901 and was subsequently elected president in his own right in 1904. Kelsey was in Washington at the time of Roosevelt's inauguration on March 4, 1905, and describes the hilarity on the streets and the "fearful congestion" at Penn Station.

president, though "overwhelmed with callers, said he would do what he could for the cause." The bill, introduced into Congress later that month, at the end of the Fifty-eighth Congress, did not move.[49]

In September 1904, as a member of the relevant committee of the AIA, Kelsey was busy preparing another bill on the preservation of American antiquities to go before Congress. But after "a long trying meeting of the American Committee of the Archaeological Institute" on December 30, when only deadlock was reached on questions of future work in the Southwest, even Kelsey's determination was dented. On the verge of resigning from the International Commission of Archaeology and Ethnology, he met with Secretary Hay on January 3–4 to discuss the matter. Hay must have been persuasive, for Kelsey did not resign. The AIA and the American Anthropological Association had decided to work in tandem on the matter of antiquities preservation, and on January 10, their committees met together in Washington, D.C. Kelsey was in attendance. The joint committee, of which Edgar Lee Hewett[50] was the influential secretary, decided to put together a draft bill that would incorporate such proposals of the various pending bills as were deemed agreeable.[51]

Subsequent to these events and underscoring his standing as a philologist as well as an archaeologist, Francis Kelsey was elected vice president of the American Philological Association in December 1905. He was further buoyed by the act incorporating the AIA, passed by both houses of Congress and approved by President Roosevelt on May 26, 1906. There were forty-two members of "this body corporate and politic," who included two of the three previous AIA presidents (Seth Low and John Williams White)[52] and the current

49. Though strongly supported by scientific and academic constituencies, the bill (by Senator Henry Cabot Lodge of Massachusetts and Congressman William Rodenberg of Illinois) was rejected by Congress: it was the old story of the rival claims of private ownership and public trust and of bickering between the interested academic parties.

50. Hewett was an American archaeologist and close associate of Kelsey in efforts to promulgate interest in American archaeology in the Southwest. For more on Hewett, see chapter 5, "Kelsey, Hewett, and the School of American Archaeology."

51. The Antiquities Act was finally passed and signed by Theodore Roosevelt in June 1906, after six years of struggle. Introduced by Representative Lacey of Iowa, it was largely Hewett's work. On Hewett's key role, see Hal Rothman, *Preserving Different Pasts: The American National Monuments* (Urbana: University of Illinois Press, 1989). See also chapter 5 nn. 27, 30.

52. Low, a New Yorker born and bred and a Columbia graduate, was a very successful businessman and politician. Twice mayor of Brooklyn and once mayor of New York City, he served as president (1890–1901) of Columbia College (which became Columbia University during his tenure) as well as president of the Archaeological Institute (1890–96). White, professor of Greek at Harvard, was chair of the first managing committee of the American School of Classical Studies at Athens (1882–87), before becoming president of the AIA (1897–1902).

president, Thomas Day Seymour. Francis Kelsey was another member of this distinguished group. At year's end, he was elected president of the American Philological Association for 1907. That he would succeed Seymour in the presidency of the AIA could not have been hard to imagine.

Research and Publication

Kelsey was constantly improving and revising the textbooks that Allyn and Bacon were publishing for him. New plans, new maps, new photographs, new engravings, new sections on historical and archaeological matters were all grist to his mill. In 1904 he completed a revision of *Select Orations and Letters of Cicero*. In August 1905, he was working on another edition of the Caesar, correcting proofs on the train to St. Louis and mailing them in from stations en route. May 1906 finds him at work on the seventh edition of his Ovid, June on the sixth edition of the Lucretius. There were also articles and papers. After Thanksgiving dinner in 1906, he finished his article "The Value of Greek and Latin as Educational Instruments,"[53] and a month later, he was completing his papers for delivery at the annual meetings: "A Pompeian Illustration to Lucretius" and "Codrus's Chiron and a Painting from Herculaneum," the latter subsequently published in the *American Journal of Archaeology*.[54]

His belief that research and publication should play a major role in the life of a prestigious university was echoed by other faculty members. In 1900 the University Research Club had been established to allow faculty engaged in research to share their activities and to promote efforts to find support for their work. It was now clear that the university would engage as eagerly in the hunt for new knowledge as in teaching; and Kelsey himself led efforts to emphasize and publish research. In 1900 he had asked the Board of Regents to support the publication of research; referred to a committee, this request vanished. Undeterred, in 1902 he approached the University Senate and urged them to set up a series of University Studies; this request, too, was referred to a committee for study and report. This committee did its work, however, and reported that "it was expedient for the University to issue a series of publications from time to time when in the judgment of a Senate committee suitable material is offered and provision is made by the Regents or otherwise to meet expenses." In a second resolution, the committee went on to say that the work submitted by Professor Kelsey was suitable for publication in a volume and

---

53. This article was published (as chapter 2) in F. W. Kelsey, ed., *Latin and Greek in American Education, with Symposia on the Value of Humanistic Studies* (New York: Macmillan, 1911), 17–39.

54. *AJA* 12 (1908): 30–38. His "Pompeian Illustration" was announced as to be published in the journal (see *AJA* 11 [1907]: 65), but it does not in fact seem to have appeared.

that Kelsey should be authorized to publish these papers under the series University of Michigan Studies, in a suitable subseries. The first subseries to appear was the Humanistic Series. Such were the hesitant beginnings of the University of Michigan Press.

The first volume of the Humanistic Series of the University of Michigan Studies bears the title *Roman Historical Sources and Institutions* and was edited by Professor Henry A. Sanders: it contained seven papers (four written by colleagues at other institutions—Swarthmore, Mount Holyoke, Cincinnati, and Princeton; two by Sanders himself; and one by his Michigan colleague Joseph Drake) and appeared in 1904. Funded by the authors and by private money raised by Kelsey (an advance of three hundred dollars from Regent Arthur Hill),[55] it set the precedent for most of the future funding of the series. A second volume appeared in 1906, aided by five hundred dollars from the regents. But their financial support for the series over the years, though warmly welcomed by Kelsey, was unpredictable: apart from their contribution to volume 2, the direct costs of the first four volumes were met by the authors and by benefactors. For example, on April 28, 1906, Franklin H. Walker of Detroit "took under consideration a request to raise $600 for a volume of University Studies" and followed this up on June 20 by saying that "he would be responsible for the payment by December 15th of $500 for volume 3 of the University of Michigan Studies, Humanistic Series." The major contributors to other volumes published or completed during Kelsey's lifetime were William Murphy[56] and Charles Freer of Detroit.[57]

Most of the seventeen volumes of the Humanistic Series that appeared before his death were edited by Kelsey himself, with the help of Henry Sanders. They worked in cramped and difficult conditions, either at home or in

---

55. University of Michigan, *Proceedings of the Board of Regents (1901–1906)*, "October Meeting, 1904" (October 13), 426. Hill would leave two hundred thousand dollars to the university in his will; ibid., "October Meeting, 1910" (October 7), 815.

56. William H. Murphy (1855–1929) was a member of a wealthy family whose interests included the Murphy Power Company, the Murphy Oil Company, and the Murphy Lumber Company. Early investors in automobile research and manufacture, the Murphy family, along with the McMillans, owned most of downtown Detroit; friends such as the Algers, the Buhls, and the Ferrys owned the rest. Educated at the University of Michigan and passionate about music, William was a great supporter of the Detroit Symphony, gladly covering the orchestra's annual deficits. See Sidney Olson, *Young Henry Ford* (Detroit: Wayne University Press, 1997), 116.

57. Other contributors included Regent Peter White, J. M. Longyear, J. Pierpont Morgan, and Mrs. E. W. Pendleton.

Kelsey's office on campus. Not content with editing the Humanistic Series and his other academic work and publications, Kelsey also edited the Macmillan Company's Handbooks of Archaeology and Antiquities series with Percy Gardner. It is thanks to this relationship that the imprint of the Macmillan Company appeared on early volumes of the Michigan Humanistic Series. The series was not restricted to topics concerning classical antiquity in the strictest sense but ranged widely over the humanities. In the wake of the Humanistic Series, other series followed: the Scientific Series in 1914; the Papers of the Michigan Academy of Science, Arts, and Letters in 1921. When departments began to issue their own individual series, it became clear that this proliferation of publications should be brought together and centrally organized. Accordingly, the University of Michigan Press was formally inaugurated in 1930.

A common theme in Kelsey's published work was the relationship between literature and the material world. His mind saw the value of written documents equally with that of archaeological materials. Accordingly, during his sojourn in Italy, he had kept his mind open to acquiring suitable objects for the university's collection. Not all of Canon de Criscio's collection of antiquities at Puteoli had been secured by Walter Dennison in 1899.[58] In 1905 Kelsey was able to negotiate the purchase of nine inscriptions, some inscribed tiles, building materials, and a marble basin from the collection. Some years after de Criscio's death, his sister wrote to Dennison offering to sell what was left. But Dennison himself had died, and the letter was passed to Kelsey. Francis went to work at once, consulted with University of Michigan president Marion LeRoy Burton (1920–25), and, after a while, identified donors. Professor John Winter, on leave in Italy, saw to the shipping of another varied batch of antiquities to Ann Arbor, all valuable for the light they throw on daily life in Roman provincial townships. They included more inscriptions, fragments of marble reliefs, storage vessels, and examples of fine wares. Thus, over many years, the major part of the important de Criscio collection came to be housed in Ann Arbor.

The Family Man

Kelsey's busy schedule might lead one to think he had little time for family life. On the contrary, his family plays an important role in his diaries, which

---

58. See chapter 3, "Italy."

reveal much about him as father, brother, husband, and son. At the turn of the century, Francis and Isabelle Kelsey had been married fourteen years and were the proud parents of two girls, Ruth and Charlotte. Francis's parents, Henry and Olive Kelsey, were still alive, on the home farm at Churchville, New York, as were Isabelle's father and stepmother, Edward and Emma Badger,[59] at their home in Niles, Michigan.

Kelsey visited his parents at Churchville as often as he could, frequently stopping on his way east to a lecture tour or for consultations with his publishers. In 1901, not having seen his parents for some time (he had been in Italy for the best part of a year), he spent Thanksgiving at the family farm, returning by overnight sleeper from Rochester to Ann Arbor. The diaries tell us he was there twice in 1902—his father was now over ninety years of age and his mother over eighty—and that he knew his parents were failing: on a visit in May 1903, he found his "father feebler, mother better." In 1904 he went to Churchville three times: in April with his sister, Harriet, when the snow was deep enough (six feet) for him to mention it in his diary, and briefly in July and November, when he was again en route to Washington. The following year, sensing the end, he stopped more often. On February 26, after he had asked the West Shore dispatcher to order the express to stop at Churchville for him, he found "all better than anticipated"; and he stopped again on April 16 on his way east. He took Charlotte along to see his parents on Independence Day and Ruth a month later, on each occasion continuing east himself and leaving the girls with their grandparents. On September 13, he was in the Southwest on business when his father died. It took a week for Harriet to get the news to him; but that year at Thanksgiving, he made a point of being with her and his mother at Churchville. Isabelle and the children—there were now three: a son, Easton, had been born on June 21, 1904[60]—held Thanksgiving at home in Ann Arbor with Isabelle's parents.

Eleven months to the day since his father's death, on August 13, 1906, his mother, too, died. At the beginning of the month, Francis had found her "very ill": he had been at Churchville on and off since then. Harriet was there, too. Fred arrived from Lake Placid on August 12; so, too, did Ida, Henry's wife.[61]

---

59. Emma was Edward's second wife. His first wife, Charlotte Augusta Colby, Isabelle's mother, had died when Isabelle was only three years old.

60. The genealogies date Easton's birth to June 22, but the diary is clear: on June 21, "six minutes before midnight was born a son."

61. Henry, the eldest of the children and a farmer near St. Joseph, Missouri, had died in 1895, leaving a widow, Ida Florence, and three children.

Francis noted, "Mother knew us all." She died on the evening of the thirteenth, with Francis, Isabelle, Harriet, Fred, Ida, Lena (the cook), and Dr. Vail nearby. The funeral took place on the fifteenth, "on a beautiful, beautiful day." Charlotte, though only nine years old, was there and remembered it clearly. In a 1957 document, which she herself characterizes as "random notes,"[62] she describes the farmhouse ("little with a glorious red trumpet vine over the front porch"), the apple orchard, the meadows, the horse, the cellar door suitable for sliding down, and her experiences at the funeral. She was present, mystified, at the brief service in the parlor, was driven in a carriage to the cemetery by her father, and was at graveside. She never forgot the sight of the closed casket lowered into the "hard brown" earth.

Olive Kelsey's brother, John Townsend Trowbridge, the prolific writer, editor, and antislavery agitator, lived near Boston. Francis shared his love of the written word and always endeavored to keep in touch. Trowbridge, though in his seventies when Francis lectured in Boston in 1902, made sure to hear his nephew speak. Since many of the leading figures in the field of archaeology were in New England, where the meetings of the AIA were often held, there were good reasons for Francis to travel there frequently.

Francis also kept in touch with his brother Fred and family, in Orange, New Jersey. He often stayed with them when visiting New York. It was an easy ferry ride from Manhattan, and he enjoyed the ease of home life, not least the evenings of music making, distinguished (notes the diary) by Fred playing the viola. He saw the family of his elder brother, Henry, less often. Henry had died in 1895, and the farm near St. Joseph, Missouri, was not near a route that Francis traveled much. But in April 1906, on his way from Kansas City to a meeting in Chicago, he stopped off at St. Joseph. His nephew Harry met him at the station and drove him out to the farm. There he spent "a delightful day" with Ida, Harry, and his two nieces, Hattie and May, by now young women twenty-five and twenty-three years of age.

But of the three siblings, he was closest to his sister, Harriet. His childhood schoolbooks show how close the only daughter and the youngest son were at this stage of their lives,[63] and his diaries confirm that from 1901 their friendship was firm. Harriet had married the Reverend Eli Fay, a man some twenty-four years older than she, in 1889 in San Francisco, and they lived in Los Angeles and Pasadena. After her husband's death in 1899, Harriet returned east,

---

62. "RNMF," 11.
63. See chapter 1, "Ogden and Beyond: Educating Francis."

living sometimes in upstate New York, occasionally in New York City, and sometimes in Ann Arbor. She invested money in Francis's business ventures, and the diaries record their meetings. In January and February 1904, in particular, there were several occasions when Francis broke his journey in Buffalo and met Harriet at the Berkeley Hotel.

Pastimes and Hardships

Music played an important role for the Kelseys, individually and as a family. Charlotte recalled musical evenings of songs and hymn singing at home: Isabelle played the piano, Ruth the violin; and Francis and Charlotte sang the parts.[64] Ruth played her violin in recitals at the School of Music and at informal receptions, too, from an early age, and Charlotte sang both at their church, First Presbyterian, and at the local German church. Francis and Isabelle attended concerts of the Sinfonia Society of the School of Music, symphony concerts in University Hall, and faculty concerts. They were critical concertgoers, but after the concert given by the university orchestra on April 10, 1905, Francis's diary comments that they "did well." The highlight of the year was the annual May Festival. In 1904 Elgar's *The Dream of Gerontius* and Bizet's *Carmen* took center stage;[65] in 1906 the focus was on Dvořák.

It fell to Francis, as president of the University Musical Society, to entertain guests, who often included sympathetic regents and other visiting dignitaries. The children were always expected to be present, to join and learn from the conversation. Their favorite guests at these meals at home were important figures from the music world in Chicago: Frederick Stock, conductor of the Chicago Orchestra;[66] Frederick T. Wessels, the manager of the

---

64. "RNMF," 3.

65. Edward Elgar's setting of Cardinal Newman's poem "The Dream of Gerontius" had received its first performance only in 1900, so its performance in Ann Arbor in 1904 is a remarkable testimony to the modernity of musical appreciation in Michigan. Georges Bizet's *Carmen*, first performed in 1875, had been hailed by Nietzsche as a paradigm of what he termed "Mediterraneanism" and likewise speaks to the wide range of musical sensibility in and around Michigan at this time.

66. Born and raised in Germany, Stock joined the orchestra as violist in 1895. Appointed assistant conductor in 1899 and then music director pro tempore in 1905, upon the death of Maestro Theodore Thomas, he was confirmed as music director in his own right in 1911. The orchestra, then renamed for Thomas, became known as the Chicago Symphony Orchestra in 1913. An avid modernist, Stock promoted the music of Richard Strauss, Holst, Mahler, and others and commissioned work from other composers, including Stravinsky (Symphony in C) and Prokofiev. See "About the CSO: Frederick Stock," http://www.cso.org/main.taf?p= 7,3,1,4,2 (accessed September 26, 2008).

orchestra; and Herbert Witherspoon, the operatic bass. Opera was a source of great pleasure to the family, especially to Francis, and the Metropolitan in New York was a favorite opera house for him. On New Year's Eve in 1904, after a busy day in Allyn and Bacon's New York office discussing new engravings for the next edition of the Cicero, Francis hurried off to a performance of *Rigoletto*.[67]

Then there was the theater. Traveling companies visited Ann Arbor, and no opportunity was missed, especially when it came to Shakespeare. On the evening of May 26, 1905, Isabelle and Francis saw *Twelfth Night,* and they would have gone to another play the next night if work had not kept Francis at his desk until two in the morning. The children were introduced to plays at an early age.[68] Charlotte recalled that, from the age of eight, she and Ruth were taken to see the annual performances put on by Ben Greet's Company, such as *A Midsummer Night's Dream, The Tempest,* and *The Merchant of Venice*. They were stagestruck by the costumes, sets, lights, actors, and stories; but their parents also impressed on them that the plays reflected human experiences and had much to teach.

For the children, reading was obligatory. Isabelle and Francis allowed Annie Fellows Johnston's Little Colonel series and books at that level but also introduced them early to the classics: as a family, they read the Bible almost every evening. The *Iliad* and the *Odyssey, Beowulf,* and the *Niebelungenlied* were on their reading list, as were the myths and legends of Greece and Rome. Books by Ernest Seton Thompson, Charles Dickens, and Sir Walter Scott were all to be digested. Less demanding, but also read with approval, were Andrew Lang's fairy tales and popular books like *Little Women* and *Black Beauty*. It was impressed on them that it was important to read, and read they did.[69]

Gardening played an important role in Francis's life. The yard behind the house was big, with a well-grassed lawn, trees, flower beds, fruit bushes, and a vegetable patch. Three seasons of the year, Francis could be found working in the garden before breakfast every day. He always wore the same gardening clothes: an undershirt, a ragged old pair of pants, a handkerchief around his

---

67. The New York Metropolitan Opera, founded in 1880, enjoyed its inaugural season in 1883–84. But the beginnings of opera in the United States are to be found in the 1830s, in the opera companies brought to New York by Lorenzo Da Ponte, librettist to Mozart, Salieri, and others. See Sheila Hodges, *Lorenzo Da Ponte: The Life and Times of Mozart's Librettist* (Madison: University of Wisconsin Press, 2002).

68. "RNMF," 4.

69. Ibid., 2, 3.

neck, and a battered straw hat.[70] Did he see a parallel between the garden, with its mix of discipline and imagination and its demands on stamina and patience, and the life of the scholar? More probably he simply enjoyed the slow process of nature and the fresh fruit and vegetables the family relished. The year 1903 offered a bumper crop that lasted until the end of October, when his diary records (October 23), "Heavy frost last night: up to this time we have had squash, cucumbers and tomatoes from the garden in abundance." In the garden, he was in his element, his green fingers testimony to his early life on the farm at Ogden. It was in part his love of nature and in part his wish for the family to be in the country during the summer that induced him to rent a cottage for $5 a week at Lake Cavanaugh, some fifteen miles west of town, for the month of July 1906.[71] Access by rail and shank's mare was easy; and there was always the possibility of more gardening.

As to holidays, Christmas Day was spent at home, though diary entries for that holiday are often short. In 1901 he comments that "Fraulein had prepared a tree in the German fashion" and adds "Christmas particularly merry";[72] "A Merry Christmas again!" appears in 1903, "A Happy Christmas at home" in 1904. In 1902, however, Francis was in the hospital, and in 1905 he worked most of the day on a paper to be given at the annual conference. At Thanksgiving he was often away from home: in 1903, for example, he was in California. He himself did not make a fuss about birthdays, but his diary does record one year when he returned unexpectedly early from Washington and surprised Charlotte "in the midst of her birthday party with Ruth and nine other little girls. Took supper with the children."

Illness struck family members from time to time, and Francis himself was not immune. On a visit to Detroit in October 1902, he felt "so badly that I

---

70. Ibid., 6. He was fastidious about his clothing in other circumstances and records shopping excursions to Hudson's department store in Detroit, where, in 1903, for example, he bought a spring overcoat "and had it pressed for me by 6 o'clock ($25). I also secured a stack of collars and cuffs." Again in 1906, he purchased a suit at Hudson's, "for $22 plus $6 for an extra pair of pants." Aside from his gardening outfit, Charlotte records other foibles: late-night suppers of apple sauce, bread, and milk; a taste for peanut brittle and Turkish delight; and rock candy and whiskey as his remedy for a cough. See ibid., 8, 12, 14.

71. According to his diary, he moved to the cottage with Isabelle, the family, and the governess on June 30 and returned himself to Ann Arbor the next day. This was the pattern for the month of July: the family at the lake, Francis there at the weekends. See diary, June 30 and July 1, 1906.

72. The records for Washtenaw County from the twelfth census of the United States (1900) list the residents at 826 Tappan Street in Ann Arbor as Francis, Isabelle, Ruth, and Charlotte Kelsey; a "boarder" (James Richmond); and a German "domestic," whose name is not clearly legible (Bertha Brock?).

came out by train at 4.35 instead of the motor." On the eleventh, a "dull abdominal pain commenced in the morning"; he adds, "Kept up work." The next day, he reports that "the pain kept me awake all Sunday night. Paroxysm so severe in the afternoon called the Doctor." Though the condition was not at first thought to be serious, the pains returned, and he underwent surgery on November 13. The operation was performed by Dr. Nancrede and was of sufficient medical interest for four other doctors to be in the hospital amphitheater. As Kelsey explained later, in a letter to AIA president Thomas Day Seymour explaining his inactivity, his operation was extensive and severe: "[It] effectively removed from under my liver that colony of Italian parasites the invisible ovum of which was probably introduced into my system on a leaf of Roman lettuce early in the winter of 1900–1. The cyst containing them was as large as one's two fists."[73] On Christmas Eve, he was still not fully mobile and had to be wheeled into the ward to hear the carols, but the outlook brightened when Isabelle and the children were with him on Christmas Day and New Year's Day. Finally allowed home on January 10, he resumed work at the university on February 9. It had been quite a scare.

The other major worry was his eyesight. In Washington in 1905, he consulted a Dr. Seibert, who prescribed drops of Adrenalin and Argyrol[74] and penciled his eyelids with 1 percent nitrate of silver. It is hardly surprising, given the hours and hours he spent poring over proofs, that over the years he continued to have trouble with his eyes.

Ruth had a serious bout of pneumonia in 1904—just a month before her brother, Easton, was born. Since Isabelle did not feel able to cope with her daughter's illness and the birth of another child at the same time, Francis—after sitting up all night with his sick daughter—engaged a nurse. The nurse stayed with them in the house until the end of May and came in for a few hours daily after that. The night of June 21 saw plenty of unusual activity at the house: Dr. Sanders arrived at 8:00 p.m., Dr. Herdman at 10:00, and the

---

73. AIA Archives, Archaeological Institute of America, Boston University, Boston, MA (hereinafter AIA Archives), box 10.7. On November 18, Isabelle had written to Seymour to explain that her husband was out of action: "for the first day we had very little hope of his recovery."

74. Adrenalin was a trademarked, commercial form of epinephrine (Parke-Davis); Argyrol was a topical antimicrobial agent developed commercially (and quite successfully) by Dr. Albert Coombs Barnes, whose art collection is at the Barnes Foundation. See David S. Goldstein, *Adrenaline and the Inner World: An Introduction to Scientific Integrative Medicine* (Baltimore: Johns Hopkins University Press, 2006), 61; Arthur Williams, "Alfred Barnes, Argyrol, and Art," *Pharmaceutical Journal* 265.7128 (December 23/30, 2000): 933–34.

nurse, Mrs. Mayhew, shortly afterward. "At six minutes before midnight was born a son," the Kelseys' third child, Easton Trowbridge Kelsey.

The Business Man

The Hays Consolidated Mining, Milling, and Lumber Company

Kelsey's diary not only brings to light the minutiae of daily family life, accounts of expenses large and small, and the highs and lows of health; it also reveals a surprising aspect of this professor of Latin: his business interests. Early in 1903, the diary begins to mention his participation in the Hays Company, a mining, milling, and timber concern.[75] The diaries' narrative suggests that he soon became a member of the company's board of directors, an unusual appointment for a high-risk enterprise with Western interests. Kelsey is sometimes described in the literature as a man of "independent means,"[76] but this cannot be taken to refer to inherited wealth. As we have seen, he was brought up in tight circumstances on the farms, first at Stony Point, Ogden, and then at Churchville, and the terms of his parents' wills show that he received only $115 from his father's estate and $500 from his mother's. Moreover, these sums did not come to him until 1907. To command a seat on the board of the company, however, he must presumably have invested a considerable sum, had influential friends, or both.

By 1899 he and his wife and their children lived in a comfortable house (fig. 10),[77] employed a cook and a governess, and entertained well. While Isabelle apparently had a small private income of her own, the diary implies that they kept their money separately: there is mention of his loaning her money from time to time (she tangled with a tax man once or twice), and she consulted him on other money matters, not least when they concerned rents and sales of small properties in Chicago. So what was the source of his extra income?

Royalties from the sale of his textbooks provide the answer. Four of the six textbooks appeared in the 1880s, including the popular *Caesar's "Gallic War,"*

---

75. As far as I have been able to work out, there were two branches to the company: the American branch, incorporated in the territory of Arizona; and the Mexican branch (a subsidiary?), licensed by Mexican authorities to operate in Sonora Province.

76. Dyson, *Ancient Marbles to American Shores*, 43.

77. The Kelseys lived in rented accommodations in the early 1890s, but the birth of the children doubtless prompted their move to the house at 826 Tappan Street (telephone extension "Michigan 114," according to the *Ann Arbor City Directory* for 1899).

10. House at 826 Tappan Street, Ann Arbor, 2010. Extended since Kelsey's day, this was the house in which Ruth, Charlotte, and Easton were brought up. Photo: Mary Pedley.

first published in 1886 and already in its tenth edition by 1900. The other two (the editions of Ovid and of Cicero's orations and letters) appeared first in the early 1890s. All enjoyed republication in multiple new editions, and some sold like hotcakes. This was a period of great expansion of secondary education in the United States, and Latin enrollments were large both in high schools and in college courses. The figures tell the tale: total enrollments in U.S. high schools rose from 202,963 in 1890 to 915,061 in 1910, Latin enrollments from 70,429 to 448,330.[78] Francis's diary occasionally records his income for the year. In 1906 his salary from the University of Michigan was $2,700, while his royalties from Allyn and Bacon amounted to $2,158.08. In 1907 the figures are similar, with a university salary of $3,000 and royalties of $2,288.42. John Allyn will have reflected smilingly on his decision in 1885 to commission a new Caesar from the young Lake Forest scholar. The partner-

78. Susan Shapiro, "Cicero and Today's Intermediate College-Level Student," *Classical Outlook* 84.4 (2007): 148.

ship had paid handsome dividends, and it is logical to suppose that Francis put a good percentage of his royalties into investments.

How he came to choose the Hays Company for investment is another matter. He may have consulted his father-in-law, a businessman involved in milling enterprises in Michigan and Chicago. It is also possible that he was guided by some of his more wealthy acquaintances in Detroit, men of affairs from whom he often solicited funds for university projects[79] and whom he knew socially.[80] It is easy to envisage a circumstance in which the conversation strayed to investments. Two incidents provide clues. When he first visited the office of the Hays Company in Washington in May 1903 (before he had acquired any shares), the vice president of the company mentioned a letter from General Russell A. Alger, the former Michigan governor who was a Detroit acquaintance of Kelsey. More telling, perhaps, when Kelsey went to Mexico in December 1903 to attend Hays Company shareholders' meetings, he was accompanied by the University of Michigan secretary James H. Wade.[81] Could it be that the university or Wade himself had invested in the Hays Company?[82]

On May 3, 1903, Kelsey and his sister, Harriet, visited the offices of the Hays Company in Washington, D.C.[83] There, the president, Mr. Charles W. Hays, "spoke of the policy of the company in respect to the development of mining, grazing and lumber interests." Two days later, they were in the office of Mr. Whelpley of the American Security and Trust Company, the treasurer of the Hays Company, who, Francis reports, "gave me facts regarding the sale of stock and the stability of the company." At some moment between May 5 and July 9, both Harriet and Francis invested in the company; on that latter date, Walter Weed, one of the foremost geologists in the United States, ad-

---

79. He solicited funds for fellowships, publications, memorials (such as the Frieze Memorial Organ), and acquisitions of books, inscriptions, and antiquities.

80. Isabelle's cousin Fred Colby and his wife, Frances Berry, would have provided one entrée into the richer world of Detroit.

81. A long-standing and influential member of President Angell's administration, especially with regard to financial matters, James Henry Wade served as university secretary for a quarter of a century. He was also an elder and member of the Board of Trustees of the First Presbyterian Church in Ann Arbor, Kelsey's church, and treasurer of the Tappan Presbyterian Association, in which Kelsey, too, was involved.

82. Records of the university's investments before 1920 are sketchy, according to personal communication from Russell Fleming, financial manager, Financial Operations, University of Michigan, May 2008.

83. After her husband's death in California in 1899, Harriet had returned to the East Coast: was she perhaps looking to invest a legacy?

vised Francis against further investment in the company "till further returns should be had from the properties."[84]

In the course of his Western lecture tour in the fall of 1903, Kelsey met James Wade at Colorado Springs. They traveled together through Colorado, Nevada, and California, Kelsey lecturing at almost every city they visited. They then went on to northern Mexico to attend meetings of the stockholders of the Hays Company, first at the Hotel Edwards in Magdalena and then at the Hotel Montezuma at Nogales. Mr. Whelpley also attended the meetings, as did, among other shareholders, General Sherman Bell, a Colonel Blount, and a Mr. Duncan. Kelsey, Wade, Bell, and Duncan then spent a couple of rough days at Camp Hays, in the hills near Magdalena, outlining development plans for the properties, securing samples at several of the company's claims, and talking with the "assayer Castanedo." Most of these claims lay in the hills and canyons about seventy miles from the U.S.-Mexico border and roughly forty miles west of Cananea, the site of the vast copper mining and smelting complex owned by the Cananea Consolidated Copper Company. On December 11, they visited the Vera no. 1 and no. 2 claims in Arizona.[85] There is no indication in the diary that trouble was brewing. On their way back to Ann Arbor, Kelsey and Wade looked over the sawmills that were the property of the American Lumber Company at Thoreau near Albuquerque.[86]

Toward the end of December, however, it was clear that the company's affairs were in a tangle. In Washington, D.C., Francis had a long interview with Mr. and Mrs. Hays—he being the company's president, each being a major shareholder—in the parlor of the house "in which they were boarding." On

---

84. Weed, a graduate of Columbia University in mining engineering, worked for the U.S. Geological Survey and became a consulting geologist specializing in ore deposits, an editor, and a publisher. He was one of the founders of the Geological Society of Washington, D.C.

85. It is hard to know which of these claims may actually have been working mines and which were not. Many were not. Operating capital to translate a claim into a mine was not easy to come by. Prospectors' plans seem often to have involved filing a claim, digging out some ore, and having it assayed. On the basis of assay reports, a prospector or a company had to decide whether to find the working capital to start a mine, look for a buyer, or extend or abandon the claim. Claims did not remain uncontested for long, and to hang on to a claim, the individual or company needed to pay more fees to the government or open the mine. In the case of the Hays Company (from the evidence of the diaries), there seems to have been little extraction of ore (details of which Kelsey would surely have mentioned). I am much indebted to Professor Samuel Truett of the University of New Mexico for many of details about mines, mining, and other Mexican and borderland material.

86. While they were visiting these operations of the American Lumber Company, Wade received telegrams from Ann Arbor that told him first of the illness (December 16) and then the death (December 17) of the wife of university president James Burrill Angell.

the following day, two days before Christmas, at a meeting with General Bell, Francis urged him to form "some plan of cooperation with Mr. and Mrs. Hays." Early in the new year, the diary records that Kelsey was hard at work on a "scheme of reorganization of the Hays Company" (January 4, 1904).

Lawsuits were being threatened from all quarters. A group of disgruntled bondholders in Baltimore were talking litigation, as were General Bell and a handful of followers in Washington and a Mr. W. T. Hand in Hot Springs, Arkansas. In Mexico a Mrs. Brooke had set her attorneys to work. Mismanagement was the prime source of alarm, with enough whispers of fraud to cause the value of the shares to be precarious (see fig. 11).[87] It seems likely that by this time Francis must have been on the board, since he was authorized to persuade the Baltimore litigants to withdraw their suits and agree to a reorganization of the company. The meeting in Baltimore was inconclusive, but at a meeting of the board of directors in Washington the same day (January 5), Mr. Hays offered 250,000 shares "to help the reorganization." A letter of agreement, signed by the directors and by Mr. and Mrs. Hays, was sent to General Bell, who refused to sign it. At a further directors' meeting on January 9, Francis put before the board an administrative reorganization of the company "by committees." When this was approved by the directors, he was asked to reconcile the litigants and empowered to do so. After the board agreed to pay his travel expenses, he said he would try. The task would be harder than he thought.

In mid-February, he traveled to Hot Springs to meet Mr. Hand and his attorney, Colonel Collier. For two days, he discussed with them the possible terms of a settlement of Mr. Hand's suit. Still straining for an agreement on the third day, they skipped lunch and settled on a proposition just in time for Kelsey to catch the train to Washington, where the directors delved into the value of the Hays properties, disputed claims, and the control of the company. Mr. Hays averred that "he could not control the company even if he would, and would not even if he could." He would have left, he said, only about 240,000 shares when the distribution should be completed. It is reasonable, then, to conclude that the reorganization involved a distribution of shares (though the diary does not reveal what the basis for the distribution was to be) as well as a new committee structure.

Shortly afterward, another litigant, a Mr. Woodward, a Washington resi-

---

87. It is possible to extract from the diaries that the directors valued the company's shares at $2.50 (par value at issue was $5) in May 1904, and one claimant was ready to settle at that; but a year later, a director bought 8,100 shares for $2,025 (25¢ a share) by private arrangement, and on August 8, 1905, he bought a further 11,900 shares for $5,000 (42¢ a share).

11. Share certificate of the Hays Consolidated Mining, Milling, and Lumber Company. Issued with a par value of five dollars, each share was worth about a quarter by the time Kelsey acquired his (May 24, 1905). Private collection of Easton Kelsey Jr., Rochester, NY. Photo: Mary Pedley.

dent, threatened another suit against the Hays Company "on old matters." Claiming to be "desirous of safeguarding the interests of the Company," Woodward hinted at the possibility of an injunction at the shareholders meeting when the new arrangements were to be proposed. Better news resulted from Kelsey's visit to Baltimore on February 25, when some suits were dismissed. Moreover, acting both for himself and Harriet, Kelsey had agreed to take some shares off General Bell's hands.

Mr. Joseph Earlston Thropp, the prosperous owner of the Earlston Furnaces in Everett, Pennsylvania, and a previous Republican representative from Pennsylvania to the Fifty-sixth Congress (1899–1901), emerged at this juncture as the leading figure on the board.[88] Discussions among the direc-

---

88. Thropp was trained as a civil engineer at the Polytechnic College of Pennsylvania; built docks at Duluth, Wisconsin; and became a railroad division engineer. After moving back to Pennsylvania, he turned to the manufacture of pig iron, became the owner of the Earlston Furnaces, and was elected a Republican congressman.

tors continued throughout the spring and early summer. Knowledgeable people were consulted. Francis conferred with the Honorable Wilson A. Jones, the commissioner of Indian affairs,[89] and asked his advice. When Mrs. Hays proposed the sale of two hundred thousand shares, her attorney spent two days in Ann Arbor with Kelsey on the matter, which went to a committee in Washington. At meetings on July 7 and 8, the board considered the situation in Mexico, Mrs. Brooke's lawsuit, and other disputes. It was a matter, at the very least, of the adjustment of conflicting claims on the ground and the transference of titles. Once again the board turned to Kelsey to go to Mexico and thrash things out.

Mexican Affairs

Leaving Ann Arbor on July 13, Kelsey first traveled to Colorado Springs for talks with Mr. and Mrs. Hays. Taking affidavits about Mrs. Brooke's suit from them, he arrived in Magdalena on July 18. There he met Mr. James H. Henley, general manager of the Hays Company in Mexico, and interviewed at length a Mr. Albert M. Conard,[90] from whom he "secured an important written statement." He also met, for the first time, Colonel Emilio Kosterlitzky, whose home was in Magdalena and who Francis said "treated me very pleasantly." It must have rapidly become clear to him that there were disputes between Hays and Conard and between Hays and Kosterlitzky. Were these just honest differences of opinion, or were they signals of more serious difficulties to come?

Kosterlitzky's was a name to conjure with in Mexico. A renowned "Indian fighter," a high-ranking officer in the Sonora National Guard, and simultaneously a hard-nosed lieutenant in the Gendarmería Fiscal, he was, thanks to his relationship with President Díaz, one of the more influential members of

89. Jones and his brothers owned the Mineral Point Zinc Works in Wisconsin, and he was a regent at the University of Wisconsin and chairman of its College of Agriculture. He served as commissioner of Indian affairs under both McKinley and Roosevelt. See Don Gander, "The Man behind the Unusual House: A Biography of the Honorable William Arthur Jones," http://www.jonesmansion.com/history/biography.htm (accessed September 26, 2008).

90. Conard ran a brewery and ice plant in Williams, Arizona, but moved to Nogales in 1899. In Mexico he made his fortune in the copper industry, and in 1908 he was president and general manager of the Sonora Copper Smelting Company. See Horace Jared Stevens and Walter Harvey Weed, comps., *The Copper Handbook: A Manual of the Copper Industry of the World*, vol. 10 (Houghton, MI: Horace J. Stevens, 1911), 1575. See also the genealogical posting by Chris Klukkert of Lompoc, California, at http://archiver.rootsweb.ancestry.com/th/read/AZSANTAC/2008-02/120187 (accessed September 26, 2008), which, inter alia, links Conard with the huge mining and milling works at Cananea.

the Mexican army in the state of Sonora.[91] On July 19, Kelsey "took statements of Conard and Kosterlitzky regarding boundary survey," in the course of which telegrams were exchanged with Mr. Hays. After conferring with Henley until 12:30 a.m., Kelsey "decided it was best for Kosterlitzky to go with me to the city of Mexico." On the following day, at the offices of the Mineral Agency—where he discovered that the clerk held Mrs. Brooke's power of attorney—he helped arrange the transfer of the claims at La Paz and El Pinito and obtained a copy of the records relating to the claim known as "The Smugler" (*sic*). Conard, Henley, and Kelsey left for Quijano, whence they continued by horse and mule to reach Camp Hays.

For the next three days, Henley (Conard evidently continued to Nogales, where he lived) took Francis on a tour of the company's properties, including the dam, the stamp mill, and the "workings of Ind.no.2." On July 24, Mr. Castañedo (the assayer) makes a sudden reappearance in the diary: Francis had a "long talk with Castanedo" prior to dinner with Mr. and Mrs. Henley.[92] The next day, Francis, Castañedo, and Henley, traveling on horseback, rode up and down more canyons and hills, visiting several claims.[93] On July 26, the three of them set off with pack animals, camping gear, and a young Mexican helper to visit the Sierra Azul properties. They passed by the ruined mission at Cocóspera, had lunch at Proto's ranch, visited the nearest claims, and pitched camp near a spring.[94] On July 27, they visited the Providenzia claim and then the Gran Fortuna, where, Francis reports, "in the tunnel near the entrance was a rattlesnake 3 feet 5 inches long. Henley struck its head with his pick." From another claim, the Esperanza, they took samples. They reached Proto's ranch once more and spent the night there. On July 28, after visiting

---

91. Porfirio Díaz was president of Mexico from 1877 to 1880 and again during 1884–1910. His interest in strengthening the Gendarmería Fiscal stemmed in large part from his wish to pacify the border regions to attract American investment. Such was Kosterlitzky's reputation as a fearless antagonist of the Indians, intrepid horseman, and ruthless soldier that he was one of the first to receive a commission in the new and improved Gendarmería.

92. Isidro Castañedo, a judge and notary public based in Nogales, was sympathetic to American mining enterprises and adept at negotiating the sale or lease of land. I am most grateful to Professor Truett for identifying this legal expert.

93. These were, in order, according to the diary, Independenzia no. 1; Emole no. 2; Independenzia; Oro Bonito no. 3; Oro Bonito no. 2; Emole no. l.

94. These adventures, with their themes of mining, camping, hardtack, firearms, and burros, cannot fail to prompt in many moviegoers images of Humphrey Bogart, Walter Huston, and high drama in *Treasure of the Sierra Madre* (1948, from B. Traven's 1927 novel of the same name). Kelsey and his two companions were not exactly in the Sierra Madre mountains, but they were close.

yet another claim, they passed "the furthest workings of the Greene Company, some 12 miles from Cananea," and reached Cananea itself at 6:30, "having ridden about 40 miles." It seems clear that the majority of the Hays Company's claims and workings were in the area to the north and east of Quijano, over toward Cananea.

Cananea was the headquarters of the Cananea Consolidated Copper Company, established in 1899 by an American magnate, Colonel William C. Greene.[95] Greene employed hundreds of workers; brought in the railroad, telegraph, and telephone; opened the mines; built the town; and bought up huge tracts of surrounding land for exploration, farming, and raising cattle. The town grew at lightning speed. At first it presented a ramshackle appearance, but in the course of a decade, it expanded into a substantial town with upward of twenty thousand inhabitants. The houses of Americans were built with spacious gardens on wide, well-planned streets in the more salubrious air of the upland mesa, free from industrial smoke and grime, while Mexican workers were relegated to a ghetto where drunkenness, noise, gunshots, and mayhem were nightly occurrences. Living arrangements did little to dispel ethnic and social differences. The railroad's gigantic locomotives and countless wagons, the huge lumberyards, and the immense smelting plant made visiting corporation officers gaze in astonishment. According to Francis's diary, the smelting plant handled five to six hundred tons of ore a day and produced five million pounds of copper a month. The cost in coke and coal was on the order of twenty-five hundred to three thousand dollars a day.[96] The day following their visit to Cananea, one of the horses was lame, so Francis offered to take the circuitous train ride back to Quijano while Henley and Castañedo rode across country. Delayed in Fairbank by a storm that washed out part of the rail line, Kelsey took a break from business and spent the day writing about the dreams he had when in the hospital in 1902 (though his diary is mute on their substance).

This trip had allowed Kelsey a good look at the company's properties and let him satisfy for himself which were simply claims and which were active

---

95. A vivid description of the development of Cananea, and Greene's part in it, may be found in Samuel Truett, *Fugitive Landscapes: The Forgotten History of the U.S.-Mexico Borderlands* (New Haven: Yale University Press, 2006), 83–99.

96. The workforce of this huge operation comprised a mix of Mexicans and Americans, though the large majority were Mexicans. The Mexicans worked more days and longer hours for less pay than the Americans—a state of affairs they naturally resented. When they later went on a strike (in 1906) resulting in a riot, it was Kosterlitzky's Rurales who restored order.

workings. It also allowed him to understand the property lines and disputed claims more clearly. It broadened his awareness of nature, too. His diary comments both on the wonderful views and on the scarcity of wildlife: occasionally they spotted deer, at which they took potshots, sometimes with success; and there were rattlesnakes, which they killed. As his father had done for him on the farm at Churchville years before, Kelsey cut off the rattles to take for the children back home. In the evenings, he wrote reports and letters for the company.

Kelsey spent all August and the first half of September in Mexico. During August, he worked much of each day on company business in Magdalena, in Nogales, or at Camp Hays. On August 4, he was busy "working over correspondence between Hays and Kosterlitzky kindly copied for me during my absence last week by Mrs Castanedo," while Castañedo shot a couple of foxes. The diary's description of the henhouses, the cabins, and the camp's inhabitants sitting about chatting leaves no doubt that Camp Hays was a considerable installation. In the evening, Kelsey worked away at his Latin, in particular at his edition of Cicero's first oration against Catiline. It is oddly fitting that he should have been working on this first-century BC diatribe against corruption at the same time as he was investigating irregularities and suggestions of fraud in the Hays Company.

On August 21, he went to El Paso to meet Mrs. Hays's mother, Mrs. Wright, who had arrived from Colorado Springs to review documents, contracts, and assay reports. Conard and Colonel and Mrs. Kosterlitzky joined them on August 22, to go the following day to Juárez. At the headquarters of a Mexican army lieutenant (whose name the diary does not mention), Mrs. Wright handed over an agreed three thousand dollars to Kosterlitzky. The diary records part of their conversation: "Colonel Kosterlitzky in answer to direct questions explained to Mrs. Wright several phases of the immoral conduct of Mr. Hays of which she had not heard, and it became clear that he had cruelly deceived her and Mrs. Hays." Mrs. Brooke's lawsuit made it necessary for Kelsey to go to Mexico City (or the "City of Mexico," as Kelsey often called it) at the end of the month. With the necessary documents and an offer of settlement in hand, he met Mrs. Brooke's attorney at the office of the American consul general. The attorney recommended that she accept twelve hundred shares; Kelsey dealt with affidavits and hired Adolfo Fenochio as company lawyer in Mexico at a rate of fifty dollars a month. He wrote a long letter to Mrs. Hays, noting in his diary, "evening commenced at 9.30 a letter to Mrs. Charles W. Hays, finished at 3.15 am."

All during his Mexican stay, Kelsey was befriended by Kosterlitzky. He went to the theater with him and his wife on several occasions and visited the shrine of Guadalupe with the Kosterlitzky family. He watched military exercises at Chapultepec Castle (the presidential palace) with them. He was even invited to an audience with President Porfirio Díaz (doubtless engineered by Kosterlitzky). On his departure for the United States on September 15, it was Kosterlitzky who came to the station to see him off.

Kelsey acknowledged the power that Kosterlitzky wielded in northern Mexico, and understood that he could achieve little without Kosterlitzky's help. In his turn, Kosterlitzky saw in Kelsey a representative of the Hays Mining Company who had the authority to settle claims, including his own. It was important to both that they cooperate. It is probably fair to say that when it came to the intricacies of the Mexican bureaucracy and the intrigues of Mexican politics, Kosterlitzky was utterly indispensable to any settlements that Kelsey might agree to make.

Kosterlitzky's colorful background perhaps explains some of Kelsey's appreciation of him. Raised mostly in Russia (with a short German sojourn) and trained in a Russian military academy, Emil Kosterlitzky reveled in military and especially in cavalry tactics and learned six or seven European languages as he grew up. In somewhat bizarre circumstances, he emigrated to Mexico, where he enlisted as a cavalryman in the army and acquired a reputation as an Indian fighter. Promoted to captain in the Guarda Nacional, he changed his name to Emilio and became a Mexican citizen (see fig. 12).

Thereafter assigned by President Porfirio Díaz to revive the Gendarmería Fiscal, soon known more familiarly as the Rurales, Kosterlitzky and his group were to patrol the border with the United States and to capture and deal with any outlaws or desperados. They were an arm of the law, whose task it was to preserve the peace and to ensure the confidence of foreigners investing in northern Mexico. As a leading figure in the Gendarmería, Kosterlitzky was responsible for monitoring the movement of people, property, trade goods, and equipment across the border, sorting out the legal from the illegal, in a manner somewhat comparable to a modern customs officer. In this capacity, he was responsible for facilitating the activities of American capitalists in Sonora.

Epitomized by the boomtown of Cananea and the resources committed to mining and lumber by the Cananea Consolidated Copper Company, American investment in Mexican natural resources was at its peak in the first decade of the century. The belief of American corporations in the stability of

12. Colonel Emilio Kosterlitzky, commanding officer of the Sonora Province Gendarmeria Fiscal, a Mexican Cossack. Arizona State Library, Archives and Public Records, History and Archives Division, Phoenix, #97-6862.

the country was important to Mexico and was continuously bolstered by President Díaz. Strikes and riots would not be tolerated, and company claims would be protected. These policies led Kosterlitzky and the Rurales to intervene in the 1906 strikes at Cananea and had led to his involvement in 1904 with Francis Kelsey and the Hays Company. With his military bearing, his bold and decisive character, his disciplined riders, and his fluency in English, Kosterlitzky was a firm favorite with his American counterparts, whether soldiers, corporate executives, or Latin professors.

It is clear from the diaries that Kelsey appreciated Kosterlitzky's help, and a genuine friendship seems to have developed between the two. Kosterlitzky appears again in the diary entry for September 1905 (when Kelsey is in Mexico once more), but he then fades from view.[97]

With the memories of his time in Mexico still fresh in mind and his knowledge of the company's affairs much increased, Kelsey resumed attendance at board meetings of the Hays Company in Washington in November. On November 19, he had dinner with the Fleming brothers (T. W. and A. H.), substantial shareholders, and "in my room after dinner unfolded the iniquitous management in Mexico and presented proofs of the guilt of Hays. They stood for what is right." Business meetings continued for the next three days. On Thanksgiving Day, Kelsey met General Manager Henley when he arrived from Mexico. Together they went to see Thropp, the most influential board member. After reading through a detective's report on "irregularities in the Mexico Hays Company," Thropp recommended "committing of criminal matters to a Committee of Three for adjustment." Kelsey and Henley then went to Henley's room, "where I for the first time saw the reports of the detective whom we had set to work on the irregularities in the Mexico Hays Company."

The next day, the board met from ten o'clock until noon and from seven o'clock until midnight. Kelsey gave an "outline of my work on the Brooke case, titles, mineral concessions etc., Henley read his report." On November 26, the Committee of Three (Thropp, Kelsey, and Isaac Baker Greene, soon to be appointed secretary of the Hays Company) met with Hays's attorneys, McLean and Ford, and then without them. When the evidence against Hays convinced Thropp and Greene, Kelsey drew up a proposition for action. Thoroughly prepared, he had this ready by 5:30 and typed by 6:10, and he still managed to catch the 7:15 overnight train. He was home in Ann Arbor the next afternoon.

In early December, Henley and Conard—the mining engineer and specu-

97. Kosterlitzky continued to be an influential presence in Sonora and remained loyal to President Díaz throughout the Mexican Revolution (1910–13), until Díaz was forced to leave the country. Kosterlitzky, too, crossed the border into the United States, with a large group of his Rurales, and was interned in California. His new life, putting his knowledge of languages to good use as a secret agent in the interests of the United States, is a whole other story. On Kosterlitzky and the U.S.-Mexican borderlands, see Dane Coolidge, *Fighting Men of the West* (New York: E. P. Dutton, 1932); Cornelius C. Smith, *Emilio Kosterlitzky: Eagle of Sonora and the Southwest Border* (Glendale, CA: Arthur H. Clark, 1970); Samuel Truett, "Transnational Warrior: Emilio Kosterlitzky and the Transformation of the U.S.-Mexico Border, 1873–1928," in Samuel Truett and Elliott Young, eds., *Continental Crossroads: Remapping U.S.-Mexico Borderlands History*, ed. Samuel Truett and Elliott Young, 241–70 (Durham, NC: Duke University Press, 2004); idem, *Fugitive Landscapes.*

lator who Kelsey had met at Magdalena on his first arrival in Mexico and who had lodged a claim against the company—came to visit Kelsey in Ann Arbor. Henley arrived on the third, Conard on the eighth. In their discussions, Conard "was unyielding." On December 10, Kelsey "began to reach an understanding with Conard in regard to the character of his evidence, speaking in hypotheses." On the next day, Sunday, "Mr. Conard and Henley were in our pew at church. So far reached an understanding that I became convinced of the guilt of Mrs. Hays as being as great as her husband's." The results of these discussions were telegraphed to Thropp and others, Kelsey suggesting a meeting of the Committee of Three at once. Henley, Conard, and he traveled together on December 13 to Washington, where things were heating up. On arrival, he went to Mr. Thropp's house. Warned of threats made against him by Mrs. Hays, he left Thropp's at midnight and went directly to Henley and Conard's hotel; there "he woke up Conard to warn him to be careful as Mrs. Hays would like to put him under arrest." An afternoon meeting the next day in the offices of the attorney Corcoran Thorn, at which there was animated discussion among Thropp, Greene, Burchell (the new vice president of the company),[98] Kelsey, McLean, and Ford, produced no outcome beyond agreement to a conference in Thorn's office the next day, to confront Mrs. Hays and Mrs. Wright with the evidence. Kelsey spent the morning of December 16 working on the evidence in Thorn's office, while Greene and McLean read no fewer than thirty-three letters to Mrs. Hays and Mrs. Wright. In the afternoon, a long meeting took place at which Thorn, Greene, Burchell, McLean, Ford, Mrs. Wright, Mrs. Hays, Conard, and Henley were present. The diary records that Kelsey "wrote till 2 o'clock on a statement of Mr. Conard."

Early the next day, taking the Hays's threat seriously, Kelsey sought permission from the district attorney to carry a revolver. A meeting held at noon, at which McLean, Ford, Kelsey, Greene, Burchell, and Thorn were present, was fractious: "They objected to paying the $8000 required by the proposition. I declared there was no alternative in the way of reduction and left the room." The members of the board were in a difficult position, needing to extricate themselves from threatened lawsuits while dealing simultaneously with allegations of fraud; at the same time, the lawyers for the Hays group were digging in their heels. McLean, Ford, and Kelsey had a further conference, at which "they agreed to recommend the proposition to their clients."

---

98. I have obtained much of the information about the identity of the company's officers from old share certificates originally in Francis Kelsey's possession, which are now owned by his grandson, Easton Trowbridge Kelsey Jr.

Later McLean brought word "that it had been accepted, and collapsed. Thorn dictated a proposed resolution which was unanimously approved at a special meeting of the board called at Mr. Thropp's house at 5 pm." Once again Kelsey hurried to the station to catch the 7:15.

He was followed to Ann Arbor two days later by Conard, who spent all available time on December 21 and 22 with him, "preparing statements" before leaving for Kansas City on the evening of the latter. Francis happily spent Christmas Day at home. On December 26, he left to visit his parents en route to the archaeological meetings in Boston. Thereafter he went on to Rochester, where he spent the night in a hotel and "completed the preparation of Affidavit no. 38 (Weed's first report)," the expert opinion of an eminent geologist. The next day, he mailed two copies of the affidavit to Conard from Boston, one to Kansas City, one to Nogales.

Gradual Extrication, 1905–6

The company's affairs were still in a dreadful tangle. Mrs. Brooke's and Mr. Hand's suits had been settled, as had those of some of the Baltimore litigants, and General Bell had been pacified. Progress had also been made toward settling with Mr. Conard and Colonel Kosterlitzky. But evidence of mismanagement involving the fabrication of contracts and fraudulent intent had been unearthed. The reports of the Pinkerton men were in hand; Mr. and Mrs. Hays and Mrs. Wright were angry; Kelsey and Conard had been threatened. The directors had in their hands Kelsey's and Henley's reports about affairs on the ground, the assay reports from the claims, and the views of geology experts like Walter Weed on the value of the properties. They also had the evidence supplied by Kosterlitzky, whose familiarity with the terrain and the activities of the miners and their bosses was second to none. But it is apparent that there had been too much room for disagreements and confusion over claims, property lines, contracts, and sales and leases of land and too many opportunities for sleight of hand.

Early in January, Thropp and Kelsey met in Washington with Mr. Adolph A. Hoehling Jr.,[99] the attorney for some of the Baltimore litigants, whom they met the following day in Baltimore. They found some more willing to compromise than others: Kelsey describes Hambleton as "hard and cold-blooded," White as "uppish," Lyon and Handley as "more sympathetic." There

---

99. Hoehling (b. 1868) would serve as a justice in the U.S. District Court for the District of Columbia (1921–28) and was one of the judges during the Teapot Dome trials. His father was Rear Admiral Adolph August Hoehling.

was no resolution, but there was enough promise for Kelsey to return to Baltimore a few days later to try to settle Lyon's suit. On January 11, the Committee of Three conferred with Walter Weed and went over many of the company's books.

February was filled with Hays business. On the fifth, Señor Torres of the Mexican Embassy, about to return to Mexico City to take his seat in the Mexican House of Representatives, reported that the company's concession would come before his nation's congress in April. On February 9, Francis asked the Pinkerton chief of detectives, who was in possession of an "important report from 'Op.no.6,'" to come to Washington, and General Bell announced that "he wanted rid of the Mexican company." Discussion with McLean and Ford on February 11 reached deadlock, prompting Kelsey to declare that he would "use my efforts to stop all litigation." He wrote in his diary for the twelfth that Mrs. Wright seemed "anxious to settle, but not to comprehend the situation fully." He reported the next day that she said "she was ready to settle but hadn't brought the money, that she could raise $3,000 or $4,000 and give notes for the remainder." Although there was no settlement, matters seemed to be moving that way, and Kelsey returned to Ann Arbor. However, it was not going to be that easy.

Summoned by an urgent telegram, Francis attended a meeting with McLean, Ford, and Mrs. Wright called for 8:30 a.m. on February 27 in Corcoran Thorn's office in Washington. Mrs. Wright was "obdurate, advised by Holmes Conrad not to settle but to pack up and go home";[100] Kelsey reports, "At noon the case seemed hopeless." Thorn, preoccupied with preparations for the inauguration of President Roosevelt, finally advised "destruction of the evidence, if so a settlement could be arranged." McLean and Ford resolved to make one more effort, and at a conference at 10:30 p.m., they and Greene and Kelsey (Thropp was sick) "agreed the destruction of the evidence with Conard's consent. McLean and Ford prepared a telegram which I sent to Conard." The agreement to destroy the (presumably incriminating) evidence was a breakthrough. More meetings followed. McLean and Ford tried to get the necessary thirteen thousand dollars from Colorado Springs in time to close before the inauguration. A full understanding was reached with Mrs. Wright whereby she agreed to permit the saving of copies of nonincriminating letters, "to look them over and select which I could keep." On March 2, the

---

100. Holmes Conrad was an eminent presence in legal circles, having been appointed assistant attorney general of the United States in 1893 by President Cleveland and solicitor general in 1895. In 1904 he had served as special prosecutor in postal fraud cases.

money was received from Colorado Springs, and a form of agreement was worked out. The day before the inauguration, the Committee of Three recommended twenty thousand shares for Conard; the board approved the settlement and voted the stock for Conard.

In April the Hays business took Kelsey back to the Rockies. In the Denver office of the Pinkerton National Detective Agency, Kelsey met Superintendent J. C. Fraser; Mr. G. C. Prettyman, who was in charge of the case; and Mr. Jesse Erb, the agent who had been "shadowing Mr. C. W. Hays in Colorado Springs."[101] In Colorado Springs, agents who were convinced of "fraudulent intent" introduced him to Judge Gunnell, who agreed to serve as company counsel. Negotiations with Hays continued until he agreed to turn over 260,000 shares of stock to the company, to give McLean and Ford 1,000 shares apiece, to surrender 25,000 shares of Goldfield-Columbia stock,[102] and to provide a note for five thousand dollars payable in four months but so endorsed that it could be cashed at the time of settlement. Hays yielded only inch by inch, reluctant to offer any cash. Kelsey was adamant. Judge Gunnell told Spurgeon, Hays's attorney in Colorado, that "his clients were guilty." At the last moment, Hays balked again, but "after a stormy afternoon," agreement was reached.

In May the plan for company reorganization was put to the shareholders: the company was to be "in Thropp's hands," with I. B. Greene as company secretary and B. R. Green as vice president. On June 22, a telegram confirmed the details of the settlement with Hays. In early July, Francis visited Holmes Conrad at his office in the Home Life Building, to put him in the picture, and two days later, the company's name was changed to the Columbia Consolidated Mining Company (incorporated in the territory of Arizona). A new board and officers were elected. Though the diaries do not reveal the names of all the directors and officers in the reorganized company, it is clear that Thropp was the leader (and had most at stake) and that Kelsey, if not a member of the board, was an involved shareholder. In August matters with Conard came to a head. After several wrangles of the sort to which Francis was by now inured, Conard agreed to accept Thropp's offer of five thousand dollars (he had wanted more) "for stock in settlement, $2000 to be on Kosterlitzky's order, and $3000 for 20,000 shares of stock," with the stock to

---

101. The use of agents to keep tabs on Mr. Hays is an eerie echo of Cicero's use of spies to follow Catiline.

102. The Goldfield-Columbia Gold Mining Company had mines at Goldfield, Nevada, and was incorporated under the laws of the state of Wyoming.

be allocated to Thropp and Kelsey. Francis wrote in his diary, "I expressed the desire to see him [i.e., Thropp] have control and said the stock I represent should be treated the same as his own." Kelsey settled with Conard, Thropp with Kosterlitzky.

September found Kelsey in Mexico again. He talked with potential partners (Raines and Cunningham) about work near Llano and the purchase of nearby properties. At Magdalena he reviewed titles of the Hays and Llano claims at the Mineral Agency with Kosterlitzky and took samples at various sites near the company camp (now renamed Puerto Camp). Near Llano, with Raines, Cunningham, and Conard, he investigated several claims and again took samples. At Nogales he agreed to terms with a Mr. Sandoval for the lease of various claims in the Llano region. Two days later, visiting the "Oro Fino" claims from Nogales and poking about a prospect hole, Raines struck "good ore": everyone was cheered.

Back at Magdalena, there was more time-consuming riffling through documents and leases, among which the record of the incorporation of the Hays Company was found. Certificates arrived from Mexico City; titles were transferred. A last-minute flurry of activity meant a sleepless night for Francis: the diary for September 26 records laconically, "worked till 4 a.m., bath, breakfast at 4.30, train at 5.05." On the way home, he had a long interview in Denver with Mr. Prettyman of the Pinkerton Agency and "gave him photographs of the Anderson forged draft."

This hectic September, consumed with the business of the Hays Company (now the Columbia Company), contrasts sharply with October–December, during which the diary makes mention of work on the papers of the Columbia Company only twice and only briefly. The company may not have been prosperous, but evidence of fraud had been rooted out, wrongs had been remedied, and it had been saved from public scandal. The complexities of the law, of the disputed claims and leases, and of the personalities involved were almost insurmountable, and the responsibilities of stewardship must have weighed heavily. Yet only with difficulty could others budge Kelsey from positions he had taken: he was nothing if not determined, and he drove things forward. Given the amount of time, energy, stamina, and tenacity he had spent on the Hays Company's affairs, it comes as no surprise to find in the diary at the end of the year these heartfelt remarks:

The year from July 1, 1904 to July 1, 1905 was far the hardest that the discipline of an overruling Providence has called upon me to pass through. I believe, however, that my appearance has not revealed to anyone the state of my thoughts and feelings, and I hope that the effort put forth may not prove to have been wholly without beneficial result.

The New Year came, and there were still the "fag ends of the Hays business" to deal with. In the first week of January 1906, Francis sounded out opinions. He described Thorn as "out of sympathy with the company," Birch as "courageous but not hopeful," and Reeside as "hopeful and determined." A sense of the value of the properties may be gauged from the fact that a certain Mr. Coale put an ad in the *Star* offering seven thousand shares at forty cents. Francis sought the views of the U.S. assistant secretary of the Treasury, Charles Hallam Keep, about "Hays forgery and government vouchers" and of Wickersham, a distinguished mining man, about "the company's condition and possible relief." Wickersham was not a man to pull his punches: on the basis of Henley's report, he saw no hope for the company. Saying that there were much better prospects, costing little or nothing, to be had in Colorado, he noted that "your sister has lost her money." He doubtless meant that Francis had lost his, too. Francis was at a directors' meeting the next day, at which, in an attempt to raise new money, a Finance Committee was appointed. Later in the year, at another meeting of the board, it was agreed that Reeside, who had been proposed as the new president of the company, should visit Kosterlitzky.

Kelsey's involvement was on the wane. In the course of the year, he must have realized that this business venture—for all its drama, excitement, and the stormy arguments that he does not seem to have shirked—had cost him and Harriet money. He must also have realized that the Hays Company had been too slow in getting on board the borderland copper bonanza and that Hays had bamboozled many of his American investors. But all was not lost, by any means. His university salary for the year was $2,700 (with a further $150 for summer school), the royalties from his publications amounted to $2,188.08, and one of his investments (the American Lumber Company) flourished and paid him a dividend of $280.[103] He had learned firsthand something of ruthless business practices, life on the edge of civilized society, and the precariousness of investment. His pragmatism, energy, and

---

103. Share certificates once owned by Kelsey and now in the possession of his grandson, Easton Trowbridge Kelsey Jr., reveal that in 1911 Kelsey owned 1,845 shares of the American Lumber Company. Other certificates reveal that in 1905 he owned 2,000 shares of the Hays Company (and Isabelle had 1,000) and that in 1908 he had 20,000 shares of the Columbia Consolidated Company. These hitherto valueless certificates have now reclaimed a fraction of their original value and appear for sale at current auctions of Americana.

willingness to work hard were further honed—and ready to serve his community, too.

Community Involvement

One of Francis Kelsey's oldest friends at Michigan was Albert A. Stanley, professor of music, who had been appointed to the faculty in 1888, just one year before Francis and Isabelle arrived. They worked together in the context both of the university, as, for example, in the acquisition of the Frieze Memorial Organ, and of the University Musical Society. That society, as we have already seen,[104] brought together university members and members of the general public in a joint effort to bring concerts and recitals to Ann Arbor for the benefit of all, town and gown; it also aimed to support the Ann Arbor School of Music (replaced in 1891 by the University School of Music), and the Choral Union, both of which were within its purview.

As president of the UMS, Kelsey tried repeatedly, formally and informally, to have the School of Music taken officially under the university's wing. For example, in April 1904, he prepared for the Board of Regents a proposal "to take the School of Music into the University," which went nowhere. A year later, after discussing the matter with Regents Barbour and Dean and the secretary of the university, James H. Wade, he invited to his home the two regents, ten faculty members, and a local businessman, Mr. Allmendinger, whose family had a long relationship with the university.[105] The issue discussed was, again, the relationship between the School of Music and the university—Kelsey was nothing if not persistent. It was a genial occasion, though no agreement was reached on "the best method of attaining the result."

Kelsey presided over the meetings of the UMS board held monthly during the academic year. Items on the agenda were routine for the most part—concerts and their programs, the May Festival, budgets (expenses for 1907 were to be limited to $6,750, including the May Festival), the hiring of orchestras and soloists, the availability of auditoriums. Stanley looked after the performance

---

104. Regarding the UMS and the music school, see chapter 3, "The University Musical Society."

105. Regent Levi L. Barbour was the donor not only of the women's gymnasium named after him but also of a dormitory and scholarships for Asian women. Regent Henry S. Dean was a distinguished Civil War veteran and successful businessman. Among the faculty were Professors Stanley, Isaac Newton Demmon, Arthur Graves Canfield, Moritz Levi, Max Winkler, Richard Hudson, and Robert M. Wenley. George F. Allmendinger was a member of the family that had founded the Allmendinger (later, Ann Arbor) Organ Company in 1872.

and technical side, Kelsey the administrative. They put together magnificent concerts, the costs of which were met by subscriptions and ticket sales, and they brought world-renowned musicians to Ann Arbor. Occasionally Kelsey would address the orchestra directly if there was a special problem, but normally he and Stanley operated successfully in their separate spheres, in tandem. They were always on the lookout for opportunities to improve and broaden interest in music at Michigan, and it was partly at least through their initiatives that the Stearns Collection of Musical Instruments came to Ann Arbor in 1899. They were on good terms with Mr. Frederick Stearns,[106] Kelsey's diary mentioning several occasions on which, Stearns having come out to Ann Arbor, "he and Mr. Stanley took lunch with us." In 1903 they took up with him the question of the publication of a catalog of the instrument collection[107] and "the proposed purchase of more instruments." The university had been slow to provide adequate accommodation for the instruments, so on a visit to Detroit in the fall of 1905, Kelsey, nothing if not direct, took up with Stearns the question of the cost of providing a suitable building. The sum discussed was one hundred thousand dollars: Stearns did not bat an eyelid; but the university did not respond, and no space proper for the display of the instruments was provided until the 1980s.[108]

Kelsey's other contributions to Ann Arbor included assistance to his church, First Presbyterian. He spoke regularly in church: on May 31, 1903, for instance, he took for his topic the imagery of Revelation. He also often addressed the Tappan Presbyterian Hall Association: on his return from Rome in 1901, for example, he spoke in McMillan Hall for three quarters of an hour on the topic of the church's relations with state universities. Kelsey attended church business meetings and, with the monitory effect of the Hays Company saga on his mind, did not hesitate to say his piece. After the service on November 13, 1904, at which the Reverend David Howell alluded positively to Francis's 1895 speech before the Michigan Synod,[109] there was a conference at-

---

106. Stearns was the founder of Frederick Stearns & Company in Detroit, one of the leading pharmaceutical companies in the nation. He was an inordinately successful manufacturer of drugs, a pharmacist, a philanthropist, and man of wide interests.

107. Stanley wrote the *Catalogue of the Stearns Collection of Musical Instruments* (Ann Arbor: University of Michigan, 1918).

108. There are more than 2,200 instruments in the collection, of which about five hundred are on display in the Stearns Galleries in the Margaret Dow Towsley wing of the Earl V. Moore Building in the School of Music. The remaining instruments are kept off campus, awaiting their turn in the galleries. For a more recent reckoning than Stanley's, see James M. Borders, *European and American Wind and Percussion Instruments: Catalogue of the Stearns Collection* (Ann Arbor: University of Michigan Press, 1988).

109. See chapter 3, "The Presbyterian Church."

tended by trustees of the Tappan Association, followed the next day by a long and fruitful discussion between them and representatives of the synod.[110]

In this collaborative spirit, James Leslie French was appointed general secretary and pastor of the Tappan Association in 1905. He was given the responsibility of meeting the spiritual needs of Presbyterian students at the university while working in full cooperation with the First Presbyterian Church. He and his wife, Edna Cummings French, were both Michigan graduates and so knew their way about campus and were familiar with student problems. French's theological and academic credentials were impeccable. After undergraduate work at Michigan, he had gone on to Hartford Theological Seminary for his doctorate, and his theological credentials were underscored by his fluency in Hebrew and Hellenistic Greek. Both husband and wife were indefatigable workers. While James focused on the needs of the male students, relations with the local church, and the YMCA, Edna concentrated on the women. One of her great successes was persuading Mrs. Katherine McGregor of Detroit to give $13,500 to buy a professor's house close to Sackett Hall for use as a residence for Presbyterian women. They renamed it Westminster House.[111] The nucleus of buildings on Huron Street for the benefit of Presbyterian students was growing steadily.

In 1900 Kelsey had been elected to the board of directors of the prestigious McCormick Theological Seminary (established in 1829) in Chicago. A considerable feather in his cap, this involved going to the seminary from time to time for meetings, where typical institutional matters—appointments, budgets, programs, and such—were under discussion. It also gave him a chance to hobnob with Cyrus McCormick Jr. and family.[112] By 1904 Kelsey was recognized outside Ann Arbor as a leading Presbyterian.

On Thursday, October 19, 1905, the day after representing his university at the inauguration of President James at the University of Illinois at Champaign, he attended a conference on religious education and mounted his Presbyterian hobbyhorse again. His was the lead paper in the afternoon. Entitled "The State Universities and the Churches," it stressed the importance of keeping religious and secular education together. He did not favor,

---

110. Representing the Tappan Association's trustees were the Reverend Gelston, Dr. Herdman, Judge Lane, Dr. Prescott, and Kelsey. Representing the committee of the Synod were the Reverend A. C. Carver, Dr. W. B. Jennings, and the Reverend Jones (from Tecumseh).

111. L. Miller, R. M. Warner, and C. R. Geider, eds., *The First Presbyterian Church of Ann Arbor, Michigan 1826–1988, Incorporating "A Sesquicentennial History," 1976* (Ann Arbor: First Presbyterian Church, 1988), 12.

112. Cyrus's father, an inventor, had developed and patented a horse-drawn reaper and founded the McCormick Harvesting Machine Company.

he said, the increasing isolation of theological faculties. State universities were strategic points, and theological studies should be integrated in them; close association of advanced religious and secular education could only be advantageous.[113] On his return to Ann Arbor, he gave a report on the Illinois conference at church, and a week later, at a university meeting to review and discuss the Illinois conference, he was again on the podium. The importance of this meeting may be gauged by the fact that President Angell himself was in the chair and that representatives of seven Ann Arbor churches were present.

Kelsey continued in the same vein early in 1906, when he gave a talk at Newberry Hall, the meeting place of the Student's Christian Association. In March, however, when speaking in the chapel at Orchard Lake on the eighteenth, he began to vary the subjects of his church-related talks; he took "Christian lamps" as his topic. Visiting Kansas in the spring, he spoke at Washburn University on April 19, both in the morning in chapel and in the evening, on archaeological topics related to Pompeii; at the University of Kansas at Lawrence the next day, however, he balanced the Pompeian lecture with a chapel address on recent educational tendencies.

His involvement with the world of the McCormicks continued. He went to Detroit in April to discuss with the Reverend Alfred H. Barr[114] of the Jefferson Avenue Presbyterian Church the possibility of Barr's coming to work for the McCormick Theological Seminary "in the chair of Homelities and Christian Sociology," and he reported on their conversation at an extended board meeting in Chicago on May 2 and 3. In the afternoon of the third, he attended the inauguration of Dr. James G. K. McClure[115] as president of Lake Forest University, and at the alumni dinner following, he spoke on behalf of the University of Michigan.

Kelsey's energetic engagement in community affairs and business dealings went hand in hand with his passionate belief in the value of education as a

---

113. Francis W. Kelsey, "The State Universities and the Churches," in "Proceedings of the Conference on Religious Education," *University of Illinois Bulletin* 3.8, pt. 2 (January 8, 1906): 39–45.

114. Reverend Barr was an early convert to the combustion engine, using an automobile in 1906 to visit members of his congregation. His son, Alfred H. Barr Jr., was the famed art historian and administrator, first director of the Museum of Modern Art (1929).

115. McClure was pastor of the First Presbyterian Church in Lake Forest, well known and well liked locally. Born in New York and educated at Yale and Princeton Theological Seminary, he was independently wealthy and had married well. Socially, the McClures were fully the equals of the McCormicks and the Farwells.

positive democratic force, of hard work and determination as the keys to progress, and of the family as an instrument of human benevolence. He had had to deploy all his skills and vision in the arduous tasks of the years since his arrival in Michigan. But there were to be more difficulties and more responsibilities ahead, and he was not about to betray President Angell's trust in him.

CHAPTER 5

A National Profile

*Kelsey and the Archaeological Institute
of America, 1902–12*

꧁

ON THE NATIONAL SCENE, Francis was becoming more visible. In 1907 he represented the University of Rochester at the semicentennial of the Agricultural College in Lansing, where he enjoyed the company of the presidents of the University of Oklahoma and of the University of California at Berkeley.[1] In April 1909, at the invitation of Professor W. P. Dickey and President Boatwright, he gave three lectures at Richmond College. He and Isabelle were lavishly entertained.[2] At commencement exercises at the University of Rochester in 1910, he was "presented for the degree of Doctor of Laws" and spoke briefly. In 1911, between meetings in Boston at his publishers and others at the Boston Museum of Fine Arts, he was one of five invited speakers at dinner at the Twentieth Century Club.[3] On May 10, 1912, he and Mr. and Mrs. Mitchell Carroll were guests at a garden party at the White House.

---

1. Diary, May 30, 1907. (As noted in chapter 4, Kelsey's diaries are among the Francis Willey Kelsey Papers at Bentley Historical Library, University of Michigan.)

2. Kelsey's diary makes a point of remarking that his lecture on Pompeian wall painting used "colored slides" for the first time and that he received an honorarium of three hundred dollars for these lectures (April 12–14, 1909).

3. Diary, March 17, 1911. According to the online organizational history of the club, "Club activities centered around Saturday Luncheons. Begun [in January 1894] as men-only affairs, they were opened to women by 1895. These informal gatherings were meant as forums for the sharing of ideas and viewpoints across the political spectrum" ("Twentieth Century Associa-

Although these invitations all testified to Kelsey's scholarship and reputation, it was his leadership of the American Philological Association and the Archaeological Institute of America that would bring him national prominence during these years. His energy and vision would become particularly apparent in the context of the AIA. Kelsey's brief experience as president of the APA and his negotiations with large philanthropic organizations were only the backdrop to his wholehearted involvement in this organization, which absorbed much of his professional attention.

THE AMERICAN PHILOLOGICAL ASSOCIATION
AND THE CARNEGIE INSTITUTION

In 1905 Kelsey had been elected vice president of the American Philological Association for 1906, with the expectation that he would become president in 1907. While serving at the same time (incredible as it may seem) as secretary of the AIA,[4] Francis, as APA president, went to Washington, D.C., to talk to Carnegie Institution president Robert S. Woodward on February 2, 1907, about the formation of a Classical Department there. The two discussed what projects such a department might undertake, including a "Thesaurus of the Greek Language," an "Atlas to illustrate the History of Ancient Wall Painting," a "Corpus of Ancient Figured Lamps," and a "Collection of materials for the study of the History of Greek and Roman Cults." They also mentioned a possible budget of thirty thousand dollars a year for ten years; President Woodward was encouraging.[5]

Kelsey next traveled to Princeton to discuss the matter with Professor Andrew Fleming West,[6] and thereafter he contacted other classicists, including James Egbert of Columbia[7] and Benjamin Ide Wheeler, president of the Uni-

---

tion Records, 1894–1964," http://www.masshist.org/findingaids/doc.cfm?fa=fa0022 [accessed November 24, 2008]).

4. On these dual positions, see chapter 4, "The Archaeological Institute of America and the International Commission of Archaeology and Ethnology."

5. Diary, February 2, 1907.

6. Andrew Fleming West (1853–1943) graduated from Princeton in 1874, taught Latin at a Cincinnati high school for six years, and returned to Princeton as the Giger Professor of Latin in 1883. The first dean of the Graduate School at Princeton and dean for twenty-seven years, he was a prolific fund-raiser, a founder of the American School of Classical Studies in Rome, a president of the American Philological Association, and editor of the important conference volume *Value of the Classics* (Princeton: Princeton University Press, 1917). He was also a great ally and friend of Francis Kelsey.

7. James Chidester Egbert Jr. spent his whole academic life at Columbia, as undergraduate, graduate student, professor of Latin, and subsequently dean of the School of Business (1916–32).

versity of California at Berkeley.[8] The resulting conference brought no fewer than twenty-five men at short notice to New York on February 9 to discuss "Carnegie projects." Thomas Day Seymour, professor of Greek at Yale and, at the time, president of the AIA, was elected chair. The inevitable committee, which included Seymour, Wheeler, and Mitchell Carroll, associate secretary of the AIA, was set up. By February 11, Kelsey was able to report this successful conference to Woodward, who seemed particularly enthusiastic about the thesaurus project.

In March Kelsey used an opportune meeting with Professor Paul Shorey[9] in Chicago about an honorary degree from Michigan to discuss the Carnegie Classical Department idea. Shorey's assent led to a draft statement to be prepared in New York and a tentative budget to be sent to West at Princeton for his consideration. The committee adopted the list of projects at a meeting on April 13, following which Kelsey reported again to Woodward at a meeting described in Kelsey's diary as "fruitful" (April 18).

The philanthropic interests of Andrew Carnegie extended well beyond the establishment of libraries and his scholarly institution. In 1906 he had given ten million dollars to his Carnegie Foundation for the Advancement of Teaching to provide pensions for retiring college professors, and the trustees, one of whom was Robert A. Franks,[10] were thrashing out the complicated administrative details, of which eligibility for a pension was only one. Hearing of this in fall 1908, Kelsey—in his first year as president of the AIA—called together the chairs of the managing committees of the institute. After a preliminary meeting attended by Professors Marquand,[11]

8. Benjamin Ide Wheeler, educated at Brown University, served as professor of Greek at Cornell before becoming president of the University of California at Berkeley (1899–1919).

9. Shorey, a native of Iowa and graduate of Harvard, taught classics, mainly Greek poetry and philosophy, first at Bryn Mawr and then at Chicago. Professor in the American School of Classical Studies at Athens (1901–2), he was Roosevelt Professor at the University of Berlin in 1913–14. For a vigorous defense of the ancient languages, see Paul Shorey, "Philology and Classical Philology," *Classical Journal* 1.6 (1906): 169–96; see also idem, *The Roosevelt Lectures of Paul Shorey (1913–1914)*, trans. Edgar C. Reinke, ed. Ward W. Briggs and E. Christian Kopf (Hildesheim: Georg Olms, 1994).

10. Franks, president of the Home Trust Company of Hoboken, New Jersey, was Carnegie's personal financial agent, acted for the Carnegie Trust Company, was one of the two managers of the great Library Building Program, and was a trustee of the Carnegie Endowment for International Peace. See chapter 6, "Fund-Raising and Acquisitions."

11. Allan Marquand graduated from Princeton in classics and joined the faculty in 1881 to teach Latin and logic. He was the first person to be appointed professor of art history at Princeton and served for more than forty years (1883–1924).

Torrey,[12] and Wheeler, they called on President Henry Smith Pritchett at the Carnegie Foundation to express their concern that directors of the AIA's schools in Athens, Rome, and Jerusalem be put on the pension list. Pritchett thought "it might be possible." Francis was also thinking of someone closer to home when he met again with Pritchett (January 26, 1909) and was very pleased when "Dr. Pritchett authorized me to say to President Angell that a retiring allowance of $4000 would be available to him." Later in the year (June), Kelsey could be seen assisting University of Michigan secretary James H. Wade, who also was close to retirement, preparing drafts for "application for a Carnegie pension."[13]

THE AIA: FOUNDING AND CONTEXT

The Archaeological Institute of America was founded in 1879 (during Kelsey's final undergraduate year at the University of Rochester) by a group of New England intellectuals, whose purpose was threefold: to promote archaeological and artistic inquiry, both at the professional level and at the level of interested nonprofessionals; to sponsor scientifically conducted expeditions; and to publish the results of archaeological work.[14] It was founded in response to similar national institutes that had sprung up in Europe and to a cultural climate in the United States that was more and more materialistic and less and less attuned to the values of history, the humanities, and the life of the mind. Accordingly, it aimed both at the promulgation of creative scholarship and at raising the level of public discourse: it wore two hats from the start. From the start, too, it claimed adherence to American archaeology as well as to Mediterranean, and the very first explorations it sponsored were in the American Southwest and Mexico.[15]

---

12. Charles Cutler Torrey was professor of Semitic languages at Yale University and the first director (1900–1901) of the American School for Oriental Study and Research at Jerusalem.

13. We can perhaps see here the origins of the TIAA-CREF (Teachers Insurance and Annuity Association—College Retirement Equities Fund) system.

14. For a lucid and valuable series of papers, including one by the editor, on the history of the Archaeological Institute of America, see *EOP*, with good bibliographies. See also Stephen L. Dyson's comprehensive overview, *Ancient Marbles to American Shores: Classical Archaeology in the United States* (Philadelphia: University of Pennsylvania Press, 1998). Equally useful, with respect to the AIA, is Nancy Thomson de Grummond, ed., *An Encyclopedia of the History of Classical Archaeology* (London: Routledge, 1996).

15. See Charles H. Lange and Carroll L. Riley, *Bandelier: The Life and Adventurers of Adolph Bandelier* (Salt Lake City: University of Utah Press, 1996).

The AIA was the brainchild of Charles Eliot Norton, professor of art history at Harvard, whose experience in archaeological work in the United States, membership in the American Oriental Society, familiarity with European museums, knowledge of European learned societies, and widespread travels had alerted him to the cultural weakness of the United States.[16] Alongside his broad, global view of the importance of archaeological research ran his admiration of Hellenism, the intellectual construct that idealized ancient Greece as the *fons et origo* of Western culture. The Hellenism of the time was most clearly exemplified in Germany, by scholars and governmental officials who established schools, at home and abroad, to study the achievements of the ancient Greeks through the discipline of classical archaeology. Alongside the establishment of scholarly institutes and foreign schools came the construction of museums to hold and display the materials recovered through exploration, as well as other objects deemed characteristic of the refinement and high aesthetic sense of the Greeks.

As Norton saw it, by comparison with Europe, the United States was culturally impoverished. Two ways to redress this were, on one hand, to establish museums for public benefit—the Boston Museum of Fine Arts (founded in 1870), the Metropolitan Museum of Art in New York (1872), and the Art Institute of Chicago (1879), for example—and, on the other hand, to establish institutes such as the AIA. A further step was the founding, through the agency of the AIA, of foreign schools: the American School of Classical Studies at Athens (founded 1881), the American School of Classical Studies in Rome (1895), and the American School for Oriental Study and Research in Jerusalem (1899). In these foreign schools, students and professors worked together to become familiar with ancient sites and museums, to meet and learn from foreign scholars and students, and to engage in detailed and precise scientific research. It was Norton's intellect and aspiration that set the AIA and the foreign schools in motion, and it was he who served as the institute's first president. Though the AIA was rooted in Boston and populated at first almost solely by East Coast scholars, Norton was clear that the organization should be broadly "American": a national organization, it should welcome

---

16. On Norton, see James C. Turner, *The Liberal Education of Charles Eliot Norton* (Baltimore: Johns Hopkins University Press, 1999); Elizabeth Lyding Will, "Charles Eliot Norton and the Archaeological Institute of America," in *EOP,* 49–62. It is perhaps worth mentioning that his cousin, Charles William Eliot, was president of Harvard at the time of Norton's appointment to the Harvard faculty and was also a founding member of the AIA.

members from all over the country; it should link local groups (societies) of professional archaeologists and interested amateurs through a lecture program of distinguished speakers dispatched nationwide; and it should incorporate every kind of archaeology.

SECRETARY OF THE AIA, 1902–7

In the spring of 1902, fresh from his year in Rome, Kelsey was invited by President John Williams White to become secretary of the AIA.[17] White could hardly have chosen better. Kelsey had the academic credentials for the job: professor of Latin at Michigan since 1889; widely known for his innovative Latin textbooks, his translation of Mau's *Pompeji in Leben und Kunst;* arguably more knowledgeable than any other American about the then-popular archaeological work at Pompeii and Herculaneum; and close associate of many European scholars and thus alert to the direction and progress of European scholarship and educational thought. Moreover, Kelsey's appointment as secretary recognized that the affiliated Detroit Archaeological Society was (in 1902–3) the third-largest archaeological society in the nation, after only Boston and New York. What is more, Kelsey was not a member of the Eastern elite: he was new.

Bearing in mind the vote passed at a recent meeting of the AIA's governing council and carried into effect by its executive committee at its meeting of May 10, 1902, "committing the establishment of new Societies and the increase of the membership of the Institute to the Secretary," Kelsey accepted. His duties were clear: to expand overall membership, to organize the program of lecturers (the integrating link between the central organization and the local groups) to be sent to the affiliated societies, to collect dues and pay lecturers, to arrange for the publication of approved works, to organize the annual general meeting, to facilitate fieldwork, and to support the foreign schools. He was not, however, in the best of health (though in May he did not know it), and in November he succumbed to an intestinal infection that put him in a hospital for nine weeks and almost cost him his life. Isabelle wrote in November to Thomas Day Seymour, the new AIA president, to explain why Francis had not been able to keep up his work, explaining that "for the first day (after a long operation) we had very little hope of his recovery."[18]

---

17. AIA Archives, box 10.6, executive committee minutes, meeting of May 10, 1902.
18. AIA Archives, box 10.7.

The indefatigable Francis rallied, and by the middle of February 1903, he was able to resume work. In April he at last turned his attention to the AIA, making his immediate objectives and those of the institute known in a letter sent to chosen individuals in communities in the West.

> University of Michigan
> April 23, 1903
>
> Dear Sir,
>
> The Council of the Archaeological Institute of America proposes to establish, in several Western cities, Affiliated Societies similar to those which, by means of public lectures and other instrumentalities, have contributed so much to the intellectual life of the East.
>
> I enclose a circular relating to the work of the Institute. Among the alumni of the University of Michigan there must be many who are already interested, or would become interested in archaeological studies.
>
> On behalf of the Archaeological Institute, I am expecting in the near future to visit Denver, San Francisco and other cities in which there may be manifested a sufficient degree of interest in our work. Will you kindly send me within a week or ten days a list containing the names of any persons who have an interest in any branch of Archaeology or in the History of Art? I desire to have the names of those who would probably be pleased to associate themselves with an Affiliated Society in case one should be organized in your state.
>
> Sincerely yours
> Francis W. Kelsey
> Secretary of the Archaeological Institute of America
> 826 Tappan Street
> Ann Arbor, Michigan

It is worth drawing attention to the language of the penultimate sentence—"interest in *any branch* of Archaeology or in the History of Art." The promised visits took place in fall 1903 (as described in chapter 4).[19] It had, however, been President White who, following Norton's plan of expansion, had earlier instigated the trip, as Kelsey subsequently (1906) wrote to Mitchell Carroll.

> The suggestion of the extension of the work of the Institute to the Pacific coast originated with Professor John Williams White who brought the

---

19. AIA Archives, box 11. See "The Professor."

matter to my attention in the spring of 1902 suggesting that I should go as far as San Francisco to see whether it would be practical to establish Affiliated Societies of sufficient size and vigor to warrant the putting forth of effort in this direction. I said to Mr. White that I should be pleased to make the trip provided he would arrange in advance for the engagements which might be made at different points.[20]

Kelsey remarked at the time, "It has become evident that there is a large body of cultivated people in San Francisco, Oakland and Berkeley who have an interest in archaeological matters; and the prospects for organizing an Affiliated Society of the Institute next fall seem bright."[21] The trip was a great success: there were large audiences everywhere he went and much enthusiasm for the future of archaeology. On his return, he reported to President Seymour the existence of newly formed, though as yet unofficial, societies in Colorado and Utah and at San Francisco and Los Angeles.[22] Of these, the unofficial society at San Francisco had a stuttering start, even though it had as its president the redoubtable Phoebe Apperson Hearst, mother of the newspaper publisher William Randolph Hearst and generous benefactor of George Reisner's explorations in Egypt, and as its vice president the eminent classicist and president of the University of California at Berkeley, Benjamin Ide Wheeler. The Southwest Society (Los Angeles) was to be the most successful and obstreperous, led by a man of enormous energy and drive, Charles Fletcher Lummis.[23]

KELSEY, HEWETT, AND THE SCHOOL OF AMERICAN ARCHAEOLOGY

As well as finding that the societies in the West were enthusiastic about archaeology and about being a part of the AIA, Francis also learned that members' interest was primarily directed toward the archaeology of America, rather than toward the Mediterranean, and in particular to the archaeology of their local districts. They rapidly formed and funded their own expeditions,

---

20. AIA Archives, box 12.20.

21. AIA Archives, box 11.7

22. AIA Archives, box 11.6.

23. For a perceptive analysis of the institute's early efforts in the West, see James E. Snead, "The 'Western Idea': Local Societies and American Archaeology," in *EOP*, 123–40. Lummis, a friend of Theodore Roosevelt's from Harvard, was a journalist and photographer who documented the culture of the Southwest and its Native Americans (e.g., the Pueblo village of Isleta, New Mexico).

demonstrating their independence. No society was more vigorous in this re-spect than the Los Angeles society, led by Charles Lummis. This society grew rapidly, as did the dollar value of the dues it raised and the number of repre-sentatives it was entitled to send to the meetings of the council[24] at the annual AIA gathering. Tension increased as the delegates from the eastern societies saw their voting majorities wither and as the Westerners began to resent the dues they had to send to head office.[25] Moreover, those in the East tended to view the Westerners as less interested in professional scholarship and more interested in excavating artifacts with which to fill the museums they were building, to the detriment of "scientific progress."

By this time, two influential figures emerged to catalyze the East-West ten-sions. Charles P. Bowditch, a Boston entrepreneur and a vice president of the AIA, had given the institute funds for a fellowship in Central American stud-ies. With the advice of Franz Boas (Columbia University) and Frederick Put-nam (Harvard) and with the agreement of Bowditch, Alfred M. Tozzer was appointed to this fellowship, which he held until 1905.[26] Faced in 1905 with a vacancy in the fellowship and few candidates to fill it, the institute's Commit-tee on American Archaeology (Boas, Bowditch, and Putnam) was disap-pointed when their first choice withdrew, leaving them with Edgar Lee Hewett.

Hewett, a forty-year-old educator from New Mexico, was conducting fieldwork in the Southwest for the Bureau of American Ethnology. Stronger in organization than in scholarship, he did not seem the right man for the job to Boas and Bowditch. Their enthusiasm waned even further when Hewett, appointed a fellow in American archaeology at the council meeting in De-cember 1905, began to lobby Congress in support of two bills rather than con-centrating on his research. One bill was a revised version of the ill-fated 1904 Lodge-Rodenberg Bill protecting antiquities on government lands.[27] The

---

24. The council consisted of the officers of the institute, themselves elected by the coun-cil, and the delegates of the affiliated societies, each society being entitled to send one delegate for every twenty-five members.

25. For example, in 1912, the Southwest Society requested an abatement of dues in order to build the SW Museum, a request denied by the institute (AIA Archives, box 19).

26. Alfred Marston Tozzer, who would have a long association with Harvard, began as an anthropologist-linguist, studying Native American languages of California and New Mexico. His fellowship took him to Yucatán for fieldwork among the Maya and at Chichen Itza. See S. K. Lothrop, "Alfred Marsten Tozzer, 1876–1954," *American Anthropologist*, n.s., 57.3, pt. 1 (June 1955): 614–18.

27. The new bill was entitled "A Bill for the Preservation of American Antiquities."

other was the act incorporating the AIA.[28] Hewett was also working for the Colorado, Utah, and Southwest societies, rather than on the intensive scholarly research in Mexico that the committee, particularly Bowditch, had had in mind. Only after completing his work in Washington, D.C., and the Southwest did Hewett begin his archaeological survey in Mexico. What is more, while in Mexico, he was spending time researching the possibility of establishing a School of American Archaeology in Mexico similar to the institute's schools in Athens, Jerusalem, and Rome—another project that did not have the wholehearted support of Bowditch or the committee.

By this time, Hewett's and Kelsey's views of the future of American archaeology had begun to overlap. Kelsey's vision of increasing the number of AIA societies and members and uplifting the general cultural level in the country (through the institute's lecture program) had joined Hewett's awareness of the new Western societies' local pride, unharnessed enthusiasm, and driving leadership. It was manifested most plainly in the activities of the Southwest Society—"the new and remote western brat," as Charles Lummis described it in a letter to Norton in late 1906.[29]

Moreover, they shared the same view of the importance of the preservation of ancient sites in the American Southwest, a priority not shared by Boas and Bowditch, who gave first place to scientific inquiry and national professionalization. In this context, Hewett, as secretary of an American Anthropological Association–AIA joint committee (of which Kelsey had been a member), had played a leading role throughout 1905 in the political maneuverings, adjustment of views, balancing of prejudices, and refining of language that finally saw passage of the Antiquities Act—the more comprehensive and less controversial version of the Lodge-Rodenberg Bill.[30] It was he who put together the compromises that the bickering constituencies were able to accept, and he had Kelsey's full support in this work.

---

28. Chap. 2560, 34 Stat. 203 (1906), signed by President Roosevelt on May 26.

29. AIA Archives, box 12. On Kelsey's enthusiasm for reinforcing the AIA's identity as a national institution that would include the study and promotion of Native American archaeology as well as Mediterranean archaeology, see Dyson, *Ancient Marbles to American Shores,* 44–46.

30. This was passed at long last on June 5, 1906, and signed into law by President Theodore Roosevelt on June 8, with the formal title "An Act for the Preservation of American Antiquities" (16 USC 431–33). Cf. chapter 4 n. 51. President Roosevelt used this act to safeguard both archaeological sites and intact natural environments, including the Grand Canyon, which, over the objections of many Arizonans, he declared a national monument on January 11, 1908.

But when Bowditch heard, in mid-1906, of Hewett's activities in Washington, D.C., and California, he was enraged. He attacked Kelsey for usurping what he took to be the AIA committee's authority.

> If the Secretary is to be allowed to dictate how the Fellow in American Archaeology shall occupy his time, or what shall be the relations of the Southwest Society to the Institute, the Committee on American Archaeology might as well abdicate.... Neither in delaying his entry upon his Mexican work nor in supervising the work of the Southwest Society has Mr. Hewett any authority from the American Committee.[31]

Kelsey retorted more calmly.

> When I saw Mr. Hewett in Washington early in January he was very hard at work, not only with the literature of his special field, but also devoting such time as might be necessary to carrying out the wishes of the American Committee, as expressed at the meeting in Ithaca, regarding the formulating and introducing of the general bill for the protection of American antiquities; and my belief is that in the same connection, as a special service to Colorado friends of American Archaeology, whom he expected shortly to visit, he was doing something for the bill for the setting aside of the Mesa Verde Park.[32]

Kelsey went on to make the case for encouraging initiative rather than holding appointees to the letter of their instructions: "in the aggregate the best results for any good cause are secured by giving the right sort of man a full opportunity." In answer to the suggestion that he was going out of his way to build the Western membership (though this was plainly the mandate of the council), Kelsey stated, "The movement for the establishment of a Colorado Society of the Institute came from that state, and that prepared the way for the extension of the Institute's work elsewhere in the West and Southwest."[33]

There were some hard feelings here, which did not soften. Bowditch wrote to Seymour about what he perceived as the negative effects of the increase in numbers of Western societies' representatives at council meetings: he questioned the motives behind their eagerness for fieldwork, thinking that they only wanted materials for their museums and that they were devoid of "higher motives." At this point, to add fuel to the fire, Hewett's work received

---

31. Bowditch to Kelsey, May 25, 1906, AIA Archives, box 12.19.
32. Kelsey to Bowditch, six-page letter of June 1, 1906, AIA Archives, box 12.19.
33. Ibid.

support from an authoritative source. Alice Cunningham Fletcher, a revered figure in American archaeology, after reading Hewett's report of the survey in Mexico in the summer, wrote to Bowditch of Hewett's "sterling qualities."[34] Kelsey also warmly praised Hewett. In 1906 he declared to Seymour, "The magnitude of Hewett's services directly to American Archaeology, and indirectly to the Institute, in accomplishing the passage of the general archaeological bill and the Mesa Verde park bill cannot easily be overestimated."[35] He wrote to Carroll on February 26, 1907, "Mr. Hewett spent Saturday and Sunday with me, and I was more than ever impressed with his strength, good judgment and preparation to do a great work for the Institute."[36]

By the beginning of October 1907, at a time when President Seymour was in ill health and did not have long to live, Bowditch's dislike of archaeological trends in the Southwest and in the AIA under Secretary Kelsey's guidance led him to resign the chair of the American Committee. He was, however, warm in his praise for Alice Fletcher: "I know of no one better fitted to occupy the position than Miss Alice C. Fletcher of Washington. I hope that she will be willing to take it."[37] In a letter to Seymour of November 1, Fletcher replied that she would. She said that she regretted Bowditch's resignation but averred that "the work of the Committee is critical at this time; the present is a very vital period in the history of the Institute and a greater influence and usefulness in the world of scholarship awaits it."[38]

---

34. Bowditch to Seymour, 1906, AIA Archives box 13.5. Fletcher to Bowditch, August 29, 1906, as cited in C . M .Hinsley Jr., "Edgar Lee Hewett and the School of American Research in Santa Fe, 1906–1912," in *American Archaeology Past and Future: A Celebration of the Society for American Archaeology, 1935–1985*, ed. David J. Meltzer, Don D. Fowler, and Jeremy A. Sabloff (Washington, DC: Smithsonian Institution Press, 1986), 225. Alice Fletcher, a New Englander and early member of the AIA (1879), came to anthropology later in life than most. Beginning her studies at the age of forty-six with Frederick Putnam at Harvard's Peabody Museum, she lived and worked with the Plains Indians, became a prominent ethnomusicologist, served as an agent for the Bureau of Indian Affairs, was a passionate advocate of Indian entitlements, and ultimately became a Harvard fellow at the Peabody. A prolific writer, she brought a rigorous logic to ethnomusicology in the early years of the discipline.

35. AIA Archives, box 12.17.

36. AIA Archives, box 13.12.

37. Bowditch to Seymour, October 2, 1907, AIA Archives, box 13.12.

38. AIA Archives, box 13.12. An index of the high regard in which Alice Fletcher was held is the fact that she served as vice president of the Anthropology Section of the British Association for the Advancement of Science at its meetings at Sheffield in 1910. (VPs of other sections were scholars as distinguished as J. L. Myers, W. H. R. Rivers, and A. F. Dixon.) She also gave an address, "Archaeological Activities in the United States," which was enthusiastically received. She wrote that it was "a red letter day," not least because she met famed English Egyptologist Flinders Petrie.

The AIA's annual report for 1907 recorded significant changes in the leadership and composition of the Committee on American Archaeology. Fletcher replaced Bowditch as chair. Now numbering five with the addition of Fletcher and Hewett (Boas, Bowditch, and Putnam remained), the committee put together a scheme for unifying the work of the societies. Hewett, elected director of American antiquities, was hard at work consulting with the U.S. government about the regulation of excavations, lecturing to the Western societies, and conducting field schools in Colorado, the Southwest, and Utah. The Western societies were putting archaeological teams in the field at their own expense and with Hewett's help and advice.

At the end of this momentous year, at the council meeting in December 1907, Francis Kelsey was elected president of the AIA.[39] The council established the School of American Archaeology with a nine-member managing committee (all five members of the American Committee plus Lummis, Carroll, Kelsey, and Walter Fewkes of the Bureau of American Ethnology). Shortly afterward (in April 1908), Hewett issued a mission statement in which he included a list of prospects for fieldwork, with opportunities for student participation, in Colorado, Utah, New Mexico, and Central America.[40] Throughout 1908, however, relations between the Bowditch-Boas-Putnam group and the Hewett-Fletcher-Kelsey group continued to deteriorate, until, at a meeting of the American Committee in October, an attempt was made by the Bowditch group to halt the progress of the school. It was thwarted only by Fletcher's determination that the votes of two absent members of the committee (Hewett and Kelsey) should be counted. Finally, on February 19, 1909, New Mexico House Bill No. 100, entitled "An Act to Establish a Museum for the Territory of New Mexico," was passed: it provided for the institute's School of American Archaeology within the newly authorized Museum of New Mexico in Santa Fe.[41]

The Bowditch group continued to inveigh publicly and privately against Hewett's fieldwork, regarding it as superficial and discounting his contributions to the welfare of American sites and antiquities. The Hewett group failed to understand why the Bowditch people saw no value in outreach and attempts in the interest of general cultural as distinct from professional education. Both sides exhibited shortsightedness, inability to see the whole picture, and reluctance to compromise. Bowditch, exasperated, wrote to Hewett

39. See below, "President of the AIA, 1907–12."
40. Edgar L. Hewett, *Archaeological Institute of America: The School of American Archaeology,* [Report on establishment of] *Bulletin* no. 1 (Washington, DC: [AIA], 1908).
41. AIA Archives, box 16.15.

at the beginning of 1909, "The time has come for me to say to you that I have lost my confidence in you. Probably this is a matter of indifference to you, but if you should ever care to regain my confidence, it will not be by the methods which you and Miss Fletcher have adopted during the past year." These were harsh words, which Kelsey, informed about them, could not let pass. Writing to Bowditch in March, he said, "You have done both Mr. Hewett and Miss Fletcher a grave injustice by your attitude of suspicion and harsh letters: and no insistence upon the letter of the agreement can bridge the chasm your inconsiderate course has opened up."[42] In Boston on AIA business in June, Kelsey called on Bowditch in an attempt to smooth ruffled feathers, only to find his "attitude hostile and uncompromising."[43] What was initially an intellectual disagreement about the purposes of archaeology had descended into personal unpleasantness.

Differences of opinion on the managing committee of the School of American Archaeology and the Committee on American Archaeology sharpened through 1909, to the point that a letter from Kelsey to Bowditch of July 10, 1909, made plain that Bowditch had been casting aspersions on Kelsey's motives for accepting the presidency of the institute. Kelsey had felt obliged to reply.

> Professor Seymour knew well of my desire to be relieved from the administrative details[44] and at the end of November 1907 we met in New York to make final arrangements for my complete withdrawal. At a conference at the Murray Hill Hotel it was arranged that my resignation should be presented and accepted at the Chicago meeting, and it was my purpose, as Professor Seymour understood, in seeking relief, to devote myself to my scholastic work which has suffered years of interruption on account of the Institute's work. When the Chicago meeting came at the end of December 1907 Professor Seymour was very ill. Word was brought to the Chicago meeting that the physicians insisted that his resignation from the presidency of the Institute should be presented and accepted. I had nothing whatever to do with the nomination and election of myself as his successor.[45]

It did not take long for Bowditch's temperament to get the better of him. He resigned from the American Committee. Boas soon followed his lead, sending his resignation to Kelsey on Christmas Eve. Resigning also from the managing committee of the School of American Archaeology and from the

---

42. Kelsey to Bowditch, March 10, 1909, AIA Archives, box 15.13.
43. Diary, June 24, 1909.
44. At the time, Kelsey was the secretary of the AIA.
45. AIA Archives, box 15.14.

institute itself, Boas repeated his assertions of the need for "careful and broad academic method" and not "superficial work."[46] Appreciation of Hewett's work, however, remained firm in both Kelsey's mind and Loomis's. "What a wonder he is," Kelsey writes to Loomis on May 4, 1910, a view endorsed by Loomis (May 8, 1910): "[H]e is the very best man in America for the very work that needs doing."[47]

The rift between the two groups grew wider. The correspondence in the AIA archives does not make genial reading: hearsay, misunderstanding, and misrepresentation became all too prevalent. At the annual meetings in Providence in December 1910, Kelsey was buoyed by a "brilliant address" of welcome given by Chicago's Paul Shorey at the joint meeting of the AIA and APA, but he spent much of his time in "conferences before and during lunch trying chiefly to keep out of public meetings the bitter discussion of the American work."[48]

Correspondence from Hewett to Kelsey in 1911 gives a sense of the distance the groups were apart.

> In conversation with Dixon I have no doubt I stated that Dr. Boas was damaging himself by such publications as that directed against the secretary of the Smithsonian Institution, but that I said that I could, or in any way intended, to damage him, is untrue. Dixon has absolutely misrepresented any remarks that I may have made on the subject, just as Tozzer seems to have misrepresented Miss Fletcher judging from the correspondence which she has sent me. . . . What we were charitable enough to consider petty personal pique in those fellows seems to be something of a much graver character. Their efforts to incite others into trouble, as for example, Bowditch, Spinden and Boas, disclose a vindictiveness of character that ought to disqualify men from the teaching privilege in a great University.[49]

This was hardly a productive use of time.

Despite the protestations of the Eastern elite professionals, the school prospered for a while. Its creation had been made possible by the dogged determination of Kelsey and Hewett, their willingness to absorb brickbats from colleagues, and the zeal of the Western societies. Its contributions mark the

---

46. Boas to Kelsey, December 24, 1909, AIA Archives, box 17.7.
47. AIA Archives, box 19.12.
48. Diary, December 28, 1910.
49. Hewett to Kelsey, May 11, 1911, AIA Archives, box 19.4.

zenith of the institute's involvement in American archaeology. But the divisions within the institute and the growth of more single-mindedly professional organizations like the American Anthropological Association were bound to weaken it. National interest slowly drifted away from locally based work in American archaeology under the aegis of the AIA, and with its diminution went much of the interest in the School of American Archaeology in Santa Fe.[50]

PRESIDENT OF THE AIA, 1907–12

In the fall of 1907, Kelsey was exhausted by the volume of administrative work of the institute, and at a November meeting in New York with President Seymour, he asked for relief. They arranged that his resignation as secretary should be accepted at the meeting the following month in Chicago; Kelsey made it clear to Seymour that he wished to spend more time on his scholarly work. But a month later, Seymour was seriously ill, and Mrs. Seymour told Francis that it would be a load off Seymour's mind if he could know that Kelsey had not left the work of the institute at that moment. So he promised he would not resign while Seymour was ill. The doctors then insisted that Seymour should resign the presidency, the news of which came as the Chicago meetings were about to open.

On December 27, Kelsey presided at the opening session of the APA, attended an AIA meeting at the Art Institute, and delivered his forty-five-minute address to the two organizations in joint session in the evening. On December 30, a crowded room heard David George Hogarth[51] speak on Knossos and Henry Sanders on Freer's biblical manuscripts; in the afternoon, the council of the AIA met to address the usual agenda—the budget, membership, regulations, officers, and so on. On the matter of the presidency, now presumed vacant after Seymour's offered resignation, Professor Harold Fowler of the Cleveland Society nominated Marquand, and West nominated Kelsey. "We both withdrew," Kelsey wrote in his diary, "I saying I wished to be

---

50. The school's mission broadened, as reflected in its 1917 name change to the School for Advanced Research. For helpful narratives of the events, ideologies, and personalities involved in the founding of the school, see Hinsley, "Edgar Lee Hewett"; cf. Snead, "The 'Western Idea.'"

51. Hogarth, who was also on the AIA Cyrene Commission (with Arthur Fairbanks and Allison V. Armour), had been director of the British School of Archaeology at Athens (1897–1900) and would long be associated with the Ashmolean Museum at Oxford.

released from the work of the Institute, and asking release. The vote 30–22 informal, then made formal and afterward moved to make the vote unanimous, Fowler alone objecting."[52] The AIA had a new president—and not a moment too soon: on New Year's Eve came a telegram announcing Seymour's death.

Administration

Between 1902 and 1907, the number of affiliated societies of the AIA had grown from ten to eighteen, and the institute's total income from $10,368 to $14,593. Expenses rose proportionately, due both to the costs of the lecture program and management. Faced with the proliferating details of the business of the institute, Kelsey expanded the administration to share the burdens and streamline executive decisions. Mitchell Carroll became secretary of the AIA, thus cementing the partnership between the two men, and to assist him, three associate secretaries, representing strong societies and different geographical areas, were appointed: George H. Chase of Harvard, Henry Rushton Fairclough of Stanford University in California, and Frederick W. Shipley of Washington University in St. Louis. They were soon joined by a fourth: George Johnston of Toronto. Kelsey's presidency was characterized by three major initiatives—membership, foreign schools, and expeditions.

Membership

The clarion call for all organizations of business or philanthropy or art or any aspect of the humanities in these years was growth. What was true for others was also true for the AIA. The institute's president, John Williams White (1897–1902) of Harvard, first suggested its westward expansion; his successor, Thomas Day Seymour (1903–7) of Yale, moved the scheme forward. That the societies in the West were actually founded was thanks largely to Secretary Kelsey's hard work, tireless correspondence, and stimulating lectures, allied to the manifest enthusiasm and ambitions of local groups.

The institute was able to nurture these Western societies through the actions of the head office, with Kelsey's involvement lasting for an entire decade (1902–12). The decisions of the Committee on American Archaeology became increasingly effective once Alice Fletcher took its chair and ensured the acceptance of the value of Edgar Hewett's work. After the departures of Bowditch and Boas, things progressed much more smoothly. Committee

---

52. Diary, December 30, 1907. On Freer's biblical manuscripts, see chapter 6.

member Hewett, director of the School of American Archaeology, published regular bulletins on the school's progress[53] and encouraged the participation of both other learned groups and the general public; also, he emphasized that the school's staff was active in supervising the investigations of local societies. *Bulletin* no. 3, for example, lists the 1911 fieldwork plan involving local communities and scholarly research centers:

1. Central America: excavations at the ancient Maya city of Quiriguá, Guatemala under the auspices of the St. Louis Society.

2. Arizona and California: study of the Yuman tribes of the Colorado Basin in cooperation with the Bureau of American Ethnology and with the participation of the University of Colorado.

3. Utah: exploration in the southern part of the state under the auspices of the Utah Society and in cooperation with the University of Utah.

4. New Mexico: Rio Grande Valley in cooperation with the Bureau of American Ethnology.[54]

The *Bulletin* also announced a summer session for interested laypersons and students, with lectures on the peoples in the U.S. Southwest and northern Mexico prior to the arrival of the Spanish, on ancient Pueblo art, and on the native languages and methods of recording them. The summer session would include visits to sites and opportunities for fieldwork experience. The school was clearly in full swing.

The AIA and its members, both in the West and elsewhere in the country, were joined in three main ways: the annual meetings for the reading and discussion of archaeological papers, at which all members were welcome, and those of the council, at which representatives of all societies were present; the *American Journal of Archaeology,* published quarterly and sent to all members;[55] and the lecture program, organized for the first time in 1895, which sent distinguished speakers to all societies. Some sense of the caliber of these scholars—who needed plenty of stamina as well as good material, a loud voice, and, with any luck, a stereopticon—may be gleaned from a list published in 1907, which included Benjamin Wisner Bacon (Yale), Howard

---

53. By 1911 the School of American Archaeology was housed in the adobe Palace of the Governors, a centuries-old seat of New Mexican government, in Santa Fe.

54. Edgar L. Hewett, *Archaeological Institute of America:* [Report on the character, aims and programs of] *The School of American Archaeology, Bulletin* no. 3 (Santa Fe, NM, 1911).

55. Founded in 1885 as the *American Journal of Archaeology and the History of the Fine Arts* and edited by Arthur Frothingham, its title was subsequently abbreviated to the *American Journal of Archaeology.*

Crosby Butler (Princeton), George H. Chase (Harvard), Arthur Fairbanks (Michigan), Henry Rushton Fairclough (Stanford), Hewett, Gordon J. Laing (Chicago), and Charles H. Weller (Iowa). Also joining the lecture program were important overseas visitors, such as David G. Hogarth and George Horton, the U.S. consul general at Athens.[56]

Lecturers' travel expenses were paid by the institute, and their local expenses were met by the societies they visited, but they received no honoraria. The AIA's budget was tight, so the idea arose of raising money to endow lectureships. In this area, too, Kelsey led the way. In 1907, at a conference with President Seymour in Washington, D.C., he proposed that the institute pursue such a plan, and Seymour worked out a circular to be submitted to AIA treasurer William Sloane. Though Sloane experienced a false start securing funds from the Carnegie people, in 1909 James Loeb, once a student of Norton's at Harvard, transferred twenty thousand dollars in U.S. Steel bonds to the institute for the endowment of the Charles Eliot Norton Memorial Lecture Fund.[57] Since Kelsey knew Loeb and corresponded with him at length, it is hard not to see Kelsey's hand in this development.[58]

Kelsey continued to press Sloane about the endowment of a lectureship in honor of Seymour, in conversations early in 1910: "Sloane said he would see Stokes in New Haven on February 22 about a Seymour Lectureship; advised to see Ed. Robinson about project of endowing monographs. . . . [A]t 5.30 Robinson called at the hotel. Talk about possibility of interesting Mr. Morgan in the project."[59] In New York later in the year, he persisted in putting before Sloane the desirability of finding twenty-five thousand dollars to endow a Seymour lectureship.[60] A year later, he continued to urge the desirability of endowments with Sloane, without any apparent success.[61] After Sloane's res-

---

56. Thomas Day Seymour, "Twenty-eighth Annual Report of the Council of the Archaeological Institute of America," in "Annual Reports, 1906–1907," supplement, *AJA* 11 (1907): 7.

57. Diary, November 10, 1909. James Loeb, a New York banker (of Kuhn, Loeb, and Company, before leaving the United States to live in Germany) and philanthropist, was a well-known supporter of the humanities. A friend of Charles Eliot Norton, he was a generous benefactor of classical studies, the Archaeological Institute of America, and the Boston Museum of Fine Arts. Instrumental in the founding of the American Institute of Musical Art (later the Juilliard School of Music) in New York, he was also a founding member of the German Institute for Psychiatry in Munich.

58. KMA Papers, box.21.9.

59. Diary, January 31, 1910.

60. Diary, June 16, 1910.

61. Diary, April 10, 1911.

ignation in July 1911, his replacement, Willard V. King, president of the Columbia Trust Company, took up the matter and suggested Charles Harkness, a director at Standard Oil and manager of his father's huge fortune, as a possible sponsor for a Seymour endowment. But nothing seems to have come of this initiative either. When Kelsey left the presidency at the end of 1912, his report issued a plea for at least three more endowed lectureships, stating that only the Norton Endowment was in place.

The Department of Canada

Just three months into his presidency, at the meetings of the Michigan Classical Conference in Ann Arbor, Kelsey discussed with Canadian colleagues the prospects for establishing AIA societies in Montreal and Toronto. It may be these discussions, together with his belief in the expansion of the scope of the AIA's activities, as well as his friendship with Canadian scholars in the United States,[62] which prompted him to launch the institute into Canada. After discussions with Secretary Carroll, he asked Harry Langford Wilson to go to Canada in the spring of 1908 to sound out prominent interested persons about the chances of setting up societies of the AIA there. Wilson was more than successful: on his return, he told Kelsey that interest was high enough to warrant the formation of societies in Ottawa, Toronto, Kingston, and Montreal and that more would follow. Greatly encouraged by these developments, the institute determined to hold its annual year-end meetings in Toronto, and Kelsey volunteered to deliver a series of lectures in Canada in early December. His diary records the logistics and pace of the tour.

Kelsey was in Washington, D.C., on Thanksgiving Day for talks with Carroll and Thanksgiving dinner with him, his wife, and three boys. He also spent the next two days on AIA business with Carroll, culminating in "supper at a small restaurant" with Carroll and Hewett before Kelsey boarded the overnight train. The next day, he sent off the "copy" for the Toronto meeting program from the station at Niagara Falls, and on November 30, in the hall of the public library at Hamilton, Ontario, he delivered the lecture "A Roman Farmhouse and Its Buried Treasure" (on the Boscoreale treasure). Arriving in Toronto on December 1, he found thirty letters and a telegram waiting for him at his hotel; he spent much of the afternoon conferring with

---

62. These included Professors Harry L. Wilson at Johns Hopkins, Henry Rushton Fairclough at Stanford, and Frederick W. Shipley at Washington University in St. Louis.

officials of the University of Toronto about the upcoming joint AIA-APA meetings and about the Toronto Society of the AIA, before lecturing at eight o'clock. On December 2, he lectured at Kingston ("responsive audience"); on the next day, his lecture at Ottawa saluted the formation of the local society; and on December 4, he was again on the podium, in Montreal, before returning via Toronto and the ferry at Windsor, Ontario, to reach Ann Arbor on December 6.

Preparations for the annual meeting and university obligations took much of his time in December. He worked most of Christmas Day before entertaining guests to Christmas dinner, then caught the 9:30 p.m. train to Detroit and onward to Toronto. The following day passed in relatively tranquil meetings, but December 28 was complicated. After a breakfast meeting with the Canadian societies, the meeting of the executive committee of the AIA is described in the diary as "stormy," with a "troublesome" Alfred M. Tozzer loudly giving voice to the disagreements in the American Committee. At the meeting of the governing council of the AIA, however, Kelsey's address was well received, as were the four new Canadian societies, alongside newcomers New Jersey and Rhode Island. The Canadian organization was to be known as the Department of Canada of the AIA and to comprise societies in Canada affiliated to the AIA, all having the same officers, procedures, rights, and responsibilities as societies in the United States.

The Department of Canada was a huge success at the start, eagerly welcoming speakers from south of the border and from Europe, not least those bringing the latest archaeological news from the spectacular British work on Crete and in the Aegean. By the end of 1909, there were already seven active societies; by 1912 there were thirteen. The largest of these was the Winnipeg Society with 93 members, followed by Montreal with 85, Toronto with 69, and Vancouver with 64. Total membership was 760, almost one-quarter of the membership of the whole of the institute. Its growth in five years had been remarkable, much due to the fast start made under the impetus of Kelsey himself and of Harry L. Wilson and to the enthusiasm of the secretary of the new department, Professor A. Judson Eaton of McGill University.

But it was all too meteoric, and the decline of the Department of Canada in 1914–15 may be attributed in the first place to administrative (power and control) arguments and personality clashes between the two secretaries, Mitchell Carroll and Eaton. Kelsey did his best to save the day, traveling to Montreal on July 13, 1912, to confer with Eaton and again on September 28 for talks with Eaton and Sir William Peterson, president of the department. He also undertook a long lecture tour to the Northwest in October and November, after which he wrote to Eaton of his optimism for the future: "I see no reason why, in Canada, as in the United States, the Societies located in these thriving cities[63] should not develop with the country and become increasingly fruitful as centers of cultural activities, contributing considerably to the general uplift." His efforts were to no avail. Sparring continued between Carroll and Eaton until the onset of World War I put an end to this imaginative enterprise. Canadians turned their attention to the war, and men were drawn away to the battlefields in droves. Membership in the department withered so quickly that the institute had little option other than to declare the Department of Canada's activities "suspended" in June 1915. After the war, an attempt to hold the AIA-APA meetings in Toronto again and thereby resuscitate the department was thwarted by an outbreak of smallpox in the city. It seemed that the Department of Canada was well and truly jinxed. The fortunes of the Canadian societies did not really improve until the 1960s.[64]

The Foreign Schools

Although the School of American Archaeology at Santa Fe was not a foreign school, it had been patterned after the AIA's foreign schools, and its purposes were similar. Prior to its establishment in 1907, there were already three other schools sponsored by the AIA outside the United States. The oldest of these were the American School of Classical Studies at Athens and the American School of Classical Studies in Rome. These two schools were established partly in a spirit of nationalism to compete with the resident schools of other countries—such as, for example, the French School of Athens, founded in 1846, or the German Archaeological Institute at Athens, founded in 1874— and partly to answer the educational needs of the United States. The members of the schools' managing committees were drawn from various institutions, as were the students, with the result that the schools were cooperative ventures embodying the common educational purpose of the participating universities and colleges. Their goals and arrangements were fully in line with the thinking of Charles Eliot Norton.

Like their umbrella organization, the AIA, they from the first catered to two constituencies, one favoring specialized professional and preprofessional

---

63. He meant Winnipeg, Edmonton, Calgary, Victoria, and Vancouver, all of which he visited on this tour (see chapter 6, "The Department of Latin").

64. For an admirable and sympathetic account of the Department of Canada, see James Russell, "The Dream That Failed: The AIA's Department of Canada (1908–1915)," in *EOP*, 141–55.

scholarship, the other preferring the broad humanistic learning characteristic of American college education, which depended on knowledge of Greek and Latin literature and philosophy to train civilized and cultivated citizens. Not all students at the schools went on to careers in scholarship, but many did, and some became leaders in their fields. The curricula provided for teaching the languages and literatures, on the one hand, and the contexts and conditions in which the languages and literatures had thrived, on the other. Thus, archaeology—the study of art, architecture, and artifacts—was recognized as a rewarding way to study antiquity. The visual record was slowly coming to the forefront as a reliable source of information.[65]

The schools in Athens and Rome were followed by one in Jerusalem, founded in 1899. Known as the American School for Oriental Study and Research,[66] it was jointly underwritten by the AIA, the American Oriental Society, and the Society for Biblical Literature. Though ostensibly following the curricula of the Athens and Rome schools in placing literature and archaeology side by side, its main objective became biblical study. According to its constitution, it existed to offer "graduates of American theological seminaries, and other similarly qualified persons, opportunities to prosecute biblical and linguistic investigations under more favorable conditions than can be secured at a distance from the Holy Land."[67]

Though the school in Jerusalem differed in mission from the other schools and from his own scholarly interests, Kelsey worked hard in its interests. In 1909 he appealed to President Woodward of the Carnegie Institution for funds for two research associates for the school,[68] and in New York the following year, he discussed the matter of an endowment for the school with

---

65. Charles Eliot Norton was the first to introduce art history to the American curriculum at Harvard in 1874; this seems to have caught on quite rapidly, since Francis Kelsey took a course in art history at the University of Rochester in his senior year (1879–80). Henry Simmons Frieze taught art history at Michigan in the 1870s, but it was not until 1910—and thanks largely to the agitation of the classicists, Professors Kelsey and D'Ooge, and of Dean Cooley—that a Department of Fine Arts and, with it, a faculty appointment in fine arts were inaugurated.

66. Renamed the American Schools of Oriental Research (ASOR) in 1921, it became the W. F. Albright Institute of Archaeological Research (AIAR) in 1970.

67. On the conditions surrounding the beginning of the school in Jerusalem and subsequent developments, see Neil Asher Silberman, "Between Athens and Babylon: The AIA and the Politics of American and Near Eastern Archaeology, 1884–1997," in *EOP*, 115–22; the quotation from ASOR's constitution is on 118.

68. Kelsey to Woodward, November 5, 1909, AIA Archives, box 16.17.

President Caleb Gates of Robert College[69] and, months later, with James Loeb.[70] When he was in Chicago a fortnight later and at lunch with Edward E. Ayer,[71] Martin Ryerson,[72] H. W. Harris, and William Anderson at the exclusive, private Chicago Club, the group tried to identify "in Chicago some person who would equip and endow the School in Palestine."[73] The consensus favored an approach to Mrs. McCormick, wife of Cyrus McCormick, a trustee of the McCormick Seminary and Lake Forest College, a man known to Kelsey since his days at Lake Forest and a colleague on the board of the seminary. Meanwhile, he was in correspondence with the American chargé d'affaires in Constantinople and others about difficulties the school was having with the Ottoman government with respect to taxation.[74]

Endowing the school in Jerusalem occupied much of his final year of presidency (1912), beginning with a "conference on a Palestine endowment" in New York.[75] In Washington, D.C., later in the year, at a meeting in the office of secretary of state Philander C. Knox, at which William Coffin, the American consul in Jerusalem, was present, discussion turned to possible endowments for the school and the question of excavations in Palestine.[76] Back in Chicago on April 26, he called on Rabbi Emil Hirsch at 3612 Grand Boulevard, seeking advice as to how best to approach Mr. Julius Rosenwald[77] on the matter of building and endowing a library in Jerusalem. He had already pre-

---

69. Diary, February 8, 1910. Robert College is a private university-preparatory school in Istanbul, founded in 1863.

70. Diary, December 9, 1910.

71. Edward Everett Ayer (1841–1927) was an American lumber magnate who made his fortune supplying timber to the railroad industry. He was an early benefactor and first president of Chicago's Field Museum of Natural History and a charter trustee of Chicago's Newberry Library.

72. Martin Ryerson served as president of the Board of Trustees of the University of Chicago and was a generous supporter of the Art Institute. The Ryersons and the Ayers were close friends: see Frank C. Lockwood, *The Life of Edward E. Ayer* (Chicago: A. C. McClung, 1929), 137.

73. Diary, December 23, 1910.

74. Gates, president of Robert College, to Kelsey, June 23, 1910, and chargé to Kelsey, August 16, 1910, AIA Archives, box 17.1.

75. Diary, February 15, 1912.

76. Diary, April 15, 1912.

77. At the time, Julius Rosenwald was the president of Sears, Roebuck, and Company. He was a prominent businessman and philanthropist, whose Rosenwald Fund, set up in 1917, contributed over seventy million dollars to educational projects, not least significant of which were gifts, actively encouraged by Rabbi Hirsch, to build schools for African American children in the Deep South.

pared the outlines of a budget in gross figures: the building would require $100,000, the stacks $10,000, books $40,000, and the endowment $350,000. In Washington, D.C., two weeks later, he asked Coffin to stay in the United States to help with a campaign for the school and the library,[78] to which Coffin agreed. Together they called an organizational meeting in New York on May 11; the same day, at a meeting of the managing committee of the American School of Classical Studies at Athens, Professor Abigail Leach[79] suggested (somewhat parenthetically, but interestingly enough for Kelsey to note it in his diary) that the proposed Jerusalem library be called the Strauss Memorial Library in memory of Mr. and Mrs. Isidor Strauss; these members of a well-known philanthropic Jewish-American family had perished when the *Titanic* went down. Two days later,[80] Coffin and Kelsey together went to see Rabbi Wise[81] at 36 West Sixty-sixth Street to see whether he thought they might be able to interest Mr. Adolph Lewisohn[82] in endowing the school in Palestine. Returning to New York two weeks later to meet architect Rutherford Mead,[83] Kelsey saw Coffin once more and prepared a full prospectus for all the projects in Jerusalem. Despite these tireless efforts, at the end of his presidency, the AIA had failed to identify a major donor. Nevertheless, Kelsey's work for the school in Jerusalem provides a good example of his tenacity and willpower. Once he had the bit between his teeth, there was little chance of shaking him off.

He found greater prospects for success with the American School of Classical Studies in Rome. Early in 1911, the school's executive committee proposed a consolidation with the American School of Architecture in Rome, the two units becoming the American Academy in Rome.[84] The academy was to be housed in a new building on the Janiculum Hill. This amalgamation,

---

78. Diary, May 9, 1912.

79. Abigail Leach (1855–1918) was professor of Greek at Vassar (1886–1918) and a president of the American Philological Association (1899–1900).

80. Diary, May 13, 1912.

81. This was almost certainly Rabbi Stephen Wise, founder of the Free Synagogue, which had purchased several brownstone houses nearby, on West Sixty-eighth Street, in 1911.

82. Adolph Lewisohn, a New York financier with interests in banking and mining, was a noted philanthropist, after whom Lewisohn Stadium at City College of New York was named; he also made significant contributions to Columbia University.

83. Kelsey was looking over the plans and elevations prepared by the architectural firm of McKim, Mead, and White for the new American Academy in Rome, discussed in the next paragraph.

84. Diary, February 11, 1911.

confirmed by the AIA's managing committee, allowed work to begin on a building designed by the prestigious New York firm of McKim, Mead, and White. The new founders of the academy included Andrew Carnegie, Henry Clay Frick, Charles F. McKim, J. P. Morgan, John D. Rockefeller, and William K. Vanderbilt, capitalist giants whose names and money lent enormous prestige to the project. Kelsey attended the first meetings of the new academy in New York in 1912,[85] and the American Academy in Rome opened its doors for the first time in 1914.

Kelsey also worked to found new schools. A plan to open a school in Constantinople was shelved because of resistance from the Athens school.[86] Another, for a school in Egypt, failed of support; and yet another, for a school in China, was supported by influential scholars and philanthropists, including Charles Lang Freer,[87] but fell victim to the economic depression after World War I.

Expeditions

From the very start, the AIA had favored participation in research projects, and its first foray in this direction had been to support fieldwork in the Americas: for five years in the 1880s, it had backed Adolph Bandelier's research in the American Southwest and Mexico. Simultaneously, its commitment to the worlds of Greece and Rome had led to the excavation of a site in the classical world. This evenhanded approach did not last long, however, and the preponderance of fieldwork at sites around the Mediterranean since the AIA's foundation indicates the major interests of the institute. The AIA excavations of 1881–83 at Assos in the Troad, in an area hotly contested by the European countries and their research centers, gave a rather halting start to American archaeological work in classical lands: the work was carried out by an inexperienced team with good intentions but limited skills, and the results were predictably mixed. The fieldwork went forward intermittently, the site on the slope of a hillside was difficult to handle, and there were arguments among the staff. But architectural blocks were retrieved, some of which found their way to the Boston Museum of Fine Arts and were admirably drawn. The

---

85. Diary, February 13, 1912.
86. Kelsey to Hoppin, April 8, 1910, and Hill to Kelsey, May 29, 1910, AIA Archives, box 17.26.
87. Diary, December 13, 1912.

shame was that publication became such a long, drawn-out affair. Twenty-five years later, Kelsey was wrestling with problems of the publication of the site, and the final volume of plates did not appear until 1921.[88]

Shortly after the Assos expedition, in 1887, another project began at the Temple of Hera Licinia at Croton, in the Calabria region of southern Italy, but it was short-lived. All eyes thereafter turned to securing the permit to work at the Panhellenic Sanctuary of Apollo at Delphi. Much effort and energy went into this attempt, but it failed for two reasons. First, the superior influence of the French in Greek governmental circles, which has allowed them to excavate and study the site to this day, was a major factor. Second, disagreement between the AIA and the American School of Classical Studies at Athens over control of the site did not enhance American prospects.[89] The American reaction to this failure was to launch a three-year project at Argos, led on the research side by the American School at Athens and funded by the institute. The work at Argos between 1892 and 1895, under the leadership of Anglo-American archaeologist Charles Waldstein, was successful and was followed in 1895 by excavations at Corinth conducted by the school alone. The excavations at Corinth continue to this day and have been very productive, serving along with the excavations in the ancient Athenian Agora as high points of the American contribution to the archaeology of Greece. In retrospect, the trend was clear: moving away from the institute's direct undertaking of fieldwork itself and toward handing responsibility for excavations and other fieldwork to the schools under its aegis, while allowing universities, museums, the affiliated societies, and other educational institutions to go their own ways. But this was not exactly Kelsey's view during his presidency.

Already at the meetings in Chicago in late December 1907, at which he was elected president, Kelsey was leading discussions about prospective sites for an expedition led by the AIA. David G. Hogarth, the English scholar who was to lecture about Knossos, and whose knowledge of classical lands was second

88. For an excellent account of the events, work, and personalities at Assos, see Susan Heuck Allen, "'Americans in the East': Francis Henry Bacon, Joseph Thacher Clarke, and the AIA at Assos," in *EOP*, 63–92.

89. A territorial dispute had broken out between Charles Waldstein, the director of the American School, and the AIA as to whether the school or the institute was to be in control of the work at Delphi. Waldstein claimed that he had resigned the directorship of the Fitzwilliam Museum and his readership in classical archaeology at Cambridge University on the understanding that, as the new director of the American School of Classical Studies at Athens, he would be the director of American work at Delphi (Waldstein to Low, November 28, 1890, AIA Archives, box 7).

to none, took part in these talks. When the discussion turned to the question of possible sites for excavation, Sardis in Asia Minor emerged as a major candidate: it had been sequentially the capital of the Lydian kings, the seat of a Persian satrap, a major Seleucid center, and one of the more distinguished cities of the Roman province of Asia. For work at this site, Hogarth, who had extensive experience of fieldwork in Asia Minor, provided on request a tentative budget, suggesting "$20,000 a year for 4 years a fair sum" to have in mind.[90] In the course of 1908, interested parties discussed possibilities and funding arrangements for work at Sardis, and the participation of both the Baltimore Society and Princeton was under discussion. Meanwhile, a new candidate for excavation emerged: Cyrene in Libya. This site appealed as a hugely wealthy and well-watered city that had regularly sent victors to the Greek games, was famous in the Greek period for its horses and silphium (a medicinal plant of great popularity but uncertain properties), and was well-known in Roman times for its size, amenities, and climate (in the summer) up on the high Jebel Akhdar (Green Mountain). Hogarth had mentioned Cyrene, knew the site, which he had visited in 1904 as a guest on Allison V. Armour's yacht,[91] and thought that the pickings would be rich: "they cannot fail, if they search at all, to find, and to find largely."[92]

In 1909 the pace of discussions quickened. On January 22 and 23, Kelsey was in Boston in conference with Arthur Fairbanks, his old classical colleague from Michigan and now director of the Boston Museum of Fine Arts, about a cooperative venture at Cyrene between the institute and the museum. On the second day, they reached an agreement, and "contracts were typed up by Miss Blanche Levy." The next day, over lunch in New York, Kelsey persuaded Allison Armour to put up five thousand dollars for Cyrene on behalf of the AIA, and on January 25, the chairs of the managing committees of all the institute's schools agreed to recommend the Cyrene project to the council. A further two days of incessant meetings, culminating in an evening at the Metropolitan Opera (*Die Meistersinger*) that Francis was "too exhausted to en-

---

90. Diary, December 29, 1907.

91. Allison V. Armour, a wealthy scion of the Chicago Armour meatpacking family, was well known for his generous contributions to archaeology, botany, and zoology and for his commodious yacht, the *Utowana*, which he used as a base for his botanical expeditions to the islands of the Caribbean and his archaeological enterprises in the Mediterranean. See Thomas Barbour, *Allison Armour and the Utowana: An Appreciation of Allison Vincent Armour and of the Services Which He Rendered to the Sciences of Archaeology, Botany, and Zoology* (Cambridge, MA: privately printed, 1945).

92. D. G. Hogarth in the *Illustrated London News,* March 18, 1911.

joy,"[93] were followed, on January 28, by breakfast with Armour at Delmonico's on Fifth Avenue. There they agreed details of the Cyrene enterprise. Kelsey then journeyed to Princeton for dinner at the Armours' home with Professors Andrew Fleming West and Howard Crosby Butler.[94]

At midyear, he was in Boston again for meetings about Cyrene with Fairbanks[95] and Richard Norton:[96] Norton agreed to search for funds, and Kelsey agreed to write to James Loeb for help.[97] Kelsey returned to Boston once more in the fall for a meeting of the Cyrene Commission with Fairbanks, Norton, Armour, and Gardiner Lane,[98] the president of the Boston Museum and trustee for the subscribers to the Cyrene Fund. Lane declared that he was unable to sign the agreement, as the representative of subscribers of five thousand dollars, unless ten thousand dollars more was "in sight." Finally, Armour offered to "find the expenses of himself and Norton to go to Constantinople to obtain the concession, and I agreed to get $5000 from the Societies." James Loeb provided the five thousand to make up the fifteen thousand dollars of the budget.[99] At the annual meetings in Washington, D.C., in December, the council voted in favor of the Cyrene contracts. At the same meeting, Butler outlined plans at Sardis, which Princeton was ready to undertake independently, and W. H. Buckler of the Baltimore Society[100] spoke of opportunities in Spain.

By mid-April of 1910, Norton, in London, wrote to Fairbanks that he had a telegram from Constantinople offering no legal objection to the excavation: "This means, I suppose, that the firman [the permit] will be granted before

---

93. Diary, January 27, 1909.

94. On Andrew Fleming West, see n. 6 above. Butler (1872–1922), already encountered in the 1907 list of AIA lecturers (see above, "Membership"), was professor of the history of architecture and first director of the School of Architecture (1920).

95. A graduate of Dartmouth (1886) with a Ph.D. in classics from the University of Freiburg (1890), Fairbanks was appointed professor of Greek and Greek archaeology at Michigan in 1906 and became director of the Boston Museum of Fine Arts in 1908.

96. Richard Norton was a son of Charles Eliot Norton, had served as director of the American School of Classical Studies in Rome during 1899–1907, and was director designate of the Cyrene excavations.

97. Diary, June 24, 25, and 26, 1909.

98. Gardiner M. Lane, a director of many corporations, including the U.S. Steel Corporation, was treasurer of the Massachusetts Red Cross, treasurer of the American School of Classical Studies at Athens, and president of the Boston Museum of Fine Arts.

99. Diary, October 22, 1909. There is a list of subscribers in AIA Archives, box 17.

100. William Hepburn Buckler (1867–1952), an archaeologist, linguist, lawyer, and diplomat, would also serve as secretary of the Board of Trustees of Johns Hopkins University.

long."[101] On May 6, Fairbanks wrote to Kelsey that "the firman has been granted and Norton is going down to make arrangements for a campaign in the early autumn."[102] The Armour yacht, the *Utowana,* then made its way from Southampton, via Algiers, Malta, and Tripoli, to Cyrenaica, with the survey group, led by Armour, Norton, and Bates, aboard.[103] From Malta, Norton signaled to Fairbanks on May 20, "All well so far. Send dollars."[104] In July Kelsey heard from Fairbanks that Norton and his team had been in Libya briefly scouting around and that Norton was busy writing up a report.[105] By the end of the summer, the report, upbeat in tone and content, was complete, and preparations for the upcoming season's work were well advanced. Work began at the site at the end of October.

Meanwhile, Kelsey was pushing Lane to come up with subscribers' funds, requests reiterated in September and October. On September 1, Armour set up a credit line of ten thousand dollars in London for the Cyrene project, and two days later, the dollars promised by James Loeb were in hand. Lane produced the list of Boston subscribers, forty-eight in all, in November and wrote to try to convince Senator Henry Cabot Lodge of Massachusetts about the desirability of appointing a U.S. consul for Cyrenaica at Benghazi.[106] Loeb seemed fully involved in all arrangements, even expressing his concerns about quality control, and in conversation with Kelsey in New York on December 9, he did not hesitate to express reservations.

> [C]alled on James Loeb at the home of Paul M. Warburg,[107] 17 East 80th St. Mr. Loeb gave me information in regard to R. Norton, and expressed his anxiety in regard to the standard of the scientific work at Cyrene, also in regard to the necessity of having an architect "on the spot." Raised question also in regard to the standard of work in American archaeology.[108]

101. Norton to Fairbanks, April 19, 1910, AIA Archives, box 17.31.

102. Fairbanks to Kelsey, May 6, 1910, AIA Archives, box 17.31.

103. A distinguished archaeologist and historian, Oric Bates was a curator at the Peabody Museum at Harvard University. Well known for his work in Egypt and Libya, he was perhaps most admired for his book *The Eastern Libyans* (1914).

104. Norton to Fairbanks, May 20, 1910, AIA Archives, box 17.31.

105. Fairbanks to Kelsey, July 27, 1910, AIA Archives, box 17.31.

106. Lane to Lodge, November 1910, AIA Archives, box 18.

107. Paul Moritz Warburg (1868–1932) was a German-born banker who settled in New York City in 1902 as a partner in the investment firm Kuhn, Loeb, and Company. His wife, née Nina J. Loeb, was the founder's daughter and sister to James Loeb.

108. Diary December 9, 1910. It is unclear who had placed these doubts in Loeb's mind.

The day after Christmas, Fairbanks met Kelsey in Boston: "We went together to the Museum of Fine Arts where we conferred on the Cyrene undertaking and settled that the publication of Norton's preliminary report should be in the Bulletin of the Institute. We discussed also financial questions of the Cyrene undertaking."[109]

The Cyrene site itself was hugely promising in what it could reveal about a wealthy Greek and Roman city, but in retrospect, those who organized the expedition might have been more alert to the international situation. Italy, not to be left out entirely from the European landgrab in Africa, was eager to follow the example of other European colonizing countries, and clear signals—to be confirmed by events in September 1911, when Italian troops landed at Tripoli and Benghazi to take possession of Libya—were recognizable in Rome. Undeterred, Norton and his team, the leading members of which were his old friend, the expert epigrapher Herbert Fletcher De Cou,[110] C. Densmore Curtis,[111] and Joseph Clark Hoppin,[112] worked steadily through the fall of 1910 and early 1911. On the morning of March 11, 1911, however, the whole enterprise was stopped in its tracks. De Cou was leading the workmen up to the acropolis to begin work when he was shot by assassins at close range. It was a stroke of atrocious luck, for normally it was Norton who assembled the workers and took them up to the site; but that morning, he was detained in camp and had asked De Cou to take his place. The assassins evidently did not single De Cou out: they were probably hired to kill Norton.

On March 13, Norton sent telegrams to Armour, Fairbanks, and Kelsey.[113] Kelsey's read, "De Cou killed March 11th by Arabs sent here for this purpose according to report by Italian influence. Notify mother. Norton." Francis immediately phoned the De Cou home in Chicago, offering to come at once, but was told by Louis F. De Cou that the "mother was too prostrated to see

---

109. Diary, December 26, 1910.

110. De Cou had taught at Michigan intermittently and had assisted Kelsey and the group from the American School of Classical Studies in Rome during their tour of Greece.

111. Educated in California and Colorado, Charles Densmore Curtis (1875–1925) pursued studies at both the American School of Classical Studies in Rome and the American School of Classical Studies at Athens. An expert in ancient jewelry, coins, lamps, and terra-cottas, he is best known for his publication of the Bernardini and Barberini tombs at Praeneste.

112. A graduate of Harvard (1893) with a Ph.D. from Munich (1896), Hoppin had gained valuable field experience at Argos (1894–96) and was associated with the American School of Classical Studies at Athens for several years. An expert in Greek pottery, he taught for many years at Bryn Mawr College.

113. Norton's two-day delay in sending the telegrams seems inexplicable, unless perhaps he was overwhelmed by the tragedy and the press of arrangements for the funeral. The burial, at which Norton himself read the service, took place at Cyrene on the twelfth.

me."[114] The next day, he sent an official notification to the State Department in Washington, D.C., and on March 19, he met with the Cyrene Commission in Boston. Armour summarized what evidence they had of Italian interference. In brief, it consisted of remarks made by the Turkish governor of Benghazi to Norton; remarks made to Armour by Halil Bey, soon to be appointed the Turkish minister for foreign affairs, and by the German emperor;[115] and the attitude of the Italian ambassador in London. According to Armour, George Reisner had told him that "Arabs excavating in Egypt had said to him that someone at Cyrene would be shot."[116] Despite this undercurrent of Italian hostility, the committee agreed that the work should continue if security could be established and that everything should be put in Armour's hands: he had already arranged to sail on March 22.

Meanwhile, Norton had written Kelsey, on March 12, that "the murderers were seen and two of them recognized as outsiders. The Council of Sheikhs was called together today. They say the murderers are shepherds in Italian employ and were instigated by Italians. Bernabei the Italian consul at Benghazi has constantly tried to thwart us and Italian influence has been repeatedly used against us."[117] Two days later, Curtis wrote to his "Folks" of the strict actions undertaken by the Turks in the immediate aftermath of the killing.[118] Gardiner Lane made an appointment to see Secretary of State Knox on April 11 in Washington, D.C., and asked Kelsey and Senator Lodge to go along. Secretary Knox was unable to meet them, but in his absence, they spoke to Mr. Arthur N. Young. In the discussion, Gardiner represented the consortium of the AIA and the Boston Museum of Fine Arts; on their behalf, he demanded security for the excavators, protection for U.S. property, the arrest of the assassins, and the dispatch of an American warship to Cyrene.[119] Kelsey phoned Senator William Alden Smith of Michigan, and the two men prepared a resolution to be put before the Senate; meanwhile, Lane spoke in person to President Taft, who told him that he would send a warship as soon as possible and would call in the Turkish and Italian ambassadors. Back in the Midwest, on

114. Diary, March 14, 1911.

115. Armour evidently moved in the loftiest social and political circles. He annually spent part of the summer in Germany and frequently was a guest of the kaiser at military and social happenings.

116. Diary, March 19, 1911. George Andrew Reisner was professor of Egyptology at Harvard, director of the excavations at Samaria in Palestine, and famous for his explorations of the pyramids and cemeteries at Giza.

117. Norton to Kelsey, March 12, 1911, AIA Archives, box 19.

118. Curtis to "Folks," March 14, 1911, AIA Archives, box 19.7.

119. Diary, April 11, 1911.

April 26, a saddened Kelsey called on Mrs. Margaret F. De Cou at 843 North State Street in Chicago.[120] We may imagine what messages of condolence he brought, with difficulty, to her in her grief.

On August 5, Kelsey sent a report of the season's work and of De Cou's death to Halil Bey in Constantinople.[121] In Washington again in September, he went to the Navy Department to see the acting secretary, Beekman Winthrop,[122] about the dispatch of a warship, seeking definite orders for it to go to Tripoli, Benghazi, and Derna and for officers to visit Cyrene. On September 13, he saw the completed plans for the movements of the cruiser USS *Chester*, and at the State Department, he "spent two hours reading dispatches and correspondence in regard to the murder of De Cou and in conference with MacMurray, a young and promising man." Between meetings, he worked through Norton's report of the first season's work, revised it, and had the text typed and the photographs prepared. Finished on September 12, he sent it all off to Norton in London.[123]

In Cyrene, Norton continued working through May, if only to demonstrate that the murder would not abort the expedition. In late May, however, he and the team left Libya on Armour's yacht. Norton spent the summer in Europe, preparing for the next season's work, and was heartened to hear from Kelsey in September that the USS *Chester* had sailed to meet the *Utowana* at Gibraltar and escort the archaeologists to Cyrene. The U.S. government had acted, the diplomatic wheels were turning, and things seemed on the upswing. It was all to no avail: the outbreak of war between Italy and Turkey forced the suspension and then cancellation of the project. Italian warships appeared off the coast of Libya at the end of September and landed troops to occupy Tripoli and Benghazi. Though they did not trouble themselves with Cyrene for over a year, there was no place for Americans in the new Africa Italiana.[124]

Who was responsible for De Cou's death? The murderers were never brought to justice, so there was no chance to cross-examine them as to purpose and motivation. At their first meeting after the assassination, the Cyrene Commission assessed the little evidence they had (the remarks, the attitude) and pointed the finger squarely at the Italians as the instigators of the murder.

---

120. Diary, April 26, 1911.

121. AIA Archives, box 19.5.

122. Winthrop (1874–1940), a lawyer, had been appointed governor of Puerto Rico (1904–7) and later assistant secretary of the Treasury (1907) by his friend Theodore Roosevelt.

123. Diary September 11, 12, and 13, 1911.

124. For a convenient discussion of this episode, see Dyson, *Ancient Marbles to American Shores*, 76–82.

It is a commonplace of precolonization that colonizing countries soften up their targets by liberal distributions of cash to susceptible individuals and groups. The Arabs in Cyrene had no doubt that the assassins had received money for the murder. When the dust settled after a year of sometimes harsh diplomatic words, an indemnity of twenty-five thousand dollars was paid by the Italian government to the AIA.[125] In view of this, it seems logical to conclude that the assassins were supported by the Italians. This payment was the nearest the Italians came to an admission of culpability.

They had denied responsibility from the first and even put about a rumor to the effect that De Cou had been chasing an Arab woman and was killed by her husband. Anyone who knew De Cou saw this as a ridiculous idea. De Cou was a quiet, modest, shy scholar and a bachelor, more at ease with his inscriptions than in society, let alone operating as a ladies' man in a totally alien foreign culture. Yet even the normally responsible Gaspare Oliverio,[126] an Italian archaeologist who took a leading role in Italian excavations in Libya after 1914, repeated the outrageous story years later. A complicating factor was Italian dislike of Richard Norton. While director of the American School of Classical Studies in Rome, Norton had taken a high-handed approach to the Italians, openly criticizing their treatment of newly discovered archaeological sites. Moreover, in agreeing to direct the American work at Cyrene in 1911, he put himself in direct competition with Federico Halbherr,[127] an Italian archaeologist whose eye was already set on Cyrene. The Italian press claimed that Norton accused Halbherr of instigating the De Cou murder, an accusation that Norton strenuously denied, even asking Kelsey to assure Halbherr that this was not the case.[128]

Norton also did not think that officials in Rome would have suggested anything as drastic as a murder. He laid the blame at the door of the Italian consul in Benghazi, Vincenzo Bernabei.[129] Certainly someone had been stir-

---

125. *Detroit Free Press*, February 26, 1913.

126. Gaspare Oliverio (1887–1956) was a student of Halbherr's. An archaeologist and epigrapher, he became professor of classical archaeology at the University of Florence and pursued excavations at Locri Epizephyrii, a site in his native Calabria.

127. Halbherr (1857–1930), of the Università di Roma (La Sapienza), had led the first scientific excavations on Crete in 1884–86 and had been chosen by the AIA governing council to head up new work there in 1893. See "American Expedition to Krete under Professor Halbherr," *American Journal of Archaeology and of the History of the Fine Arts* 9.4 (October–December 1894): 538–44.

128. Norton to Kelsey, October 24, 1911, AIA Archives, box 19; R. G. Goodchild, "Death of an Epigrapher: The Killing of Herbert De Cou," *Michigan Quarterly Review* 8.3 (1969): 153.

129. Norton to Kelsey, March 24, 1911, AIA Archives, box 19.

ring things up. Apparently random shots had already been fired at the American camp on six separate occasions, beginning right at the start of the work in October and most recently on March 1. In a letter to his sister Sara some five days before the assassination, Norton spoke of "troubles with the natives." He added that he "had to handle all questions pretty delicately" and remarked that "one of the soldiers tried to club me with his gun the other day." He went on, "We can manage fairly comfortably should the Arabs show their teeth as they have done once or twice."[130] His inability to see the danger doubtless sprang from the same condescending attitude that provoked resentment at the American presence. Such a personality would have made any inhabitant who was already disposed to object to Europeans and Christians also susceptible to inducements to make trouble. Thus, Norton himself may have been partly responsible for the disaster.[131]

Disappointed and shocked by this disastrous setback in Libya, Kelsey tried to engage interest in other possible sites for the institute. Writing in November to Ernest Jackson, a member of the AIA's executive committee and the secretary of the Boston Society, he lamented the suspension of work in Cyrene and suggested working in Malta, Knidos, or conceivably the Sanctuary of Zeus Ammon in Egypt.[132] There were no takers. He was more successful in efforts on behalf of the School of American Archaeology in Santa Fe. In a letter dated December 25, 1911, to the United Fruit Company, he requested support for excavations at the Maya city of Quiriguá in Guatemala, to which he received a positive reply early in the New Year.[133] Hewett's work in the Americas was moving forward.

Kelsey and AIA Publications

The AIA had assumed responsibility for the publication of the results of expeditions conducted under its sponsorship. Thus, in the decade of Kelsey's involvement in the administration, as secretary (1902–7) and president

---

130. Norton to sister, March 6, 1911, AIA Archives, box 19.

131. For an excellent assessment of this aspect of the story and more, see Goodchild, "Death of an Epigrapher"; cf. idem, "Murder on the Acropolis (1904–1911)," in *Libyan Studies: Select Papers of the Late R. G. Goodchild,* ed. J. Reynolds (London: Paul Elek, 1976), 290–97 (these pages written not later than 1960). Cf. also F. W. Kelsey, "The Tragedy at Cyrene," *Bulletin of the AIA* 2.3 (June 1911): 111–14.

132. Kelsey to Jackson, November 25, 1911, AIA Archives, box 17.9.

133. United Fruit Company to Kelsey, January 12, 1912, AIA Archives, box 18.16.

(1907–12), he inherited two major publications: the excavations at Assos in Asia Minor (1881–83) and those at the Heraion at Argos in Greece (1892–95). The work at Assos and the long, drawn-out period of its publication have already been mentioned.[134] That work had been organized directly by the institute; at Argos, it had been organized by the American School of Classical Studies at Athens—under the umbrella of the AIA—and directed by Charles Waldstein. In effect, Waldstein chose the staff and arranged the fieldwork, while the institute found the funds. Miraculously, this dual leadership was successful. It speaks well for Waldstein that he was able to work so constructively with the AIA in the aftermath of the failure to get the permit for Delphi. Moreover, the excavations at the Argive Heraion allowed him to train the next generation of American classical archaeologists.[135] The results of the expedition were published in two volumes, also with funds raised by the institute.[136]

The 1910–11 Cyrene expedition, in whose organization Kelsey had played a leading role, was published in 1911. Following the appalling murder of Herbert De Cou, Norton and the members of his team worked up the report of the excavations and made arrangements for work to resume in the fall. In September (as noted earlier), Kelsey read through and revised the manuscript of the report, arranged for the illustrations, and sent the whole package off to Norton. James Loeb was once again a generous contributor to the costs of production.[137]

Funds for the publications of Assos and Argos were raised by subscription, and subscription lists for both publications may be found in the institute's archives.[138] But pledges often took long to arrive. As with his other fund-raising efforts, Kelsey proposed funding AIA excavation reports and monographs by endowment. In 1911, for example, he drew up a prospectus

---

134. See above, "Expeditions." For the publications, see Joseph T. Clarke, *Report on the Investigations at Assos, 1882, 1883,* pt. 1, AIA Papers, Classical Series 2 (New York: Macmillan, 1898); Joseph T. Clarke, Francis H. Bacon, and Robert Koldewey, *Investigations at Assos: Drawings and Photographs of the Buildings and Objects Discovered during the Excavations of 1881–1882–1883,* Expedition of the AIA (London: Bernard Quaritch and Henry Sotheran; Cambridge, MA: Archaeological Institute of America; Leipzig: Karl W. Hiersemann, 1902).

135. This included De Cou, as was noted in chapter 4 "The American School of Classical Studies in Rome."

136. Charles Waldstein et al., *The Argive Heraeum,* 2 vols. (Boston: Houghton, Mifflin, 1902–5).

137. R. Norton et al., *The Excavations at Cyrene: First Campaign 1910–1911* (New York: Macmillan, 1911), extract from the *Bulletin of the AIA* 2 (1911): 141–63.

138. AIA Archives, box 10.

for an endowment to fund scholarly publications, comparable to those of the Fondation Piot,[139] and sent it to several men of means, including Andrew Carnegie and Otto Kahn.[140] Such publications would and did appear irregularly.

Of equal, if not more, importance to the institute were its *Bulletin* and the *American Journal of Archaeology.* Excavation reports and monographs spoke only intermittently to the AIA's commitment to fieldwork research; but the *Bulletin,* which provided an annual report of activities, and the *American Journal of Archaeology,* the institute's professional periodical, sent to all members, were its lifeblood.

The *American Journal of Archaeology* started life as the *American Journal of Archaeology and the History of Fine Arts* in 1885. Owned by Arthur Frothingham Jr. and Allan Marquand of Princeton University and sponsored by the institute, it was edited by Frothingham, with the support of Charles Eliot Norton as advising editor. In 1897 it became the official, professional periodical of the institute, with a new editor, John Henry Wright of Harvard. A decade later, in the year Kelsey was elected AIA president (1907), Harold North Fowler became its third editor.[141]

While the journal served professional scholars of the institute well, it had less appeal for the interested amateur members, especially when more and more articles tended to focus on Mediterranean antiquity while increasingly few focused on topics in the archaeology of the Americas or periods from Late Antiquity to the Renaissance. To answer a growing demand for less technical articles, the council voted in 1912 to publish another periodical with a more popular focus alongside the journal. The Washington Society, with the wholehearted approval of President Kelsey, was instrumental in pushing this initiative. The new periodical was to appeal to a wider audience, to be richly illustrated, and to broadcast all the latest news. It was fully in line with Charles Eliot Norton's (and Kelsey's) identification of archaeology as an attractive vehicle of humanistic education that would lift the tone of American

---

139. Eugène Piot (1812–90) left his estate to the Académie des Belles-Lettres et Inscriptions in Paris for research in art and archaeology from antiquity to the Renaissance. This resulted in the appearance of the academy's publication series Monuments et Mémoires de la Fondation Eugène Piot.

140. AIA Archives, box 19. Otto Hermann Kahn (1867–1934)—investment banker, philanthropist, collector, arts patron—was, like Paul M. Warburg, a partner in the investment firm Kuhn, Loeb, and Company.

141. Fowler had been one of the first students at the American School of Classical Studies at Athens and was the longtime (1893–1923) professor of Greek archaeology at Western Reserve College in Cleveland. He served as editor until 1916.

public discourse. It was to be called *Art and Archaeology: An Illustrated Magazine,* and to make way for it, the *Bulletin* was to be suspended[142]—though in fact, when the first issue appeared in July 1914, the *Bulletin,* too, continued. Motivated by Norton's ideals, the original incarnation of *Art and Archaeology* owed much to the presidency of Francis Kelsey and the energy and drive of AIA secretary Mitchell Carroll, as well as to the influence of the large Washington Society that Carroll nourished.

Among the rank-and-file members, *Art and Archaeology* was an instantaneous success. However, there were many leading figures in the profession who opposed it, viewing it as a step in the direction of popularization—which indeed it was. These detractors' negative assessment was based on the assumption that popularization necessarily implied the lowering of academic standards and that such reaching out to the intelligent general public was not in the best interests of archaeology. During World War I and throughout the 1920s, *Art and Archaeology* was a focus of debate between those who wished to exclude the interested layperson from the institute and those who favored encouraging a wider membership. Under assault from conservative, not to say authoritarian, elements, who pleaded funding difficulties, *Art and Archaeology* issued its final number in 1934. Its cancellation mirrored a rapid fall in membership, a decline rectified only by its reincarnation in 1948 as *Archaeology,* a popular magazine that has gone from strength to strength. Since 1948, *Archaeology* has become a full partner with the *American Journal of Archaeology* in publishing archaeological research and in furthering the work of the AIA.

THE LEGACY OF KELSEY'S TENURES

The decade 1902–12, during which Francis Kelsey shouldered a major share of the administrative and leadership work of the AIA, first as secretary and then as president, was a time of great accomplishment and growth. The membership almost tripled, leaping from 1,052 to 2,987. By the end of 1912, the number of affiliated societies had increased from eighteen (in 1907) to forty, and the organization's income had jumped from $14,593 to more than $21,000.[143] The Department of Canada, which by 1912 numbered thirteen affiliated societies with 760 members, was up and running.[144] The burden of work had increased hugely, and administrative changes were needed.

---

142. "The Proposed Non-Technical Magazine," *Bulletin of the AIA* 4.1 (March 1913): 7.
143. The figures are from Francis W. Kelsey, "Thirty-third Annual Report of the President of the Archaeological Institute of America," *Bulletin of the AIA* 3.4 (October 1912): 195–96.
144. Ibid., 198 (table).

The act incorporating the AIA had been passed by Congress and approved by President Roosevelt in May 1906.[145] The desirability of having the AIA's offices and records within easy reach of the country's legislators and of the institute's secretary, Mitchell Carroll, resulted in them finding a home at George Washington University, where Carroll was a professor. This space rapidly proved too cramped, however, and in January 1911, the office was moved to a room in the Octagon House.[146] The increase in workload that necessarily accompanied the growth in the membership and the complexity of the lecture program had called for the appointment of associate secretaries, of whom there were four by 1909.[147] By the end of 1911, when Kelsey agreed reluctantly to continue as president for a further year, two working vice presidents were elected by the council.

Of the institute's established schools, the School of American Archaeology flourished under the leadership of Edgar Hewett and Alice Fletcher; the American Academy in Rome had grown from the amalgamation of the American School of Classical Studies in Rome and the American School of Architecture; the school at Athens continued to flourish; and the school in Jerusalem was straining to steady itself in difficult times. As for research projects and publications, the institute had collaborated with the Boston Museum of Fine Arts and Arthur Fairbanks, its director, in the exploration of Cyrene in Libya. In Guatemala, excavation was conducted on behalf of the institute by the St. Louis Society and the School of American Archaeology; and in Greece, the American School of Classical Studies continued its admirable work at Corinth. The publication of the work at Assos was pushed forward, and the *American Journal of Archaeology* continued to attract favorable comments from European as well as American scholars. To satisfy the preferences of interested but not necessarily learned members, the council voted to publish a new, nontechnical periodical, *Art and Archaeology,* which appeared in 1914 for the first time.

Francis Kelsey could leave the presidency with plenty of cause for satisfaction. In his final report, he pleaded for more endowments—for the schools, for the lecture program, and for publications. He ended on a personal note, which encapsulates his belief in archaeology as a beneficial discipline.

---

145. See n. 28 and, for the act, *Bulletin of the AIA* 3.2 (March 1912): 155–56.

146. In 1899 the Octagon House (built 1798–1800) in Washington, D.C.—designed by the architect of the U.S. Capitol, William Thornton—became the home of the American Institute of Architects, who granted the AIA space.

147. See above, "Administration."

In relinquishing the responsibilities which the Council entrusted to me, I cannot refrain from voicing the conviction that the Institute has only begun to realize the possibilities of its twofold mission, the advancement of knowledge in a most important field of human achievement and the wide dissemination of the highest ideals of art and learning. . . . In many centres, there are those who find in it an effective instrument for the combating of philistinism and for the advancement of culture, as well as those who look to it for the encouragement and support of work of investigation. In the well balanced union of the two interests lies its strength. Rash would he be who, at the present time, would essay to forecast the range and limits of its influence.

> Francis W. Kelsey
> Ann Arbor, Michigan
> October 31, 1912[148]

---

148. Kelsey, "Thirty-third Annual Report," 201.

CHAPTER 6

A Regional Presence

Kelsey Close to Home, 1907–12

৶

WHILE THE AIA AND ITS PROGRAMS were taking much of Kelsey's time
and executive abilities in these years, much was happening in Ann Arbor, too.
Only a person of unusual aptitudes could attend to developments in the university and town, as well as important moments in his and his family's private
lives, in addition to the policies of the AIA. In Kelsey, both Michigan and the
AIA were fortunate to have a leader of exceptional talents.

THE UNIVERSITY OF MICHIGAN

The Presidency

By 1907 James Burrill Angell was nearing the end of his presidency. The tasks
before him had increased hugely in number and complexity. He was seventy-
eight years old; his energy levels were diminished; his wife had died in 1903,
and she was badly missed. The university, meanwhile, had grown at a tremendous rate. Enrollments were rising continuously, having increased from 3,303
in 1900 to 5,339 in 1910, making Michigan the third-largest college in the
United States that year, surpassed only by Columbia and Chicago. When Angell was appointed president in 1871, there had been thirty-five faculty mem-

bers; at his retirement in 1909, there were more than four hundred.[1] Administrative problems had therefore multiplied, with increasing demand for new buildings and equipment, more faculty, and improved salaries. All too clearly, more administrators were needed to work closely with a president whose duties were expanding on what seemed an almost daily basis.

In early 1905, he had submitted his resignation to the Board of Regents. They had not seen it coming and were taken aback. Though they declined at once to accept his resignation, they instantly offered more administrative help. In the face of their apparent confusion, offer of help, and affection for him, Angell agreed to continue. Just four years later, however, after celebrating his eightieth birthday in January 1909, he was again feeling the pressure of the office, the changing times, and his age, so he wrote to the regents once more. It is worth quoting his letter in full for its eloquence, modesty, sense of propriety, and generosity of tone.

> Ann Arbor
> February 17, 1909
>
> To the Board of Regents:
>
> Four years ago I tendered my resignation to you in the belief that the interest of the University would be subserved by the appointment to the presidency of a younger man. You declined in such kind words to accept my resignation that I have continued at my post and rendered the best service of which I was capable.
>
> But as I have now passed my eightieth birthday, it is fitting that I should renew the tender of my resignation. I therefore do so with the urgent request that you accept it to take effect at the end of the academic year.
>
> May I take this occasion to express to you again my sincere thanks for all your courtesy and kindness to me?
>
> Yours very truly
> James B. Angell

This time the regents were ready. Regent Loyal Edwin Knappen[2] of Grand Rapids at once voiced the unanimous assent and gratitude of the regents, in the most generous terms. The following resolution was passed:

---

1. J. L. Marwil, *A History of Ann Arbor* (Ann Arbor: University of Michigan Press, 1987), 56–57.

2. A University of Michigan graduate (B.A. 1873, M.A. 1876), Knappen had been a prosecuting attorney for Barry and Kent counties, served as U.S. district judge for the Western Dis-

> That the Board of Regents hereby tenders to James Burrill Angell the appointment of Chancellor of the University of Michigan, the duties of the office to be such as, at the request of the President, he may be willing and able to perform, the salary for such office to be $4000 per year with house rent, light and fuel, as long as he sees fit to occupy his present residence; said appointment to take effect at the close of this academic year.[3]

They could hardly have expressed in more genuine a manner or more meaningful terms the profound sense of appreciation they and all Michigan felt for the work of the man who had provided such successful and distinguished leadership to the university for no fewer than thirty-eight years.

Angell continued to live in Ann Arbor, providing help in numerous ways, including to Francis Kelsey, to whom he often gave sensitive advice (not least in the area of fund-raising) and at whose home he was a welcome visitor and guest. At his death at the age of eighty-eight in 1916, his funeral cortege was accompanied by widespread scenes of public mourning. The procession wound its slow way from the president's house to the cemetery, the streets lined by students two deep, hats off and heads bowed to honor the great leader who had given his life to the university and had brought it to maturity.

It would be no easy task to find a successor to Angell. At the end of the summer of 1909, the regents decided they would not be rushed and appointed the dean of the Law School, Harry Burns Hutchins,[4] as acting president for one year. They continued their national search, making unsuccessful overtures to the governor of New York, Charles Evans Hughes;[5] to David

---

trict of Michigan, and would soon (February 1910) become a U.S. circuit judge for the Sixth Circuit. See Burke Aaron Hinsdale, *History of the University of Michigan,* ed. Isaac Newton Demmon (Ann Arbor: University of Michigan, 1906), 212–13; University of Michigan, *Proceedings of the Board of Regents (1910–1914),* "June Meeting, 1913," 764.

3. *Michigan Alumnus,* 15 (1909): 222.

4. Harry Burns Hutchins (b. 1847), a University of Michigan graduate (B.Phil. 1871), practiced law for eight years with his father-in-law, Thomas M. Crocker, as Crocker and Hutchins. Appointed professor of law in 1884 and subsequently dean of the Law School, Hutchins had been named acting president in President Angell's absence as minister to Turkey in 1897. See "Michigan's New President: The New Hampshire Head of a Great University," *Granite Monthly,* n.s., 5 (1910): 249–52.

5. Following his governorship (1907–10), Hughes (1862–1948) was to serve as associate justice of the U.S. Supreme Court (1910–16), the Republican candidate for president (1916), U.S. secretary of state (1921–25), and chief justice of the United States (1930–41).

Jayne Hill,[6] former president of the University of Rochester; and to Woodrow Wilson, president of Princeton.[7] They were aiming high; but as is generally the case, the competent had many opportunities before them. Finally, twelve months later, they voted to offer the presidency to Hutchins for a five-year term. There were misgivings on the board, but the hesitations of one or two regents rapidly dissipated once they saw Hutchins in full swing as president. When, at the end of his term, he agreed to serve for a further five years, they were only too pleased, and Hutchins was president of the University of Michigan for the full decade of 1910–20. Although Kelsey did not have the same close relationship with Hutchins as he had had with Angell, he continued to be involved in many aspects of the university not directly related to the classics or to archaeology—among them, the physical expansion of the campus.

Campus Expansion

Since the turn of the century, the noise of construction crews had been heard across campus almost without pause.[8] The Barbour Gymnasium, a gymnasium for the exclusive use of women students, opened its doors in 1902, thanks to the generosity of Regent Levi Lewis Barbour. This building provided ample space for exercise and was also equipped with a swimming pool, a dining room and kitchen, and a large hall suitable for assemblies, lectures, concerts, or plays. It was a welcome addition to the architecture of the campus.[9] The New Engineering Building,[10] located at the corner of East Univer-

---

6. Hill (1850–1932), a historian and diplomat, was University of Rochester president from 1888 to 1896. Thereafter he served as assistant secretary of state (1898–1903), the U.S. minister to Switzerland (1903–5) and to the Netherlands (1905–8), and ambassador to Germany (1908–11).

7. Remarkably, both 1916 candidates for U.S. president, Hughes and Wilson, were offered the university's presidency during this search.

8. For a splendid pictorial review of the physical development of the campus, see Anne Duderstadt, *The University of Michigan: A Photographic Saga* (Ann Arbor: University of Michigan, Bentley Historical Library, 2006).

9. President Angell had remarked in his 1895 annual report that the gymnasium built in 1894, funded in large part by a gift from Detroit lawyer Joshua W. Waterman, was all very well but that a separate facility was needed for the women students. Women students did have access to Waterman Gymnasium at specific and restricted times, but everyone thought the arrangement wholly unsatisfactory. Ruth Bordin, *Women at Michigan: The "Dangerous Experiment," 1870s to the Present* (Ann Arbor: University of Michigan Press, 1999), 28–29.

10. In 1923 the New Engineering Building was renamed the West Engineering Building; a new structure, on East University Avenue south of East Hall, was to be called the East Engineering Building.

sity and South University streets and completed in 1904, was provided with the most up-to-date tackle. Reflecting the interests of Dean Cooley,[11] a graduate of Annapolis whose expertise was in mechanical engineering and naval architecture, it was equipped with a naval testing tank, the only one in the country outside Washington, D.C. The medical faculty, too, was not slow to voice its needs, and a sympathetic legislature responded by authorizing the construction in 1904 of a big new Medical Building that housed the many laboratories required, amphitheaters, lecture halls, and administrative offices. Also brewing were the demands of the Dental College.

Kelsey's interest in campus planning was well known to President Angell. In May 1907, he was invited to participate in discussions about campus development, particularly about proposed new science buildings: one for biology, botany, forestry, and psychology and another for geology and mineralogy. Kelsey favored placing one of these on the north side of the campus and the other on the south. He was also concerned about a proposed new building for the College of Dental Surgery, which he did not think should be placed on campus.[12] His objections may have been based on his wish to see other new buildings related to the humanities and the Literary College located on campus; he did not want the College of Dental Surgery to limit the options. At the time, he was in discussion with Andrew Carnegie's people about the need for funds to erect three such buildings: a Music Building, an Art Museum, and a Hall of Humanities. He evidently hoped that one or another of the Carnegie trusts might be sympathetic.[13] After talking with Angell and university secretary James H. Wade, Francis prepared a resolution for the Board of Regents "raising a committee of six, three from the Board and three from the Senate, on the arrangements of the campus." At the invitation of Regent Barbour, he spoke on this matter at their May 8 meeting. Present were Regents Barbour,

---

11. Dean of engineering Mortimer Elwyn Cooley had been appointed to the faculty in 1881 and became dean in 1903. Long critical of the facilities provided for engineering students and faced with rapidly expanding enrollments, he had at last persuaded the regents of the need for improvements. (For more on Cooley, see Hinsdale, *History*, 263–64, and below, "The Weldon Gold and Copper Company.")

12. Diary, May 7, 1907.

13. Carnegie had set up a number of charitable trusts—after he sold the Carnegie Steel Company to J. P. Morgan for $480 million—in line with the ideas outlined in the essay he published in 1899 entitled "The Gospel of Wealth," in which he argued that the rich had an obligation to act as the stewards of society. The purpose of the Carnegie trusts, managed by trustees as adept at making money as spending it, was to help people and communities. The trust that assisted the building of more than three thousand libraries may be the best known.

Knappen, Dean,[14] Hill,[15] and White,[16] President Angell, and Mr. Wade.[17] On May 9, the board passed the resolution and appointed Regents Knappen, Hill, and Fletcher,[18] Deans Cooley and Hutchins, and Professor Kelsey to the committee, with Professor Lorch as secretary.[19] On May 23, according to Kelsey's diary, this "Special Grounds Committee" walked around campus debating various proposals. On the question of the location of a new building for dentistry, the diary claims that "with the help of Cooley, he blocked the proposed location of the Dental Building on the Penny property."[20] However, at a subsequent meeting of the committee on June 13, when Kelsey proposed an idea of Lorch's placing the Dental Building at another location further away on North University Avenue, the meeting "seemed to drift toward the Penny lot"—until Cooley intervened to urge adjournment until the following day, for "more time."[21]

At 6:45 the next morning, Francis called Professors Hoff and Hall[22] of the

---

14. Henry Stewart Dean (b. 1830), a lieutenant colonel in the Civil War and a prominent Ann Arbor businessman, joined the board of the University School of Music in 1895 (Hinsdale, *History*, 208–9).

15. After graduating from the university as a civil engineer in 1865, Arthur Hill (1847–1909) enrolled in the Law Department. A successful businessman (in lumber and steel) in mid-Michigan, he was three times the mayor of Saginaw. See ibid., 211.

16. One of the first settlers of Marquette, Michigan, and quick to take advantage of the newfound mineral resources of the Upper Peninsula, Peter White (1830–1908) served in the Michigan legislature (both House and Senate). He founded American history and classical fellowships at the university, serving as regent from 1904 to 1908. See ibid., 213–14. On his connection to Kelsey's business affairs, see nn. 156 and 168 below.

17. Diary, May 8, 1907.

18. Frank Ward Fletcher (b. 1853), a University of Michigan graduate (B.Phil. 1875; postgraduate at MIT), worked as a mining chemist before entering the lumber business; by 1899 he was president of Fletcher Paper Company in Alpena. Fletcher long served as chairman of the university's Committee on Buildings and Grounds. See Hinsdale, *History*, 207–8.

19. Appointed in 1906, Emil Lorch was professor and chair of a new curriculum in architecture attached to the School of Engineering. In due course, he became head of the School of Architecture and Design, serving the university until his retirement in 1938. Lorch designed Barton Dam on the Huron River (built 1912) and Belle Isle (renamed Macarthur) Bridge in Detroit (completed 1923).

20. The Penny property was at 919 North University, the last member of the family to live there being Henrietta Penny, who had removed to California in 1900 (*Ann Arbor City Directory*, 1899 and 1900).

21. Diary, June 13, 1907.

22. Nelville Soule Hoff, a Cincinnati dentist, moved to Ann Arbor in 1888 as the College of Dental Surgery's assistant professor of practical dentistry; in 1903 he became professor of prosthetic dentistry. He later served as acting dean (1907–11) and dean (1911–16). Louis Phillips Hall graduated from the College of Dental Surgery in 1889 and became professor of operative and clinical dentistry in 1903. See Hinsdale, *History*, 289, 318–19, respectively.

dental faculty—those most directly affected by the decision about the building's location—and met with them and Lorch at 7:45 to inspect several sites, including three lots on North University Avenue. All agreed that these three lots between the Homeopathic Hospital (at the extreme eastern end of North University) and Mr. Prettyman's boardinghouse would provide a satisfactory site.[23] Prettyman "said he thought the lots could be secured for $15,000 or thereabouts," and all these activities were reported to the committee, which thereupon voted unanimously "to recommend this course." Mr. L. D. Carr[24] was authorized to secure options and, on discovering that one of the owners was in Bay City and another in St. Louis, was advised by Kelsey to go and see these parties at once. Subsequent discussions among Prettyman, Carr, a Mrs. Campbell, and Kelsey resulted in terms being agreed for two of the properties (six thousand dollars and fifty-five hundred dollars).[25]

At a regents' meeting on June 27, the board addressed two planning matters. After listening to the Memorial Committee, it voted to put $50,000 toward a "Memorial building" to be built on the southwest corner of campus, "if the committee could raise $132,000."[26] The board also voted to put the Dental Building where the committee suggested. Kelsey's view had prevailed. The next day, his salary was raised to thirty-five hundred dollars.[27] Although this is unlikely to have been a case of *post hoc, ergo propter hoc* and was more likely the result of long deliberations about all faculty salaries, it is nonetheless a striking coincidence.

In 1865 the Alumni Association had promised fifty thousand dollars toward the cost to construct a memorial building to honor those who had died in the Civil War. Though the Board of Regents had agreed to provide the necessary land on campus, the plan had stalled. Money continued to be raised,

---

23. The Prettyman family was well established in Ann Arbor. Horace G. Prettyman, captain of the Michigan football team (1884–86), was the Ann Arbor postmaster in 1907 and a vice president of the Farmers and Mechanics Bank. He was the proprietor of the Campus Club, a boardinghouse at 1005 North University, where he also resided (*Ann Arbor City Directory*, 1907).

24. Lauren D. Carr was a reputable real estate and insurance agent in town (*Ann Arbor City Directory*, 1907).

25. Diary, June 14 and 18, 1907.

26. This building, Alumni Memorial Hall, functions now as the University Museum of Art, echoing one of its earliest functions. Still standing, it has recently (2009) been modernized and enlarged.

27. Diary, June 27 and 28, 1907.

but no construction was begun until the events and casualties of the Spanish-American War provided new impetus. Over one hundred thousand dollars was in hand by the turn of the century, but it took the fifty thousand offered by the regents in 1907 to get things going. Additional money was needed and found.[28] The building went up on the southwest corner of the campus, as the regents had stipulated. The inauguration of the building in 1910 was marked by the opening of a grand exhibition of Oriental and American art, of which all the Oriental art and a handful of the American paintings were generously loaned by Charles Freer.

As well as housing the Alumni Association, Alumni Memorial Hall effectively became an art museum, when the university's art collections were immediately transferred there from the 1883 library building. It was also the home of the newly established Department of Fine Arts. Space was even found—admittedly, in the basement—for a faculty club. Francis Kelsey was among the faculty members from the Literary College (hard pressed as ever for office space) who successfully scrambled for the larger office spaces available. His claim was justified partly by the archaeological collections that he had been instrumental in bringing to the university and that, up to this point, had been kept in and around his office in the Library; by his practice of enthusiastically teaching aspects of Roman art and art of all periods; and by his consequent support for the establishment of the Department of Fine Arts. Approaches to the regents about the need for such a department and for an appropriate faculty appointment had been made on several occasions. They were finally convinced by the 1910 proposal, which was signed by Dean Cooley and Professors Kelsey, Lorch, and Martin D'Ooge of the Greek Department and nominated Herbert R. Cross for the position of assistant professor of fine arts.

In August 1910, the archaeological collections were moved from the Coin Room in the Library to the faculty's "Club Room" in the new building's basement. Not every faculty member, however, was pleased by the move of these collections. In September, Professor D'Ooge was annoyed at finding that they

---

28. Familiar names among the major donors are Dexter M. Ferry (see chapter 3 n. 6), for whom the building's south upper gallery was named, and Arthur Hill of Saginaw, whose name graces the lower north front room. Perhaps less well known, in the context of the university, are Simon J. Murphy of Detroit (for whom the north upper gallery was named), a businessman with extensive interests in timber, oil, power, and railroad companies; and Ezra Rust (for whom the main gallery was named), who, like Hill, was a successful Saginaw businessman (in lumber and iron).

were no longer in the Library, and it took a good deal of tact on Kelsey's part and several days of deliberation between the two for an agreement to be reached.[29] In the course of the next year, under Francis's supervision, groups of the sculpture casts of the Arch of Trajan were placed on the west wall on the second floor, and some Latin inscriptions were mounted on the wall in the gallery: this made reading them and teaching from them much easier. Provision was also made for the public exhibition of suitable objects in display cases in the gallery.

Kelsey's general enthusiasm and interest in campus space continued. In the meantime, his opportunity to become completely immersed in the design and construction of a major campus building had come with his role as the president of the University Musical Society. Along with Albert Stanley and other members of the UMS, he had been remarking for years that the university needed an auditorium suitable for orchestral concerts, plays, and other grand events. Plans and lists of possible benefactors had been drawn up in the 1890s, to no avail. Regent Arthur Hill, however, quietly latched onto the idea and, by the terms of his will (made public in 1910), left two hundred thousand dollars for the construction of such an auditorium. No one had been aware of his intention. Discussions began immediately as to architects, the shape and size of the building, and its location. Albert Kahn, chosen to be the architect, was asked to prepare plans.[30]

As president of the UMS, Kelsey was in his element. By September 1911, he was in conference with President Hutchins about where the auditorium should be built, and with Hutchins's blessing, he went to Detroit to talk with Kahn.[31] At the end of the month, he was in discussion again with Hutchins,

---

29. Diary, September 20–24, 1910.

30. Albert Kahn (1869–1942) arrived in the United States in 1880 at the age of eleven. He served his architectural apprenticeship with the firm of Mason and Rice in Detroit, and in 1890 he remodeled a summer residence for Dexter M. Ferry, a wealthy Detroit businessman and generous benefactor of the University of Michigan. He worked with partners at first but struck out on his own in 1902 and was involved in the planning of a growing variety of buildings, including industrial structures such as the Packard Motor Car Company plant in 1903. His first building on the Michigan campus (with George D. Mason, his mentor at Mason and Rice) was the New (later West) Engineering Building, completed in 1904 (Kahn was only thirty-five). Thereafter he was in great demand for all manner of buildings—residential (including a home for William L. Clements [see n. 32 below] in Bay City in 1908), institutional, commercial, and industrial. For a convenient summary of his accomplishments, see W. Hawkins Ferry, *The Legacy of Albert Kahn* (Detroit: Detroit Institute of Arts, 1970).

31. Most travelers between Ann Arbor and Detroit went either by the Detroit United Railway (the interurban trolley known also as "the electric" or " the motor") or by the Michigan Central Railroad. The Michigan Central was faster (taking one hour versus two) but less

who declared that "Regent Clements[32] was in favor of reviving the campus committee," which had been somnolent. Hutchins said that he, too, was in favor of a "campus plan" and approved Kelsey's "further conference with Mr. Kahn." Perhaps seeing difficulties ahead, Hutchins was careful to praise Kelsey, describing him, to Kelsey's pleasure (obvious in his diary), as "visionary."[33] On October 2, after conferring with Lorch, Kelsey again discussed with Kahn two possible locations for the building: one on the north side of campus (the Winchell lot), the other on the west. Of these, Kahn preferred the site on the north side of North University Avenue, bounded by North University, Washington, South Thayer, and South Twelfth Street. Blueprints were examined, and tracings were brought back to Ann Arbor.[34] Kelsey received Kahn's plan for the auditorium on October 10 and, three days later, presented it to a small group of interested faculty members.[35] The UMS committee then met with Kahn and Lorch and "convinced him [Kahn] that by deepening the stage, room could be made to mount operas. He agreed to take the matter up."[36] It is not difficult to see Kelsey's hand in this. A great fan of the opera, he

---

frequent and more expensive (costing seventy-four cents one way versus forty-five cents). The costs, recorded in Kelsey's diaries, did not vary between 1908 and 1912. He normally took the interurban. Other expenses of his visits to Detroit sometimes included ten cents for a streetcar ride and about thirty-five cents for lunch. In terms of travel, the wealthy were experimenting with the newfangled automobile (Henry Ford produced his first car in 1903: the Model T did not arrive until 1908), and Kelsey records in his diary that on November 3, 1904, Charles Freer and Colonel Hecker "came from Detroit in an automobile guided by Henry Hecker—made the run in 2 hours and 15 minutes." Much useful information may be found in Milo S. Ryan, *View of a Universe: A Love Story of Ann Arbor at Middle Age* (Ann Arbor: Ann Arbor Historic District Commission, 1985), esp. 116, a reference I owe to the kindness of Jean Wedemeyer.

32. On graduating with a degree in engineering from the University of Michigan (B.S. 1882), William L. Clements (1861–1934; regent 1909–33) went into the family firm in Bay City. The firm prospered by turning out massive equipment, including heavy-duty cranes, for large-scale projects, notable among which was the Panama Canal. Clements would also become president of Bay City's First National Bank and a large stockholder in its successor, the National Bank of Bay City.

33. Diary, September 25, 29, and 30, 1911.

34. Diary, October 2, 1911.

35. These included Albert A. Stanley, professor of music and director of the Men's Glee Club; Charles Albert Sink (1879–1972), secretary and business manager of the School of Music and secretary of the UMS; and Emil Lorch, professor of architecture.

36. Diary, October 10, 13, and 19, 1911. Members of the UMS committee included Kelsey, Stanley, Sink, and George F. Allmendinger, a prominent local businessman and member of an extended Ann Arbor family with a long-standing connection to the university (see chapter 4 n. 105).

visited the Metropolitan Opera in New York whenever he could. Over time, he had become acquainted with many members of its administrative staff and many of its leading singers, some of whom he brought to perform in Ann Arbor under the auspices of the UMS. To stage operas in Ann Arbor would have been a huge accolade for the university and an enormous pleasure to him.

On October 26, at the request of President Hutchins, Kelsey addressed a meeting of the regents. He urged the creation of a new campus plan, the placement of the new auditorium "on the axis of North Ingalls Street" (i.e., aligned on the site Kahn preferred), the fitting of the stage for opera, and the revival of the campus committee. At a meeting with Kahn in Detroit on November 3, it was agreed that Kahn should send Kelsey new plans and elevations of the proposed auditorium, which Kelsey would then take to New York to go over with his friends at the Metropolitan Opera.[37]

On this subject, the diary then goes quiet; but wheels had evidently been turning at a higher level. At a meeting of the revitalized campus committee in January, the plan for the auditorium stage to accommodate opera was vigorously opposed by Regent Clements and "failed of support."[38] The reasons for Clements's objections are not known, but not even Kelsey's determination and dogged hard work could prevail against the will of the regent who was to become the leading figure in the planning and management of building projects on campus for the next twenty-five years.[39] Construction went ahead, and this splendid building, with its excellent acoustics—the result of an astute combination of engineering and architecture—went up, under Clements's demanding eye, on North University. The Frieze Memorial Organ, in the acquisition of which Kelsey had played such a singular role, was transferred here, and the building was dedicated in June 1913. It was placed, as Kahn had wished, on the Winchell lot, where it still stands. Recently refurbished, Hill Auditorium continues to be recognized as a cultural center of the university.

---

37. Diary, October 26 and November 3, 1911.

38. Diary, January 11, 1912.

39. In later life, Clements became a bibliophile and subsequently both gave his collection of rare books to the university and provided a library to house them. The plans for the Clements Library were drawn by Albert Kahn to specifications laid down by Clements himself, and the building remains one of the architectural delights of the Michigan campus. It opened for business in 1923.

THE PROFESSOR

The Department of Latin

Kelsey's work for the university on large building projects and campus planning should not, of course, keep us from recalling the work for which he was hired: teaching Latin. Thanks to the growing number of high schools, the students enrolled in Latin courses in them, and the continued popularity of Latin at the college level,[40] enrollments in the department remained steady and even grew, despite the curricular shocks earlier in the decade. New courses continued to attract students, as did new faculty. In 1908 Professor Joseph Drake left the department for a full-time appointment as professor of law and was replaced by Albert Robinson Crittenden—the man whose wedding Francis and Isabelle had attended on the Capitoline in June 1901. Now a recent Michigan Ph.D., Crittenden's interest in Latin pedagogy and in training teachers was critical in the development of a Latin teaching certificate program. In 1910 Walter Dennison left for Swarthmore, and his Latin classes were picked up by John Garrett Winter, who had been teaching in the Department of Greek since 1908 and was now promoted to assistant professor, with responsibilities in both departments. In 1912, to help with the growing interest in archaeology and art, Miss Orma Fitch Butler was appointed assistant in Roman archaeology and instructor of Latin.[41]

The university solidified its connection to Latin teachers in secondary schools by hosting the meetings of the Michigan Classical Conference and the Michigan Schoolmasters' Club in Ann Arbor annually. Attendance was invariably large and enthusiastic; many papers were read, and there was much entertaining. Kelsey himself was often on the program, speaking in 1911, for example, about the archaeological collections and in 1912 about the excavations at Cyrene. Professor D'Ooge also claimed the limelight, lecturing at the 1910 meeting about Crete and giving the keynote address in 1912. There were always distinguished speakers from outside the university, too. Such was the success of the conference—as many as a thousand said to be attending a con-

---

40. See Susan Shapiro, "Cicero and Today's Intermediate College-Level Student," *Classical Outlook* 84.4 (2007): 147–52, esp. 148.

41. A graduate of the University of Michigan (A.B. 1897, Ph.D. 1907), Butler taught in several colleges in Michigan, Ohio, and Illinois before returning to Ann Arbor, where she served for twenty-five years. She died in 1938.

cert of ancient music in 1911—that President Emeritus Angell himself agreed to take the chair in 1912.[42] Cooperation and continuity of instruction between high schools and the university remained strong.

Visiting lecturers happily broke departmental routines. Among those who came at Kelsey's invitation and spoke to attentive audiences were Esther Van Deman, the first American woman to specialize in Roman field archaeology;[43] Franz Cumont, a Belgian philologist, historian, and archaeologist;[44] and George Arthur Plimpton, a New York publisher, dealer of rare books, and generous-minded philanthropist.[45] Of special interest were the lectures in 1912 of W. H. D. Rouse, a fellow of Christ's College at the University of Cambridge, one of the founding editors of the Loeb Classical Library, a translator of Homer and Plato, and an ardent advocate of the Direct Method of teaching Greek and Latin.

Francis played a leading role in all these activities and was busy in other ways as well, assuring the visibility of the department in the university. He took part himself in all the academic ceremonies. On Commemoration Day (June 26, 1912), marking the seventy-fifth anniversary of the founding of the university, he walked prominently in the procession, attended the exercises at which the presidents of various universities spoke, entertained many visitors in the afternoon at home, and was present at a reception given by the Senate in the evening. As if that were not enough rubbing shoulders, he was present

---

42. Angell presided for the final session, on the afternoon of Friday, March 29. See Francis W. Kelsey, "The Eighteenth Michigan Classical Conference," *School Review* 21.3 (March 1913): 198.

43. Diary, July 28, 1911. Esther Boise Van Deman was a Michigan graduate (A.B. 1891, A.M. 1892) with a Ph.D. (1898) from Chicago. A native of Ohio, she is best known for her studies of techniques of Roman architectural construction and of the important Atrium Vestae. She taught at various times at Wellesley, Bryn Mawr, Mount Holyoke, and Goucher, but she chafed under the demands of college administrators and was happier in an independent research role—which, toward the end of her career, thanks in no small part to the interventions of Francis Kelsey, she achieved with an appointment as a Carnegie Research Professor of Roman Archaeology at Michigan.

44. Diary, December 15, 1911. Born and educated in Belgium, Cumont received his Ph.D. from the University of Ghent in 1887 and taught there for many years. Famous for his studies of Mithraism and early excavations at Dura-Europos, he was an expert on mystery religions and their impact on Rome. Denied the chair of Roman history at Ghent for religious reasons (he was a Protestant), he resigned from Ghent and spent most of the rest of his active career in Rome.

45. Plimpton, a member of a well-known New England family and a discriminating collector of rare books and manuscripts, was for many years president of Ginn and Company, publishers in Boston. He served as treasurer of Barnard College for no fewer than forty years and as chair of the Board of Trustees of Amherst College for thirty.

the very next day at commencement exercises—another procession, more speeches, and another dinner.

He often taught his classes at home—his Juvenal class in 1907, for example, meeting regularly between 7:30 and 10:00 p.m., the Lucretius class in the winter of 1912 meeting between 7:00 and 9:00 p.m. He entertained the Classical Club at home, too—students and faculty. On these occasions, he frequently provided a speaker from outside (in 1907 Professor John K. Lord of Dartmouth spoke about the wall at Phaleron, "controverting Gardner's view") or refreshments served by his daughters for the thirty-five members (January 1908). Similarly, ice cream was sometimes offered to the summer students[46] poring over their Cicero at 9:30 in the evening. There were dinner parties for faculty members, too: on March 18, 1910, he and Isabelle entertained the Drakes, the Dennisons, the Meaders, the Crittendens, and Mr. Sanders; it was "a pleasant occasion."[47] He kept pushing for promotions for others and exclaimed with relief in his diary entry of June 27, 1911, "Regents promoted Sanders, thus ending a three year agitation."[48]

Much of his outside lecturing in these years was done away from Michigan on behalf of the Archaeological Institute of America, a series of lectures in the Northwest in 1912 being a highlight. In the space of two weeks in the fall, he lectured at major Canadian and American cities, sometimes in high schools, sometimes at meetings of local societies of the institute, whether in a chamber of commerce (Seattle) or a museum of art (Portland). Rooms were crowded everywhere. In addition to giving his formal lecture, Kelsey, as AIA president, always drew attention to the aims and programs of the institute.[49]

Research and Publication

Writing. Kelsey's scholarly work proceeded on several fronts. He published articles on topics concerning Julius Caesar,[50] on matters to do with Herculaneum,[51] on the assassination of Herbert Fletcher De Cou and the excavations

---

46. He often taught summer school, generally two courses: for example, Roman Art and Tacitus in 1910, Topography of Rome and Cicero in 1911.

47. Diary, May 18, 1910.

48. Diary, June 27, 1911.

49. For his comment to Secretary A. Judson Eaton after this tour, see chapter 5, "The Department of Canada."

50. Francis W. Kelsey, "The Cues of Caesar," *Classical Journal* 2.2 (December 1906): 211–38; idem, "Hirtius' Letter to Balbus and the Commentaries of Caesar," *Classical Philology* 2.1 (January 1907): 92–93.

51. Francis W. Kelsey, "Codrus's Chiron and a Painting from Herculaneum," *AJA* 12 (1908): 30–38.

at Cyrene,[52] and on religious teaching in state universities.[53] The article most cited, however, was published in *Classical Philology* (1908) and entitled "Is There a Science of Classical Philology?"[54] Faced with the popularity of science in colleges and universities and the usefulness of scientific training exemplified by the obvious material success of engineering and industrialism, some classicists countered that rather than seeming to offer less than the sciences, the humanities in fact offered more. The humanities, they said, offered a route, through a new regime linking the liberal arts with the concept of culture, to the cultivated, contented, and enlightened life. In the same breath, they claimed that the word *science* should be used for the humanities as well as for the physical and natural sciences. "Science" was to be interpreted as a method. In his article, Kelsey linked the study of classics as a humanizing experience with a scientific approach that he defined as a "critical attitude" to the ancient authors. In a science of classical philology, the authors and their sources would be disentangled, rigorously examined for their reliability, and dissected word by word. Scientific, word-by-word scrutiny was valuable as an interpretive method, to be sure, but it could not be allowed to distract from appreciation of the larger picture, the purpose of which was the promotion of refinement of thought and discrimination.

The reformulation of the claims of classical studies was given a wider focus in a volume published in 1911 under the title *Latin and Greek in American Education*,[55] in which Kelsey drew together papers written by himself and various colleagues and friends, most of them delivered at the meetings of the

52. Francis W. Kelsey, "The Tragedy at Cyrene," *Bulletin of the AIA* 2.3 (June 1911): 111–14; Francis W. Kelsey and Arthur Fairbanks, "The Excavation of Cyrene," *Classical Weekly* 4.6 (November 5, 1910): 46–47.

53. Francis W. Kelsey, "The Problem of Religious Instruction in State Universities," in *Education and National Character* (Chicago Religious Education Association, 1908), 1–22.

54. Francis W. Kelsey, "Is There a Science of Classical Philology?" *Classical Philology* 3.4 (October 1908): 369–85.

55. Francis W. Kelsey, ed., *Latin and Greek in American Education, with Symposia on the Value of Humanistic Studies* (New York: Macmillan, 1911). The volume comprises four chapters—of which three, addressing the current situation of Latin and Greek, the value of Latin and Greek as educational instruments, and Latin and Greek in courses of study, were written by Kelsey himself—and seven symposia. Of the symposia, four addressed the usefulness of the classics for training in medicine, engineering, law, and theology, and three addressed their value and/or utility in practical affairs (i.e., as training in business), in the "new education," and in the context of formal discipline. The publication was supported once more by Detroit donors: Frederick M. Alger, James B. Book, Lem W. Bowen, Mrs. Theodore D. Buhl, Dexter M. Ferry Jr., F. J. Hecker, J. L. Hudson, Jere C. Hutchins, Clarence A. Lightner, Philip H. McMillan, W. H. Murphy, John R. Russel, Walter S. Russel, and Charles B. Warren. On these worthies, see Albert N. Marquis, ed., *The Book of Detroiters* (Chicago: Marquis, 1914).

Michigan Classical Conference. In the preface, Kelsey states that the book's purpose was "to set forth, from different points of view, the just claims of classical study."[56] Its titles—for example, "The Value of Humanistic, Particularly Classical, Studies as a Training for Men of Affairs" (comprising letters from James Bryce, James Loeb, and William Sloane)[57] or R. M. Wenley's "The Nature of Culture Studies"[58]—speak for themselves.

In response to the steady demand for the Kelsey textbooks, Francis was always at work on new editions for Allyn and Bacon. He was by now well acquainted and on good terms not only with John Allyn but with the whole Bacon family, parents and children, and he worked hard and successfully at cementing these relationships. On April 13, 1911, for instance, he was in New York when Mrs. George Bacon and her daughter were about to leave for Germany for the summer. He bought an azalea in bloom for their cabin on the ship and joined John Allyn and Carl in seeing them off. On returning to the office with the two men, Allyn suggested that Kelsey might like to put together thirty pages of Caesar for a junior Latin book. Francis acted with his usual alacrity, going to a bookstore, finding the texts, and making selections, which he then left at the office. It had taken him the best part of an afternoon.

Editing. His editorial work continued apace, largely divided between work for Macmillan in his capacity as coeditor (with Percy Gardner) of their Handbooks of Archaeology and Antiquities series and work for the Humanistic Series of the University of Michigan Studies.[59] Among the Macmillan volumes on which Kelsey worked were Arthur L. Frothingham's *The Monuments of Christian Rome: From Constantine to the Renaissance* (1908) and Charles Heald Weller's *Athens and Its Monuments* (1913). Another manuscript on his desk was by Richard Norton, which he undertook to edit partly out of respect and friendship for the Norton family and partly out of obligation to Norton for his work at Cyrene.[60] The book, entitled *Bernini and Other Stud-*

---

56. Ibid., v–vi.

57. Ibid., 210–19. The Honorable James Bryce (1838–1922) was the British ambassador to the United States (1907–13); William Sloane (1873–1922) was president of W. and J. Sloane in New York, a high-end furniture and home furnishings store (see n. 132). For Loeb, see chapter 5, "Membership."

58. Robert Mark Wenley (1861–1929), who had received his degrees from and taught at the University of Glasgow, was professor of philosophy at the University of Michigan (since 1896) and a good friend of Kelsey's. See Hinsdale, *History,* 303–4.

59. See chapter 4, "Research and Publication."

60. Richard Norton was the leader of the ill-fated AIA expedition to Cyrene during Kelsey's presidency of the institute; see chapter 5.

ies in the History of Art, was finally published by Macmillan in 1914. Since
Kelsey had been helping put final touches to it in 1911,[61] this gives some idea
of the length of time required for a book to pass through the press at this
time. Another book on which Macmillan asked for Kelsey's comments, perhaps because of his farming background, was the unusual *Roman Farm Management: The Treatises of Cato and Varro Done into English, with Notes of Modern Instances* (1913), by "a Virginia farmer" (Fairfax Harrison).[62]

The preponderance of Kelsey's editing energies went toward the Michigan
Humanistic Series, a task shared with Henry A. Sanders. Three volumes appeared between 1907 and 1912. Scholars vary in the speed at which they work,
making it difficult to predict when a volume might appear; this was particularly the case when a volume had many authors. Volumes did not, therefore,
appear in the order in which they had been planned. In 1907 volume 6 appeared, *Athenian Lekythoi, with Outline Drawing in Glaze Varnish on a White
Ground,* by Arthur Fairbanks, recently appointed professor of Greek and
Greek archaeology at Michigan. It was followed in 1910 by volumes 3 and 4:
Latin Philology, edited by Clarence L. Meader of the Michigan faculty (in four
parts, one written by Meader), and *Roman History and Mythology,* edited by
Sanders (in three parts, two of which were written by Michigan faculty Orma
Fitch Butler and J. G. Winter).[63] Many more volumes were in the works, their
publication already approved by the University Senate committee now over-
seeing these activities. Of particular interest was the publication of manuscripts acquired in Egypt by Charles Freer. Four Greek biblical manuscripts,
written on parchment, and a Greek papyrus manuscript of the Minor
Prophets were to be published by Sanders; part of a Coptic Psalter was assigned to Professor William H. Worrell of the Hartford Seminary Foundation. Kelsey had more than an editorial interest in these manuscripts: he had
helped Freer recognize their importance a few months after their acquisition.

The Freer Manuscripts. In December 1906, Charles Freer, on the lookout
for objects of art, visited a dealer called Ali Arabi, purchased a number of objects from him, and was shown four parchment manuscripts. His bid of half

---

61. Diary, September 11, 1911.

62. *The Virginia Carys: An Essay in Genealogy* (1919) was also written by a Fairfax Harrison. Since the introduction is signed F. H. [i.e. Fairfax Harrison], as is *Roman Farm Management,* it is likely that the same man wrote both books.

63. The third was by Alvin E. Evans of Washington State College. An advertisement for
volumes 3 and 4 appears in Ralston Hayden, *The Senate and Treaties, 1789–1817* (London:
Macmillan, 1920), 239.

the asking price was accepted, and the manuscripts were sent to Detroit. There they sat for six months, until Kelsey, on a visit to Freer to ask for a contribution toward the cost of the memorial building, was told about them. Expressing great interest, he was invited to lunch at Freer's a few days later, with professors D'Ooge and Sanders, to examine them. All three were amazed to find that the documents were written on parchment and not on papyrus. It did not take them five minutes to be able to assure Freer that "they were genuine and valuable."[64]

These four Greek manuscripts comprise a copy of Deuteronomy and Joshua of fifth-century date, a rather fragmentary fifth-century manuscript of the Psalms, a fifth-century manuscript of the four Gospels that is entire except for three leaves, and a badly damaged sixth-century manuscript of the Epistles of Paul. These documents were evidently of great significance for scholars of the Greek Old Testament and the New Testament. Subsequent discussions among Kelsey, Sanders, and Freer about the condition and content of the manuscripts led to meetings between Freer and Kelsey in Detroit and Ann Arbor in January, at which a plan of publication was discussed. Seven professors came to Kelsey's house for tea, and at 8:00 in the evening, Sanders gave a lecture about the discoveries. In mid-March, when Kelsey was again in Detroit to talk to Freer about the costs, Freer offered to pay all the expenses of publication and distribution, exclaiming, according to the diary, "I am not a Christian; but my feeling is such that I cannot do business with the Bible."[65] He doubtless meant that he was disinclined to negotiate. It was somewhat later that he purchased the surviving part of a sixth-century Coptic Psalter and the third-century papyrus of the Minor Prophets.[66] In January 1909, on a visit to Ann Arbor, Freer told Kelsey that he would take care of the publication costs of the Coptic materials, too; but he also voiced concerns about the proposed color of the morocco binding of the Joshua and Deuteronomy fascicule: he was keeping an eye on things. During the winter of 1910, Freer's in-

---

64. Diary, September 4, 1907.On these remarkable documents, see now Larry W. Hurtado, ed., *The Freer Biblical Manuscripts: Fresh Studies of an American Treasure Trove* (Atlanta: Society of Biblical Literature; Leiden: Brill, 2006); for the cordial relationship between Freer and Kelsey, Kelsey's generosity to younger scholars, and international recognition of the importance of the manuscripts, see 29–30.

65. Diary, March 17, 1908.

66. On Freer and his interests in Egypt, see Ann C. Gunter, *A Collector's Journey: Charles Lang Freer and Egypt* (Washington, DC, Freer Gallery of Art: Arthur M. Sackler Gallery, Smithsonian Institution, 2002).

terest in the work intensified. He spent the whole of one January morning with Kelsey in Detroit. On February 17, he was with Francis the whole day in Ann Arbor. On March 1, at a meeting of the Detroit Society of the AIA at Freer's house, the opportunity to discuss the manuscripts was not missed. On August 30, Francis learned from Mr. Alger, son of the former governor of the state, that "the total charged to the publication account on Mr. Freer's books was above $19,500."[67]

Francis was as engaged with technical problems as he was with the costs and the progress of the scholarship. He spent two days in the fall of 1908 in conference in Cambridge, Massachusetts, with the University Press (forerunner of Harvard University Press, founded five years later) about the printing of the front matter and about the binding; and in Franklin, Massachusetts, he "spent the forenoon in a heliotype establishment, inspecting processes, and arranging for dummies and proofs," before spending the evening with Uncle John and Aunt Ada at Arlington and then taking the midnight train for New York.[68] March 1911 saw him in Boston at the offices of Allyn and Bacon in talks with Oliver J. Barr of J. S. Cushing and Co., in Norwood, about the difficulties of composition in Coptic and costs per page. A few days later, he and Worrell met at the offices of the American Type Founders' Company to discuss further with Joseph W. Phinney, an experienced type designer and senior vice president of the company, questions of dies and type for the Coptic volume, as well as Arabic type.[69]

The Morgan Manuscripts. In the fall of 1911, Kelsey heard of an extraordinary collection of Coptic manuscripts for sale in Paris, one that had been authenticated by Professor Henri Hyvernat of the Catholic University of America.[70] Francis was eager for these materials to come to America, and so, Freer being unavailable at the time, he put the matter before J. P. Morgan. He wrote to Miss Belle da Costa Greene,[71] librarian at the J. Pierpont Morgan Library

67. Diary, August 30, 1910.

68. Diary, October 28 and 29, 1908.

69. Diary, March 19, 1911. Kelsey had already written to Colonel Hecker about the process of making a Coptic font and its costs. The charge to be made for each character was $5.50, plus $40 for trial casts. In trying to minimize the costs, Kelsey stressed that Coptic had only thirty-five characters (Kelsey to Hecker, January 20, 1911, KMA Papers, box 15.14).

70. The Right Reverend Eugene Xavier Henri Hyvernat (1858–1941), born in France, was a leading authority in Coptic studies and editor of the *Corpus Scriptorum Christianorum Orientalium*. He had been on the faculty of the Catholic University of America since 1889.

71. Born Belle Marion Greener in modest African American circumstances in Alexandria, Virginia, in 1879, Belle da Costa Greene (1879–1950), who passed as white, changed her

in New York,[72] describing the Coptic materials in Paris and mentioning Freer's manuscripts. Miss Greene replied instantly by wire and letter, notifying Kelsey that Morgan was already in negotiations for this collection, expressing interest in Freer's material, and inviting Kelsey to visit the library.[73] Kelsey's reply, on September 30, expresses his excitement about the new Coptic material.

> I am much interested in the illuminations and when I come to New York I shall show you a chromo-lithographic reproduction of the covers of the Freer Gospels which has been made to accompany the facsimile of the Gospels manuscript. The Coptic manuscripts of Mr. Freer are of slight importance in comparison with the collection which you are on the point of obtaining. I enclose a bit of proof showing samples of the two new fonts of Coptic type which are being cut for our work from designs prepared by Dr. Worrell.

After receiving sample pages from Miss Greene, he wrote to her again on October 24.

> We are amazed to find here the first page of a manuscript of the Gospels in the Sahidic dialect. No complete manuscript of the Gospels in Sahidic has previously been known. This manuscript will be as important for the determination of the original Coptic form of the text as is the Freer codex of the Gospels for the Greek text.

---

name after her parents' separation. Moving to Princeton, she went to work in the University Library. Introduced to J. P. Morgan by his son, a student at Princeton, she became Morgan's personal librarian in 1905 and, ultimately (after his death), the first director of the Pierpont Morgan Library. Blessed with a sharp memory, a quick intelligence, good looks, and a tough attitude toward dealers, she spent millions of Morgan's dollars on rare books, incunabula, manuscripts, and art. A stylish dresser, she carried herself well and was at ease at all levels of society. Morgan left her well provided for, with a lump sum of fifty thousand dollars plus ten thousand dollars a year for life. She had come a long way. See Heidi Ardizzone, *An Illuminated Life: Belle da Costa Greene's Journey from Prejudice to Privilege* (New York: W. W. Norton, 2007).

72. The J. Pierpont Morgan Library was at 33 East Thirty-sixth Street, New York, just east of Morgan's home. Designed by Charles Follen McKim in 1903, it was recently renovated by architect Renzo Piano and reopened in 2006 as the Morgan Library and Museum.

73. Letters of September 27 and 29, 1911, KMA Papers, Correspondence series, box 14, folder 12. The same folder contains all the correspondence cited below between Kelsey and Miss Greene.

In New York on December 11, at the Morgan Library, Francis met Miss Greene and Miss Thurston,[74] another librarian, and talked with them about publishing the manuscripts. We cannot know whether he had in mind their publication in the Michigan Humanistic Series, but he was evidently interested in facilitating their appearance in the public domain, and he soon discovered that Hyvernat saw himself as being in charge. Miss Greene told him that Hyvernat had sailed for America on December 9 with the fifty Coptic manuscripts and that as soon as they were received, "she would telegraph me suggesting I spend 3 or 4 days examining them." Francis was then introduced to J. P. Morgan himself and was shown, in the vault, some of Morgan's prized possessions, including "a letter of Lord Cornwallis offering to surrender to George Washington, addressed as General now for the first time" and "part of a manuscript of Milton's *Paradise Lost* in the handwriting of one of his daughters."[75]

Back in New York the day after Christmas, Francis went to the Morgan Library with Worrell, who had come in from Hartford, and met Hyvernat there. The Coptic manuscripts had just come in and were down in the cellar. Hyvernat opened a few packages for them ("not eagerly," the diary says). They paid their respects to Morgan and lunched together at the Murray Hill (Francis's favorite hotel). Kelsey noted in his diary, "We urged on Hyvernat a spirit of cooperation." The meal and the conversation seem to have mollified Hyvernat: he met Miss Greene in the afternoon and told Kelsey later that the manuscripts were to stay in New York (he had initially wanted to take them back to Europe with him) and that he would return from Europe in three months; Kelsey wrote in his diary that Hyvernat "would cooperate in the matter of publication and assured me Worrell should have a full share."[76] Miss Greene had evidently impressed on him the value of Francis's experience and expertise in the details of publishing illustrated material. At the annual meeting of the AIA in Pittsburgh during December 27–30, Kelsey, newly reelected AIA president, was pleased to see the following resolution passed by the institute's governing council:

---

74. This was undoubtedly Ada Thurston, who, with Curt F. Bühler, compiled the *Check List of Fifteenth Century Printing in the Pierpont Morgan Library* (New York: Pierpont Morgan Library, 1939). See George K. Boyce, "The Pierpont Morgan Library," *Library Quarterly* 22.1 (January 1952): 29.

75. Diary, December 11, 1911.

76. Diary, December 26, 1911.

The Council of the AIA with lively interest and profound satisfaction had learned of the acquisition, by Mr. J. Pierpont Morgan, of the most valuable collection of Coptic manuscripts yet discovered; and it desires to express to Mr. Morgan its sincere appreciation of the distinguished service which he has rendered to American letters and learning by bringing this unique collection to the US.

Throughout 1912, Francis had both the Morgan and the Freer materials on his mind. In April he discussed both the Morgan Coptic material and Freer's "illuminations" with Princeton art historian Charles Morey,[77] promising that if it could be arranged with Mr. Freer and with Professors Sanders and Cross of Michigan, he would try to give Morey the chance to write up the Freer illuminations and those of the Morgan Coptic manuscripts, too. Later in April, he met with Professor Richard J. H. Gottheil of Columbia University, with whom he had already discussed publishing in the Michigan Humanistic Series the fragments from the Cairo Genizah in the Freer Collection; these would finally appear in 1927 as volume 13 of the series.[78] On May 28, with his attention focused on the Morgan manuscripts, he had a long conference with Hyvernat in New York; there, Hyvernat agreed to give Worrell all the help he could and revealed that he had Mr. Morgan's consent to take manuscripts abroad for repairs if Miss Greene would consent. It was becoming apparent to Francis that Morgan was increasingly dependent on Miss Greene's judgment and that many decisions at the Morgan Library were made by her. The following day, he was back in Ann Arbor, having traveled overnight. Arriving at 8:10 a.m., he gave a lecture at 9:00 and then had a long talk with Morey, who

---

77. Charles Rufus Morey (whom we met seeing off the Kelsey family in chapter 4, "The American School of Classical Studies in Rome") was by now establishing himself as an authority in early Christian art. His major publications would come to include the influential *Early Christian Art* and *Medieval Art* (both 1942).

78. Richard James Horatio Gottheil (1862–1936) was educated at Columbia (A.B. 1881) and Leipzig (Ph.D. 1886). Professor of Semitic languages at Columbia and chief of the Oriental Department of the New York Public Library, he served as head of the American School of Archaeology at Jerusalem (1909–10). He was a noted Syriac scholar and ardent Zionist. On this occasion at Gottheil's New York home, Kelsey met Gisela Richter, who was to become curator of Greek and Roman art at the Metropolitan Museum of Art (1925–48). The first woman to hold that position, she was one of the foremost connoisseurs and scholars of Greek art in the twentieth century. For a convenient narrative of the discovery of the Cairo Genizah, arguably the most important deposit/archive of medieval Jewish documents, see Janet Hoskice, *The Sisters of Sinai: How Two Lady Adventurers Discovered the Hidden Gospels* (New York: Alfred A. Knopf, 2009), 220–21, 226–30.

had "come out to study the Byzantine illuminations in Freer's manuscripts. He agreed to have a statement with regard to the Gospels covers ready by July 1. I arranged the payment of his expenses from the deposit of $100 by Mr. Freer."[79] At a meeting with President Hutchins on July 19, Francis was asked to succeed D'Ooge as chair of the committee "in charge of Michigan Studies." It was a welcome endorsement of his efforts to promote research and publication at Michigan and to raise the profile of the university.

At the end of July, publication costs were again under review. Francis "finished working out and typing estimates of costs of the Freer publications,"[80] and the following day, in Detroit, he "was with Charles L. Freer from about 2.45 to 4.40. Presented and left with him an outline of 'Ideal Complete Plan' of his publications, said that I came not to argue or persuade, but left with him the outline worked out as if for myself under similar conditions."[81] On August 19, Sanders reported good progress, and in November, Freer was back in Ann Arbor looking things over.

The parallel interests of Freer and Morgan were exemplified in another way. At the Morgan Library in September, Francis saw the "gold treasure lately obtained in Egypt which belongs to the same lot as that acquired by Charles L. Freer years ago."[82] Two days later, Francis took Sanders to the Morgan Library. They were greeted by Miss Thurston and had a good viewing of the "treasure" and of the manuscripts, which Sanders particularly wanted to see. At the beginning of October, Francis had lunch with Freer in Detroit, made arrangements for the Hebrew-Arabic matter to be sent to Gottheil, and took away photographs of the Freer gold for Walter Dennison's use. That Dennison, now at Swarthmore, had agreed to work on the Freer gold is clear from a letter written by Kelsey to Miss Greene, in which he alludes to the Freer material on which [Dennison] "is now at work."[83]

In New York on October 12, Francis accompanied Freer to the Morgan Library. Freer was obviously interested in the "gold treasure" and said that "he would supply the missing pendant to the necklace but for the fact that he had deeded it to the US for the new National Museum." They also had a chance to

79. Diary, May 29, 1912.
80. Diary, July 31, 1912.
81. Diary, August 1, 1912.
82. Diary, September 19, 1912.
83. Kelsey to Greene, October 17, 1912, KMA Papers, Correspondence series, box 14, folder 12.

look at the "golden gospels" and met J. P. Morgan (who had been delayed on his boat by the fog), before leaving to have lunch at George A. Plimpton's, "where we saw his wonderful collection of books and manuscripts."[84] Six weeks later, Walter Dennison met Francis in New York to look over the Morgan gold at the library: there they met Miss Thurston and Miss Greene. "Started Dennison at work," says Kelsey's diary. "Arranged to have Dennison help photograph the treasure."[85] Provisional publication arrangements were that the treasure should appear as a volume in the Humanistic Series and that the costs should be divided equally between Freer and Morgan. On December 21, Kelsey was able to write to Miss Greene that "work on the Byzantine treasure is progressing very well."[86]

Fund-Raising and Acquisitions

Kelsey was deeply engaged in the activities of the American Philological Association and of the Archaeological Institute of America in this period, and many of his fund-raising efforts were given over to them. He was, however, also busy seeking support for his publication projects, including the Humanistic Series, and he broached these needs with many of the most illustrious leaders in Detroit. These included John W. Anderson, Henry Ford's personal attorney.

He always looked to find fellowships for students, too, and was careful to keep in touch with the Buhl family. In June 1907, he had a meeting about the Buhl fellowships with Franklin Hiram Walker,[87] who said that "he would take up the continuation and possible endowment"; later that summer, Kelsey arranged for Mr. Walker and his sister, Mrs. Theodore Buhl, to lunch with President Angell. The following year, Kelsey called on Mrs. Buhl in Detroit and was invited to spend a day at their residence and on their yacht. He did not fail to give them copies of the volumes of the Humanistic Series.[88] The Buhl fellowships were renewed every year.

---

84. Diary, October 12, 1912.

85. Diary, November 23, 1912.

86. The volume, Walter Dennison's *A Gold Treasure of the Late Roman Period*, appeared in 1918 as part 2 of volume 12 of the Humanistic Series.

87. Franklin Walker, the brother of Mrs. Theodore Buhl, was the first member of the prodigiously wealthy Canadian Club family to attend university—as it happens, the University of Michigan.

88. Diary, October 14, 1910.

Francis's involvement in the planning of the campus led him to try to raise money for university building projects, too. His concern for funds for projects of the APA had led him, as vice president (1906) and then president (1907), to be in touch with the Carnegie Institution.[89] Having come to know some of Carnegie's people pretty well, he did not hesitate to broach with them the question of the need for various buildings on the Ann Arbor campus. On February 6, 1907, he had a long talk with Robert A. Franks, Andrew Carnegie's confidential financial agent, about the range of Carnegie gifts, including possible pensions for faculty members of state universities.

Later that month, in a meeting with Regent Knappen, Francis took up the question of the siting on campus of an auditorium and an art gallery, "should funds be forthcoming,"[90] and he urged Knappen to ask the state legislature for one-half a mill tax and a flat five hundred thousand dollars for these purposes. On April 3, he went to Jackson, Michigan, for a further meeting with Knappen about the data and arguments to be used with Franks. En route to New York two days later, at the lunch counter at the railroad station in Rochester while waiting for the overnight train, he sketched out for Franks a brief on University of Michigan attendances and resources. On arriving in New York the next morning, he went straight to 542 Fifth Avenue, "the offices of the Carnegie Foundation," where he fleshed out the brief and had it typed up in four copies.

On April 8, he had a long conference with Franks over lunch at the Lawyer's Club and afterward, "in regard to the possibility of securing from Mr. Carnegie a gift of buildings for Music and Art for the university. Gave Mr. Franks a copy of the brief and on the back of an envelope drew a plan to illustrate the location and relation of the buildings." Franks replied, "I will take the matter up with Mr. Carnegie but you mustn't hurry me."[91] The urgency with which Francis pursued these objectives cannot be mistaken, and his hopes were high. Several months passed until at last, in November, Francis decided to write to Franks. When the reply came, the letter was from James Bertram, Carnegie's private secretary and a fellow Scot, who managed the building grant program with Franks. Carnegie declined to entertain the Michigan proposal. Francis's hopes were dashed. The remarks he confided to

---

89. See chapter 5, "The American Philological Association and the Carnegie Institution."
90. Diary, February 21, 1907.
91. Diary, April 8, 1907.

his diary were heartfelt: "no one was permitted to know of the deep inner disappointment which made the day seem dark."[92]

The matter did not end there, however. A year later, at the offices of the Home Trust Company in Hoboken, Francis broached the subject with Franks again. It seemed that the sticking points for Carnegie had been the costs of maintenance and the sustainability of audience participation.

> Mr. Carnegie's reluctance to accept our proposal due largely to certain disappointment in the Pittsburgh enterprise. I pointed out that such an enterprise as was contemplated at Ann Arbor would have the maintenance of the state for the buildings, and of a constantly changing public for the audiences. He said he would take up the matter with Mr. Carnegie again.[93]

Back home in Ann Arbor the very next day (Thanksgiving), "early in the morning," Francis drafted another letter: "prepared and mailed to Mr. R. A. Franks a 'memorandum' in regard to the Carnegie proposal." Again, nothing came of it. A year later, Franks voiced his conclusion that "the only chance now with Mr. Carnegie is a personal presentation by Dr. Angell."[94]

Francis continued to badger the Carnegie people for money. In early 1910, he was on the phone to Franks, again searching for funds for building projects at Michigan. Having been rebuffed three years earlier in his requests for support for buildings for art and music (i.e., a gallery and an auditorium), he turned now to what he thought might be more promising ground: he inquired "about the possibility of securing a Carnegie Library for the university."[95] Here again he was disappointed. Nothing daunted, he waited a couple of years before trying to resurrect the old request for an art or music building. He did this in a series of meetings with George Plimpton in New York[96] and in Ann Arbor in November, when Plimpton came to lecture. On the day of Plimpton's arrival, Francis took him to call on President Emeritus Angell and held a reception, attended by over a dozen callers, for him at 826 Tappan Street. The next day, Francis took Plimpton around the campus, showing him the collections, the manuscripts, the publications, the School of Music,

---

92. Diary, December 9, 1907.

93. Diary, November 25, 1908. It is unclear what is meant here by "certain disappointment in the Pittsburgh enterprise." Might this allude to cost overruns in the great expansion of the museum in 1907?

94. Diary, November 11, 1909.

95. Diary, February 11, 1910.

96. Diary, September 20, October 12, and December 15, 1912.

McMillan Hall,[97] the Library, and so on. After lunch with faculty members, Plimpton lectured at 4:30 on "Education in the time of Shakespeare, illustrated by the books that Shakespeare in all probability studied," and he dined in the evening at the Kelseys' home, with President Hutchins and four other guests. When the big topic in Francis's mind finally came out, Plimpton said that he would try to help "with access to Carnegie." Francis confided to his diary, "I mentioned three buildings needed: Museum of Arts, Hall of the Humanities, Music Building."[98] But once more, Francis drew a blank.

In this period, Francis did not altogether abandon the acquisition of objects for the teaching programs of the department. When Walter Dennison was on leave from Michigan and serving as professor at the American School of Classical Studies in Rome (1908–9), he was asked by Kelsey to keep his eyes peeled for any suitable acquisitions. So Kelsey was hardly surprised to hear from him, in the fall of 1908, that batches of inscriptions were coming up in the course of excavations for the foundations of a new palazzo on private property near the Porta Salaria in Rome and were available for purchase. Kelsey trusted Dennison's judgment as to the content of the inscriptions and immediately went about finding the necessary funding. In the course of the fall and winter, Dennison acquired, from various sites in Rome, some one hundred inscriptions, most of which were funerary in character and had marked the burial places of slaves or freedmen or soldiers of one rank or another (some were members of the Praetorian Guard).[99] They were shipped to Ann Arbor on May 31, 1909, the gift of M. E. Farr[100] and Charles F. Freer of Detroit.

Charles Freer comes into the picture again the same year. While abroad, he had met Giovanni Dattari, a fellow collector, and learned that he was interested in giving his collection of ancient Greek and Roman coins to a responsible university. Knowing of Kelsey's enthusiasm for building up Michigan's collections of ancient materials, Freer persuaded Dattari to give them to the University of Michigan. The coins, which range in date from the fourth

---

97. On this large gabled structure—a well-equipped meeting place for Presbyterian students, donated by Senator James McMillan—see chapter 3, "The Presbyterian Church."

98. Diary, November 25, 1912.

99. See Martha Baldwin and Mario Torelli, eds., *Latin Inscriptions in the Kelsey Museum: The Dennison Collection*, Kelsey Museum Studies 4 (Ann Arbor: University of Michigan Press, 1979).

100. Merton E. Farr was the president of the American Shipbuilding Company, a huge concern owning shipbuilding facilities and dry docks around the Great Lakes.

century BC to the fourth century AD, were duly dispatched to Ann Arbor and received by President Emeritus Angell. He promptly invited Francis and his family to dinner[101] to see the four boxes that had arrived and their contents.

THE FAMILY MAN

At New Year's in 1907, Ruth was twelve and a half years old, Charlotte nine and a half, and Easton just two and a half. Easton was still a toddler, but the girls' formal education was well in hand: they were enrolled in the Ann Arbor public schools. Opinion among Michigan faculty members was divided about the merits of these schools. Professor Wenley—who had joined the faculty in 1896 from Glasgow University and who had two daughters, Kitty and Jemima—did not like the public schools at all. The Wenley girls were friends with Ruth and Charlotte and were often seen at the Kelsey house on Tappan Street; but Professor Wenley's views about public education hardly chimed with Kelsey's, and they caused some amusement. Charlotte recalled one occasion when Professor Wenley announced in her presence that the public schools were "the hog pens of civilization." When she told her father this, he "wiped tears of laughter from his eyes and chuckled." "Poor Wenley," he said, "he'll learn, and some day he'll see without English blinders." The Wenley girls themselves "sighed over the fact that their father had sent them to that small private school of Miss Waples, and not public school," and Charlotte herself remarked that "they would have found University work so much easier."[102]

Ruth, the more musically minded of the two girls, had taken to the violin. Francis roamed the pawnshops of New York and Boston to find an instrument for her and finally bought a "violin and bow" for $175.[103] Delighted, she took every opportunity to play it: in orchestras at faculty concerts, at the annual performances of the *Messiah,* and at "at homes" given by her parents. Both girls enjoyed dancing: at a party given at home by their parents for the "young ladies of the Teachers' Course" in the spring of 1908, the class played violins and danced, and the girls joined in (in costume). Ruth joined a minuet and a handkerchief dance, Charlotte a Swedish polka and a Highland fling.[104]

---

101. Diary, November 28, 1909.

102. "RNMF," 2.

103. Reasonably priced musical instruments were hard to find outside the big cities in the East, and when Ruth's violin needed repair two years later (in 1909), it had to be taken back east to be fixed.

104. Diary, May 29, 1908.

Despite their belief in public education, Francis and Isabelle decided in early 1911 to send Ruth to boarding school in New York. In January Francis interviewed Miss Lois Adelaide Bangs, principal of the "Bangs and Whiton School" in Riverdale, and agreed to Miss Bangs's offer to take Ruth "in an upper room at $650."[105] At the end of September, Ruth left Ann Arbor for Riverdale and her New York adventure. Though Francis accompanied her only as far as Detroit on that occasion, she knew she would see a good deal of him during the year in the course of his business visits to New York. In December they caught a glimpse of the new main branch of the New York Public Library together[106] on the way to a matinee performance (*Tristan und Isolde*) at the Metropolitan Opera;[107] in February he surprised her at a reception at the school and took her to Harriet's for supper; in April he took her to see the new store of W. & J. Sloane,[108] for a tour of the public library, and for dinner at an old haunt (the Lion d'Or on Twenty-fourth Street); in May he moved her to Harriet's apartment on account of a measles scare at school; later that month, he "had a lovely walk with Ruth at Riverdale, in the moonlight!"[109]

While Ruth was the more reserved sister—"a little lady," as Charlotte described her[110]—Charlotte, by her own admission, was more of a chatterbox, opinionated and argumentative, and more socially inclined. She enjoyed parties. In 1909, she entertained as many as thirty-five guests at home, an experience repeated when Ruth was home from school at Christmas 1911. On that occasion, a supper and dancing party at 826 Tappan Street involved forty guests and employed two musicians—at a cost of five dollars, as Kelsey wryly

---

105. Diary, January 3, 1911. Both a boarding and day school, Miss Bangs and Miss Whiton's School for Girls was located "on a well-wooded estate on the highest land between the Hudson River and Van Cortlandt Park opposite the Palisades," on Riverdale Avenue near 252nd Street in the Bronx; it offered not only sports and riding instruction but also "easy accessibility to museums, libraries, concerts" (Porter Sargent, *The Handbook of Private Schools* [Boston: P. Sargent, 1916], 171, 536).

106. The library, on Fifth Avenue between Fortieth and Forty-second streets, had opened to great fanfare and in the presence of President Taft on May 23, 1911.

107. Diary, December 9, 1911.

108. The Scottish brothers William and John Sloane established a firm of rug and carpet importers, furnishers, and interior decorators at Broadway and Nineteenth Street, where they purveyed items for the top end of the market. By 1911 their clientele was the wealthiest in New York, and they had become wealthy themselves.

109. Diary, February 14, April 13, and May 26, 1912.

110. "RNMF," 2.

commented to his diary.[111] Charlotte was also somewhat stagestruck. She enjoyed playing parts and clowning around with her father and, more publicly, taking small parts on the stage: for example, a gingerbread girl in a performance of *Hansel and Gretel*.[112] In her early years, she was a close friend of Constance (Connie) Winsor McLaughlin, whose father, Andrew, was a professor of history at the university, and whose mother, Lois, was the daughter of President Emeritus Angell.[113] McLaughlin moved to the University of Chicago in 1906, thus separating the two girls, who nevertheless kept up their friendship. For some summers, Connie came to stay at the Kelseys' Lake Cavanaugh cottage; for others, Charlotte stayed with Connie at their summer place at Charlevoix.[114]

The success of the rental of the Lake Cavanaugh cottage in 1906 persuaded Francis and Isabelle to get a cottage there for themselves. After discussion with Mr. Merchant (Merch) Brooks, from whom they had rented the cottage in 1906,[115] they bought one of the lakeshore lots of Hall's Addition on the Lake Cavanaugh Club Grounds. They then invited Emil Lorch, professor of architecture at the university,[116] and his wife for a picnic at the lake, and together they drew plans for the cottage. A few days later, Francis engaged a Mr.

---

111. Diary, January 1, 1912.

112. "RNMF," 3. See also diary, May 7, 1910. The diary entry does not make clear whether this *Hansel and Gretel* was the opera written by Engelbert Humperdinck, first performed in America in 1895; but Ann Arbor's enthusiasm for new music has been noted (see chapter 4 n. 65).

113. Andrew Cunningham McLaughlin (1861–1947), who had taken a leave of absence to be director of historical research at the Carnegie Institution during 1903–5 (Hinsdale, *History*, 292), would win the 1936 Pulitzer Prize in History for his book *A Constitutional History of the United States*.

114. Constance, who had four sibs, graduated from Smith College, married Donald Green, was awarded her Ph.D. by Yale University, and became an expert in urban history. In 1963, like her father before her, she was awarded the Pulitzer Prize in History, for her book *Washington: Village and Capital, 1800–1878*.

115. Merch Brooks lived in Chelsea, Michigan, and, among other activities, worked as a crossing guard at the Michigan Central railroad tracks on North Main Street in Chelsea. He built five summer cottages at Lake Cavanaugh, which he rented out on a weekly basis. I owe this information and much else regarding Lake Cavanaugh to Mr. John P. Keusch, attorney at law of the firm of Keusch, Flintoft, and Conlin in Chelsea, whose family rented one of the cottages on several occasions and who remembers seeing "Professor Kelsey walking from the Kalmbach Road station on the Detroit United Railway and walking the one or two mile distance to his place at Cavanaugh Lake" (letter to author, September 20, 2007).

116. For Lorch, see above, "Campus Expansion."

Howe from Chelsea to build a cottage for $600 (finally settled at $625).[117] Within ten days, the floor was laid, the sides were up, and the roof was on: the building was insured for five hundred dollars, the contents for two hundred. Just seventeen days after Mr. Howe began the work, a large load of furniture and household goods was moved from Ann Arbor to the cottage, using drays to haul the load to the station and using the interurban railway to carry it to the stop on the Jackson line from which Lake Cavanaugh was reachable (fig. 13).[118] By the end of the month, the cottage was finished and the furnishings were in. Just one item was missing—a boat. In early August, Francis remedied this by purchasing a rowing boat for fifty dollars (ten dollars down and forty payable in October).

From then on, summer months at the lakeside cottage (fig. 14) became a fixture for the family, though Francis, often busy teaching summer school or with business matters, would spend only the occasional weekend at the cottage. But the appeal of the countryside, the fresh air, the lake, the woods and hills, and the birds and animals were irresistible to both the children and the parents. To the farm boy in Francis, the physical work that the cottage afforded was a welcome balance to his academic work. In 1908 he bought an addition to the lot from a Mr. Babcock and, despite the heat that summer (one day it was "so hot I didn't go out to the Lake"),[119] made the first clearing himself. He started digging the foundations for an outhouse and began turning over the earth in readiness for plantings. The next year, he planted three apple trees, three plum trees, and black raspberry bushes, and at the invitation of Andrew Smith, a fellow elder in the First Presbyterian Church, he biked

---

117. Diary, July 6 and 27, 1907.

118. The interurban trolleys of the Detroit United Railway connected the towns and cities with the townships and rural communities and could even be flagged down by farmers in the open fields. The cars were larger than the streetcars in use within town and city limits, faster, and sometimes more comfortable (on the more prestigious lines, some cars might have heated bathrooms, and there might be a separate smoking car), but the operating system was similar, including rails, cars, trolleys, and electric overhead cables, with each car controlled by a motorman and a conductor. Tracks for the interurban cars ran alongside roads or the railway tracks; within city limits, they often used the same tracks as the streetcars. See Jack E. Schramm, William H. Henning, and Richard R. Andrews, *When Eastern Michigan Rode the Rails*, book 3, *Detroit to Jackson and across the State* (Glendale, CA: Interurban Press, 1988); George W. Hilton and John F. Due, *The Electric Interurban Railways in America* (Stanford: Stanford University Press, 1960); H. Hildebrandt and Martha Churchill, *Electric Trolleys of Washtenaw County* (Charleston SC, Chicago IL, Portsmouth NH, San Francisco CA: Arcadia, 2009).

119. Diary, August 16, 1908.

13. Sylvan Road Cavanaugh Lake Station (interurban line), early twentieth century. Image courtesy of the Chelsea Historical Society, Chelsea, Michigan.

over to his farm in another part of Ann Arbor, dug up "shoots of red raspberry bushes," took them out to the cottage, and planted them.[120] In the summer of 1910, he managed to spend only two weekends in the country (see fig. 15); but in mid-October, he was able to write, "Beautiful day at the Lake. Slept late. Rowed across."[121]

The lake itself was an enormous source of pleasure. Charlotte recalls that when a business colleague of Kelsey's, Bernard Granville,[122] visited in 1909, he "cajoled" her and Connie McLaughlin to swim the length of the lake, a distance of about a mile and a quarter. Neither of them had to turn for help to the boat that went with them. As a result, Francis gave Charlotte a canoe, since "he now felt that I could really swim if tipped over." Charlotte rhapsodizes rather wildly over her adventures in her red canoe.

---

120. Diary, May 3 and 19, 1909.

121. Diary, October 16, 1910.

122. Granville was a consulting engineer; see below, "Columbia Consolidated Mining Company (ex Hays Company)."

14. Cavanaugh Lake cottages, 1907. Image courtesy of the Chelsea Historical Society, Chelsea, Michigan.

15. Holiday makers at Cavanaugh Lake, 1910. Image courtesy of the Chelsea Historical Society, Chelsea, Michigan.

I spent countless hours in it, exploring all the tiny, fascinating nooks along the shore all the way around; and armed with a lighted lantern at night, I glided out under the stars on the smooth, black, glass lake which reflected moon and milky way more wonderfully than any other place I have ever seen, I think. The white water lilies were lovelier when approached so close in my red canoe, the long reaching green under water plants lured with more mystery than from a rowboat.[123]

Francis's enthusiasm for Lake Cavanaugh was recognized by his election as a "Director of the Lake Association," an event he celebrated by walking around the lake with his young son Easton. Easton, seldom mentioned in the diary in these years, puts in an appearance again in 1912, when we get a surprising glimpse of a domesticated Kelsey. The day after picking a bushel of wild grapes and a basket of elderberries at the cottage, he and Easton took jelly glasses out from Ann Arbor to "work on the fruit with Isabelle." Over the course of the next few days, Kelsey packed up the jelly and grape juice in five baskets and "scrubbed sitting room, two sleeping rooms and kitchen with mop."[124] There was no reason to doubt his affection for the place. If the main purpose of the cottage was to offer outdoors experiences in the country for the children, it was the opportunities for walking, gardening, planting, picking, and rowing that appealed to him personally.

His other great enthusiasm was for music. This manifested itself in his continuing commitment to the University Musical Society as its very active president, in attendance at every possible musical event in Ann Arbor, in the practice of music with his family at home, and in his passion for the opera. When in New York, he could often be seen at the Metropolitan.[125] In the course of three February days in 1907, he went on a spree, taking in four operas: *Tannhäuser, Hansel und Gretel, Pagliacci,* and *Aida.* In 1910 he saw a performance of *Aida* featuring Caruso as Radames, as well as Richard Strauss's *Elektra;* in 1912, *La Gioconda* and a *Manon Lescaut* in which Caruso again was the star. When there was no opera, there was always the theater: in 1910 he saw *The Thunderbolt,* "a play satirizing the greed of the modern middle class," at the New Theater;[126] in 1911 he went "to Belasco theater to see Williams in mu-

---

123. "RNMF," 11.
124. Diary, September 7–11, 1912.
125. As noted in chapter 4, "Pastimes and Hardships."
126. Diary, November 16, 1910. The playwright was Sir Arthur Wing Pinero.

sical 'A German Prince[.]' Thin!"[127] In 1912, after lunch at the Plimptons, he went in the evening to *Daughter of Heaven* by Pierre Loti and Judith Gautier (translated by Helen Davis) at the Century Theatre, remarking to his diary, "following Dido? Love and duty. Impressive performance, drama conceived on broad lines, developed with power, gorgeously staged. At close Loti appeared after repeated calls, said with delicious accent 'I don't speak English'!"[128]

As pleasurable for the affable Kelseys as music was the almost constant round of social events: there were dinners to attend and parties to give. In 1911, for example, Francis took all three children to the "wedding of Anice Haightcox, cook, part Indian, and Andrew Johnson, negro, Junius E. Beal's coachman, at his house."[129] Beal, a local editor and newspaper publisher, was a regent and frequent supporter of the University Library and of Kelsey's interest in research and publication.[130] Shortly after Anice and Andrew's wedding, Beal invited the family to dinner: this time, Isabelle was in town and went along, too. Charlotte recalled the wide circle of Francis's friendship, which included businessmen and tradesmen, and his view that there "should never be a division between town and gown, that the business part of Ann Arbor was as worthy of respect as the university."[131]

Birthday parties are mentioned infrequently; though after lunch on his own birthday in 1907, a birthday cake with fifty candles appeared—"a Surprise! With pop-corn balls and fudge to the great delight of the children."[132] Thanksgiving is treated perfunctorily—once when Harriet was visiting (1911) and another time (1908) when he was in Washington, D.C., and dined with Mitchell Carroll and family. Christmas was a different matter and always hectic. In 1907 Francis took the part of Santa Claus, recording in his diary,

---

127. Diary, September 12, 1911. *A German Prince,* which was touring the country in 1911, starred singer and German-dialect comedian Al H. Wilson (might this be the actor to whom Kelsey was alluding?). See Dixie Hines and Harry Prescott Hanaford, eds., *Who's Who in Music and Drama* (New York: H. P. Hanaford, 1914), 325.

128. Diary, October 12, 1912.

129. Diary, May 30, 1911.

130. Regent Junius Emery Beal was also an ally of Kelsey's in his push for an auditorium large enough to handle operatic performances. See Charles A. Sink, "Michigan Memories and Personalities," in *Our Michigan: An Anthology Celebrating the University of Michigan's Sesquicentennial,* ed. Erich A. Walter (Ann Arbor: University of Michigan Press, 1966), 29.

131. "RNMF," 5. For entertaining, there was always the help of a resident servant, who doubtless pitched in both as cook and maid. Records for Washtenaw County from the thirteenth census of the United States (1910) show five Kelsey family members and one servant (Viola Wright) resident at 826 Tappan Street.

132. Diary, May 23, 1907.

Easton a little afraid—Santa Claus song, sung on the landing upstairs; then as I came downstairs and into the drawing-room (air from *Pinafore*

"I am the venerable Santa Claus
And I give no presents without cause
I drive all night with my 4 reindeer
And so in the morning I am here" (repeat)
"And down the chimney now I've come
Because this is a children's home
My book says there are children there
And so I'll go downstairs and see"

[verses for each member of the family][133]

Since the annual meetings of the AIA and the APA were held directly after Christmas, Francis often worked part of the holiday. On Christmas Day 1908, he worked all the time between entertaining guests at both dinner and supper, before taking the 9:30 train for Toronto. The next year, the turkey was large enough to warrant mention (fifteen and a half pounds), after which he wrote, "worked all p.m. Train at 9:30 for Washington."[134] In 1910 Harriet was with them, but again Francis left for Boston after dinner, and in 1911 he had a business meeting at the main Ann Arbor post office building before taking the 2:40 train for New York. Since the 1912 meetings were his last as president of the AIA, the annual address was much on his mind. The related diary entries make interesting reading: he wrote on December 21, "pressed by correspondence accomplished little"; on December 22, "started for church but getting an idea went to Moran's office and wrote a few paragraphs"; on December 24, "work on my address much interrupted." Christmas dinner was moved to Christmas Eve to free him for work: "at about 6 pm started with the address and finished at 4:30 am Christmas morning." He left for Washington, D.C., by the 11:30 a.m. train on Christmas Day.

THE BUSINESS MAN

Columbia Consolidated Mining Company (ex Hays Company)

After all his efforts in Mexico, countless discussions in New York, Washington, D.C., and Baltimore, and the reorganization of the Hays Company into

133. Diary, December 25, 1907.
134. Diary, December 25, 1909.

the Columbia Company, Kelsey probably thought that prospects for the company looked brighter. In early 1907, he successfully proposed that his AIA colleague Mitchell Carroll join Columbia's board of directors. Thereafter he seems to have slowly withdrawn from much of the company's activities. Yet, in the summer break, after organizing the construction of the Lake Cavanaugh cottage and the move of family and furniture, he spent four days arranging "two volumes of documents relating to the administration of the Hays Company"[135] and writing memoranda to be attached to them. After attending meetings in Washington in November, he sent these volumes to Isaac Baker Greene, the secretary of the company, in care of the American Security and Trust Company in Washington, "to secure affidavits of certification."[136] Duly certified, these books returned to Ann Arbor with him after a board meeting in February 1908. On this visit to Washington, he was invited to dinner with the Thropps[137] and shared the table with Admiral and Mrs. Schley, ex-senator and now governor (of Panama) Joseph Blackburn and Mrs. Blackburn, Senator and Mrs. Daniel—a company of the powerful by which he was probably flattered.[138] He attended company board meetings when they coincided with AIA meetings. Things seemed to be going smoothly, until he and Thropp had a meeting in August with the Mexican ambassador, who remarked that "he feared we had a weak case against the Government for the recovery of the lands."[139]

Board opposition to Thropp voiced itself in November. In the New Year (1909), in the face of the continued agitation of the bondholders, a consulting engineer, Bernard Granville, was hired to assess the company's properties and

---

135. Diary, August 10–14, 1907.

136. Diary, November 30 1907. Old share certificates, kindly loaned by Easton Kelsey Jr., reveal the names of other officers of the company. In 1907 W. Taylor Birch was first vice president; in 1908 Wallace Donald McLean was first vice president, and Herbert E. Smith was second vice president. In 1907 Francis Kelsey held 5,000 shares, to which he added 14,999 in 1908; Harriet acquired 12,630 in 1908.

137. Joseph Earlston Thropp had been the senior member of the board of the Hays Company (see chapter 4, "The Hays Consolidated Mining, Milling, and Lumber Company") and had emerged as the leader of the new company (Columbia Consolidated) after the reorganization.

138. Diary, February 11, 1908. Admiral Winfield Scott Schley, whose career was not without criticism, published his memoirs under the title *Forty-five Years under the Flag* (New York, D. Appleton and Company, 1904). Joseph Clay Styles Blackburn (1838–1918) was the military governor of the Panama Canal Zone in 1907–9, and John Warwick Daniel was a U.S. senator from Virginia.

139. Diary, August 14, 1908.

propose courses of action. His report, delivered at a board meeting on March 28, did not come soon enough to allay the fears of the Baltimore bondholders, who were threatening "foreclosure under mortgage due April 1."[140] The promise of a 20 percent payment on June 15, however, persuaded them not to "press foreclosure on the Columbia bonds." By now Thropp was unpopular with the board again, and a conspiratorial phone call to Kelsey prompted the latter's indignation. "I hung up," Kelsey's diary for April 19 records. In response to a visit to Ann Arbor by Granville, who complained that "he was disgusted with the lack of energy shown by the Board of the Columbia Company,"[141] Kelsey met the Baltimore bondholders on two consecutive days in Baltimore: at the first meeting, they were "discouraging"; at the second, they said that "they expected payment of 1/5th on June 15 as agreed and did not propose to abate their rights in any respect."[142] After consultations at the American Security and Trust Company in Washington, D.C., Kelsey persuaded Thropp to offer seventy-five cents on the dollar up to twenty-five thousand dollars for the Baltimore people, an offer promptly rejected. At a conference at Everett, Thropp then agreed to the formation of a Committee of Four "with absolute authority,"[143] which at least pacified the board. Finally, Granville proposed to form a new company "and buy in Columbia."[144] Though obviously a stalling tactic, this maneuver appealed to the bondholders, who in September agreed to extend the mortgage one year. A year later, Thropp "renewed notes for $850,000 for interest on the Baltimore bonds,"[145] but emergency measures were in the air. In September Granville proposed "in case of complete loss to make good to deserving stockholders (say to the extent of 50 or 60,000 shares) in another company."[146] The situation did not improve. One experienced businessman "advised the abandonment of Columbia, proposing that Granville 'make good' to Columbia people deserving consideration from another source";[147] another, Wallace Donald McLean (formerly attorney for Mr. Hays), favored putting the company in the hands of a receiver.[148] The following year, when McLean proposed another reorga-

---

140. Diary, April 10, 1909.
141. Diary, May 2, 1909.
142. Diary, June 10, 1909.
143. Diary, July 20, 1909.
144. Diary, August 25, 1909.
145. Diary, July 14, 1910.
146. Diary, September 19, 1910.
147. Diary, February 10, 1911.
148. Diary, April 11, 1911.

nization of the company, Kelsey wrote in his diary, "I agreed to cooperate with Thropp clearing titles and handling properties with an understanding that deserving people would have a share in the reorganization."[149] Meanwhile, the board decided to send two colleagues to Mexico to investigate the company's mines and disputed claims. To Kelsey's ears, this all sounded alarmingly like a recurrence of events in 1904: disputed claims, troublesome bondholders, emissaries to Mexico, reorganization. The emissaries (McLean's law partner, Ford, and a Mr. Barker) came to Ann Arbor on March 21 to confer with Kelsey over the four large boxes of the company's files before departing for Nogales. There is no further mention of the Columbia Company in the diary for the year 1912.

This silence is hardly surprising. Kelsey's days were enormously busy. He was president both of the AIA and of the UMS in Ann Arbor, whose activities required much of his extracurricular attention. He was busily engaged in the affairs of the university campus committee involved with key decisions about the Hill Auditorium, the Alumni Memorial Hall, and other projects. Moreover, he had become embroiled in another business adventure: the Weldon Gold and Copper Company.

The Weldon Gold and Copper Company

In early 1908, Kelsey visited the office of George H. Russel, president of the newly consolidated People's State Bank in Detroit, to ask his opinion about two companies: the Parke-Davis Company (founded in Detroit in 1886, later to become a subsidiary of Pfizer) and the Weldon Mining Company, "in regard to which he had no direct knowledge."[150] Undeterred, after talking at length in Ann Arbor on March 9 with Ferris S. Fitch (secretary, treasurer, and general manager of the Weldon Company) and "learning about the Weldon property and his trials in getting it developed," he gave Fitch $750 to purchase one thousand shares of the Weldon Company for Harriet.[151] By March 27, he had acquired a thousand shares for himself, too.[152] Kelsey's confidence in the

---

149. Diary, January 6, 1912.

150. Diary, January 29, 1908. Russel (b. 1847) had been involved for decades in the iron manufacturing industry. See Charles Moore, *History of Michigan*, vol. 2 (Chicago: Lewis, 1915), 1127.

151. Diary, March 9, 1908.

152. Much information about the company and its operations comes from old share certificates, notices of location, annual work affidavits, powers of attorney, mining deeds, agreements, stationery, and so on spanning the years 1899–1909, now in the possession of Easton Kelsey Jr. and generously made available to me.

company was no doubt bolstered by his friendship with one of the directors, University of Michigan dean of engineering Mortimer Cooley—an ally in more than one campus battle—and by Ferris Fitch's reputation in Ann Arbor.[153] Nevertheless, Kelsey was uneasy enough about the company early in 1909 to spend "an evening with Fitch going over affairs of Weldon."[154] At a meeting the next day in Detroit with businessman F. M. Alger,[155] all three agreed to ask Bernard Granville (who was already acting as a consultant for the Columbia Company) to visit the properties.

In early April, a representative of Mr. H. B. Ledyard[156] came from Detroit to Ann Arbor to discuss the Weldon situation with Kelsey. Two days later, at a meeting of the Weldon stockholders at which the thirty present "displayed much interest," Granville gave a stereopticon talk on the company's properties and prospects. Though two directors were present, the meeting was chaired by Kelsey.[157] Although Kelsey's name does not appear on the company's letterhead in 1909,[158] his activities in a leadership role are interesting: he attended many directors' meetings (sometimes, as the diary notes, "by in-

---

153. Fitch had been appointed principal of Pontiac High School in 1870, superintendent of Pontiac schools in 1881, and state superintendent in 1890, the same year that he had become editor and publisher of the *Oakland County Post* and embarked on a business career that took him to Arizona, where he was appointed a regent of the University of Arizona in 1902.

154. Diary, February 18, 1909.

155. Frederick Moulton Alger (b. 1876) was a son of General Russell A. Alger, a former governor of Michigan. The secretary and director of his father's lumber manufacturing firm, Alger, Smith, and Company, he was also a director of several other Detroit firms. See Moore, *History of Michigan*, 1108–9.

156. Henry Brockholst Ledyard (1844–1921), president of the Michigan Railroad Commission and a director of a dozen or so railroad companies in the state, was a major stockholder in the Great Lakes Engineering Works. Others who took large positions in this ambitious venture included fellow Detroiters George H. Russel, Charles Freer, and Henry M. Campbell (who had been a director of the Michigan Air Line Railroad Company when Ledyard was its president), along with leading capitalists in Saginaw, Pittsburgh, Buffalo, Cleveland, and New York. (Ledyard and Campbell were also directors of Russel's People's State Bank, as was R. A. Alger.) Ledyard and Campbell represented the interests of the estate of Peter White, former president (1904–6) of the Weldon Company, who had died June 6, 1908, of a heart attack on the steps directly outside city hall in Detroit. See "Peter White Drops Dead," *New York Times*, June 7, 1908, 9. On White, see also nn. 16 above and 168 below.

157. He wrote "I presided" in his diary entry for April 7, 1909.

158. The 1909 company letterhead reads: "The Weldon Gold and Copper Company, Ann Arbor, Michigan. Officers: Frank R. Osborne, President; George M. Stellwagen, Treasurer; Ferris S. Fitch, Secretary. Directors: Frank R. Osborne, Cassopolis, Mich.; Mortimer E. Coo-

vitation") and was recognized as an influential and contributive member of the company.

When Granville was back in Ann Arbor at the end of the month, he went with Kelsey, Fitch, and George Stellwagen, the company's treasurer, to a meeting in Detroit in the offices of Russel, Campbell, Bulkley, and Ledyard[159] in the Union Trust Building, to discuss the company's difficulties. A complicated agreement involved "surrendering 825,000 shares to the Treasury of which those present underwrote 52,000 shares at 25 cts, with the general understanding that 180,000 shares should be underwritten before announcement should be made to stockholders."[160] On May 1, Granville's report and a letter from the directors went out to the company's 443 shareholders. Though the situation was far from dire, Weldon's situation evidently needed regularization; and since subscription blanks for stock were among the documents sent to the shareholders, the company apparently was short of cash. These events occurred at about the same time as the crises in the other mining company—the Columbia Consolidated Company—in which Kelsey was involved.

The Weldon directors continued to meet fortnightly in June, and in July Ledyard began to attend the meetings. Those at a meeting in Detroit on the twenty-sixth agreed to the formation of the Wayne Development Company along lines suggested by Granville, to bring about some kind of partnership with the Weldon Company.[161] Three Weldon directors were at the meeting (Cooley, Fitch, Stellwagen), with other Weldon investors (Alger, Granville, Kelsey) and several newcomers, who included another Michigan faculty member, Frederick G. Novy.[162] Another faculty member, Horace L. Wilgus,[163] joined the discussions in August. Kelsey's remark in his diary for August 20 that the board of directors of the Wayne Development Company "completed

---

ley, Ann Arbor, Mich.; Ferris S. Fitch, Ann Arbor, Mich.; Samuel W. Smith, Pontiac, Mich.; Geo. M. Stellwagen, Wayne, Mich."

159. This company, founded in 1878 by Henry Russel and H. M. Campbell as Russel and Campbell, survives as Dickinson Wright PLLC of Detroit.

160. Diary, April 28, 1909.

161. Diary, July 26, 1909.

162. Frederick George Novy (b. 1864), a University of Michigan graduate (B.S. 1886, M.S. 1887, D.Sc. 1890, M.D. 1891), joined the faculty in 1887, became a distinguished bacteriologist and dean of the Medical School, and served until his retirement in 1935. He died in 1957 at the ripe old age of ninety-two. See Hinsdale, *History*, 314.

163. Horace LaFayette Wilgus (b. 1859) became acting professor of law in 1895 and professor in 1897, serving on the University of Michigan Law School faculty until 1929. See Hinsdale, *History*, 308–9.

the organization and transfer of stock" was premature, since talks were still being held in November about "Weldon and adjustment between Wayne and Weldon interests."[164] Details of the deal are unknown but evidently entailed a partnership or takeover of some sort, with a stock swap and overlapping directorships; at year's end, however, the directors of each company were still meeting separately, and what Francis Kelsey's role was is uncertain.[165]

Throughout 1910, Kelsey attended meetings dealing with the Wayne Company once or twice a month. In the first six months of the year, the major items on the docket were contracts for hauling ore, disputed claims, boundaries, and the sale of stock;[166] by September the state of the company's affairs had deteriorated to an extent that the question before the directors was whether to sell the company or "make another attempt to finance the company and go ahead."[167] Kelsey hurried to Cleveland to talk with William Gwinn Mather, president of the Cleveland-Cliffs Iron Company, about the Weldon Company's prospects and the disposition of Peter White's estate.[168] Mather could offer no help.

A ray of hope emerged for the company in February of the following year: George Shiras III[169] agreed that he would meet the stockholders in April, and

---

164. Diary, November 19, 1909.

165. I have not been able to discover any formally stated details of the Wayne Development Company's organization or operations, though it is logical to suppose that its purposes were similar to, if not identical with, those of the Weldon Company. *The Copper Handbook*, however, is skeptical: "Property [i.e., Weldon] now said to be under the management of the Wayne Development Co is not regarded favorably notwithstanding the fact that some men of excellent standing are included in the directorate" (Horace Jared Stevens and Walter Harvey Weed, comps., *The Copper Handbook: A Manual of the Copper Industry of the World*, vol. 10 [Houghton, MI: Horace J. Stevens, 1911], 1806).

166. Diary, February 22, 1910.

167. Diary, September 8, 1910.

168. Mather (1857–1951) had bought land in Marquette County, Michigan, in 1901 for his company's mining operations. White was a former president of the Weldon Company (see n. 156) and one of the founders of Marquette, Michigan, where some of the earliest operations of the Cleveland-Cliffs Iron Company were located. White not only invested in this and other mining enterprises in the Upper Peninsula of Michigan but also had widespread banking, insurance, and shipping interests. A firm believer in the power of education, he was a good friend to the Northern Michigan College of Education and served as a regent of the University of Michigan (see n. 16). See Herbert J. Brinks, *Peter White* (Grand Rapids, MI: W. B. Eerdmans, 1970), 63.

169. Born on New Year's Day, 1859, Shiras was educated at Cornell and Yale. The son of a U.S. Supreme Court justice, he was elected to the Pennsylvania House of Representatives in 1889 and to the U.S. House of Representatives in 1903. A son-in-law of Peter White—which doubtless accounts for his interest in the Weldon Company—he developed a keen interest in

Samuel Smith, one of the directors and a Michigan member of the U.S. House of Representatives, agreed, after a visit to Panama and the close of Congress, "to take off his coat and see what could be done to save the Weldon Company."[170] Yet April brought a directors' meeting "throwing the Company into bankruptcy," and Wilgus dictated "three night letters containing instructions and a long letter with details containing certified resolutions passed by the Weldon directors."[171] Monthly meetings revealed the worsening of the company's position until it became clear, in November, that it was doomed.[172] There is no further mention of the Weldon Company in the diaries, confirmation that it was effectively under the management of the Wayne Development Company.

COMMUNITY INVOLVEMENT

If Kelsey's contacts in the wider world of business proved to be unsteady, he found a deeper satisfaction in the town of Ann Arbor, not only with his academic work, but also with his efforts on behalf of Presbyterianism and the University Musical Society.

The University Musical Society continued to demand Francis's attention. There were the regular administrative agendas with which, as UMS president, he had to deal, as well as some unusual challenges. The outcomes were most often positive; occasionally they were not. Once, he tried but failed to persuade the Chicago Opera to come to Ann Arbor; another time, in the face of fractious concertgoers, he successfully settled problems of seating in University Hall and of selling standing-room tickets.[173] His UMS presidency also made him president of the School of Music, in which ca-

---

the biology of wild animals and birds and pioneered the use of flash photography. He died at Marquette, Michigan, in 1942 ("George Shiras, 83; Noted Naturalist," *New York Times*, March 25, 1942, 21).

170. Diary, February 8, 1911. A graduate of the law department of the University of Michigan (1878), Samuel William Smith (1852–1931) practiced law in Pontiac, Michigan, was prosecuting attorney of Oakland County during 1880–84, served as a legislator in the Michigan Senate in 1885–87, and was elected to the U.S. Congress in 1897, where he served until 1915, when he returned to the practice of law in Detroit (Biographical Directory of the United States Congress, 1774–Present, http://bioguide.congress.gov/scripts/biodisplay.pl?index=S000613 [accessed December 20, 2008]).

171. Diary, April 25, 1911.

172. Diary, November 4 and 20, 1911.

173. Diary, May 10, 1909.

pacity he presided at the annual commencement exercises, gave out certificates and diplomas, and delivered an address. With Isabelle, he regularly attended the school's concerts.

He had to pay most attention to the society's budget. In 1907 he led discussions aimed at improving profits and reducing the debt. By 1909 he was able to note that the "UMS has been the means of securing for the University gifts amounting to $100,000—the great organ reckoned at $25,000, Stearns Musical Collection at $70,000"; he further noted, "after all debts paid, surplus cash in bank about $5000."[174] When good financial results were again reported in 1911, a new five-year contract was voted by the board for Charles A. Sink, secretary and business manager of the School of Music, at a salary rising from twenty-six hundred dollars to three thousand.[175]

During the annual May Festival, initiated in 1894 by Albert Stanley,[176] the university's professor of music, Kelsey attended as many events as he could and entertained lavishly. Not every concert was a success. With reference to Haydn's *The Seasons* performed at the 1909 festival, Kelsey comments, "Perceval Allen (did poorly), Beddoe, tenor, ill and sang like a sick man; choral work fine."[177] In 1912 Elgar's *Dream of Gerontius* and Saint-Saëns's *Samson and Delilah* were the highlights. Programs for concerts by visiting artists and local musicians were subjects of long and sometimes highly imaginative debate. Discussions in 1912 in which Charles Sink was always involved included a "long talk about possible drama [opera] of Vercingetorix," in which Kelsey "suggested to him a libretto."[178] Discussions with Albert Stanley centered on a production of Euripides's *Alcestis*. Of this performance in front of Alumni Memorial Hall on June 24, 1912, Kelsey reported to his diary, "costuming brilliant, music by Stanley exquisite, immense crowd."

Kelsey was always ready to support music faculty, whether they held appointments in the university or in the School of Music. He reported in his diary May 13, 1909, that, during the 1909 May Festival, "Stock[179] urged on President Angell and me to have Mr. Stanley go to Vienna to attend the meetings of the International Musik Gesellschaft May 26ff at which he had been invited

---

174. Diary, June 15, 1909.

175. Diary, June 15, 1911.

176. See chapter 3, "Community Involvement."

177. Diary, May 13, 1909.

178. Diary, February 21, 1912. Vercingetorix was Julius Caesar's most dangerous adversary in Gaul, so it is easy to see how Kelsey might warm to this project.

179. Frederick Stock, music director of the Theodore Thomas Orchestra, which later became the Chicago Symphony Orchestra (see chapter 4 n. 66).

to read a paper." Kelsey wrote, "Dr. Angell and I took the matter up; he offered to put in $25 toward expenses, I started subscriptions and got an appropriation of $125 from the directors of the Musical Society. Dr. A. spoke of the matter to Lawrence Maxwell who drew his check for $250."

Kelsey was instantly involved, in his role as school president, when the news arrived that Regent Arthur Hill had left money in his will for a new auditorium, a building for which the UMS and others had badgered the university for years. As we have seen, Francis had his own ideas about the building and its location.[180] Although he was not successful in having an opera-sized stage included in the plan, Hill Auditorium's ultimate location was favored by the architect Albert Kahn and by Kelsey.

In the sphere of church activities, his visibility as a leading Presbyterian only increased. In September 1907, the Board of Education of the Presbyterian Church invited him to address them in Philadelphia on religious education in state universities.[181] The following winter, he gave a paper on religious instruction at the meetings of the Religious Education Association in Washington[182] and was elected chair for the following year. Heavily engaged in this association's affairs, he presided at the 1909 meetings,[183] and the next year, he attended an all-day conference in Chicago on February 19. On March 26, again in Chicago, he worked on the program for a nationwide meeting on religious education with fellow committee members, all high-level university administrators.[184] At the General Assembly of the Presbyterian Church in Atlantic City in May 1911, he was once more at the podium to address the Board of Education.[185]

Kelsey was busy with Presbyterian activities in Ann Arbor, too. At the university, he read a paper at the joint session of the Interdenominational Guild Conference and the Michigan Classical Conference on "the Study of Classics as

---

180. See above, "Campus Expansion."

181. Diary, September 24 and 25, 1907. The board paid his expenses, which were duly noted in the diary: "railroad $30.02, sleeper two nights $4, meals, 6 at 50cts = $3, for a total of $37.02."

182. Diary, February 13, 1908. Founded in 1903 by William Rainey Harper, the first president (1891–1906) of the University of Chicago, as an association of teachers, professors, researchers, and the religious-minded, the REA aimed to promote conferences, research, and publication.

183. Diary, February 10, 1909.

184. Diary, March 26, 1910. The administrators were Presidents James H. Baker (University of Colorado), George E. McLean (University of Iowa), Franklin B. Gault (University of South Dakota), and Frank L. McVey (University of North Dakota) and Chancellor Frank Strong (University of Kansas).

185. Diary, May 20, 1911.

preparation for the Study of Theology,"[186] and during this period, he regularly attended board meetings of the Tappan Presbyterian Association. At the First Presbyterian Church, a major concern in 1910 was the election of a new pastor. After several meetings of the search committee and a visit and sermon by the Reverend W. Merrill, the church committee nominated Merrill on August 3, authorizing a salary of thirty-five hundred dollars. Kelsey was commissioned by the elders and the trustees to take the call to Merrill, who visited again on August 10 and 11 but declined.[187] It was not until the following year that the Reverend L. A. Barrett, a graduate of the McCormick Seminary, arrived.

Kelsey continued his lectures at church[188] and attended other churches on special occasions. On February 19, 1910, he spoke at the First Congregational Church on "professional training for religious work," and on November 9 he went to the First Baptist Church for the "baptism by immersion of Mr. Redden, graduate in Law, formerly captain of football and now assistant coach."[189] Two highlights of the 1912 church year were the October visit of Bishop Williams, who gave "a masterly address," and a talk delivered a little later by the Reverend Hall, on the study of theology.[190]

The McCormick Seminary[191] benefited from Kelsey's regular attendance at meetings of its board of directors during these years and is especially prominent in what the diary records of Kelsey's church activities in 1911. In April, at a two-day meeting of the board regarding proposed changes to the curriculum, Kelsey took a strong position against a "reduction of the requirement in Hebrew." Buttonholed by Cyrus McCormick Jr. after the meeting, he was asked, in the context of the search for a Princeton University president, about "the religious life and activities of James R. Angell" (the son of Michigan's president).[192] Kelsey reported in his diary that when at the seminary

---

186. Diary, April 1, 1908. This was published as "Greek in the High School, and the Question of the Supply of Candidates for the Ministry," *School Review* 16.9 (November 1908): 561–79.

187. Diary, August 3, 10, and 11, 1910.

188. According to his diary, he delivered the speech "The Pagan Background to Corinthians" on January 16 and 23, 1910.

189. Diary, February 19 and November 9, 1910. Curtis Redden had been football captain in 1903.

190. Diary, October 6 and December 1, 1912. The bishop was Charles David Williams of the Diocese of Michigan (1905–23).

191. For more on Kelsey and the seminary, see chapter 4, "Community Involvement."

192. Diary, April 26 and 27, 1911. James Rowland Angell graduated from the University of Michigan (A.B. 1890, A.M. 1891) and, after receiving a master's in psychology from Harvard (1892), taught at both Minnesota and Chicago, becoming department head at the latter in 1905. He eventually became president not of Princeton but of Yale (1921–37).

again on October 20 for an appointment with McCormick, "I presented the memorial to him. He said he would read it on the train to New York."[193]

That Francis had time to attend to church and seminary matters in his final year as president of the AIA is remarkable testimony to his interest and to his stamina and staying powers. This had been a busy decade, and by the end of 1912, he was ready to make the more customary professorial activities the focus of his professional life. At the same time, his ever-active mind would continue to register developments in the business world, and his successes in the more public world of Washington would not allow him to withdraw entirely from the national scene. That he would be a serious candidate for appointment as American ambassador to Italy in 1913 is a sure sign of his high reputation among men of rank in the country.

---

193. Diary, October 20, 1911. Kelsey does not tell the reader what this memorial was about. If, however, the term *memorial* may here be taken in the old sense of "memorandum," it may be that the document represented Kelsey's views on the importance of instruction in Hebrew to the seminary's mission.

CHAPTER 7

Leading the Way,
1913–18

❧

IN JANUARY 1913, Francis Kelsey's mind began to turn to the more mundane aspects of professorial life—teaching, research, and publication—and to his family. Yet information about his other activities by no means vanishes from the diaries, nor does he disappear from the national and international stage.

Business recedes into the background. Since the Wayne Development Company's board of directors met only once in 1913 and once in 1914, it is evident that business was not exactly booming. In fact, toward the end of 1914, Granville told Kelsey, on a visit to New York, that no more Wayne assessment work was needed.[1] Again in 1915, there was only a single meeting, attended by Granville, at which matters appeared to be "more encouraging."[2] Once more, in 1916, only a single meeting was recorded.[3] A board meeting held on August 3, 1917, preceded a stockholders' meeting on August 17, where it had seemed to Kelsey that "Simpson and Wilgus worked out a settlement of Simpson's claim"[4]—a view that would prove to have been too optimistic. What was discussed at another meeting on October 5 is unclear, but the meetings' infrequency suggests clearly enough the lack of business activity and even the apathy of investors.

Toward the end of 1918, Mr. H. H. Simpson brought suit against the com-

---

1. Diary, December 8, 1914.
2. Diary, December 22, 1915.
3. Diary, January 3, 1916.
4. Diary, August 17, 1917.

pany on a grievance concerning the old Weldon Company. The board met about this on December 6 and 10 and separately with Simpson on December 14: the meeting took place in Kelsey's office in the Alumni Memorial Hall, and Kelsey wrote in his diary of Simpson's "preposterous claims," declaring that "he contradicted himself frequently."[5] On December 16, Kelsey went to the offices of Campbell, Bulkley, and Ledyard in Detroit to consult former University of Michigan regent Harry C. Bulkley about Thomas W. Butter, Simpson's attorney; he learned only that Butter was on record as a corporation lawyer. He also went to see Russell A. Alger Jr., millionaire son of General Alger, about the Simpson suit; Alger said that he had best refer the matter to Ledyard. In Detroit again on December 21, Kelsey and Wilgus met first with H. B. Ledyard and one-time Weldon director George Stellwagen about the old matter and then with Simpson, Butter, and his brother-in-law, R. S. Smith: "Butter seemed to have no great desire to have the law or the facts, but rather to get for HHS what he could—best offer we could get was $3000 for his stock (about 30,000 shares) and receipt in full."[6] A week later, Stellwagen told Kelsey in conversation that "he had decided to pay no attention to the Simpson notice."[7]

The year 1919 saw virtually the end of Kelsey's business entanglements. In March Ledyard advised a cash payment of four hundred dollars to Simpson to "close up that matter of the Wayne Company," a recommendation accepted by the directors.[8] In April a Mr. C. H. Thomas was engaged to "work on Wayne matters."[9] Kelsey conferred with Thomas twice in July, after which, immediately prior to Kelsey's departure for Europe and the Near East, Charles Sink of the School of Music took Kelsey's place on the board.[10] Of Kelsey's other business venture, the Columbia Company, there is no mention in his diaries of 1913–18.

ON THE NATIONAL SCENE

The AIA

Though released at the end of 1912 from the heavy burden of the presidency of the Archaeological Institute of America, Kelsey continued to serve on one

---

5. Diary, December 14, 1918.
6. Diary, December 21, 1918.
7. Diary, December 28, 1918.
8. Diary, March 18 and 19, 1919.
9. Diary, April 10, 1919.
10. Diary, July 4 and 26 and August 28, 1919.

or two of the institute's committees and remained engaged in projects that were close to his heart. On February 1, for example, he wrote to AIA treasurer Willard V. King about the proposed American School of Archaeology in China: "I have withdrawn from association with all other undertakings of the Archaeological Institute, but I am much interested in this project and am a member of the Committee."[11] A Canadian, Harry L. Wilson, professor of Roman archaeology at Johns Hopkins University,[12] had succeeded Kelsey as president; early in the year, Kelsey began turning over files and equipment owned by the institute to him.[13] In New York on February 17, the two had a long meeting: "in conference almost continuously with Wilson till he left for his train at 2.40."[14] It was therefore with great consternation that he received a night letter from Frederick W. Shipley in Pittsburgh a week later, telling him of Wilson's sudden death the night of February 23.[15] A meeting of the executive committee in New York on March 24 voted unanimously to ask Vice President Shipley to act as president until the next meeting of the council. Called into action once more, Kelsey spent the evening of April 11 in Indianapolis with Shipley and prolonged his stay to confer for most of the following day with him and AIA secretary Mitchell Carroll "upon matters of the Institute."[16] At the next annual meetings, held in Montreal, Shipley was elected to succeed Wilson in the presidency and did Kelsey the great courtesy of asking him to preside at the evening session on January 2.[17]

The institute's schools were the projects that most keenly held Kelsey's interest, and of these, the School of American Archaeology at Santa Fe, the American School in Jerusalem, and a proposed school in China were fore-

---

11. AIA Archives, box 19.28.

12. A graduate of Queen's University, Kingston, Ontario (A.B. 1887), Harry Langford Wilson had continued his studies at the University of Bonn and at Johns Hopkins (Ph.D. 1896). A faculty member at Johns Hopkins from 1902 to 1913, his scholarly work includes his published dissertation, *The Metaphor in the Epic Poems of Publius Papinius Statius* (Baltimore: John Murphy, 1898).

13. Diary, January 3 and February 8, 1913.

14. Diary, February 17, 1913.

15. Diary, February 24, 1913: "As I had committed to Wilson the last responsibilities of the presidency of the Institute in New York the previous Monday, the shock was great."

16. All three were attending the meetings of the Classical Association of the Midwest and South. A graduate of the University of Toronto (A.B. 1892), Frederick W. Shipley had received his doctorate from the University of Chicago in 1901 and taught at Washington University in St. Louis (where we first encountered him in chapter 5) until his retirement in 1941. The most conspicuous among his publications may be *Compendium of Roman History: C. Velleius Paterculus–"Res Gestae divi Augusti,"* with his English translation (New York: G. P. Putnam's Sons, 1924; London: W. Heinemann 1924; Cambridge, MA: Harvard University Press, 1924).

17. Diary, January 2, 1914.

most in his mind. At discussions in 1913 about the Jerusalem school, held at Columbia University, agreement was reached on the importance of appointing a permanent director for the school, and renowned biblical scholar C. C. Torrey nominated William H. Worrell, the editor of Freer's Coptic manuscripts, for the post. There was further agreement that this group should try to raise five thousand dollars a year for five years by subscription; Kelsey moved on this matter immediately and, two days later, urged Willard King to provide a subvention to this end.[18] Yet Kelsey's interest in this school seems to have dissipated, and he submitted his resignation at a meeting of the managing committee at the close of 1915, nominating Leroy Waterman to take his place as the Michigan representative.[19] Due to the military and economic complications of World War I, the school in Jerusalem ceased operations in 1915: whether Kelsey's withdrawal was caused by disappointment at the school's closure, however temporary, or other pressures is unclear.

The establishment of a school in China, a project given added impetus by the enthusiasm of Charles Freer, had occupied the closing months of Kelsey's presidency.[20] Toward the end of 1913, happily continuing his advocacy for this undertaking, he called in New York on Mr. F. C. Marston, who reported a contribution of ten thousand dollars "for the School in China."[21] The next year, Kelsey asked Jerome D. Greene, the secretary of the Rockefeller Foundation, for support.[22] Later the same year, a meeting of the committee tasked to establish such a school was held in New York, at the home of Eugene C. Meyer Jr.[23] Dr. Charles D. Walcott, secretary of the Smithsonian Institution, was chair; members in attendance were Meyer, Charles Freer, and Langdon Warner, with Kelsey and Mitchell Carroll present by invitation. Kelsey notes,

---

18. Diary, December 8 and 10, 1913.

19. Leroy Waterman (1875–1972) was educated at Hillsdale College (A.B. 1898), Oxford, Berlin, and Chicago (Ph.D. 1912) and taught at Michigan from 1915, where he headed the Department of Oriental Languages and Literatures, until his retirement in 1945. Director of archaeological work at Seleucia on the Tigris (1928–31) and at Sepphoris (1931), he was an experienced biblical scholar, a prolific author, a member of the Chicago committee (1922–27) responsible for *The Bible: An American Translation,* and among the thirty-one scholars (1938–52) that produced the *Revised Standard Version of the Bible.*

20. See chapter 5, "The Foreign Schools."

21. Diary, December 10, 1913. This may well have been Fred Carver Marston (b. 1875), a New York lawyer who would be elected treasurer of the Columbia Trust Company in 1916.

22. Diary, February 16, 1914.

23. Eugene C. Meyer Jr., educated in finance at Yale (B.A. 1895), was a banker with offices on Wall Street. He was the son of E. I. Meyer, chairman of the Board of Governors of the Federal Reserve System (1930–33), who may be equally well known as the father of Katherine Graham, publisher of the *Washington Post.*

"Carroll, Warner and I were asked as a sub-committee to work out a budget for one year for the proposed school."[24] Kelsey continued to look for funds, approaching Cyrus McCormick and Charles Freer once more in 1915, but all to no avail. The economic crisis precipitated by World War I put an end to this exciting prospect, just as it had caused the Jerusalem school to close its doors.

The situation in which the School of American Archaeology found itself was much brighter. Established at the 1907 meeting of the AIA governing council, it had found a home for itself in 1909 in Santa Fe. Even after Kelsey's AIA presidency ended, its director, Edgar Hewett, kept in touch, visiting Ann Arbor annually; and he asked Kelsey to give an address at the dedication of the school's new building in 1917.[25] Kelsey gladly agreed. Consequently, he and Isabelle spent several pleasant days in New Mexico in the fall.

Arriving on November 23, they were "quickly installed in the guest room of the newly fitted director's house."[26] The following day, the American Committee of the AIA enjoyed a conducted tour. Alice Fletcher herself was present. Hewett then made the formal presentation of the building to the state; Governor Washington E. Lindsey accepted; and, on behalf of the institute, Kelsey said a few words. On the morning of November 26, he presented to the conference a paper entitled "Sidelights on Virgil." Writing to his sister, Harriet, that afternoon, with reference to his imminent keynote speech, he remarked, "It comes this evening, and I cannot foretell how it will be received; but I feel as if I had a *message,* and I hope I am not self deceived." He ends his letter, all too humanly, by saying, "I shall breathe more easily after tonight."[27] After speaking briefly at a dinner at the museum, he delivered his address "The New Humanism" to a joint session of the state teachers association and museum members, held in the Scottish Rite Cathedral. There were, so Hewett said, fifteen hundred in the audience.[28] Stressing the importance of the expansion of knowledge, his talk included the following salient passage:

> The earlier humanism felt no necessity of passing beyond the domain of the languages and literatures of ancient Greece and Rome. The new humanism must be broader, taking account of a half-millennium of progress since the earlier movement. Upon a foundation of the ancient classics, it

24. Diary, December 5, 1914.
25. Diary, April 21, 1916.
26. Diary, November 23, 1917.
27. Francis Kelsey to Harriet Fay, November 26, 1917, private collection of Easton Kelsey Jr., Rochester, NY.
28. Diary, November 26, 1917.

will base a superstructure of knowledge concerning man in the Orient, in the Occident, in those phases of development and activity that shall best reveal the capabilities of man as man, and fit youth to live in accordance with ideals in a world of humankind.[29]

There was a further session of the conference in the museum the following morning. The next two days were for relaxation. On November 28, Francis and Isabelle visited the impressive archaeological site at Pecos, winding their way through the awe-inspiring "Apache canyon." The next day, they were treated to a day trip with spectacular views of the Rio Grande—with Isabelle exclaiming that "she should count the excursion in the same class as the trip through the Langhada Pass"[30]—and to a "bountiful Thanksgiving Dinner," after which they enjoyed "an indescribably beautiful drive home."[31]

The AIA's publications were also of continuing interest to Kelsey. An early supporter of *Art and Archaeology*, initiated at the last meeting of the council (in December 1912) , he remained eager for news. The first issue appeared in July 1914, thanks to guaranteed subscriptions that raised four thousand dollars, guided by its first editor, David Robinson of Johns Hopkins University.[32] Also on the editorial board was Mitchell Carroll, one of the proponents, among members of the Washington Society, of the new publication. Carroll consulted with Kelsey in Ann Arbor in August and again in December 1915 about several aspects of *Art and Archaeology*, not least about details of the periodical's contract. Kelsey was impressed enough with Carroll's grasp of production problems to write in his diary that he "seemed to have a clear idea of the manufacture of a 1st class publication."[33] Subsequently, at a meeting of the executive committee of the AIA on December 27 in New York, the contract was agreed after what Kelsey described as "a spirited but not acrimonious dis-

---

29. *AIA Annual Bulletin* 1919: 41, cited by Stephen L. Dyson, *Ancient Marbles to American Shores: Classical Archaeology in the United States* (Philadelphia: University of Pennsylvania Press, 1998), 160.

30. Their journey through the Langhada Pass had taken place during the trip around the Peloponnese in 1901; see chapter 4, "The American School of Classical Studies in Rome."

31. Diary, November 29, 1917.

32. A graduate of the University of Chicago, David Moore Robinson joined the faculty at Johns Hopkins in 1905. An early president of the College Art Association and editor of the *Art Bulletin,* he is perhaps best known for the exploration over a period of ten years (1928–38) of Olynthus in northern Greece. He joined Kelsey and Sir William Ramsay in 1924 in the excavations at Antioch in Pisidia.

33. Diary, December 5, 1915.

cussion."[34] On December 15 of the following year, he continued his solicitation of publication funds, encouraged by Willard V. King's remark that "he thought the time was propitious to secure endowment for our publications if someone would only take up the matter heartily."[35]

Ambassador to Italy

Kelsey's growing eminence—both nationally, through his recent presidency of the AIA, and internationally, as an expert on Roman history and archaeology—and his skills, both rhetorical and administrative, made him an obvious candidate for a possible diplomatic post. What better position for him could there be than American ambassador to Italy? His name was put forward to the White House by Charles Richard Williams.[36] An old acquaintance of Kelsey's as a Latin scholar and participant in the symposia on Humanistic Studies held in Ann Arbor, Williams dined with Kelsey when in Ann Arbor, as Kelsey did with him when in Indianapolis.[37] A series of letters between the two documents the discussion prior to Williams's submitting Kelsey's name to President Wilson. The nomination was supported by a distinguished cadre of letter writers that included the Right Reverend Edward D. Kelly of Ann Arbor; Presidents Angell and Hutchins of the University of Michigan; George P. Brett, president of the Macmillan Company; William Sloane, president of W. & J. Sloane; Willard V. King, president of the Columbia-Knickerbocker Trust Company (and also a trustee of Columbia University and treasurer of the AIA); and William K. Bixby, former president of the American Car and Foundry Company and a trustee of Washington University. The aid of politicians—Congressman S. W. Beakes and Governor Woodbridge N. Ferris, whose political loyalties were with "the same wing of Democracy as the Pres-

---

34. Diary, December 27, 1915.

35. Diary, December 15, 1916. He had appealed to the Rockefeller Foundation for assistance earlier (on February 16, 1914), without success.

36. A graduate of Princeton University (A.B. 1875), Williams (1853–1927) was a distinguished author and editor. A college professor in his early career, he served as assistant general manager of the Associated Press (1883–92) and subsequently as editor of the *Indianapolis News* (1892–1911). As an author, he is best known perhaps for *The Life of Rutherford Birchard Hayes, Nineteenth President of the United States*, 2 vols. (Boston and New York: Houghton Mifflin, 1914). Like Kelsey, he was born in New York State, attended the University of Rochester (before Kelsey's days), and published Latin texts (Lucian) for Allyn and Bacon.

37. Diary, April 12, 1913.

ident and Mr. Beakes"—was also enlisted. It was an impressive group representing the worlds of the church, academe, banking, business, and politics.[38]

Kelsey wrote to President Wilson on May 26, "My long-time friend, Mr. Charles Richard Williams writes that he nominated me to you for the post of Ambassador to Italy. . . . While I am not seeking the appointment, I should accept it if offered and should put forth every effort to discharge the duties in a way to occasion no regret."[39] Unfortunately, he was up against strong opposition for the post, as a letter to Williams three weeks later shows.

> My dear Williams,
>
> Your good letter is at hand. The "Virginian" is Thomas Nelson Page whom you probably know. My understanding is that his name was proposed before mine, that the Italian government, consulted, pronounced him persona grata, and that a dinner is to be given him shortly by the Italian Ambassador in Washington. He outranks me in literary standing, being a successful novelist and well known "club man" being a member of the leading Washington and New York clubs; also socially, having behind him the Field millions (his wife, if I remember correctly, was the wife of Marshall Field's son). So the President has made an admirable choice—and if I chance to meet him I shall congratulate him on his good judgment, and good fortune; for literary gifts and princely wealth are not often joined in one house, or available for public service.
>
> I should keenly regret, my dear friend, that I have occasioned you so much fruitless trouble, were it not that you have given proof (tho' proof were not needed) of that loyalty to early associations which has always been a conspicuous and endearing trait of your character. With heartfelt appreciation of your kindness, and most cordial greetings von Haus zu Haus, I remain,
>
> Faithfully yours
> Francis W. Kelsey[40]

The letter reveals, with only a hint of disappointment, Kelsey's recognition of the ambassador designate's qualities and, by its warmth, Kelsey's appreciation of Williams's generosity and efforts.

---

38. Kelsey to Williams, May 20, 27, and 31, 1913, etc., KMA Papers, box 36, folder 2.
39. Kelsey to President Woodrow Wilson, KMA Papers, box 36, folder 5.
40. Kelsey to Williams, June 17, 1913, KMA Papers, box 36, folder 2. In fact, Kelsey's memory let him down. Page's wife was not the former wife of Marshall Field's son but was Marshall Field's widowed sister-in-law.

Speaking Engagements

Throughout these years, Francis continued to be in great demand as a public speaker, always to audiences attentive and appreciative. He spoke to college and university audiences, to civic groups and church groups, to Latin clubs and classical clubs, at inauguration ceremonies, in art museums, in capacious auditoriums and smaller settings, in state and out. Any audience interested in the ancient world or susceptible to the claims of the classics, as well as any group of listeners concerned about the relationship between the church and education, provided grist to his mill. He was a commanding presence, a robust speaker, and a knowledgeable scholar and churchman.

At the 1913 meetings of the Classical Association of the Midwest and South in Indianapolis, Kelsey gave an illustrated lecture entitled "The Plimpton Manuscript of Caesar."[41] Two months later, President Hutchins, detained at a meeting of the regents, asked Francis to stand in for him and say a few words at the inauguration of President Charles McKenny at Michigan State Normal College in nearby Ypsilanti. Happy to oblige, Francis delivered the speech "The Significance of the Normal School as Educational Type."[42] Later in the year, he spoke in Columbus, Ohio, to the state university's Latin club, about Roman farmhouses,[43] and twice at the Detroit Museum of Art: on the first occasion, he delivered to a capacity audience his speech "Fifty Minutes in the Roman Catacombs"; on the second, he spoke to an audience of 273 on "St. Peter and St. Paul in Rome."[44] In early December, he undertook a lecture tour in northern New York, repeating the St. Peter and St. Paul talk at Buffalo in the lecture room of a Presbyterian church and at the University of Rochester, after dining with President Rush Rhees and other faculty, for a meeting of the local AIA society in the university's Eastman Building.[45] On December 5, in the auditorium of Syracuse University, the audience that came to hear him was "estimated at 1800."[46] During December 6–11, he was in New York and

---

41. Diary, April 12, 1913.

42. Diary, June 24, 1913. Michigan State Normal College, formerly Michigan State Normal School, is now Eastern Michigan University.

43. Diary, October 25, 1913. Kelsey rarely mentions whether or not he received an honorarium or whether his expenses were paid. Since the diary notes that his expenses were paid on this occasion and that he received an honorarium on others, perhaps the implication is that if he does not mention either, then he paid his own way.

44. Diary, November 9 and 22, 1913.

45. Diary, December 2 and 3, 1913.

46. Diary, December 4 and 5, 1913.

Washington, D.C.—conferring with Charles Freer at the Plaza, visiting the Metropolitan Museum, lunching with brother Fred and his family, attending meetings to raise funds for a religious foundation for state universities, and in discussion with Mitchell Carroll and Willard King on AIA matters[47]—before going to Northampton, Massachusetts, to speak at Smith College. At Smith he was greeted by Professor John Everett Brady, well known in the profession for his *Women in Roman Literature;*[48] met President Emeritus and Reverend Laurenus Clark Seelye and other faculty members; lectured in the evening to an audience of four hundred; and received an honorarium of fifty dollars for his pains.[49]

His program in 1914 was less congested but equally varied. After speaking at the University of Pennsylvania in February on St. Peter and St. Paul in Rome, he traveled with Dennison to Swarthmore, where he gave a talk on archaeology and literary studies to the classical club.[50] On a day excursion to Monroe, Michigan, he repeated the Peter and Paul lecture at the First Presbyterian Church, arriving back in Ann Arbor shortly after midnight—a long day.[51] In the fall, at the inauguration of the Reverend J. L. French as education director at a Presbyterian church in Toledo, his talk was "The Church and Secular Education."[52] His popularity as a speaker, whether in a church forum or before an audience of scholars, undergraduates, or high school students, remained strong throughout these years. In 1917, for example, at Grand Rapids, he gave two talks to the state teachers association: "Latin and Greek in Michigan Colleges" and "Sidelights on the Study of Virgil."[53] Later in the month, en route to the dedication of the new building at the School of American Archaeology in Santa Fe, he lectured in Denver, Colorado Springs, and Pueblo. All went well except at Denver, where "the operator cracked several slides and I had to telegraph to Mr. Swain to send on duplicates."[54] After the

---

47. He also found time to visit the Shubert Theater on December 10, seeing Shaw's *Caesar and Cleopatra,* which was playing in repertory and starred Johnston Forbes-Robertson and Gertrude Elliott.

48. John Everett Brady, *Women in Roman Literature* (Florence, MA: Bryant Printing, 1894). Brady (1860–1941), who graduated from the University of North Carolina (A.B. 1881) and studied at Leipzig, Göttingen, Paris, Athens, and Heidelberg (Ph.D. 1888), was professor of Latin at Smith during 1888–1926.

49. Diary, December 12, 1913.

50. Diary, February 9, 1914.

51. Diary, March 8, 1914.

52. Diary, October 13, 1914.

53. Diary, November 2, 1917.

54. Diary, November 19, 1917. A graduate of the University of Michigan (A.B. 1897, A.M. 1900), Swain had been a high school teacher and administrator for sixteen years before re-

stay in New Mexico, he spoke on three consecutive days in southern California, sometimes speaking twice on the same day.[55] In northern California, he gave talks at the "Hopkins School of Fine Arts" in San Francisco and at Stanford University in Palo Alto, where they were hosted by Professor Henry Rushton Fairclough and his wife.[56] He spoke in Portland at a meeting of classical teachers at Lincoln High School and to the classical club at Reed College, and he spoke in Seattle the following day at the Fine Arts Rooms.[57] Some of his topics were old favorites, such as St. Peter and St. Paul; some were variations on familiar refrains; others were quite new. "Is modern civilization a failure?" he asked at Reed. At Palo Alto, he commented on present attitudes to classical studies, and at Portland he offered vigorous justifications in "The Present Condition of Classical Studies." After Kelsey spoke at Whitman College,[58] he and his wife were on their way home and, on December 22, "passed Lake Forest and other North Shore towns familiar to our earlier life."[59]

Everywhere they went, he and Isabelle remarked on the delights of nature. In San Francisco they enjoyed "a long walk with views of rocks and sea-lions" and "a glorious sunset over the Golden Gate"; at Dunsmuir (northern California) it was the sight of the twin peaks of Mount Shasta, "which stands out, snow covered, with indescribable brilliancy in the glorious sunlight," and where he enjoyed "one of the most inspiring walks I have ever had—all the happier because Isabelle was with me"; in Seattle it was the "superb view over the city, the sound and snow covered Olympic mountains."[60] The sight of Mount Olympos itself, experienced in 1885, will not have been far from his thoughts.

---

turning to Ann Arbor in 1913 as assistant in photography in the Latin Department. He served as assistant professor of Latin from 1820 and as the university's staff photographer from 1913 to 1947.

55. Diary, December 2–4, 1917. He spoke at Claremont, where he and Isabelle were the guests of professor and Mrs. H. E. Robbins; at San Diego, in the First Congregational Church; and to the Friday Morning Club at Los Angeles, after visiting the Southwest Museum. While in Los Angeles, Isabelle took the opportunity to visit her uncle and aunt, Mr. and Mrs. H. F. Badger.

56. Diary, December 6 and 7, 1917. Fairclough, a Canadian and graduate of the University of Toronto, was professor of Latin and department head at Stanford for many years. A longstanding member of the AIA and APA, he had served as associate secretary of the AIA during Kelsey's presidency and had done much to advance the institute's interest. A distinguished Latinist, he may be best known for his translations of Virgil and Horace.

57. Diary, December 12 and 13, 1917.

58. Diary, December 17, 1917.

59. Diary, December 22, 1917.

60. Diary, December 9 and 14, 1917.

As engaged in all aspects of humanistic study and as alert to his environment as Kelsey was, he would clearly be susceptible to the attractions of the Chautauqua Institution. Lake Chautauqua, in northern New York State, lends its name to a cultural, literary, religious, and scientific institution that, in the late nineteenth and early twentieth centuries, in an era when radio was in its infancy and television unheard of, held out to rural populations opportunities for learning and betterment. It continues today as an important center for lifelong learning. At Chautauqua, an annual meeting, which began in 1874, grew over time into a conference lasting about two months that offered opportunities for education, instruction, and the discussion of current topics in almost all branches of learning. It came to attract adherents from all walks of life but appealed in particular to those leading isolated lives in areas where learning was sparse and company infrequent. Such was the popularity of this experiment in the dissemination of knowledge that leading literary and political figures, such as Mark Twain and Theodore Roosevelt, enlisted in the crusade, came to Chautauqua, and took part in lecture and debate. Programs at these gatherings expanded after a while beyond instruction in language, arts and crafts, music, journalism, physical training, and domestic science, as well as the discussion of broad cultural issues, to include performance, theater, mime, dance, and recitation. By 1904 the annual assembly at Chautauqua had spawned numerous itinerant "Circuit Chautauquas": summer schools that traveled about the country as small-scale adaptations of the upstate New York Chautauqua, met in hastily erected canvas tents, and offered entertainments and enlightening programs for about a week before moving on. These experiments in adult education and self-help went some way toward assuaging the thirst for knowledge and the desire for new experiences and improved lives felt, above all, in the rural areas of the country.[61] In giving expression to a pervasive mood of curiosity, inquiry, optimism, growth, and shared values, they echoed the climate of the times.

The meetings were supported by publications; these included the *Chautauquan,* a periodical put out by the Chautauqua Literary and Scientific Circle (the institute's book club) and described as a monthly magazine for self-education, in which articles appeared on topics catering to every imaginable current interest—for example, agriculture ("Farmers' Institutions"), politics ("Cooperation in International Reforms"), literature ("Critical Studies in

---

61. On the value of the Circuit Chautauqua to those living in rural communities, see Charlotte Canning, "The Platform versus the Stage: Circuit Chautauqua's Antitheatrical Theatre," *Theatre Journal* 50.3 (1998): 303–18.

German Literature"), matters of social concern ("The Chautauqua Reading Course for Housewives"), travel ("The Land of Luther"), and history ("Diplomatic Incidents of the Mexican War"). The *Chautauqua Quarterly,* also issued by the institute, published the catalog for the summer schools, listing the various offerings and the names of the leading participants. In 1916 Francis Kelsey was invited to join in "humanistic conferences" discussing how to make the classics and archaeology more accessible to high school and college students and more visible and relevant to the general public: other participants included Frederick Shipley, president of the AIA; John A. Scott,[62] president of the Classical Association of the Midwest and South; Charles E. Bennett,[63] president of the Classical Association of the Atlantic States; Mitchell Carroll, secretary of the AIA; and Professor James Henry Breasted[64] of Chicago.[65]

Leaving Ann Arbor on July 10, Kelsey traveled to Toledo and thence to Westfield and Chautauqua, writing all day in the train and at stations. The next day, he delivered his lecture "St. Peter and St. Paul in Rome" in the evening before an audience of about two thousand. On July 12, after giving a morning talk, "Glimpses of Pompeian Walls," to Mitchell Carroll's class, he went at noon to a lecture by Breasted on prehistoric archaeology. On the evening of July 13, Breasted delivered an illustrated lecture entitled "Our Rediscovered Ancestors by the Nile and the Euphrates," highlights of which—to Kelsey, at any rate—were the examination of new discoveries in an ancient sculptor's studio and a broader discussion of Egyptian art. Kelsey's next (and last) day at Chautauqua was especially busy: after giving his address "The

62. John Adams Scott, who earned his Ph.D. from Johns Hopkins and his LL.D. from Illinois College, taught Greek at Northwestern University for some forty years, beginning in 1897; he would be appointed John C. Shaffer Professor of Greek in 1923. He would also serve as president of the APA during 1918–19.

63. Charles Edwin Bennett (1858–1921) graduated from Brown University (1878) and later studied both at Harvard and in Germany. After teaching in secondary schools (1878–89), he became professor of Latin at the University of Wisconsin–Madison (1889). By 1892 he was at Cornell, eventually becoming Goldwin Smith Professor of Latin. His publications include editions of Tacitus and Cicero and translations of Horace's *Odes* and *Epodes.*

64. Breasted, professor of Egyptology and Oriental history at the University of Chicago, was already a well-known scholar famous for his work on Egyptian hieroglyphics and history and for his books, including *A History of Egypt from the Earliest Times to the Persian Conquest* (New York: Charles Scribner's Sons, 1905) and *Development of Religion and Thought in Ancient Egypt* (New York: Charles Scribner's Sons, 1912). He later became so illustrious and his work so widely appreciated that he appeared on the cover of *Time* magazine in 1931 (December 14).

65. "Summer Schools Catalogues, July 10–August 18," *Chautauqua Quarterly* 16.2 (April 1916).

Classics in School and College" in the morning and presiding at a humanistic conference in the afternoon, he attended a reading of Benjamin Bickley Rogers's translation of Aristophanes's *The Clouds* at 4:45[66] and took the chair at the dinner at the Hotel Athenaeum in the evening. He arrived back in Ann Arbor later in the afternoon of July 15: in the diary, he remarks laconically, "Very hot trip; in fact whole week hot." He goes on to list his expenses.[67]

KELSEY IN ITALY, 1915

The routine of teaching, lectures, and life in Ann Arbor would be altered once again by a trip to Italy, this time not for research but to sort out the affairs of a University of Michigan benefactor, T. S. Jerome. In July 1908, Kelsey had been visited in Ann Arbor by Thomas Spencer Jerome,[68] and in the course of supper with Francis and Isabelle at the Cutting Café, Jerome had spoken of "his desire to leave a trust fund for a lectureship in ancient history, or rather, in the historical field, saying that he would arrange to put the matter into the hands of Mr. Freer and Mr. Mann to arrange in case of his decease."[69] By the terms of his will, Jerome had established an endowment for such a series of lectures, to be given both at the University of Michigan and at the American Academy in Rome, and to be published.[70] Jerome was on good terms with Presidents Angell and Hutchins, who doubtless cleared the way for the establishment of this lectureship (for which Jerome's name is now famous) and encouraged his friendship with Kelsey. It seems that prior to Jerome's death,

---

66. Rogers was a British classicist, born in Somerset and educated at Wadham College, Oxford. A successful barrister, he transferred his professional allegiance to literature and became famous for his translations of all the plays of the Athenian comic playwright Aristophanes, rendered into English verse.

67. Diary July 10–15, 1917. Kelsey lists his expenses as follows: hotel five nights, $6; board four days, $5; typing, $2; railway Ann Arbor–Toledo, $1.14, Toledo–Westfield, $5.82, Westfield–Chautauqua, $0.35, parlor car, $1.15. The entire cost (travel, board, incidentals) was $37.25, against which he received $100 from the Chautauqua Institution.

68. See chapter 4, "The American School of Classical Studies in Rome."

69. Diary, July 29, 1908. Frederick Wharton Mann was, with Freer and Jerome, a member of the exclusive (and, for half a century, exclusively male) Yondotega Club in Detroit, founded in 1892 and known for fine dining and card playing.

70. Jerome set out broad criteria for the lecturers. Themes he mentioned include the circumstances or causes determining the rise or fall of peoples, the application of the biological sciences to the solution of historical problems, aspects of Roman history and historical method, and the relevance of ancient history to modern problems. On the amalgamation of the American School of Architecture in Rome (founded 1894) and the American School of Classical Studies in Rome (founded 1895) to form the American Academy in Rome (in planning from 1911, opened in 1914), see chapter 5, "The Foreign Schools."

only Angell and Kelsey (of those in Ann Arbor) were aware of Jerome's intention to fund this lectureship.[71]

After Jerome's death on Capri on April 12, 1914, Francis was sent a copy of the will[72] and was visited in Ann Arbor on June 23 by William Savidge, an old friend of Jerome's, who, on behalf of the Union Trust Company of Detroit, the executor and trustee of the will, was handling the sections of the will concerning Jerome's manuscripts and the lectureship.[73] Early the following year, he was in Ann Arbor again to tell Kelsey that Jerome's villa on Capri had been sold and to ask him if he could go as soon as possible "to fetch the unfinished manuscript by Jerome and oversee the division of the library according to the will." Together Savidge and Kelsey called on President Hutchins, who, according to Kelsey, agreed to a leave of absence for "the time I preferred (six weeks) though Savidge had said two or three months offering to pay my expenses."[74] These circumstances brought Francis to Italy in the midwinter of 1915.

Thomas Spencer Jerome and Charles Lang Freer

Thomas Spencer Jerome was a rich, academically gifted, rather retiring and bookish member of Detroit's elite, a friend of Charles Freer and other clubmen. His family was well placed politically and socially: his father, David Howell Jerome, was the governor of Michigan from 1881 to 1883; and his mother, Lucy Peck, was a member of a prominent Saginaw family and a leading figure in the town's literary and artistic circles. By the time his father left the governorship of the state, Thomas, born in Saginaw in 1864, was a teenager enjoying undergraduate life at the University of Michigan, from which he graduated in 1884. After pursuing legal studies in Ann Arbor for a further year, he transferred to Harvard, where he took an M.A. degree in 1887. On his return to Detroit, Jerome practiced law and led the leisurely life of a wealthy bachelor, supported by his family with an ample allowance.

It was inevitable that he would cross Charles Freer's path. Despite their different backgrounds—Freer grew up in modest circumstances in Kingston,

---

71. Kelsey to Angell, January 3, 1913, PTSJ, box 1, folder 4, sheet 49: "I suppose you and I are the only persons who know of Mr. Jerome's bequest of a historical lectureship for the University."

72. Diary, June 9, 1914.

73. William Savidge (b. 1863), of Spring Lake (Ottawa County, Michigan) and Detroit, graduated from Michigan the same year as Jerome (1884) and, like Jerome, also attended Harvard University, before becoming a successful lawyer and lumberman. A friend of University of Michigan regent Loyal Edwin Knappen, he served as a Michigan state senator in 1897–98.

74. Diary, January 5, 1915.

New York, and was a self-made millionaire—their intellectual interests, social tastes, and artistic inclinations were similar. Neither was married. It was also inevitable that, sooner or later, Jerome should get to know Francis Kelsey—whose arrival in Michigan all but coincided with Jerome's return from Harvard—especially since Jerome's interests were leaning away from law toward history, particularly Roman.

Neither Freer nor Jerome was in robust health. The neurasthenic Freer, older than Jerome by eight years, had retired entirely from his business activities in 1899 to devote himself and his fortune to the collection of art,[75] and Jerome was plagued throughout his life with stomach disorders. Traveling together in Europe in pursuit of their interests (Jerome's in ancient Rome and Freer's in art), they were captivated by Capri. The island's landscape, its location at the southern extremity of the Bay of Naples, the warmth of its climate, and its cosmopolitan population beguiled them.[76] They decided to acquire a property on the island together, and, as luck would have it, a choice villa came on the market in the summer of 1899.

Built on top of the ancient city wall, the Villa Castello occupied part of one of the high points of Capri, commanding glorious views of the coast, the mountains, and the sea. Incongruous and asymmetrical in plan, the villa benefited from spacious verandas and balconies and a large terraced garden. The garden—traversed by straight walkways, from which narrow paths descending by means of steps meandered this way and that—was planted with dozens of trees, shrubs, and flowers. Climbing plants encircled trellises forming sheltered courtyards and loggias. Recycled fragments of ancient architecture and brickwork evoked the antiquity of the place and the antiquarianism of its owner, another American, Allan McLane Hamilton.[77] During Jerome

---

75. Freer had begun his collection in the 1880s by acquiring paintings of American artists, in particular those of James McNeill Whistler. He then widened his attention to the work of European masters and, as his taste intensified and his connoisseurship ripened, finally to the collection of Asian art. But he was always susceptible to any art, antiquities, or manuscripts that took his imagination, as was the case with his acquisitions in Egypt.

76. On the literary and artistic temper of the island in these years, on its international and sexually adroit inhabitants, and on Jerome, see Carlo Knight, *L'avvocato di Tiberio: La tormentata esistenza e la quasi tragica morte di Thomas Spencer Jerome* (Capri: La conchiglia, 2004), esp. (for letters from Freer to Hecker in this period) 51–58. Knight evidently believes that Freer and Jerome enjoyed a homosexual relationship.

77. Dr. Allan McLane Hamilton, a renowned New York psychiatrist whose patients included the elderly socialite Caroline Webster Schermerhorn Astor, was the author of *The Intimate Life of Alexander Hamilton* (New York: Charles Scribner's Sons, 1910)—a portrait of his paternal grandfather (vii)—and *Recollections of an Alienist* (New York: George H. Doran, 1916), which devotes a chapter to Capri (172–83, with references to Jerome, as "the new tenant," on 174 and 176).

and Freer's visit to the island, he agreed to the sale of the villa, which—after Jerome and Freer returned to Michigan—was finalized, in February 1900, by another American resident on Capri, Charles Caryl Coleman.[78] In April Jerome gave a farewell party in Detroit at which he shocked his guests by announcing his intention to abandon the practice of law in Detroit in favor of life on Capri.[79]

With the help of Michigan's U.S. senator James McMillan,[80] Jerome had contrived to be appointed for the year 1900–1901 as American consular agent in Sorrento (on the coast of the Amalfi [or Sorrentine] Peninsula, a short boat ride from Capri), an office that McMillan persuaded the State Department to transfer to Capri in the following year. Freer joined Jerome at the villa in the late summer of 1900 but was surprised to find that Jerome was not alone: with him was a young and attractive American woman. Henrietta Sophia Rupp (known as Yetta) was officially installed at the villa as the housekeeper, and though the distance between housekeeper and owner was ostensibly maintained, it soon became plain to everyone living on the island that she was Jerome's mistress.[81] This arrangement did not seem at first to trouble Freer, nor does he seem to have guessed at the implications (or worried about them) during a visit in 1901, in the course of which he and Jerome entertained Isabelle Kelsey and Kelsey's brother Fred and his wife, Ella.[82] Freer visited again briefly and peacefully in 1903; but an argument between him and Yetta two years later, perhaps concerning her conduct (more as mistress than

---

78. A distinguished painter of landscapes and portraits, Coleman lived at the Villa Narcissus, scarcely a stone's throw from the Villa Castello.

79. It seems that he was already planning to follow the life of an independent scholar; but that this was uncharacteristic and seemed quixotic may be judged from the surprised reaction of his socialite Detroit friends when they learned later of his intention to write a history of Rome. See *Detroit Tribune*, May 5, 1905.

80. McMillan (1838–1902), who served as U.S. senator from 1889 to 1902, was succeeded in that office by none other than General Alger (1902–7).

81. Given the relaxed approach to sexual matters for which Capri was well known and that had induced many Europeans and Americans to take up residence on the island in the wake of the trial of Oscar Wilde (1895), it seems strange that Jerome should not have introduced her openly on the island. But he did not, and the ambiguity of her position brought considerable tension to the villa. Her dark complexion has led some commentators to speculate that she was of mixed blood, but this suggestion seems contradicted by the discovery that she lived in what was, to all intents and purposes, a segregated white neighborhood when she returned to Detroit after Jerome's death (first on Euclid Avenue, then on Grand Boulevard; Knight, *L'avvocato*, 233 n. 9). Nevertheless, it is possible that there was a social aspect to their reluctance to socialize with other members of the expatriate intelligentsia. Might Yetta have been another reason for Jerome to leave America for Italy?

82. Diary, June 28, 1901.

housekeeper?), led to a break between the two men. This came to a head in 1906 when, after a meeting in London, Jerome bought Freer's share of the villa and became the sole owner. Yetta was to remain at the villa until 1915, the year after Jerome's death.

On Capri Jerome spent his days reading, writing, and thinking about problems in Roman history and historical method. He assembled a large library, cataloging each book as it came in from the booksellers with whom he spent a lot of money.[83] His work oscillated between consideration of the methods of inquiry of different Roman historians; more general themes such as the reliability of evidence, the gullibility of readers, and authors' propensities to lie; and a more precise focus on the reputation of the Roman emperor Tiberius, who also had lived on Capri. The Roman writers Tacitus and Suetonius painted Tiberius's activities on Capri in a nefarious light; there was, they said, hardly a vice he did not practice. Jerome wished to refute this malevolent view of the emperor. As he pursued reports of the emperor's conduct, teased out implications, and explored authors' motives, his voluminous notes on all these topics grew and grew, until the book he had in mind to write broadened into what would have become an extensive treatise on Roman morals. The manuscripts retrieved from Capri by Kelsey in 1915 were finally gathered together by Professor John Winter into a posthumous book, *Aspects of the Study of Roman History*.[84]

Along the way, Jerome published articles, gave a series of lectures at the American School of Classical Studies in Rome on the use of historical method, and traveled to London to deliver a paper at the 1913 International Congress of Historical Studies, at which he represented the University of Michigan.[85] At leisure, he and Yetta profited from the sun and the sea, swimming and sailing in the summer months, but he was often under the weather with gastritis, turning morose and irritable. Bouts of drinking were not un-

---

83. In the two years 1900 and 1901, he spent more than forty-five hundred dollars to acquire two thousand books. Knight (*L'avvocato*, 94) gives a full list.

84. It is noteworthy that, like Kelsey, Jerome stressed the importance of archaeology to historical studies (e.g., *Aspects of the Study of Roman History* [New York: G. P. Putnam's Sons, 1923], 424). Shortly before his death, Jerome also published *Roman Memories in the Landscape Seen from Capri* (London: Mills & Boon, 1914), a memoir combining personal observation with historical and mythological recollections. The book is illustrated with images oddly juxtaposing actual landscapes with reconstructed ancient buildings and mythological creatures, by Morgan Heiskell (b. ca. 1885), an American photographer and artist on Capri and friend of Jerome.

85. Jerome to Kelsey, December 16, 1912, PTSJ, box 1, folder 4, sheets 44–47; Kelsey to Jerome, congratulatory note, May 10, 1913, PTSJ, box 1, folder 1, sheet 33.

known. Isolation from a society that both accepted their eccentricities and caused untold stresses and strains did not help. The raffish flavor of this privileged society may be discerned in a novel published by the celebrated author Compton Mackenzie, himself a resident on the island and an acute observer of its inhabitants and their foibles.[86] At his death in 1914, Jerome left Yetta well provided for, with a trust fund of twenty thousand dollars, five hundred dollars a year to pay for her custodianship of the villa pending its sale, and travel money for her return to the United States; she was also free to choose five hundred (nonclassical) books from his library.[87]

Kelsey in Capri

Two weeks after the meeting with Hutchins, Kelsey received from Savidge a letter of credit for five hundred pounds and Savidge's power of attorney; on the same day, he met Hobart B. Hoyt, vice president of the Union Trust Company, who explained the situation in Capri and gave Francis the company's power of attorney as well.[88] In New York he conferred with George Haven Putnam, president of G. P. Putnam's Sons, about the handling of Jerome's unfinished manuscript and with Cyrus McCormick about the AIA's proposed school in China, and he attended a performance of Massenet's *Manon* at the Metropolitan Opera. The following two days give further evidence of his determination never to lose a moment. After retrieving his luggage, checked direct from Ann Arbor to the White Star wharf, he had it loaded on board the SS *Canopic*,[89] bought "a heavy Scotch rug for $6.75 'Special Sale,' regular price

---

86. Compton Mackenzie, *Vestal Fire* (London: Cassell; New York: George H. Doran, 1927); Jerome is easily recognized in the recondite scholar Scudamore (93, 134, 144, 295, etc.). During his visit, Kelsey called on Mackenzie and was told by the eminent author that he wrote fifteen hundred words a day (diary, February 24, 1915). Mackenzie maintained a residence on Capri for much of the period 1913–20 but saw action at the battle of Gallipoli in 1915 and served as head of British intelligence in Athens and the Cyclades for much of the remainder of World War I. He tried to recruit David Hogarth (see chapter 5) for work in Greece, but Hogarth opted for the Arab Bureau in Cairo, in whose (not-so-clandestine) activities one of his protégés in the excavations at Carchemish, T. E. Lawrence (Lawrence of Arabia), was to play a prominent role.

87. For more on Jerome, see Elaine K. Gazda, ed., *In Pursuit of Antiquity: Thomas Spencer Jerome and the Bay of Naples (1899–1914)* (Ann Arbor: Kelsey Museum of Archaeology, 1983), a concise and informative booklet prepared in connection with the exhibition of the same name.

88. Diary, January 19, 1915.

89. He thought his steamship ticket of ninety-five dollars plus five dollars tax exorbitant.

$10" at the London Leather Store on Fifth Avenue, took drawings to be pre-
pared for publication to the National Photo Engraving Company, attended a
matinee performance of *Fidelio* at the Met, and conferred with other trustees
of the American Academy in Rome in the evening at the Century Club, before
taking the 1:00 a.m. train to Boston.[90] Arriving in Boston, he established himself at the Brunswick Hotel, where Carl Bacon and John Allyn brought him
proofs of the next *Caesar* edition. The SS *Canopic* arrived from New York
about noon, to sail from Boston at four o'clock, Kelsey aboard. In the ship's
mail, Francis found to his great delight the gift of a book from his Horace
class in Ann Arbor. The excitement of the activity of these days comes flying
off the diary's pages.

Francis occupied himself profitably enough during the voyage, reading
through the proofs of his *Caesar*. After arriving in Naples on February 13, he
crossed two days later to Capri, where he immediately bumped into Morgan
Heiskell[91] on the street and later met the new owners of the Villa Castello,
Mrs. Alice Tweed Andrews and her daughter Edith. In the course of the next
few days, he visited the villa, finding much to disturb him. With Heiskell he
called on Yetta, who was living in a small house nearby, and met Dr. Camillo
Feo, a Neapolitan doctor, with whom Yetta was in difficulties and for whom
Kelsey came to have a low regard.[92] The situation at the villa was worse than
he expected: damage had been done to the interior, and furnishings had vanished; there were mountains of documents and some evidence of the burning
of papers. The minute news of his arrival circulated, swarms of people appeared claiming to be creditors.

Moreover, there was a legal problem concerning the sale of the property.
The sale had been ratified in the United States—Mrs. Andrews's money had
been transferred to the Union Trust in Detroit, and she had the keys in her
possession. But in Italy the estate was not free of obligations, which should
have been discharged prior to the signing of the contract. The debts seemed
genuine, but Francis was unable to consult all the relevant papers, which were
divided among six people: Mrs. Andrews, Morgan Heiskell, and four attorneys—two of whom were not on speaking terms and another of whom
would not let Francis see the papers he claimed to have. Francis worked
twelve-hour days, gradually making progress in the matter of the estate. To

---

90. Diary, January 30, 1915.
91. On Heiskell, see n. 84 above.
92. Diary, February 15–18, 1915.

complicate matters further, he found Feo intransigent, reporting "conferences seeming without end" and that he made an "attempt to arrange compromise with Dr. Feo, but failed."[93] Between meetings, he endeavored to put Jerome's papers and manuscripts in some kind of order. Finding it necessary to confer directly with Mrs. Andrews's attorney, Raffaele Acquaviva, in Naples, he crossed to the mainland to meet with him, Roberto Serena (attorney for the Jerome estate), and Miss Andrews for long, tedious sessions. He found Miss Andrews sympathetic, however, and spent an evening with her at the "theater of Sannazaro 'La Resa di Berg-op-Zoom' a four act comedy by Sacha Guitry, most entertaining."[94]

By the terms of Jerome's will, his three-thousand-volume library was to be divided between the University of Michigan and the American Academy in Rome. So, after spending a few days in Naples—in the course of which he called on the American consul, hired a stenographer to type up Jerome's manuscripts, and arranged with the American Express manager for the shipment of the books—Francis went to Rome, "taking a card catalogue of Mr. Jerome's library made by Miss Andrews when her mother took possession of Villa Castello": "Delivered the cards to A. W. Van Buren at the American Academy asking him to select out all dupes of titles in the Academy library, and took up with Carter the matter of the accounts."[95] For the next week, he worked on the academy's accounts, called on Ambassador Thomas Nelson Page (his onetime rival for the position) with Carter, and cabled back to New York the results of his scrutiny of the academy's accounts. With funds from the bank and certificates of government stock with which to meet the Jerome estate's outstanding debts, he returned to Capri accompanied by Van Buren and began the division and packing of books.

Yetta's health was cause for concern. On March 14, she suffered what the diary described as a "brainstorm," and elsewhere Kelsey expresses the opinion

---

93. Diary, February 20, 1915.

94. Diary, February 27, 1915. Kelsey wrote at length to Savidge and Hoyt in Michigan about the plethora of problems he encountered during his first fortnight on the island (Kelsey to Savidge, March 1, 1915, PTSJ, box 3, folder 3, sheets 5–22). The play was an Italian translation of Guitry's *La prise de Berg-op-Zoom* (The Surrender of Berg[en]-op-Zoom), which had premiered in October 1912 at the Théâtre de Vaudeville, Paris, and ran in English translation at London's Garrick in 1913 as *The Real Thing*.

95. Diary, March 3, 1915. An American archaeologist, epigrapher, and historian, Van Buren was a longtime resident of Rome and the American Academy's librarian. Jesse Benedict Carter was director of the academy during 1913–17.

that she suffered from mental confusion, a kind of hysteria[96] resulting in un-predictable behavior and temper tantrums that, however, he did not think a medical board would consider insanity.[97] There were stories that she began giving away items of furniture after Jerome's death and that she continued to allow the removal of fixtures even after the villa's sale was agreed; certainly furniture and fixtures were missing, and walls were damaged. Consequently, Kelsey was glad to be able to arrange passage home for her on the SS *Finland*, due in Naples on March 21. She left Capri, "bag and baggage," two days before its expected arrival, and "relief that she was no longer on the island was expe-rienced by many persons."[98]

Work continued on the books and manuscripts, Van Buren and carpen-ters packing up the books, Kelsey and Heiskell organizing the manuscript into chapters. Finally, on March 24, thirty-five cases of books (seventeen for the University of Michigan, eighteen for the American Academy) were ma-neuvered down to the marina and thence to Naples. In Naples Kelsey dis-cussed with Mrs. and Miss Andrews a settlement of the damage to the villa. They agreed "to leave it all in my hands since the amount was so large I felt I ought to have special authorization from Yetta before making payment."[99] The SS *Finland* belatedly came in on March 25. In the pouring rain, Kelsey ushered Yetta on board. The bill for her freight was settled there and then. She was gone.

Francis spent the next week in Naples, working for five consecutive days on Jerome's papers, setting them in order while Miss Steinman, the stenogra-pher, began to type them up. He settled the matter of the damages at the villa with Miss Andrews and, at a meeting with Acquaviva, Serena, and Miss An-drews, agreed to a provisional final settlement of the estate papers. Cables were dispatched to Savidge in Spring Lake and to Hoyt in Detroit. In the evenings, if fine, he went for walks, sometimes with the American consul, Mr.

---

96. Even when she visited Ann Arbor later in the year, she seemed unbalanced: "Yetta's condition about as bad as it was in Capri" (diary, November 19, 1915). She was evidently living in Detroit at the time (see n. 81), but what happened to her thereafter remains unclear. A Hen-rietta Sophia Rupp was buried on April 18, 1944, in the columbarium at Oakland's Mountain View Cemetery in Alameda County, California. Is this she?

97. Knight, *L'avvocato*, 218; Kelsey to Savidge and Hoyt, March 1, 1915, PTSJ, box 3, folder 3, sheets 8–9. Others were less critical: Gale to Kelsey, PTSJ, box 3, folder 22, sheet 8. Thomas B. Gale, chairman of the American Relief Committee in Naples, vouched for her good sense and rational conduct.

98. Diary, March 19, 1915.

99. Diary, March 24, 1915.

Jay White, or to the theater.[100] Before going to Rome on April 4, he sent the typed chapters of Jerome's work to G. H. Putnam in New York and arranged for the balance of Jerome's account at the Credito Italiano to be sent to Rome: there was just time for a brief visit to his beloved Pompeii. In Rome he worked through the Jerome accounts, wrote up a report of his activities, had it typed in four copies, and sent it to Savidge and Hoyt.

Not neglecting his own scholarly pursuits, he called on foreign scholars of his acquaintance.[101] But the wishes of his fellow trustees also obliged him to spend two days in long conferences at the American Academy. The first problem was the condition of some of the academy accounts; the second, friction between Carter and other members of the staff. The reader senses the weariness in his comment to his diary: "favorable outcome but extended and painful discussion."[102] Two days later, however, with Carter and Stevens[103] still at loggerheads, Francis could do no more. On April 10, he made his farewells at the bank to Mr. Sebasti, "whose courtesy I much appreciated," and the next day, in heavy rain, he took the train for Naples, boarded the SS *Canopic,* and cabled Isabelle. In the evening, he "stayed up late at night watching the lights of the receding shore and the increasing lights of Capri as we swept by in the darkness. The weather was wet and raw."[104] Though doubtless exhausted, he had the satisfaction of a job well done and the prospect of the addition of fifteen hundred important books for the Michigan library.

Kelsey spent the twelve-day voyage from Naples to Boston working on his reports and the *Caesar* proofs. On arrival, he did not waste a minute: he conferred with his publishers about the *Caesar* edition and, in New York, attended meetings at the American Academy offices; he visited his relatives in Massachusetts and New Jersey; he arranged payment for the drawings of the Morgan jewelry for Dennison and took drawings of the Freer jewelry to the

---

100. He went to the Teatro Bellini for *Finalmente Soli,* a two-act comedy by Ivano Montano, which he described as "highly amusing"; and to the San Carlo for the opera *Le Donne Curiose,* by Ermanno Wolf-Ferrari (diary, March 26 and 31, 1915).

101. One day he had tea with Walther Amelung, the German scholar long associated with the Deutsches Archäologisches Institut in Rome and the Vatican collections; on another he walked around the Palatine with Giacomo Boni, the Italian excavator of the Roman Forum; and on another he visited Thomas Ashby, director of the British School at Rome, in the school's quarters in the Odescalchi Palace (diary, April 5, 6, and 10, 1915).

102. Diary, April 7, 1915.

103. Gorham P. Stevens was director of the School of Fine Arts at the time and subsequently director of the American Academy overall.

104. Diary, April 11, 1915.

National Photo Engraving Company.[105] He discussed the revision (a third edition) of Mau's *Pompeii* at the Macmillan Company[106] and took up with G. H. Putnam the publication of Jerome's material: "he suggested a limit of 100,000 words. I advised rather a limit of 125,000–140,000 which he seems disposed to accept."[107] When he arrived in Ann Arbor, so, by chance, did the seventeen cases of books sent from Naples.

This episode figures prominently in Kelsey's diary, but neither Jerome's gift of his library nor his own work are as well known as the lectureship that bears his name. It took time for the funds to accumulate sufficiently for the endowment to become operative, and Kelsey did not live to see the first lectures delivered in 1929–30 by his colleague John G. Winter, the scholar who brought the Jerome papers to publication under his aegis. From that day to this, the Thomas Spencer Jerome lectureship has continued to attract some of the most distinguished historians.

THE UNIVERSITY OF MICHIGAN

Faculty and Students

Kelsey's work on Capri placed him in a Europe embroiled in a conflict that directly engaged the United States only in April 1917. Yet the entry of the United States into World War I had an obvious and immediate impact on the university. The number of students enrolled fell from 7,517 (1916) to 6,057 (1917), a number further eroded when four hundred students left for the war in early fall.[108] High school enrollments had continued to rise, but at college level, the declining numbers meant smaller classes. At Michigan the Department of Latin was not immune.

Nonetheless, the faculty was not reduced and had been cheered by recent appointments: Arthur Boak had been appointed to teach ancient Greek and

---

105. See chapter 6, "Editing," "The Freer Manuscripts," and "The Morgan Manuscripts," The jewelry items owned by Mr. Morgan and the item owned by Mr. Freer came from the same hoard and were published together, in Walter Dennison, *A Gold Treasure of the Late Roman Period*, University of Michigan Studies, Humanistic Series, vol. 12, pt. 2 (New York: Macmillan, 1918).

106. Diary, February 11, 1914.

107. Diary, April 27, 1915.

108. Howard H. Peckham, *The Making of the University of Michigan, 1817–1992*, ed. Margaret L. Steneck and Nicholas H. Steneck (Ann Arbor: University of Michigan, Bentley Historical Library, 1994), 144.

Roman history in 1914,[109] the same year Leroy Waterman, a prime mover in Near Eastern archaeological work, joined the faculty as professor of Semitic studies. The following year, William Warner Bishop came from the Library of Congress—where he had been superintendent of the Reading Room—to be the university librarian. Soon after his arrival, he presided over an ingenious and large-scale extension of the University Library, aided by the architect Albert Kahn. Throughout his tenure, Bishop worked determinedly to expand the library's holdings and cooperated closely with Kelsey in the acquisition of many manuscripts and papyri.[110]

The academic calendar continued in its familiar pattern: courses taught, examinations taken, faculty meetings, and commencement exercises. Visitors came and went, some as learned as Théodore Reinach[111] or as scholarly as Henri Hyvernat.[112] The Michigan Classical Conference met every year in conjunction with the Michigan Schoolmasters Club in early spring, enlivened now not only by visiting speakers—one year Princeton's Andrew F. West,[113] another Johns Hopkins University's Ralph Van Deman Magoffin[114]—but also

---

109. Arthur Edward Romilly Boak was to become author of several volumes in the Michigan Humanistic Series and a significant participant in Kelsey's archaeological exploration of the site at Karanis in Egypt.

110. A product of Detroit High School and graduate of the University of Michigan (A.M. 1892), Bishop corresponded with Kelsey at length during 1892–93, lamenting Kelsey's absence in Europe. A fellow of the American School of Classical Studies in Rome in 1898–99, he taught and was a part-time librarian at Brooklyn Polytechnic before finding employment in the Princeton University Library. From there he moved to the Library of Congress in 1907. On architect Albert Kahn, see chapter 6 n. 30.

111. A famous French editor, archaeologist, numismatist, and historian, Reinach spoke on the contributions of France, through excavation, to the advancement of the study of Greek art (diary, November 27, 1918).

112. Hyvernat (see chapter 6 n. 70) was attentively feted at a dinner party at the Kelseys, at which other guests included the Bishops, the Crittendens, and the Winters, followed by a luncheon the next day at the Michigan Union, with President Hutchins and Deans John Robert Effinger (Literary College) and Alfred Henry Lloyd (Graduate School) all present (diary, October 22 and 23, 1917).

113. Among his other accomplishments (see chapter 5 n. 6), Andrew Fleming West was the principal founder of the American Classical League (1919).

114. An undergraduate at Michigan and a graduate student at Johns Hopkins, Magoffin (1874–1942), the nephew of archaeologist Esther Boise Van Deman (see chapter 6 n. 43), had been a fellow at the American School of Classical Studies in Rome in 1907. A faculty member first at Johns Hopkins and then at New York University (from 1923), he served as president of the AIA during 1921–31. Fully in the Kelsey tradition, he was a firm believer in expanding the membership to the interested public and in the value of *Art and Archaeology;* as such, he came under searching criticism from the Eastern elite.

by student performance of a Greek or Latin play. Big lunches at the Michigan Union were always a feature of these gatherings, as was the entertainment provided at the Kelsey home. Typical was the meeting of the state teachers association in Ann Arbor in the fall of 1913, when 130 attended a classical roundtable for which Kelsey (with the help of others) prepared much-admired exhibits on late classical books, biblical manuscripts, Greek inscriptions, Latin inscriptions, and ancient lamps, all from the Michigan collections.[115]

The Classical Club met regularly to hear reports from students or faculty: for example, President Emeritus Angell's report on his experiences in Italy or Francis Kelsey's presentation "Constellations and Landscapes in Vergil and Horace."[116] Not a term passed that Kelsey did not invite students and faculty to his house for refreshment and talks—to hear, for example, Henry Sanders speak on the Mithraeum underneath the Baths of Caracalla or, on other occasions, just for conversation and refreshment.[117] He was not alone in welcoming students: Albert Crittenden and his wife frequently held receptions for the undergraduates.[118]

Francis was constantly alert to the welfare of Crittenden and Sanders as faculty members at the heart of the Department of Latin. He worked side by side with Sanders in publishing the volumes of the Humanistic Series, persistently urged the regents to improve Sanders's salary, introduced him to the University Research Club, and gave a dinner for him at the Union on the eve of his departure for Europe in 1913[119] to pursue further research on the Freer manuscripts in Paris and Rome and to discover more about the precise provenance of the manuscripts in Egypt.[120] If Sanders represented the research excellence of the department, Crittenden spoke for its commitment to undergraduates. Keenly engaged in problems of pedagogy, he kept in touch with the Latin teachers in the state (many trained by him), sustaining close ties between the university and the high schools. He and his wife, Lisla,[121]

---

115. Diary, October 31, 1913.

116. Diary, March 7, 1913, and January 11, 1917.

117. Diary, October 18, 1913, and August 18, 1916 (for the summer school).

118. Kelsey's diary mentions one day for freshmen and the next for upperclassmen on December 7 and 8, 1915, as well as a reception for freshmen attended by Francis, Isabelle, Ruth, and Charlotte on November 14, 1916.

119. The dinner was a gala affair. There were fourteen guests, who included Presidents Angell and Hutchins, Deans Effinger and Karl E. Guthe (Graduate School), librarian Theodore Wesley Koch, and all the members of the Department of Latin.

120. In a letter to Freer on March 11, 1913 (KMA Papers, box 67, folder 7), Sanders describes his visit with Worrell to the site of Dimay—explored in 1896 by Bernard Grenfell—and his doubts that the manuscripts came from the site.

121. Their wedding is mentioned in chapter 4, "The American School of Classical Studies in Rome."

were longtime residents of Ann Arbor and were deeply rooted in the town; but their lives were not without heartbreak. On a cold January morning in 1913, Francis Kelsey was at the railroad station at 6:00 a.m. awaiting the arrival of Crittenden "with the caskets of the two young children," offering support in a comfortless moment. He was also at the burial in Forest Hill Cemetery at 3:00 that afternoon, "two little caskets in one grave."[122]

Despite his frequent absences from campus, Kelsey kept up a full teaching load, often anticipating or making up missed classes in the evenings or on Saturdays, when he occasionally would double classes up. He seems to have favored author-based courses (on Cicero, Lucretius, Ovid, Juvenal, Persius)— always taught in a cultural and historical context, alongside courses in coins, inscriptions, and artifacts. He was especially pleased by the courses he taught in summer school in 1916.[123] He covered classes for other faculty in their absence, did his share of directing and examining doctoral candidates, and even arranged extra makeup work for students preparing to enter the university.[124]

Fund-Raising and Acquisitions

Francis continued his fund-raising activities, seeking help primarily for students, for the School of Music, and for publications. For student support, he carefully nursed the department's connection with the Buhl family, which, after the death of Theodore Buhl in 1907, generously kept up its annual fellowship grant. He did not hesitate to approach others in Detroit: Fred Alger, John R. Russel, Philip McMillan, and William H. Murphy,[125] among others. Many were Michigan graduates whom he had come to know either through their association with the university, their enthusiasm for the University Musical

122. Diary, January 8, 1913. The headstone, legible today, reads on the front "CRITTEN-DEN," on the top "James Albert" followed by "May 7, 1910–December 20, 1912" and "Alice Elizabeth" followed by "August 18, 1911–December 24, 1912." Happily, three other children survived: Charles, Edward, and Faith.

123. He wrote in his diary, "Last session of class on coins and inscriptions—best class in these subjects I have had" (August 19, 1916); "Most satisfactory summer work I have yet had—perhaps the highest average ability in any class of graduate students; 9 men and 3 women completed the course in the *Fasti*" (August 23, 1916).

124. The sons of Mr. and Mrs. Abner Larned, Bradford and Cortland, whose preparation Francis supervised personally, offer a good example (diary, May 30 and June 7, 1918). Abner Larned was a member of an old established Michigan family initially involved in the lumber business. A successful businessman in his own right, Larned served as president of the Detroit Board of Commerce, was prominent in the activities of the YMCA and the Michigan Humane Society, and was one of the founders of the Detroit Athletic Club.

125. These four had been among the funders of Kelsey's edited volume *Latin and Greek in American Education* (1911). John Ross Russel (1857–1932), a Michigan graduate (B.A. 1879,

Society and the May Festival, their membership in the Presbyterian Church, or his business involvements. That he was gregarious, courteous, knowledgeable about Europe, enjoyed conversation, and was an affable host smoothed the way.

He visited Detroit three or four times a month, following a regular, predictable pattern. He took an early "electric," or train, into the city. After a prearranged meeting, he would drop by the offices of one or two potential donors, who were sometimes in and sometimes not. He would have lunch with one or more of them, always turning the conversation to the university's needs. Sometimes he would persuade President Hutchins to accompany him. On June 30, 1914, for instance, he went with Hutchins to ask William Murphy for funds to help publish two volumes of the Humanistic Series and for the preparation of an atlas to accompany his *Caesar,* a total of one thousand dollars a year for five years. After Kelsey's presentation of the facts in Hutchins's numinous presence, Murphy agreed.[126]

Two years later, Kelsey approached Murphy again for help on his project concerning Caesar's battlefields in France and elsewhere—a project he was already planning for after the war. His shopping list also included a subsidy for the publication of some of Professor Stanley's music and—a fearless request—funds for a new building for the School of Music.[127] Leaving Murphy pondering, he called at Frederick Kimball Stearns's office, where, in Stearns's absence, he found his secretary, a Miss Anna Francis, with whom he broached the question of funding the publication of a catalog of the Stearns Collection, adding an invitation to see it.[128] When she arrived at Hill Auditorium to in-

---

M.D. 1882), was a vice president and a director of Russel Wheel and Foundry Company and vice president of Great Lakes Engineering Works (see also n. 205 below). Philip Hamilton McMillan (1872–1919) was the third son of Senator James McMillan, for whom the university's McMillan Hall was named. After Yale (1894) and Harvard (LL.B. 1897), he initially practiced law in New York, returning to Detroit in 1899 as a partner at Wells, Angell, Boynton, and McMillan. Lumber baron William H. Murphy (1855–1929) financed the short-lived Detroit Automobile Company (whose chief engineer was Henry Ford), organized the Murphy Power and Liberty Motor companies, and helped underwrite the Detroit Institute of Arts and Detroit Symphony Orchestra.

126. Diary, June 30, 1914.

127. Murphy had been an amateur musician, joining the Detroit Musical Society in 1873 (as second violin) while in high school, as well as the orchestra and Men's Glee Club of the University of Michigan (though he left for Boston after two years). Given his support of the Detroit Symphony Orchestra (to which he contributed a pipe organ), Murphy might have seemed to Kelsey an excellent fit for music-related philanthropy. See J. Bell Moran, *The Moran Family: 200 Years in Detroit* (Detroit: Alved, 1949), 78.

128. Diary, March 11, 1916. The idea of a catalog had been broached with Stearns back in 1903; see chapter 4, "Community Involvement."

spect the collection, he proposed a program of repair of the instruments as well as the catalog (three volumes, four hundred pages apiece), including photographs, drawings, engravings, plates, and so on: "say 1200 pages at $12 a page, prefer $250 per month for five years."[129] But Stearns himself remained elusive.

He continued to pursue Murphy, again accompanied by President Hutchins, about a building for the School of Music (Murphy said he was "interested") and approached Charles B. Warren about the need of five thousand dollars a year for three years for the Humanistic Series:[130] "He suggested 100 subscribers at $50 each for three years and offered to send out a letter asking for the subscriptions if we would furnish the data. President Hutchins agreed to write him a letter."[131] Kelsey was indefatigable in these pursuits and, though often turned away, never defeated; over time, he raised enormous sums of money.

As to acquisitions, World War I obviously put a damper on travel and research. And the sinking of the RMS *Lusitania*, torpedoed by a German submarine in May 1915 with catastrophic loss of passenger life,[132] exacerbated difficulties. Consequent disruption of shipping did nothing to encourage American researchers looking to acquire ancient artifacts in Europe. But Kelsey's mind was already turning to different objectives—the acquisition and study of manuscripts and the opportunities that fieldwork might offer both for research and for the acquisition of materials. These thoughts culminated in the university's accession of countless papyrus manuscripts—among which a letter written by a soldier to his mother is of particular human interest (see figs. 16 and 17)—and to an ambitious program of excavation that would carry Michigan archaeologists to Turkey, Tunisia, and Egypt.[133]

In the latter part of the nineteenth century, Egyptian farmers digging for fertilizer in the houses and rubbish dumps of ancient settlements in the Fayoum, a fertile area in the Egyptian Western Desert some forty miles southwest

---

129. Diary, March 18, 1916. The catalog was finally published in 1918; see chapter 4 n. 107.

130. Charles Beecher Warren, attorney and businessman, served as a colonel in the U.S. Army in 1916 and subsequently as U.S. ambassador to Japan (1921–22) and Mexico (1924).

131. Diary, December 5, 1916.

132. This attack significantly turned American public opinion against Germany. Among passengers who lost their lives was the niece of Robert Franks, Andrew Carnegie's confidential financial adviser (see chapter 5 n. 10).

133. By the time of the armistice at the end of World War I, Kelsey was already planning an expedition in Asia Minor and had approached Abner Larned about the possibility of support (diary, December 7 and 8, 1918). For more on the soldier's letter, see chapter 10.

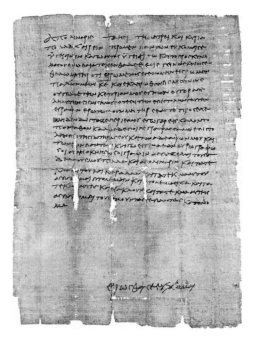

Apollinarius to Taesis, his mother and lady, many greetings. Before all else I pray for your health. I myself am well, and I make obeisance on your behalf before the gods of this place. I wish you to know, mother, that I arrived in Rome in good health on the 25th of the month Pachon and was assigned to Misenum. But I have not yet learned my century, for I had not gone to Misenum when I wrote you this letter. I beg you then, mother, take care of yourself, and do not worry about me, for I have come into a fine place. Please write to me about your welfare and that of my brothers and all your kinsfolk. And for my part, if I find someone <to carry the letters>, I will write to you; I will not delay to write to you. I salute my brothers often, and Apollinarius and his children, and Karalas and his children. I salute Ptolemaios, and Ptolemais and her children, and Heraklous and her children. I salute all your friends, each by name. I pray for your health.

(Verso) Deliver to Karanis, to Taesis, from Apollinarius, her son, of Misenum.

16. Private letter on papyrus from Apollinarius to his mother, Taesis, at Karanis, second century AD, found at Karanis. P. Mich. inv. 4528, Papyrus Collection, Hatcher Graduate Library, University of Michigan.

17. Translation of the papyrus letter in figure 16 (P. Mich. inv. 4528).

of Cairo, discovered scraps of inscribed papyrus stalk (sliced into strips and flattened), which they then sold to dealers, who in turn passed them on to museums and collectors. Much of the writing on these seemingly worthless scraps of papyrus proved to contain invaluable information about the social history of Greco-Roman Egypt (documentary papyri), while some preserved lines of the work of early Greek authors (literary papyri). The publication of the first of these papyri in the 1890s had made them desirable acquisitions, and the supply very shortly became scarce. This dearth prompted two Oxford scholars, Bernard Grenfell and Arthur Hunt, to think of retrieving papyri through direct excavation rather than through dealers in Cairo. The success of their work at Oxyrhynchus, where they found about half a million papyri in six seasons of excavation up to 1907, had reverberated around the academic world, not least among those interested in documents written in Greek, Latin,

Coptic, Demotic Egyptian, or Arabic.[134] The importance of this research was not lost on Francis Kelsey.

His work for the AIA, his research projects and teaching, and then World War I all effectively curtailed new initiatives. Yet his interest in manuscripts and papyri (papyrus manuscripts) had been roused by Charles Freer's acquisitions in 1906, and in 1909 he had been approached by the Egyptian dealer Nahman.[135] When, in later years, he began the systematic acquisition of manuscripts and papyri, he bought them from dealers, privately and through a collaborative venture with the British Museum and other universities. Subsequently, he began the Michigan excavations at the site of Karanis, one of the objectives (following the example of Grenfell and Hunt) being the recovery of papyri.

To purchase papyri, he worked through an American who lived in the Fayoum, Dr. David Askren. In 1920 Kelsey recollected his first meeting with Askren.

> By pure accident on the way over I overheard a gentleman make reference to the Fayoum in such a way that I inferred that he knew the region in which the Freer Greek Manuscripts and Morgan Coptic Manuscripts are said to have been discovered. This gentleman proved to be Dr. David L. Askren, a missionary physician and surgeon, living at the capital of the Fayoum, and I found that among his patients were the fellaheen who handled the Morgan Manuscripts. He had acquaintance also among the fellaheen who were proposing to excavate for fertilizer on the ancient site of Dimay where the Freer manuscripts were said by Ali Arabi, with solemn assurance to Mr. Freer, to have been found. He said he would most gladly do anything possible to assist in solving the problem of the place of discovery of these mss, and would keep close watch for us in case any others were discovered.[136]

---

134. The papyri, packed in about seven hundred boxes, were dispatched to England in biscuit tins. See P. J. Parsons, *City of the Sharp-Nosed Fish* (London: Weidenfeld and Nicolson, 2007), 17; J. Soskice, *The Sisters of Sinai: How Two Lady Adventurers Discovered the Hidden Gospels* (New York: Alfred Knopf, 2009), 262; Bernard P. Grenfell and Arthur S. Hunt, eds. and trans., *The Oxyrhynchus Papyri*, 17 vols. (London: Egypt Exploration Fund, 1898–1922), of which the first thirteen volumes are by the two together, the last four by Hunt alone. The publication of the papyri from this site continues, with no fewer than seventy-two volumes in print as of 2009.

135. Maurice Nahman (d. 1948) was a banking official in Cairo and (on the side) a leading antiquities dealer. Kelsey was introduced to him by Freer.

136. Kelsey to Hecker, March 15, 1920, KMA Papers, box 15, folder 14. On the Morgan and Freer manuscripts, see chapter 6.

Since this letter suggests that Francis simply introduced himself to Askren, the incident reveals, once again, his readiness to seize opportunities. It is clear that their conversations continued and that Francis asked Askren to acquire papyri for Michigan. The day after the ship passed Gibraltar, Francis described the gist of an agreement between them: that Askren would keep manuscripts or well-preserved papyri until "we have an opportunity to examine a photograph or sample page or section. In case a mss of value is recovered I agree to come or send for it and to reimburse you." He went on, "My interest in all this is purely scientific having as its aim the advancement of learning, particularly in America; any mss of value you may be instrumental in recovering will be suitably published under American auspices and have permanent place in some library where they will be available for study."[137] Thus began, aboard a transatlantic steamer, a friendship that contributed significantly to the papyrological collection at Michigan, still regarded as among the best in the Western Hemisphere.

In 1916 J. P. Morgan and Charles Freer bought from Nahman a batch of Coptic manuscripts and a papyrus book in Greek later discovered to be a book of the Minor Prophets. Morgan took the Coptic materials, Freer the Greek. Since any means of moving these acquisitions was risky in the middle of the war, they were given to the American consul in Cairo for safekeeping; sealed in a large tin box, the manuscripts were placed in a safe-deposit vault in the National Bank of Egypt. Smaller batches of papyri were also coming to light in the hands of the fellaheen and making their way to Askren or Nahman, who informed Kelsey. When Kelsey phoned Freer to ask about Nahman's reliability, Freer said that "Nahman is a banker in Cairo, dealing in antiquities as a side line" and "that he is responsible and if we should remit him under an agreement we could rely on him keeping the agreement."[138] Francis's knowledge of the network of Cairo's dealers and their workings was growing.

Research and Publication

During this period, Kelsey undertook a major overhaul of his Caesar text, inspired partially by his own and contemporaries' interest in comparison

---

137. Kelsey to Askren, aboard *SS Canopic,* February 11, 1915, KMA Papers, box 1, folder 8.
138. Diary, April 10, 1916.

between Caesar's maneuvers and those of the ongoing world war.[139] A new introduction, new notes, new illustrations, new maps, and new commentaries were highlights, and the process of passing galleys and proofs back and forth to his publisher was long and complex. The result was essentially an entirely new book: *C. Iulii Caesaris, Commentarii Rerum Gestarum; Caesar's Commentaries: The "Gallic War," Books I–IV, with selections from Books V–VII and from the "Civil War"* appeared in 1918. Over eight hundred pages in length, it testified to the enduring appeal of Caesar in American classrooms, to Kelsey's absorption in Caesar's life and times, and to his commitment to improving the teaching of Latin. As the demands of writing and supervising the preparation of the illustrations for *Caesar's Commentaries* diminished, Kelsey found time to publish a couple of articles for *Art and Archaeology*,[140] but his other great scholarly preoccupation in these years was the Humanistic Series.

In 1912 President Hutchins had asked Kelsey to succeed Martin D'Ooge as chair of the committee "in charge of Michigan Studies." During the academic year 1911–12, however, the regents had established a Graduate School, distinct from the Literary Department, with the physicist Karl E. Guthe as its first dean. There was at once the possibility of differences of opinion between the publishing arm of the university (Michigan Studies) and the new Graduate School, with its emphasis on graduate and faculty research and publication. Faced with "friction in the committee on Humanistic Studies," Kelsey consulted President Emeritus Angell about the best course of action.[141] Shortly afterward, Kelsey attended a meeting of the regents' executive committee to show them Sanders's *The New Testament Manuscripts in the Freer Collection* in proof, with plates of manuscript pages in facsimile (thus demonstrating the success of the Humanistic Series), and to request funding for a visit to the East Coast to arrange the engraving and printing of no fewer than four further volumes of the series that were at that moment in progress.[142] The request was granted. Five days later, Kelsey was careful to invite Hutchins, An-

139. See, e.g., Arthur L. Keith, "Two Wars in Gaul," *Classical Weekly* 8.6 (November 14, 1914): 42–43; Roland G. Kent, "The Military Tactics of Caesar and of To-day," *Classical Weekly* 8.9 (December 12, 1914): 69–70; B. L. Ullman, "German Trenches on a Roman Battlefield," *Classical Weekly* 9.19 (March 11, 1916): 152.

140. "The New Humanism," *Art and Archaeology* 7.1–2 (1918): 14–29; "The Tomb of Virgil," *Art and Archaeology* 7.9 (1918): 265–71.

141. Diary, January 14, 1913.

142. Diary, February 4, 1913.

gell, and Guthe, as well as members of the Department of Latin and a handful of others, to the farewell dinner he gave for Henry Sanders at the Union.

On June 5, the Michigan Studies committee met in the president's office.
"All went smoothly," and the committee approved the publication of volume
5 of the series. So Kelsey was unprepared for the University Senate's decision
shortly thereafter that "the handling of the Humanistic Series of the Studies
be left to the Executive Board of the Graduate Department in place of the
present Committee."[143] The motion had been put, at the request of President
Hutchins, by Professor Isaac Demmon, about whom Charlotte comments
somewhat caustically in her memoir.[144] This transparent territorial maneuver, behind which one might detect Guthe's hand, resulted in a "very unsatisfactory" meeting of the Graduate Department's executive board a month
later.[145] The tensions were not relieved until, at a meeting of a new committee "on Freer publications," Francis objected to the red tape delaying Freer
vouchers, Guthe's signature being required. Hutchins broke the impasse by
declaring that he would sign them himself.[146] This apparently was acceptable
to Guthe, who was "more reasonable"[147] at subsequent meetings and, along
with the others, approved the granting of permission to Harvard University
Press to have access to the fonts of Coptic type prepared from Worrell's de-
signs. Nor did Guthe object to the committee's authorization of the manufacture of volume 5 with a contract given to the University of Chicago
Press.[148]

It was not all smooth sailing, however, and a year later, Kelsey felt obliged to
make a "frank presentation to the President of the difficulties under which the
administration of the Humanistic Series is carried on."[149] Whereas one of
Guthe's objections had been to the handling of the Freer volumes, Kelsey now
talked directly with Guthe about his own objections concerning "the adminis-

143. Diary, June 10, 1913.

144. Isaac Newton Demmon (1842–1920), a University of Michigan graduate (B.A. 1868,
A.M. 1871) and briefly an instructor in mathematics there (1872), returned as assistant professor of rhetoric and history in 1876. In 1881 he became Professor of English and Rhetoric, and
from 1903 Chair of the Department of English. On the difficulties between him and Kelsey,
see "RNMF," 10; Charlotte writes loosely of Demmon's "constant attempt to interfere with father's accomplishments" and so on.

145. Diary, July 11, 1913.

146. Diary, January 17, 1914. Members of the committee were Hutchins, Guthe, Kelsey,
Sanders, and Wenley.

147. Diary, March 4, 1914.

148. Diary, July 1 and 17, 1914. On the Coptic type, see chapter 6, "The Freer Manuscripts"
and "The Morgan Manuscripts."

149. Diary, June 29, 1915.

tration of the non-Freer volumes of the Humanistic Series."[150] Despite what resulted in a "friendly confidential talk," the productivity of the Humanistic Series
gathered pace only after Guthe's death on September 11 and his replacement as
dean by Professor Alfred H. Lloyd from the Department of Philosophy.[151]

There was much shuttling back and forth among Ann Arbor, Boston, and
New York in the interests of both *Caesar's Commentaries* and the Humanistic
Series during these years.[152] It was worth it. The outcome of the work of the
authors in the Humanistic Series, most of whom were Michigan faculty, and
of the editors, Kelsey and Sanders, was prodigious and brought the university
great acclaim. Indeed, when a delegation from Germany arrived in 1914 for
the celebrations marking the seventy-fifth anniversary of the university, one
of two faculty members they asked about was Kelsey. When shown into his
study, they took off their hats and declared, "So this is where the Humanistic
Series was born!"[153] Much of the work of the series authors focused not on
the heartlands of the classics (Athens and Rome) but, rather, on the edges,
where cultures overlap—as the following list of volumes that appeared between 1913 and 1918 shows:

1913

Edward L. Adams, *Word-Formation in Provençal.* xvii + 607 pages.
Volume 2.

1914

Arthur Fairbanks, *Athenian Lekythoi with Outline Drawing in Matt Color
on a White Ground.* x + 275 pages, with 41 plates. Volume 7.

---

150. Diary, July 2, 1915.

151. Alfred Henry Lloyd received his undergraduate and graduate degrees from Harvard
(Ph.D. 1893), having also studied at Göttingen and Heidelberg. He began at the University of
Michigan in 1891 as an instructor in philosophy and was promoted to professor in 1906. In
1915 he became dean of the Graduate School, which blossomed under his leadership. Emerging during the next decade as a major figure in the university's upper echelons, Lloyd served
as acting president after the death of President Marion L. Burton in 1925.

152. For example, Francis was in Boston in early 1914 consulting with Mr. W. C. Ramsay,
treasurer and clerk of the Heliotype Printing Company, about the reproduction of the Freer
gold treasure; and again toward the end of the year, he records that "he (Ramsay) can do the
plates (for volumes IX part ii and XII part ii) of gold and jewelry satisfactorily at perhaps $200
a plate; admitted he lost money on the colored plates of volume XII part I" (diary, February
13 and December 12, 1914). On the high quality of Ramsay's work, see Larry W. Hurtado, ed.,
The Freer Biblical Manuscripts: Fresh Studies of an American Treasure Trove (Atlanta: Society
of Biblical Literature; Leiden: Brill, 2006), 31 with n. 37.

153. "RNMF," 12. The other scholar they wanted to see was Moses Gomberg (1866–1947),
discoverer of organic free radicals and founder of the field of organic free-radical chemistry.

Charles R. Morey, *East Christian Paintings in the Freer Collection*. xii + 87 pages, with 13 plates (10 colored) and 34 in-text illustrations. Volume 12, part 1.

1915

Carl S. Patton, *Sources of the Synoptic Gospels*. xiii + 263 pages. Volume 5.

Louis C. Karpinski, *Robert of Chester's Latin Translation of the "Algebra" of Al-Khowarizmi, with an Introduction, Critical Notes, and an English Version*. vii + 164 pages, with 4 plates and 25 in-text diagrams. Volume 11, part 1.

1916

John G. Winter, trans., *The Prodromus of Nicolaus Steno's Dissertation Concerning a Solid Body Enclosed by Process of Nature within a Solid*. 118 pages, with 7 plates. Volume 11, part 2.

1917

Henry A. Sanders, *The Old Testament Manuscripts in the Freer Collection*. viii + 357 pages, with 9 plates. Volume 8.

1918

Henry A. Sanders, *The New Testament Manuscripts in the Freer Collection: The Washington Manuscript of the Epistles of Paul*. vii + 247 pages, with 5 plates. Volume 9, part 2.

Walter Dennison, *A Gold Treasure of the Late Roman Period*. 86 pages, with 54 plates and 57 in-text illustrations. Volume 12, part 2.

The achievement of the Humanistic Series in publishing works that emphasized the edges of the Greek and Roman world was driven partly by Kelsey's enthusiasm for broadening fields of knowledge, partly by the accidents of discovery (Freer's acquisitions in Egypt). This emphasis aptly foreshadows Kelsey's interest, when considering prospects for archaeological fieldwork, in exploration at the perimeter of the classical world. If he was to be a transformative figure in his methods of archaeological research, he was a visionary in his desire to expand disciplinary boundaries in the interests of both scholarship and the general public.

All the books in the Humanistic Series were published by the Macmillan Company, which also published, separately, Richard Norton's book on Bernini. Norton was back in America in September of 1912, putting the final touches to the manuscript that Francis had helped revise in the previous year. At first the Humanistic Series was proposed as a suitable outlet—an idea scotched when President Hutchins opposed the book, saying "it might stir up comments unfavorable to the University."[154] A month later, after discussing the matter with Allison Armour[155] in New York, Kelsey took the matter up with the Macmillan Company, which, he noted, "thought the firm would be willing to take Norton book if I would superintend manufacture and pay for same, the firm to handle the book on commission."[156] Here is another instance, then, of Kelsey being willing to provide, on someone else's behalf, the administrative, technical, and financial means to get a job done. By September he had proofs in hand, which he sent to Arthur Fairbanks at the Boston Museum of Fine Arts for his comments.[157] The book appeared the next year.

In the summer of 1918, the Carnegie Endowment for International Peace asked Kelsey whether he would undertake a new translation of the rare 1646 edition of the great treatise *De Jure Belli ac Pacis* by Hugo Grotius, in the hope that it might be ready by the time of the peace negotiations at the end of the Great War.[158] The Clarendon Press in Oxford had already agreed to publish it. This was a tall order, entirely beyond Kelsey's range of legal competence—though the approach was evidently made to him in his capacity as an eminent scholar of Latin. After consultation with several colleagues—Boak, Sanders, and Reeves[159]—who all agreed to participate, Kelsey accepted the invitation on the university's behalf, more, it seems, out of a sense of moral duty than with direct academic interest.[160] In a letter to Bernard Allen,[161] Kelsey explained the reasons that lay behind the project.

---

154. Diary, January 13, 1913. No reason for this ungenerous view is given in the diary.

155. On Armour see chapter 5 n. 91. Recall Armour's involvement with the Cyrene project; see chapter 5, "Expeditions."

156. Diary, February 17, 1913.

157. Diary, September 22, 1913.

158. Hugo de Groot (1583–1645), best known by his Latin name Hugo Grotius, was a seventeenth-century Dutch scholar of law and philosophy and a poet. His disquisition *De Jure Belli ac Pacis* (About the Law of War and Peace), first published in 1625, has stood for centuries as the preeminent work on international law and the morality of war.

159. Jesse Siddall Reeves was head of the Department of Political Science. Author of *American Diplomacy under Tyler and Polk* (Baltimore: Johns Hopkins University Press, 1907) and noted scholar of international law, Reeves served in the war in the department of the judge advocate general and later as a U.S. representative to the Pan-American Commission of Jurists meeting in Rio de Janeiro, Brazil, and president of the American Political Science Association (1926–27).

160. Diary, June 21, 22, and 28, 1918.

161. Bernard Melzar Allen of Phillips Academy in Andover, Massachusetts, was the coauthor (with John L. Phillips) of *Latin Composition* (Boston: Allyn & Bacon, 1909), from which were drawn the exercises in Latin composition for Kelsey's 1918 edition of *Caesar's Commentaries.*

Carnegie Peace Endowment decided to bring out a new English version of the foundation work of International law, the *De Jure Belli ac Pacis* of Hugo Grotius. The thought was that if a fresh reading of this masterpiece could be distributed slightly in advance of the peace negotiations, its insistence upon absolute justice and the regard for fundamental principles would serve to reinforce the proper attitude of deliberation against the selfish and commercial trend of such negotiations for the last century.[162]

Francis made a start on the *Prolegomena* in July and on chapter 1 in August. He involved other faculty when necessary, consulting Waterman on Grotius's use of Hebrew words and Lloyd on philosophical terms. In September he was working on chapter 2, and by November he and Sanders were completing revisions and sending drafts to Dr. James Brown Scott, the secretary of the Carnegie Endowment. However, given the press of other business and the complications of multiple authorship, the team of scholars was not able to complete this huge undertaking in time for the Paris Peace Conference of 1919, and the book did not emerge from the Clarendon Press until late 1926 (with a 1925 title page).[163]

FAMILY MATTERS

By the fall of 1915, both Ruth and Charlotte were enrolled in the university. As a rule, they were at ease with their parents; but occasionally Francis had to let his sterner side show. One year, for example, there was serious talk about their allowances and about punctuality at meals: "today was inaugurated, by agreement, the practice of having breakfast together at 7.15."[164]

In 1917 (and perhaps earlier), a certain William Edward Howes began paying attention to Charlotte. The two were together a good deal that summer at Lake Cavanaugh, so much so that Isabelle felt obliged in September to have a heart-to-heart with Charlotte about "plans." In June of the following year, Francis and William had a conversation in Francis's office: "in regard to his engagement with Charlotte, I suggested first that he give his father a chance to resume cordial relations, and, second, that he give the religious side of his

---

162. Kelsey to Allen, August 30, 1918, KMA Papers, box 1, folder 3.
163. Francis W. Kelsey, ed. and trans., with the collaboration of Arthur E. R. Boak, Henry Sanders, Jesse S. Reeves, and Herbert F. Wright, *Hugo Grotius, "De Jure Belli ac Pacis," Libri Tres* [1646], vol. 2 (Oxford: Clarendon, 1925).
164. Diary, October 4, 1915.

nature a chance to develop."[165] Despite these reservations, the announcement of the engagement appeared in the *Detroit Free Press* a week later.[166] The proposed wedding between Charlotte and William never happened; when and where the breakup took place remains unclear.

Ruth and Charlotte, now both in their early twenties, graduated from the Literary Department together. Within a month, Ruth was offered a fellowship to study "Indian Art and Dramatics" at Santa Fe, and she departed a week later.[167] Francis wrote shortly afterward, "Charlotte informed me of prospect of appointment in chemical work for the government in a munitions laboratory."[168] There had earlier been a clash of wills between father and daughter over Charlotte's interest in chemistry: at the start of her sophomore year, her announcement that she was switching from classics to chemistry had not pleased Francis, provoking him to say that he would not allow her to remain in college and would no longer support her. When she replied, "Very well, I will make my own living," and he saw that she meant it, he relented.[169] At this moment, the prospect of success in her chosen area gave him great pleasure, and on September 13 in Detroit, Charlotte was sworn in for government service.

Easton was nine and a half years old in January 1914, an eager companion in summer expeditions with his father,[170] but also a worry: there was little progress at school, and his health was poor. In the spring of 1916, we glimpse him at Lake Cavanaugh, bird-watching with friends (identifying forty-five species) and later enjoying a house party with them over a long weekend. For long periods in the spring and summer of 1917, he was sick: in May he was seen by two doctors, pneumonia was diagnosed, and a nurse was brought in. He was not up and about until June 18, only to be admitted to the hospital six weeks later for an operation.[171]

With Ruth and Charlotte no longer living at home (they were in rooms in

---

165. Diary, June 2, 1918.

166. *Detroit Free Press,* June 9, 1918.

167. Diary, July 30, 1918. Kelsey wryly notes that her rail ticket cost $66.50.

168. Diary, August 30, 1918.

169. "RNMF," 7.

170. They traveled together by train to Isabelle's parents' cottage at Gun Lake, where they rode around the lake in Mr. Freer's launch; then they later took a trip to Battle Creek to visit the "immense establishment of Kellogg's Cornflakes and the 'Postum' cereal products" (diary, August 8–11, 1914).

171. His father stayed with him, commenting to his diary that the experience was "severe but the boy showed fine grit" (diary, August 6, 1917).

town), Isabelle and Francis, anticipating their western trip, decided to close the house at 826 Tappan and send Easton to boarding school. He left for the Hill School in September and did not see his parents again until the family dinner at his Uncle Fred's at the end of the year. On vacation in late March 1918, he again fell ill and was told not to return to school until his appendix had been removed. After a long delay and an operation in May, he spent the summer at the lake, making up his studies under his father's supervision. In September, now fourteen years old, he enrolled in Ann Arbor High School. The next day, he was back at the lake enjoying a walk with his father.[172]

Francis's time at the lake, however, was restricted by summer school and other duties; Isabelle, too, was away occasionally, visiting her parents at Gun Lake, and Ruth preferred life in town. But Charlotte enjoyed the open air and liked to invite friends to stay for a week or so. Easton took walks with his father, through marshes, around lakes, through farms, and down the railroad track to the cement works at Chelsea.[173] But some days, it was just too hot: "Loafed all day," said Francis to his diary.[174]

There was work to be done on the lot, too. One year, with the help of Merch Brooks,[175] Francis "pulled down the oak tree back of the house that was struck by lightning three years ago." There was fruit to be gathered: "Charlotte gathered, alone, wild grapes, and made 23 quarts of grape juice and about 40 glasses of grape jelly."[176] Francis trimmed and grafted trees and gathered wild artichokes.[177] Isabelle canned pears and made grape jelly. In 1915 Francis bought two more cottages on adjacent properties: noisy neighbors had disturbed his work (for which, each year, he transported large numbers of books and papers from Ann Arbor to the lake). Most summers passed calmly enough. By 1917 the sale of the house at 826 Tappan was already in the wind, with approaches with a view to purchase made by a fraternity in 1913 and by a sorority in 1914. Until 1919, however, Kelsey could not consider such a sale, despite the pressure of keeping up all his properties.

In addition to the practical pleasures of the garden at 826 Tappan Street and life at the lake, music, the theater, and opera remained reliable sources of recreation for Francis. Whenever he was in New York, he looked for seats at the Metropolitan Opera and was so successful that Charlotte was sure he was

---

172. "Glorious walk with Easton" (diary, September 15, 1918).
173. See, e.g., diary, August 3 and 24–27, 1913.
174. Diary, September 3, 1913.
175. See chapter 6 n. 115.
176. Diary, September 11–12 and 22, 1914.
177. Diary, May 6, 1916.

well known to the scalpers.[178] He was not averse to the theater. On New Year's Day 1913, he went to the Belasco Theater in Washington, D.C., to see Franz Lehár's *The Merry Widow* and found it "much more entertaining than I had anticipated."

Gregarious and talkative, he enjoyed the company of others, whether academic colleagues, business acquaintances, chance encounters while traveling, parents of students, fellow music enthusiasts, Presbyterian church folks, or family members. So there was always plenty of activity at 826 Tappan Street and plenty to occupy the cook. He took real pleasure in special occasions, sharing in the entertainment when William Follett, "whom I had not seen since we attended the Lockport Union School in 1875,"[179] came from El Paso to receive an honorary degree in engineering. It was a joyous occasion also when, on the fifteenth anniversary of their wedding, Albert and Lisla Crittenden held a reunion of those who had been in Rome in 1901; Francis, Isabelle, Ruth, and Charlotte joined W. W. Bishop, recently appointed university librarian, and his family in the celebrations.

His Detroit friends invited him to grand places: the Hotel Pontchartrain, where he dined in the company of Abner Larned and Governor Albert Sleeper in April 1917,[180] or the Detroit Club, where he dined with his fellow Presbyterians Bethune Duffield and John R. Russel.[181] In June of the following year, he was in Detroit enjoying the company of the Buhls, the Murphys, and the Pendletons.[182] After Armistice Day brought the end of the war, he attended the Victory Dinner at the Detroit Athletic Club as a guest of Abner Larned.[183]

COMMUNITY SERVICE

As we have come to expect of a man of such high energy, Kelsey did not neglect his obligations in Ann Arbor. The University Musical Society's year revolved around major fixed points: a winter directors' meeting, the May Festival, and the School of Music commencement exercises. At the directors' meeting, generally held in January, the state of finances, plans for the May Festival, and arrangements for other concerts topped the agenda, along with

---

178. "RNMF," 9.

179. Diary, June 23, 1914.

180. Albert Edson Sleeper, governor of Michigan during 1917–20, was instrumental in setting up the state parks system and the Michigan State Police.

181. Diary, April 30 and June 5, 1917. On Duffield, see chapter 4 n. 34.

182. The Pendletons were Edward Waldo (see chapter 4 n. 34) and his wife, the wealthy Catherina Berry. They had married in 1901.

183. Diary, June 23 and November 19, 1918.

the election of officers and directors.[184] The School of Music's commencement was regularly well attended by students, parents, teachers, relatives, friends, and well-wishers, and President Kelsey gave an address each year.

By 1913 the School of Music's activities were too numerous to be accommodated in the Maynard Street building, a problem the directors faced by taking options to buy on two other properties. However, their views were too evenly divided for a decision to be reached, so nothing happened, and the school soldiered on.[185] Three and a half years passed before the issue came up again, this time with extension and renovation of the existing property on the docket. Plans were rapidly approved, a budget of $17,500 was set, and the project was completed in timely fashion.[186] This solution was marginally satisfactory, but Francis still had hopes for an entirely new building, and 1918 brought positive signs. During a lunch in Ann Arbor, President Hutchins, John R. Russel, and he examined a sketch of a proposed new School of Music building, discussed a budget, and talked over the means to stimulate William Murphy's already keen interest. After lunch they visited the site proposed for the building,[187] but there was no immediate consequence.

Francis continued to press for the incorporation of the School of Music into the university and for a suitable building, as well as to emphasize the fundamental value of music to humanistic education. But he did not live to see the full acceptance of his ideas. It was not until 1929 that the School of Music was integrated into the university and not until 1963 that adequate buildings were found for it. It is clear that Kelsey was visionary in his realization of the centrality of the arts in education, a realization to which, in some respects, Michigan and other universities have been slow to come.[188]

The May Festival continued its great success, relished by Francis for the social activity and entertainment as well as the music. However, there were hiccups. When Hill Auditorium was first used in 1913, there were complaints about the visibility of the stage; Francis toured the auditorium and adjusted the podium himself. The following year, the organ was out of tune, so he had the temperature in the building raised and put thirty-pound weights in each

---

184. For instance, in 1916 a business associate of Kelsey's and long-standing Ann Arbor resident, H. G. Prettyman (see chapter 6 n. 23), was elected a director.

185. Diary, November 3 and December 20 and 23, 1913.

186. Diary, June 4, 1917.

187. Diary, November 25, 1918.

188. With respect to premises, the situation has been remedied with excellent facilities for the School of Music and School of Art and Architecture on North Campus (1960s and 1970s) and with the renovations and extensions to the Museum of Art and the Kelsey Museum of Archaeology completed in 2009.

of the bellows "so there was no discernible discord."[189] As a rule, however, the festival's concerts were greeted with applause, and there were some exhilarating moments: in 1916 a performance of Saint-Saens's *Samson and Delilah* delighted the audience, and Elgar's *Dream of Gerontius* was the high point the next year; each had been a highlight of the 1912 festival. The 1918 performance of César Franck's oratorio *The Beatitudes* was described by Francis as "the greatest religious work I ever heard" (Diary, May 16, 1918). Immediately after the May Festival of 1918, Kelsey heard of a legislative threat to levy a tax on tickets sold for the society's concerts. This educationally perverse proposal sent Kelsey to the Detroit office of Regent James Murfin, a Michigan graduate and successful Detroit attorney.[190] Murfin promised he would look into it, inviting Kelsey to come back the next day, on which Murfin told him "not to worry. He'd sort it out with Washington."[191] Such was Michigan's confidence and clout in the first part of the century.

The UMS's occasional and extra concerts were always well received. A performance in Hill Auditorium in February 1914 held the audience enthralled, and the recital given there by Ignacy Paderewski the following month made for a day to remember.[192] When Paderewski returned to Ann Arbor two years later, he performed, according to the diary, with not quite the same verve: "all the family attended. There lacked something of the all-sweeping enthusiasm of the other appearances of Paderewski here—but it was a great concert."[193] Another star performer in Kelsey's sights was Enrico Caruso. Arrangements for an Ann Arbor concert were postponed in October 1918 because of the outbreak of the worldwide influenza epidemic,[194] but Caruso's arrival was not long delayed: he appeared at Hill in March of the following year.

189. Diary, May 15 and 16, 1913, and May 14, 1914.

190. James Orin Murfin Jr. (1875–1940) graduated from Michigan with literary and law degrees (1895, 1896), becoming partner at Bowen, Douglas, Whiting, and Murfin (1897–1908) and serving in the Michigan State Senate (1901–3) and on the Detroit Circuit Court (1908–12). Newly elected regent in 1918, he would remain one for nearly twenty years. A professorship of political science at the university was established in his name in 1940.

191. Diary, May 23 and 24, 1918.

192. Diary, March 3, 1914. Paderewski was born in the village of Kurylowska in the province of Podolia, then in the Russian Empire (now Ukraine). Virtuoso pianist, ardent patriot, and political activist, he traveled widely in America on concert tours, everywhere received by rapturous audiences. Fifty-four years old when he visited Ann Arbor in 1914, he would become prime minister of a reconstituted Poland five years later, after the Treaty of Versailles.

193. Diary, January 20, 1916.

194. Kelsey's diary entry for October 17, 1918, reports, "all public meetings restricted—influenza."

To the work of the UMS, Kelsey added his commitment to his church. Kelsey's prominence as a churchman was underscored at the May 1914 meeting of the General Assembly of the Presbyterian Church in Chicago.[195] On the first day, he and his old Lake Forest colleague Professor A. C. Zenos[196] lectured on "religious workers in state universities." On the second, after assisting in the communion service at the first session of the assembly,[197] he took part in discussions aimed at reconciling the work of the university's Tappan Association with that of the assembly's Board of Education.[198] The major issue was funding: churches around the state could see little reason to support students (albeit Presbyterian) in Ann Arbor, about whose conduct and theology they were more and more dubious. The expense of the upkeep of the buildings the association owned was a particular concern, and generous donors could not be expected to continue plugging the gap.

On the sixth and last day of the General Assembly, at the request of the moderator, Kelsey spoke at a meeting of the Board of Education on the attitude of state universities to the board, followed by an evening conference on the particular problem presented by the Tappan Association, at which a provisional agreement was reached. On his final day in Chicago, he called on Mrs. De Cou, mother of his old colleague who was killed at Cyrene,[199] and at the offices of Allyn and Bacon, before returning to his hotel and taking a taxi: "reaching the Michigan Central station at 5.30, I had one minute on the train before it left at 5.40."[200] This was unlike Kelsey, who rarely left things to the last moment.

In Ann Arbor his energies were divided, as before, between the needs of the Tappan Association and the First Presbyterian Church. He constantly worked to strengthen the links between them and to advocate greater participation by the Ann Arbor church and the Michigan Synod in ministering to the student population. The recently appointed pastor at the church, the Reverend Leonard A. Barrett, was sympathetic to the students and himself a vigorous proponent of Presbyterianism in both the association and the Ann Ar-

---

195. Diary, May 20–25, 1914.

196. Kelsey and Zenos had been coeditors of the 1889 *Xenophon's "Anabasis."*

197. "Dr. Bailey of Philadelphia and I headed the processional in the middle aisle" (diary, May 21, 1914).

198. On the Tappan Association, see chapter 3, "The Presbyterian Church."

199. See chapter 5, "Expeditions."

200. Diary, May 26, 1914.

bor church,[201] but the cooperative spirit of the 1890s and 1900s was melting away.

Throughout 1913 the executive committee of the Tappan Association and the trustees (eight in number, four appointed by the synod) met—sometimes alone, sometimes together, sometimes with members of the Ann Arbor church and/or members of the Presbyterian Board of Education—to try to hammer out a new agreement. On one occasion, they met in the evening at Kelsey's office in Alumni Memorial Hall.[202] Finally, in a series of meetings in March 1914, a new contract between the association and the Presbyterian board seemed to have been agreed.[203] Yet tensions remained, as the Chicago discussions in May attest. Kelsey conferred privately with Barrett and with individual members of the board and continued, through 1916, to put his conciliatory views to the executive committee of the association,[204] but problems mounted.

Faced with declining student interest in Presbyterianism, many rooms in McMillan and Sackett halls were rented out to the YMCA, but the shortfall in revenue continued, and the condition of the buildings deteriorated. In 1917 Francis attended meetings diligently and conferred privately with Bethune Duffield and George Russel[205] more than once, but no solution was in sight. After the entry of the United States into the war, McMillan and Sackett halls were taken over by the university's Student Army Training Corps, which did not treat the buildings kindly, leaving them in tatters.[206] By midyear 1918, the

---

201. During his tenure of the Ann Arbor pulpit (1911–24), the membership of the church more than doubled. See Lila Miller, Robert M. Warner, and Carl R. Geider, eds., *The First Presbyterian Church of Ann Arbor, Michigan, 1826–1988, Incorporating "A Sesquicentennial History,"* 1976 (Ann Arbor: First Presbyterian Church, 1988), 13.

202. In his diary entry for February 25, 1913, Kelsey reports that he "served cocoa and sandwiches at 9."

203. Diary, March 15, 22, and 23, 1914.

204. Diary, July 7 and 8, 1916.

205. On George H. Russel, see chapter 6, "The Weldon Gold and Copper Company." George was one of four Russel brothers whose father, Dr. George B. Russel (1816–1903) had founded the Russel Iron Works in Detroit (later the Gaylord Iron Works, then the Detroit City Iron Works), of which George H. was president, Walter S. vice president, and John R. (see n. 125 above) secretary-treasurer. On the fourth brother, Henry, see n. 222 below. See Fred Carlisle, comp. and ed., *Chronography of Notable Events in the History of the Northwest Territory and Wayne County* (Detroit: O. S. Gulley, Bornman, 1890), 459–61, esp. 461. See also Clarence Monroe Burton, *Compendium of History . . . Detroit and Wayne County* (Chicago: H. Taylor and Co., 1909), 189, 364.

206. Miller, Warner, and Geider, *First Presbyterian Church,* 14.

strain on resources was such that the trustees voted to close Westminster House, the university's residence for Presbyterian women.[207]

Francis continued to volunteer his talks at First Presbyterian Church each year—to the Sunday school, the Bible class, and the men's class—and spoke at other churches, too. He prepared the lecture "Thirty Minutes in the Roman Catacombs" for the Unitarians and spoke to the Congregationals on St. Augustine.[208] He also entered into discussions about possibilities for a new church. Indeed, he voiced the need for a new building and a fund drive as early as 1914 and persisted in this plan, at one stage producing tentative plans and elevations.[209] Poignancy was added to this proposal when the church boiler blew up and services had to be held in the high school auditorium,[210] but action was slow to materialize.[211] Personally, Francis was pleased to note in his diary that Easton "graduated" in 1914, receiving a diploma and a Bible on Children's Day, and that the Pew Committee offered the family a more convenient spot "on the aisle" (Diary, June 7, October 4).

The humanitarian interests that grew from Kelsey's church affiliation also spurred his charitable work during and after the war. As the United States was slowly drawn toward the war in Europe, the plight of the civilian populations there attracted popular concern, with many funds established to provide support. Among the first were the Polish Relief Fund (with Mr. and Mrs. Paderewski leading the charge) and the Alliance Française, which sent speakers around the country urging action. Responding to the many appeals, American volunteers served in the ambulance corps on the Western Front as early as 1915, their presence in the war zone brought home to Ann Arborites by the death of one of their own. On Christmas morning 1915, Richard Hall, one of the earliest volunteers in the American Field Service, was killed by German shelling of the road on which he was driving an ambulance in the Vosges Mountains.[212] Charlotte Kelsey was among those who attended the memorial service for him in St. Andrew's Episcopal Church.[213] But most attention in Ann Arbor focused on the situation in Belgium.

---

207. Diary, June 8, 1918. On Westminster House, see chapter 4, "Community Involvement."

208. Diary, March 5 and October 22, 1916.

209. Diary, October 14, 1916.

210. Diary, January 7, 1917.

211. Diary, November 1, 1915.

212. "Richard Neville Hall, Killed in Alsace, Christmas Morning, 1915," *Michigan Alumnus* 22 (1916): 222–31; cf. *Detroit Free Press*, December 26, 1915.

213. Diary, January 16, 1916.

Already in the fall of 1914, members of the American Red Cross were visiting schools in Ann Arbor, appealing for clothing and money (for food) for
orphaned Belgian children. There were many tales of German brutality and
heartlessness. It was hard for Ann Arbor children to make sense of: they had
no idea where Belgium was, but they did have classmates of German extraction, or blood, in their everyday lives.[214] Paul van den Ven, professor of philology and classics at Louvain University in Belgium, came to Ann Arbor in
March 1916 to give a talk about Constantinople and, at a reception at 826 Tappan Street, drew attention to the terrible events in Belgium.[215] Following his
visit, Francis met with a group of Ann Arbor women "to talk about relief
work" and went the next day to Detroit to talk to Rev. E. H. Henri Amaat Jan
Baptist "Henry" Syoen, "the Belgian priest who brought over the Belgian children."[216] An address given by members of the Belgian Protestant Church at
the General Assembly of the Presbyterian Church in Atlantic City in May kept
the problem at the front of his mind.[217] But it was not until 1917 that he took
the bit between his teeth.

In January he swung into action. Spurred by a meeting with Harriet and
their friend Miss Crocker, he telephoned around to recruit members for a
Committee for the Relief of Belgian Children and prepared a circular for the
printer. At a meeting with President Hutchins in his office on February 2,
Kelsey, three other faculty members, and several ladies from the Ann Arbor
community established a Dollar-a-Month Club, and distribution of circulars
in Manchester and Detroit was arranged.[218] Further meetings with this committee and with other representatives of the town culminated in a lightning
visit to Lansing to talk with Governor Sleeper, who agreed to be chairman of
a statewide committee and suggested several names. In Ann Arbor the next
day, Kelsey spoke about the Dollar-a-Month-Club at the Rotary Club, which
voted "to spread the idea to the branches."[219] His effort was handsomely endorsed early in the month by the chairman of the Commission for Relief in

---

214. For a child's view, see Milo S. Ryan, *View of a Universe: A Love Story of Ann Arbor at
Middle Age* (Ann Arbor: Ann Arbor Historic District Commission, 1985), 186.
215. Toward the end of the war, van den Ven, acting as a representative of the Belgian government, was notable for his efforts to raise funds for charitable organizations faced with the
demands of the refugee problem, which increased in intensity as the German army withdrew.
He also advised the Belgian contingent at the Paris Peace Conference.
216. Diary, April 4 and 5, 1916.
217. Diary, May 25, 1916.
218. Diary, January 28 and 29, February 2, 1917.
219. Diary, February 26, 27, and 28, 1917.

Belgium, Herbert C. Hoover, who wrote from New York to congratulate and commend him.[220]

On March 3, in the university's Lane Hall, Kelsey addressed a ladies' meeting that then handed out circulars and organized further distribution. On March 23, he was in Detroit at the Twentieth Century Club, drumming up interest and recruiting for the state committee. Toward the end of the month, he spent three whole days on "the Belgian work." Throughout April, there were conferences, committee meetings, correspondence, lectures in Monroe and Plymouth, and a dinner in Detroit at which thirty were present to meet Mme Léon Dupriez of Louvain.[221] Henry Russel[222] introduced Mme Dupriez, "who spoke forcefully" on the Belgian situation. "I was called on," the diary adds.[223] At the end of the month (April 30), a meeting of the state Dollar-a-Month Club in Detroit was followed by a banquet at the Pontchartrain Hotel, where the speakers were Governor Sleeper, Mme Dupriez, and Professor Kelsey. The press reported that two hundred Detroit citizens present donated over $120,000 to the Belgian Relief Fund, continuing, "Professor Francis W. Kelsey of the Latin Department, who started the movement in this state, emphasized the worthiness of the cause. Governor Albert E. Sleeper, Mayor Oscar B. Marx and a score of Detroit's prominent citizens were present."[224]

There was more Belgian work after the May Festival. Mme Dupriez attended a ladies' lunch given by Isabelle before she gave a talk in Hill Auditorium, graphically outlining conditions in Belgium—a talk described by Francis as "very successful."[225] In Lansing on May 11, the executive committee of the statewide Commission for Relief in Belgium met to discuss the success of the fund-raising effort and the pros and cons of continuation.[226] Three days

---

220. Hoover concluded his letter, dated February 8, 1917, with these apposite words: "Hoping that your 'Dollar-a-Month Club' may spread its influence throughout Michigan, and put the state in the front rank of patriotic and humanitarian giving, believe me, etc." (private collection of Easton Kelsey Jr., Rochester, NY).

221. Mme Dupriez was married to Professor Léon H. Dupriez, the social and political historian of Louvain University, who was a visiting professor at Harvard at the time.

222. Detroit native Henry Russel (b. 1852), who graduated from the University of Michigan (A.B. 1873, A.M. 1875) and its law school (LL.B. 1875), was one of the founding partners in the law firm Russel and Campbell (1878) and a director and/or president of numerous banking, railroad, manufacturing, and real estate firms.

223. Diary, April 19, 1917.

224. *Ann Arbor News*, May 1, 1917.

225. Diary, May 8, 1917.

226. Members of the committee who were present were Governor Sleeper; Messrs. Blodgett (Grand Rapids), Staebler (Kalamazoo), Ottaway (Port Huron), and Beal (Ann Arbor); ex-governor Woodbridge N. Ferris; and Kelsey.

later, Francis "began to close up the Belgian work."[227] This should be taken to mean closing up the first phase of activity, since the diary reveals that the work of collecting clothing and money to provide meals for Belgian children continued in 1918.[228]

With the successful launch of the Belgian Relief Fund in Michigan and the approach of the end of the war, Francis could look back with some satisfaction on the events and accomplishments of the six years since he relinquished the presidency of the AIA. The Latin Department had emerged relatively unscathed from the curricular changes and downturn in enrollments caused by the war, and his fund-raising for student fellowships and for his and others' research and publication projects had met with continued success in Detroit. He had transformed his *Caesar's "Gallic War"* into *Caesar's Commentaries* with great skill and much industry and had organized the technical, manufacturing, and editorial aspects of nine volumes (or parts of volumes) of the Michigan Humanistic Series. He had contributed convincingly to the work of the Chautauqua Institution; he had completed the division of Thomas Spencer Jerome's library on Capri and the other pertinent provisions of Jerome's will with patience and aplomb. He had seen his daughters, Ruth and Charlotte, graduate from the university and blossom into active and thoughtful young women; he had seen his son, Easton, suffer troubling illnesses with resilience and in good heart. Lake Cavanaugh had continued to provide the place and space where he could both enjoy nature and work.

But his mind had already turned to the opportunities that the postwar situation in Europe and the Near East might offer. He looked forward to the study of Caesar's (and the recent Great War's) battlefields in Europe and to the acquisition of manuscripts and papyri from the Near East and Egypt for the university's library. In particular, he foresaw the possibilities that new methods of archaeological fieldwork, refocused with new objectives, might yield, in terms of retrieving papyri and other materials and of reconstructing social history. At the war's end, he was already planning long-term expeditions, waiting—with some impatience, we may be sure—for 1919 and the postwar world.

---

227. Diary, May 14 and 15, 1917.
228. Diary, March 20, 1918.

CHAPTER 8

The First Expedition (1919–21)

Battlefields and Manuscripts

৯৯

OUTWARD BOUND

Through August of 1919, Kelsey's energies were divided between routine academic business and preparation for the expedition he had long had in mind. Since he was granted leave for two years as of September 1919,[1] replacements were needed to cover his courses. James E. Dunlap was appointed instructor in Latin for 1919–20 and Bruno Meinecke for the following year.[2] Kelsey had been mulling over the expedition throughout the war years, and though financing was not yet in hand, the expedition's objectives were clear enough.

There were four major projects. One was a survey and restudy of Julius Caesar's battlefields, primarily in Gaul in light of the recent war, but also in Greece, Asia Minor, North Africa, and Egypt.[3] Another was collecting photographs of ancient sites and monuments for teaching purposes, some by

---

1. Kelsey to Spaulding, December 8, 1920, KMA Papers, box 31, folder 2. Kelsey continued to receive 80 percent of his university salary during his leave.

2. James Eugene Dunlap (b. 1889), previously at Ohio State University, would soon write "The Office of the Grand Chamberlain in the Later Roman and Byzantine Empires" (the second study in *Two Studies in Later Roman and Byzantine Administration,* University of Michigan Studies, Humanistic Series, vol. 14 [Ann Arbor: University of Michigan, 1924]). University of Michigan graduate Bruno Meinecke (b. 1888; A.B. 1917; Buhl Fellow in Latin) authored *Consumption (Tuberculosis) in Classical Antiquity* (New York: Paul B. Hoeber, 1927), edited a revision of Kelsey's Cicero (1933), and was a symphonic conductor and composer to boot.

3. Cf. *Ann Arbor Times-News,* July 8, 1919.

purchase, others by on-the-spot photography, for which he could call on George Robert Swain.[4] Another was the study of manuscripts, especially biblical manuscripts, in European libraries and in monastery collections in Greece, Constantinople, Palestine, and Egypt. The fourth was the acquisition of ancient artifacts and manuscripts, more especially papyri, for research and teaching. One ancillary goal was the gathering of photographs of indigenous peoples in Asia Minor and Syria for the Smithsonian Institution and of architecture of all periods and of contemporary cultural phenomena for social and historical research. Another was inquiry for the Board of Commissioners for Foreign Missions—with the American Red Cross being one of the missions most heavily involved—into the current state of the missions in Turkey and Syria after the collapse of the Ottoman Empire.

In his professorial role, Francis followed the familiar rhythms of teaching, research, and administration, journeying for lectures,[5] entertaining students at home, supervising the college preparation of the Larned boys,[6] and paving the way for the Michigan Classical Conference, which met, as usual, in early April. Early in the year, he published an article on Theodor Mommsen, the German scholar whose work had strongly influenced the study of ancient history, epigraphy, law, numismatics, and linguistics and under whose eagle eye August Mau had studied the inscriptions from Pompeii.[7] Though his own research centered on the Grotius project, the Michigan Humanistic Series commanded much of his attention, too: three volumes were in progress—those of Arthur Boak (volume 14, part 1), William H. Worrell (volume 10), and Albert Stanley (volume 15)[8]—and two others were on the drawing boards.[9] In March he took Stanley's manuscript to the Theodore Presser Publishing Company in Philadelphia (which specialized in music) for an estimate and discussed Boak's and Worrell's books at the Macmillan Company in New York, finding that estimates needed to be increased by 25 percent.

---

4. On Swain, see chapter 7 n. 54.

5. Diary, January 19 and March 9 and 26, 1919.

6. Diary, February 19 ("they agreed to do better work") and April 9, 1919. On Abner Larned and his sons, see chapter 7 n. 124.

7. Francis W. Kelsey, "Theodor Mommsen," *Classical Journal* 14.4 (1919): 224–36.

8. Arthur E. R. Boak, *The Master of the Offices in the Later Roman and Byzantine Empires* (New York: Macmillan, 1919); William H. Worrell, *Two Homilies and a Magical Text* (New York: Macmillan), pt. 2 of *The Coptic Manuscripts in the Freer Collection* (1923); Albert A. Stanley, *Greek Themes in Modern Musical Settings* (1924).

9. Nicomachus of Gerasa, *Introduction to Arithmetic,* trans. Martin L. D'Ooge, with studies by Frank E. Robbins and Louis C. Karpinski, vol. 16 (New York: Macmillan, 1926); Leroy Waterman and Robert F. Harper, trans. and commentary, *Royal Correspondence of the Assyrian Empire,* vols. 17–20 (Ann Arbor: University of Michigan Press, 1930–36).

Earlier in March, devotees of the University Musical Society had been thrilled by the voice of Enrico Caruso, whose sold-out concert at Hill Auditorium was the high point of the musical year, a "success in every particular." The noted impresario and secretary of the Metropolitan Opera Company, Francis C. Coppicus, who accompanied Caruso to Ann Arbor, admired the auditorium and was heard to exclaim, "I am sorry I did not come before."[10] As the summer approached, Francis concentrated more on arrangements for the expedition, not least its funding. He had written in March to Mr. J. M. Longyear, asking his support.[11] In 1911 and 1913, Longyear had contributed heavily to volume 7 of the Humanistic Series,[12] and a cordial relationship had developed. Knowing the deeply Christian cast of Longyear's mind, Francis hoped that he would be sympathetic to at least some of the expedition's aims. In a long letter to Longyear, Francis described the venture as "an expedition to the Near East, particularly Asia Minor and Syria, to search out and save from destruction Biblical manuscripts still remaining in neglected corners." He added that "while upon this quest the same expedition should study and also photograph the battlefields of Caesar." He also mentioned that the American Red Cross was eager to have a report of conditions in the Near East and that the budget for the whole project was twenty-five thousand dollars.[13] Longyear replied that he regretted he could not help.

We can only imagine, then, the delight and surprise with which, a few days later, he received a letter from Longyear's wife, Mary Beecher Longyear, saying, "Mr. Longyear forwarded your very interesting letter to me, and I am inclined to help you in your project."[14] Two weeks later, a check for ten thousand dollars arrived,[15] the beginning of a prolonged correspondence. In the course of the expedition, Francis sent Mrs. Longyear reports from London, Paris, Constantinople, and Patmos—indeed, from everywhere they went— and often included packets of photographs, which delighted her. Francis was

---

10. Diary, March 3, 1919. Coppicus and Caruso stayed at the Allenel Hotel.

11. John Munro Longyear (1850–1922) made an immense fortune in mining and timber enterprises in Michigan, being one of the first to recognize the ore-bearing possibilities of the Upper Peninsula. He and his wife may be equally well known for the magnificent stone house they built in Marquette on a ridge (now Ridge Street) overlooking Lake Superior, which they dismantled block by block, transported by rail, and reconstructed in Brookline, Massachusetts.

12. Longyear to Kelsey, June 15, 1911, and June 24, 1913, KMA Papers, box 21, folder 11. Volume 7 was Arthur Fairbanks's *Athenian Lekythoi with Outline Drawing in Matt Color on a White Ground* (New York: Macmillan, 1907).

13. Kelsey to Longyear, March 11, 1919, KMA Papers, box 21, folder 11.

14. Longyear to Kelsey, March 26, 1919, KMA Papers, box 21, folder 12.

15. Diary, April 12, 1919.

also, of course, trying to identify donors in Detroit, and on a visit in April, he found Standish Backus sympathetic.[16] A month later, Backus came to Ann Arbor with his father-in-law, Joseph Boyer, chairman of the Burroughs Adding Machine Company, to talk with Kelsey; Boyer was impressed enough by what he heard to give Backus bonds with a face value of ten thousand dollars to deliver to Kelsey.[17]

In June Francis was on the East Coast, again attending to his many interests—lunching with Mr. and Mrs. Longyear "in their beautiful home in Brookline"; talking to printers about the Humanistic Series volumes and to Allyn and Bacon about his textbooks (they proposed a new edition of the *Xenophon*); working on the index to *Caesar's Commentaries* in his hotel room; visiting the Tremont Theatre in Boston for a performance of the musical *Flo-Flo*;[18] and conferring with Dr. W. E. Strong of the American Board of Commissioners for Foreign Missions, who provided him with introductions. In New York he became involved in AIA business again. The animosity between those who disliked the extension of the membership to the general public and those who favored it, Edgar Hewett told him, continued to color much discussion. Hewett had visited James Egbert, the AIA president, but told Kelsey he "got little out of him"; Hewett claimed that Egbert "was possessed with the notion of the value of his service as a peacemaker and seemed unconscious of the failure of his administration of the Institute."[19]

In the same year (1914) that his initial requests for funding went out, Kelsey intensified his search for help with the battlefields project. Captain Oliver Lyman Spaulding Jr.—elder son of former regent General Oliver Lyman Spaulding[20]—had an interest in Julius Caesar as a military tactician and,

---

16. A graduate of the University of Michigan (A.B. 1898) and of the Detroit College of Law (LL.B. 1901), Backus had been secretary of the General Motors Company and became its general counsel in 1917.

17. Diary, May 27 and June 6, 1919.

18. Kelsey called it the "most vulgar and least amusing of the musical travesties I have heard, notwithstanding lavish expenditure on scenic effects and costumes" (diary, June 9, 1919). Produced by John Cort, the musical featured many shopgirls and the song "Lingerie."

19. Diary, June 12, 1919.

20. General Spaulding (1833–1922), after his term as regent (1858–63), also served as Michigan secretary of state and in the U.S. House of Representatives. His younger son, Thomas M. Spaulding (1882–1973), also served in the army and, after retiring in 1936 with the rank of colonel, became an author, best known perhaps for a book cowritten with Louis C. Karpinski, *Early Military Books in the University of Michigan Library* (Ann Arbor: University of Michigan Press, 1941). Thomas was also known as a prolific book collector: his only son, Stephen, died while an undergraduate at Michigan, after which the parents established a memorial collection of books at the University Library, known now as the Stephen Spaulding Collection and numbering more than six thousand volumes.

knowing Kelsey's interests, had sent him a copy of the second edition of his book on field artillery.[21] Francis lost no time in writing to thank him for the book and to ask his advice. He tried to interest Spaulding in lending his military expertise to the part of the expedition investigating Julius Caesar's military movements and battle sites,[22] but Spaulding replied that he was otherwise committed at the moment.[23]

Though one or two letters were exchanged during the war, it was when Spaulding was posted to the American Expeditionary Force in Europe in 1919 that the pace of the exchanges picked up. Kelsey mentioned to Spaulding that the expedition's plan had now been expanded to include the Near East, and he asked about the ease of travel in Europe and about the availability of automobiles. Spaulding said that traveling in France and Italy would be easy "if you have authority from the War Department; but that anything in the Balkan country or Asia Minor was out of the question now." Spaulding also recommended that Kelsey "ask the War Department for authority to buy gasoline, food and other stores from the AEF" and "also ask to be accredited to headquarters here, so that you may have a claim upon the assistance of billeting officers, town mayors etc."[24]

When Francis was in Washington in June, he met Spaulding, already back from France, at the War Department on several occasions and was introduced "to many generals,"[25] introductions that were to stand him in good stead. At first the proposal that Colonel Spaulding join the expedition in a formal capacity seemed favorably received, and when both General Spaulding and Colonel Spaulding came to Ann Arbor for commencement exercises later in the month, the tenor of discussion was positive. On June 30, Francis received

---

21. O. L. Spaulding Jr. (1875–1947), *Notes on Field Artillery for Officers of All Arms* (Fort Leavenworth: U.S. Cavalry Association, 1914; 1st ed., 1908). Spaulding's other written works reveal him as a military historian of some distinction and include *The United States Army in War and Peace* (New York: G. P. Putnam's Sons, 1937) and O. L. Spaulding Jr., Hoffman Nickerson, and John Womack Wright, *Warfare: A Study of Military Methods from the Earliest Times* (London: George G. Harrap, 1924).

22. Kelsey to Spaulding, December 29, 1914, KMA Papers, box 31, folder 1.

23. Spaulding to Kelsey, January 10, 1915, KMA Papers, box 31, folder 1. Later in the year, he was posted to the Philippines, remaining there until 1917.

24. These letters of February 26 and March 15 and 31, 1919, are in KMA Papers, box 31, folder l.

25. Diary, June 14–19, 1919. Spaulding had arranged for the privileges of the Army and Navy Club to be extended to Kelsey. A colonel by 1919, Spaulding remained in the army until 1939, when he retired with the rank of brigadier general.

a telegram declaring, "Memorandum approved," only for the decision to be reversed the following day, when another telegram read, "information yesterday unofficial and erroneous, detail disapproved."[26] He was encouraged, however, by a note from Spaulding in July to the effect that the following spring or summer might offer "a possibility." At the university, Francis discussed arrangements in the Latin Department with Dean Effinger, the campaign for the Music School Building and funding for three Humanistic Series volumes with President Hutchins,[27] and the UMS's plans with Professor Stanley. With H. B. Hoyt and Union Trust officer Joel H. Prescott, he prepared a final memorandum on the Jerome lectureship, to go to both the American Academy in Rome and the University of Michigan. On a flying visit to New York, he saw Charles Freer at the Gotham Hotel and found him in generous mood: Freer coughed up the funds required for the Coptic volume and added fifteen hundred dollars to enable expedition members to get to Dimay in the Fayoum, the putative findspot of Freer's biblical manuscripts.[28]

On the domestic front, the question of what to do with the house at 826 Tappan remained. There being no takers when Francis put it up for sale with an asking price of twenty-two thousand dollars,[29] the house was "leased to Miss Hills as residence for girls, $150 a month for 2 years, furniture included."[30] Charlotte came from Glenolden near Philadelphia (where she was working at H. K. Mulford and Company's laboratory) to help with the packing and moving for two weeks; Isabelle's grand piano went into storage, and books and household items were moved to the cottages at Lake Cavanaugh, "the old Churchville bookcase in pink cottage, four large beds in white cottage."[31] Easton lent a willing hand. Now approaching his fifteenth birthday, he was a big lad but had struggled with his schoolwork. His exam results were mixed: he got As in Greek and Latin but failed both Algebra and English. This lack of academic aptitude played a significant part in Francis and Isabelle's decision to take him along on the expedition; another reason was George Swain's need for help in handling the photographic equipment.

Typhoid shots were administered. Four new suitcases were bought at Wilkinson Luggage Shop, on Ann Arbor's South Main Street, for thirty-five

---

26. KMA Papers, box 31, folder 1.
27. Diary, July 2, 1919.
28. Diary, July 19, 1919.
29. Diary, May 22, 1919.
30. Diary, August 2, 1919.
31. Diary, August 22, 1919.

dollars.[32] Visas for the United Kingdom, steamer reservations, and two letters of credit for fifteen hundred pounds apiece were picked up in Detroit. On September 1, Francis, Isabelle, and Easton headed east. After one night at Niagara Falls and three in New York—where Kelsey attended to last-minute publishing matters and visited Freer at the Gotham Hotel, finding him "very feeble and in bed, mind not altogether clear"[33]—they were joined by Swain and went aboard the SS *Columbia* on September 6. The weather was glorious; Charlotte, Fred, and Ronald, Fred's younger son, were at the pier to see them off.

EUROPE

After ten days at sea, they arrived in Glasgow none the worse for wear (though Isabelle and Easton missed several meals). Francis instantly shipped most of his books to the American Academy in Rome and the photographic equipment to his London agents, Brown, Shipley, and Company, at 123 Pall Mall. Afterward, they took a train to Edinburgh. They left the next day for London, spending a night in York, where Swain and Easton walked around the city walls and the Minster, establishing a pattern that was to last throughout the expedition: Swain and Easton working together at the photography or sightseeing, while Francis and Isabelle were otherwise occupied.

In London on September 19, they took rooms opposite the British Museum, where Francis went at once to make arrangements for the photography of manuscripts, not least of the Beatus manuscript, in which Henry Sanders had a particular interest.[34] Much of the following week was taken up in conversations at the American Embassy; visits to the British Foreign Office, where officials were telegraphing on their behalf to the military authorities in

---

32. This shop, founded in 1904, finally closed in March 2008. (It had relocated to Scio Township in 2005.) See Stefanie Murray, "Ann Arbor's Wilkinson Luggage Shop Closes Its Doors," *Ann Arbor News,* April 14, 2008, available online at http://blog.mlive.com/annar bornews/2008/04/ann_arbors_wilkinson_luggage_s.html (accessed June 1, 2009).

33. Diary, September 5, 1919. Freer died on September 25.

34. Beatus was an eighth-century monk who wrote a long commentary on the book of Revelation, the Christian Apocalypse, while in the monastery of San Martin de Turieno at Liébana in northern Spain. Copied and illuminated in the early twelfth century at the monastery of Santo Domingo de Silos, near Burgos, the British Museum example—the "Silos Apocalypse"—is famous for the beauty of its images, its state of preservation, and the depiction of an early Christian *mappa mundi*. It was acquired in 1840 from Joseph Bonaparte. Sanders's work on Beatus appeared in 1930 in the edited volume *Beati in Apocalipsin libri duodecim,* American Academy in Rome, Papers and Monographs, vol. 7 (Rome: American Academy in Rome).

Palestine and Egypt; or trying to work out what route to take to Constantinople. The Thomas Cook Agency favored an overland route, suggesting that the Mediterranean steamers from Marseilles to the East were unpredictable in their scheduling and, when functioning, crowded beyond belief.[35] Progress on these fronts was then halted by the nationwide strike of railway workers, which paralyzed communications from September 27 until October 6. Fortunately, they were so close to the British Museum that work on manuscripts and photography could go forward, and Francis could continue reading through the proofs that had been brought to him in New York from Boston. He also enjoyed a cordial conversation with the museum's director, Sir Frederic Kenyon;[36] acquired the services of a stenographer, Miss Louise Jacobs; and was able to crank out memoranda and reports for President Hutchins and much other correspondence. In more relaxing moments, he and Isabelle toured the city, visiting Westminster Abbey and taking meals at the Swiss restaurant at Tottenham Court Road.

They collected their visas for Palestine and Egypt on October 9 and left the next day, heavily burdened, for Paris.[37] They were bowled over by the sights and sounds of the city: "view of Notre Dame in the setting sun and of the Seine in the afterglow, an abiding and glorious memory." They spent a month in and around Paris. General Connor, the officer commanding American forces in France, put a car and a chauffeur at their disposal, so that they were able to tour the area west and north of Reims, a sector that had been the site of battles between Caesar and the Gauls and between Germans and the Allies in the recent war.[38] Swain took photographs; Kelsey examined the terrain, walking wherever he could.

---

35. Diary, September 22–26, 1919. The overland route required a discouraging visit to the Serbian chargé d'affaires at 195 Queens Gate.

36. Educated at Oxford, Frederic George Kenyon was a classical and biblical scholar, director of the British Museum, president of the British Academy, and president of the Society of Antiquaries, famous for his 1891 translation of Aristotle's *Constitution of Athens*. He had a particular interest in papyri. His eldest daughter, Kathleen Kenyon, would be the excavator of Jericho during 1952–58 and appointed dame in 1973.

37. "Up at 5.45, tea and bread at hotel at 6.30, train at 8.45 (3 trunks, 8 suitcases and cameras etc.), taxi one pound 15 shillings, 4 tickets ten pounds nine shillings and four pence (2nd on train, 1st on boat), boat at 11.15, train at 1.30, Paris at 7.30 Hotel St. James" (diary, October 10, 1919).

38. In particular, they visited the zone around Berry-au-Bac and along the river Aisne (Axona in Latin). See Francis W. Kelsey, *C. Iulii Caesaris, Commentarii Rerum Gestarum; Caesar's Commentaries: The "Gallic War," Books I–IV, with selections from Books V–VII and from the "Civil War"; with an Introduction, Notes, a Companion to Caesar and a Vocabulary*

They were shocked by what they saw: residues of battles, trenches, barbed wire, gas cylinders, unexploded shells, shrapnel everywhere, shell craters, trees reduced to splinters, shattered tanks and field guns, and German prisoners. Curious as ever, Francis asked hoteliers about their experiences, learning from one who had served for eighteen months in the trenches before Verdun that casualties had reduced his company's complement from 165 to 22.[39] The city of Reims itself was little more than heaps of rubble—"like the ruins of Pompeii," wrote another visiting American professor.[40]

Writing to Captain Spaulding on November 1, Francis remarked "the military men most cordial" and, stressing "the value of aeroplane photographs in studying the movement of forces," noted that "I have asked General Connor to request the French government to let us have duplicate aeroplane photographs."[41] Not everyone was so helpful. At the Bibliothèque Nationale one day, "an attendant spent an hour trying to locate Napoleon's *Caesar* but failed to find it either in the catalog or on a shelf."[42]

Francis spent a day at the American Embassy, where Ambassador Hugh Wallace provided a letter of introduction to Admiral Mark L. Bristol, the American high commissioner in Constantinople; he spent another day at the Hôtel de Crillon, where James Brown Scott was staying, as was the noted American archaeologist, epigraphist, and historian W. H. Buckler.[43] Kelsey took up with Scott remaining issues concerning the Grotius project.[44] With Buckler he turned to logistical matters: since he needed to study and photo-

---

(Boston: Allyn & Bacon, 1918), xx–xxvii. Kelsey wrote there that "when the Belgians tried to ford the Aisne in the face of Caesar's archers, the stream was choked with dead (II.10); dead and wounded again clogged the Aisne in 1914 when French and English troops near Berry-au-Bac built pontoon bridges within range of a murderous artillery fire" (xxi).

39. Diary, October 16, 1919.

40. James T. Shotwell, *At the Paris Peace Conference* (New York: Macmillan, 1937), 234–39, cited in Margaret MacMillan's authoritative and prizewinning *Paris 1919: Six Months That Changed the World* (New York: Random House, 2002), 149, originally published as *Peacemakers: The Paris Peace Conference of 1919 and Its Attempt to End War* (London: John Murray, 2001).

41. Kelsey to Spaulding, November 1, 1919, KMA Papers, box 31, folder 1.

42. Diary, October 25, 1919.

43. See chapter 5 n. 100.

44. At issue were the proposed publication date (now determined to be best associated with the three hundreth anniversary of the publication of the first edition, 1925), the character of the footnotes, and the need for a chapter on the life and letters of Grotius. At the time of the publication, Scott (whom we first encountered in chapter 7, "Research and Publication") had served as a delegate to the Paris Peace Conference in 1919 and was president of both the Institute of International Law and the American Institute of International Law.

graph the manuscript of the Revelation of St. John in the monastery on the island of Patmos, both for his own interest and for Sanders's, Kelsey asked Buckler about the monastery's ecclesiastical relationships and was told he would need to consult the patriarch in Jerusalem. Most days, Kelsey was in the Bibliothèque Nationale working on Grotius or Caesar or writing up his notes on the battlefields and dealing with correspondence. Swain and Easton were kept busy with photography and the printing of the seven-by-eleven-inch negatives.

On the evening of November 13, Francis and Isabelle left Paris by train for Bucharest. Swain and Easton, unable to find a place on the same train, were to follow as soon as possible; as it was, Francis had enough difficulty getting tickets for Isabelle and himself. The agent made a fuss, caused delays, and issued the tickets only when stamped "aucune responsibilité" (absolutely no responsibility). The crush of people and bags on the platform was so thick that Swain and Easton had to push the seven pieces of luggage through the window to get them into the compartment.[45] Arriving in Zagreb very late on November 15, the train pushed on through Hungary the next day, in the course of which Francis and Isabelle met two "well-groomed" German-speaking Romanians who regaled them with jokes, several ridiculing the reduced size of Austria after the war.[46] They arrived in Bucharest on November 17. Since all the hotels were full, they went to the prefect of police, who threw up his hands; there was nothing he could do. Seldom reluctant to call on the help of American authorities, Francis hurried to the American Legation, which sent him back to the prefect with an official request. At this, the prefect sent them with a soldier to the Hotel Bristol "with orders to clear a room for us."[47] Swain and Easton caught up with them late the next day, neither of them in good shape. Francis and Isabelle, however, visited the Archaeological Museum and were able finally to locate elsewhere the metopes (carved panels) from the Tropaeum Traiani at Adamclisi,[48] which were no longer in the museum. Since both Swain and Easton were sick and since the weather was foul, only a little

---

45. Devotees of the movie *Casablanca* (1942) will recall the scene of Rick's departure from Paris in somewhat similar circumstances.

46. For example, "Tomorrow's Sunday what shall we do?" "Oh let's walk around Austria," "Oh, alright but what shall we do in the afternoon?" (diary, November 16, 1919). Kelsey frequently noted such tales in his diary.

47. Diary, November 17, 1919.

48. Conrad Cichorius, *Die römischen Denkmäler in der Dobrudscha* (Berlin: Weidmannsche Buchhandlung, 1904), in which the Tropaeum Traiani is mentioned briefly, would have been well known to Kelsey.

photography was possible; but Swain did contrive one day to photograph the Adamclisi sculptures and some street and market scenes. After a week, both invalids were better, Francis paid the hotel bills, and they moved on.[49]

Their plan had been to go from Bucharest to Constanţa by rail and take a boat down the Black Sea to Constantinople. But when Swain spotted a U.S. Army Cadillac on the street in Bucharest, he spoke to the officer in charge, who, it turned out, was the American military attaché at Sofia in neighboring Bulgaria. He, Captain Erickson, advised them to avoid Constanţa and instead go to Constantinople by train though Bulgaria. Following this advice and armed with a letter from the American minister to the prefect of police at Giurgiu on the Danube (which marked the Romanian-Bulgarian border), they took a train there and found a city as ruined and derelict as Reims, thoroughly looted by the Bulgarians during the war. After staying two nights and enjoying "plaintive songs in a minor key" in restaurants, they were escorted by a police officer to the ferry across the Danube. Their baggage was waved through customs, and they reached Sofia five hours late on the next day.[50]

During the four days they were in Sofia, they secured permits to photograph the Roman baths and in the museum. Swain photographed, Easton again came down with a cold, and Francis called on Charles Wilson, the American chargé d'affaires. Francis's interests had taken yet another tack: the state of European politics after the Paris Peace Conference and the conditions in the countries through which he was passing captured his attention, so that he was sympathetic when Wilson encouraged him "to make some effort to obtain a better hearing for the Bulgarian side in the United States. The *New York Times* has been quoting the *Paris Temps* in those matters and 80% of stock of the *Temps* is owned by Greeks who also control *Figaro* and have ways of influencing newspapers in New York and London as well as Paris."[51] Not all of Francis's energies were involved with antiquity, as Wilson's request and his own well-known concern for refugee populations indicate.

A few days later, they arrived in Constantinople.[52] Francis's agenda was predictable. He went directly to the American Embassy to meet Admiral Bristol—the American high commissioner and officer commanding the fleet in the Eastern Mediterranean, to whom he had introductions from the army generals and the American ambassador in Paris—to ask for help arranging

---

49. Francis thought the hotel costs reasonable, except for the charge for firewood.
50. Diary, November 28, 1919.
51. Diary, November 29, 1919.
52. Diary, December 4, 1919.

transport through Turkey and Syria to Jerusalem. Also high on his to-do list were consultation with leaders of the American relief efforts, particularly the American Committee for Relief in the Near East (ACRNE);[53] discussion with the Greek and Armenian patriarchs about permission to study manuscripts in monastic libraries; the acquisition of Greek manuscripts from dealers; and photography of the city's architecture, antiquities, and any other evidence of social and historical change.

Immediately after his interview with Admiral Bristol, Kelsey called at Bible House, the headquarters of the American Bible Society and the local business office of the American Board of Commissioners for Foreign Missions, to confer with Dr. James McNaughton, a Canadian missionary who had worked for many years in Turkey. Shortly afterward, he met Major Davis Arnold, the head of all American relief work in the Near East, with whom he came to an arrangement by which "as opportunity offered he would endeavor to serve the interests of the ACRNE in any way possible."[54] Armed with introductions from Bristol to both the Greek and Armenian patriarchs,[55] he was able to meet the Greek patriarch's secretary, who prepared letters to the monks on Athos and Patmos that permitted photography and allowed Kelsey access to the library to look for manuscripts.[56] One day, he made his way to the Grand Bazaar, where, simply by asking who had Greek manuscripts, he located the premises of Andronikos Kidaoglou, from whom he subsequently bought several fragments of lectionaries and a late Greek manuscript "with 8 leaves palimpsest," the total cost of which was less than five hundred dollars.[57]

---

53. Few Americans had been left unmoved by the efforts of Ambassador Morgenthau (Bristol's predecessor in Constantinople) to mitigate the effects of the deportation of Armenian, Greek, and Syrian Christians. The main American agency through which help was funneled to Turkey was the American Committee for Relief in the Near East. Through its missions in Anatolia, the ACRNE organized orphanages, hospitals, and schools and distributed enormous quantities of food and clothing, tents, cots, ambulances, X-ray equipment, stoves, sewing machines, and so on. More than a hundred thousand orphans, many of whom were resettled in missions in America, came into its care.

54. Kelsey to Bristol, March 4, 1920, private collection of Easton Kelsey Jr., Rochester, NY.

55. Kelsey had written formally to Bristol with his requests (Kelsey to Bristol, December 8, 1919, KMA Papers, box 4, folder 7). Bristol wrote not only to the Greek and Armenian patriarchs but also to the director of the Imperial Ottoman Museum and to the other Allied high commissioners.

56. Diary, December 19 and 23, 1919.

57. Diary, December 9, 1919. For a stimulating account of Kelsey's activities on this day, see Artemis Leontis and Lauren Talalay, "A Day's Journey: Constantinople, December 9, 1919," *Michigan Quarterly Review* 45.1 (2006): 73–98, a reference I owe to Laurie Talalay. I am grateful, too, to Artemis Leontis for a copy of her log of the whole of the Kelsey itinerary.

He sent these acquisitions directly to William Warner Bishop, the university librarian in Ann Arbor: "By permission of US High Commissioner Bristol I am sending to you by registered post from the postal station on his flagship, USS *Galveston*[58] three packages containing manuscript material, as follows."[59] With Swain and Easton, he toured the city, photographing everywhere— monuments, street scenes, panoramas, people; he went to the Archaeological Museum, where he met the director, Halil Edhem Bey, and asked permission to photograph there.[60] Christmas Day was spent with the archbishop of Jerusalem, the personal representative of the patriarch, after which the Kelsey party was ready to move on.

A TRAVELER IN ANTIQUE LANDS

Western Asia

Major Arnold had made arrangements for the Michigan team to accompany him and a group of ACRNE officials and missionaries heading south. On December 27, after Arnold had sent a truck to pick up their luggage, a launch took the whole party to the destroyer USS *Biddle* (DD-151), which carried them down the Sea of Marmara some sixty miles to Derindje (see fig. 18), the Asiatic railhead of the Berlin-Baghdad Railroad, where a makeshift train was waiting for them.[61] There were just four cars for their group, modified freight cars in fact: a kitchen and dining car; a car for the ladies (three missionaries and Isabelle); a car for Francis, Swain, Easton, and a Mr. Seeley, an ACRNE man; and a fourth for Major Arnold, an accountant, an interpreter, and a staff member from the International Film Service (fig. 19).

---

58. After convoy service in World War I, the *Galveston* became Bristol's flagship at Constantinople, where her duties included transporting refugees, Red Cross officials, and American officers.

59. Kelsey to Bishop, December 26, 1919, FWK Papers, box 1, folder 8,

60. Diary, December 16 and 17, 1919. Kelsey took a letter from Halil Bey to be sent by diplomatic pouch to Howard Crosby Butler, the Princeton professor whose excavation at Sardis had been interrupted by the war.

61. Kelsey wrote in a letter, "Without such assistance the trip across Asia Minor by rail at this time would have been quite out of the question for us" (Kelsey to family from Jerusalem, January 28, 1920, private collection of Easton Kelsey Jr., Rochester, NY). The same letter also contains interesting details about the railway line, tunnels, freight cars (Belgian) and engines (German), much touristic geographical and historical material, and the disposition of the European troops—British (in the northwest), Italian (on the Anatolian plateau extending to Konya), and French (in the Taurus, Cilicia, and western Syria).

The train took them by way of Afyon to Konya (ancient Iconium), where they visited the museum and ruined Armenian buildings. According to Easton, there were two ACRNE orphanages there—looking after about four hundred orphans, almost all Armenian (half boys, half girls)—and a hospital. Attached to the boys' orphanage was a trade school.[62] On December 30, they crossed the Taurus Mountains, "snowcapped peaks either side, high and precipitous," to arrive in bright moonlight at Adana in the heart of what had once been Armenian Cilicia.[63] Wherever the journey took him, Kelsey documented whatever remains of Armenian culture he encountered, as well as the work of the American missions. The party stayed three days in Adana, one day visiting a refugee camp accommodating about six hundred Armenians and three hundred Greeks, the Armenian Red Cross Hospital, the YMCA, a school for girls, and a rug-making factory where more than a thousand women were at work—the last a project funded by the lord mayor of London's fund.

On New Year's Day 1920, they went by local train (tickets payable in Egyptian piastres) to Tarsus, birthplace of St. Paul. There Swain photographed "St Paul's Gate," and Francis and Isabelle visited "St Paul's College." They then pressed on—an all-day journey through the mountains—to Aleppo, the headquarters of ACRNE for southeast Asia Minor and northern Syria, where they parted company with Major Arnold and the freight cars.

Leaving Isabelle and Easton in Aleppo, Francis and Swain drove northeast some ninety miles to Aintab, another center of relief work. There, as at Konya and Adana, they documented the work of the missionary orphanages and schools and toured the mission hospital, the Armenian Relief shop, and the shattered Armenian quarter of the town. Returning to Aleppo, Kelsey found antiquities for sale "at high prices" in the souk (among other items, an Arab astrolabe), and Swain took photographs at an orphanage populated mostly by Armenian girls.[64] After a rapid visit to Baalbek to see and photograph the Temple of Zeus, they continued to Damascus for a stay of four days. In the

62. For a fifteen-year-old's perspective, containing much geographical, agricultural, architectural, and human-interest material on the whole of this trip, see Easton T. Kelsey, "At 15 I Look at '19: Letters to Alfred MacLaren White of Ann Arbor, Michigan on European Trip in 1919–1920," typescript, private collection of Easton Kelsey Jr., Rochester, NY.

63. For Kelsey's interest in Armenia, see Thelma K. Thomas, *Dangerous Archaeology: Francis Willey Kelsey and Armenia (1919–1920)* (Ann Arbor: Kelsey Museum of Archaeology, 1990).

64. Diary, January 1–12, 1920. See also Kelsey to Family, January 28, 1920. private collection of Easton Kelsey Jr., Rochester, NY.

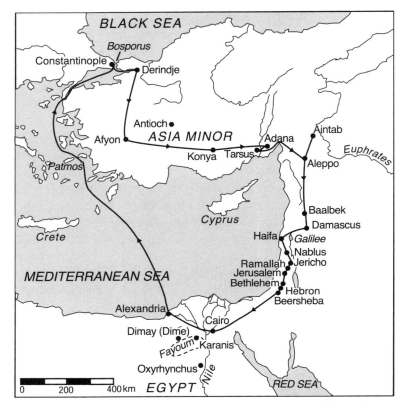

18. Map of the Eastern Mediterranean showing the route of the Kelsey party's tour. Drawing: Lorene Sterner.

course of their stay there, in addition to their regular activities, Swain photographed the arrival of Emir Faisal from the peace conference in Paris, and Francis attended the emir's speech in which he outlined the Arab objectives, in the aftermath of the Ottoman Empire, of independence for Syria and Arabia.[65]

Authorized by the military governor, Mustafa Pascha, who had commanded the Turkish army in the Caucasus, the party proceeded to Haifa and

65. For a discursive account of the journey through Europe, Turkey, and north Syria, see "The University's Expedition to the Near East: A Letter to the President from Professor Kelsey," *Michigan Alumnus* 26 (1920): 443–47, 498–503. For interesting comparison to Kelsey's 1919–20 expedition to the Near East and Egypt, detailing the similar activities of Professor

19. Train taking F. W. Kelsey, his party, and personnel of the American Committee for Relief in the Near East across Turkey to Syria, at Konya, January 1920. The modified cattle cars numbered in pencil (by Easton, whose photograph this is?) are identified in ink on the back of the photograph as follows: "1. the cook house; 2. the ladies car; 3. F.W.K, G. R. Swain and E.T.K.; 4. Near East Relief personnel." Private collection of Easton Kelsey Jr., Rochester, NY.

thence onward to Jerusalem.[66] They stayed a little more than two weeks, visiting the Mount of Olives, Gethsemane, and other major sites; at the American School, they met W. H. Worrell, who (the reader will recall) was working on Freer's Coptic manuscripts. Francis conferred with Major Nichols, a Presbyterian missionary who opined that "relief work will soon be wound up except for orphanages and rescue work";[67] bought a Hebrew scroll (the book of Esther) for one pound; and, with Dr. Robert Glover, an Evangelical missionary, visited Bethlehem, Hebron, and Beersheba. All the while, Francis wrote letters and reports, and Swain photographed. With A. G. Dana of the Stan-

James Henry Breasted, see G. Emberling, ed., *Pioneers to the Past: American Archaeologists in the Middle East, 1919–1920*, Oriental Institute Museum Publication 30 (Chicago: Oriental Institute of the University of Chicago, 2010).

66. Diary, January 20, 1920. This Mustafa Pascha should not be confused with Mustafa Kemal Pasha (Ataturk), who was in Angora (Ankara) at this time.

67. Diary, January 25, 1920.

dard Oil Company, to whom he was introduced by Worrell, Francis went (in Dana's Cadillac) to Ramallah, where they toured the Friends' School, Nablus, and Samaria.[68] Turning from the documentation of relief activities and archaeological sites to antiquities, Francis purchased some lamps and amphora stamps, which he sent at once to Ann Arbor. At this point, Isabelle fell ill for several days; her physique had held up well through the arduous journeys, but now there were worrying signs. Francis had dental problems but was otherwise as strong as a horse, and Easton and Swain had recovered from their earlier troubles.[69]

Egypt and Italy

When Isabelle rallied, they moved on to Egypt. Kelsey's first item of business in Cairo was with the local manager of the Eastman Kodak Company, a Mr. Nassibian, to make arrangements for Swain and Easton to develop and print the large number of seven-by-eleven-inch negatives and to get more film. The second was to retrieve the manuscripts that Morgan and Freer had purchased from Maurice Nahman in 1916 and that Dr. David Askren had delivered to the American consul for safekeeping until the end of the war.[70] Askren came up to Cairo from the Fayoum, and he and Kelsey duly took possession of the manuscripts—the Coptic materials for Morgan, which Kelsey had agreed to deliver in Rome to Professor Hyvernat (who was handling all of Morgan's Coptic manuscripts); and the Greek for Freer, which Kelsey planned to send direct to Ann Arbor from Italy.[71] In the meantime, Francis scurried around getting permits from various authorities (the Egyptian Museum, the British General Headquarters), deflecting the attentions of Nahman, and enduring sessions in the dentist's chair, but also lunching with James Breasted, meeting the staff of the Metropolitan Museum's excavations at Luxor, and enjoying *Tosca* at the Teatro Sultaniale de Opera.

---

68. Diary, February 2, 1920.

69. Francis was constantly bothered by his teeth. In November a dentist in Paris "had replaced the cap of rear right molar and crowned next tooth." Barely two months later, when the toothache attacked again, a dentist in Aleppo subjected him to four fillings. A week after that (now in Damascus), the diary notes "teeth hurting." Consul Young took him to a dentist who filled three more teeth, only to be persuaded later in the day by Mrs. Ellen Norton, a nurse from the ACRNE eye hospital in Aleppo, to remove the fillings, under which an abscess appeared. This was dentistry in its infancy, Francis might have thought.

70. See chapter 7, "Fund-Raising and Acquisitions."

71. Diary, February 19, 1920.

He spent the next four weeks either visiting the ancient sites accompanied by Swain or in the search for papyri, for much of the time in the company of Bernard Grenfell, who rapidly became a good friend. Grenfell was seeking papyri for the British Museum and the John Rylands Library in Manchester, while Kelsey was acting for Michigan and for the University of Wisconsin. Since Grenfell was looking for Ptolemaic material and Kelsey for Roman, a partnership was formed, with Kelsey happy to let Grenfell select papyri for them both. In Cairo they bought from Nahman; they relied on Grenfell's identifications and sense of quality and struck hard bargains.[72] A few days later, they were together at David Askren's house in the Fayoum, purchasing papyri he had acquired and buying directly from local dealers: Mohammad Rafar, Andreas Gurgis, Mohammad Abdullah, and others. They visited sites together—Oxyrhynchus, Heracleopolis, Theadelphia (see fig. 20), Karanis—Kelsey thinking about suitable sites for excavation. Back in Cairo, there were more purchases from Nahman;[73] Francis was so pleased by the acquisitions that when he left Egypt at the end of April, he asked Askren and Nahman to get hold of whatever good-quality papyri they could and said that he would buy them "at a fair price."

Since Grenfell had agreed to identify and evaluate the papyri and be responsible for the division of the Roman material between Michigan and Wisconsin, taking into account the funding each provided and the kind of papyri each wished to have, all the papyri were sent to Oxford. It was a stroke of great good fortune that the Americans were able to call on Grenfell's skills and those of his colleague, Arthur Hunt,[74] and this owes a good deal to Kelsey's genial personality. The partnership was so successful that, later in the year, Francis proposed to Harold Idris Bell, a curator of manuscripts at the British Museum who became a key member of the team and a good friend to Kelsey,[75] that they form a consortium—consisting of the British Museum, the

---

72. Diary, February 21, 1920.

73. Diary, March 6, 10, and 12, 1920.

74. Grenfell commented to Kelsey that Hunt was married and "not disposed to travel," whereas he (Grenfell) was "otherwise, and ready to excavate for papyri" (diary, March 1, 1920). For a journalistic view of the recovery of papyri, Michigan's acquisitions in 1920, and Kelsey's relationship with Grenfell, see "Damming of Nile Enabled University to Get Papyri," *Ann Arbor Times-News*, October 21, 1920. For more on Grenfell and Hunt, see chapter 7, "Fund-Raising and Acquisitions."

75. Educated at Oxford, Harold Idris Bell joined the Department of Manuscripts at the British Museum as an assistant in 1903. Appointed deputy keeper in 1927 and keeper in 1929, he was knighted in 1946. A prolific scholar, he was both a distinguished papyrologist and a discerning critic of Welsh poetry.

20. Francis Kelsey and Bernard Grenfell at Theadelphia, spring 1920.
Private collection of Easton Kelsey Jr., Rochester, NY. Photo: Easton Kelsey.

Rylands Library, the University of Michigan and the University of Wisconsin, and others[76]—which would send a representative to Egypt each year to find papyri. The consortium continued in existence as long as Kelsey was alive— and, indeed, sporadically thereafter—succeeding in keeping the prices asked by Nahman and others to a reasonable level, since the interested parties were not bidding against one another.[77]

---

76. Columbia, Cornell, Princeton, and the University of Geneva participated from time to time.

77. As an example of the moderating power of the consortium and of its principal nego-tiator, Idris Bell, see the comparison of the prices asked by Nahman and those offered by Bell

It was agreed that the British Museum should be the nerve center of this alliance, since it alone had staff capable of dealing expertly with and conserving the papyri, many of which were often in precarious condition when on offer in Cairo—tangled together, folded up, and fragile. Painstaking sorting, cleaning, and flattening had to take place before identification of content and evaluation of quality. It was therefore also agreed that the British Museum should have first choice among the papyri best suited to its collection. Further division took place on the basis of the size of each institution's financial contribution and the interests of its scholars—whether they were studying Coptic, Greek, or Latin, literary or documentary papyri. In most years, the consortium sent a representative to Egypt to buy papyri, and annual division took place in London.[78]

By the end of 1926, the dealers' supply of papyri was running dry; but a new, more legitimate source had come into existence, at least for Michigan. In the excavations at Karanis, papyri came to light in the very first season of work (1924–25). These documents came to Ann Arbor in accordance with the regulations then in force governing the export of antiquities and with the blessing of the authorities of the Egyptian Museum.[79]

During these early months of 1920, Swain was taking and developing photographs, assisted by Easton, while Kelsey, in addition to searching for papyri, was dealing with correspondence: reports to ACRNE and to Michigan and letters to the main supporters of the expedition, Mrs. Longyear and Mr.

---

in his *First Report on Papyri Sent by Nahman: July 1923,* available online at http://www.lib .umich.edu/pap/exhibits/MPC/Reports/1923/7_20_23_bell.html (accessed June 9, 2009). Acquisition reports for the years 1920–26, most written by Bell, may be found in the Papyrus Collection at the Hatcher Graduate Library, University of Michigan; see http://www.lib .umich.edu/pap/exhibits/MPC/Reports (accessed June 9, 2009).

78. For activities prior to the division that took place in the summer of 1921 and details of the division itself, see the September 21, 1921, letter sent (according to the online version) by Frederic L. Kenyon (incorrect initial if intended to be that of the director of the British Museum) to the Princeton and Cornell members of the consortium, with details of the distribution of the papyri. The electronic version of this letter may be found online at http://www.lib.umich.edu/pap/exhibits/MPC/Reports/1921/9_21_21_kenyon.html (accessed June 9, 2009). However, this letter written from New York cannot have been written by the director of the British Museum, since he was not there at the time. Kelsey, however, was, and the language of the letter is his. The electronic version is due to be changed accordingly (personal correspondence with T. Gagos).

79. For a concise history of the early years of the growth of the Michigan collection, see Arthur E. R. Boak, "The Building of the University of Michigan Papyrus Collection," *Michigan Alumnus Quarterly Review* 66.10 (Autumn 1959): 35–42; for more recent developments, see Traianos Gagos, "The University of Michigan Papyrus Collection: Current Trends and Future Perspectives," in *Atti del XXII Congresso Internazionale di Papirologia, Firenze 1998,* ed. I. Andorlini (Florence: Istituto Papirologico "G. Vitelli," 2001), 511–37.

Boyer. He also prepared two documents for Admiral Bristol: a memorandum of his impressions of the Arab response to Emir Faisal's arrival in Damascus after the peace talks in Paris and of the failure of the French administration in Cilicia and Syria and a report of information available to him about the murder of two American relief workers, James Perry and F. L. Johnson, on the road between Aleppo and Aintab on February 1, 1920.[80] He sent these documents from Alexandria via the destroyer USS *Du Pont* (DD-152).[81]

Having promised to deliver Morgan's manuscripts to Professor Hyvernat in Rome, Kelsey made arrangements to travel to Italy on the SS *Sicilia* on March 17. After staying up writing and typing until 3:00 a.m., he caught the morning train to Alexandria and was on board, carrying both the Morgan and the Freer manuscripts with him, when the *Sicilia* sailed at 4:00 p.m. Among the passengers was an ailing Mrs. Petrie, wife of the renowned Egyptologist Flinders Petrie,[82] whom Kelsey had visited at his site at el-Lahun in February. Although he remarked that "the younger French woman was the center of attraction on board,"[83] the voyage to Italy repeatedly evoked classical associations for Kelsey. When the steamer passed Syracuse, his thoughts turned to the Cyclops, and "Lucretius' description rang in my ears," while Syracuse itself "quickened memories of Thucydides VI and VII, of Cicero's story of Dionysius and Damocles, and the view of Etna the first day of my visit in 1883." The diary becomes quite rhapsodic: "In the straits of Messina I seemed to see again Nasidius, Pompey's general, filch a ship from the naval base of Messana, escaping Curio and sailing off to Massilia to fight Brutus"; "Stromboli with memories of Vergil's Aeolus and Pliny the Elder; Capri with a flood of associations and all the recollections, innumerable, associated with the shore back of the Bay of Naples."[84] But arrival in Italy brought him back to earth: the train to Rome was crowded,

---

80. Kelsey to Bristol, March 4 and 5, 1920, private collection of Easton Kelsey Jr., Rochester, NY.

81. Diary, March 4, 1920.

82. Diary, March 17, 1920. Excavator of many Egyptian sites for the Egyptian Exploration Fund and professor of Egyptology at University College, London, Sir Flinders Petrie (knighted in 1923) revolutionized archaeology in Egypt by his introduction of stratigraphic recording, the study of typology, and the use of the comparative method. Well known for his work at the Great Pyramid of Giza, at Thebes, and at Naukratis, he had briefly investigated Karanis in 1890.

83. Diary, March 19, 1920.

84. Diary, March 20 and 21, 1920.

and since he had no reservation, the Pensione Boos could only fix up a cot for him in the bathroom.[85]

He immediately took the Morgan manuscripts to Professor Hyvernat and touched base at the American Academy, where Director Stevens provided him with a workroom. After spending a couple of days with Hyvernat, going over details of the transaction and the accounts, he made arrangements at the American Embassy to have Freer's Greek manuscripts sent by diplomatic pouch to the State Department and from there to the University Library at Michigan. He then set about his correspondence: letters to Mrs. Longyear and to President Hutchins, Henry Sanders, W. W. Bishop, Regents Beal and Hubbard, and others in Ann Arbor. A major item was a report for the executors of the Freer estate, documenting the purchases of papyri, the intention to acquire others, discussion of the will's provision of fifty thousand dollars for the University of Michigan, and the use of the fifteen hundred dollars given by Freer to test the site where (the dealer claimed) the Freer manuscripts had been discovered.[86] Tireless, he also wrote an article to be submitted to the *New York Times* and the *Detroit Free Press,* "A Message from Emir Faisal."[87] After a week, he had accomplished what he wanted done and set out on the return to Egypt. The train to Naples was again so crowded that he had to sit on his suitcase in the aisle of the carriage, but he was nevertheless surprised to hear a departing soldier make the uncomplimentary remark, "Ecco Roma, capitale del mondo, capitale muco." All the same, his spirits rose when, having found a dining car on the train, he enjoyed what he described as "a good dinner, as times are—macaroni, omelet, roast, small bottle of wine."[88]

Unsure when the steamer—the *Sicilia* again—would arrive and almost instantly depart, he busied himself with correspondence, including a letter of condolence to Mrs. Alice Tweed Andrews on the death of her son Vernon on Capri,[89] about which Stevens at the American Academy had informed him. He also called on the American consul, Homer Morrison Byington, a friend

---

85. For an American, however, living was cheap. Whereas there were five lire to the dollar before the war, there were now twenty-one (Easton T. Kelsey, "At 15 I Look at '19," 17).

86. Diary, March 27, 1920. Freer had died the previous September (see n. 33).

87. Other newspaper articles he wrote in the course of the expedition included "A Rainbow on the Sea of Galilee," "A Speed Run on a Destroyer in the Sea of Marmara," "The Battlefield of Berry-au-Bac," and "Aspects of American Relief Work in the Near East."

88. Diary, March 31, 1920; April 1, 1920. "Take a look at Rome, capital of the World, capital of slime." I am most grateful to Daniela Gobetti for help with the translation.

89. Mrs. Andrews was the American who had bought Jerome's villa on the island.

of Jerome's, with whom he took walks and shared breakfast and who agreed to mail his letters for him. The return voyage to Egypt was uneventful, Kelsey again stirred by the sight of the mountains as they passed Crete: "in 1885 Eckfeld and I with muleteer riding north over the shoulder of Parnassus caught sight of the dazzling brilliance of Olympus; such glimpses no doubt suggested to more distant folk the idealization of snow-capped mountains as home of the gods; nearer folk would have been more conscious of the cold."[90]

For the balance of the month, he continued negotiations with Nahman, worked on the accounts, wrote several newspaper articles,[91] and toured sites in the Fayoum with Askren and Swain. On one day, he enjoyed a conversation with Clemenceau[92] in the hotel garden; on another, a chat with Flinders Petrie, thinking it worth noting in his diary Petrie's remark that "the excavator is the salvage man, rescuing for the future before it is too late"—a rather obvious observation doubtless prompted by the ongoing destruction of ancient sites by farmers seeking fertilizer and by developers. Swain and Easton were occupied with photography and developing; Isabelle fell ill but recovered. Having asked Admiral Bristol in Constantinople about a ride to the island of Patmos, where he wished to study and photograph manuscripts in the Monastery of St. John the Divine, he was delighted to receive a telegram on April 26 telling him of the arrival in Alexandria of a destroyer that could help him.

Patmos

The destroyer USS *Smith Thompson* (DD-212), under the command of Captain J. H. S. Dessez, took them on board on the evening of May 2 for the two-day journey to Patmos, a small island off the coast of Asia Minor.[93] Kelsey was amused to find a Michigan alumnus among the officers, Lieutenant McDonald, whose brother had been editor of the *Michigan Daily* in 1917–18 and whose father was a graduate of the dental school. They were greeted on ar-

---

90. Diary, April 6, 1920.

91. Diary, April 16, 1920.

92. Georges Benjamin Clemenceau was prime minister of France in the closing stages of World War I and a dogged negotiator in the talks leading to the Treaty of Versailles in 1919. On his crafty, demanding, stubborn, in-your-face manner of negotiating, see MacMillan, *Paris 1919*, 198–203.

93. Among Christians, Patmos is the most sacred island in the Aegean, the one where St. John experienced the apocalyptic visions that became the New Testament book of Revelation.

rival by the commander of the Italian occupying force, Tenente Armonoto Cozzi, their way smoothed by a letter from the Italian high commissioner in Constantinople.[94] They spent a fruitful month on an island "still in the Middle Ages—no roads, no newspapers, no carts."[95] The very first day, the Italians sent a messenger up to the Monastery of St. John with the letter of introduction Francis had brought from the patriarch of the Greek Church in Constantinople. The following morning, they were escorted by priests from the monastery, first to see the mayor, then further up the hill to visit the monastery,[96] where they met the prior. The whole party (including Isabelle) was then, to Francis's obvious delight, invited to stay at the monastery itself, with the twenty-two resident priests and ten monks.[97]

The monastery's church, to which is attached the Chapel of St. Christodoulos (named after the monastery's founder), faces the central court, and there are seven other chapels dotted around the complex. Francis attended early morning mass in the church twice during their stay and the vespers more frequently, noting the "glorious rituals" and the complex music.[98] The guest apartment, furnished with a sitting room, three bedrooms, and a kitchen, was comfortable without being commodious. Their meals, mostly cooked for them by the mother of one of the monks outside the monastery and sent in, were simple "but adequate."[99] Once or twice, they were invited to dine outside the monastery with the Italians, who provided more ambitious fare: antipasti, macaroni, fish, partridge. But the library, with its many valuable ancient manuscripts and lectionaries, was the principal object of Francis's attention. Swain was occasionally allowed, under close supervision, to

---

94. After the war between Italy and Turkey in 1911–12, Patmos (whose population of some thirty-five hundred was entirely Greek) and eleven other islands were transferred from Turkish control to Italian. The Italian force on Patmos in 1920 comprised four officers, seven soldiers, and two signal corpsmen.

95. Diary, May 13, 1920.

96. The monastery is equipped with mighty towers and battlements as well as belfries and domed roofs, making it visually an impressive document of Byzantine military and ecclesiastical architecture.

97. The rule at the similar monasteries on Mount Athos that women are not allowed inside was here relaxed. Indeed, Isabelle found herself welcome wherever she went; when outside the monastery, she was often greeted by women and children bringing her bunches of roses.

98. Diary, May 12 and 22, 1920.

99. Further details about the apartment, the monastery as a whole, the countryside, and activities may be gleaned from a letter written by Isabelle to Ruth and Charlotte dated "May, 1920" (private collection of Easton Kelsey Jr., Rochester, NY).

photograph critical pages while he pursued his research on the manuscripts of the Gospels and the Greek text of the Apocalypse.[100] He also took many photographs of the monastery itself and its inhabitants. As usual, Francis also kept up his correspondence, writing and sending photographs to Mrs. Longyear and Mr. Boyer.[101] In his gregarious way, he conversed with some of the monks and other locals, who do not seem to have appreciated the presence of the Italians: "It was better under the Turks, they were cordial to us."[102]

When Swain and Easton were occupied in hauling the photographic equipment all over the island (admittedly with the help of a mule) and taking pictures of panoramas, the more than 350 small chapels with which the island is dotted, and contemporary buildings, Francis and Isabelle would sometimes take walks admiring the landscape and the views—to the west, the Cyclades, visible on a clear day; in other directions, the islands of Ikaria and Samos and the coast of Asia Minor. Among sites they visited was the Cave of the Apocalypse, the grotto, transformed into a chapel, in which legend has it that John experienced his visions recorded in the book of Revelation.

Constantinople and Athens

After four weeks on the island, their work done, they were picked up by the destroyer USS *Biddle* (on regular patrol in the Aegean) and taken to Constantinople. Exchanging the tranquillity of Patmos for the hustle and bustle of the city, their two-week stay in Constantinople was as hectic as ever. There were consultations with and reports for ACRNE, as well as reports for the YMCA, along with the delivery of photographs of relief activities (hospitals, schools, housing, industries). There was exhilarating photography with the help of the subchaser USS *SC-338*, which towed a motorboat up the Asiatic side of the Bosporus and down the European, allowing the party to land wherever they wanted to take photographs of sites, ruins, or views. There were visits to Robert College, first to request and be granted use of the college's photography lab and then to attend the baccalaureate exercises, and to

---

100. More recent studies include Canon J. P. M. Sweet, *Revelation* (Philadelphia: Westminster Press, 1979), in which the author suggests that parts should no longer be thought of as Christian but should be considered more like scenes from opera.

101. An eight-page chatty letter to Mrs. Longyear gives interesting perspectives and sidelights on life on the island (Kelsey to Longyear, May 19, 1920, private collection of Easton Kelsey Jr., Rochester, NY).

102. Diary, May 16, 1920.

Constantinople College for Women, also an American foundation.[103] At Constantinople College, Francis examined a collection of antiquities before attending commencement exercises, where the international character of the students was emphasized by the presence among the graduates of "9 Greeks, 9 Armenians, 3 Turks, 2 Bulgarians, 1 Hebrew."[104] Admiral Bristol gave the address.

There was the usual mountain of correspondence, for which Kelsey was fortunate to get the help of a stenographer (Mrs. de Bouvier) at the ACRNE headquarters and to be able to use the postal facilities on the USS *Galveston*. He wrote an article on contemporary Constantinople (particularly the areas destroyed by fire), with proposals for the future;[105] he visited the dealer Kidaoglou again in the bazaar and purchased a lamp and a brick stamp; he dined with Admiral Bristol, "who thinks the Greeks will get Constantinople," and Sir William M. Ramsay, "who thinks the Greeks will fabricate an excuse and just seize Constantinople."[106] On June 7, he lodged a request with Admiral Bristol for transport to Samsun on the Black Sea coast, wishing to see conditions in that part of the country, only to be told a week later that Mustafa Kemal (better known these days as Atatürk) wanted no Americans going about anywhere in the country.[107] So Francis decided to go to Greece for more manuscript and photography work in Athens, and since Admiral Bristol could not help with transport, no naval vessels being due to go to Piraeus, passage was booked on the SS *Milano*, leaving on June 19.

By the evening of June 21, they were installed at the Hotel Minerva, and

---

103. A university preparatory school, Robert College was founded by American philanthropists in the 1860s to offer American-style education; Constantinople College for Women was founded similarly a few years later. In a letter later sent from Patras to his sister, Kelsey mentions that Swain and Easton spent a whole week at Robert College on photographic work in the lab, staying with Professor Theodore Fowle (a Michigan graduate) and his wife (Kelsey to Harriet, June 28, 1920, private collection of Easton Kelsey Jr., Rochester, NY).

104. Diary, June 11, 1920.

105. "The Burnt Areas of Constantinople and Proposal for a City Plan," *Art and Archaeology* 10.5 (1920): 163–70. Kelsey had asked Admiral Bristol to read over and comment on a draft of this article (Bristol to Kelsey, January 13, 1920 and May 21, 1920, KMA Papers, box 4, folder 7).

106. On Ramsay, see n. 136.

107. Mustafa Kemal knew better than anyone that the Greek assault on the interior of Asia Minor was imminent. By August the Greeks were 250 miles inland; a year later, they were close to Angora (Ankara). Once the Turks had settled their problems in the east, they counterattacked against the Greeks, on August 26, 1922, taking just fourteen days to drive the Greeks into the sea. The Turks had many scores to settle.

Francis had already called at the American School of Classical Studies, looking unsuccessfully for Carl Blegen.[108] They remained in Athens a week. On one day, Francis was at the National Library, searching for a manuscript of Nicomachus, and at the Academy of Sciences, wishing to see John Svoronos, the famous numismatist; on another, he saw the ephor general, to request access to museums and permissions to photograph (granted), and was then back at the National Library with Swain, to photograph Nicomachus manuscripts (nos. 1115, 1238, and 1187). Another day was spent with Swain and Easton, shooting panoramas from the Panathenaic Stadium and Philopappos Hill, as well as street scenes; Francis noted, "only European costumes seen— the red fez common on the street 35 years ago has entirely disappeared."[109] All done, they left for Patras by train, crowded as usual, the discomfort softened by glorious views of arable land around Eleusis, vineyards beyond Corinth, and the many cypresses. Their ship for Naples, the SS *Presidente Wilson,* was late, giving them a free day in Patras for walks, letter writing, and shopping and for Francis and Isabelle to reminisce about their visit in 1901 with the group from the American School of Classical Studies in Rome.[110]

Boarding the steamship on June 29, they were in Rome two days later, spending just six days there. Francis took care of major business quickly. There were arrangements to make for "next year" at the American Academy, including the storage of books and packages that had arrived for him and the reservation of a study; then there was correspondence, largely with colleagues at Michigan. He also wrote to Ruth, enclosing a birthday gift, a check for twenty-five dollars.[111] There was time for walks with Easton to the basilica and catacombs of San Sebastiano and the tomb of Caecilia Metella on the Appian Way, with "Soracte visible, and vistas over the Campagna with stalking aqueducts"; and there was even time for the purchase of a dark serge suit for Francis.[112] On July 7, they were on the move again. As they approached Paris,

---

108. Carl William Blegen, assistant director of the American School of Classical Studies (1920–26) and then professor at the University of Cincinnati for thirty years (1927–57), became a renowned excavator, perhaps best known for the discovery and excavation (1939, 1952–69) of the so-called Palace of Nestor at Pylos in the Peloponnese.

109. Diary, June 25, 1920.

110. Diary, June 28, 1920.

111. Diary, July 5, 1920.

112. Soracte is an often snow-capped mountain some twenty-five miles from Rome, celebrated by the poet Horace. The suit cost 375 lire, which Francis reckoned the equivalent of $23.31.

the farmer in him noted that they had followed the harvests—Egypt in April, Patmos in May, Greece at the end of June, Italy in early July, and in the "Paris environs just beginning." Twenty-four hours after leaving Rome, they were in the Hôtel Saint James in Paris.

Paris and London

For the next month, among all the time-consuming business of correspondence, requests for permits, and other bureaucratic problems, Francis was busy with his Caesar studies and with the acquisition of manuscripts from Parisian dealers. Wishing to make arrangements for another trip to the battlefields, he had conversations with Major General Henry T. Allen,[113] the commander of American forces in Germany, who promised help at Coblenz. On the lookout for manuscripts, Francis, accompanied by Yale professor Albert T. Clay,[114] visited the offices of I. E. Géjou, a recognized dealer, where he saw and bought a Greek lectionary. Géjou, a native of Baghdad whose wife was French, followed up by sending a batch of manuscripts around to the hotel, three of which Francis also purchased. In free time, Francis took walks with Isabelle in the Tuileries; and on July 14, he enjoyed the Bastille Day illuminations and fireworks at the Hôtel de Ville, where he was impressed by the conduct of the crowd—"no jostling, no intoxication."

Family matters were, as ever, on his mind. On July 28, Francis and Isabelle received a letter from Ruth "regarding the arrangements for her marriage on July 17th to Fred C. Diel" (this is the first mention of the event in the diary), to which they replied with a cable noteworthy for its brevity: "Diel, Kirkland Apartments, San Diego, California. Our Blessings. Kelsey." Ruth had always had a mind of her own. Telegrams were exchanged with Charlotte, about whose health there was some worry.[115] Wondering how to proceed with Easton's schooling—in light of his unsuccessful year at the Hill School in Penn-

---

113. Henry Tureman Allen (1859–1930), who had led an exploratory expedition in Alaska during 1885, had also served in the Spanish-American War and led the Nintieth Infantry Division in World War I.

114. Albert Tobias Clay (1866–1925) was a Semitic archaeologist who, after teaching at the University of Pennsylvania and the Chicago Lutheran Seminary, became an Assyriologist in Yale's Department of Near Eastern Languages and Civilizations and fostered an archaeological research center in Baghdad. Among his writings are *Amurru, the Home of the Northern Semites* (1909) and *Neo-Babylonian Letters from Erech* (1919), both recently reprinted (Whitefish, MT: Kessinger, 2009).

115. Diary, July 30 and August 2, 1920.

sylvania, his struggles with learning in Ann Arbor, and now his unconventional year abroad with no formal instruction whatever—they decided to send him to Phillips Exeter Academy in New Hampshire. He was to take lodgings at Mrs. Rowe's house, 40 High Street, for the academic year 1920–21, while they remained in Europe. Meanwhile, on July 16, Francis sent him to London with Swain to complete the photography of the large Beatus manuscript (more than four hundred pages), a task involving eleven-by-fourteen-inch photographic plates and three weeks' work. They arrived back in Paris on August 4.

But mostly Francis was anxious about Isabelle's health. She had felt uncomfortable and sick on several occasions on the journey through Asia Minor and Palestine and in Egypt, and he feared the worst. On July 19, they consulted Dr. T. G. Jarvis, who, after reassuring Isabelle about "the cancer she feared," nonetheless referred her to Dr. Charles Dubouchet, a distinguished surgeon and stalwart of the American Hospital in Paris during the war, who suggested a short stay for tests at the Clinique Médicale de Paris at 6 rue Piccini. She entered the clinic a few days later. After the tests and a brief operation, "no indication of abnormal growth" was reported; all the same, tissue samples were sent to the lab for analysis. On August 1, to the enormous relief of them both, Dr. Dubouchet declared "the report wholly favorable—no trace of abnormal tissue revealed by curetting."[116] Isabelle's birthday party on August 6 was particularly joyous.

While Isabelle was in the clinic, Francis visited almost every day, on occasion spending whole days at her side. When not visiting the clinic, he worked on a version of his *Caesar;* at the Bibliothèque Nationale; or at the Louvre, examining Assyrian material with Professor Clay. But now it was time to move on. An overnight journey took them to Coblenz, where an army officer met them and took them to their billet at the Hotel Traube. Dining that evening with General Allen, they met a Captain Minuth, who had been assigned to the expedition as "assistant in research." For the next three weeks, he accompanied them as they traveled by automobile, covering some fourteen hundred miles in Germany, Belgium, and eastern France, studying the terrain and its relevance to Caesar's campaigns.

By riverboat, Francis reconnoitered the banks of the Rhine between Coblenz and Andernach, following up by having Swain photograph possible

---

116. Isabelle was in the clinic for nine days, and the bill for the clinic was 707 francs, while Dr. Dubouchet's fee was a round 1,000 francs (diary, August 1, 1920).

sites for Caesar's bridge over the river, as well as the sites of Roman camps near Andernach. The river is narrow at this point, and the riverbanks on either side are flat and spacious, so it was unsurprising that this had been the spot chosen by the German army for a railway bridge in the recent war. They visited Bonn, where they saw the statue of Julius Caesar (close to the bridge there) and the museum with a map display showing the Roman fortifications. Then they went to Cologne (visiting a museum with Roman glass, plates, and lamps), Cobden (seeing milestones and wooden bridge piles), Düren, and Aachen. Crossing into Belgium, their route took them close to Liège (where Francis noted the land divided into small fields by thick hedges, just as in Caesar's day)[117] and to Brussels, Louvain, and Malmedy. In their Opel car, which Francis described as "sound" but "tires weak" (reduced to shreds at one point), they ranged as far in France as Sens (Agedincum) to the southwest and Besançon (Vesontio) to the southeast. At Alise-Sainte-Reine (Alesia), they saw and photographed the statue of Vercingetorix. Francis walked over and inspected what were thought to be the sites of Roman camps, battlefields, and siegeworks, considering lines of march and approach and not always agreeing with others' observations.[118] After saying good-bye to Captain Minuth and the car at Colmar, they made their way to Strasbourg and, from there, back to Paris, arriving at the end of the month. The value of their survey was thought by Kelsey to be fourfold: it provided visits to "sites now to be understood more intelligently"; it gave a good idea "of the countryside in which Caesar's and other military operations took place"; it had made available "rapid comparison of remote sites" impossible other than by car; and driving had meant that "earth features could be viewed and comprehended" better than by train travel.[119]

Delaying only a single day in Paris for Francis to write to contributors— principally Mrs. Longyear and Mr. Boyer, but also John R. Russel, Dexter Ferry Jr., and Paul, David, and Philip Gray[120]—they pressed on to London.

---

117. *De Bello Gallico* 2.17.

118. Near Liège, Kelsey thought "the depression at Koninxheim not in close agreement with Caesar's description"; and at Mont-Falhize, between Huy and Namur, he found it "difficult to reconcile the site with Caesar's account of his approach with siegeworks" (diary, August 20, 22, 1920).

119. Diary, September 28, 1920.

120. Paul Gray, who graduated from Michigan (A.B. 1890) just one year after Francis Kelsey arrived on campus, became a successful banker and manufacturer in Detroit. David was a director of the Ford Motor Company. All three Gray brothers were the sons of John S. Gray, president of the German American Bank in Detroit and one of the initial investors in (and first president of) the Ford Motor Company in 1903.

Two matters were at the front of Francis's mind. Swain and Easton were due to leave London for their return to the United States on September 4, and Francis needed to write letters to people in New York—William Sloane, Otto Kahn, Willard King, George Plimpton, and Belle da Costa Greene—for Swain to deliver. From New York, Swain would accompany Easton to Phillips Exeter, delivering a letter (and a check) to the principal, and then go on to Ann Arbor. The other matter was the examination and division of the papyri sent from Cairo to Hunt.

Francis and Isabelle went with Swain and Easton, loaded down with photographic plates as well as their bags, to the railway station to see them off to Liverpool.[121] Everything went according to plan; two days later, they received letters from Easton and Swain, mailed from Queenstown, the port in Ireland where the RMS *Caronia* had stopped to pick up passengers. Francis had called at Brown, Shipley, and Company to pick up his mail, pleased to find that the materials sent from Cairo to London had arrived, as had the packages and trunks from Constantinople. However, there was no news from Hunt in Oxford of the arrival of the papyri; this was an instant worry, and Francis wrote Hunt at once. Meanwhile, there were countless letters to be written, accounts to be tallied, arrangements to be made, and people to see.

Francis arranged for Swain's photographic equipment to be stored in London (pending other expeditions already taking shape in his mind) and for the regents of the university to send a vote of thanks to Admiral Bristol and General Allen. At the British Museum, he met Idris Bell in person for the first time and spent hours in the library and the manuscript room, witnessing the unrolling and mounting of papyri. In his spare time, he and Isabelle visited St. Paul's Cathedral, Westminster Abbey, Westminster Cathedral, and Hampton Court and attended the theater.[122] Flinders Petrie was not at University College the day that Francis sought him out; when he did catch up

---

121. Summarizing the photographic results of their work in a letter to his old friend Charles R. Williams (see chapter 7 n. 36), Kelsey wrote: "I might say that the photographs number upwards of 600 11″ × 14″ negatives (manuscript material in the British Museum), upwards of 900 negatives 7″ × 11″ (field studies of several kinds, manuscript material on Patmos and in Athens) and more than 3,000 small photographs showing details" (Kelsey to Williams, January 29, 1921, KMA Papers, box 36, folder 2, copy in private collection of Easton Kelsey Jr., Rochester, NY).

122. He attended *Chu Chin Chow*, a musical comedy that had been running at His Majesty's Theatre since 1916. Based on *Ali Baba and the Forty Thieves* and starring Oscar Asche and Lily Brayton, its record-breaking run lasted into 1921, for 2,238 performances. Francis comments, tolerantly, on the "swing and rhythm" and "good orchestration" (diary, September 18, 1920).

with him on September 26, Petrie remarked, in the course of conversation, that he avoided theft at his excavations by paying the workmen "the market value of anything they found on top of their wage."

Hunt messaged that there was "no light on the missing papyri," at which Kelsey cabled Mr. Firth at the Egyptian Museum in Cairo ("Can you locate shipment left your charge May first. No trace. Non-arrival upsets plans")[123] and wrote to Campbell Cowan Edgar, the head of the museum. Three days later, a cable in reply stated that the "shipper was Congdon," and a follow-up letter said that the "shipper had given receipt for insurance." Somewhat mollified but still without the precious papyri, Kelsey decided to handle this himself. Visiting the shipping agent in Fenchurch Street, he was directed to the docks, only to be told that there were always undesignated "mysterious packages" there and to help himself. Stumbling about among these boxes, suitcases, and packages, by some stroke of fortune, he found the boxes with the papyri. Two days later, he was on the train with them to Oxford. Making his way to Grenfell's rooms in Queen's College, he found Grenfell sick, but Hunt was there, too, and eager to examine the papyri and make the division. He left them to it.[124]

Exhilarated by the recovery of the papyri, he invited Idris Bell and two other papyrologists he had met recently at the British Museum, Walter E. Crum and Hugh G. Evelyn-White, to lunch at the Authors' Club at Whitehall Court in London to discuss difficulties in the acquisition and publication of papyri.[125] Alarmed at the possible loss in transit of the papyri and by the damage done to the other boxes that had arrived in Ann Arbor and fearful of possible problems with U.S. customs officers, who might not treat the papyri as deferentially as he thought they should, Kelsey decided to transport them across the Atlantic himself.[126] Learning that Mrs. Abner Larned and her son Bradford—for whom, the reader will recall, Francis had arranged special tu-

---

123. Diary, September 20, 1920.

124. Diary September 29, 1920.

125. Educated at Eton and Oxford, Crum was the most eminent Coptic scholar of his generation. Evelyn-White, a professor at Leeds University, was a classical scholar known for his knowledge of Egypt and of Arabic.

126. Writing to David Gray at this time, he explained his anxieties: "The wooden case in which were the tin boxes containing them bore the seal of the Egyptian government, affixed at the Museum in Cairo; yet conditions of transport are bad, and the box was completely lost sight of for three months, and only recovered by me last week. Some smaller boxes which I sent to Ann Arbor arrived in bad condition—had they contained papyri, these would have been a complete loss; in this case the mischief was likely done at the Customs House" (Kelsey to Gray, October 8, 1920, KMA Papers, box 14, folder 7, copy in private collection of Easton Kelsey Jr., Rochester, NY).

ition in Ann Arbor—were not only in London but were returning to the United States on the RMS *Aquitania* on October 23, he booked passage on the same vessel, urging Hunt and Grenfell to work as fast as they could.

He was also pushing forward with plans for future expeditions in which he hoped to involve Captain Spaulding. To this end, he planned to circumvent the generals who had blocked Spaulding's appointment to the Michigan expedition in the past by going straight to the secretary of war, Newton D. Baker,[127] in Washington. He knew that the help of General Allen would carry weight in any discussion with Baker, so he decided on a lightning trip to Germany. Leaving from Folkestone on October 14 and traveling via Boulogne, Brussels, and Cologne, Francis and Isabelle were in Coblenz the following day.[128] Allen received him the next day and provided him with a sealed letter to the secretary of war the following morning. They then returned to London.

Grenfell and Hunt had meantime done their work. They had flattened out the papyri, put them in folders, made two inventories and transcripts, and decided on a division (534 items for Michigan, 81 for Wisconsin)—all in the space of three weeks. Kelsey could not have asked for more. Hurrying to Oxford, he returned to London with the papyri just three days before the *Aquitania* was due to sail. Isabelle was to stay in London and go about with her friends while Francis was away.

TO THE UNITED STATES AND BACK

Boarding ship on October 23, Francis enjoyed the journey, chatting with anyone he met (including his steward, on such topics as the relative merits of oil and coal, the number of stokers, and their food), dining each day with the Larneds,[129] noting the number of passengers and crew (1,474 third-, 700 second-, and 650 first-class passengers, plus 900 crew), and recording speeds and distances. The ship docked on October 30, and by evening he was at his brother's house in Orange, overjoyed to find Charlotte there with the new man in her life, Frank J. Hubley. Charlotte, now assistant to the head of re-

---

127. Newton Diehl Baker Jr. had been mayor of Cleveland (1912–15) and cofounded the Cleveland law firm Baker and Hostetler (1916) before serving as Wilson's secretary of war (1916–21).

128. Diary, October 15, 1920.

129. Diary, October 27, 1920.

search at the Mulford Laboratory, told her father that her duties were "diverse and of much interest on account of variety and contact with people"; what is more, University of Michigan president Marion LeRoy Burton[130] had asked her to represent the university at the fiftieth anniversary of the founding of Wilson College (Chambersburg, Pennsylvania) a few weeks earlier.[131]

The next day, Francis left for Ann Arbor, where he stayed a week. He reserved a room at the Union; gave a lunch for interested faculty and regents (attended by eleven), after which he showed them the papyri; and gave another the next day for President Burton, former President Hutchins, and the principal benefactors. In Detroit one day, he lunched with Backus, now president of the Burroughs Adding Machine Company, and Boyer (Backus's father-in-law and the company's chairman), telling them of the funds needed for an excavation in Egypt, about which they were not sanguine: "the money market is on the edge of panic."[132] He had supper twice with Harriet (on one occasion in the Nickels Arcade, a covered downtown shopping district), who had a room at 323 Packard. He put the house at 826 Tappan on the market again (asking twenty-five thousand dollars); he visited the dentist; he bought a new hat. Most important, he delivered the papyri to W. W. Bishop: "It is a relief and satisfaction to commit the papyri and other materials to the care of the University Library, thus shifting the responsibility. The more I have handled the papyri, the more evident their value has become to me."[133]

On the train to Washington, D.C., with President Burton, the conversation turned to Henry Frieze's contribution to education at Michigan and, through the university, to a wider public: "when trustees representing the new foundation of Johns Hopkins came on a tour of institutions, President Angell presented them to Professor Frieze who urged them to found a real university and cut away from the college idea then generally in vogue."[134] Francis did not let slip the opportunity to harangue Burton about the needs of the School of Music and the Humanistic Series. On arrival, they went to the secretary of

---

130. Educated at Carleton College and Yale, Burton (1874–1925) served as president of Smith College (1910–17) and of the University of Minnesota (1917–20) before becoming president at Michigan in 1920. A charismatic presence and eloquent speaker, he was chosen to nominate President Calvin Coolidge for a full term at the 1924 Republican National Convention.

131. Diary, October 30, 1920.

132. Diary, November 8, 1920.

133. Diary, November 6, 1920.

134. Diary, November 11, 1920.

war's office to see the army chief of staff, General Peyton C. March,[135] about the possibility of Colonel Spaulding's secondment to the next expedition— only to receive "an immediate rebuff." Not to be turned away so brusquely, Francis returned the next day, questioning March's statement; began lobbying congressmen, who seemed disbelieving ("what Michigan wants, Michigan gets," said one); and went, in the company of a Treasury Department official, to the War Department, where he was told, "General March has antagonized many." When he finally got to see Secretary Baker, it was no use: Colonel Spaulding was not to be released. The outcome of the journey to Washington was not wholly negative, however. Kelsey attended two lectures by Sir William Mitchell Ramsay, with whom he was to be closely associated in the coming (1924) Michigan excavations at Antioch in Pisidia, where Ramsay had worked before the war.[136]

In Boston on November 18, he spoke with Heliotype Printing Company treasurer W. C. Ramsay about the Coptic plates for part 2 of volume 10 of the Humanistic Series; with Oliver J. Barr about the printing; with Paul and Carl Bacon about the new edition of Cicero's orations; and with M. O. Henning, music engraver, about the needs of volume 15, by Stanley. He then went on to Exeter, New Hampshire, to see Easton, whom he found in good heart. Satisfied with the individual attention given the students at the school, as well as with Mrs. Rowe's boarding arrangements, Francis returned to Boston for meetings with his publishers.[137]

After a couple of nights with Fred in Orange, he boarded the SS *Carmania*—"less impressive than the *Aquitania*," he thought—for the return to England. The sea was smooth, and on arrival in Liverpool on December 3, he noted "the most comfortable voyage I have had." The train from Liverpool landed him in London in the afternoon for the short walk to 1 Taviton Street,

---

135. Peyton Conway March had served in the Philippines during the Spanish-American War and commanded the First Infantry Division's First Field Artillery Brigade for the American Expeditionary Forces in World War I before becoming army chief of staff (1918–21). Among those he antagonized was General John J. Pershing, who wanted the AEF conducted as an independent command. March published a War Department memoir, *The Nation at War* (Garden City, NY: Doubleday, 1932), in which he criticized Pershing.

136. A noted archaeologist, epigrapher, and historian, the Scots-born Ramsay was educated at the universities of Aberdeen, Oxford, and Göttingen. A research fellow at Exeter College, Oxford, and a fellow of Lincoln College, he served briefly as Lincoln Professor of Classical Archaeology and Art at Oxford before moving to Aberdeen to become regius professor. A specialist in Early Christian history who was famed for his knowledge of the geography, topography, and history of Asia Minor, he was the dominant English-speaking scholar in his field for most of his lifetime (1851–1939).

137. Diary, November 19, 1920.

where he found Isabelle "more vigorous and getting about than at any previous time since we left the United States."

Two weeks of a London December were enough. He wrote letters, letters, and more letters; went to the British Museum one day, to ask Kenyon if Bell could go to Egypt in place of Hunt, were Hunt indisposed or disinclined; and dealt with packages, boxes, church, and the usual diversions. Fog one day and snow on another saw Francis in Smithfield Market "prowling about this interesting neighborhood."[138] By December 17, they were in Paris, where Francis visited Kalebdjian Frères (12 rue de la Paix) and saw two lectionaries—one Greek, the other Coptic—the look of which he liked. Four days later, they were in Rome, installed in a Pensione Boos so busy that, though a room was found for Isabelle and a Miss Heine with whom they had traveled from Paris, Francis had to manage on a cot in the lounge. It did not matter; he had wanted to be in Rome since September and set to work at once.

ITALY AGAIN

After rounding up the trunks from the railway station and checking on the packages from Cairo and Paris at the American Academy, he began work on the Grotius volume, one of four projects that would occupy most of his time in Italy, the others being the Patmos manuscripts, the new edition of Cicero's orations, and the updating of the Mau-Kelsey *Pompeii: Its Life and Art.* Dinner on Christmas Eve at the academy was a treat, with fifty-eight people tucking in and with Francis speaking on behalf of the trustees amid much merriment—"glorious moonlight, Rome astir on the mild air." On Christmas Day, they enjoyed a picnic in the theater at Frascati—"a perfect day." They were both happy to be in Rome, revisiting a city they had come to know twenty years before, and they had a visit from Charlotte to look forward to.[139] On a courtesy visit to American ambassador Robert Underwood Johnson,[140] the

---

138. Diary, December 12, 1920.

139. Ruth, also invited, opted for the one thousand dollars offered by Francis should either of them prefer money to a European trip. In early 1921, she was settled in a library job for the San Diego art and natural history museums and was shortly to move to Missoula, Montana, complications that might have made any European trip difficult. See *Michigan Alumnus,* 27 (1921): 264, 462.

140. Robert Underwood Johnson (1853–1937), who had succeeded Thomas Nelson Page (see chapter 7, "Ambassador to Italy"), was a poet and translator and had been editor of *Century Magazine.* The Italian government had earlier honored him for his work in promoting international copyright law. His memoirs were published as *Remembered Yesterdays* (Boston: Little, Brown, 1923).

latter commented to Francis that he had expected "to sit with my feet up and have an easy time—I wanted to write some poetry; but I never worked so hard in my life."[141] On New Year's Eve, Francis confided to his diary, "Here ends with a prayer of thankfulness the most diversified year of my life."

They settled easily into life in Rome, lodging at the Pensione Boos, Isabelle taking Italian lessons and Francis working at the academy: "These walks across Rome from the Pensione Boos to the American Academy are a delight."[142] Indeed, for the first three months of the year—with the exception of five January days in Pompeii—he could be found daily at the academy. At the start of the year, amid the usual high volume of correspondence, Francis wrote two memoranda to President Burton in Ann Arbor: one, twenty-two pages long, about the School of Music (on a new building and the school's incorporation into the university); the other, not quite so long, on the Humanistic Series. He could not escape academy affairs (nor did he want to), and since the faculty were overstretched, he volunteered to help with the course on Pompeii, saying that he would teach "what no one wanted as all parts of the field are of interest to me." So he took on the public architecture and the fora, while others dealt with the inscriptions, the private houses, and the paintings. He attended lectures by distinguished scholars here and there: by Calza on Ostia and Rome ("slides taken from a dirigible"), by Lugli ("very fine slides"), and by Amelung on the Vatican storerooms.[143] He and Isabelle dined often with the Van Burens and the Magoffins at the academy and with the Amelungs, with whom, as with Mau, Kelsey seemed to have a special rapport. Almost every week, he and Isabelle attended the opera. But a performance of Strauss's *Salome* was too much for Francis: his remark to his diary that "Strauss seems to me musically and morally a degenerate. Strauss for me—never again!" strikes a discordant note in one whose devotion to opera appears total, yet it confirms the conservative streak in a nature otherwise open to innovation.

Research was at the center of his thinking. Beginning in December, he worked away steadily at the translation of Grotius, switching to Cicero's orations in early February. In March he switched to the Patmos manuscripts, for

141. Diary, December 28, 1920.

142. Diary, January 29, 1921.

143. Guido Calza directed excavations at Ostia and in the Roman Forum; Giuseppe Lugli was professor of topography at the University of Rome; and Walter Amelung, a member of the German Archaeological Institute, was an expert on Roman sculpture and the Vatican collections.

which he found the library at the French School, housed in the Palazzo Farnese, most helpful—these days found him there as often as at the academy. Volumes of the Humanistic Series, too, demanded his editorial eye. Proofs of volume 15 (Albert Stanley's *Greek Themes in Modern Musical Settings,* to appear in 1924) came to hand in January, as did part 2 of volume 10 (William Worrell's *Two Homilies and a Magical Text,* to appear in 1923) in March—not to mention Jerome's manuscript, now reworked by Winter (*Aspects of the Study of Roman History,* to appear in 1923), which needed his comments before going on to G. P. Putnam's Sons in New York.

Late in March, his attention switched from Patmos to Pompeii—to the lectures he was to give and the proposed new edition of *Pompeii: Its Life and Art.* Since Charlotte was due to arrive in Naples, he and Isabelle went down to Pompeii on March 26. He delivered some of his talks in Pompeii in front of the buildings themselves—leading the academy party around the site and the new excavations, discussing town planning, housing, and the frescoes—and others in the Naples Museum. He "especially enjoyed two half days spent in the ruins with the Fine Arts men of the Academy of whom four were architects" (see fig. 21).[144] Separately, he took Charlotte and Isabelle around Pompeii, to sites near Naples (Cumae, Avernus, the cave of the Sibyl), to the Naples Museum, and to Vesuvius. But there was also an excursion to Naples for "shopping," and there was discussion of Charlotte's upcoming wedding, mentioned now for the first time in the diary.[145]

Francis, having trouble with his teeth, went to Rome for a few days, leaving his wife and daughter to enjoy each other's company. At the Cunard Company office, he got the last three berths for Isabelle, Charlotte, and himself on the SS *Albania,* sailing from Liverpool for New York on September 7. After returning to Pompeii, Francis took them to Amalfi, Ravello, and Positano and then to Capri, where they lunched with Mrs. Andrews at the Villa Castello. They saw Freer's apartment, where Kelsey let slip, "he told me that he said to Jerome that he would not set foot in the Villa Castello when Yetta was there. Jerome had his choice and kept Yetta."[146] On the last day of the month, they parted company, mother and daughter to Rome and points north, Francis to his work in Pompeii.

---

144. Diary, April 7, 1921; Kelsey to Harriet, April 11, 1921, private collection of Easton Kelsey Jr., Rochester, NY.

145. Diary, April 15, 1921.

146. Diary, April 27, 1921.

21. Francis Kelsey with a group of architecture students at Pompeii,
April 7, 1921. Bentley Historical Library, University of Michigan HS 5257.
Photo: Jack Skinner.

And work he did. He hired a draftsman and a photographer, and for most
of May, he was busy compiling reports on the houses, baths, and public buildings, taking measurements on site, studying the wall decorations, at pains to
include the results of the latest excavations and research. In blank books, he
"laid off" chapters of the third edition, with memoranda and references for
several chapters, arranging notes and memoranda in envelopes according to
subject matter. He contemplated writing a booklet on Pompeii in English,
One Day in Pompeii, with routes from the Porta Marina shown in red, and
was urged to do so. But he also wrote many letters (no surprise),[147] went for
long walks,[148] and visited the Naples Museum, where he met a Dr. Holger Ny-
gard of Copenhagen, who (ahead of his day) was working on hygiene in Pompeii. He bought photographs and books (*pompeiana*) from a Mr. B. Johan-

---

147. These included important communications with Nahman; see below, "The Papyri."
148. He wrote in his diary on May 15, 1921, "How beautiful this landscape is!"

nowsky at the bookstore of Detken and Rocholl[149] and inquired as to the price of the residue of the de Criscio collection,[150] now available for purchase. Expecting to meet Isabelle and Charlotte at the Pensione Boos on May 28, he traveled to Rome in a crowded train, standing all the way, only to meet with disappointment—"table set for Isabelle and Charlotte and me with lovely bouquet; they decided to remain another week in Florence."[151] In fact, they would not be reunited for another month.

Making the most of it, Francis stayed in Rome a week. At the academy, he cleared his correspondence, which included letters to President Burton and to Frank J. Hubley in Philadelphia, and worked in the library on Pompeii references and illustrations for the Cicero. When a strike in Rome paralyzed the mails, he was lucky to be able to ask Bishop Kelly to take his thirty-two letters to mail in Paris; but he entrusted the Grotius manuscript to the American Embassy, to go to Washington by diplomatic pouch. Sample papyri arrived from Nahman, about which he instantly wrote to Bell in London. Returning to Pompeii, he visited and studied the new excavations (shops) and resumed work on Chapter XLIII, the House of the Golden Cupids, whose excavator incurred his rather severe displeasure: "Why didn't Sogliano have the plans correctly and nicely drawn? There is no excuse for such slovenly work. It will take me 30 or 40 hours to complete all the measurements and have a new plan drawn and engraved."[152]

The next week, he was in Naples again, buying more books from Johannowsky; meeting Vittorio Spinazzola,[153] the director of the museum, who promised to send him proofs of his new work at Pompeii; and trying unsuccessfully to find a dentist. In Pompeii he worked on the houses, keeping his photographer busy, and entertained Mrs. Andrews to tea.[154] As the end of the

---

149. Diary, May 12, 1921. Johannowsky's son, Werner, later served as superintendent of antiquities for Salerno, Avellino, and Benevento.

150. See chapter 3, "Italy."

151. Diary, May 28, 1921.

152. Diary, June 17, 1921. Antonio Sogliano was director of works at Pompeii from late 1905 to 1910.

153. Spinazzola was the director of the National Archaeological Museum of Naples and of works at Pompeii during 1910–23, after serving as superintendent of archeological works for Campania and curator of the San Martino Museum in Naples (1889–1910). He is known for redirecting the excavation to the southern sector of the city and for his recovery of the Via dell'Abbondanza, the city's main road.

154. Diary, June 22, 1921. Mrs. Andrews told him she went all the way to Florence if she needed to see a dentist.

month approached, he returned to Rome and, to his relief and delight, found Isabelle and Charlotte at the Pensione Boos. For much of the past four weeks, they had been in Venice. Since their time in Italy was growing short, he went back to Pompeii for a final ten days. Finding Gisela Richter and Mary Swindler in the forum, he spent a pleasant evening with them.[155] For the rest of the time, he was at work on the houses, mosaics, and frescoes or on photographs and memoranda for the new edition or was in Naples buying more books and photographs. For the final ten days in Rome, he was busy with travel arrangements, packing up his room at the academy, sending off packages of books, packing trunks and suitcases, and tying up loose ends. He and his family left Rome on July 27.

HOMEWARD BOUND

Their route took them to Bologna, Milan, and Verona in "hot but endurable" weather (thirty-four degrees Celsius in Milan), which did not deter them from touring around. The onward journey to Innsbruck was difficult, and accommodations there left much to be desired, so they were glad to push on to Munich. Here, on four nights between August 2 and 7, they were present at performances of *The Ring*. During the day, they visited museums, the Pinakothek and the Glyptothek, but it was the opera that commanded their attention. "To see the *Ring* in Munich is the experience of a lifetime," wrote Francis.

> One can hardly have the full effect of *The Ring* unless one hears the four operas in succession, and near together. Also, here more than in the ordinary opera it is necessary to make oneself familiar with both the text and a certain number of the motifs before each performance. The overwhelming power of the Wagner operas is in no small degree due to the fact that the text and the music emanated from one mind, different means of expression for the same fundamental concepts.[156]

From Munich they went on to Dresden and Berlin, where the main attractions for Francis were the huge second-century BC Pergamon Altar, excavated in Turkey in the last decades of the nineteenth century, and the

---

155. For many years a well-known and well-liked professor of classical archaeology at Bryn Mawr College, Mary Swindler served for more than a decade as editor of the *American Journal of Archaeology*. Her special expertise was in ancient painting. On Richter, see chapter 6 n. 78.

156. Diary, August 7, 1921.

Hildesheim Treasure, a hoard of early imperial Roman silver vessels; for Isabelle and Charlotte, it was the "movies."[157] They continued by night train to Cologne. Taking a steamer down the Rhine to Coblenz, Francis called on General Allen. Explaining that his Caesar studies had to go on the back burner next year in favor of work on Grotius, he heard from Allen that "the Polish question will give trouble for the next 200 years and that the Allied Commission is keeping strict neutrality on the war in Asia Minor."[158] Francis, with the help of a YMCA vehicle, toured the region around Urmitz, walking the fields and pondering the problem of Caesar's bridges.

By August 19, they were in Paris, Francis admiringly noting in the diary, "there is a kind of breadth in the boulevards and spaces of the city which has a charm all its own and the more one sees of the architecture of the public buildings the more pleasing it becomes. No other city can present so many attractive vistas or so impressive an array of public monuments felicitously placed." They went to the opera—*Rigoletto* one night, followed on the same program by Léo Delibes's *Lakmé*, an opéra comique; on another night, Berlioz's *Les Troyens*[159]—and they visited the Louvre and Notre Dame. Francis went to Kalebdjian Frères to examine Greek and Coptic lectionaries, and Charlotte got a wedding dress, fur stole, and muff from Jehan Duchesne at 37 Boulevard Malesherbes. After ten days in Paris, they crossed to London. Staying at 1 Taviton Street, Francis went at once to the British Museum, for talks with Kenyon and Bell about the papyri. There was time for walks, letters, and discussions with Hugh Evelyn-White about future work in Egypt and with W. W. Bishop (staying at the Savoy!) about the papyri, before the Kelseys headed north to Liverpool to catch the SS *Albania* for New York.[160] The journey was uneventful. Francis was happy to find Gisela Richter and her sister on board, and all three Kelseys were delighted to be met at the Cunard pier by Fred, Ronald, and Charlotte's fiancé, Frank Hubley.[161]

Charlotte's wedding was only a week away. To ease a few problems, Francis immediately gave some cash to Frank for wedding announcements and to Charlotte for "furnishings." There were problems, too, with the customs

---

157. Diary, August 13, 1921.

158. Diary, August 16, 1921.

159. This was the Grand Opéra's first staging (premier on June 10, 1921) of both parts of this monumental work (*La prise de Troie* and *Les Troyens à Carthage*).

160. Their luggage was considerable: for the hold, two box trunks with papers and books and one large box; for the cabins, five suitcases, three toilet bags, one blanket roll, two large packages of papyri, two small square boxes with *pompeiana*, and two cabin trunks.

161. Diary, September 17, 1921.

people, but these were ironed out quickly enough for Francis to deliver the papyri allocated to Cornell and Princeton to their respective librarians, in New York. Relatives began to assemble, Easton arriving with his cousin Fred and Fred's wife, Anna.[162] The wedding took place at Fred and Anna's house in South Orange, Fred himself playing the wedding march on the violin. The whole party then moved to Fred senior's house for the wedding breakfast. Francis wrote in his diary, "Charlotte looked very pretty—I have never seen her look so pretty. A happier family wedding can hardly be imagined; all the arrangements were favored. Charlotte and Fred took a late afternoon train for Atlantic City."[163] The next day, Francis and Isabelle took the train home, both in a contented frame of mind: "we were both very happy—it is the last stage in our return to Ann Arbor after an absence of slightly more than two years— since September 1, 1919. How much we both have to be thankful for!"[164] Efforts to sell the house at 826 Tappan had failed, but Miss Hills had leased it for another year; in the meantime, Albert Stanley had moved from his house at 810 Oxford Road and agreed to rent it to Francis. So, on arrival in Ann Arbor—after asking the train conductor at Detroit to mail numerous letters to his Detroit friends—it was to their new home that they went (see fig. 22). At 8:00 a.m. the following day, Francis was in his classroom on campus to greet the new students.

THE PAPYRI

The afternoon of his first day back, Francis and Sanders checked the papyri he had sent from Cairo to Oxford, lost sight of for a while, recovered from the London docks, and hand-carried himself to Ann Arbor the previous year. Two days later, with the help of Boak and Bonner, he began opening the boxes of papyri about which Nahman had written excitedly to him in May and that he had just brought with him.[165]

Writing in December 1920, he had asked Nahman to hold anything valuable for him, and by letter again in January 1921, he had told Nahman that

---

162. Fred Trowbridge Kelsey, Francis's nephew, had married Anna Whitney in 1913.

163. Diary, September 24, 1921. For details of the wedding, see "South Orange is the Scene of Hubley-Kelsey Wedding," *Newark (NJ) Sunday Call,* September 25, 1921; "Michigan Girl Bride in Orange," *Newark (NJ) Star-Eagle,* September 26, 1921.

164. Diary, September 25, 1921.

165. Diary, September 29, 1921. Campbell Bonner (1876–1954), educated at Vanderbilt University and Harvard, joined the University of Michigan Greek faculty in 1907, becoming department chairman in 1932.

22. Kelsey's second home in Ann Arbor, 810 Oxford Road, 2009. Photo: Mary Pedley.

Dr. Budge of the British Museum would look over anything he had and that he looked forward to hearing either from Evelyn-White or Budge.[166] It was in May, while in Naples, that he had received an urgent message from Nahman saying two things: first, that he had given all the papyri he had to Budge on approval; and second, that more had just come in, which Evelyn-White had seen and recommended for Kelsey. There were a hundred manuscripts, small rolls, and one large roll "of two and a half yards written on both sides."[167] They were documents, not accounts.

Francis had cabled at once (May 20), asking the price and the exact number. Nahman had replied that the asking price was two thousand pounds. By return (May 26), Francis cabled "probabilmente prendiamo" (we'll probably take them) but asked Nahman to send samples. Nahman replied by asking Francis to go to Egypt to look at them, repeating a few details—there were

---

166. E. A. Wallis (later Sir Wallis) Budge, an expert on Assyrian antiquities, noted Egyptologist, and prolific author, was keeper of the Oriental Department of the British Museum during 1894–1924.

167. For the correspondence cited here and immediately following, see KMA Papers, box 84, folders 7 and 8.

two bilinguals, a will, and other legal and business documents. Five days later, Nahman had written again to say that he was sending four samples to the British Museum for inspection; and a week later, Francis reported to him that they had arrived. On June 23, Nahman wrote that he was expecting Francis's arrival (though Francis never said he would go), a letter that crossed with another sent by Francis advising that the four sample papyri were entirely satisfactory and that he had cabled the United States "recommending an appropriation." His cable to President Burton read, "Nahman sent four. British Museum report says if typical of whole collection find one of best ever made. Business documents. Reigns Tiberius and Claudius."

In July the correspondence had turned to questions of price and payment. Francis wrote, "sample very satisfactory but British Museum thinks price too high," adding that the four papyri were safe in London and that he was still waiting to hear from the United States about the money; Nahman said that, against his will, he would stay in Cairo in the summer heat in case Francis came, that he was bothered by the involvement of the British Museum (not knowing of the existence of the consortium), that he needed to know if Michigan was going to buy, and that he was short of cash. On July 15, agitated, not having heard anything from Francis, he wrote again, "requesting an answer." The day before he left Italy (July 26), Francis had replied at length: that the university was short of cash, that he was asking friends in New York for help, that if Nahman would send the papyri to London to arrive by September 3, "I agree to take the whole collection and pay for it with reasonable promptness after reaching the US. I can take the collection as insured baggage when I sail on September 7th." He had added that if Nahman preferred, he would alert his friends at the Louvre about the opportunity, though he preferred to keep it "confidential with the British Museum."

The level of trust between the two and of Nahman's admiration for Charles Freer is plain in what he wrote next: that he agreed to send the papyri in registered packages to London "in memory of my regretted friend" and that he was aware that Kelsey knew of the friendship between him and Mr. Freer. Francis wrote from Paris on August 23 that the British Museum had received the packages, adding, "Were Mr. Freer living you would have had your money before this." In another long letter on the eve of departure for America, he had written that the museum technicians had "damped out" the papyri and that Bell had examined them.

> The long roll is a record of the business of a record office in or near Tebtunis for 41–42 A.D. It is one of the finest rolls I have ever seen, and the content is interesting. The other rolls are chiefly legal documents with a few letters written in the reign of the Roman emperors Tiberius, Caligula

and Claudius. The rolls are exactly as you represented and we are very glad to have them. I have a very small balance here but without waiting till I reach the US I enclose a check for 100 pounds on account.[168]

This was hardly satisfactory to Nahman, but he did not complain, and in October Francis sent him a further 650 pounds. But it was January 1922 before Francis wrote again to say he hoped to send the balance soon and that in future he would pay cash, and it was February before he had actually sent a check for 150 pounds. At this point, Nahman's patience ran out. He wrote both remonstrating and offering new materials, cabling also, "Your Delay is Disaster." Things suddenly fell into place. On March 3, Francis sent 100 pounds, and nine days later, he cabled 1,000 pounds, adding that he would pay whatever interest Nahman thought right. It was now almost a year since Nahman had shown the papyri to Evelyn-White.

These papyri are of high historical importance. They represent the contents of a single archive of the records office of the village of Tebtunis in the Fayoum in the first century AD and reveal many details of the workings of the office, the law, the government, and the lives of individuals. They include quantities of tax receipts, public oaths, sales and deeds, petitions, leases, dowries, rents, guild memberships and receipts, and regulations, as well as some single documents—a partnership agreement, a guarantee of immunity, an apprenticeship to a weaver, a contract for service to a weaver, a marriage contract, a contract for work, a release of an inheritance. They bring history to life: the arrangements documented in these papyri affected the lives of ordinary people, living real lives in an Egyptian village long ago.[169]

---

168. Kelsey to Nahman, September 6, 1921, KMA Papers, box 84, folder 7.

169. A. E. R. Boak, *Papyri from Tebtunis*, pt. 1, 2 vols., University of Michigan Studies, Humanistic Series, vol. 28 (Ann Arbor: University of Michigan Press, 1933); Elinor M. Husselman, A. E. R. Boak, and William F. Edgerton, *Papyri from Tebtunis*, pt. II, 2 vols., University of Michigan Studies, Humanistic Series, vol. 29 (Ann Arbor: University of Michigan Press, 1944). Grenfell and Hunt had poked about Tebtunis in 1899 and pulled out some papyri, including some used as wrapping for crocodiles buried in the cemetery they excavated (Bernard P. Grenfell, Arthur S. Hunt, and J. Gilbart Smyly, *The Tebtunis Papyri*, vol. 1 [London: Henry Frowde, 1902], v–viii), but Italian expeditions discovered many more papyri at the site in the 1930s. For a revealing discussion about the contributions of Gilbert and Stewart Bagnani to this work and about the controversy that engulfed these expeditions, see D. J. I. Begg, "The Canadian Tebtunis Connection at Trent University," *Echos du Monde Classique/Classical Views*, n.s., 17.2 (1998): 385–405. See also idem, "Fascism in the Desert: A Microcosmic View of Archaeological Politics," chapter 2 of *Archaeology under Dictatorship*, ed. M. Galaty and C. Watkinson (New York: Kluwer Academic/Plenum Publishers, 2004). For more on the Tebtunis papyri, the generosity of donor John W. Anderson, and the state of the papyri collection in winter 1923, see *Michigan Alumnus* 29 (1923): 533–35.

In mid-October 1921, Kelsey prepared an exhibit of the materials he had acquired on his travels. Inviting donors to the expedition to view it, he put on display parchments bought in Constantinople and Paris; Roman glass from Cologne; twenty-five papyri under glass; photographs of Palestine, Patmos, and Athens; some of Swain's panoramic shots; and photographs of the Beatus manuscript in the British Museum. Afterward, he and Isabelle hosted a lunch for Mr. and Mrs. D. M. Ferry, Standish Backus and his mother and sister, Joseph Boyer, Miss Elizabeth Russel (daughter of John), Paul Gray, President and Mrs. Burton, and Mr. and Mrs. Sanders. After lunch, Kelsey and Sanders gave talks, and Swain offered a slide (stereopticon) show. Kelsey noted in his diary, "All expressed themselves with no slight enthusiasm."[170]

The resounding success of the expedition of 1919–21 and the richness of the information and materials it yielded left Francis and his colleagues on the Committee for Near East Research at Michigan and throughout the university eager for a second such undertaking. This would come to involve exploration of three archaeological sites in Mediterranean lands and engage not only Kelsey and Swain but also Evelyn-White, Ramsay, and Robinson. This endeavor would first require several years of planning, and Kelsey would need to find donors to fund it, especially now that longtime benefactor Charles Freer was gone.

---

170. Diary, October 11, 1921.

CHAPTER 9

The Second Expedition (1921–27)

Kelsey on the Move

❧

THE INTEREXPEDITIONARY YEARS

For the balance of 1921, Francis resumed his usual academic life. He was teaching three courses (including Cicero on Saturdays at 10:00 a.m.). There was the normal round of staff meetings, which had to cope this year with arrangements for the annual concurrent meetings of the AIA and APA to take place in December in Ann Arbor. He was involved, as ever, in meetings of the campus planning committee, which was wrestling with the placement of new buildings and the proposed route of a freight railroad through Ann Arbor.[1] He conferred with Dean Effinger (Literary College) about the identification of potential donors, salaries, possible successors to Professor Stanley (now seventy), and the whole question of the future of the School of Music,[2] and he returned to the problem of finding a suitable successor to Stanley in conference with President Burton, ex-president Hutchins, and Deans Effinger and Lloyd (Graduate School) on November 12. With Effinger, Boak, and Sanders, he took up the tantalizing prospect of future work in Egypt, whether of excavation in a Roman urban context (and if so, what would staffing arrangements be?) or of work at a Coptic site under the direction of Evelyn-White

---

1. Diary, October 17 and 25, 1921.
2. Diary, October 7 and 26, 1921.

and with the cooperation of the Metropolitan Museum.[3] He presented lectures in Indianapolis, Grosse Pointe, Detroit, and Buffalo ("New Light from Roman Egypt"); to Ann Arbor's First Presbyterian Church ("American Relief and Mission Work in the Near East"); and to the Congregationalists ("Congregational Missions in Turkey"). From such an accomplished lecturer, it is surprising to read in his diary, "How I dread and dislike lecturing!"[4] He pursued his work on Pompeii, on the Grotius translation, and with the Humanistic Series. Routines were interrupted by the Michigan-Ohio football game, which caused "fearful congestion of automobiles,"[5] and by the visit of Marshal Foch, which caused cheers to be heard on campus all the way from the railroad station, stimulated as much perhaps by the cancellation of classes as by his appearance.[6]

Boak's volume in the Humanistic Series had appeared in 1919, but others were still in the works. To speed these up (and for other reasons), Francis traveled to Washington, D.C., New York, and Boston in November. In Washington he inquired at the Smithsonian about Charles Freer's will, about which there seemed to be some ambiguity;[7] at the Carnegie Institution, he discussed with President John C. Merriam[8] the issue of the wall paintings of Pompeii (regarding reproductions?); and at the Carnegie Endowment, he reviewed the Grotius project with Dr. James Brown Scott. He had lunch with Mitchell Carroll, Ralph Magoffin, and David M. Robinson, talking over problems of the AIA.[9] In New York he first met with Worrell, proofs in hand, then with Putnam's to discuss Jerome's manuscript. He conferred with Herman Charles Hoskier[10] at 14 Wall Street about the publication of the Patmos manuscripts and with Gisela Richter at the Metropolitan Museum about the Boscoreale

---

3. Diary, November 14, 1921.

4. Diary, November 22, 1921.

5. But it did not stop Francis from holding his class (diary, October 22, 1921).

6. Diary, November 7, 1921. General Ferdinand Foch, promoted Marshal of France in 1918, was the French general in command of the Allied armies in the final year of World War I.

7. Diary, March 13 and 28, 1922.

8. John Campbell Merriam had assumed the presidency in 1920, leaving his new appointment as dean of the Department of Paleontology at the University of California to do so. He was perhaps best known for his studies of vertebrates at the La Brea Tar Pits.

9. Diary, November 23–26, 1921.

10. Hoskier, born in England and educated at Eton College, was both an expert on Greek biblical manuscripts—particularly on the book of Revelation (the Apocalypse)—and a banker with the Foreign Finance Corporation. His father was the merchant banker Herman Hoskier, a founder of Brown, Shipley, and Company (Kelsey's agents in London) and later a director of the Guinness Brewery.

frescoes. With George P. Brett at Macmillan, he took up the question of a third edition of the Mau-Kelsey book on Pompeii (under contract since February 1914); with Otto Kahn, he broached the question of the urgent need of funds for the German Archaeological Institute in Rome.[11] By December 1, he was in Boston, looking over proofs of volumes 10 and 15 of the Humanistic Series (Worrell's and Stanley's), visiting John Allyn in Cambridge, and dining with Mr. and Mrs. Carl Bacon. After a quick visit to Easton at Phillips Exeter Academy, he returned to Boston, called on Mrs. Longyear in Brookline, and gave a talk to a group of her friends. With queries about Stanley's Greek music manuscript, he visited the John Worley Company; later, at the Boston Museum of Fine Arts, Arthur Fairbanks showed him the recently acquired Greek gold bowl.[12] On the way home, he stopped in Detroit to speak to Joel Prescott at the Union Trust Company about a subsidy for Jerome's book.

In Ann Arbor Isabelle returned from visits to Ruth in Missoula, Montana, and to relatives in California and Hot Springs, Arkansas; Easton, too, arrived for the holidays. Harriet joined them for Christmas dinner and festivities. With the AIA meetings in Ann Arbor, the year drew to a close. The meetings went off without a hitch; Egbert stood down from the presidency and was replaced by Magoffin. There was some difficulty between Egbert and Kelsey, caused by Francis's forthright attitude, but this was dissipated swiftly by his equally direct diplomacy.[13] For the next two years, against the backdrop of his daily routines—teaching, research, and editorial work (Grotius, Caesar, the Beatus manuscript, the Humanistic Series), committees, appointments, promotions, lectures up and down the country, the First Presbyterian Church, and the University Musical Society—and amid the interruptions of academic life,[14] there were some notable developments.

Horace Rackham, Family News, and Gustav Holst

In 1922 Francis was in need of a new donor to take Charles Freer's place. Roy Dikeman Chapin, one of the founders of the Hudson Motor Company, to whom Francis was referred by Standish Backus, suggested an approach to the

11. Diary, November 28–30, 1921.

12. This must be the later seventh-century BC libation bowl dedicated by the sons of the tyrant Kypselos (inscription just below the rim).

13. Diary, December 27, 1921.

14. Among these interruptions was, on the plus side, a concert by the famous Austrian-born violinist Fritz Kreisler, who attracted a huge and appreciative audience; on the minus side, fraternity rowdyism reached new heights, with students firing revolvers and other types of gun when girls appeared for sorority rush (diary, January 9 and October 1, 1922).

"Ford people"—those who had invested in and now taken their money out of the business—mentioning specifically James Couzens, Paul Gray, Mrs. John F. Dodge, Mrs. Henry Ford, and Horace H. Rackham. Former president Hutchins also mentioned John W. Anderson, Rackham's law partner,[15] who replied quickly to Francis's request with a check for seventy-five hundred dollars, which he used at once to discharge the debt to Nahman.[16]

Shortly afterward, Herman C. Hoskier told Francis about a sale at Sotheby's in London of manuscripts from the library of Baroness Burdett-Coutts.[17] After seeking information from Wilfrid Voynich, an antiquarian book dealer,[18] Francis arranged for Hutchins and himself to meet Rackham in Detroit.

> [W]e arrived about 11 o'clock and went to the office of H. H. Rackham 1715 Dome Bank Building, Mr. Hutchins spoke of early associations with Mr. Rackham's family at Mt. Clemens; the father was a farmer and the son walked to High School in Mt. Clemens. Mr. Rackham has a kindly face, and is of my age, born in 1858. He was very sympathetic. Mr. Hutchins spoke of our request, and I set forth the need of purchasing the Chrysostom ms of which we had had possession since 1919 (Homilies on the Acts, 55 homilies, complete costing about $3000) and of $12000 to enable us to bid on the Greek Biblical mss in the Burdett Coutts library (acquired by her traveling in Albania in 1870–1871). He asked whether the securing of the mss would be for the good of humanity, and I told him about the work on the Freer mss. He drew his check for $15000, and handed it to Mr. Hutchins who handed it to me.

Thus began a relationship between the two farm boys Rackham and Kelsey—philanthropic on one side, scholarly on the other—which was to benefit the university for many years and culminate in the construction of the Rackham School of Graduate Studies.

---

15. John Wendell Anderson, a University of Michigan graduate (LL.B. 1890), was a director of its Alumni Association, served on its Board of Governors, and once (1911) ran for its Board of Regents. Anderson and Rackham, which specialized in commercial law, was founded in 1896 in Detroit. On Rackham himself, see the upcoming paragraphs.

16. Diary, March 12 and 16, 1922. On Anderson's donation, see "In the Name of Law Class of 1890," *Michigan History Magazine* 6.4 (1922): 500; "A Gift of $7,500 for Papyri," *Michigan Alumnus* 28 (1922): 729.

17. At one time the richest woman in England, Angela Burdett-Coutts (1814–1906) was known for her widespread philanthropy and wild parties. The peerage conferred on her by Queen Victoria in 1871 was in recognition of the former.

18. Voynich (né Micha Habdank-Wojnicz) was a well-known and experienced European dealer with bookshops in both London and New York.

A modest man, Rackham made no show of his wealth, preferring his home to social activities and always remaining an anonymous donor.[19] A country boy whose education began in a one-room schoolhouse, he had made his way, by means of various odd jobs, to the study of law at night school in Detroit. By chance, he happened to have been a neighbor of Henry Ford at the time that Ford was experimenting noisily with his engines. Needing a legal mind to write the papers of incorporation of his business, Ford turned to Rackham, who joined John Anderson in preparing them and in investing in Ford's company.[20]

With the new influx of cash, Francis went over the catalog of the Burdett-Coutts sale with Bishop and Sanders, deciding on bids. Telegrams went off to London, and Voynich reported to Bishop, "at the sale we came off well, the total value of assignments to us (41 mss) was 1829 pounds."[21] In the course of 1922, other manuscripts were bought from Géjou in Paris, as well as papyri from Nahman in Cairo.[22]

On the family scene, Ruth came to stay for a month before going on to see Charlotte in Philadelphia.[23] Charlotte had news of her own, announcing on July 7 by telegram, "Francis Kelsey Hubley arrived 2 o'clock today, weight 7 lbs." Easton, though more successful at Phillips Exeter than at the Hill School, was obliged to enroll for summer school before entering the University of Michigan in the fall. In January Francis sold one of the cottages at Lake Cavanaugh, and 826 Tappan, too, was sold at last. Work always had a high priority. Though invited out to dinner on his birthday, he preferred to stay at

---

19. Diary, August 21 and September 9, 1922. Rackham is easily identifiable in the frequent mentions of an "anonymous" donor in the publications of the Karanis expedition and of the Humanistic Series.

20. Rackham's fortune came from an initial investment in 1903 of $5,000 in the Ford Motor Company. When Edsel Ford bought up all the stock in 1919, Rackham's investment was worth $12.5 million; in the interim, he had received over $4 million in dividends. (Anderson also invested $5,000, borrowed from his father, and likewise sold his shares for $12.5 million.)

21. Diary, May 15, 1922.

22. Aside from raising funds for the purchase of manuscripts, Francis persuaded another Detroit acquaintance, Henry G. Stevens, secretary of the Stevens Land Company, to contribute five thousand dollars for the American School of Classical Studies at Athens, and he persuaded Mrs. James Inglis, wife of the president of the American Blower Company, to pay for the education of one of Askren's sons at Phillips Andover. He was also actively pursuing support for the German Archaeological Institute in Rome and for the German *Thesaurus Linguae Latinae,* both threatened by lack of funding. See diary, October 31 and November 10 and 17, 1922.

23. Kelsey wrote in his diary on May 5, 1922, "What a joy to see Ruth again! She seems so vigorous in health and so happy."

home.[24] But he enjoyed the company of the rich: he and Isabelle were treated to lavish social events in Detroit—to the wedding of one of Mr. and Mrs. Abner Larned's sons to a daughter of Mr. and Mrs. Oliver Hutchins[25] and, later in the year, to a reception given by Mr. and Mrs. James Couzens for their son and his bride, "the largest and most brilliant affair I ever attended."[26] But trouble was brewing. Two days after a happy family Christmas—"great happiness though we missed dear Ruth. How much we have to be thankful for"— Isabelle was taken ill in the middle of the night and whisked off to the hospital, where she was to remain for over a month.

An operation early in 1923 was followed by a long period of recuperation. By March Isabelle was up to looking at houses they might possibly buy, and by May she was happy to be driven in a "Dodge car" to Detroit to the society wedding in Grosse Point of Elizabeth Russel, daughter of John R. Russel.[27] But she had not completely recovered: six months later, she was in the hospital again for another operation, after which the surgeons reported "the cancer entirely eliminated."[28] Charlotte was in Ann Arbor with "wee Francis" for much of the first six months of the year (while her mother was under the doctors' care), but she was not at Lake Cavanaugh in the summer to witness the sale of her red canoe.[29] Ruth visited at Thanksgiving, as did Harriet. Easton's academic work was not going as his parents hoped, culminating at the start of his sophomore year in a talk with his father at which he "agreed to give up smoking of cigarettes for the semester, and to do better work at his studies."[30] He did not. A few weeks later, the dean called him in and warned him.[31] As to

---

24. He wrote in his diary on May 23, 1922: "Isabel and Ruth went to A. H. White's for dinner and came back after I had retired, about midnight. I declined because too busy and had a more healthful supper at the Baltimore Lunch (beef stew and prunes!) thus celebrating my 64th birthday. How little I have accomplished in my 63 years!—though I have worked as hard as I could; but I see so many and so alluring opportunities that I cannot embrace! However, few men have so much to be thankful for!" White was a professor in the School of Engineering.

25. Diary, June 3, 1922.

26. Diary, December 21, 1922. Waved over to the Couzens's table, they joined some of the better-known names in Detroit: Mr. and Mrs. Murphy, Mr. and Mrs. Henry Ford, Mr. and Mrs. Abner Larned. James J. Couzens, having cashed out his Ford shares in 1919 for roughly thirty million dollars, became mayor of Detroit (1919–22) and then a U.S. senator (1922–36).

27. Diary, May 26, 1923.

28. Diary, June 29, 1923.

29. Kelsey wrote in his diary on August 31, 1923, "In a way sorry to see the pretty red canoe go—last association of Charlotte's girlhood at the lake: it was a pretty sight, Charlotte in her red canoe paddling in the afternoon light."

30. Diary, October 8, 1923.

31. Diary, November 12, 1923.

their houses, Isabelle and Francis agreed to buy 810 Oxford from Stanley (after looking at several other properties on Ferdon and Lincoln) and continued to enjoy their times at Lake Cavanaugh in the summer months.[32]

In the search for a successor to Stanley as professor of music, Gustav Holst emerged as a leading contender.[33] Already in 1922, Kelsey had proposed his name in conference with President Burton, and Holst had agreed to take part in the 1923 May Festival. Arriving with his wife on May 1, he gave a rehearsal a few days later, at which Francis was struck by his "thoroughness, tact, sympathy."[34] There was much entertaining—a grand "tea" with forty guests, a small dinner party for the interested Detroit elite, and a larger dinner given by Francis at the Barton Hills Country Club. In the afternoon on the second day of the festival, Holst conducted his new Fugal Concerto for strings, oboe, and flute, begun on his journey from England and completed in Ann Arbor; he conducted his *Hymn of Jesus* in the evening. Mr. and Mrs. William H. Murphy, escorted by the Kelseys, were in the audience. Holst declared that he was "much interested in the possibility of a professorship," and generous terms were suggested;[35] but after taking a break from Michigan to visit friends in Toronto and Chicago, he declined to pursue it. The invitation had been a bold move, and the appointment of Holst at Michigan would have put music at Michigan on the world map, but it was not to be. On June 14, Earl Moore,[36] director of the University School of Music, was appointed in Stanley's place.

The Near East Beckons: Money and Manpower

Since the question of expeditions was inextricably tied to that of funds, Francis hoped to find donors to support the acquisition of manuscripts and papyri, either from dealers or—in the case of papyri—from controlled excava-

---

32. Kelsey wrote in his diary on August 28, 1923, "How good it seems to be at the Lake again!"

33. Holst, the son of musician Adolph and singer Clara von Holst, was born and bred in England. Though the family was Swedish, not German, in origin, he dropped the "von" from his name during World War I. A prolific composer (best known for his 1916 orchestral suite *The Planets*) and a gifted teacher, he was for many years director of music at St. Paul's Girls' School in London.

34. Diary, May 6, 1923.

35. Diary, May 24, 1923.

36. A University of Michigan graduate (A.B. 1912, A.M. 1915), Earl V. Moore had cowritten the popular Michigan 1911 field song "Varsity" before heading to Paris to study organ and theory.

tion, which would have the great benefit of the recovery of the cultural context in which the papyri were found. In the first half of the year, John Anderson contributed another seventy-five hundred dollars, and Paul Gray gave two thousand for acquisitions.[37] But the breakthrough that made all things possible came when Horace Rackham wrote to President Burton offering one hundred thousand dollars over two years, "to permit the University of Michigan to conduct archaeological work in the Near East."[38] Two days later, a meeting attended by Deans Effinger and Lloyd and Professors Boak, Bonner, Kelsey, and Winter began discussions. On the table were three items: (1) work in Egypt, to be supervised by Hugh Evelyn-White; (2) an expedition across Asia Minor to identify and excavate a site or sites recommended by Sir William Ramsay, with David Robinson in charge; and (3) the purchase of manuscripts and papyri.

Evelyn-White, Ramsay, and Robinson were well known to Kelsey, and all were well aware of what was in the wind. Following a meeting with Evelyn-White in London in 1920, there had been letters back and forth, and in 1921 they had talked over the possibilities of work in Egypt.[39] He had met and dined with Sir William Ramsay in Constantinople in the summer of 1920, had attended lectures given by him in Washington in the fall of that year, and had already engaged in a considerable scholarly correspondence with him;[40] and in June 1923, he was about to send former Michigan student Enoch Peterson[41] to study epigraphy with Ramsay in Scotland. Similarly, Kelsey had known and corresponded with Robinson over many years.[42] At the 1923 Michigan Classical Conference, Robinson had given two lectures on classical sites in Asia Minor, after which he and Francis had talked over prospects for archaeological work there, one of which might be an expedition to track and record Xenophon's journeys.[43] Though sure that work in Egypt at a Greco-Roman urban site would be rewarding, correspondence and conversations both sug-

---

37. Money was coming in for other purposes, too: in the summer, Mrs. E. W. Pendleton promised to fund "four scholarships," and brothers Richard H. and Oscar Webber (see nn. 194, 208) offered one thousand dollars toward the education of the Askren boys.

38. Diary, June 26, 1923.

39. KMA Papers, box 35, folder 14.

40. KMA Papers, box 27, folder 1.

41. Enoch Ernest Peterson (M.A. 1922) had taught Latin at Luther College and served as its assistant librarian. Coming to the University of Michigan to study in the summer of 1918, he became a Buhl Fellow in Latin in 1921.

42. KMA Papers, box 28, folder 1. On Robinson, who had also been the first general editor of *Art and Archaeology,* see chapter 7 n. 32.

43. Diary, March 30, 1923.

gest how ready Francis was to explore opportunities and how broad his interests were.

The first meeting of the staff of this second expedition was held in November, and duties were assigned. Francis would be in charge of policy; Swain, photography and equipment; Professor Thomas Callander, inscriptions;[44] Robinson, Asia Minor excavation; Peterson, bibliography; Boak, Egypt excavation and papyri. Ramsay's advice was sought, and a permit request was prepared for Antioch (in Ramsay's name) and nearby Sizma (in Kelsey's).[45]

In the meantime, yet another opportunity was in the offing. A certain Count Byron Khun de Prorok had been in the United States in 1922, casting about for resources with which to buy a plot of land in Carthage where Punic inscribed stone stelae (markers) were coming to light (a sanctuary of Tanit?). With this in mind, he had contacted Kelsey as an archaeologist with an obvious scholarly interest in Carthage and as a possible source of funds.[46] In 1923 de Prorok succeeded in buying the land, and in December he renewed discussions with Kelsey. Quite early in 1924, the Washington (D.C.) Society of the AIA asked Francis his views on the desirability of work in Carthage along lines proposed to them by de Prorok.[47] Meeting with them, Francis pointed out the complexities of work on a site not yet built over but being rapidly developed (e.g., high prices for land) and suggested a season of preliminary work to test working conditions. Agreeing with this, they later asked Francis to lead such a project. De Prorok had meantime shown his mettle by engaging the interest of leading French scholars, including Reverend Père Delattre, an archaeologist resident in Carthage,[48] and the Abbé J.-B. Chabot, a leading

---

44. Callander, a professor of classics at Queen's University, Canada, had worked with Ramsay at Antioch before the war.

45. Diary, November 23, 1923. Sizma was a mound some thirty miles from Antioch, where Ramsay suspected an ancient sanctuary could be found. See Francis W. Kelsey, "The Second Michigan Expedition to the Near East," *Michigan Alumnus* 31 (1925): 459.

46. De Prorok, educated in England and Switzerland, more (one might say) of a dilettante than a scholar, claimed a Polish title and Polish estates. In the United States, he was looking not only for funds but for an established senior figure to lend credibility to the Carthage project. How far his objectives were commercial rather than scholarly is unclear. Nothing came of his initial overtures to Kelsey, though Francis lunched with him in New York and discovered that he was scouting about in Carthage with funds provided by the Singer family in Paris.

47. Diary, January 5, 1924.

48. Alfred Louis Delattre (1850–1932), a member of the White Fathers (Pères Blancs) order, was a founder and director of the Musée Lavigerie de Saint-Louis de Carthage.

French scholar interested in Carthaginian matters,[49] who joined him in exploring the site in 1924.

NEW YEAR, NEW EXPEDITION

Throughout 1923, Francis had continued teaching a full load and lecturing widely. In his research and editorial life, he had been busy the whole year with the Grotius project, kept up work on the Humanistic Series (the complexities of which may be gauged by a diary entry for the last day of the year),[50] managed to write an article,[51] and acquired more papyri. As the new year opened, Francis's hopes centered on the upcoming expedition, due to begin soon after the end of March. Meanwhile, Ann Arbor life resumed: teaching, correspondence (the pace and volume of which did not slacken),[52] churchgoing, UMS concerts and meetings, and committee work. One of his newer committees, in which he took great interest, was the Jerome Lectureship Committee, which announced on February 22 that the first Jerome Lecturer would be John Winter.[53]

Long-standing projects continued to demand attention: the Grotius translation, proceeding in fits and starts, section by section, proofs by proofs; the Humanistic Series, four volumes of which were on the drawing boards; fresh editions of the Cicero and Ovid texts for Allyn and Bacon; the third edition of Mau-Kelsey for Macmillan; and Caesar's battlefields, each waiting its

---

49. A highly respected historian and archaeologist, Jean-Baptiste Chabot (1860–1948) was an expert in Semitic inscriptions and on the Phoenician presence in the Western Mediterranean. An editor of the *Corpus Inscriptionum Semiticarum* and of the *Corpus Scriptorum Christianorum Orientalium* (with others, including Baron Carra de Vaux, Louis Cheikho, Ignazio Guidi, and Henri Hyvernat), he was a leading member of the Académie des Inscriptions et Belles-Lettres of the Institut de France.

50. He wrote in his diary on December 31, 1923, "Boston. Hotel Brunswick . . . then came T. W. Small of John Worley Company, he will print the music for vol. XV, the plates to be delivered to him by M. O. Henning, the paper by Mr. Barr. The printed sheets are to be sent to Norwood and there bound with pages of text printed at Norwood Press." No fewer than five volumes of the series were in the works in the course of the year.

51. Francis W. Kelsey, "A Waxed Tablet of the Year 128 A.D.," *TAPA* 54 (1923): 187–95.

52. Diary, February 23, 1924: no fewer than forty-five letters went out this day.

53. The two Michigan members of the committee were Francis Kelsey and Alfred Lloyd; representing the American Academy in Rome were James Egbert and William Linn Westermann; the fifth member was the president of the AIA, Ralph Magoffin. Westermann, a professor of classics at Columbia (1923–48), had attended the Paris Peace Conference in 1919 as a member of a U.S. government agency responsible for advising the politicians as to the practicality of the proposed new frontiers in Europe and of the states expected to be established in the Middle East.

turn.[54] Some of this work involved travel: in Norwood he looked over the proofs of volume 15 of the Humanistic Series and was given an estimate of thirty-two thousand dollars for four further volumes; in Boston he talked over his ideas for freshening up the Latin texts with Paul and Carl Bacon; in New York he discussed with Richard Gottheil and Heliotype Printing's W. C. Ramsay the question of the heliotype photographs for volume 13.[55]

Also occupying Kelsey was the ongoing search for funds—for students, for those in need (individuals or institutions), for promoting research, and for improving the university's collections of books, manuscripts, art, and artifacts. Francis continued his efforts to raise money for German scholarly institutions and projects—for the German Archaeological Institute in Rome and for the German *Thesaurus Linguae Latinae,* both seriously hampered by lack of funds and the collapsed German economy. Although Indianapolis and Milwaukee, whose German communities might be expected to help, did not produce much support, Americans of German extraction elsewhere were more helpful. For the University of Michigan, funding looked brighter: Horace Rackham contributed $12,500 in January and Joseph Boyer $5,000 in March for research fellowships, and in March Francis heard from the Detroit Trust Company that the Pendleton fellowships would also be renewed.[56] Around this time, he began to propose in university circles a suitable memorial for Edward Waldo Pendleton, a committed supporter of the university (and friend of the Latin Department) who had served as secretary to the building committee of Alumni Memorial Hall: a Pendleton Library on the second floor of the Union building.[57]

Even though Francis could successfully juggle several projects at the same time, the new expedition occupied most of his thoughts. At its meeting on January 15, the newly formed Advisory Committee on Near East Research[58] discussed the organization of the expedition, staffing arrangements, provisions for publication, and the question of participation at Carthage. They

---

54. Diary, February 11 and March 6–8 and 12–15, 1924.

55. Diary, January 3 and March 21, 1924. The plates were for Richard Gottheil and William H. Worrell, eds., *Fragments from the Cairo Genizah in the Freer Collection,* University of Michigan Studies, Humanistic Series, vol. 13 (Ann Arbor: University of Michigan, 1927).

56. Diary, January 7 and March 3 and 10, 1924.

57. Diary, February 29, 1924. On Pendleton, see chapter 4 n. 34.

58. The advisors were President Burton; assistant to the president Frank E. Robbins; Deans Effinger and Lloyd; Professors Boak, Bonner, Winter, and Sanders; and librarian Bishop. (Semitics professor Leroy Waterman joined the committee two weeks later.) Robbins (1884–1963), who had entered the University of Michigan faculty in 1912 as a teacher in Greek, would become director of the University of Michigan Press in 1930.

also welcomed the gift of two vehicles for the expedition's use: a Dodge sedan, donated by Mr. and Mrs. Howard Bloomer of Detroit, and a Graham truck, the gift of Joseph, Robert, and Ray Graham.[59]

In February the press carried announcements of the membership of the expeditionary team (and responsibilities): Boak (Egypt), Robinson (fieldwork), Callander (inscriptions), Evelyn-White (Coptic), Swain (photography and equipment), Enoch Peterson and Orlando Qualley (fieldwork students).[60] A Turkish student at Michigan, Hussein Shefik Feizy, whose brother happened to be chief of police in Konya (within striking distance of the site proposed for excavation at Antioch), was later to be added as a surveyor, as were architects to be named.[61] It was understood that Sir William Ramsay, who was expecting a renewal of his permit for Antioch, would be on site some of the season, working on inscriptions while the Michigan team excavated. It was hoped that he and the Michigan team would work together harmoniously and that a permit would also be granted for *sondages* at the ancient site at Sizma, near Antioch, in which Ramsay had expressed an interest.[62]

The objectives of the expedition were as follows:

1. the photography of manuscripts, which might easily be destroyed in the unsettled conditions of the Near East, and of ancient sites and architectural monuments of all periods, for which purpose Swain was taking along no fewer than four cameras;

2. the acquisition of manuscripts and papyri; and

3. fieldwork
   (a) in Turkey, on the assumption that Ramsay's reputation, experience in Asia Minor and at Antioch, and undoubted clout could get permits;
   (b) at Carthage if agreements could be reached, and
   (c) at a suitable site in Egypt, yet to be determined.

The team was to gather in Paris as soon after April 1 as possible, proceed across Europe, and then divide into two groups, one to work in Asia Minor, where they would link up with Ramsay, the other to work in Egypt.

---

59. Howard R. Bloomer was a lawyer in the Detroit firm of McGregor and Bloomer. The Grahams owned the car manufacturing firm Graham Brothers in Detroit.

60. Diary, February 13, 1924. Orlando Warren Qualley, like Peterson (see n. 41 above), had taught at Luther College (math, Norwegian, Latin, Greek) and come to study at the University of Michigan (summer 1920), becoming a fellow in Latin in 1922.

61. Though he was to be a help to Swain and participated in other ways (e.g., transport), Easton's name did not appear.

62. See n. 45 above.

Enthusiasm for work in Carthage was growing, as vigorously in the Washington Society of the AIA as anywhere.[63] A lecture (with films) given by de Prorok, which had been well received at Harvard and in Baltimore, was a success in Ann Arbor, too. But some scholars preferred other sites: the English archaeologist A. J. B. Wace, visiting on January 9 to give a lecture about Mycenae, was asked his opinion and suggested that Olynthus in Greece, for which he had the permit, might be a better bet.[64] When Francis asked him the next day if he would be willing to direct the work in Carthage, Wace replied by urging the claims of Olynthus, the permit for which (he said) could easily be transferred. The problem of identifying competent field directors under whose guidance young Americans could learn the ropes was constantly a worry to Francis; as far as Turkey was concerned, he was confident enough in the skills of David Robinson, who had excavated at Corinth and Sardis; but Carthage was problematic, and Egypt was soon to present difficulties.

With the house rented, books returned to the library, and farewells made, Francis left Ann Arbor on March 19 for Washington, where he conferred—all on this single day—with Mitchell Carroll about the AIA and Carthage, at the State Department with Allen Welsh Dulles, at the Carnegie Endowment about the Grotius work, and even for a few hours with Charlotte before leaving for New York.[65] On March 22, he and Isabelle boarded the SS *President Roosevelt*. After a wrangle over cabins and staterooms, they were upgraded to a luxurious suite (no. 202, equipped with a maid's room, trunk room, sitting room, bedroom, and bathroom) and seated at the captain's table—from which Isabelle, seasick most of the journey, sadly was unable to profit.

In London, after checking at Brown, Shipley, and Company for his mail, Francis met W. H. Buckler, who had worked in Turkey as a member of the Princeton excavation team at Sardis before the war and knew well both the inscriptions of Asia Minor and conditions in the country.[66] He also conferred with Kenyon at the British Museum, to ask if Edward Edwards, a Persian

---

63. Other sponsors, as well as the University of Michigan, were to include the University of Rochester, McGill University, the French Institute in Carthage, and the Canadian government.

64. Educated at Cambridge, Alan John Bayard Wace (1879–1957) was director of the British School at Athens during 1914–23, a deputy keeper in the Victoria and Albert Museum in London during 1924–34, and Laurence Professor of Classical Archaeology at Cambridge during 1934–44. A remarkably versatile and prolific scholar, he developed a particular interest in Greek prehistory and excavated in and around Mycenae for many years.

65. Swain and Easton had left earlier but separately (diary, February 18 and 27, 1924).

66. Buckler (see chapter 5 n. 100), was an experienced lawyer and diplomat as well as being a consummate classicist.

manuscripts expert on the museum's staff,[67] could go to Egypt to assess a group of Islamic manuscripts from the collection of Sultan Abdulhamid II that Nahman was offering for sale, as well as to ask Kenyon's thoughts about material that another Cairo dealer, a Dr. A. N. Kondilios, had on offer. Further conferences ensued: with Ramsay and Peterson (on Asia Minor); with publisher George Macmillan, who was chairman of the management committee of the British School at Athens (on Olynthus); with Evelyn-White (on work in Egypt); and with Kenyon, Edwards, and Bell at the British Museum (on manuscripts and papyri).[68] On April 12, he cabled Nahman, "Can we examine Abdulhamid Collection early May?"

Isabelle, meanwhile, was in touch with Mrs. Catherina Pendleton (whose sister lived in Surrey) and invited her to dinner. Thereafter, Francis spoke with her about the proposed Pendleton Library in the Union; and on April 6, he was able to cable President Hutchins, "Mrs. Pendleton raises Union subscription to $21,500 with three conditions—completion this year, bronze tablet honoring Mr. Pendleton, pay $15,000 as needed, balance after January 1. Cable if accepted." It took Hutchins just forty-eight hours to reply: "All accepted. Thanks. Hutchins."[69] Isabelle, however, was again not feeling well, and a nurse was engaged. Catherina stayed with Isabelle a whole day; once Dr. Maxwell Chance declared there "was no organic trouble," she also took the rallying Isabelle for a ride in a limousine. When Isabelle seemed brighter and Dr. Chance vouched for her progress, the Kelseys left for Paris.[70]

Settled in the Grand Hôtel de Malte, 63 rue de Richelieu, they learned that Swain and Easton and the cars were blocked by customs in Brussels. Unfazed by the news, Kelsey went to meet Alfred Chester Beatty (whose collection of manuscripts was among the best in Europe),[71] to find out whether he might join in the purchase of the Abdulhamid Collection, and he visited the dealer Géjou's office, where he bought two manuscripts; that evening, at the theater, Isabelle and he enjoyed a performance of Édouard Lalo's opera *Le Roi d'Ys.*

---

67. Diary, April 1 and 2, 1924. Edwards's *A Catalogue of the Persian Printed Books in the British Museum* (London: British Museum) had appeared in 1922. (This Edwards [1870–1940] is not to be confused with an earlier cataloger there of the same name [1812–86], who wrote *Lives of the Founders of the British Museum,* 2 vols. [London: Trübner, 1870].)

68. Details of all these conferences are in exhaustive memorandums submitted by Kelsey to the Advisory Committee on Near East Research at Michigan (April 1924, FWK Papers, box 1, folder 28).

69. Diary, April 9, 1924.

70. Diary, April 14, 1924.

71. Beatty (1875–1968) was an American-born mining millionaire (and the so-called King of Copper). His collection, the Chester Beatty Library, is now housed in Dublin Castle.

After four days in Paris, they took the Orient Express for Milan, where they met Professor and Mrs. Stanley. But here Isabelle fell ill once more, a Swiss doctor was summoned, and she was moved to the Clinica Internazionale (the hospital of the foreign colony in Milan) at 12 via Monte Rosa. Together they decided that she should not continue the trip but stay in Milan until Francis returned. Francis left for Constantinople on April 22, arriving three days later, after joining up with Robinson in Venice. He learned at once from Admiral Bristol, the American high commissioner, that there were permit problems.

From Turkey to Egypt to Italy to London

The difficulties Admiral Bristol reported were caused by the presence in the Metropolitan Museum in New York of fifty-eight cases of archaeological objects from the excavations at Sardis, exported from Turkey during the period when the Greek army controlled this part of Asia Minor (1921–22); the objects were now claimed by the Turkish government as Turkish property illegally exported.[72] Carl Blegen of the American School at Athens had written to Robinson in 1923 that work in Asia Minor was impossible, conditions being utterly unstable; but Buckler, in sync with, if not ahead of, the times, had written him more positively, stressing that Robinson's survey should "note all sites, prehistoric or otherwise," that sites should be "thoroughly examined," and that there was no time for "rapid excursions to promising inscription sites of the type Ramsay used to do." When Callander took the view, in a message to Kelsey, that Egypt was a better prospect, Robinson, too, had written him that Olynthus—as Francis already knew from Wace—presented a good opportunity, since he had heard that the British, concentrating on Sparta, could not afford it.[73] When news filtered through that the uncooperative reaction of the Metropolitan Museum in the matter of the antiquities from Sardis was blocking permits for American archaeological work in Turkey, some reactions were unrestrained. Buckler wrote to Kelsey that the Metropolitan's board was "a stiff-necked and stupid crowd," and Harold Wilmerding Bell, the numismatist working on the coins from Sardis, confided to

---

72. In the merciless carving up by the Allies (France, Britain, Italy) of what remained of the Ottoman Empire after World War I, the Greeks were encouraged to seize a sizable portion of western Asia Minor. The ferocious reaction of Atatürk's ragtag Anatolian army against all foreigners, driven by a rekindled spirit of nationalism, is hardly surprising.

73. Robinson's interest in Olynthus foreshadows the excavations at and the publications of the site that were to make him famous (David M. Robinson, ed., *Excavations at Olynthus*, 14 vols. [Baltimore: Johns Hopkins University Press, 1930–52]).

Buckler that the board was "a bunch of crooks."[74] The arch Hellenophile Callander let loose the patently Victorian colonial comment that there was a need to "cuff the Turkish ear."[75]

In March Halil Bey, the director of the Constantinople Archaeological Museum, had refused point-blank all requests for permits, pending a decision on the Sardis antiquities in the Metropolitan, a decision confirmed to Kelsey by Feizy after his arrival in Turkey. Faced with this situation in April, Kelsey, Ramsay, and Bristol met with Adnan Bey, the representative in Constantinople of the Angora (now Ankara) government, who referred them back to the influential Halil Bey. With the utmost courtesy, Halil said no. A day of visits followed—to Constantinople College and Robert College and to Feizy's wedding, where, amid much jollification, Francis appeared wearing a fez.[76] After a further conference with Admiral Bristol at the embassy, they were given visas for Smyrna—the Turkish authorities presumably would not prevent their "touring," and they would have Feizy with them. At lunch, in response to the Sardis antiquities problem, Ramsay uttered a comment that Francis recorded in his diary: "Honesty can never be presumed with reference to two classes of men—horse thieves and museum directors"—doubtless intended as a witticism. The next day, they boarded a steamer for Smyrna, a party of five: Kelsey, Ramsay, Robinson, Peterson, and Feizy.

Approaching Smyrna cautiously for fear of mines, the steamer decanted four—Ramsay, Robinson, Peterson, and Feizy—to make their way inland to Antioch, hoping day by day for news of the permit requests. The ship plowed on to the Piraeus, where Francis mailed a bundle of letters, before going on to Alexandria. At Shepheard's Hotel in Cairo, Francis found a telegram from London: "Gladly withdraw claim Olynthus. Macmillan."[77] So opened the option of Olynthus as a site for archaeological research. Askren came up from the Fayoum with the papyri he had collected for Francis and to talk about excavation prospects.[78] The site at Maabdah (Samoun) came under consideration but, with others (e.g., Medinet), was later rejected for one reason or an-

---

74. Bell (1885–1947) was also a collector of books and manuscripts relating to Sir Arthur Conan Doyle's fictional character Sherlock Holmes and was author of *Sherlock Holmes and Dr. Watson the Chronology of Their Adventures* (London: Constable, 1932).

75. For all correspondence mentioned in this paragraph, see FWK Papers, box 1, folders 23–27.

76. Robinson and Peterson did likewise (diary, April 27, 1924).

77. Diary, May 4, 1924.

78. The papyri were in two tin boxes and twelve envelopes, for which Francis paid a total of 200.5 pounds.

other. G. A. Wainwright,[79] an Egyptologist who had worked many years with Sir Flinders Petrie, was a leading candidate to be the field director; that he was not available (though he agreed to act in an advisory capacity) allowed a younger man, James Leslie Starkey, to come to the fore.[80]

Turning to some of his other sources for papyri, Francis took a twenty-minute train ride to Zeitoun to call on Dr. Kondilios—a journey in vain, as Kondilios regretted that his papyri were locked away in a bank and inaccessible: the key to the box was at his summer home on the Greek island of Leros.[81] Another day, he spent three hours in the evening at Nahman's house, looking through the Abdulhamid Collection, which he described as "in part calligraphic, in part containing miniatures—Persian, Turkish, and Arabic. I am much attracted to this material."[82] A more learned view of this collection became available when Edward Edwards arrived and spent three days examining it, concluding that four hundred of the manuscripts were "desirable." He had no doubt the manuscripts were genuine. Nahman had asked sixty-five hundred pounds, but a price of four thousand was agreed.[83] While Edwards worked on the Abdulhamid material, Francis was busy buying papyri for Michigan and Columbia from Nahman and others. The better part of a day was spent boxing up those papyri, leaving just enough time for Francis to buy two prayer rugs for Mrs. Rackham and take the train to Alexandria to catch the SS *Milano* for Naples. He had spent ten busy days in Egypt and two thousand pounds of Columbia's money,[84] agreeing to a further expenditure

79. Gerald Averay Wainwright (1879–1964) authored *Balabish* (London: George Allen & Unwin, 1920) and *The Sky-Religion in Egypt: Its Antiquity and Effects* (Cambridge: Cambridge University Press, 1938).

80. Trained as a field archaeologist by the British School of Archaeology in Egypt, Starkey (1895–1938), also a Petrie associate, spent most of his professional life in Egypt and Palestine, for the most part successfully; for instance, he was instrumental in the discovery of the Badarian culture. But his life ended haplessly—he was murdered en route to the opening of a new museum in Palestine.

81. One of the Dodecanese islands, Leros is about midway between Samos and Kos. Kelsey does not seem to have taken to Kondilios, a Greek said to have been educated in Paris and Athens, noting that he had "a shrewd face" and that Askren and Nahman agreed in regarding him as a "sharper." This description and characterization are added in Kelsey's handwriting on a page (368) left blank but with the printed title "Memoranda" at the end of his 1924 diary.

82. Diary, May 5, 1924.

83. Diary, May 12 and 13, 1924. For more on the Abdulhamid collection, see "Islamic Manuscripts at the University of Michigan: Summary of Collection History," http://guides .lib.umich.edu/data/files/30956/IslMssSummary.pdf (accessed August 31, 2009).

84. In this, he was acting for William Westermann, on whom see n. 53 above.

of four thousand pounds. And he had narrowed the choice of sites in Egypt, suitable to his purposes, and of field directors.

In Constantinople Admiral Bristol had been at work; he sent Francis a telegram, received in Naples: "Sardis matter adjusted. Granting of your permit to be facilitated and expedited."[85] Things were falling into place. Swain and Easton greeted him in Naples and traveled to Rome with him to spend one day sorting out insurance coverage for the expedition vehicles and another day photographing in the Forum and on the Palatine. It should not have come as a surprise to Francis to learn at the American Academy that Spinazzola's antifascist remarks had been noticed by Mussolini's henchmen and that he had been dismissed from the National Archaeological Museum of Naples. Leaving Rome on May 26 for Milan, he was overjoyed to find Isabelle at the Hotel Francis and in good health. He also found Mr. and Mrs. Bishop there, a meeting he had arranged at long distance, not least because he wished to discuss the Abdulhamid collection with the university librarian. Bishop's reaction to the possibility of acquiring these Persian and Arabic manuscripts was so positive that he wrote forcefully the next day to President Burton and the rest of the Advisory Committee on Near East Research, urging their purchase.[86] Francis and Isabelle left Milan on the evening of May 29 and were in their London hotel the next day.[87] Since Edwards was already back from Egypt, Kelsey and Bell immediately went into conference with him about the manuscripts. Francis also discussed with Kenyon the papyri and their division among the British Museum, Columbia, Michigan, and Princeton. With the help of Bell, he showed Mrs. Pendleton the rooms where the papyri and manuscripts were unpacked, opened, and studied. After just three days in London, they were on their way to Southampton and the SS *Leviathan,* bound for New York, Francis with the precious papyri in his bags.

In the States and Back to Turkey

Wasting no time in New York—they arrived at 2:00 p.m. and were on the overnight train to Detroit by 6:00 p.m.[88]—Francis and Isabelle took the prayer rugs bought for Mrs. Rackham to her husband's office on the morning of June 10. A pleased Rackham asked "whether we had money enough" for the

---

85. Diary, May 19, 1924.
86. Bishop to Burton, May 28, 1924, FWK Papers, box 1, folder 29.
87. Diary, May 30, 1924.
88. Diary, June 9, 1924.

work in the Near East. Francis replied, "our opportunities were greater than our means," and could not resist adding, "we need to lay out work on a 5 year basis." On arrival in Ann Arbor, the Kelseys took a room at the Union, and the next day, at a hastily convened meeting of the Near East research committee, Francis reported on events and opportunities: possible acquisitions from Kondilios, the Abdulhamid manuscript collection, work permits in Turkey and Egypt, the opportunity at Olynthus, and the papyri acquired in Egypt.

In the course of the next few days, Francis attended the commencement exercises in Ferry Field, briefed colleagues on developments, and had a conference with President Burton, who had just returned from making the nomination speech for Calvin Coolidge at the Republican National Convention. Money was short (he learned), so it was a relief when an extra ten thousand dollars came in from Rackham, on the basis of which he cabled Kenyon, "$15,000 available for purchase Abdulhamid manuscripts for UM."[89] A rapid visit to Washington, D.C., and New York entailed, in Washington, meetings with Carroll and Merriam about Carthage, with Brown Scott about Grotius, and at the State Department. At dinner with Charlotte's husband, Frank, Kelsey learned, to his considerable disappointment, that Frank's company was in trouble, that he had resigned from it and was seeking other opportunities.[90] In New York Francis scurried about trying to engage an architect for the work in Turkey and discussed the format for the revised edition of the Mau-Kelsey *Pompeii* at Macmillan.

Francis was back in Ann Arbor on June 27, and when Isabelle, ailing again, went into Dr. Cowie's private hospital for a rest, he moved from their room at the Union to another at 327 South Division (the hospital being at 320).[91] On one day, he went into Detroit for meetings with Joseph Boyer, William Murphy, and Horace Rackham. On another, Isabelle was well enough to go with him to lunch with Mr. and Mrs. Rackham, after which Francis noted some of Rackham's remarks: "I do not wish to pose as a rich man. I never wish to allow myself to have that mental attitude. I never think of it unless the idea is forced upon me." Francis added his own estimations: "He avoids publicity"; "he enjoys a simple life, as does Mrs. Rackham. They are very devoted."[92]

89. Diary, June 19 and 20, 1924.

90. Diary, June 23, 1924.

91. David Murray Cowie (1872–1940), of the Cowie Private Hospital (320 South Division), had founded the Pediatrics Department at the University of Michigan Hospital. Creature comforts were evidently not a priority for Kelsey: he did not mind where he slept. But accounts were, as his careful notation of the charge for the room on South Division (three dollars a week) testifies.

92. Diary, June 30, 1924.

Francis was about to return to Turkey, this time alone, since Isabelle decided not to risk the demands of summer life in an Anatolian village. She opted to visit Ruth in Missoula instead and left on July 2.[93] The Near East research committee met again to decide on the allocation of funds, after which Francis spent two or three days managing money matters, mailing books and papers to Rome, working on the new edition of his Ovid textbook, spending Sunday morning at church and the afternoon at Lake Cavanaugh, and writing to Isabelle almost every day. Leaving for Boston on July 10, he worked all night—"went to bed at 4, up at 6.30"; after a day in Boston working with Paul Bacon and O. J. Barr at the offices of Allyn and Bacon, he pressed on to New York and the SS *America*.

On board the ship, he read through Bell's *Jews and Christians in Egypt*,[94] a gift from Kenyon; corrected proofs of Sanders's *The Minor Prophets in the Freer Collection* (volume 21 of the Humanistic Series); and enjoyed conversations with President Ellen Fitz Pendleton of Wellesley College and Miss Agnes Goldman, sister of Hetty Goldman, the pioneering American archaeologist.[95] In London during July 20–23, though he negotiated visas for a day at the U.S. consulate, much of his time was spent at the British Museum. There Edwards reported that the Abdulhamid collection "surpassed expectations," that some 290 manuscripts were to go to Michigan, that Nahman had brought more papyri to London for evaluation, and that Francis might catch him in Paris if he was lucky. Francis fired off a cable, as a result of which Nahman joined him at the Gare de Lyon (between trains) for an hour-long meeting. Nahman exclaimed, "I see the Abdulhamid Collection was a gift at the price you paid, yes, a gift. A like collection will never be seen again. But I do not regret the transaction—the manuscripts are well placed in the British Museum and the University of Michigan." Concerning the papyri, he added that Pierre Lacau, director general of the Department of Antiquities of Egypt, had berated him in no uncertain terms: "After this, you must never expect to put through another

---

93. She also spent time with relatives in California and Denver and was not reunited with Francis until November 22. Ruth and her husband moved from Montana to California later in the year.

94. H. Idris Bell, *Jews and Christians in Egypt: The Jewish Troubles in Alexandria and the Athanasian Controversy* (London: British Museum; Oxford: Oxford University Press, 1924).

95. President Pendleton had herself been educated at Wellesley (A.B. 1886, A.M. 1891). Hetty Goldman, educated at Bryn Mawr and Radcliffe, was one of the foremost women archaeologists of the early twentieth century, famous for her excavations at Eutresis in Greece and at Colophon and Tarsus in Asia Minor.

big box of papyri so quickly. That was done as a courtesy to Mr. Kelsey: hereafter we shall examine every piece."[96]

In Venice Francis gave voice, for the first time, to a sense of failing stamina (he was, after all, sixty-six years of age), writing in the diary, "How I wish I could stay a few days and rest!" His energy and vitality returned as he passed from Sofia to Constantinople, taking delight in the sight of the countryside and the crops.[97] Once in Constantinople, however, it was all business: trouble at the customs with Swain's photographic equipment; more visas required for Anatolia; cables hither and thither, including one to Mrs. Pendleton, who was contemplating the journey to Constantinople (it is no wonder she changed her mind, after Kelsey reported to her, "Six visas required: Turkey, Greece, Bulgaria, Serbia, Italy, France").[98] On the first of the month, he left for the excavations, taking a ferry across the Bosporus and trains to Eskişehir and on to Akşehir, where he found Swain, Easton, and Feizy waiting for him with the Graham truck.

Antioch in Pisidia

Pisidian Antioch, so named when it became the capital of a new province of Pisidia in the late Roman period, is situated on the Anatolian plateau some three thousand feet above sea level, about two hundred miles due east of İzmir (ancient Smyrna), a hundred miles due north of the south coast, and some sixty miles west of Konya. Surrounded by mountains, it was linked to the rail line at Akşehir by a rough dirt road that climbed to a point some 5,800 feet above sea level, offering breathtaking views of the valley to the west and the low hill on which the ancient site was built. Water, timber, stone, and clay are abundant; the land is rich, the site easily defensible. Whether any settlement existed prior to the city named after its Seleucid founder in the third century BC is unknown; but its strategic and secure location made it a magnet for Roman interest, so much so that in 25 BC Augustus Caesar (soon to become the first Roman emperor) gave the city the standing of a Roman

---

96. Diary, July 24, 1924. The independence of Egypt in 1922 had signaled new restrictions on the activities of foreign archaeologists, and Lacau (1873–1963, director general for 1914–36), was not reluctant to implement these controls, provoking the ire, for example, of Howard Carter (of Tutankhamun fame).

97. Diary, July 27, 1924.

98. Diary, July 31, 1924.

colony, Colonia Caesarea Antiochia.[99] Antioch rapidly became a center for civil administration and a military base, furnished with typical Roman buildings and infrastructure. Visited by the apostles Barnabas and Paul (Acts 14:20, 25), the community gradually became more and more Christian, to judge by the several churches that have come to light. By the third-century reign of the emperor Maximinus Thrax, there was a bishop here.[100]

Adjacent to the ancient site is the modern village of Yalvaç. Here the expedition located its headquarters in the only so-called hotel. The expedition rented the whole of the second floor: there were four bedrooms, a storage room, and a large open space that functioned as kitchen, dining room, library, registry, darkroom, and drafting room. It was hardly ideal, especially at night, when bedbugs were active and mosquitoes feasted. The ground floor of the building was occupied by a social club and coffeehouse, boisterous at night (until the expedition threatened to leave). If the accommodations were less than comfortable, the food was good, prepared by a Russian chef hired in Smyrna. The team arrived in Yalvaç in stages; first to appear were the quartet left by Kelsey in Smyrna in early May (Ramsay, Robinson, Peterson, and Feizy). Swain and Easton, delayed by customs in Constantinople, did not arrive with the vehicles until the end of June. The architect F. J. Woodbridge[101] arrived in July and his assistant, Horace F. Colby, in August.[102]

---

99. Veterans of the Fifth and Seventh legions were among the colonists: see David Magie, *Roman Rule in Asia Minor to the End of the Third Century after Christ*, 2 vols. (Princeton: Princeton University Press, 1950), 1:459; 2:1319 nn. 30, 31.

100. For an early traveler's visit to the site, see F. V. J. Arundell, *Discoveries in Asia Minor, Including a Description of the Ruins of Several Ancient Cities, and Especially Antioch of Pisidia*, 2 vols. (London: Richard Bentley, 1834); for a more recent synopsis, see Stephen Mitchell and Marc Waelkens, *Pisidian Antioch: The Site and Its Monuments* (London: Duckworth and Classical Press of Wales, 1998). See also Lauren E. Talalay and Susan E. Alcock, *In the Field: The Archaeological Expeditions of the Kelsey Museum* (Ann Arbor: Kelsey Museum of Archaeology, 2006), 12–15. A reevaluation of the site was conducted in 2004 by Professor Elaine Gazda and a team from the University of Michigan. The resulting catalog of the stunning 2006 exhibition of the site morphed into a book of essays: Elaine K. Gazda, Ünal Demirer, and Diana Ng, eds., *Building a New Rome: The Imperial Colony of Pisidian Antioch* (Ann Arbor: Kelsey Museum of Archaeology, 2011). See the online version of the exhibition at http://www.lsa.mich.edu/Kelsey/exhibitions/pastexhibitions.

101. Frederick James Woodbridge (1900–74) was educated at Amherst (B.A. 1921) and the Columbia University School of Architecture (B.A. 1923) and received an honorary M.A. in architecture from Amherst in 1951. Initially with the famous McKim, Mead, and White in New York during 1921–25, he later became a partner first in Evans, Moore, and Woodbridge (1928) and then in Adams and Woodbridge (1945).

102. Colby, educated at Cornell (B.F.A. 1924) and the son of Frederick Lee Colby (see n. 191), was to become a successful sculptor: "Horace F. Colby II was recently awarded a prize of

Francis had become aware that difficulties between Ramsay and Robinson had arisen almost from the beginning. Since the permit for Antioch was given to Ramsay and the permit for nearby Sizma was slow to arrive from Angora, both were at Antioch for the first part of the season, with Robinson in charge of the excavation and Ramsay, if present, the éminence grise.[103] Arguments over objectives, procedures, and territory doubtless ensued. Ramsay wrote to Francis of problems with Robinson; Robinson wrote to Francis of work progressing well although he was at odds with Ramsay; Ramsay wrote again that "he had had it out" with Robinson. None of this was good for camp morale.[104] By mid-June, Ramsay was back in Edinburgh, writing to Francis in exasperated mood; but work continued at Antioch until Robinson left to scout around the site at Sizma, some thirty miles away, in accordance with the permit issued to Kelsey. After digging trial trenches there across the mound but finding no evidence he thought worth pursuing—the mound was little more than a slag heap—Robinson returned to Antioch to find that Francis had arrived. In Ramsay's absence, difficulties had arisen with the Antioch fieldwork permit, causing Kelsey to cable Halil Bey, "Sizma unfruitful. Work there stopped. Kindly telegraph permission to resume excavating here immediately."[105] Halil replied with a cable to the mayor of Yalvaç granting the request, only for this permission to be withdrawn the next day by officials in Angora.[106] Faced with this situation, Francis sent Robinson off to Angora with Easton and the car to ask for a permit at the source, while he himself returned by train as quickly as he could to Constantinople to talk to the embassy and Halil Bey. These maneuvers proved successful, and Robinson returned from Angora with permit in hand.[107] The intervening ten days had not been wasted in Yalvaç or at the site, with Peterson hard at work at the registry and Woodbridge persevering with his architectural drawings. Excavation resumed at once, though hampered by sickness in the team: Robinson and Easton, not feeling well after their exhausting journey (including escape from an

---

one hundred dollars by the Founders' Society of the Detroit Institute of Arts for a bronze bust of a negro child. . . . He is now studying at the American Academy in Rome and expects soon to do some traveling in Egypt and Greece" (*Cornell Alumni News* 27.21 [February 19, 1925]: 266). The statue of Captain Charles E. Belknap in Belknap Park, Grand Rapids, is a work by Colby (1931).

103. Cf. the June 23, 1923, meeting at which it was determined that Robinson was to be in charge of one or more sites selected by Ramsay (see above, "The Near East Beckons").

104. May 1924, FWK Papers, box 1, folder 29.

105. Diary, August 7, 1924.

106. Diary, August 11, 1924.

107. Diary, August 23, 1924.

Angora hotel in flames), were treated with liberal doses of aspirin, quinine, and castor oil.[108] The palliative medicines given to ailing members of the team took effect, and work continued at full throttle for the final few days of the excavation, stopping on September 1. Robinson and Easton left the following day.

Before Easton left, there was family business to attend to: Francis had a heart-to-heart talk with him, laying out conditions on which he would be allowed to return to university. These tell us much about both father and son. As recorded in the diary, the pledge ran as follows:

1. Enter classes first day if I possibly can and attend without an absence except for sickness. University work always first.

2. Room alone and turn out visitors who interfere with studies.

3. Prepare lessons with a view to attaining perfection in every class as nearly as possible; cultivate mastery from the first day.

4. Cut out waste of time in idle talk.

5. Go to bed early nights and get up in good season regularly.

6. Attend Presbyterian Church two Sundays a month.

7. Cut out all smoking and drinking.[109]

Apparently Easton, now aged twenty, took more readily to social life than to the life of the mind, and if these conditions make Francis appear more of a martinet than an indulgent parent, it may have been what the playful Easton needed. At the same time, Easton's help and energy on the excavation and his fondness for foreign life boded well for his later career in the State Department.

The next few days were spent in packing up, completing notebooks and drawings, and fighting off the clouds of mosquitoes.[110] After Francis had made his courtesy exit calls on the local authorities, the remaining members of the team dispersed. Kelsey, Peterson, and Haidan Bey, the Turkish commissioner at the site, made for Angora. At the Ministry of Education, Francis—with the help of Haidan Bey, who had earlier declared that "Ram-

---

108. Some detail in this passage is drawn from Easton T. Kelsey, "Digging for Ruins Centuries Old," *Michigan Chimes* (University of Michigan), January 1925, 15–18, 45–46; and idem, "Exploring Where Paul Preached: Notable Architectural and Art Treasures Unearthed on the Site of Ancient Antioch," *Dearborn Independent*, September 4, 1926, 13–14.

109. Diary, September 1, 1924.

110. Diary, September 6 and 7, 1924.

say was too old to conduct excavations"[111]—prepared an application for an excavation permit for Antioch for 1925; at the Ministry of Finance, he sought a refund of the customs duty paid on the vehicles, which were now to be exported. By September 14, he and Peterson were in Constantinople, where Francis, though ill, wrote his memoranda for the Advisory Committee on Near East Research from a hospital bed. After five days in the hospital, he was up and about, calling on Halil Bey, offering help with the restoration of the seraglio, and buying manuscripts (plus another Persian rug for Mrs. Rackham).

The fieldwork at Antioch had concentrated on three main areas: a city gate, a large Christian basilica, and a sanctuary of the imperial cult—with emphasis on the architecture and sculptural decoration, to enable the buildings to be reconstructed on paper. Attention was also paid to the huge aqueduct that had brought water into the city (materials, fabric, capacity, and source) and to any epigraphic evidence—in particular any fragments of the *Res Gestae* of Augustus, the official version of the emperor's achievements, posted on public buildings all over the empire as political propaganda, of which Ramsay had recovered several pieces in his prewar excavations.

As the blocks of the city gate were uncovered and disentangled from the collapsed mass of the structure, the plan and elevation of the structure slowly revealed themselves and were drawn by Woodbridge. About fifty meters broad and thirteen meters high, the gate comprised four piers supporting pilasters and three arches, with fasciated architrave, frieze, and cornice above. The order is Corinthian. The frieze is carved on one side with spiral and vegetal motifs and on the other with weapons in relief; standard-bearers, *erotes,* captives, and Victories enrich the spaces above the arches, and the cornice is decorated with lions' heads. The architrave carried an inscription in bronze letters (fig. 23) recording the name of the benefactor who built (or restored) the gate: Caius Julius Asper, proconsul in AD 217.[112] It was an imposing threshold.

Much of the masonry of the Christian basilica, almost two hundred feet in length, had been robbed away for use in modern roads or houses. But blocks of a couple of courses of the north wall and the apse had survived, with enough of the rest of the structure to allow the drawing of a restored plan of walls, nave, aisles, apse, and narthex. Beneath the floor, evidence of an earlier

111. Diary, August 29, 1924.
112. Magie, *Roman Rule in Asia Minor,* 2:1585.

23. Architect Frederick James Woodbridge demonstrates placement of the inscription's bronze letters on the architrave block at the city gate of Antioch, 1924. Kelsey Museum of Archaeology, University of Michigan KR 107.12. Photo: George R. Swain.

church came to light in the shape of a polychrome tessellated mosaic, datable to the fourth century AD by Greek inscriptions in the mosaic.[113]

Several architectural features contributed to the impact of the sanctuary. On the approach was a long, narrow, axial piazza, leading to a staircase supporting an entrance gate, a so-called propylon, consisting of piers from which sprang three arches. This entrance, like the city gate, was richly ornamented, the piers in all probability emblazoned with the lettering of the *Res Gestae*. The staircase led to a large, rectangular, colonnaded court and, at the furthest point from the visitor coming up the staircase, the Temple of Augustus itself, placed in front of a semicircular, colonnaded exedra (figs. 24 and 25).[114] Note-

---

113. The ruined remains of another, Byzantine church were also found within the city walls.

114. For the results of the 1924 expedition's work, see David M. Robinson, "A Preliminary Report on the Excavations at Pisidian Antioch and at Sizma," *AJA* 28 (1924): 435–44; idem, "Roman Sculptures from Colonia Caesarea (Pisidian Antioch)," *Art Bulletin* 9.1 (1926): 5–69.

24. Semicircular exedra at the sanctuary of the imperial cult at Antioch, 1924, with excavation in progress. Kelsey Museum of Archaeology, University of Michigan 7.1116. Photo: George R. Swain.

25. Ruins of the Temple of Augustus in front of a colonnaded exedra at Antioch, 2004. Kelsey Museum of Archaeology, University of Michigan A 87. Photo: Benjamin Rubin.

worthy among objects recovered was a striking large-scale marble head of Augustus; among inscriptions were some two hundred more fragments of the *Res Gestae,* as well as an interesting legal document recording measures taken by Lucius Antistius Rusticus, the governor, to regulate the activities of grain profiteers in ca. AD 90. Perhaps the most successful and satisfying outcome of the work, however, was the drawn reconstructions of the public buildings.[115]

Through Europe

Leaving Constantinople the evening of September 20, Francis reached Venice three days later. His reaction to the city was upbeat: "Venice is unique. For one thing the city seems not so poverty stricken and abject as in the summer of 1883. Shops are brilliant and tourist traffic is manifestly greater than in past years."[116] The next day, he was in Rome, feverish again. When, once more, there were delays about the vehicles, which were in Naples with Swain but not admitted to the country, he went down there to get help from the American consulate in dealing with the customs officials. Armed with a letter from the director of fine arts in Rome to the superintendent of antiquities in the National Archaeological Museum, he also requested permission to photograph in Pompeii. This granted, he set Swain to work on the site and, when the vehicles were released, returned to Rome.[117]

In Rome, he received effusive thanks at the German Archaeological Institute for his part in finding funds to enable the library to reopen, and he bought and sent some books off to Easton in Ann Arbor. In connection with his work at Pompeii on the new edition of the Mau-Kelsey book, he had studied the wall paintings from the Villa of the Mysteries, discovered in 1909, and wished to have replicas of the fresco cycle made to add to the collections in Ann Arbor. Accordingly, he paid a visit to Professor Maria Barosso (at 15 via Tre Cannelle) and, after admiring the work in her studio, asked if she would go to Pompeii to look at the paintings in the Villa of the Mysteries, whether she might be willing to prepare a set of watercolor replicas of them, and, if so, if she would please give him an estimate of the costs. She said she would.[118]

---

115. Adrian Ossi, "Architectural Reconstruction Drawings of Pisidian Antioch by Frederick J. Woodbridge," *Bulletin of the University of Michigan Museums of Art and Archaeology* 16 (2005–6): 5–29.

116. Diary, September 23, 1924.

117. Diary, October 1–5, 1924.

118. Diary, October 8, 1924. A well-known artist, illustrator, and archaeologist, Barosso became head of drawings for the Superintendency of Monuments of Rome and Lazio.

Arriving in England two days later, Francis spent a little over three weeks in the country, based in London. His first item of business was the fieldwork in Egypt. Having heard positive things about Starkey in Egypt in May, he had met him in London in July, and correspondence, including discussion of the cash needed for an expedition of 120 days' duration, had followed.[119] In the course of this correspondence, Starkey had been one of those who informed Francis of Evelyn-White's unexpected death on September 9, a suicide at age forty. At dinner one evening and in a more formal setting the next day, discussion ranged over staffing, salaries, equipment, and a site. Starkey agreed that Qualley should be a student assistant, Francis that Starkey might have Samuel Yeivin[120] as assistant field director and that Starkey should receive a salary of five hundred pounds, Yeivin four hundred. Starkey also agreed to "make a reconnoiter on the north side of the lake (of the Fayoum) such as was arranged with Evelyn-White."[121]

Francis now wanted to retrieve the money advanced to Evelyn-White. To avoid possible difficulties, he took the trouble to travel to Leeds (in Yorkshire) for a talk over tea at the Queens Hotel with Arthur Armitage, the solicitor involved,[122] and the Reverend K. V. Evelyn-White, the executor. Things went so smoothly that Francis was able to tell the accountants at Michigan that the money would be reimbursed by October 25. From Leeds he went to Oxford, where, at the university press, he talked with the man in charge of the Grotius project, John de Monins Johnson, who would shortly become printer to the university (1925–46), but he could not find either Hunt or Buckler. He then went to Cambridge, where, despite the crowds (it was a race day at nearby Newmarket), he found his way to the university press; there Mr. W. Lewis gave him estimates for the Hebrew proofs needed for Gottheil's Humanistic Series volume.

In London he took Starkey and Yeivin to dinner, after which the two left for Egypt. At the British Museum, he had productive talks with Kenyon (on division of the manuscripts and papyri and on payments) and with Crum (on the Coptic materials). Ramsay appeared on the scene and, though "bitter towards Robinson," agreed to "transfer the Antioch concession" to Francis.[123]

---

119. Diary, May 6 and 12, 1924; Starkey to Kelsey, July 1924, FWK Papers, box 1, folder 31.

120. Samuel (Shmuel) Yeivin (1896–1982) was to remain a staff member of the Michigan expedition for the first four seasons. Years later, he would become the first director of the Israeli Department of Antiquities (1948–61).

121. Diary, October 10 and 11, 1924.

122. This man is not to be confused with the solicitor Arthur Llewellyn Armitage (1916–84), who lectured in law at Queens' College, Cambridge.

123. Diary, October 17 and 18, 1924. The transfer of the concession to Kelsey meant that Robinson would be clearly in charge at the site, under Kelsey's authority.

When Mrs. Pendleton, too, put in an appearance, Francis accompanied her to church one day and lunched with her on several occasions. After days at the British Museum, busy with accounts and the division, at last everything was arranged: of the papyri, Columbia received 267, Princeton 128, and Michigan 489. All was packed up, bills were paid, and early on November 4, Francis traveled to Southampton and the SS *Leviathan*. Meanwhile, Arthur Boak was in Cairo, writing that the expedition staff was assembling and that the request for a permit had gone in: attention was turning from all other sites to the mound at Kom Aushim (Karanis), explored briefly by Hunt and Grenfell long ago as a promising site but abandoned by them in favor of Oxyrhynchus.[124]

Back Home

In New York and Washington, the Carthage project was picking up steam. The press was in attendance at the pier for the *Leviathan*'s arrival, cameras at the ready. Francis, snapped in a group shot with child film star Jackie Coogan, who had just turned ten, was mentioned (with many others) in the *Herald Tribune* the next day. Unsurprisingly, rather more attention was paid to Coogan, Rudolf Valentino, and Nita Naldi.[125] De Prorok joined the press on the quayside, and the following day, he took Francis to lunch and then introduced him at dinner to his father-in-law, William F. Kenny,[126] and Mrs. Kenny at their Fifth Avenue home. Two days later, after visiting Fred and the family in Orange, Francis met de Prorok at Kenny's office, and the three went over a Carthage budget. There were two parts to the project, excavation in the Punic sanctuary and raising a sunken Roman galley three miles off the coast and a hundred miles southeast of Carthage, the total budget amounting to ninety-four thousand dollars.[127] The Canadian government had pledged five thousand, Kenny offered eighteen thousand to buy land, and he and Francis un-

---

124. October 1924, FWK Papers, box 1, folder 35.

125. Diary, November 11, 1924. Nita Naldi was a top star of the silent movies, a notorious vamp, and had worked with Valentino before. They were slated to shoot another film together, *The Hooded Falcon,* and had just been fitted for costumes in France; but then Ritz-Carlton Pictures terminated the deal.

126. Kenny, of William F. Kenny Construction Company and other building, contracting, and realty firms, was a personal friend of Governor Alfred E. Smith. His brother, Edward J. Kenny, was honorary deputy chief of the Fire Department of New York.

127. Diary, November 14, 1924. The purchase of land was thirty thousand dollars, operating costs were twenty-nine thousand, and the cost of raising the sunken galley was thirty-five thousand. See also Kelsey to Merriam, February 1925, FWK Papers, box 2, folder 2. Kelsey was evidently thinking of the hull and keel of the Mahdia wreck, discovered in 1907, from which much of the cargo had been removed. See Gisela Hellenkemper Salies, Hans-Hoyer von Pritwitz und Gaffron, and G. Bauchhenß, eds., *Das Wrack: Der antike Schiffsfund von Mahdia,*

derwrote twelve thousand each, totaling 50 percent of the budget's needs. In Washington, D.C., on the morning of November 17, Francis and Mitchell Carroll attended a meeting of the AIA Society's research committee, at which the society agreed to underwrite the other forty-seven thousand dollars needed. In the afternoon, Francis met David Robinson, and they agreed on a number of points: to omit work in Asia Minor in the next season to concentrate on publication, to try for a permit for Olynthus, to urge Peterson to finish his doctorate before further fieldwork, and to have Robinson join the Carthage project.

Back in Michigan, Francis was reunited with Isabelle, and together they visited Rackham's office, only to find that the Rackhams had left for their winter home.[128] However, a letter from Rackham, bearing the statements "we are very proud of what you have accomplished" and "we are very glad to have a part in the work with you," must have cheered Francis to no end.[129] The Advisory Committee on Near East Research discussed the season's results and prospects at a preliminary meeting on December 1; the advisors approved the plan for Antioch but expressed reservations about Carthage, distrustful of de Prorok's methods.[130] At an extended meeting later in the month, the printed agenda—a carbon copy of which was pasted into the diary—included the following:

1. Antioch in Pisidia: results, publication

2. Carthage: proposed UM staff for spring 1925: Kelsey, Swain, Woodbridge, Peterson

3. Pompeii: progress of students' work; photography, Barosso's paintings of the Villa of Mysteries frescoes

4. Olynthus, yes or no

5. Letters of credit: for various staff members

6. Miscellaneous reports: papyri, program of excavation in Egypt, parchment leaves from Coptic manuscripts and Georgian and Aramaic manuscripts in Berlin, offer of Greek manuscripts in Munich, duplicate set of electrotypes of coins and medals exhibited in the British Museum, etc.

Francis noted that "all went well."[131]

exhibition catalog, 2 vols. (Cologne: Rheinland-Verlag, 1994–95); cf. Kelsey to Poinssot, March 1925, FWK Papers, box 2, folder 3.

128. Diary, November 22, 1924.

129. November 1924, FWK Papers, box 1, folder 36.

130. Diary, December 1, 1924.

131. Diary, December 20, 1924.

The minutes recorded that a team for Carthage should include Kelsey, Swain, Peterson, and Woodbridge; that three thousand dollars should be appropriated for Professor Barosso; and that consideration of Olynthus as a potential site was premature.[132] Wrote Francis to Robinson, "our committee will not listen to proposals for excavation at Antioch or Olynthus until what has been done has been properly worked up." To Rackham, explaining that work at Karanis was about to begin, he wrote that he would go "to inspect the work, as I did at the end at Antioch" and, proudly, that "the work has given the University of Michigan a new place among American universities: Harvard, Yale and even the University of Chicago started this kind of work in foreign lands a number of years ago."[133]

For most of the month, Francis carried on with his habitual tasks: proofs of the Ovid textbook for Allyn and Bacon and photographs of Syracuse for the Cicero; plans with Bishop to bring to Ann Arbor the contributors to the purchase of manuscripts and papyri destined for the library, especially Standish Backus, Paul Gray, and Lawrence Buhl; and schemes for more acquisitions, Bishop having his eye on a fifteenth-century manuscript of Juvenal and a twelfth-century Latin Apocalypse.[134] John W. Anderson came out from Detroit to see the papyri, whereupon Francis proposed to former president Hutchins that they visit him in Detroit to ask for help with the publication of two Humanistic Series volumes (16 and 17) under preparation by Professors D'Ooge and Waterman.[135] When Horace Rackham wrote of arrangements to continue his subscription for Near East work for the third year, Francis prepared a list of his gifts to the university over the past four years and proposed a resolution of appreciation for the regents to consider. They did this at their December meeting, along with offering votes of thanks to the British Museum and Turkish officials. They went further, passing a requisition for volume 13 of the Humanistic Series and extending Francis's leave of absence through the academic year 1925–26. In a few spare moments that day, Regents Beal and Hubbard visited the papyri.[136]

The Bishops agreed to rent 810 Oxford from the Kelseys for one hundred dollars a month. The Stanleys invited Francis for dinner on December 22 (when Dora cooked a Christmas goose) and again for Christmas Day break-

---

132. December 1924, FWK Papers, box 1, folder 37.
133. Ibid.
134. Diary, December 2 and 22, 1924.
135. Diary, December 5 and 12, 1924.
136. Diary, December 18, 1924.

fast, after which the industrious Francis went to work. At his desk by eight o'-clock, he wrote notes for the Cicero all day, taking lunch at the Union and supper at the Baltimore Lunch—"an interesting and happy day instead of a big dinner."[137] Isabelle had gone to New York the previous week, presumably to spend Christmas with Charlotte and her grandson.

TO CARTHAGE

The pattern of a life alternating between traditionally academic/administrative pursuits and family life, on the one hand, and travels abroad in the search for books, manuscripts, papyri, and artifacts and to engage in archaeological fieldwork, on the other, continued for the rest of Kelsey's life. As 1925 opened, news arrived in Ann Arbor from the annual AIA-APA meetings: Robinson reported, "Everyone said what a remarkable man Kelsey is, and what wonders he has done for Classics!" Less welcome was evidence of the continuing spat between Robinson and Ramsay, which was casting a cloud over any prospects for future work at Antioch and becoming so disagreeable and widely known that Francis wrote to the Advisory Committee on Near East Research in explanation.[138] It also was not smooth sailing with respect to Carthage. The dean of the Literary College, John Effinger, had been warned against de Prorok—Francis should make sure that a permit was in hand—and de Prorok's publications had met with criticism in the English press; yet he had the support of Abbé Chabot in Carthage and of Louis Poinssot.[139] Moreover, Woodbridge was eager to serve as architect; a check for ten thousand came in from Rackham; the University of Rochester's contribution also arrived; and Swain, enthusiastic as ever, set off for Europe and Carthage with his son Robert as assistant, before the end of January.[140]

In Boston in early February, Francis met Paul Bacon to review the proofs of the Cicero and Ovid books and the revisions needed for the Cicero and the Xenophon.[141] He also received updated estimates from W. C. Ramsay for the Humanistic Series volumes in his care. In New York he was troubled to hear

---

137. Diary, December 25, 1924.

138. January 1925, FWK Papers, box 2, folder 1.

139. Diary, January 13, 1925. A well-placed French archaeologist, Poinssot (1879–1967) was the director of antiquities of Tunisia (1921–41) and excavator of the important Roman site at Dougga.

140. Diary, January 25 and 31, 1925.

141. The texts continued to provide handsome royalties: $3,569.86 in 1925, for instance.

26. Francis Kelsey and colleagues aboard the SS *George Washington,*
February 14, 1925. *From left,* Horton O'Neil, Byron de Prorok, Francis
Willey Kelsey, unidentified, F. C. Shorey, C. E. Barriere. Bentley Historical
Library, University of Michigan HS 5258. Photo: Mrs. Maurice
Kellerman.

from brother Fred of his daughter-in-law Anna's serious illness (diagnosis
uncertain), but he was pleased to find Isabelle with Charlotte and their
grandson at Charlotte's home on Long Island and all well. On February 11,
they set off again: he, Isabelle, and de Prorok boarded the SS *George Washing-*
ton for the transatlantic trip. At sea (see fig. 26), they heard the frightening
news about young Dennis Kenny—brother of de Prorok's wife, Alice—who
had been shot by a taxi driver in a dispute over a fare and died in a hospital
ten days later, a day after the steamship left. There was even worse in store: the
news of the death of Anna, aged a mere thirty-two.[142]

Changing their plans in midvoyage, to go to Paris before London, they
disembarked at Cherbourg and by nightfall were in the Hôtel Saint James in

---

142. Diary, February 12 and 14, 1925.

Paris, where a cable from Ann Arbor informed them that President Burton had died on February 18.[143] In the course of the following day, Francis, moving with his usual alacrity, had an interview with Edward R. Stoever,[144] an architect and engineer who had worked for several years at the Sardis excavations, about survey work at Carthage; discussed at the American Embassy the prospects for getting U.S. Navy assistance with the underwater opportunities presented in Tunisia (the submerged walls of Carthage, the sunken galley, the underwater settlement near Djerba); and engaged Alfred Merlin, éminence grise of Tunisian archaeology, to act as consultant on Greek and Roman antiquities.[145]

The next day, they were in London, where the first news they received was that Mrs. Pendleton was sick but under the care of a Dr. Russell, who seemed to Francis "keen, concise, clear and sure of himself—hence convincing."[146] Needing to sort out some problems with Ramsay, Francis set off for Edinburgh, where he stayed with Peterson (who was in Edinburgh studying inscriptions with Ramsay) in his arctic digs, "two hot water bottles in bed." There he thrashed out with Sir William the arrangements for the publication of the Antioch inscriptions.[147] He was back in London, with Peterson, the next day. After meeting at the British Museum with Kenyon and Bell (on papyri), they left on February 28 for Paris, where they picked up Stoever and his wife and took the train to Rome. There they found Swain (with his son) and Woodbridge (with a pair of assistants) waiting for them. Two days later, traveling via Palermo (see fig. 27) and Tunis, they were in Carthage.[148]

---

143. Diary, February 20, 1925. Burton had suffered a serious heart attack in October and never fully recovered. He was succeeded in the presidency by the president of the University of Maine, the thirty-six-year-old Clarence C. Little.

144. Edward Royal Stoever, a 1908 Princeton University graduate, served at Sardis in 1911–14 under H. C. Butler of Princeton (see chapter 5 n. 94). After, he was with the War Relief Commission and represented the Rockefeller Foundation in Turkey, reporting on conditions there, including those in the internment camps.

145. Merlin (1876–1965), onetime director of the Tunisian Department of Antiquities (1906–21) and then a conservator of Greco-Roman antiquities at the Louvre (1921–46), was the author of *Inscriptions Latines de Tunisie* (Paris: Presses universitaires de France, 1944) and coauthor (with Louis Poinssot) of *Bronzes trouvés en mer près de Mahdia (Tunisie)* (Paris: Leroux, 1909), as well as other materials from the Mahdia wreck.

146. Diary, February 23, 1925.

147. Diary, February 25, 1925.

148. Diary, March 4, 1925.

27. Isabelle and Francis on the quay at Palermo, Sicily, en route to
Carthage. Bentley Historical Library, University of Michigan HS 5259.
Photo: Enoch Peterson.

Carthage

Carthage is probably best known for the mythical Queen Dido, for the wars
she fought with Rome, and for the phrase "delenda est Carthago."[149] The first
of these wars, fought over twenty years in the middle of the third century BC,
resulted in victory for Rome and the capture of Sicily. In the second, despite
Hannibal, his elephants, and the invasion of Italy, Rome was again tri-
umphant, the war ending in the defeat of the Carthaginian army on African
soil.[150] In the third brief war, in 146 BC, Carthage was reduced to ruins.

---

149. In the period between the second and third Punic wars, Cato the Elder, the author
of the *De re rustica,* is said to have ended his speeches with the phrase "Ceterum censeo
Carthaginem esse delendam" ("But it's my opinion that Carthage should be destroyed"). Cf.
Plutarch *Cato* 27.

150. The defeat occurred at the battle of Zama, fought some 150 kilometers south and
west of Carthage, at the very end of the third century.

Abandoned for many years, the site nonetheless inevitably attracted new settlers because of its rich agricultural land and strategic location. The Romans themselves could not leave so advantageous a site empty for too long and planted a colony there. Expanded in the time of Augustus into a whole new urban complex, over time it became the leading city of the province of Africa and an important center of Christianity, known for famous churchmen—Tertullian, for example—and the number of its churches.[151] For centuries Roman Carthage flourished, but it fell on hard times when taken by the Vandals. Recaptured a hundred years later (in AD 533) by the Byzantines, the city enjoyed 150 years of prosperity, only to be cruelly treated by the Arab conquest. Thereafter the masonry blocks of the collapsed buildings became fodder for merchants and builders, who hauled them away for use in the construction of the new city of Tunis and other, more distant structures.[152]

Prior to the wars with Rome, Carthage had been the most powerful and prosperous city in the Western Mediterranean, wealthy by reason of its agriculture and commerce. Founded, according to tradition, in the ninth century BC by Phoenicians from Tyre, the settlement grew up at the head of a great bay (now the Gulf of Tunis) on the north coast of Africa where the continent points most directly at Europe, only a short distance away. It rapidly developed as the leading Phoenician colony in the west, outpacing nearby Utica and Hadrumetum. Before long, equipped with a merchant fleet as well as a war fleet, each provided with its own harbor, Carthage came to dominate the whole of the western Mediterranean and, by trade and colonization, established control over large parts of Spain, Sardinia, and Sicily.

With its complex history and archaeology, the site was ripe for exploration. But what approach should be taken? Francis's view, as put before the research committee of the AIA's Washington Society, was that a preliminary season should assess the situation on the ground before formulating any more comprehensive project. This view accepted, Kelsey proposed as an initial step that exploration should begin where Punic (Carthaginian) votive monuments and cinerary urns had appeared in 1921[153] and where more had

---

151. It is perhaps this aspect of Carthage that, after the establishment of the French protectorate of Tunisia in 1881, drew many French clergy interested in archaeology to the country, eager to rebuild Christianity.

152. Columns from Roman Carthage may be identified, for example, in the Great Mosque of Sidi-Uqba, in Kairouan. For an entertaining slant on ancient Carthage, see the historical novel by Gustave Flaubert, *Salammbô* (Paris: Michel Lévy frères, 1862; rev. ed., G. Charpentier, 1883).

153. François Icard, "Découverte de l'area du sanctuaire de Tanit à Carthage," *Revue Tunisienne* 29 (1922): 195–205; Louis Poinssot and Raymond Lautier, "Un Sanctuaire de Tanit à Carthage," *Revue de l'histoire des religions* 87 (1923): 32–68.

been found by de Prorok and Chabot in 1924—the Sanctuary of Tanit. Such
was the historical and cultural importance of Carthage that Kelsey later concluded that the whole city should be surveyed, excavated, and protected as an
archaeological park; that the undertaking was so huge and would be so costly,
given the rising cost of land, that only a governmental intervention could
handle the scale of it; and that France should take this in hand.[154]

After disembarking in Tunis, Francis went with Isabelle and Mrs. Stoever
to take rooms at a hotel, while others went straight out to Carthage, which
could be reached by a light rail system after a journey of about twenty minutes. After lunch, the ladies made a tour of Tunis while Francis proceeded to
Carthage. Once there he lost no time in visiting the site, where he was
shocked to find two volunteers, Horton O'Neil and Gerard de Villette, acquaintances of de Prorok, busily excavating. He did not mince matters but
declared, "if another spade of earth is turned without my approval I will leave
in 24 hours."[155] Stoever approved of Kelsey's stand on this matter and had already protested against the start made before Kelsey arrived. Within a week,
the team was assembled: the chef came in from Paris and servants were hired,
though "one of the Arab boys refused to scrub the floor on the ground that it
would ruin his pants."[156] Isabelle caught a bad cold; Francis called on the director of antiquities, Poinssot; Swain and the vehicles arrived; Chabot appeared; workmen were hired, and serious excavation began. The news that
Mitchell Carroll had died suddenly on March 3 came as a dreadful blow. The
loss of a good friend was bad enough, but there was much time-consuming
busywork, too: cables back and forth to the United States about the reorganization both of the project and of the AIA.[157] Meanwhile, de Prorok was starting work at Utica, also on the Gulf of Tunis, where his expectations ran high.
At Utica the land was owned by the Count de Chabannes, a French friend of
de Prorok's, and though Francis had an interest in the site (what Romanist
would not?), de Prorok was acting on his own behalf.

Francis spent much of his second week in Carthage in conferences—with

---

154. Francis W. Kelsey, "Carthage, Ancient and Modern," *Art and Archaeology* 21.2 (February 1926): 55–67, esp. 62–63. It finally fell to the Tunisian government to engage teams from
various countries in an international effort (with the United States represented by Michigan
and Harvard) in 1972, in the UNESCO-sponsored project Sauvegarde de Carthage.

155. Diary, March 4, 1925.

156. Diary, March 6, 1925. With his own experience of scrubbing floors at Lake Cavanaugh, Francis may well have reacted with more than a smile.

157. Though George Meason Whicher had taken over as general secretary of the AIA in
1919, Carroll was still a trustee and, of course, a leading figure in the AIA's Washington Society.

Chabot, de Prorok, and Stoever about the conduct of the fieldwork and with Woodbridge and his two assistants, Douglas and Calder, about the architectural drawings.[158] He visited the site frequently, examined the finds, and attended the daily reports of activities. On one day, he was at the Bardo Museum in Tunis ordering photographs of the Roman mosaics; on another, he was preoccupied with correspondence and reports. Boak wrote him about progress at Karanis; he wrote to the Advisory Committee on Near East Research about Carthage.[159] Since the season's work at Karanis was coming to a close and he wished to see the results, Francis made plans to abandon Carthage for a few days. He cabled Askren about his arrival in Egypt, and leaving Carthage in the hands of Chabot and Stoever, he and Isabelle boarded the SS *Italian Prince* for Alexandria. Traveling with, inter alia, a cargo of eleven hundred bags of bark (used for tanning) and a textile merchant from Manchester, England, they arrived in Egypt four days later.[160]

Remaining in Egypt no more than a week, they visited the pyramids of Giza, spent a day in the Fayoum with Askren—from whom Francis bought a few papyri—and drove to the Michigan camp at Karanis. They met Boak, Starkey, Yeivin, and Qualley there; stayed two full days; inspected the excavation; examined the papyri, ostraca, glass, baskets, rope, lamps, coins, terracottas, and woodwork—all evidence retrieved from domestic contexts; and, pleased with the results, returned to Cairo.[161] Francis visited Nahman to see what Greek and Coptic material he had and, with Boak, made courtesy calls on the authorities at the Egyptian Museum of Antiquities, before heading back to Alexandria and the return voyage.

The SS *President Adams* docked at Naples on April 5, allowing them time to get to Rome that evening. After checking at the American Academy for his mail,[162] using the library, and conferring with Director Stevens, Francis cabled Swain, "Excavation Results Surpass Expectations." He also called on

158. William Douglas was later (1928) a fellow of the American Academy in Rome. Perhaps he was the William Douglas who became director of the Lyman Allyn Art Museum in New London, Connecticut, in the 1930s. Ralph Russel Calder, who received his architecture degree at Michigan (B.S. 1923), was the first recipient of the Booth Traveling Fellowship in Architecture; he later designed several buildings for Michigan State and Western Michigan, as well as a 1955 addition to Albert Kahn's housing on East Ann Street for the University of Michigan Training School for Nurses.

159. Diary, March 18 and 19, 1925; March 1925, FWK Papers, box 2, folder 3.

160. Diary, March 25, 1925.

161. Diary, March 28, 1925.

162. A letter from W. M. Calder (the epigraphist and historian), on the subject of the Antioch inscriptions and Sir William Ramsay, cautioned that "in the public eye our friend wears a very bright halo" (April 1925, FWK Papers, box 2, folder 4).

Maria Barosso, who was working on the reproductions of the frescoes at the Villa of the Mysteries; he listened patiently to her complaints about the cost of cloth and paint from Germany. A cable arrived from an anxious Stoever: "Service insists on purchase outright of all ground for excavation and claims permission given only on that condition apparent complete misunderstanding our plans this season. Please wire instructions." Unruffled, Kelsey replied, "Continue until unreasonable restrictions removed or I come 15th."[163] They were in Naples on April 13 and in Carthage two days later.

Accompanied by Chabot and Stoever, Francis immediately called on Poinssot. Chabot did most of the talking. As Francis noted in his diary, Poinssot was "in a very bad humor, stiffly maintained the position that we could only excavate ground which had been bought and paid for etc." Speaking of the Americans, he said, "Mon seul desir est qu'ils partent" (My only wish is that they leave). "C'est fou" (It's madness), said the abbé, touching his forehead.[164]

Despite Poinssot's attitude, work did not stop. There were, however, long discussions about policies and procedures: major issues at the site were the damage done by the workmen, as they were excavating, to the all-important urns and the need for closer oversight. Since more "inspectors" were needed, volunteers were co-opted, notably Dr. Orma Fitch Butler, assistant in Roman archaeology at Michigan, and Isabelle herself.[165] Specialists arrived from time to time, conspicuous among them an instructor at Aberdeen University, Donald B. Harden, whose expertise in pottery became key to the interpretation of the site and whose subsequent knowledge of Roman glass, including that from Karanis, made him famous.[166] Work continued day by day until, at midmonth, it was time to leave: calls were made on Père Delattre, Chabot, and the de Proroks before the Michigan contingent—Francis and Isabelle, the Swains, Dr. Butler and her sister, and Peterson—left by boat to Palermo.[167]

---

163. Diary, April 10, 1925.
164. Diary, April 15, 1925.
165. Diary, April 18, 20, and 21, 1925. On Butler, see chapter 6 n. 41.
166. D. B. Harden, "Punic Urns from the Precinct of Tanit at Carthage," *AJA*, 31 (1927): 297–310; idem, "The Pottery from the Precinct of Tanit at Salambô, Carthage," *Iraq* 4.1 (1937): 58–59; idem, *Roman Glass from Karanis Found by the University of Michigan Archaeological Expedition in Egypt, 1924–1929*, University of Michigan Studies, Humanistic Series, vol. 41 (Ann Arbor: University of Michigan Press, 1936); idem, *The Phoenicians* (London: Thames & Hudson, 1962). Harden would spend 1926–27 at Michigan on a grant, begin cataloging Askren's collection of ancient glass in 1927, and participate in the Michigan Archaeological Expedition to Egypt during 1928–29.
167. Diary, May 15, 1925. Dr. Butler's sister's name is Nita.

When Francis, accompanied by Chabot, paid his departing salute to Lucien Saint, the resident-general (representative of the French government), he noted with interest Chabot's remarks about Poinssot—as well as Saint's response that "he had twice tried to have Poinssot removed and failed because he had influential relatives in Paris, that just now he had made trouble at a conference in Tripoli, that undoubtedly he was sick." Saint concluded by asking Chabot to write him "a confidential report on Poinssot's treatment of the American mission."[168] Two weeks before this meeting, de Prorok had gone with the Swains and others on an archaeological and photographic reconnaissance of southern and western Tunisia and Algeria, in the course of which they had met Professor Stéphane Gsell.[169] Gsell had painted a rather rosier picture of Poinssot, giving assurances regarding him that were "less discouraging" and adding that "he and the Resident were at odds."

The successful excavation of the Sanctuary of Tanit site fostered Francis's conviction that the historical importance of Carthage warranted a large-scale expedition far beyond the resources of a single institution. Still, even with start-up problems and numerous difficulties with the French authorities, much had been accomplished in a single season.

The Sanctuary of Tanit (the Tophet)

The plot of land from which stelae decorated with symbols of the Punic goddess Tanit had first appeared and that subsequently was purchased by de Prorok lies in an urban area now densely populated (and with buildings and streets on all sides in 1925). It is an irregular rectangle measuring about sixty-five meters in length and varying in width between fifteen and thirty meters. Located close to the harbors of Carthage, it emphasizes connection with the sea and with commerce; as with many sanctuaries at Punic sites, its placement in the context of the seashore is far from accidental.[170]

The excavation (see fig. 28) revealed three levels of Punic activity (named

---

168. Diary, May 13, 1925.

169. Diary, April 30, 1925. Gsell (1864–1932) was a distinguished French historian, a member of the Collège de France, and author of *Histoire ancienne de l'Afrique du Nord,* 8 vols. (Paris: Hachette, 1913–29).

170. Francis W. Kelsey, *Excavations at Carthage, 1925: A Preliminary Report* (New York: Macmillan, 1926); Talalay and Alcock, *In the Field,* 20–22. For parallels between materials from the Carthage Tophet and other Phoenician sites, see, e.g., P. Cintas, *Manuel d'archéologie punique,* vol. 1, *Histoire et archéologie comparées: Chronologie des temps archaïques de Carthage et des villes phéniciennes de l'ouest* (Paris: Picard, 1970), 309–460.

28. View west of the Tophet excavation in full swing, Carthage, April 1925. Kelsey Museum of Archaeology, University of Michigan 7.1872. Photo: George R. Swain.

Tanit I, II, and III, a simplified stratigraphy still regarded as broadly accurate) beneath a broad band of burnt material that is taken to represent the destruction of the city in 146 BC. On ceramic evidence, use of the site as a Tophet began sometime in the middle of the eighth century BC. The lowermost level, resting on bedrock, was difficult to excavate except when pumps were working to extract the groundwater continually seeping in; at this level were found funerary urns of varying shapes, each urn surrounded by fieldstones seemingly piled up around and on top of it. The second distinct stratum (with different texture and color of earth) contained more urns, here placed in groups of three or four, their location identified by stone markers. Some of these markers take the form of stelae, upright thin rectangular stone slabs crowned by a gable, sometimes elaborated with an inscription to Tanit and Baal-Hammon and a carved symbol of Tanit. Such inscriptions, for the most part, stated that the dedicator of the stela had fulfilled a vow. Others are shaped like the facades of miniature temples, framing symbols of Tanit, or resemble altars; some of these bear traces of stucco and paint. Still others were simple large pebbles or boulders, which the excavators also thought acted as sacred markers. All were placed close to one another in this thickly populated stratum. In the topmost level (Tanit III), more urns were found: according to Harden's analysis of the pottery, this level contained fragments of Hellenistic lamps and black Campanian ware but no pottery earlier than ca. 300 BC. Closed by the thick burnt stratum, this level evidently represents the period immediately prior to the Roman sack. Massive Roman vaults (the foundations of a large villa?) later intruded into this sacred space.

Most of the urns contained the burnt or partly burnt bones of infants, while others contained those of animals (young sheep or goats) and small birds. The contents of some occasionally included items of jewelry (earrings and bracelets), beads, and amulets. Lids of unbaked clay or stone closed the mouths of these vessels, which, with their contents, give unambiguous evidence of ancient Punic rituals involving the death of children. The question the excavators then faced was whether this place was an infant cemetery or a sanctuary in which child sacrifice was practiced.

The ancient classical authors tell of the Carthaginian custom of burnt sacrifices and of sacrificing children to the gods when their city and their lives were in peril or when begging a favor—literary evidence that the archaeology seemed to corroborate.[171] Kelsey was reluctant to accept this interpretation, stating in his *Excavations at Carthage* that "we should resort to the hypothesis of sacrifice of living children only in case the facts of discovery warrant it; the burden of proof in this instance rests on the affirmative." (Unfortunately, the French authorities refused to allow the Americans to take urns out of the country for scientific analysis.) Yet the Harvard team that revisited the site in the 1970s (see figs. 29 and 30) as part of the UNESCO international project has had a good deal more archaeological evidence to consider and, with the assistance of painstaking laboratory work, appears to have reached the opposite conclusion: that infant sacrifice was indeed practiced.[172]

---

171. E.g., Diodorus Siculus 20.14.4–7; scholia to Plato *Republic* 337A.

172. Lawrence E. Stager, "The Rite of Child Sacrifice at Carthage," in John G. Pedley, ed., *New Light on Ancient Carthage* (Ann Arbor: University of Michigan Press, 1980), 1–11. The careful reexcavation of parts of the site that the Michigan Franco-American team excavated in 1925, as well as the excavation of previously unexcavated areas with more modern methods, has convincingly refined the chronological phasing of the site and reinterpreted details of the work undertaken by Kelsey's team. The final publication of the Harvard work is in the ultimate stages of preparation: Lawrence E. Stager, Joseph A. Greene, Brian K. Garnand, and Kathleen Birney, *Carthage, the "Precinct of Tanit" (Tophet)—The American Schools of Oriental Research Punic Project, The Stager Excavations (1976–1979)*, Studies in the Archaeology and History of the Levant 6, (Cambridge MA: Semitic Museum, forthcoming). It remains unclear what aspects of her personality Tanit shared with other Phoenician deities or with African, Greek, or Roman counterparts and how high she stood in the hierarchy of Carthaginian deities.

29. View west along the bottom of Kelsey's trench at the Tophet excavation, Carthage, May 1979. Pictured are members of the Punic Project of the American Schools of Oriental Research: *foreground to background*, Lawrence E. Stager (*left*), Douglas L. Esse (*right*), Joseph A. Greene (*right*), unidentified Tunisian workman (*right*), Samuel R. Wolff. Photo: Punic Project, PN n/n.

30. CT6, Carthage Tophet, under excavation, June 1, 1979. View east. Bedrock is at the bottom right of the photo, 1979 ground level (bottom of Kelsey's 1925 trench) is at upper left; funerary urns at different levels with stelae above. Photo: Punic Project, PN 1290.

Heading Home

Spirits were high as the Michigan party drove across Sicily—the Swains and Peterson in the truck; Francis, Isabelle, and the Butler sisters in the sedan. Swain took photographs of archaeological sites. Crossing into mainland Italy, the Swains and Peterson continued with the vehicles, while the others took the train. Arriving in Pompeii on May 23 (his birthday), Francis found Maria Barosso at work on the site and celebrated the day in style. His unflagging optimism is as clear as crystal.

> Today the happiest birthday I have ever had. Though now 67 I have so much to be thankful for, in the good health of Isabelle and the family and myself. And in 14 months it has been possible to acquire for the University library not only the manuscripts of the Abdul Hamid collection but also valuable classical mss (particularly the Sallust) and papyri, and to conduct three successful excavations in three countries, Asia Minor, Egypt, Africa.

They were in Italy about a week. In Naples Francis bought more books from Johannowsky and conferred at the museum with Amedeo Maiuri, the senior Italian archaeologist working at Pompeii, about Roman wall painting.[173] At Pompeii he was shown the new discoveries by other Italian colleagues.[174] In Rome he had talks at the American Academy with Director Stevens and Dr. Van Deman[175] and resolved a number of architectural questions about Antioch with Woodbridge and Calder. Leaving Swain at work in Italy,[176] he and Isabelle took the night train for London (via Boulogne) on May 29, arriving the next day. At this point, Francis wrote a brief summary of the expeditions' objectives in his diary: "first expedition in September 1919 with the aim of getting MSS pertaining to the literature of the bible, papyri and documents of early date: those now in the University Library the fruit of this effort. The second expedition set out two years ago with excavations the target."[177]

---

173. Amedeo Maiuri (1886–1963) became the director of the National Archaeological Museum in Naples in 1924 (succeeding Spinazzola), the chief of excavations in Pompeii and Herculaneum, and superintendent of antiquities for the Campania region. He also directed work at Paestum (1929–39), located what he took to be the fabled cave of the Sibyl of Cumae in 1932, and excavated the Villa Jovis on Capri during 1932–35.

174. Diary, May 24 and 25, 1925.

175. On Esther Van Deman, see chapter 6 n. 43.

176. Swain spent several weeks of June and July photographing in and around the monasteries on Mount Athos and on Patmos, then spent most of August elsewhere in Greece (mostly around Delphi and in the northern Peloponnese), before traveling across Europe to Cherbourg and the boat home.

177. Diary, May 30, 1925.

At once Francis went to the British Museum for discussions with Kenyon and Bell, about papyri that Kondilios had brought to London in the hope of a sale, and with Crum, about the Coptic manuscripts Francis had bought in Cairo.[178] By June 6, Bell had examined the Kondilios lot and put a value of thirteen hundred pounds on it; Kondilios, offered that amount, refused it on June 8 but agreed to it the next day. In the meantime, Francis met Starkey to get his report on the work at Karanis and invited him, Yeivin, and their wives to dinner one evening.[179] He and Isabelle saw Mrs. Pendleton, now recovered, in the normal course of events, enabling Francis to approach her about dollars needed for books for the Pendleton Library and for the publication of D'Ooge's Humanistic Series volume.[180] Never one to neglect his correspondence or his donors, he wrote to Rackham that

> our policy "to conduct excavations in two possibly three countries under different working conditions within two years" has been carried out. . . . For the first time in its history the University has been enabled, through the warm interest of yourself and Mrs. Rackham in this work, to place itself on a par with the Eastern universities in work of this kind, and in certain respects, as in the acquisition of papyri and manuscripts, it is surpassing the institutions which so long had the start.[181]

Francis's delight in achievement, his competitive drive, and his profound sense of gratitude are clear.

Leaving England on June 10, he and Isabelle were in New York six days later at the Murray Hill Hotel, where Charlotte joined them for dinner. In Washington, D.C., the next day, Francis reported to the Carnegie Endowment on the Grotius project and conferred at the Carnegie Institution with President Merriam, a prominent member of the AIA's Washington Society, about

---

178. The Kondilios material included papyri from the archive of Zenon found at Gerza (Philadelphia) on the eastern edge of the Fayoum. Zenon was a Greek who became a senior administrator for the finance minister Apollonius in the middle years of the third century BC. His archive, discovered in the winter of 1914–15, therefore sheds important light on social and economic conditions in the Fayoum in this period. On Zenon, see H. I. Bell, review of *A Large Estate in Egypt in the Third Century B.C.: A Study in Economic History,* by Michael Rostovtzeff, *Classical Review* 37 (1923): 32–34; idem, review of *Zenon Papyri in the University of Michigan Collection,* by Campbell Cowan Edgar, *Classical Review* 45 (1931): 180–81.

179. While in Carthage, Kelsey had received brief reports from both Starkey and Boak (April and May 1925, FWK Papers, box 2, folders 4 and 5).

180. Diary, June 7, 1925; Nicomachus of Gerasa, *Introduction to Arithmetic,* trans. Martin L. D'Ooge, with studies by Frank E. Robbins and Louis C. Karpinski, University of Michigan Studies, Humanistic Series, vol. 16 (Ann Arbor: University of Michigan, 1926).

181. June 1925, FWK Papers, box 2, folder 6.

prospects for Carthage. Returning to the United States also brought his family more closely into view. Catching a glimpse of his sister, Harriet, he told himself to make provision for her in his will. Back in New York, a family lunch brought Francis, Isabelle, Charlotte, and young Francis (nearly age three) together with the elder Francis's brother Fred, his wife, Vergilia, and his sons, Fred and Ronald.[182]

Francis and Isabelle left New York after just a few days' stay. Reaching Detroit overnight, they were in time for Francis to take up with Joel Prescott of Union Trust a Jerome estate matter: should Henrietta (Yetta) Rupp be permitted to take a surplus of seven hundred dollars from the interest on the lifetime interest of twenty thousand dollars that she had in the estate? Francis thought not, remarking that "the stripping of the plumbing and other property not properly 'moveable' cost the estate more than the surplus."[183] In the evening, they were met by Albert Stanley and Easton at the Ann Arbor station; they were home.

BACK IN MICHIGAN

There was no time to rest, however: summer school, in which Francis taught two courses—one on Lucretius, the other on Roman antiquities—began two days later. Toward the end of the month, when the Advisory Committee on Near East Research met, Francis reported on developments. The busy agenda bounced along in timely fashion as follows:

I Purchase of Manuscripts (Coptic, Armenian)

II Purchase of Papyri (Kondilios, Nahman and Askren)

III Editorial Work and Publication (Oriental manuscripts, Coptic manuscripts and papyri, Zeno papyri)

IV Excavations
  A) General Policy
  B) Special Fields:
    1. Asia Minor, obligation to complete excavation at Antioch and publication
    2. North Africa: offer to take over examination of 50 urns from area of Tanit, publication to be by Abbé Chabot

---

182. Diary, June 18 and 19, 1925. Fred's first wife, Ella, had died in 1913. The following year he married Ella's sister, Virgilia. "Kelsey-Butts Wedding Today," *New York Times*, June 5, 1914.

183. Diary, June 20, 1925. Francis also brought a Persian rug as a gift for Prescott's wife.

3. Egypt, positive progress, publication, collections

V Pompeii (Barosso)[184]

For the balance of calendar year 1925, Francis followed the customary routines of his life: presiding over the UMS, attending concerts and social events, giving lunches, going to church, keeping an eye on his family and his properties, enjoying the professorial life. His diary suggests that four major areas commanded much of his attention: publication, fund-raising, research, and family matters.

The Grotius project and the Humanistic Series remained central in his publication plans. Francis and his collaborators plugged away at the translation and editing of Grotius's magisterial work, wrestling with its legal and linguistic complexities,[185] so that by November 13, Francis was able to have an informed discussion with Brown Scott in Washington about the length and character of the introduction. In the Humanistic Series, volume 21 (Sanders and Schmidt) was progressing well,[186] but volume 13 (Gottheil and Worrell) was causing difficulties that required conferences with Worrell and Sanders.[187] It was smoother sailing with volume 16 (D'Ooge et al.'s edition of Nicomachus's *Introduction to Arithmetic*): a contribution of three thousand dollars toward the publication costs arrived from C. E. Hilton of Detroit Trust Company, acting for Mrs. Pendleton;[188] galley proofs were ready on November 2; and Francis was given page proofs and estimates in Boston on November 20. That same day, he took up with W. C. Ramsay the question of the plates (delayed) for volumes 13 and 21.

Work on the textbooks also continued. Allyn and Bacon were always keen to think about new editions and to see Francis. His visit to Boston in November ran true to form. After conferring at some length with Paul Bacon about the proposed companions to the Caesar, the Cicero, and the Xenophon, on which he had been working off and on throughout the year, and on the new editions of Cicero's *De Senectute* and letters,[189] he dined with Mr. and Mrs.

---

184. Diary, June 29, 1925. A copy of the typed agenda is pasted into the diary.

185. Diary, August 25, 27, 28, and 31, September 1, and October 6 and 12–14, 1925.

186. Diary, August 24, 1925; Henry A. Sanders and Carl Schmidt, *The Minor Prophets in the Freer Collection and the Berlin Fragment of Genesis,* University of Michigan Studies, Humanistic Series, vol. 21 (Ann Arbor: University of Michigan, 1927).

187. Diary, August 24, September 2, and November 23, 1925; Gottheil and Worrell, *Fragments from the Cairo Genizah.*

188. Diary, September 2 and 3, 1925. Charles E. Hilton, a well-known lawyer, had been made assistant secretary of Detroit Trust Company in 1914.

189. Diary, September 7, 9, and 10 and October 23–26, 1925.

Carl Bacon in the evening. Rome and Pompeii, too, were never far from his thoughts, and he wrote up and published an article on a Roman topic this year.[190]

At a meeting with President Hutchins in early July, Francis outlined his fund-raising objectives, stipulating that an income of seventy-five thousand dollars a year, of which twenty-five thousand would be earmarked for publications, would be "ideal." Immediate needs were not, however, for research but for the completion of the Edward Waldo Pendleton Library and for student fellowships. On a visit to Detroit Trust at the end of the month, he met with C. E. Hilton and Fred Colby[191] and was assured that Mrs. Pendleton would help: two separate checks, one for two thousand dollars for fellowships and another for three thousand for the publication of D'Ooge's book, would be forthcoming. Following up, Fred and Horace Colby came to Ann Arbor on August 12, visited the new Pendleton Library, and voiced their approval. Encouraged by these reactions, Francis approached Hilton again at the beginning of September about making the Pendleton fellowships permanent. This did not happen, but in late October, on a visit to Fred and Frances Colby at their home on Seminole Avenue in Detroit, Francis got the good news that "Mrs. Pendleton had authorized renewal of the Pendleton Fellowships for next year"; furthermore, he heard that "she was better [in health] than when she left the United States two years ago."[192] In the meantime, the Buhl family, loyal supporters of the department, had sent in their annual contribution (twelve hundred dollars) to the fellowship funds.[193]

By the end of September, the needs of research projects planned for 1926 were pressing. Calls in August in Detroit on Oscar Webber,[194] Howard Bloomer, Joel Prescott, and Horace Rackham (who was having tax problems),

---

190. Francis W. Kelsey, "A Picture Map of Rome in a Manuscript of Valerius Maximus," *TAPA* 56 (1925): 242–51.

191. Frederick Lee Colby (1862–1932), who began his career working for the Colby Milling Company in Dowagiac, Michigan, at the age of eighteen, married Frances Berry in 1899 and moved the following year to Detroit to work for Berry Brothers, a manufacturer of varnishes and finishes (including for automobiles), of which he became president (1920–29); Mrs. Pendleton's deceased husband, Edward, had been its vice president. Colby was first cousin to Isabelle Badger, whose mother, Charlotte, had been a Colby. It was Colby's son Horace who had assisted Woodbridge on the excavations at Antioch.

192. Diary, September 2 and October 27, 1925.

193. Diary, September 14, 1925.

194. See nn. 37, 208. Webber (1888?–1967), who graduated from Michigan in 1910, was a nephew of Joseph Lowthian Hudson (1846–1912), the founder of the J. L. Hudson department store in Detroit. Webber would become its president in 1958 and chairman in 1961.

seeking donations of thirty-five thousand dollars, had drawn a blank, so Francis settled on another maneuver. Calling on the director of the Detroit Museum of Art, W. R. Valentiner,[195] he proposed a partnership in the work at Karanis. The museum would contribute fifteen thousand dollars a year for five years and have a 50 percent share in the finds. Evidently intrigued, Valentiner visited Ann Arbor a week later and was given a tour of the campus (the Clements Library and the Martha Cook Dormitory were the highlights) before being guided to the New Library, where he was shown recently acquired manuscripts. But there was no happy outcome.[196] Returning to his Detroit friends, Francis asked Standish Backus to suggest names of possible donors, and on October 28 and 29, he visited Mr. and Mrs. Rackham. A long talk with Rackham alone preceded an evening at the Rackham home when Francis showed them examples of the papyri and manuscripts acquired with their help. He reported, "they are much pleased,"[197] but again no money was immediately forthcoming.

Suddenly things looked up when, in New York the following month, Francis was offered thirty thousand dollars by William Kenny, de Prorok's father-in-law, "for Carthage, if continued";[198] but this did not alter the fact that funds were needed for fieldwork in Egypt (Karanis), for the acquisition of papyri and manuscripts, and for publications—both of the fieldwork and of the volumes in the Humanistic Series. Francis returned to his Detroit hunting ground, asking Oscar Webber, Bryant Walker,[199] and Roy Chapin[200] for help with fund-raising methods and donor names: so hard up was the Near East

---

195. William Rheinhold Otto Valentiner (1881–1958) was a German art historian (he became a naturalized American in 1930), director of the Detroit Institute of Art (1924–45), and founder and editor of the *Art Quarterly* (1937–49). In 1932 he commissioned, with Edsel Ford's money, Diego Rivera's famed fresco cycle of murals, entitled *Detroit Industry*, in the DIA's entranceway.

196. Diary, October 2, 8, and 9, 1925. The Clements Library (opened in 1923) is a self-standing unit of the university, not to be confused with the main university library, the New Library (built in 1916–20).

197. Diary, October 29, 1925.

198. There was still doubt about further work at Carthage, and Kelsey seems to have kept consideration of the funding of Carthage separate in his mind from the needs of other projects.

199. Walker was a Michigan graduate (A.B. 1876, LL.B. 1879) and a successful lawyer in Detroit. Like Standish Backus, he was a Presbyterian.

200. One connection between Chapin, a founder of the Hudson Motor Company, and Webber is worth noting: it had been Webber's uncle, department-store magnate J. L. Hudson, who had provided most of the capital (and his name) to start up Hudson Motors.

research fund that Francis himself lent it twenty-five hundred dollars to buy the Zeno papyri.[201] Though he seemed to be getting nowhere in Detroit, he persisted, describing the "emergency in Near East Research work" to Standish Backus and Oscar Webber over lunch and specifying the need for fifteen thousand dollars at once and for two hundred thousand over five years. He conferred with Hilton and Bloomer on the same day[202] and was still soliciting names at year's end. One wonders at both his tenacity and the patience of his friends.

Research

Carthage. Views about the advisability of continuing at Carthage were mixed. In July Charles-Marie Widor, the *secrétaire perpétuel* of the Académie des Beaux-Arts in Paris, wrote urging Francis not to give up on the site. Francis's reply, however, was hesitant: there would be "no continuation at Carthage till conditions were removed," by which he doubtless alluded to the requirement to purchase property outright and the refusal to allow the urns to leave the country for scientific analysis of their contents.[203] Peterson, on his way to Egypt in October, left with Francis both the 1924 journal of the Antioch excavations and the card inventory of the 1925 Carthage finds. In November Francis gave a well-received report on Carthage to the trustees of the Washington Society of the AIA (a major sponsor of the research) and conferred on the next day with the influential Merriam at the Carnegie Institution; but the question of continuing at Carthage was still unresolved until a few days later, when William Kenny made his generous offer allowing it to go forward. At a meeting in Ann Arbor of the scholars with a direct interest in the research (Boak, Bonner, Sanders, Winter), there was a lively discussion.

> [T]he men fear the University's reputation will suffer from association with de Prorok. I took the position that I cannot desert the French scholars who have stood by us, and "play small" in allowing the misconduct of Poinssot to serve as a pretext in case the authorities remove him and make proper amends; also, that I have been cheated out of the results of the sea-

---

201. Diary, November 24 and 27, 1925.
202. Diary, December 9, 1925.
203. Widor to Kelsey, July 25, and Kelsey to Widor, September 3, 1925, FWK Papers, box 2, folders 7 and 9. Widor (1844–1937) was a composer and, for sixty-four years, the organist of Saint-Sulpice in Paris.

son's work in the refusal to allow the urns to be exported for laboratory examination, and am entitled to another chance.[204]

That Francis was undeterred by de Prorok's reputation is shown by the fact that de Prorok continued to be involved in the Michigan work in Egypt and that, two days after the Ann Arbor meeting, Francis sent money to Chabot for the purchase of land and "a receipt to Kenny for $25,000 for Tanit work 1926–1930."[205]

The situation remained in flux during the first six months of 1926, but eventually there was no further involvement. The decision ultimately not to continue at Carthage was perhaps arrived at by Francis's unwillingness to have to deal with arguments among the French and by his conviction that the importance of Carthage was not best served by a piecemeal archaeological approach but deserved an overarching, citywide exploration that could be satisfactorily handled only at a national level. Whether he was at all influenced by a report in December that the governor of Algeria would ask the U.S. government to arrest de Prorok for "illegal importation" of archaeological remains seems unlikely—though the diary mentions it.[206] A happier note had been struck by a cable arriving from France announcing his election to the Académie des Inscriptions et Belles-Lettres of the Institut de France: he was immensely pleased but too modest to agree to a celebratory dinner proposed by his colleagues, Bishop and Reeves.[207]

Karanis. After a successful season earlier in the year, hopes for further work were high. In July David Askren came to Ann Arbor for a ten-day visit, bringing several boxes of Karanis materials with him. Lengthy conversations ensued, centering both on Egypt and on Askren's sons, who were being educated in the United States with funds provided, thanks to Francis's intervention, by the Webber brothers.[208] Askren unpacked the boxes and checked the

---

204. Diary, December 5, 1925.

205. Diary, December 7, 1925.

206. Diary, December 27, 1925.

207. Diary, December 5 and 20, 1925. The cable read: "Elu Correspondent Academie Felicitations Chabot." His election was announced in the Paris edition of the *Chicago Tribune* (December 10, 1925), with the observation that "Professor Kelsey is the second American to be honored with an election to this body, the only other one being Dr. Nicholas Murray Butler, president of Columbia University. At the same meeting of the Academy last Friday, two other new members were chosen, they being Rudyard Kipling, the celebrated English novelist, and Sir John Fraser [*sic;* likely James Frazer, who was indeed, like Kipling, an associate member of one of the academies constituting the Institut de France] the English scientist." On Francis's colleague J. S. Reeves, see chapter 7 n. 159.

208. See nn. 37, 194. Richard H. Webber was the current president (since 1912) of the J. L. Hudson Company.

inventories. He dined one evening with Boak, had talks with Peterson and Qualley, and met with the Advisory Committee on Near East Research. He accompanied Francis to Detroit, where he was introduced to the Webbers and Horace Rackham. After much profitable discussion of Karanis prospects and papyri, Askren left to visit relatives in Iowa.[209]

Francis was regularly in touch with Starkey and, as funds slowly dribbled in, was able to cable him in August to say that available funds for the 1926 season had grown to three thousand pounds (subsequently increased to thirty-four hundred). The cases containing papyri, ostraca, and sherds from Karanis, sent by Starkey from Cairo, arrived safely the same month.[210] Lest there be any doubt in Starkey's mind about the purpose of the work, Francis wrote stressing that "our primary consideration is the advancement of knowledge of the cultural background of the period which produced the Greek, Roman and Coptic papyri."[211] Throughout the fall, letters were exchanged between the two about the budget, staffing arrangements (especially Dr. Askren's role in the Karanis work), and the success of the aerial photographs Boak had had enlarged.[212]

Meanwhile, with respect to the acquisition of papyri (beyond those recovered in the excavations at Karanis), Princeton had asked to join the consortium of parties involved in the search, and this was agreed. Since Yale, too, did not want to miss out, Michael (Mikhail) I. Rostovtzeff[213]—perhaps the foremost ancient historian of his generation, who had just moved to Yale from Wisconsin—had approached Westermann with the proposal (strengthened by the offer of fifteen thousand dollars for the purchase of papyri) that Westermann work with him. Yet Westermann declined, saying that he preferred working with Michigan—a decision that caused Francis to comment that "he recommended cooperation, rather than competition in the quest for papyri."[214]

209. Diary, July 15–25, 1925.

210. Diary, August 22 and 29, 1925.

211. Kelsey to Starkey, August 22, 1925, FWK Papers, box 2, folder 8.

212. E.g., Kelsey to Starkey, October 8, and Starkey to Kelsey, December 1, 1925, FWK Papers, box 2, folders 10 and 12.

213. Rostovtzeff (1870–1952) had been a professor at the University of St. Petersburg when he emigrated to the United States and joined the University of Wisconsin–Madison (1918). Moving to Yale in 1925, he would supervise all its archaeological activities, including the Syrian site at Dura-Europos.

214. Diary, November 7 and 18, 1925.

Family Matters

In the knowledge that he was to be on leave for the academic year 1925–26 and that he was likely to be away for considerable periods of time, he and Isabelle rented their home at 810 Oxford Road to Mr. and Mrs. Bishop for two years from the end of July and moved out to the cottages at Lake Cavanaugh.[215] This arrangement was satisfactory as long as the weather was good but made for unsettled situations when the cold set in—not that Francis seemed to mind the fairly frequent moves, always provided that his campus study and books were close by. To ease movement between Ann Arbor and Lake Cavanaugh, he bought a Dodge car from the Ann Arbor Garage for $175, using part of his summer school salary (nine hundred dollars) to do so.[216] Charlotte and grandson Francis came for an August visit and stayed a week; Easton went into St. Joseph Mercy Hospital for a minor operation and emerged unscathed three days later;[217] and in mid-September, Francis and Isabelle set off by train to visit Ruth in California.

Pausing in Denver to visit Isabelle's parents, they traveled via Colorado Springs, Salt Lake City, and Fresno to Los Angeles and San Bernardino, "where Fred and Ruth drove down for us" and took them to Borestone Ranch, a fox farm owned by a Mr. R. T. Moore of Pasadena and now managed by Ruth's husband.[218] Francis, however, was ominously uncomfortable and "felt the altitude," so they decided to leave after two days "because of health" and rested in Los Angeles.[219] Taking the train back east, they passed through Gallup to La Junta, where they parted company, Isabelle heading for Denver and her parents' home, Francis for Chicago and Ann Arbor, where he put up at the Union for a few days. Checking in to Dr. Cowie's hospital, he underwent a "searching examination" on September 30 and was told his heart and blood pressure were normal, after which he felt free to go to the wedding in Detroit of Fred Colby's daughter, Elizabeth. But it was with relief that he was able to settle at Lake Cavanaugh ("so glad to be here") on October 3.

---

215. Kelsey to Swain, August 1925, FWK Papers, box 2, folder 8.

216. Diary, August 14 and 15, 1925.

217. Diary, August 29, 1925.

218. All the foxes were registered and pedigreed, best blooded, and quite tame—"such beautiful creatures," comments Kelsey's diary (September 23, 1925). Robert Thomas Moore (1882–1958) was the son of wealthy Philadelphia businessman Henry D. Moore. In addition to fox farming, he was also a successful ornithologist. In 1946, drawing on his English literature education from the University of Pennsylvania (B.A. 1904) and Harvard (M.A. 1905), he founded and edited the *Borestone Mountain Poetry Awards* anthologies.

219. Diary, September 25 and 26, 1925.

Mindful of the doctor's advice, he busied himself outdoors for exercise, weeding a small, recently purchased strip of land behind one of the cottages and splitting wood with a new ax.[220] This activity did not deter him from going into Detroit to a wedding reception at John Anderson's house a few days later. Two months after his September medical exam, Dr. Cowie examined him again. In answer to Francis's questions, he commented that it was "safe for me to embark on a five year program and congratulated me on my physical condition." Having apparently no inkling that Francis's life would end within eighteen months, the doctor added only the recommendation that Francis "get weight down to 190 lbs" and, as to diet, "eat under surface vegetables."[221]

Based at Lake Cavanaugh, Francis often went into Ann Arbor for meetings with faculty or students, for concerts (when he would stay overnight at the Union), or, on one occasion, to give a lunch party, after which he showed his guests around an exhibit he had prepared of objects, manuscripts, and papyri that the expeditions had brought to the university.[222] By the end of October, the weather had taken a turn for the worse at the lake—"too cold to stay, water frozen in pitcher and pail, pump frozen, snow two meters deep at rear porches"—so that with Swain's help packing up, including bags of apples and pears, Francis moved back to Ann Arbor, renting the front parlor at Mrs. Yost's (526 Jefferson Street) for two weeks at three dollars a week.[223] On his usual fall trip to Washington, New York, and Boston, he called on Harriet in D.C., visited his brother Fred and family in New Jersey, and enjoyed a lunch with Charlotte and the young Francis in New York; back in Detroit, he was re-

---

220. Diary, October 6, 1925. The ax was bought (for $2.75) specifically for this purpose.

221. Diary, November 30, 1925. His teeth also had been showing room for improvement: on November 7, a Dr. Lyons—likely Chalmers J. Lyons (1874–1935), educated at the Michigan School of Dentistry (D.D.S. 1898, D.D.Sc. 1911), professor of oral surgery there, and consulting dental surgeon to the University Hospital—extracted a tooth crowned by a French dentist in 1917, and another dentist "worked on two other teeth."

222. Diary, October 21, 1925. His guests at the Union lunch included President and Mrs. C. C. Little (see n. 143), Mr. and Mrs. Bloomer (donors), Professor and Mrs. Sanders, Professor and Mrs. Frank E. Robbins (Robbins was now assistant to the new president), Mr. and Mrs. Swain with Robert, Easton, and two representatives of the automaker Dodge Brothers. Clarence Cook Little (1888–1971) had been president of the University of Maine since 1922 and was brought to Michigan to replace Burton. (Alfred Lloyd had served as acting president in the interim.) He was a cancer researcher, leaving Michigan in 1929 for his laboratory in Sag Harbor and becoming a director of the American Cancer Society. By 1959 he was a scientific advisor to the Tobacco Industrial Research Committee, refuting his ACS claim of a causal link between smoking and cancer.

223. Diary, October 30, 1925.

united with Isabelle.[224] He and Isabelle then settled into life at Mrs. Yost's until the end of the year, sharing a happy Christmas dinner with Easton (now living in a fraternity) at the Union, with Francis preparing most of the day for the annual meetings in Ithaca, at which he was to install a photographic exhibit of Tunisia, Algeria, Sicily, and Greece and was scheduled to deliver two papers on the same day: one for the APA on a manuscript of Valerius Maximus and the other for the AIA on Carthage.[225]

ALWAYS ON THE GO

With an eye constantly on events in Egypt, Tunisia, and Turkey, Francis spent the first half of 1926 in the United States. He had wanted to leave for Egypt—the work at Karanis was in full swing in the winter months—but was delayed by the press of business and spells of sickness in the family, so he did not leave for Europe until mid-July. From then on, apart from an eight-week period (September 27–November 24), he was out of the country until the end of the year—making no fewer than four transatlantic crossings.

In Ann Arbor he and Isabelle moved lodgings all too frequently, continuing in the rooms at Mrs. Yost's at first, moving to 337 Thompson Street (quieter and steam heated) through February and March, then taking rooms at the Union (with a connecting bathroom) until the beginning of May. While Isabelle spent most of May in the hospital—there is no mention of what her ailments were—Francis returned to 337 Thompson.[226] When Isabelle came out of the hospital, they returned to the Union rooms they had occupied before, until Isabelle left on June 7 to visit Ruth in California. She did not return until October. A peripatetic existence does not seem to have troubled Francis: as long as he had his study at the university, his papers, and his books when he was in Ann Arbor and as long as he found clubs and hotels that were amenable when he was on the road, he was fine. Though the diary records that he wrote to Isabelle almost every day, a modern view might be that such a life could threaten his marriage. What Isabelle may have made of it is harder to discern, though her frequent visits to Ruth and Charlotte, as well as obvi-

---

224. Diary, November 10–22, 1925.
225. Diary, December 30, 1925.
226. During this period, Kelsey went out for a couple of days to the cottages at Lake Cavanaugh, traveling—unusually—by bus to Chelsea and from there by taxi. One wonders what happened to the Dodge.

ous marks of her affection for her daughters and her grandchildren, speak to her way of coping with Francis's absences and his work.

Francis continued to make his usual trips to the East Coast. Staying at the Cosmos Club in Washington in January, he called on his sister, Harriet, now "pleasantly situated in a comfortable apartment with a Mrs. Knowles and a Mrs. Brown." Seeing her again on the eve of his departure for Europe in July, he remarked in his diary, "hard to realize she will be 78 years old in December."[227] On another trip in March to New York, he stayed at the Murray Hill Hotel, had Sunday dinner with Charlotte and Francis and Isabelle (who had been staying with Charlotte since late February), and lunched the next day with Isabelle and Charlotte before taking them to the Metropolitan Opera for a performance of *Lucia di Lammermoor*.[228] After finishing up his work, he spent a night at Charlotte's on Long Island and another in New Jersey with his brother Fred. On yet another day, after lunching with Charlotte, he took her to the George M. Cohan Theatre to see the movie version of *Ben-Hur:* "this is the only first class screen I have ever seen—in good taste with artistic effects and fine climaxes."[229]

The pace of life was beginning to wear on Francis, as it had on Isabelle. On the way to visit Isabelle's parents in Denver, he was taken ill on the train, a situation hardly improved by the news that Isabelle's father had died.[230] With Francis increasingly sick with a high temperature, they got off the train in Omaha and checked into the Hotel Fontenelle, where Francis spent three miserable days in bed before rallying and returning to Ann Arbor.[231] As the time for Francis's departure for Europe approached, Isabelle went off to stay with Ruth in California once again. Francis accompanied her to Chicago, where, after dealing with business matters concerning properties she owned, they parted, she heading for California, he for Ann Arbor.[232] Easton appears

227. Diary, January 31 and July 14, 1926.

228. Diary, March 14 and 15, 1926. The opera would have starred the nineteen-year-old Marion Talley as Lucia in her debut season.

229. Diary, March 20–22, 1926. The novel *Ben-Hur: A Tale of the Christ*, written by General Lew Wallace, was published in 1880, dramatized in 1899 by William Young (whose play had six Broadway productions between then and 1916), and made by Metro-Goldwyn-Mayer into a feature film, directed by Fred Niblo and starring Ramon Novarro (1925).

230. Mr. Badger's funeral, attended by Isabelle and Francis, took place on April 26 at Silverbrook Cemetery in Niles, Michigan (*Niles Daily Star*, April 26).

231. Diary, April 6–11, 1926.

232. Diary, June 7, 1926. Francis remained interested in financial minutiae throughout his life, and he records expenses for this trip in the diary: Isabelle, round trip to Los Angeles,

rarely in these pages of the diary, though Francis thought it worth mentioning one evening when "Miss Charlotte Williams came for dinner with Easton, an attractive and unspoilt girl"[233] and that Easton was at the railroad station, with Sanders, to see him off.

At the University

Though officially on leave, Francis immersed himself in academic duties. Faced with a lapse in Horace Rackham's subscriptions, he sought help from the recently appointed president Clarence C. Little, who responded by visiting the collection of papyri one day and lending a sympathetic ear to Francis's entreaties on behalf of the Humanistic Series.[234] Moreover, he agreed to preside at the commencement exercises of the University School of Music on June 9, where he was introduced by Francis. Commencement was only one area, of course, of Francis's responsibilities as president of the UMS, for which his affection only grew. He chaired meetings of its board, attended concerts regularly, and was a prominent presence at the May Festival: he attended all the concerts, taking special pleasure in a performance of Mendelssohn's oratorio *Elijah* at which "Harrison sang as one inspired."[235]

Francis's enthusiasm for the Michigan Classical Conference, meeting as usual in April, was undiminished and further energized by lectures given by Thomas Ashby on Roman aqueducts.[236] Similarly, he busied himself at the meetings of the Schoolmasters' Club, eagerly endorsing the agreed resolution of the club's executive committee that "the basic idea is the correlation of secondary education with the University."[237] He remained in contact with colleagues and dealers about the acquisition of papyri, continuing a lively corre-

---

$104.58, Pullman, $23.63; two chairs to Chicago, $3; Francis, round trip to Chicago, $17.84, couchette (his train left Chicago at 10:00 p.m.), $3.75, dinner on train, $2.45, etc.

233. Diary, May 28, 1926. Kelsey refers to Theodore Harrison who also sang in 1921.

234. Diary, January 8, February 16, and April 24, 1926. Francis showed Little (see nn. 143 and 222) pages of three of the volumes (17, 23, and 31) then in progress.

235. Diary, May 20, 1926.

236. Diary, April 2–4, 1926. Ashby was no longer director of the British School at Rome. He had been obliged by the executive committee of the school to retire in 1925—a matter of internal politics. Given his contributions to and knowledge of the archaeology and history of Rome, his retirement came as a surprise and a matter of great disappointment to Italian archaeologists.

237. Diary, May 15, 1926.

spondence with Géjou in Paris; Nahman in Cairo; Askren in the Fayoum; Kenyon, Bell, and Edwards at the British Museum; and Bishop in Ann Arbor.[238] A major result was the purchase of Oriental manuscripts, approved by Edwards, from A. S. Yahuda in Heidelberg, of which half the agreed purchase price was dispatched at the end of June.[239]

A less familiar activity was his participation in radio programs aired by the University Broadcasting Service. When asked to contribute a talk to the program *Michigan Nights,* he agreed, seeing this as another opportunity to address a larger audience and encouraged by a local farmer's comment that the programs were a welcome change from the interminable jazz on commercial stations. At 9:00 p.m. on a Tuesday evening, he gave the lead talk, "reading into the microphone," followed by talks by William Warner Bishop and Dean Alfred Lloyd. His topic was the excavations at Antioch.[240]

Fund-raising was a continuous concern. In early February, he called on William Murphy and Horace Rackham in Detroit, following up with letters to Rackham. Making amends for his delay, Rackham sent a check for ten thousand dollars.[241] Further encouragement came in the form of recognition in the newspapers of the support gathered—largely through Francis's efforts, slowly at first but finally successfully—for the German *Thesaurus Linguae Latinae* and for the German Archaeological Institute in Rome. This financial support had allowed continued work on the *Thesaurus* and at the institute through 1923, 1924, and 1925.[242] In advance of a visit by Mrs. Pendleton, the relevant committees decided how the Buhl and Pendleton fellowships should be distributed and welcomed the arrival of a portrait of the late Edward W. Pendleton.[243] Mrs. Pendleton came to Ann Arbor on April 21. After visiting the Pendleton Library, she lunched privately with Isabelle before having Francis as well as Fred and Frances Colby to tea in her rooms at the Union. In the course of the next three days, she visited the collections, met all seven of

---

238. Numerous letters back and forth, FWK Papers, box 2, folders 13, 15, 17, and 18.

239. Diary, June 30, 1926. Abraham Shalom Yahuda (1877–1951), a Palestinian Jew, was a linguist, writer, and professor (teaching Arabic at Heidelberg, relocating to the United States in 1940, and landing at the New School for Social Research), as well as a collector of rare documents.

240. Diary, January 26, 1926; "The University and the State," *Michigan Alumnus* 33 (1926): 292.

241. Diary, February 9 and March 4, 1926; Kelsey to Rackham, February 24 and 27, and Rackham to Kelsey, March 2, 1926, FWK Papers, box 2, folders 14 and 15.

242. Diary, February 26, 1926.

243. Diary, April 2 and 16, 1926.

the Pendleton fellows, lunched with former president Hutchins and Mrs. Hutchins, took tea with Professor and Mrs. Sanders, visited the oak-paneled memorial library again, and gave a tea party at the Union, where guests included Francis and Isabelle, President and Mrs. Little, and Professor and Mrs. Karpinski.[244] The importance of the care of benefactors was well understood in Ann Arbor.

Francis was in Detroit again in May, canvassing William Murphy and Howard Bloomer for help, and he returned once more in June, to visit the Rackhams. Arriving at their house with a suitcase of Karanis objects for them to see, he made the case for a subvention of fifty thousand dollars. Rackham, burdened by tax problems, "demurred at the amount and referred the matter to her; she said 'the work must go on, even if we have to trim our corners in other things.'" The following day, Rackham wrote to Francis with a pledge of forty thousand dollars.[245] Thus, in the most real sense, the excavation of Karanis, with its revelation, for the first time, of the material culture of a Greco-Roman village in Egypt, is owed to the benevolence of Horace and Mary Rackham. (At the end of the month, William Murphy also responded to Francis's pleas, with a gift of one thousand dollars for student fellowships.) But it was not only his own drum that Francis beat: late in June, he traveled to Grand Rapids to meet a Mr. and Mrs. Frederick Stevens, who were interested in giving their collection of Chinese artifacts to the university, and he invited them to Ann Arbor to meet President Little and the director of university museums, Alexander G. Ruthven.[246]

In his editing work, Francis focused on various projects in fits and starts—spending several successive days in January on his Cicero books, more in June on the illustrations and proofs of the coins to be ready for a meeting at Allyn and Bacon in Boston the day before he sailed for Europe.

---

244. Diary, April 21–24, 1926. Professor of mathematics Louis C. Karpinski (1878–1956) was, as we have seen, a contributor to the Nicomachus volume and author of *Robert of Chester's Latin Translation of the "Algebra" of Al-Khowarizmi*, University of Michigan Studies, Humanistic Series, vol. 11, pt. 1 (New York: Macmillan, 1915).

245. Diary, June 22, 1926; Rackham to Kelsey, June 23, 1926, FWK Papers, box 2, folder 18.

246. Diary, June 28, 1926. Alexander Grant Ruthven (1882–1971) taught zoology and curated at the Museum of Zoology beginning in 1906, leading to his professorship and directorship of that museum (1915–29). Director of university museums during 1922–36, he would also become Michigan's next president in October 1929, just weeks before the Wall Street Crash. He served in that capacity through 1951, his twenty-two-year tenure exceeded only by Angell's thirty-eight years.

The discussion at his publishers covered content changes in the Cicero material (the *De Senectute* and *Select Orations and Letters*) and in the companion volumes, changes needed to adjust to new college entrance requirements. Francis suggested the need for fresh photographs of the images of Caesar, Pompey, and Demosthenes, to which the publishers agreed as they handed him more proofs to keep him busy on his voyage.[247] Volume 16 of the Humanistic Series (D'Ooge et al.'s Nicomachus) was assured publication by Dean Lloyd, who provided university funds to supplement those given by Mrs. Pendleton and who also offered support for the purchase of more papyri. Advance copies of the book were in Kelsey's hands by the end of the month.[248] Batches of proofs of the Grotius book kept arriving. In late June, a flood of them washed in, resulting in long workdays immediately prior to his leaving Ann Arbor and even at the Cosmos Club in Washington, in spare moments between visits to foreign embassies (France, Italy, Britain) in the quest for visas, an evening with Hyvernat on the subject of Coptic manuscripts, discussions at the State Department about Turkey and Tunisia, a lunch with Harriet, and another with "the Carnegie people."[249] Yet he still managed to write three articles and one review on his own interests.[250]

Departure

Having secured from the regents an extension of his academic leave through 1926–27 and the appointment of Esther Van Deman as Carnegie Research Professor of Archaeology (with her salary paid by the Carnegie Foundation), he made arrangements for Donald Harden to come to Ann Arbor as a Commonwealth Fellow for the year, to work on Karanis material.[251] He attended commencement exercises, at which Harvard's Professor Kirsopp Lake, the

---

247. Diary, July 16, 1926.

248. Diary, March 8 and 29, 1926.

249. Diary, July 2, 6, 13, and 14, 1926.

250. "Carthage, Ancient and Modern"; "Mitchell Carroll," *Art and Archaeology* 21 (1926): 103–12; "Great Fires in Constantinople," *Quarterly of the National Fire Protection Association* (1926): 2–12; review of *Groma*, by Matteo Della Corte, *Classical Philology* 21.3 (July 1926): 259–62. He also prepared an assessment of the manuscript of de Prorok's *Digging for Lost African Gods* for G. P. Putnam's Sons, which was considering it for publication (and did publish it that year).

251. Diary, May 28 and 29, 1926. At the same meeting, the regents accepted twenty-four reels of film of Carthage from Pathé Exchange.

noted biblical and patristic scholar, received an honorary doctorate.[252] In conference with Lake, he proposed a joint expedition to the Monastery of St. Catherine at Mount Sinai for 1927, with Lake and Swain in the forefront, and provided Lake with introductions to Admiral Bristol, Halil Bey, and Fouad Bey[253] in Constantinople and to Stevens in Rome. With arrangements for his journey falling into place, he felt free to leave early in July for his work abroad, via Washington, New York, and Boston.

The future of the work at Carthage had been debated since the first of the year. In January Francis, apparently feeling the burden of his duties, had proposed to Henry Fairclough of Stanford, who had served as an associate secretary during Kelsey's AIA presidency, that he assume "general oversight of work in North Africa" in Francis's place; discussion with Kenny and de Prorok about Carthage and land purchases had led nowhere.[254] At the State Department, Francis was told that it was best to work through Paris, rather than Tunis, about Carthage and that the head of the French Chancellery had been amazed at the virulent controversy between Poinssot and Chabot made public in the newspapers.[255] In New York in early February, Kenny had made no bones about where his priorities lay: "his daughter's happiness was his main concern."[256] At lunch with de Prorok the following month, Francis, expressing some frustration, declared, "it's time to have done with puttering in excavation," and he outlined near- and longer-term plans to finish what had been started at Carthage and "move to Utica in a big way." At a conference with Kenny the same day, Francis took the same line—"a big thing is easier to handle than a little thing"—to which Kenny replied by promising to provide ten thousand dollars a year and saying that he knew two others who would do the same: "So there's $30,000 to begin with." Francis wanted fifty thousand dollars for five years.[257] Five days later, at lunch with Kenny in the "attractive room at the top of his block" (at 44 East Twenty-third Street), encouraged

252. Diary, June 14, 1926. Lake, a professor of early Christian literature, had also participated in a number of archaeological expeditions to the Near East. Others receiving degrees were Henry Ford and the former head of Vassar's History Department, Professor Lucy Maynard Salmon, who, in 1923, had published two books on the relationship between historians and the press.

253. Dr. Fouad Bey was a member of the Angora National Assembly and a former Turkish minister of health.

254. Diary, January 1 and 2, 1926.

255. Diary, January 29, 1926.

256. Diary, February 2, 1926.

257. Diary, March 13, 1926.

perhaps by the service and meal offered by the crew of Kenny's railway dining car (available since in town), he proposed the purchase of the site at Utica.[258] However, in Washington the day after his departure from Ann Arbor in July, Francis was told at the State Department of reluctance in Paris to endorse de Prorok for the excavation permit for Carthage. Soon after, at a conference in New York, Kelsey, Kenny, and de Prorok all decided to shelve the Carthage project and to arrange for de Prorok to join Peterson at Karanis, with a salary of twenty-five hundred dollars and all expenses paid by Kenny.[259]

OUTWARD BOUND ONCE MORE

In the early morning of July 17, Francis left the Murray Hill Hotel in New York to board the SS *Minnewaska;* once on board, he mailed his letters, taken off by the pilot as the ship cleared the harbor waters. In his cabin, he found a gift from Mr. Kenny, a basket of books. The crossing was much to his liking: "Ideal days at sea." He enjoyed the conversation at his table in the dining room and worked steadily in his cabin through the Cicero proofs given to him in Boston: the *Pro Archia,* the *Pro Milone,* the *In Catilinam I–IV,* the *Select Orations and Letters,* and the *De Senectute.* The regularity of his work and the pleasure of the journey come through clearly in remarks to his diary at the end of the voyage.

> Harris [the steward] had brought coffee, toast and two apples to my state-room usually at 6.40 a.m. I have good morning light for proofs and writing. I have a table and every convenience. This is the only voyage I have made without closing the porthole once during the voyage. I have kept the same hours of work as on land; from that point of view, as work in the cabin has been without interruption, and as I have no trace of lassitude or discomfort from the sea, this has been the best voyage I have ever made.[260]

By the afternoon of July 26, he was at his hotel in London, where he instantly went out and bought fourteen Teubner texts before meeting Egyptologist Wainwright to discuss the work at Karanis and the conduct of the participants.

From January onward, Francis had been receiving progress reports from

---

258. Diary, March 18, 1926.
259. Diary, July 12 and 15, 1926.
260. Diary, July 24, 1926.

Starkey.[261] Rumors of difficulties at the excavation camp had also filtered through, to the extent that on March 25, Francis cabled to Askren, "Stop Excavation Close Camp"; to Swain, "If Much Delayed Cable Before Arranging Trip To Egypt"; and to Maria Barosso at Pompeii, "non posso venire adesso io mando denaro oggi Kelsey" (I cannot come now I am sending money today). Askren replied urging Francis to discuss Starkey with Boak,[262] the upshot of which was a cable to Askren: "We Hereby Give You Full Authority to Settle Affairs at Camp. Kelsey Boak."[263] That same day, he sent another to Swain in Rome advising, "Cancel Egypt Get Permits through Embassy and Naples Photography Pompeii Get Help Butler, Della Corte, Barosso, Confidential Trouble Egypt. Acknowledge. Kelsey," and two days later, he wrote to Swain, "Recommend See Della Corte First Follow Della Corte's Advice in case Difficulty Advise With Barosso Much Tact Necessary Kelsey."[264] After his abortive trip to Denver and illness in a hotel room in Omaha, he cabled Swain once more: "Arrival Uncertain. Photograph Whatever You Consider Profitable. Consult Stevens Kelsey."[265] Early in May, he received a letter from Wainwright describing trouble at Karanis, others from Askren and Yeivin on the topic of salaries, and two from Peterson about the Karanis staff, about problems with Yeivin, Starkey, and Wainwright, and about "the need for more Michigan men."[266] Francis's response to these difficulties—after consulting with Boak, who also had read Peterson's report—was to write to Starkey requiring an explanation of his overspending of four thousand dollars; Starkey's response presented transparent excuses.[267] Boak's continuing concern for the work at Karanis is shown by letters to Francis outlining the problems he would have to confront in London and urging that Harden should be the one to work on the glass from the site.[268]

---

261. Starkey to Kelsey, January 14 and 20, February 3 and 23, March 12, and April 8 and 16, 1926, folders 13–16.

262. Diary, March 25, 26, 28, and 30, 1926.

263. Diary, April 3, 1926.

264. Diary, April 3 and 5, 1926. Epigraphist Matteo Della Corte (1875–1962) spent his entire career at Pompeii, from 1902 (nine years before he had a degree in archaeology) through his directorship of the site (1926–42) and beyond, when he continued to document and publish inscriptions at Pompeii.

265. Diary, April 17, 1926.

266. Wainwright to Kelsey, May 4, and Peterson to Kelsey, May 19 and 26, 1926, FWK Papers, box 2, folder 17.

267. Kelsey to Starkey, June 5, and Starkey to Kelsey, June 26, 1926, FWK Papers, box 2, folder 18.

268. Boak to Kelsey, July 12 and 16, 1926, FWK Papers, box 2, folder 19.

From London to Rome to Paris to London

Francis spent a little more than two weeks in London, where his main aims were to sort out the difficulties at Karanis and to make arrangements at the British Museum for the acquisition and distribution of papyri and manuscripts. At the British Museum, he had long talks with Sir Frederick Kenyon and Edwards about manuscripts and with Bell and Crum about papyri; in fact, he asked Kenyon whether Bell might go to Egypt to help find and evaluate papyri.[269] Nonetheless, Karanis occupied much of his time. After a long session with Askren and Peterson, who had just arrived from the Continent, and Wainwright, he took them to the theater.[270] They were all greatly encouraged when told by Flinders Petrie that "our work would fill important gaps in the Greco-Roman period" and "that our material was not the kind to stir up the Egyptians."[271] Buoyed by this endorsement, Francis was ready to face Starkey, Yeivin, and the Karanis accounts: Starkey and Yeivin delivered the drawings from the first season (winter 1924–25), and a penitent Starkey, describing his "conduct 'an error of judgment,' expressed deep regret." Harden arrived and joined the talks. To Francis's astonishment and dismay, Wainwright demanded all his salary up front. It was agreed that Askren and Peterson should run up the new budget.[272] Conferring almost daily with Askren and Peterson, Francis was careful to relay to Boak the unflattering evidence about Starkey's conduct at Karanis: his tardiness, colonial attitude toward the servants, selfishness with the whiskey supplies, and bad behavior toward his wife. Another letter informed Boak about staffing arrangements for the 1926–27 season: Peterson, director; Wainwright, technical advisor; Askren, physician and local representative; Boak, papyrologist; and minor roles for Starkey, Yeivin, Harden, and Van Deman.[273] Any spare moments Francis had were spent on correspondence or the Cicero proofs. With administrative matters clarified, Francis, Askren, and Peterson left London for Rome on August 16, arriving the following day in time to attend a performance of the *Barber of Seville* at the Teatro Eliseo.

Kelsey's three weeks in Italy were as action-packed as ever. After calling on

---

269. Diary, July 27 and 31, August 4, 1926.

270. They saw the play *The Best People,* by David Gray and Avery Hopwood, perhaps chosen by Francis because Hopwood was a Michigan alumnus. Francis called it "highly amusing" (Diary, August 3, 1926).

271. Diary, August 3 and 4, 1926.

272. Diary, August 5–13, 1926.

273. Kelsey to Boak, August 10 and 13, 1926, FWK Papers, box 2, folder 20.

Director Stevens at the American Academy, depositing books and papers "in my study," and conferring with Kirsopp Lake about the Mount Sinai project, Francis lost no time in going to Naples. There he met Swain and his son Ned, who had just arrived from Piraeus. On seeing Maria Barosso's copies of the fresco cycle of the Villa of the Mysteries unrolled, he gasped; he could only say, "They are splendid," and arrange to take Matteo Della Corte and Amedeo Maiuri to see them two days later. Barosso had them mounted in the villa itself, where Francis and the others were able to compare them with the actual frescoes and check details. Barosso told him that the manuscript of her technical study was nearly ready.[274]

Discovered in 1909, the wall paintings themselves had instantly attracted the scholarly world for their enigmatic Bacchic subject matter, the brightness and variety of their colors, their size, and their state of preservation. It is no wonder that Francis wanted reproductions made before the deterioration of the surface set in and colors faded; it is remarkable that few others were thinking along the same lines. His hope was to bring reproductions to the United States and install them in a museum he had wished for many years to see built in Ann Arbor.[275] Here, not only students and scholars but also members of the general public would be able to walk into a room—designed to be as similar as possible to that in which the originals had been found in the Villa at Pompeii—and have an experience like that enjoyed by Romans of the first century. The audacity and vision of this project are astounding.

The twenty-two watercolors that Maria painted are very large (the panels are as much as twenty feet in length, with almost life-size figures). Painted on canvas-backed paper, they are neither paintings on canvas nor paintings on paper, their medium unfamiliar to many curators of ancient art. Since arrival in Ann Arbor, they have remained out of sight and rolled up for most of the past eighty years; no provision of space large enough had been found for their display, and only a single exhibition was devoted to them.[276] At last, however, with the construction of a new wing to the Kelsey Museum during 2008–9—almost a full century after Francis's agitations for suitable buildings on campus for the display of art and artifacts—they are on brilliant display, their appearance due in large measure to the energetic work of the museum's curators and conservators in devising new techniques to deal with the warped

---

274. Diary, August 19 and 21, 1926.
275. See chapter 6, "Campus Expansion" and "Fund-Raising and Acquisitions."
276. E. K. Gazda, ed., *The Villa of the Mysteries in Pompeii: Ancient Ritual, Modern Muse* (Ann Arbor: Kelsey Museum of Archaeology and University of Michigan Museum of Art, 2000).

and, in some places, torn paper, the difficulties of mounting the panels, and the problems posed by light-sensitive watercolors.[277]

By August 25, Francis was back in Rome, happily lodged at the Pensione Boos, enjoying his walks across Rome and to the American Academy. He hired Edgar Fletcher-Allen,[278] on the recommendation and with the money of Mr. Kenny, to work at Karanis; called on both the American and Egyptian ambassadors on matters of protocol; and went out to Hadrian's villa at Tivoli—"I never enjoyed a visit so much before."[279] He made the most of his study at the academy, correcting the seemingly endless Cicero proofs, working on Pompeii, writing letter after letter, and conferring with Director Stevens about the academy's needs (added endowment of $1.5 million).[280] But he was needed in London and back home and felt obliged to leave. His diary entry testifies to his reluctance: "I never left Rome with so keen regret. I am under deep obligations to finish work which I have undertaken which I can do here to so great advantage, with the Academy study now in good order. But 'duty first' and all will turn out for the best."[281]

Traveling via Genoa and Milan, he soon reached Axenstein (a resort favored by Queen Victoria) in central Switzerland,[282] where he was met by de Prorok and introduced to Edgar Fletcher-Allen and his wife, Joy. A day of walks and talks allowed him to get the measure of the couple and calm any hesitations he may have had. Accompanied by de Prorok, he then took the overnight train to Paris. At the embassy, officials expressed frustration at the outcome of the Carthage plans—"disgusted with the way negotiations have been messed up," said one. Francis was happier at lunch with the Abbé Chabot and de Prorok and in the afternoon at the Institut de France, where

---

277. The museum has been able to call on the expertise of the Intermuseum Conservation Association in Cleveland to cope with repairs and mounting arrangements and on the Art Conservation Research Center at Carnegie Mellon University for assessment of the light sensitivity of the colors.

278. Fletcher-Allen, who had already published a novel under the pseudonym Granville Street (*Peter Was Married* [New York: G. P. Putnam's Sons, 1924]), handled notes and translations for de Prorok's 1926 *Digging for Lost African Gods*. Enlarging on his travels, he would write *Cook's Traveller's Handbook to North Africa: Morocco, Algeria, Tunisia, and Libya* (London: Simpkin, Marshall, 1933). In the late 1940s, he would translate (from the French) works by Romanian journalist-diplomat Grigore Gafencu, including *Last Days of Europe: A Diplomatic Journey in 1939* (New Haven: Yale University Press, 1948).

279. Diary, August 26 and 27, 1926.

280. Diary, August 30–September 6. On September 2 alone, he wrote fifteen letters.

281. Diary, September 7, 1926.

282. Axenstein, in the canton of Schwyz, is not to be confused with Auenstein, to the northwest, in the canton of Aargau.

he met the most prestigious of the French scholars working in North Africa—Cagnat, Cumont, Reinach,[283] Gsell, Merlin—and talked over with Gsell the idea of a joint research project (on churches of North Africa) between the American Academy and its French counterpart in Rome, the École Française. He also sought advice as to the ways and means of purchasing the site at Utica from its French landlord, the Count de Chabannes.[284] The next day, he was back in London and looking forward to a September 17 visit to the Chadwick Museum in Bolton, where twenty-seven hundred cloth fragments from Karanis were being examined.[285]

Prior to his appointment at the Chadwick Museum, Francis took a day off work (after church) to rest. On other days, he met Mr. and Mrs. Kenny at the luxury hotel Claridge's, on one occasion for dinner, on another for lunch, when the conversation inevitably turned to Egypt and de Prorok. He was glad to leave all that behind and head north, reaching the Swan Hotel at Bolton on the evening of September 16.[286] The curator at the Chadwick, Thomas Midgley,[287] told him that in terms of quality, the Karanis fragments were "on a par with the best poplin." Midgley escorted him to the Tootal Broadhurst Lee textile factory, where Francis learned many details of poplin production, and Midgley learned, about the Karanis research, that "the aim of our excavation is the scientific reconstruction of the Greco-Roman culture in Egypt: the visualization of the background of the culture which produced the papyri in our collection."[288]

Back in London, at the British Museum, he began packing papyri and manuscripts to take with him to the United States. But Karanis problems lingered. In reply to a letter from Wainwright, Francis invited him to dinner. As they talked over the question of whose authority was to take precedence at

---

283. These are René-Louis-Victor Cagnat (1852–1937), a French epigraphist and historian, specializing in Roman Africa; Franz-Valéry-Marie Cumont (1868–1947), a Belgian archaeologist, historian, and philologist who had led expeditions to Syria (e.g., Dura-Europos) and Turkey; and Salomon Reinach (1858–1932), a French archaeologist who had worked near Smyrna (at Myrina) and at Carthage. On Gsell, see n. 169; on Merlin, n. 145.

284. Diary, September 10, 1926. The idea of working at Utica was frustrated by the count selling the site to a property company (diary, March 26, 1927).

285. Bolton is some fifteen miles north of Manchester, in what used to be the heartland of the English cotton manufacturing business. The museum's archaeological textile collection is extensive.

286. Diary, September 13–16, 1926.

287. Thomas's father, William Waller Midgley, had been the first curator of the museum, which opened in 1884; Thomas succeeded him and served until 1934.

288. Diary, September 17, 1926.

Karanis, his or Peterson's, the conversation developed into an argument: Who was to be the director? Who was responsible for what? At another dinner the following day with Mr. and Mrs. Starkey, another argument developed, Starkey claiming that Askren, who had been asked by Francis and Boak to take charge of the end of the season,[289] was responsible for the deficit in the budget and that he (Starkey) had "proved his loyalty to me by cleaning up his year." With other evidence in hand, Francis could barely stomach Starkey's casuistry. Determined that Peterson should lead the excavation, and before boarding the SS *Leviathan* for New York Francis wrote to Wainwright, dismissing him: "relations with the University of Michigan terminated."[290]

The crossing was uneventful. Francis worked on the Cicero proofs; met Mr. R. J. Cuddihy, publisher of the *Literary Digest,* who had raised the magazine's fund for Belgian children during the war;[291] and attended a subscription concert for Florida hurricane sufferers, to which the largest contributors (always a source of interest to Francis) were Hershey (eight thousand dollars) and Cuddihy and Kenny (five thousand each).[292]

New York, Ann Arbor, New York, and Away Again

Based in New York for a few days, Francis took young Thomas Kenny to Yale for a talk with President James Rowland Angell, son of former Michigan president James B. Angell, with a view to his entering the college. He later reported to Mr. Kenny, who "then handed me a check for $5000 for the University." Charlotte and grandson Francis came into the city for lunch; she "spoke of her writing and her gardening" and recalled meeting John Galsworthy on the boat when she crossed to Europe in 1921. In New Jersey he saw Fred and Vergilia as well as his nephew Fred and was "delighted with the progress and appearance of the children."[293]

---

289. See n. 263.

290. Diary, September 18–21, 1926; Wainwright to Kelsey, September 15, and Kelsey to Wainwright, September 21, 1926, FWK Papers, box 2, folder 21.

291. Robert Joseph Cuddihy (1862–1952) had started as an office boy in 1878 for publishing partners I. K. Funk and A. W. Wagnalls, who put him in charge of their *Literary Digest* upon its inception in 1890. It had a circulation of 1.5 million by 1927 and 2.2 million by 1930. An appeal to readers in 1914 to help feed Belgian children had brought in more than one hundred thousand dollars; another, in 1917, more than five hundred thousand. Having assumed control of Funk and Wagnalls in 1914, Cuddihy remained its director until he retired in 1948, and he was the *Digest's* publisher until its sale in 1937.

292. This Mr. Hershey was presumably Milton S. Hershey (1857–1945) of milk chocolate fame.

293. Diary, September 29–October 3, 1926.

On his first day back in Ann Arbor, Francis took a room at the Union, went to see Easton, and had dinner with Boak, Bonner, Sanders, and Winter. Boak had already written to him of his opposition to de Prorok, as incompetent, and had received Francis's reply—which included the news that Harden had arrived in New York and was on his way to Ann Arbor.[294] Now, at dinner, "Boak said he would not go to Egypt this year because de Prorok was on the Karanis staff. Boak and Bonner disposed to be offish because appointments not submitted to the Committee. I presented the necessity of giving Peterson the responsibility of choosing the people he had to live with. I suggested to Boak that we talk it over privately." Evidently exasperated, Francis said to Bonner, "Bonner, I don't have to do this work."[295] After working through a mountain of correspondence, Francis completed his article "Great Fires in Constantinople" and took a day of "absolute rest" at Lake Cavanaugh before welcoming Isabelle back from California.[296] At lunch with President Little, he heard of fund-raising problems, conflicts between competing university units in the search for support, and was invited to join a committee to resolve the problem. This committee, to be chaired by William Warner Bishop, included some heavy hitters: assistant to the president Robbins, dean of students Joseph Bursley, Dean Edward Kraus of the College of Pharmacy, Oscar James Campbell from the English Department, and Herbert Charles Sadler from Engineering.

Isabelle and he soon moved from the Union to the recently opened, enormous, and well-appointed Book-Cadillac Hotel in Detroit, where Francis resumed his hunt for donors. For three days, he visited friends to little avail, only the Webbers offering to continue their support of the Askren boys' education; but he and Isabelle enjoyed a performance of *Abie's Irish Rose,* described in the program as a "tornado of hilarity," at the Garrick Theater.[297] Easton came for an overnight at the hotel, and Isabelle and Francis spent a couple of evenings with Mr. and Mrs. Rackham, bringing them up to date and showing them objects from Karanis. Francis shuttled back and forth to Ann Arbor for the balance of their week's stay in Detroit, attending in Ann Arbor to his correspondence, accounts, and the business of the Advisory

---

294. Boak to Kelsey, September 23, and Kelsey to Boak, September 28, 1926, FWK Papers, box 2, folder 21.

295. Diary, October 6, 1926. A week later, he withdrew the invitation to Boak to go to Egypt (diary, October 13, 1926).

296. Diary, October 11, 1926. The article is cited in n. 250 above.

297. Diary, October 16, 1926. This comedy had been the surprise hit of the 1922–23 Broadway season.

Committee on Near East Research.[298] Still eager to bolster the Karanis team for the upcoming season (1926–27), he had dinner with H. Dunscombe Colt,[299] introduced him to Harden and Winter, and telegraphed his opinion to Askren and Peterson. He sent off the final corrections to volume 13 of the Humanistic Series (Gottheil and Worrell). Mrs. Pendleton came for a visit and met the students she supported (the Pendleton fellows).[300] There were meetings almost every day. Despite his differences with Boak over Karanis, the two remained civil, conferring more than once about the publication of the ostraca and the papyri; the university committee on research and fund-raising chaired by Bishop met and wrote a report. As for library acquisitions, Bishop himself removed 314 Oriental manuscripts (those from Yahuda) to the Library, while Edwards reported from the British Museum that 96 volumes of manuscripts were ready to be brought to Ann Arbor.[301]

With scarcely two weeks remaining before his return to Europe, Francis strove tirelessly to push his plans forward. He conferred with President Little about the next meeting of the Michigan Classical Conference and the Schoolmasters' Club, Little saying that "he would do what he could to help." On receiving news from Askren that no photography was now allowed at Mount Sinai, Francis agreed with Lake to postpone the expedition. He met with Swain to discuss his duties should he not go to Egypt; they settled that Swain "prepare a full set of prints, mount in albums, descriptive material for every negative made from September 1, 1919." He cabled fifteen hundred dollars to Askren for the purchase of papyri. He also did not neglect social responsibilities: he accepted an invitation from former president Hutchins and Mrs. Hutchins to dinner ("no dress suits"); he gave a lunch at the Union for Professor Max Farrand, the former general director of the Commonwealth Fund,[302] to which he invited Sanders, Winter, and Harden and others. Among the others was Howard R. Newcomb of Detroit, who had an interest in the

---

298. Diary, October 17–22, 1926.

299. Harris Dunscombe Colt Jr. (1901–73) had worked with British anthropologist and archaeologist Margaret Murray in Malta (as had his future bride, Teresa Strickland). In 1936–37, he would lead an expedition to 'Awjâ' al-Hafîr (Nessana) that yielded thirteen Arabic papyri from AD 672–89.

300. Diary, October 23–29, 1926.

301. Diary, November 1–6, 1926.

302. The Commonwealth Fund had been formed as a charitable organization in 1918 with a gift of roughly ten million dollars from Anna M. Harkness (widow of Standard Oil silent partner Stephen V. Harkness), who added another six million a year later. Yale's Max Farrand (1869–1945), an American history specialist, took a leave of absence to lead it initially but returned to Yale in the fall of 1921, though he continued to serve as an adviser in education for the fund.

electrotype reproductions of ancient coins in the British Museum and had offered a contribution of five thousand dollars if twenty thousand were needed to acquire a set.[303]

Amid a flood of correspondence, Francis managed a telegram to President H. M. Moore of Lake Forest College, regretting that he could not participate in the fiftieth anniversary celebrations of the refoundation of the school: "Sailing immediately Europe. Keenly regret cannot accept kind invitation. Mrs. Kelsey joins me in warm congratulations on a half century of devoted and effective service and in earnest good wishes for the future. Francis W. Kelsey." In Detroit one day, he bought a new winter coat at Hudson's for fifty-five dollars; called on William Murphy and C. E. Hilton, who assured him that Mrs. Pendleton would renew three fellowships next year; and met Howard Newcomb at the Athletic Club. There were bills and other obligations to be met.[304]

On November 18, the Near East research committee had a last meeting before his departure, at which everything went smoothly. The next day, he saw President Little again, to urge the claims of the School of Music and to take up the subject of a College of Fine Arts. Francis summed up the gist of this meeting as follows:

> College of Fine Arts to be developed about the School of Music, a successful existing unit: first painting, then sculpture; a separate school not under any existing Dean because technical work must be commenced early and not be hampered by too great academic demands: cost to be $40K for 1927–1928, $55 for 1928–1929, and $15[K] to be added every year until $100K reached. Little said my estimate was lower than his. Development of a plant costing $2 million for the School of Music already in mind could be modified to include painting and sculpture.[305]

In light of such far-reaching and ambitious plans, it is hardly surprising that several colleagues described Francis as visionary.

On the morning of November 21, he and Isabelle left Ann Arbor early enough to catch the 8:40 a.m. train from Detroit to New York and were in the

---

303. Diary, November 9–13, 1916. Howard Rounds Newcomb (1877–1945), son of the founder of Detroit's first department store, the Newcomb-Endicott Company, was a well-known, published numismatist whose coin collection was deemed one of the nation's best.

304. These obligations included, for example, $133.53 to Hutzel's (plumbing and heating) for an electric pump at the house at 810 Oxford, $55 for a subscription to the Detroit Club, and $500 for a new building project at church.

305. Diary, November 19, 1926.

Murray Hill Hotel at 11:45 p.m.: "It seems remarkable to go from Ann Arbor to New York in one day." The following day, the Parisian dealer I. E. Géjou[306] brought some Gospel manuscripts and music books for Francis to see. The asking price was six hundred dollars, against which Francis offered four hundred, which Géjou accepted. Pleased with the acquisition, he and Isabelle went to South Orange for dinner and a musical evening with Fred and the family. The day before his departure, he visited the American Numismatic Society in New York to talk with President Edward Theodore Newell and Secretary Howland Wood about the British Museum's electrotype copies of ancient coins; they thought that an offer of three thousand dollars for a set would be reasonable. In the afternoon, he and Isabelle went to Charlotte's on Long Island to spend the night.

On the morning that he sailed, Francis went first to the Metropolitan Opera to buy tickets for Isabelle and Charlotte and then to the Murray Hill Hotel for a conversation with Mr. Kenny. Isabelle and Fred came to the dockside to see him off "and stood on the wharf as we swung out to sea." The pilot sent off four letters that Francis had written hastily. He had made all the necessary preparations for the journey that he could and was exhausted.

> [I]n pm Captain Cunningham and the Purser called on me and found I was not in my room; they found me fast asleep in the library and did not wake me up. Purser transferred me from rm. 167 to rm. 146, a luxurious room, double with private bath, 3 portholes. The Chief Steward seated me at the Captain's table—there was delivered a large bouquet of roses and a large basket with 6 new books and the latest magazines from Mr. and Mrs. Kenny and a fine basket of fruit from Ronald and Helen.[307]

The next day, he thanked Captain Cunningham for "his courtesy and for assigning me so luxurious a room; he said Mr. Kenny had phoned him."[308] In such comfortable conditions, secure in the high esteem of his family and friends, Francis began the final eastbound transatlantic crossing he was to make.

---

306. On Géjou, see chapter 8, "Paris and London."

307. Diary, November 24, 1926. Ronald was Fred's younger son, who had married Helen Demarest in 1922.

308. Diary, November 25, 1926.

CHAPTER 10

The Final Passage

꙾

FRANCIS'S STAMINA WAS NOT what it used to be. He uncharacteristically slept too late for church services on Sunday, and the next day, he did not even have his breakfast—café au lait and croissant in his stateroom—until eleven o'clock. He read novels and newspapers and wrote letters, remarking, "This is the most complete rest I've had for years."[1] So mild was the weather that he did not need an overcoat. This elicited from him interesting comparisons with previous November crossings he had taken: whereas each of those occasions (in 1884, 1893, and 1920) had been accompanied by two or three days of heavy seas with squalls and flurries of snow, his present (1926) trip was "the most calm and restful voyage imaginable."[2] The liner docked at Plymouth soon after midnight on December 2, and after only the most perfunctory customs inspection, he was quickly on the train. Arriving in London by noon, he cabled Charlotte, "Hubley, 76 Hudson, Bellerose, Long Island. Fine Voyage Rested Kelsey."[3]

Spending the next three days in London, he met at the British Museum with Kenyon, who told him that Bell was finding only a few papyri in Cairo (the supply was drying up), and with Cooke, who put a valuation of twenty-seven thousand pounds on a set of the museum's electrotype coins—an outrageous sum that left Francis more amused than staggered. He also met

---

1. Diary, November 29, 1926.
2. Diary, December 1, 1926.
3. Diary, December 2, 1926.

George Macmillan at his publishing offices to discuss the inclusion of the University of Michigan titles in the Macmillan Company list. He wrote his letters, made his travel arrangements, and left for Italy. Departing from Victoria Station at 9:00 in the morning, he was in Paris at 4:20 p.m., arrived in Dijon at 9:30 that night, and—after the customary hassle at the border over his bags (excess weight)—reached Genoa at 10:56 the following morning, Rome at 8:10 in the evening, and the Pensione Boos just an hour later.[4] Pausing four days in Rome, he visited the American Academy every day, conferring with Director Stevens about the trustees' decision to withdraw his authority to accept works of art, discussing their work with Michigan students, and accompanying Van Deman as she lectured on Roman aqueducts and Augustan brickwork. Twice he called at the embassy in the quest for visas. He saw Maria Barosso's paintings of the frescoes from the Villa of the Mysteries on display at the Villa Borghese and noted her request for one hundred thousand lire and expenses.[5] On December 11, he was on his way south to Brindisi and the SS *Helouan* (on the Trieste–Alexandria run), which he boarded at midnight. Amid rough seas, the boat pitched and rolled its way past Crete for most of the night and the next day, but he had the benefit of lively conversation with a Mr. Harmon (a fellow opera enthusiast) before arriving at Alexandria. Assisted every step of the way by Cook's agents, helping especially with his bags, he was at Shepheard's Hotel in Cairo by 10:00 p.m. on December 13.

IN EGYPT

His first week in Egypt was spent in the hunt for papyri. Though impressed at Shepheard's Hotel by the hall porter's recognition, Francis transferred to the Cecil House Hotel, where Idris Bell was staying. Bell had already visited Nahman with Askren, with whom he also had gone around the villages of the Fayoum buying bits and pieces of papyri, never offering more than 15 percent of the asking price (e.g., 30 pounds when 250 was asked). Now they continued the search together, visiting various dealers—Mohammed M. Elgabry, Ismail El Shaer, the Khawam brothers, and Kondilios, for example. Francis bought a few Coptic fragments from Elgabry for one pound and a thirteenth-century Greek lectionary from Kondilios for fifty pounds.[6] Visiting the antiquities collection of Mme Sickenberger, they concluded that the papyri were forg-

---

4. Diary, December 7, 1926.
5. Diary, December 10, 1926.
6. Diary, December 14, 1926. Kondilios was asking 250 pounds for the lectionary, claiming that he had paid 125 for it—the usual 100 percent markup.

eries; but Francis bought from Nahman a thirteenth-century Psalter for three hundred pounds. Bell's friendship with the Americans blossomed: "of the kindness of the American representatives I cannot speak too highly."

Diversion came in several forms. Leon Pardowitz, the concierge at the Palace Hotel in Constantinople, far from home, caught sight of Kelsey across the street and hailed him. Mr. Harmon invited him to an opera performance where a protégée of his, Madeleine Keltie,[7] was singing Mimi in *La Bohème*. After dinner the next day with Askren, Bell, and Peterson, when there was much talk of Karanis, Francis noted, "I am more than ever convinced that Peterson is the man for the place." At the Museum of Egyptian Antiquities (known colloquially as the Egyptian Museum or the Cairo Museum), Francis talked with Campbell Edgar,[8] the head of the museum, and a "chilly" Wainwright, but he was more interested in what Bell was up to as he sorted through a batch of papyri choosing fragments for Michigan.[9] When de Prorok put in an appearance, he took Francis to see Père Paul Bovier-Lapierre's[10] prehistoric collection (twelve thousand Egyptian objects), after which all three went to visit the sandpits thick with prehistoric material that the construction boom in Cairo had exposed. One day, he set aside to visit, with Bell and Westermann, the mosques and pyramids and was shown round the tombs by Dows Dunham—"a thrilling experience."[11]

---

7. Diary, December 15, 1926. Keltie (1890–1977) was an American soprano and regular performer with the San Carlo Opera Company in New York and Philadelphia.

8. Born in Scotland (Tongland, Kirkubrightshire), Campbell Cowan Edgar (1870–1938) studied at Glasgow University (1887–91) under both Richard Claverhouse Jebb and Gilbert Murray and later at Oriel College, Oxford (1891–95). A Craven Fellowship took him to Athens, allowing him to work at Kynosarges and on Melos. In 1910 he cleared the recently uncovered tomb of Khesuwer (Hsw) the Elder at Kom el-Hisn (ancient Imu). Edgar served as keeper and secretary-general of the Cairo Museum during 1925–27.

9. He chose nine Coptic fragments, one Coptic vellum fragment, two Demotic and one Arabic papyri, and a leaf of an eighth- or ninth-century Greek Psalter—all costing just nine pounds (diary, December 17, 1926).

10. In 1925 French archaeologist Bovier-Lapierre had begun to excavate the Neolithic el-Omari sites, codiscovered (with Egyptian mineralogist Amin el-Omari) during earlier surveys of the Helwan region. In the early 1930s, he was investigating the Lower Paleolithic at Abbasiyeh.

11. Diary, December 22, 1926. Dows Dunham (1890–1984), educated at Harvard College (A.B. 1913), worked under Egyptologist and archaeologist George A. Reisner in Giza, where he excavated the tomb of Queen Hetepheres that Reisner's team discovered in 1925. A highly respected Egyptian archaeologist, Dunham would become curator of Egyptian and Ancient Near Eastern art at the Boston Museum of Fine Arts. His publications include *The Royal Cemeteries of Kush*, 5 vols. (Cambridge, MA: Harvard University Press; Boston: Museum of Fine Arts, 1950–63).

After packing up boxes of papyri in a suitcase and taking them to Edgar at the Egyptian Museum for safekeeping, he telegraphed to William Kenny ("Kenus, N.Y. Everything fine. Merry Christmas to all. Do come Egypt. Kelsey"), bought boxes of chocolates for the Karanis camp, and took the train on Christmas Eve to the Fayoum, where he was met at the station by Askren, Fletcher-Allen, and Swain. They went first to Mohammad Abdullah's shop, where he thought the Coptic paper fragments he was shown were worthless, though he did purchase some Greek papyri for forty-two pounds (the asking price was 250 pounds); they then proceeded to the Michigan camp, where Francis found the housekeeping arrangements "admirable, thanks to Mrs. Allen."[12] Though Christmas Day was a holiday (see fig. 31), Francis walked around the site with Fletcher-Allen—whose workmen had found a hoard of sixty gold coins a few days before—and Peterson, discussing objectives, problems, and logistics before sitting down to a "fine Christmas dinner with gifts and good cheer."[13] Francis spent the following day almost entirely on the site, amid the throng of workers, with Fletcher-Allen and Peterson at his side. On December 27, after conferences with Fletcher-Allen and de Prorok, he was driven to Askren's house and then back to Cairo, a distance of some seventy miles, where his first stop was at the National Bank of Egypt to find a safe-deposit box for the coins. The final few days of 1926 were spent in photography (with Swain); in correspondence, including a cable to Kirsopp Lake at Harvard, announcing more promising news about the proposed expedition to Mount Sinai; in visits to the consulate; and in money matters, from which tiresome work he was relieved on New Year's Eve by the arrival of a letter from Isabelle.

As the New Year (1927) opened, Francis settled down to administrative work: reports, memoranda, and always correspondence. His diary records that in the first week alone, he wrote sixty-five letters, many by hand; began a report on the work at Karanis that, when complete, ran to sixty pages; and started writing a memorandum for the Advisory Committee on Near East Research at Michigan. Finished on January 20, this memorandum, 109 pages long, was bound for him at the consulate and dispatched.[14]

Always on the lookout for new acquisitions, Francis saw Maurice Nahman on one or two occasions in January: on one day, he bought a Coptic service

---

12. Diary, December 24, 1926.

13. "A happy and memorable Christmas—unlike any such Christmas before in my life," concludes the diary entry.

14. Diary, January 21, 1927.

31. Karanis expedition staff, Christmas Day, 1926. *From left,* Edwin L. Swain, H. Dunscombe Colt, Valeri Fausto, Harold Falconer, Joy Fletcher-Allen, Francis Kelsey, Byron Khun de Prorok, Edgar Fletcher-Allen, Enoch Peterson. Kelsey Museum of Archaeology, University of Michigan 5.2345. Photo: George R. Swain.

book from him for thirty pounds; on another, Nahman came by offering to sell three letters with Napoleon's signature; and on yet another, they went together to look over a collection of seven thousand Alexandrian coins.[15] William Westermann, too, was looking for papyri, for Columbia University, and he and Kelsey visited the dealer Kalemkarian; though Francis was unimpressed, Westermann bought fifteen papyri.

When he was not working on his reports or his letters, however, Francis often spent time at the Egyptian Museum.[16] He frequently discussed Karanis matters there with Edgar: What steps should be taken to preserve the ancient grain found at the site? How was the conservation of other Karanis materials

---

15. Diary, January 9, 14, and 24, 1927.

16. Among the distinguished Egyptologists he met there was German philologist Wilhelm Spiegelberg (1870–1930), who had been part of Flinders Petrie's team in Thebes during the late 1890s and was an expert on Demotic papyri.

at the museum proceeding? How should the gold coins be handled? With Edgar's agreement and prior to any decision about their division between Cairo and Ann Arbor, he brought the coins from the bank and worked several days on them at the museum, arranging them by emperor,[17] having them photographed, and leaving them in the care of Reginald Engelbach, the assistant keeper—being careful not to leave without a receipt.[18] A long discussion with Edgar on January 25 touched on the management of the excavation: Edgar asked "who was head of our work in the Fayoum. I told him Peterson was. He suggested de Prorok be kept as inconspicuous as possible, Egyptians always asking about administrative matters." Edgar, close to retirement, was concerned also about the publication of the Greek papyri from Karanis, which Boak had agreed to handle. These papyri were being kept at the museum under Edgar's care; but as they were in fragile condition and needed to be unrolled by an expert, he wondered whether Boak could come to Egypt soon. His successor might have his own interest in Greek papyri, so Edgar could not make commitments beyond the current year.[19]

Peterson came up from Karanis for a meeting, "half sick with a cold and worry about the younger men at camp," and took the Westermann family back with him for a few days. When Westermann called on Francis to thank him for making their Cairo visit so pleasant, his son Evan in particular expressed enthusiasm for their stay at the site.[20] Kelsey himself went to Karanis toward the end of the month, cheered to no end by a cable from Isabelle— "Granddaughter Both Fine Isabelle"—to which his reply, addressed to Ruth, was the equally laconic "Diel Congratulations Pater."[21] He spent two whole days on the site itself with Peterson, Fletcher-Allen and his wife, and de Prorok, but much attention focused on the nearby site at Dimay, which Fletcher-Allen was keen to explore. On January 29, they were up early to drive (Swain at the wheel) to the site. Francis found it largely unaltered from the time when he had seen it in 1920 and, on reflection, thought that "the temple and enclosure present a definite problem in a measure capable of solution after

---

17. For some specifics on these coins, see below, "Karanis: An Excursive Chronicle."

18. An English Egyptologist, Engelbach (1888–1946) served as chief inspector of Upper Egypt before taking the position as assistant keeper at the museum; he became head keeper in 1931. Years before, he had excavated and published a number of cemeteries in Riqqeh (1912–13) and Harageh (1913–14). Among his popular writings is *The Problem of the Obelisks: From a Study of the Unfinished Obelisk at Aswan* (London: T. Fisher Unwin; New York: George H. Doran, 1923).

19. Diary, January 25, 1927.

20. Diary, January 11 and 20, 1927.

21. Diary, January 22 and 23, 1927.

complete excavation; as regards the rest of the place, exploratory trenches should be cut from the Northeast side before definitely deciding on a future policy, and perhaps trenches from the opposite side also." After a conference with Peterson, the Fletcher-Allens, and de Prorok, at which the major topics were Donald Harden (would it be helpful to have him on site next year to help with the pottery?) and Dimay (they decided "to attack Dimay next year"), Francis returned on the last day of the month to Cairo.[22]

On his frequent visits to the Egyptian Museum, Francis inevitably met other foreign scholars. As a result, he dined with Henri Frankfort and his wife one evening, an occasion at which there were two major topics of conversation: the division of finds from excavations conducted by foreigners and the printing of color plates.[23] Francis took note of Frankfort's view that the division of finds from his work at Abydos had been unsatisfactory. Regarding printing, he thought that Frankfort "has the right idea of publication—proposing to print the frescoes of el-Amarna in colored plates, regardless of ordinary computation of cost; he thinks nine plates will be needed, costing say 80 pounds per plate. His estimate is rather low." Another scholar he met at the museum was Ludwig Borchardt, the celebrated German archaeologist and founder of the German Archaeological Institute in Cairo.[24] Also at the museum, he continued his talks with Edgar about Karanis, the conservation of the finds, and the need for the "chemical and mechanical examination of the pottery." On one day, he showed Edgar papyri from Oxyrhynchus that he had bought for thirty-five pounds; on another, they went together to visit the Bucher collection of antiquities (lamps, terra-cottas, scarabs, sculptures, inscriptions).[25] But a good deal of his time was taken up in dealing with the

---

22. No work was done at Dimay in 1928. A Michigan team, led by Peterson, explored the site in the 1931–32 season but found the logistics too difficult to contemplate a longer involvement. See Lauren E. Talalay and Susan E. Alcock, "Soknopaiou Nesos (Dime), Egypt, 1931–1932," in *In the Field: The Archaeological Expeditions of the Kelsey Museum* (Ann Arbor: Kelsey Museum of Archaeology, 2006), 32–33.

23. Educated in Amsterdam, London, and Leiden, Henri Frankfort (1897–1954) was a Dutch archaeologist, anthropologist, and linguist who directed excavations for the Egypt Exploration Society of London at Abydos and el-Amarna in the 1920s, subsequently led the Oriental Institute of Chicago's work in Iraq, and finally served as director of the Warburg Institute in London (1949–54).

24. Borchardt (1863–1938) was the discoverer of the photogenic head of Queen Nefertiti now in Berlin. Debate continues about its ownership and legitimacy (is it a twentieth-century copy?).

25. Diary, February 2, 3, 5, and 17, 1927. Can this be the collection of Franz Joseph Bucher (1834–1906), Swiss hotelier, railroad pioneer, and businessman who died in Cairo?

difficulties that had clouded the management of the Karanis excavation during the 1925–26 season and their uncomfortable aftermath.

During the first season (1924–25), as the reader will recall, Boak had been in charge as Michigan's representative on the ground, with Starkey as field director and Yeivin as his assistant. Wainwright, in the employ of the Egyptian Department of Antiquities, had served as volunteer technical adviser.[26] Things had run smoothly enough. In the second season (1925–26), however, Boak had not been present. He and Francis had evidently assumed that Starkey would cooperate well with Peterson; that Wainwright would be a judicious adviser at the practical level; and that Askren, the expedition's doctor and local representative, would be an authoritative American presence should any difficulties of diplomacy or personnel arise. But it seems that misstatements and misunderstandings had led to disagreements and arguments, so that Francis and Boak had been obliged to give overall authority to Askren toward the end of the season.[27] Ultimately, after an awkward dinner with Wainwright in London on September 19, 1926—at which Wainwright, claiming that Askren had made promises to him about the 1926–27 season, asked point-blank whether he or Peterson was to be the director—Francis had decided to let Wainwright go.[28]

By the time that Francis had arrived in Egypt in December 1926, officials in the Egypt Museum (Edgar, Engelbach, and others) were aware of the problem, doubtless informed—or, rather, given his side of the matter—by Wainwright, hence Wainwright's "chilly" attitude toward Francis when they first met in Cairo and Edgar's question to Francis at their meeting on January 25. On February 5, when Francis asked Engelbach for his advice about Wainwright's claim that Askren had made promises to him, Engelbach replied, "Get the facts," and asked, "Was Askren the official agent/representative of the University?" The very same day, Francis had a long talk with Askren about Wainwright's claims for the current year: "[Askren] understood the cable of April 3, 1926, as a warrant for closing the camp and clearing up matters for 1925–1926; the tentative agreement [with Wainwright] was an attempt to formulate a possible arrangement for the present season, as a starting point for reorganization. Askren made no promise to Wainwright about compensation."[29] Four days later, with

26. On Kelsey's visit to Karanis during this first season, see chapter 9. For a concise review of the first season's work, see Arthur E. R. Boak, "Uncovering a Greco-Roman City in Egypt," *Michigan Alumnus* 32 (1925): 205–8.

27. Cable to Askren, April 3, 1926. See chapter 9, "Outward Bound Once More."

28. See chapter 9, "From London to Rome to Paris to London."

29. Diary, February 5, 1927.

Askren's approval, Francis met Wainwright in the museum library and delivered by hand a letter in which he spoke of Wainwright's "unbridled effrontery" and declared that he was "strictly accountable for the dissemination of libelous untruths."[30] The following day, Wainwright called on him and began in conciliatory terms, saying, "we ought not to be enemies but friends." Francis's diary summarizes his understanding of the discussion.

> Conversation was very unsatisfactory since he insisted on talking about his claim and I refused to discuss it. Disputed claims on State funds need arbitration. He said he thought we were funded privately and couldn't I find his claim out of private monies? He says Starkey lied in declaring he was not invited to camp for a second season; he said also that I never said in his presence that no one but an American citizen could be our Director in Egypt though in London I emphasized this in the presence of Askren and Peterson who remember it clearly.[31]

Francis was happy to get away from Cairo to his colleagues in the Fayoum. There were long talks at the Michigan camp about the practical aspects of work at Dimay, in connection with which he had already written to Feizy in Turkey, asking him to send the Antioch equipment to Askren in the Fayoum. More immediately, details of the timetable for closing the camp at the end of the season were worked out with team members. Francis spent one morning at Askren's clinic, watching the doctor at work, at which time he also learned that Askren had a letter from Magoffin, now president of the AIA, asking him about possible excavation sites and telling him he had twenty-five thousand dollars in prospect.[32] At lunch with him in Cairo the next day to discuss his remuneration and his boys' education, Francis proposed that Askren's fee for his work for Michigan for the year be one thousand dollars, to be applied to the expenses of Leslie and Charles's education, and that Amherst might be a more convenient college than Michigan, since Mrs. Askren would be close by.[33] He also told Askren that when writing to Magoffin, he would recommend Starkey as the only good digger available.

Going from lunch to the Egyptian Museum, Francis found Engelbach,

---

30. February 1927, FWK Papers, box 2, folder 27.

31. Diary, February 10, 1927.

32. Diary, February 14, 1927. Francis remarked that Askren operated without gloves, with chloroform administered by a local helper, and with instruments sterilized in a solution of low-strength bicarbonate and carbolic acid, with the "abdominal incision some 5–6 inches, sewing rapid and strong."

33. At this time, the Askren home in the United States was at Southwell Cottage, East Northfield, MA.

who concurred in the recommendation of Starkey; but when Francis suggested Tebtunis as a site for Magoffin, Engelbach said that "Lacau was the man to take up that matter."[34] Other expedition projects were in the air. Over lunch at Shepheard's, de Prorok proposed the exploration, now that a road had made the area accessible, of the oasis of Siwa in the Western Desert and the excavation of the Temple of Zeus Ammon and its precinct—an ambitious project if ever there was one.[35] At the end of the month, Kirsopp Lake arrived from Port Said to be introduced to Askren and to visit the office in Cairo of the Monastery of St. Catherine at Mount Sinai, from which he subsequently learned that he had been authorized to visit the monastery itself.[36]

Routine business occupied Francis for the ten days prior to his departure from the country: searching for papyri, dividing the Karanis finds, pursuing the support of the Egyptian authorities for the proposed work at Dimay, and packing materials to go to Ann Arbor. Thirty-four packages of books were sent off to Michigan; Nahman brought papyri he had gathered, which Francis took to Edgar for assessment. Indeed, he saw a good deal of Edgar during these days, traveling with him and Alfred Lucas, another British Egyptologist,[37] from Cairo through Gerza (ancient Philadelphia), to the Michigan camp at Karanis, and onward to visit Dimay. Francis proposed to Edgar the exploration of unexcavated parts of that site, the clearing and plotting of the temple area, and "scouting in the neighborhood," while Lucas looked about for glazed pottery. Staying two nights at the camp, Edgar was able to inspect the site and activities and to examine the frescoes that the excavation had uncovered: the Isis and Harpocrates group, the Thracian rider god Heron, and the Mithraic fragment. Lucas took the view that all were removable and suggested alternative methods.[38]

On the question of the allocation of the sixty gold coins from the excavation, Francis was referred to the director of the Greco-Roman Museum in Alexandria, Annibale Evaristo Breccia,[39] whom he visited with the coins. Breccia agreed to refer the division back to Edgar. Thereafter, at a meeting at

---

34. Diary, February 15, 1927. On Lacau, see chapter 9 n. 96.

35. Diary, February 23, 1927.

36. Diary, February 28 and March 3, 1927.

37. Lucas's interest was in ancient Egyptian technology, particularly the coloration of the surface of pots, walls, and floors. His *Ancient Egyptian Materials and Industries* (London: Longmans, Green, 1926) has been revised and reprinted several times.

38. Diary, March 4–6, 1927.

39. A well-known Italian Egyptologist, Breccia (1876–1967) served as director of the museum during 1904–31. Returning to Italy, he would become the rector (Rector Magnifico) of the University of Pisa in 1939.

the Egyptian Museum at which Kelsey, Edgar, and Lacau were present, Lacau allotted thirty-three coins to Ann Arbor and twenty-seven to Alexandria.

Finally, there were bills to pay: taxes were owed on exported materials, and Nahman was due the equivalent of $2,342.25 for various manuscripts and papyri. A last visit to Kondilios, who had some "remarkable literary fragments" for sale, was fruitless: Kondilios said he had paid 150 pounds for them and wanted 165, and he would not listen to Francis's offer of 100 pounds.[40] Up early on March 10 and with ample help from Cook's agents with his baggage, he took a taxi to the station and the train to Alexandria, where he boarded the SS *Esperia* for the voyage to Naples.

KARANIS: AN EXCURSIVE CHRONICLE

The mound that marks the ancient site of Karanis[41] is situated close to the modern village of Kom Aushim, on the northeastern edge of the fertile area known as the Fayoum, some forty miles southwest of Cairo and fifteen miles northeast of Medinet-el-Fayoum, the leading town of the province.[42] Here, some sixty years after the death of Alexander the Great and under the direction of King Ptolemy II, Macedonian veterans were settled alongside native Egyptians in villages, of which Karanis was one (Philadelphia was another), to work the land. A program of land reclamation, the installation of a new system of irrigation, and proximity to Alexandria were significant factors in their prosperous development.

However, by the time of Augustus, when Egypt became, for most purposes, part of the Roman Empire, the irrigation systems had silted up, with

---

40. Diary, March 9, 1927.

41. For a splendid overview of the site and its excavation, see Elaine K. Gazda, ed., *Karanis: An Egyptian Town in Roman Times; Discoveries of the University of Michigan Expedition to Egypt 1924–1935* (Ann Arbor: Kelsey Museum of Archaeology, 1983; 2nd ed., with preface and expanded bibliography by T. G. Wilfong, 2004). See also Boak, "Uncovering a Greco-Roman City in Egypt"; Lauren E. Talalay and Susan E. Alcock, "Karanis, Egypt, 1924–1935," in Talalay and Alcock, *In the Field*, 16–20, with bibliography at 90–91; Terry G. Wilfong, "Fayum, Graeco-Roman Sites," in *Encyclopedia of the Archaeology of Ancient Egypt*, ed. Kathryn A. Bard and Steven Blake Shubert (London: Routledge, 1999), 309–13. A spate of articles and volumes, many of which appeared in the Michigan Humanistic Series (vols. 25, 30, 31, 41–43, 47), have published technical studies of the excavation's results. Work on the Karanis papyri continues.

42. A low-lying area of rich agricultural land west of the Nile, the Fayoum (from an Egyptian word for "lake") was initially a basin almost completely filled by the water of Lake Moeris. Early Hellenistic kings drained away much of that water and reclaimed the land; green fields, orchards, and villages replaced more than half of the lake.

consequent stagnation in agricultural productivity. Economic activity withered, improving only when the Roman army was sent in to clear the blocked ditches and waterways. Thereafter the area again flourished, Egypt became one of the breadbaskets of Rome, and Karanis prospered—even in the face of a heavy burden of taxation, to which the papyri lend eloquent testimony. The village continued to exist—with periods of depression that echoed the situation throughout the empire—until a persistent slowdown beginning in the fourth century led to impoverishment and the abandonment of the site at the end of the fifth.

Farmers had been digging about on the site for decades, searching for the fertilizer formed from disintegrating organic matter, before it attracted the attention of scholars on the lookout for papyri. Among these later nineteenth-century scholars were Bernard Grenfell and Arthur Hunt. Though they found papyri that told them, among other things, the name of the ancient site, they decided that too much of the center of the mound had been removed for a prolonged exploration to be worthwhile. Moreover, they were not alone in their lack of interest as to what other types of archaeological data could tell them about Greco-Roman Egypt: the excavation of Greco-Roman sites in Egypt continued to focus on papyri alone, even though Flinders Petrie had already pointed the way to the importance of all archaeological materials in studying typologies, establishing the phasing of sites, and understanding wider chronologies. Thus, the work of the University of Michigan at Karanis was to reflect a "modern" approach to archaeology.

On visiting Karanis and other sites in the Fayoum with Grenfell in 1920,[43] Kelsey had noted the wealth of archaeological materials exposed and instantly concluded that work at Karanis would not only gather information from papyri but retrieve many other data, all of which would help reconstruct a full picture of life in a Greco-Roman Egyptian village. Archaeology could work shoulder to shoulder with papyrology; information gleaned from one could amplify, support, or correct information supplied by the other. The Michigan team, then, had disregarded Grenfell's view of the value of the site and decided to open previously untouched areas of the mound, with two objectives in mind: the recovery of papyri and other written documents (ostraca), on the one hand, and, on the other, the meticulous recovery of every scrap of archaeological evidence with which to reconstruct the physical con-

---

43. See chapter 8, "Egypt and Italy."

text in which the inhabitants had lived their lives and the papyri had been written. An aspect of Egyptian archaeology hitherto largely ignored could therefore be examined, and a gap in our knowledge of post-Pharaonic Egyptian life could be filled.

Once the decision to excavate Karanis had been taken and permits granted, work began on the construction of the Michigan camp, on November 24, 1924. Excavation of the site followed early in the New Year. The objective of recovering every piece of archaeological evidence, entirely new to the archaeology of Greco-Roman Egypt, required a new system of fieldwork and new methods of recording that paid attention both to the objects themselves and to their places of discovery. In practice, the scheme that was worked out called for a large-scale survey of the zone to be excavated, the division of the surveyed plan into seven areas, and the further splitting of each area into large squares. As the work of excavation advanced, sections were drawn through each square, linking them across the site.

Excavation proceeded square by square, level by level. Excavators identified buildings and streets and disentangled the phasing of the site: the three phases distinguished in the early seasons' work were later refined to five. At each level, the work moved from house to house and room to room, the excavator keeping a daily notebook in which the retrieval of each object was recorded with its place of recovery. Each object was tagged with a label giving the house, the room, and the level of its origin and logged into the season's registration book. Photographs were taken of each house and group of objects in the course of excavation, and—another example of Kelsey's enthusiasm for developments in photography—movies recorded the panoramas of places and events. If the guiding intellect behind the new archaeological thrust of the excavation was Kelsey's, the recording system, both in the field and in registration, was the painstaking work of Peterson.

Kelsey had been right to select Enoch Peterson. Assuming the directorship in the third season, Peterson continued the work through 1935 with unqualified success, publishing with Boak the *Topographical and Architectural Report*.[44] A striking testimony to his character is provided by Charles

---

44. Arthur E. R. Boak and Enoch E. Peterson, *Karanis: Topographical and Architectural Report of Excavations during the Seasons 1924–28*, University of Michigan Studies, Humanistic Series, vol. 25 (Ann Arbor: University of Michigan, 1931).

Brasch,[45] a New Zealander who visited Karanis in 1932 and was a friend of Colin Roberts,[46] who was working on the papyri.

> Enoch Peterson was a classical scholar who ran his expedition with admirable smoothness, quietly spoken, friendly and hospitable, liking good American comfort, but with restraint and just a touch of Puritan rectitude; an upright, kindly, entirely trustworthy man. . . . Peterson was not only capable but a man of taste, as the camp dining room showed. For every meal the long refectory table was laid with a well-ironed cloth of spotless linen and plain good cutlery. Meals were excellent; those of an American who enjoyed good food of all kinds, more varied, rather more lavish than ours at Amarna, and with delicacies added—Bath Olivers, dry ginger. I remember little of the talk, except that it was more adult in tone than ours: it seemed open and receptive to men, to history, to ideas; a large-minded American presiding over an international team being (although no intellectual) more fully a man of his time, more aware of its currents and demands than any of us in our tight little English enclave.[47]

When work began in 1925, parts of the mound rose some fifty feet above the plain, revealing the broken or crumbling mud brick walls of houses, some three stories high. In the early seasons (see fig. 32), the excavators concentrated on the remains of buildings of the topmost level, systematically retrieving their contents; although most often only building foundations of the level survived, it could be dated to the fourth and fifth centuries AD on the basis of the coins and papyri recovered there. These house foundations were supported by the walls of earlier buildings that were better preserved, with basement and second story as well as a ground floor: coins and papyri again provide dates of the second to third centuries AD for this earlier level. These multistoried houses were built in blocks in typical Roman fashion. Mud brick was used for walls (with interior surfaces sometimes stuccoed) and for the stairways linking the different stories, with wood for roofs, ceilings, floors,

---

45. Apparently a man of independent means, Charles Orwell Brasch (1909–73) was a noted editor, poet, and supporter of the arts. In Egypt he joined John Pendlebury (1904–41)—the British archaeologist better known perhaps for his work on Crete (and as a hero of World War II on the island) than for his contributions to Egyptian archaeology—in the excavations at el-Amarna.

46. Colin Henderson Roberts (1909–90) would become lecturer in papyrology at Oxford and a contributor to *The Oxyrhynchus Papyri* (especially during 1941–57).

47. Charles Brasch, *In Egypt,* with an introduction by Margaret Scott (Wellington, New Zealand: Steele Roberts, 2007), 57–59, a reference I owe to the kindness of Larry Berlin.

32. Houses under excavation at Karanis. Kelsey Museum of Archaeology,
University of Michigan 5.2741.Photo: George R. Swain.

doors, and windows. Stone appeared only occasionally and then only in areas
of intensive use (steps leading to an entrance) or in places of visibility (jambs
and lintel of an entrance), to mark the prominence of the owner. Basement
spaces were used for storage; ground and upper floors, built around an open
court, were the focus of domestic life.

Since almost every fragment of evidence was retained and since the dry
climate helped preserve organic material, the number of objects recovered
was enormous. From the houses came furniture and furnishings (chairs,
stools, and tables in wood; textiles and mats; lamps in clay and bronze),
kitchen equipment and products (ovens, hand mills, pestles, mortars, baskets,
foodstuffs), crockery (ceramic cups, plates, bowls, jugs and jars of every shape
and size), and living room utensils (incense stands and pitchers in bronze,
lamps and goblets in glass) (fig. 33), as well as equipment for work in the fields
(pitchforks, sickles, shovels, rope, harness, hoes, cordage), for the workshop
(saws, planes, axes), and for the home (weavers' combs, spindles, whorls, nee-
dles, crochet hooks) (fig. 34). More personal items included shoes, hair combs
and pins, jewelry, cosmetic jars and application sticks, playthings (dice), and

33. Household objects found on a windowsill of House BC 61 at Karanis: glass decanter, jar, plates and dishes, wooden implements for making cloth, lamp, ceramic bowl, and basket. Kelsey Museum of Archaeology, University of Michigan n/n. Photo: Ron Baryash.

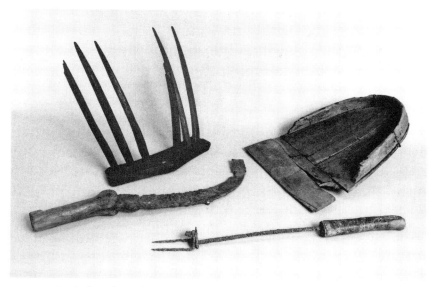

34. Agricultural implements found at Karanis: winnowing shovel, sickle, pitchfork, and cultivator. Kelsey Museum of Archaeology, University of Michigan 3355, 3420, 3738, 3740. Photo: Sue Webb.

35. Papyrus rolls found in the (wood) threshold of a door in House 5026 at Karanis. Kelsey Museum of Archaeology, University of Michigan 5.1801. Photo: George R. Swain.

children's toys (rattles, miniature animals and furniture, dolls in wood and terra-cotta). All these categories of evidence could now be set alongside the written evidence of the coins (of which the first season alone yielded more than 1,100 in bronze and 860 in silver), the ostraca (mostly accounts), and the papyri (fig. 35). Though a few literary fragments were found among the papyri, most were legal documents, contracts, or private letters. The variety is boundless.

As the excavation continued, public buildings also were uncovered. Granaries were conspicuous: ten large and seven smaller ones—resembling, in many respects, the warehouses of the Roman military—emphasized the centrality of agriculture to the life of the village. Many papyri record the receipt of grain paid as tax, and these granaries doubtless stored the tax grain. Temples and their contents lend solid confirmation to the evidence of papyri and inscriptions that speak of religious life at Karanis. Votive offerings, charms and amulets, and images of the gods in terra-cotta, bronze, and stone attest the presence of no fewer than thirty deities. The practice of Christianity came hesitantly and late, perhaps not before AD 300.

Francis had been present at the excavations for a few days during the 1924–25 season,[48] when he had traveled across from Carthage with Isabelle, but he had been unable to visit during the difficult second season. During his ten-week stay in Egypt from December 1926 to March 1927, however, he made several visits to the excavations. Striking discoveries from this third season were the wall paintings he examined with Edgar and Lucas; a pair of letters written by a Roman soldier to his mother (one sent from Portus, the harbor at the mouth of the Tiber, and one from Rome itself); and the hoard of gold coins.[49]

The oldest of the coins are from the reign of Emperor Hadrian (AD 117–38) but were struck later than 128, the year in which Hadrian assumed the title *pater patriae*, with the majority struck during the reign of Antoninus Pius (138–61). Thirty-nine carry portraits of a young Marcus Aurelius; seven, portraits of Faustina the Elder, wife of Antoninus Pius; and a further seven, portraits of Faustina the Younger, wife of Marcus Aurelius. All appear to have been struck between AD 128 and 158. Remarkably well preserved, they support the theory that they were struck in Egypt from dies sent from Rome; and although all the types were previously known and therefore bring little to numismatic research, their appearance in a dusty Egyptian village says something about the economic prosperity of the community in this period—or at least of the individual in whose room they were found.

Idris Bell, after examining the soldier's two letters during a visit to Karanis, suggested that they were written ca. AD 200. Since the handwriting of each is different, it is clear that the soldier, unable to write, made use of scribes, one on arrival at Portus and the other in Rome. The soldier's name was Apollinarius, his mother's Taesis. Sending familiar greetings in the first letter, he tells her where he is and that he has not yet been summoned to Rome but has heard that he will be posted to Misenum; the second letter confirms that he is to go there. These papyri testify to age-old family concerns (filial devotion, maternal worries). Placed alongside the archaeological evidence of daily domestic living and working, they testify to the character of daily life in Karanis eighteen hundred years ago.

---

48. Again, see chapter 9.

49. Francis W. Kelsey, "Fouilles américaines à Kom Ousim (Fayoum)," *Comptes rendus des séances de l'Académie des Inscriptions et Belles-Lettres* (1927): 81–90. The precious letters were found tied together (excavation locus 26-BIC-MI). For one of these letters, with translation, see chapter 7, figs. 16 and 17.

ACROSS EUROPE

Leaving Egypt behind him, Kelsey reached Naples on March 14. He had time to visit Director Maiuri at the museum; consult with Michigan student Nita L. Butler about her work on the houses at Pompeii; and write to Horace Rackham. He had been conscientious in writing to Rackham monthly about his activities and the progress of the work. Now he wrote in both retrospective and prospective terms: "in 1898 I commenced to have an active part in the work of humanistic research in foreign lands through membership on Committees which directed such research in the interests of national organizations in which the University of Michigan was represented." Now it was time to press forward, with the increased strength and rapidly growing reputation of the university, to highlight what Michigan, on its own initiative, was contributing to new knowledge. Francis asked for support for five more years, to the tune of one million dollars.[50] In Rome the next day, he had more consultation with students at the American Academy and discussions with Stevens and Bishop, before saying his good-byes and turning in the keys to his study. As he left Rome for the last time, the management at the Pensione Boos said they would "have a room for us with running water and private bath next year," and he confided to his diary, "Again I leave Rome on a lovely cloudless morning with deep regret. I yearn to return to that study and work there away from the telephone and other distractions of Ann Arbor." It was not to be.

Taking the noon train for Paris on a typical spring day and gazing at farmers at work in the fields, he found his agricultural interests had not deserted him: he noted the farmers "for the most part plowing, spring wheat thriving." Passing through Paris and enjoying a smooth channel crossing, he was at the Cambridge House Hotel in London before midnight on the next day.[51] He immediately resumed his normal London activities: writing letters[52] and memoranda and visiting the British Museum. There he handed over to Bell for his assessment the papyri acquired by joint purchase, the papyri from Karanis, the Coptic papyri, and the fragments of Greek manuscripts he had bought. He discussed the gold coins with Harold Mattingly, who concluded from their freshness that they had been struck in Egypt, and he talked over with G. F. Hill a collection of electrotype coins for which Hill thought that

---

50. Kelsey to Rackham, March 14, 1927, FWK Papers, box 2, folder 28.

51. Diary, March 18, 1927.

52. Among the letters was one to President Little, telling him that Kelsey had the gold coins with him in London (Kelsey to Little, March 1927, FWK Papers, box 2, folder 28).

"not a penny more than $20,000 should be offered."[53] He met with Crum to discuss the Coptic papyri and manuscripts and began packing up the materials to go with him back to the United States: the Greek Psalter and lectionary bought in Cairo, the Karanis papyri, the Greek manuscript fragments, and the Arabic manuscripts. He spent an entire day[54] preparing a paper on Karanis that he was soon due to give to the Académie des Inscriptions et Belles-Lettres in Paris.

Traveling overnight by train and boat and across Paris through the rain by taxi, he reached the Abbé Chabot on March 25 in time for lunch before the meeting of the Académie. He was not feeling well, his diary now mentioning for the first time the ailment that was to kill him: "feeling wretched on account of lameness of muscles of chest [i.e., chest pains], culminating after several days of soreness."[55] They discussed the unsatisfactory situation in Tunisia: in Carthage they were unable to come to an agreement with the landowners about property on the Hill of Juno, and at Utica the property company that had bought out the Count de Chabannes was more likely to excavate the site itself than to yield control of an excavation to Americans. In the face of these difficulties, Francis told Gsell later in the day that "now that Utica was out of the way," his preference was for a project to examine the churches of Algeria. The Académie met at 3:30 p.m., with Francis's paper, read by Chabot, the second item on the agenda after business matters.[56] All went well. Returning to London the next day, a storm in the channel made for a rough crossing.[57]

On March 27, he "stayed in all day—muscles of chest sore so that it hurts more," but the next day, he was as active as ever. Sixteen letters were mailed off and bills paid. At Spink and Son in Picadilly, he picked up three rare early Roman bronze coins (an *as, semis,* and a *sextans*) that Hoskier had left there as a gift for the university, and he was told that the Hadrianic gold coins of the

53. Harold Mattingly (1884–1964), assistant keeper of the British Museum's Department of Coins and Medals, was a prolific historian and numismatist who basically rewrote the history of Roman coinage. George Francis Hill (1867–1948), also of that department, was an expert in Greek coins.

54. Diary, March 23, 1927.

55. Dr. Michael O'Donnell, a cardiologist at St. Joseph Mercy Hospital in Ann Arbor, was kind enough to give me modern equivalents of the language Francis used to describe his complaint (personal communication, September 27, 2007). Dr. O'Donnell's medical explanations appear bracketed in the text.

56. See n. 49. Francis passed around examples of the gold coins and papyri from the recent Karanis season.

57. Diary, March 26, 1927.

Karanis hoard were worth some twenty-five or thirty pounds apiece and the Antonine between eight and ten pounds. At the British Museum, he paid his respects to Kenyon and Edwards and made arrangements for the trunk packed with the papyri and manuscripts to be sealed, roped up, and delivered to the United States Lines. Bell and Crum joined him for lunch at his hotel (Bell bringing an inventory of the papyri), before he packed up his belongings and took the train to Southampton to board the SS *Leviathan*. Once on board, "Dr. Stewart took me in hand promptly—drastic treatment."

JOURNEY'S END

The next day, he felt better—"the drastic treatment of Dr. Stewart is producing an effect—more comfortable than I have been for ten days"—and his letters were mailed when the liner picked up passengers at Cherbourg. He took his meals at the chief engineer's table, read the newspapers, wrote letters, and began a paper on Karanis for the meetings of the Classical Association of the Midwest and South (CAMWS) in Ann Arbor in the middle of the month. But the soreness and discomfort in his chest nagged at him, and the day before the liner arrived in New York, he commented, "muscular tension [i.e., tightness across the chest] worse than any previous day since starting; started the medicine again—three tablets every two hours and a capsule every four hours. Did not attend service."[58] After seeing his baggage (three trunks and two suitcases) through customs, he hurried to the Murray Hill Hotel, where a message from Fred, asking him to call, was waiting for him. Francis's diary entry tells it all—"Too ill to do so." Commenting on the journey on board, it continues, "A more comfortable room or voyage could hardly be imagined. Yet it has been a far from agreeable experience on account of the muscular tension and soreness about the chest and shoulders."

Though evidently in some pain, he moved quickly the next morning to complete his business in New York. He sent a telegram to Isabelle and a night letter to Dr. Cowie in Ann Arbor, asking whether he could see him on the morning of April 7 and explaining "the nature of the muscular trouble." Fund-raising was a matter of urgency, too. On a meeting with Dr. George Edgar Vincent,[59] president of the Rockefeller Foundation, at 4:00 p.m., he

---

58. Diary, April 3, 1927.

59. Educated at Yale and the University of Chicago, Vincent became a moving force in the Chautauqua Institution in his early career, then, successively, professor of sociology at Chicago (1904), president of the University of Minnesota (1911), and president of the Rockefeller Foundation (1917).

notes, "I asked whether if we could secure $75,000 for 5 years from other sources, the Rockefeller funds would furnish a like amount for excavation and publication. There are five boards. I am to write him a statement about the matter, and he will see what can be done. A favorable report from Breasted would help." A long conversation on the phone with Magoffin concerning Van Deman's work and the possibility of an AIA excavation at Tebtunis preceded lunch with William F. Kenny, who handed Francis one check for five thousand dollars for the university and another for twenty thousand francs for the Abbé Chabot before announcing that he would bring New York governor Alfred E. Smith and Walter P. Chrysler (founder of the Chrysler Corporation) to Ann Arbor for lunch with President Little. Coming by the hotel at four o'clock, his brother Fred accompanied Francis to the station to catch the Wolverine at five o'clock for Detroit. It was the last time he would see him.[60]

On arrival in Ann Arbor, Francis went straight to the hospital, where Dr. Cowie gave him a full physical examination followed by electrical treatment for soreness of the chest.[61] Francis noted that the treatment could be "efficacious if started at once" but "in my case it seems too late, as it is nearly a month since my soreness in the chest muscles started." After going to the University Hospital for X-rays,[62] he went to his office, delivered plaster casts of the Karanis coins to Swain for photography, and talked over with Harden his work on the Roman glass.

For his first two weeks at home, his time was divided between the hospital and the university, as far as his discomfort would allow. He did not for a moment cut back on his workload. On his second day at the hospital, Dr. Cowie prescribed a course of tablets for him, two of five grams each (though he does not tell us of what or how frequently),[63] "which relieved the soreness somewhat"; later in the evening, after a long electrical treatment, he slept better. During the day, he had delivered Kenny's check to the university secretary, written several letters, and had a long talk with Sanders. On another day, after meeting with President Little to discuss the funding of the Near East work for the next five years—when he naturally took the opportunity to mention

---

60. Diary, April 6, 1927.

61. Such electrical treatments, says O'Donnell, were intended to stimulate the muscles.

62. There he ran into Regent Clements (see chapter 6 n. 32), who was in town for his twice yearly checkup.

63. The tablets prescribed were likely, in the opinion of O'Donnell, opium or an opiate derivative, having the effect of relieving pain, dilating the veins, and bringing more oxygen to the muscle system.

Kenny's generosity and the possibility of support from the Rockefeller Foundation—he went for a walk with Easton and was given "another thorough electrical treatment before going to bed—beneficial."[64] On Palm Sunday, he attended church, wrote letters, and cabled Peterson, "Karanis financed next year. Good prospect Dimay." On another day, he conferred with Charles Sink about the School of Music and called on Dean Effinger; on another, Easton spent the evening with him; and on yet another, Swain ran through the slides of the gold coins he had prepared for the paper for the CAMWS conference. Francis wrote to Isabelle every day.[65]

On April 13, the day before the conference opened, his diary records "improvement in rheumatism but very slow."[66] He spoke too soon. After attending President Little's welcome address, Francis suffered "a severe attack of intercostal [rib] pain on the left side, long electrical treatment, ineffective."[67] In the morning of April 15, the "intercostal pain continued: afternoon Dr. Cowie strapped the ribs together with long strips of adhesive tape."[68] He was due to read his paper, "New Light on Greco-Roman Egypt," in the evening; but not feeling up to it, he asked John Winter to read it for him: "At 7.30 Dr. Cowie had a drug ready for me: this I took and went over to the Natural Science Auditorium where Winter and Swain had everything ready. On being introduced I said a few words of greeting and found it impossible to make myself heard; as I came forward the audience rose in greeting." It must have been obvious to all that his health was failing.

He stayed in all the next day, as visitors came and went. His interest in the AIA and the world of business was as keen as ever. Magoffin, telling him that his subscription for work in the Fayoum had failed, agreed that if a permit for work at Siwa was acquired, it should be in the name of the AIA. H. J. Abbott, a local businessman,[69] thought that the house at 810 Oxford would be suitable for sale to a small fraternity or sorority, and Kelsey reports that when Abbott added that he was going to buy "Mr. Earhart's share of stock in his Gasoline Company, I asked if I could get $2500 worth."[70] Although he began to decline

---

64. Diary, April 9, 1927.

65. Diary, April 10, 11, and 12, 1927.

66. According to O'Donnell, "rheumatism" was at the time a catchall term for overall aching.

67. Diary, April 14, 1927.

68. The taping, intended to shore up cracked or damaged ribs, was misguided (says O'Donnell): it would have had a negative effect, bringing more pressure on the rib cage.

69. Horatio Johnson Abbott (1876–1948), once the publisher of the *Ann Arbor Record* (1900–1902), was locally prominent in real estate.

70. Diary, April 16, 1927.

social invitations and regretted that he could not be in church on Easter Sunday, meetings continued: with A. G. Ruthven and Carl Guthe[71] about the exhibition of classical materials in the new Museum of Anthropology and Guthe's trip to Egypt to study the Karanis pottery; with Harden about work in Egypt; with Worrell (on more than one occasion) about the Yahuda collection and cooperation with Crum on a Coptic dictionary and with Spiegelberg[72] on Demotic papyri and ostraca; and with Leslie Askren, who was doing better at his college studies. Throughout, Kelsey kept up his daily visits to campus and his correspondence.

For the next week, the pattern of his life remained the same, with him shuttling back and forth between hospital and campus. Four manuscripts arrived from Géjou for consideration with the lectionary he had acquired earlier. At the Dictaphone office, he dropped off two hundred invitations, personally signed, for members of the Schoolmasters' Club.[73] He sent a cable to Fletcher-Allen that read, "Hope arrange conference New York early May"; made arrangements for a student, Sally Clarkson, to work in Paris, Vienna, Munich, and Italy; and took up with Harden his proposal to study for a Ph.D. in classical archaeology with a thesis on Roman glass. But his health was not improving. On April 24, he noted, "rheumatism went over to the right side: obliged to sit still all day long. Miss Hoskins strapped the right side, afterwards somewhat more comfortable." He recovered and the next day attended a meeting of the executive committee of the Michigan Schoolmasters' Club, followed by "dinner at the Union ($7.50)." Earlier in the day, "Dr. Canfield made inspection of nose and throat and found no source of infection to cause rheumatism." The physicians seemed baffled. On one day, a long discussion with Swain preceded a visit in the evening to former president Hutchins and Mrs. Hutchins.[74]

Francis's diary continues to intersperse comments about his health with the record of daily events. April 27 was a "dull day—no pain, but lassitude,"[75] though he was alert enough to note that "Mrs. Sanders came to the hospital—

---

71. Carl Eugen Guthe (1893–1974), the son of physicist Karl E. Guthe (1866–1915; see chapter 7, "Research and Publication"), received his B.A. from Michigan (1914) and degrees in anthropology from Harvard (M.A. 1915, Ph.D. 1917). At Michigan, he was the new museum's associate director (1922) and eventually director (1929), would cofound the Department of Anthropology in 1929, and was named director of university museums in 1936.

72. On philologist Wilhelm Spiegelberg, see n. 16.

73. Presumably there was a mailing service at the Dictaphone office.

74. Diary, April 26, 1927.

75. According to O'Donnell, "lassitude" implies myocardial infarction (heart attack).

she has the same room on the third floor which Isabelle occupied so long." The next day, a "bad day—lassitude," did not keep him from opening the meetings of the Schoolmasters' Club in Room B of the Law Building or from writing letters. The day after that, "somewhat better," he went to campus to collect his mail, to confer with Carl Guthe about Egypt, and to cable Peterson as follows: "Peterson Fayoum Approve Appointment Yeivin Commencing July 1st." Saturday and Sunday were both quiet days: he ate meals regularly for the first time in a week, Easton called, and as news of his illness seeped out, people began "sending flowers, roses and carnations."[76]

On Monday he met with Bonner and Sanders to discuss fellowship applications, on Tuesday "more roses" arrived in his room, on Wednesday he dictated pages of his memorandum to George Vincent at the Rockefeller Foundation, and he sent out his letters each day. The diary does not signal any medical event, though the handwriting (never easy to read) deteriorates. On Thursday, after Sanders and Bishop visited him in hospital for a conference that he was alert enough to mention in the diary, he described himself as "too stupid to read or write."[77] On Friday it was Swain's turn to go to the hospital. Among topics they discussed were photographs of the Karanis Demotic ostraca for Spiegelberg and what titles to give the movie films. When Francis asked him, "shall we develop movie photography in our work in Egypt?" Swain said " 'Yes,' much informed on the subject since we first considered it in 1924. If we do go into movie photography we agree that it must be on a strictly professional basis, with best equipment. 'Baby' camera not adequate."[78] Francis never stopped thinking big and never lost his interest in new technologies. The entries for this day, May 6, are the last in the diary. He was still writing letters, the very last mentioned in the diary being to his wife, "IBK."

His life lasted another week, and he was working, or attempting to work, surrounded by his books and papers in the hospital, until the very end. Swain had a meeting with him on the morning of Saturday, May 14, talking over plans for the five-year program of research Francis had in mind. Swain left at about 11:00 a.m. A few moments later, Francis passed into a coma. He died at noon. Easton was with him at the last.[79]

76. Diary, April 30 and May 1, 1927.
77. To O'Donnell, this implies very low blood pressure.
78. Diary, May 6, 1927.
79. *Detroit News*, May 17, 1927.

AFTERMATH

Isabelle arrived from California on May 16,[80] and the funeral took place at the First Presbyterian Church two days later. Shortly before the funeral, colleagues commented to reporters on aspects of Francis's life that they knew well. George Swain, for example, remarked that Kelsey "had a tremendous fund of learning at his command but when in doubt he never hesitated to call in experts to supplement his judgment" and, moreover, that "few appreciated that the man among other remarkable qualities possessed those of a consummate diplomat. Few other expeditions maintained the same cordial relations with the Egyptian and Turkish governments as did that of the university."[81] Orma Fitch Butler noted,

> It was for us to worry whether his enthusiasm would not prove too much for his physical strength. At 68 after a distinguished career which won the official recognition of three foreign governments, when he might well have devoted the rest of his life to the writing and publication of works long planned but never begun, he was preparing to direct a further expeditionary program covering five years in the field.[82]

The family had wanted a quiet event, but requests from the university community and Ann Arbor people wishing to pay their respects were so heartfelt that the funeral was opened to the public. The pastor of the church, officiating, gave a generous address, to which President Little added the following remarks:

> Francis W. Kelsey will remain in the memory of all who knew him as a tremendous source of enthusiasm and energy in the encouragement of creative scholarship wherever he found it. Combining in rare degree tact with pertinacity, broad vision with a mastery of detail and high executive ability with vivid and inspiring imagination, he has served for almost 40 years as a wise counselor and loyal friend to hundreds of Michigan students and as a commanding figure nationally and internationally recognized among scholars in his chosen field. Original, vigorous—always building, planning, organizing—his life was so interwoven with that of the university that his

---

80. She had been staying for the winter with Ruth and her infant granddaughter, Catherine Constance (1927–31).

81. *Detroit News,* May 16, 1927.

82. Ibid.

place was peculiarly his own, and no future circumstances can ever destroy or modify the impress of his strength and individuality.[83]

Immediately after the service, the funeral procession made its way to Forest Hill Cemetery, where Francis was buried—not a stone's throw from the grave of his distinguished predecessor, Henry Frieze, whose example he had so closely followed.

On the day of the funeral, the University School of Music closed at 3:00 p.m. to honor their longtime president, and the next UMS May Festival concert after his death was dedicated to his memory. On May 27, the regents wrote to Isabelle, at length and in grateful terms, of his accomplishments, capacities, and character, adopting the following resolution:

> Resolved: That the Regents hereby express their great appreciation of the unique service rendered to the University of Michigan by the late Professor Francis Willey Kelsey whose death has been a cause of great sorrow to the members of the Board, and that they extend to Mrs. Kelsey and her family their deepest sympathy.

His colleague David Robinson, in a tribute written for the *American Journal of Archaeology,* commented on "a new monumental work on Pompeii for which he and his students had been making for years special studies at Pompeii";[84] on his generosity in furnishing "so much new research material for classical scholars"; on his "unique capacity for organization and a rare faculty for raising money to further archaeological investigation"; and, from the heart, on his "loving personality who was such a help in the field as well as in the study, as I can personally testify."[85]

In Munich the German scholars responsible for the *Thesaurus Linguae Latinae* expressed their appreciation of Francis and the part he had played in saving the *Thesaurus* during the dark days after World War I, by incorporating a memorial of him—in the form of four lines of Latin verse celebrating his generosity and lamenting his death—at the front of their next issue.[86] In

---

83. *Ann Arbor Times-News,* May 18, 1927.

84. In 1949 the Italian government would award Francis a medal, commemorating the two hundredth anniversary (1948) of the first excavations at Pompeii, in recognition of his contributions to Pompeian studies. Accepted by Easton, then serving in the U.S. diplomatic corps in Lisbon, it was sent by him to Professor Winter in Ann Arbor (*Ann Arbor News,* October 11, 1949).

85. David M. Robinson, "Archaeological News, 1927," *AJA* 31 (1927): 357–58.

86. Printed on heavy black-edged cards, it was also sent to numerous prominent classical scholars.

Amsterdam representatives of the Royal Academy of Science, on hearing of the publication at long last of the translation of Hugo Grotius,[87] wrote to Kelsey,

> The literary branch begs to express to you and to your collaborators its sincerest [con]gratulations on the publication and expresses its conviction that a good new translation of Grotius' book of 1625 [*sic*] in the English language will prove to be not only of great use to scholars, but equally to those, who interest themselves in modern international organization or who occupy leading positions in that organization.[88]

Dated June 7, 1927, this letter was never seen by its intended recipient; nor did he see the volume itself (see fig. 36).

The obituaries, published rapidly, were both factual and rich in praise. John Winter spoke of Francis as a sturdy champion of the classics, of his deep interest in problems of teaching, of his energy and commitment (he "carried his full share of class work until 1920"), and of his "ceaseless activity in planning, organizing, and directing large projects," behind which lay his wish to "encourage scholarship and provide the means of research."[89] *Art and Archaeology* editor Arthur Riggs spoke of his being "one of the most indefatigable of workers, a human dynamo working with an energy, smoothness and precision in his sixty-ninth year that far outstripped the best efforts of many noted men in their physical prime."[90] Kelsey's fellow editor of the Humanistic Series, Henry Sanders, commented,

> In the University of Michigan he was conspicuous from the first for his initiative and his energy. . . . He was a most inspiring teacher, a broad and

---

87. A review by Dutch law professor and legal scholar Cornelis van Vollenhoven notes that, despite 1925 appearing on the title page, "its first part (Book I) was not published until May, 1927, its second part (Book II) not until quite recently, and its third part (Book III, and indices) is still expected" (*American Journal of International Law* 21.3 [July 1927]: 628).

88. James Brown Scott, "Editorial Comment: Francis W. Kelsey—In Memoriam," *American Journal of International Law* 21.3 (July 1927): 522–24. Kelsey's long-awaited translation was, in fact, of the rare 1646 edition of *De Jure Belli ac Pacis* (see chapter 7, "Research and Publication").

89. John Garrett Winter, "Francis Willey Kelsey," obituary, *Classical Journal* 23.1 (1927): 4, 6.

90. Arthur Stanley Riggs, "Francis Willey Kelsey," *Art and Archaeology* 23.6 (1927): 272, 284. Riggs (1879–1952) was secretary of the Washington (D.C.) Society of the AIA (1925–35), having replaced Carroll, who had followed Robinson. He was a writer of travel books and popular histories, including *With Three Armies: On and Behind the Western Front* (Indianapolis: Bobbs-Merrill, 1918).

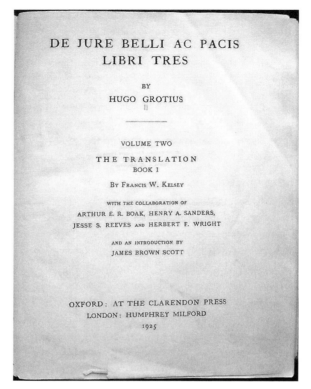

DE JURE BELLI AC PACIS
LIBRI TRES

BY

HUGO GROTIUS

VOLUME TWO

THE TRANSLATION
BOOK I

By Francis W. Kelsey

WITH THE COLLABORATION OF
ARTHUR E. R. BOAK, HENRY A. SANDERS,
JESSE S. REEVES AND HERBERT F. WRIGHT

AND AN INTRODUCTION BY
JAMES BROWN SCOTT

OXFORD: AT THE CLARENDON PRESS
LONDON: HUMPHREY MILFORD
1925

36. Title page of Kelsey's translation of Hugo Grotius's *De Jure Belli ac Pacis* (Oxford: Clarendon, 1925 [1926]). Photo: Mary Pedley.

accurate scholar, an investigator of ability, but even more conspicuous as an organizer and director of research. Always kindly and generous in his attitude to others, he harbored no resentment at criticism, even when unfair and undeserved, but he was never influenced by it to abandon plans and projects which he believed were right.[91]

LEGACY

A sense of the value of international collaboration is one component of Francis's legacy. Speaking eloquently to this point are the positive results of his

---

91. Henry A. Sanders, "Francis Willey Kelsey," obituary, *Classical Philology* 22.3 (July, 1927): 308–10.

work with Mau and Della Corte in Italy; with Grenfell, C. C. Edgar, and Lacau in Egypt; with Halil Bey and Feizy in Turkey; and with Delattre and
Chabot in Tunisia. Moreover, his cooperation with Kenyon, Edwards, and
Bell at the British Museum brought to the University of Michigan manuscripts and papyri of enormous educational and historical value. Another
telling part of his international legacy is the unprecedented approach to excavation at Karanis, at his initiative and direction, which effectively revolutionized Greco-Roman archaeology in Egypt.[92]

At the national level, his legacy is most evident in the increased strength of
the AIA, in the movement for the conservation of ancient sites, in new ways
of teaching the ancient languages, and in educational outreach. The AIA grew
rapidly under his leadership, his support for the Antiquities Act of 1906
identified him as a proponent of archaeological conservation, his introduction of fresher ways of teaching was widely accepted, and his advocacy of
teaching programs that reached out to the general public—whether nationwide (such as those on behalf of the AIA), regional (Chautauqua Institution),
or more local—proved popular.

At the University of Michigan, his leadership set the Latin Department in
directions in which it arguably still leads the country: unswerving support for
research and publication, the development of new teaching methods, its great
strength in archaeology and papyrology. His teaching populated high schools
throughout the Midwest with teachers of competence and flair and provided
graduate programs with soundly based and contextually alert Latinists. His
enthusiasm for graduate work paved the way for doctoral programs in Greek
and Latin that go from strength to strength and for an interdepartmental program in classical archaeology—incorporating the study of art, archaeology,
history, language, and anthropology—in which he would have rejoiced. In a
sense, too, the very existence of the Department of the History of Art today is
due to him, since he was instrumental in persuading the regents to appoint
the first professor of fine art and to authorize the organization of a department.

Kelsey's dogged agitation for support from the university for the publication of research, not only research by Michigan faculty members but that by
other scholars as well, resulted in the launch of the Michigan Humanistic Series, which formed the springboard for the University of Michigan Press.
Similarly, from the moment of his arrival in Ann Arbor, he had stressed the
centrality of music in education and pushed presidents and regents year after

---

92. See above, "Karanis: An Excursive Chronicle."

year to incorporate the Ann Arbor School of Music into the university. Recognition of the legitimacy of music as a key component in the humanities and of the importance of its formal presence in the curricula of the university would finally be achieved two years after Francis's death.[93] Another musical legacy from Francis—one to the city of Ann Arbor and indeed to the state of Michigan as much as to the university—is the University Musical Society, under whose aegis the School of Music had originally operated. Organizationally and financially independent of the university and struggling at the time of founder Henry Frieze's death, the UMS had found a true champion in Francis, who helped drive it forward during his long presidency.

On campus, his hand can be detected in many places. A member of the president's Special Grounds Committee, his grand plan was for a nucleus of buildings for the arts on the north side of campus—a museum of art, an auditorium, a school of music, and a hall of the humanities. He had striven to raise funds for these projects and, for one tantalizing moment, had been close to a commitment from the Carnegie people. He did see the creation of one of these buildings: Hill Auditorium, in whose architectural plans he had been directly involved. In addition—after plans for a new building adjacent to Hill Auditorium in 1957 were shelved for lack of funds—in 1963 the School of Music moved into a visually spectacular and well-equipped complex designed by Eero Saarinen. Moreover, Alumni Memorial Hall, which, from its opening in 1910, had in part served to house the university's art, became wholly an art museum in 1966.[94] Another mark of his presence on campus is the collection of manuscripts and papyri in the Hatcher Graduate Library, the most remarkable and possibly the very best such collection in America. In this context, it is worth quoting at length from a letter written to him by university librarian Bishop.

> I cannot close this letter acknowledging the receipt of this material without expressing my very keen sense of the extraordinary service which you have rendered not only to the University of Michigan and its library, but to the cause of historical and classical scholarship the world over, by securing these papyri and manuscripts for careful editing and publication. The possession of this material of itself is sufficient to put the Library of the University of Michigan in a class with the great university libraries of

---

93. That the university possesses the remarkable Stearns collection of musical instruments is likewise due to Francis's vision.

94. After three years of work, a restored and greatly expanded University of Michigan Museum of Art reopened in March 2009.

Europe. While there are a number of manuscripts in American libraries, they are chiefly late manuscripts in Latin—mostly Books of Hours—and only occasionally possessing any literary or historical value. The papyri which you have gathered are extremely important from both a historical and literary point of view. The parchment manuscripts are undoubtedly of significance in the textual criticism of the New Testament and for an understanding of the liturgy and music of the Orthodox Greek Church. My long acquaintance with you, dating in fact from the first year of your service as Professor in the University of Michigan, perhaps gives me the right to dwell longer on the service to American scholarship which will result from the mere possession of these documents, in addition to their intrinsic value. It is a great thing to have saved them from destruction for publication to the learned world. It is a further service, and one no less worthy, to have given to this University the means of publishing a series of documents of first rate importance to the world of letters. The work on the Freer manuscripts has already shed distinction on the University of Michigan; the work on the manuscript of the Minor Prophets, now in my custody thanks to your activity and zeal, will add further distinction; and the publication of the papyri and of a competent treatise on the liturgical and musical manuscripts will, I am sure, increase the repute not alone of the scholars performing it, but of the University in which they serve. I am happy to be the custodian of this material, and to realize that thanks in great part to the studies begun under your direction and continued under your friendly counsel, I am enabled to value them as they deserve and to give some aid in their proper care and publication.[95]

The most visible mark of Kelsey's legacy, however, is the museum that bears his name. At the time of his death, the archaeological objects he had collected for the university over the years primarily as teaching aids were kept in different places around campus: in his office, in rooms and corridors in Alumni Memorial Hall, and in the University Library. To these materials had been added the increasingly imposing collection of papyri and the excavation materials from Karanis. They were so numerous and scattered by 1927 and so awkward to use that the regents were obliged finally to acquiesce to Francis's long-standing demand for a suitable building for them. So Newberry Hall—though originally constructed in 1890–91 for the use of members of the Students' Christian Association and far from ideal for museum purposes—was designated the Museum of Archaeology, John Winter was appointed its first

---

95. Bishop to Kelsey, November 8, 1920, FWK Papers, box 1, folder 10.

director, and the materials were gathered together there. It did not, however, bear Kelsey's name until 1953, when, at the urging of Peterson and belatedly, to mark the twenty-fifth anniversary of Francis's death, the regents endorsed the renaming of the building.[96] Today, the museum—by housing and caring for its collections of Greek, Roman, Near Eastern, Coptic, and Islamic materials; by conducting fieldwork in Mediterranean lands; by bringing ancient objects to life in exhibitions for the benefit of the general public as well as the university; by promoting vigorous programs of outreach in innovative ways; by offering archaeological data to scholars and students to study and publish and for instructors to use in teaching situations; and by housing the students of the graduate program in classical art and archaeology—is bringing to life Francis W. Kelsey's vision of multifaceted humanistic education in a productive, vibrant university, a legacy truly worthy of the man.

---

96. Three years earlier, in 1950, the regents had also designated one of the residence halls in the newly erected South Quadrangle in his memory ([Herbert] Watkins to Diel, March 21, 1951, private collection of Easton Kelsey Jr., Rochester, NY).

Bibliography

SELECTED WORKS BY FRANCIS WILLEY KELSEY

1881. "The Study of Latin in Collegiate Education." *LFUR* 2.6 (April): 54–56. Expanded and modified in *Education* 3.3 (January–February 1883): 260–70.

1881. "The Political Character and Aims of Julius Caesar." *LFUR* 2.9 (September): 95–96.

1882. Ed. *Cicero, "De Senectute" and "De Amicitia," with Introduction and Notes*, by James S. Reid. Boston: John Allyn. 7th ed., 1896.

1883. Editorial. *LFUR* 3: 36, 69, 134.

1884. Ed. *Lucretius, "De Rerum Natura," with an Introduction and Notes to Books I, III, and V.* Boston: John Allyn. 6th ed., 1906.

1886. Ed. *Caesar's "Gallic War," with an Introduction, Notes, and Vocabulary.* Boston: John Allyn. 7th ed., Boston: Allyn & Bacon, 1895. 10th ed., 1899. 21st ed. 1927.

1889. Ed., with Andreas C. Zenos. *Xenophon's "Anabasis," Books I–IV, with an Introduction, Notes, and Vocabulary.* Boston: Allyn & Bacon. 3rd ed., 1892.

1889. *An Outline of Greek and Roman Mythology.* Boston: Allyn & Bacon.

1890. "Outlines in Roman Archaeology and Life by Members of the Class in Horace, 1st Semester, 1889–1890." Ann Arbor: Register Press.

1891. *Fifty Topics in Roman Antiquities, with References.* Boston: Allyn & Bacon.

1891. *Topical Outline of Latin Literature, with References.* Boston: Allyn & Bacon.

1891. Ed. *Selections from Ovid, with an Introduction, Notes, and Vocabulary.* Boston: Allyn & Bacon.

1892. Ed. *Select Orations and Letters of Cicero, with an Introduction, Notes, and Vocabulary.* Boston: Allyn & Bacon.

1896. "The Presbyterian Church and the University of Michigan." Address before the Michigan Synod, Adrian, October 9, 1895. Published the next summer as a supplement to the *Michigan Presbyterian* (August 13).

1897. Ed. *The Religious Census of the State Universities and of the Presbyterian Colleges in the Collegiate Year 1896–97.* Ann Arbor: Wesleyan Guild of the Methodist Episcopal Church.

1899. Ed. and trans. *Pompeii: Its Life and Art,* by August Mau. New York: Macmillan, 1899. 2nd ed. 1902.

1906. "The State Universities and the Churches." In "Proceedings of the Conference on Religious Education," *University of Illinois Bulletin* 3.8, pt. 2 (January 8): 39–45.

1906. "The Cues of Caesar." *Classical Journal* 2.2 (December): 211–38.

1907. "Hirtius' Letter to Balbus and the Commentaries of Caesar." *Classical Philology* 2.1 (January): 92–93.

1908. "Codrus's Chiron and a Painting from Herculaneum." *AJA* 12 (January): 30–38.

1908. "Is There a Science of Classical Philology?" *Classical Philology* 3.4 (October): 369–85.

1908. "Greek in the High School, and the Question of the Supply of Candidates for the Ministry." *School Review* 16.9 (November): 561–79.

1910. With Arthur Fairbanks. "The Excavation of Cyrene." *Classical Weekly* 4.6 (November 5): 46–47.

1911. "The Tragedy at Cyrene." *Bulletin of the AIA* 2.3 (June): 111–14.

1911. Ed. *Latin and Greek in American Education, with Symposia on the Value of Humanistic Studies.* New York: Macmillan. 2nd ed., 1927.

1912. "Thirty-third Annual Report of the President of the Archaeological Institute of America." *Bulletin of the AIA* 3.4 (October): 191–201.

1913. "The Eighteenth Michigan Classical Conference." *School Review* 21.3 (March): 191–200.

1918. "The New Humanism." *Art and Archaeology* 7.1–2:14–29.

1918. *C. Iulii Caesaris, Commentarii Rerum Gestarum; Caesar's Commentaries: The "Gallic War," Books I–IV, with selections from Books V–VII and from the "Civil War"; with an Introduction, Notes, a Companion to Caesar and a Vocabulary.* Boston: Allyn & Bacon.

1918. "The Tomb of Virgil." *Art and Archaeology* 7.9:265–71.

1919. "Theodor Mommsen." *Classical Journal* 14.4:224–36.

1923. "A Waxed Tablet of the Year 128 A.D." *TAPA* 54:187–95.

1925. "The Second Michigan Expedition to the Near East." *Michigan Alumnus* 31 (1925): 459.

1925. "A Picture Map of Rome in a Manuscript of Valerius Maximus." *TAPA* 56:242–51.

1925. Ed. and trans., with Arthur E. R. Boak, Henry Sanders, Jesse S. Reeves, and Herbert F. Wright. *Hugo Grotius, "De Jure Belli ac Pacis," Libri Tres* [1646]. Oxford: Clarendon.

1926. "Carthage, Ancient and Modern." *Art and Archaeology* 21.2 (February): 55–67.

1926. *Excavations at Carthage, 1925: A Preliminary Report.* New York: Macmillan.

1927. "Fouilles américaines à Kom Ousim (Fayoum)." *Comptes rendus des séances de l'Académie des Inscriptions et Belles-Lettres,* 81–90.

COLLECTIONS

Archaeological Institute of America, Boston University, Boston, MA
    AIA Archives, boxes 10–19
Bentley Historical Library, University of Michigan, Ann Arbor, MI
    Board of Regents (University of Michigan), *Proceedings*
    Francis Willey Kelsey Papers, 1894–1928 (including diaries)
    Henry Simmons Frieze Papers
    Kelsey Museum of Archaeology Papers (including correspondence)
    Thomas Spencer Jerome Papers
Lake Forest College, Lake Forest, IL
    Special Collections, Donnelley and Lee Library (includes copies of *LFUR*)
Private Collection of Easton Kelsey Jr., Rochester, NY
    Diel, Ruth Kelsey. "Francis W. Kelsey in Lighter Vein." 1952. Typescript. Includes personal reminiscence of Ruth and others.
    Kelsey, Charlotte Badger. "Random Notes on Memories of Father." January 25, 1957. Typescript.
    Kelsey, Easton T. "At 15 I Look at '19: Letters to Alfred MacLaren White of Ann Arbor, Michigan on European Trip in 1919–1920." Typescript.
Rush Rhees Library, University of Rochester, Rochester, NY
    Rare Books and Special Collections: Alumni Files, Letters, Annual catalogues

OTHER SOURCES

Adams, Charles Francis, Jr. *A College Fetich: An Address Delivered before the Harvard Chapter of the Fraternity of the Phi Beta Kappa in Sanders Theatre, Cambridge, June 28, 1883.* Boston: Lee & Shepard; New York: Charles T. Dillingham, 1884.

Allen, Susan Heuck, ed. *Excavating Our Past: Perspectives on the History of the Archaeological Institute of America.* AIA Colloquia and Conference Papers 5. Boston: AIA, 2002.

"American Expedition to Krete under Professor Halbherr." *American Journal of Archaeology and of the History of the Fine Arts* 9.4 (October–December 1894): 538–44.

Ammerman, Rebecca Miller. *The Sanctuary of Santa Venera at Paestum.* Vol. 2, *The Votive Terracottas.* Ann Arbor: University of Michigan Press, 2002.

Angell, James Burrill. "A Memorial Discourse on the Life and Services of Henry Simmons Frieze, LL.D., Professor of Latin Language and Literature in the University from 1854 to 1889." Address delivered at University Hall, University of

Michigan, Ann Arbor, March 16, 1890. In *Selected Addresses,* 155–87. New York: Longmans, Green, 1912.

Angell, James Burrill. *The Reminiscences of James Burrill Angell.* New York: Longmans, Green, 1912.

Arundell, F. V. J. *Discoveries in Asia Minor, Including a Description of the Ruins of Several Ancient Cities, and Especially Antioch of Pisidia.* 2 vols. London: Richard Bentley, 1834.

Ashby, Thomas. *The Aqueducts of Ancient Rome.* Ed. I. A. Richmond. Oxford: Clarendon, 1935.

Ashby, Thomas. *The Roman Campagna in Classical Times.* London: E. Benn; New York: Macmillan, 1927.

Barbour, Thomas. *Allison Armour and the Utowana: An Appreciation of Allison Vincent Armour and of the Services Which He Rendered to the Sciences of Archaeology, Botany, and Zoology.* Cambridge, MA: privately printed, 1945.

Boak, Arthur E. R. "The Building of the University of Michigan Papyrus Collection." *Michigan Alumnus Quarterly Review* 66.10 (Autumn 1959): 35–42.

Boak, Arthur E. R. "Uncovering a Greco-Roman City in Egypt." *Michigan Alumnus* 32 (1925): 205–8.

Bodel, John P. *Roman Brick Stamps in the Kelsey Museum.* University of Michigan, Kelsey Museum of Archaeology, Studies 6. Ann Arbor: University of Michigan Press, 1983.

Borders, James M. *European and American Wind and Percussion Instruments: Catalogue of the Stearns Collection.* Ann Arbor: University of Michigan, 1988.

Bordin, Ruth. *Women at Michigan: The "Dangerous Experiment," 1870s to the Present.* Ann Arbor: University of Michigan Press, 1999.

Boyce, George K. "The Pierpont Morgan Library." *Library Quarterly* 22.1 (January 1952): 21–35.

Brasch, Charles. *In Egypt.* With an introduction by Margaret Scott. Wellington, New Zealand: Steele Roberts, 2007.

Brinks, Herbert J. *Peter White.* Grand Rapids, MI: W. B. Eerdmans, 1970.

Brown Scott, James. "Editorial Comment: Francis W. Kelsey—In Memoriam." *American Journal of International Law* 21.3 (July 1927): 522–24.

Canning, Charlotte. "The Platform versus the Stage: Circuit Chautauqua's Antitheatrical Theatre." *Theatre Journal* 50.3 (1998): 303–18.

Clarke, Joseph T. *Report on the Investigations at Assos, 1882, 1883.* Pt. 1. AIA Papers, Classical Series 2. New York: Macmillan, 1898.

Clarke, Joseph T., Francis H. Bacon, and Robert Koldewey. *Investigations at Assos: Drawings and Photographs of the Buildings and Objects Discovered during the Excavations of 1881–1882–1883.* Expedition of the AIA. London: Bernard Quaritch and Henry Sotheran; Cambridge, MA: AIA; Leipzig: Karl W. Hiersemann, 1902.

Coolidge, Dane. *Fighting Men of the West.* New York: E. P. Dutton, 1932.

Cooper, Florence Hopkins Kendrick. *American Scholar: A Tribute to Asahel Clark Kendrick, 1809–1895.* New York: n.p., 1913.

de Grummond, Nancy Thomson, ed. *An Encyclopedia of the History of Classical Archaeology.* London: Routledge, 1996.

Dennison, Walter. "Some New Inscriptions from Puteoli, Baiae, Misenum, and Cumae." *AJA* 2 (1898): 373–98.

Dobbins, John J., and Pedar Foss, eds. *The World of Pompeii.* London: Routledge, 2007.

Douglas, Norman. *Old Calabria.* Boston: Houghton Mifflin, 1915. 6th ed. New York: Harcourt Brace, 1956.

Duderstadt, Anne. *The University of Michigan: A Photographic Saga.* Ann Arbor: University of Michigan, Bentley Historical Library, 2006. Available as a multipart PDF download from http://umhistory.dc.umich.edu/history/publications/photo_saga/Saga.html (accessed September 19, 2008).

Dyson, Stephen L. *Ancient Marbles to American Shores: Classical Archaeology in the United States.* Philadelphia: University of Pennsylvania Press, 1998.

Ellis, Franklin, Crisfield Johnson, et al. *History of Berrien and Van Buren Counties, Michigan.* Philadelphia: D. W. Ensign, 1880.

Fay, Harriet Kelsey. "The Kelsey Family." In *Ogden Centennial Pioneer Reminiscences, 1802–1902,* comp. Augusta E. N. Rich, with Sarah Flagg Smith and H. H. Goff, 58–59. Rochester, NY: John C. Moore, 1902.

Gagos, Traianos. "The University of Michigan Papyrus Collection: Current Trends and Future Perspectives." In *Atti del XXII Congresso Internazionale di Papirologia, Firenze 1998,* ed. I. Andorlini, 511–37. Florence: Istituto Papirologico "G. Vitelli," 2001.

Gazda, Elaine K., ed. *In Pursuit of Antiquity: Thomas Spencer Jerome and the Bay of Naples (1899–1914).* Ann Arbor: Kelsey Museum of Archaeology, 1983.

Gazda, Elaine K. *Karanis: An Egyptian Town in Roman Times; Discoveries of the University of Michigan Expedition to Egypt, 1924–1935.* Ann Arbor: Kelsey Museum of Archaeology, 1983. 2nd ed., with preface and expanded bibliography by T. G. Wilfong, 2004.

Goodchild, R. G. "Death of an Epigrapher: The Killing of Herbert De Cou." *Michigan Quarterly Review* 8.3 (1969): 149–54.

Goodchild, R. G. "Murder on the Acropolis (1904–1911)." In *Libyan Studies: Select Papers of the Late R. G. Goodchild,* ed. J. Reynolds, 290–97. London: Paul Elek, 1976.

Gottheil, R., and W. H. Worrell, eds. *Fragments from the Cairo Geniza in the Freer Collection.* Ann Arbor: University of Michigan, 1927.

Grenfell, Bernard P., and Arthur S. Hunt, eds. and trans. *The Oxyrhynchus Papyri.* 17 vols. London: Egypt Exploration Fund, 1898–1922.

Hellenkemper Salies, Gisela, Hans-Hoyer von Pritwitz und Gaffron, and G. Bauchhenß, eds. *Das Wrack: Der antike Schiffsfund von Mahdia.* Exhibition catalog. 2 vols. Cologne: Rheinland-Verlag, 1994–95.

Hilton, George W., and John F. Due. *The Electric Interurban Railways in America.* Stanford: Stanford University Press, 1960.

Hines, Dixie, and Harry Prescott Hanaford, eds. *Who's Who in Music and Drama.* New York: H. P. Hanaford, 1914.

Hinsdale, Burke Aaron. *History of the University of Michigan.* Ed. Isaac Newton Demmon. Ann Arbor: University of Michigan, 1906.

Hinsley, C. M., Jr. "Edgar Lee Hewett and the School of American Research in Santa Fe, 1906–1912." In *American Archaeology Past and Future: A Celebration of the Society for American Archaeology, 1935–1985,* ed. David J. Meltzer, Don D. Fowler, and Jeremy A. Sabloff, 217–36. Washington, DC: Smithsonian Institution Press, 1986.

Hodges, Sheila. *Lorenzo Da Ponte: The Life and Times of Mozart's Librettist.* Madison: University of Wisconsin Press, 2002.

Hurtado, Larry W., ed. *The Freer Biblical Manuscripts: Fresh Studies of an American Treasure Trove.* Atlanta: Society of Biblical Literature; Leiden: Brill, 2006.

Kelsey, Easton T. "Digging for Ruins Centuries Old." *Michigan Chimes* (University of Michigan), January 1925, 15–18, 45–46.

Kelsey, Easton T. "Exploring Where Paul Preached: Notable Architectural and Art Treasures Unearthed on the Site of Ancient Antioch." *Dearborn Independent,* September 4, 1926, 13–14.

Kelsey, Frederick Wallace. *The First County Park System: A Complete History of the Inception and Development of the Essex County Parks of New Jersey.* New York: J. S. Ogilvie, 1905.

Kelsey, H. N., et al. *A Genealogy of the Descendants of William Kelsey.* Vols. 1–4. Bridgeport, CT: Marsh, 1975.

Kendrick, Asahel C., with Florence Kendrick Cooper. *Martin B. Anderson, LL.D.: A Biography.* Philadelphia: American Baptist Publication Society, 1895.

Knight, Carlo. *L'avvocato di Tiberio: La tormentata esistenza e la quasi tragica morte di Thomas Spencer Jerome.* Capri: La conchiglia, 2004.

Lanciani, Rodolfo. *Forma Urbis Romae.* Issued in 8 parts. Milan: U. Hoepli, 1893–1901.

Lanciani, Rodolfo. *The Roman Forum: A Photographic Description of Its Monuments.* Rome: Frank, 1910.

Lanciani, Rodolfo. *Ruins and Excavations of Ancient Rome: A Companion Book for Students and Travelers.* Boston: Houghton Mifflin, 1897.

Lange, Charles H., and Carroll L. Riley. *Bandelier: The Life and Adventures of Adolph Bandelier.* Salt Lake City: University of Utah Press, 1996.

Leontis, Artemis, and Lauren Talalay. "A Day's Journey: Constantinople, December 9, 1919." *Michigan Quarterly Review* 45.1 (2006): 73–98.

Lothrop, S. K. "Alfred Marsten Tozzer, 1876–1954." *American Anthropologist,* n.s., 57.3, pt. 1 (June 1955): 614–18.

MacMillan, Margaret. *Paris 1919: Six Months That Changed the World.* New York: Random House, 2003.

Magie, David. *Roman Rule in Asia Minor to the End of the Third Century after Christ.* 2 vols. Princeton: Princeton University Press, 1950.

Mau, August. *Geschichte der decorativen Wandmalerei in Pompeji.* Berlin: G. Reimer, 1882.

Mau, August. *Katalog der Bibliothek des Kaiserlich Deutschen Archäologischen Instituts in Rom.* 2 vols. Rome: Löscher, 1902. Rev. ed. by Eugen von Mercklin [and Friedrich Matz], Rome: Löscher, 1913–14; reprint, Berlin: Walter de Gruyter, 1930–32.

Mau, August. *Pompeji in Leben und Kunst.* Leipzig: W. Engelmann, 1900. Ed. and trans. Francis W. Kelsey as *Pompeii: Its Life and Art.* New York: Macmillan, 1899.

"Michigan's New President: The New Hampshire Head of a Great University." *Granite Monthly,* n.s., 5 (1910): 249–52.

Miller, Lila, Robert M. Warner, and Carl R. Geider, eds. *The First Presbyterian Church of Ann Arbor, Michigan, 1826–1988, Incorporating "A Sesquicentennial History," 1976.* Ann Arbor: First Presbyterian Church, 1988.

Miller, William. "The Marquisate of Boudonitza (1204–1414)." *Journal of Hellenic Studies* 28 (1908): 234–49.

Mitchell, Stephen, and Marc Waelkens. *Pisidian Antioch: The Site and Its Monuments.* London: Duckworth and Classical Press of Wales, 1998.

Montoya, María E., and Roderick M. Hills Jr. *First Presbyterian Church and the Larger World.* Ann Arbor: First Presbyterian Church, 2005.

Moore, Charles. *History of Michigan.* Vol. 2. Chicago: Lewis, 1915.

Moran, J. Bell. *The Moran Family: 200 Years in Detroit.* Detroit: Alved, 1949.

Norton, Richard, Joseph C. Hoppin, Charles D. Curtis, and A. F. S. Sladden. *The Excavations at Cyrene: First Campaign, 1910–1911.* New York: Macmillan, 1911. Extract from *Bulletin of the AIA* 2 (1911): 141–63.

"Ogden Town." Map (plat book) after *Gillette's Map of Monroe Co.: From Actual Surveys by P. J. Browne.* Philadelphia: John E. Gillette, 1858.

Peckham, Howard H. *The Making of the University of Michigan, 1817–1992.* Ed. Margaret L. Steneck and Nicholas H. Steneck. Ann Arbor: University of Michigan, Bentley Historical Library, 1994.

Pedley, John G., and Mario Torelli, eds. *The Sanctuary of Santa Venera at Paestum.* Vol. 1. Rome: Giorgio Bretschneider, 1993.

Platner, Samuel B., and Thomas Ashby. *Topographical Dictionary of Ancient Rome.* London: Humphrey Milford; Oxford: Oxford University Press, 1929.

Richard, Carl J. *The Founders and the Classics: Greece, Rome, and the American Enlightenment.* Cambridge, MA: Harvard University Press, 1994.

Richardson, Rufus B. *Vacation Days in Greece.* New York: Charles Scribner's Sons, 1903.

Riggs, Arthur Stanley. "Francis Willey Kelsey." Obituary. *Art and Archaeology* 23.6 (1927): 272, 284.

Robinson, David M. "Archaeological News, 1927." Note in tribute to Kelsey. *AJA* 31 (1927): 357–58.

Robinson, David M. "A Preliminary Report on the Excavations at Pisidian Antioch and at Sizma." *AJA* 28 (1924): 435–44.

Robinson, David M. "Roman Sculptures from Colonia Caesarea (Pisidian Antioch)." *Art Bulletin* 9.1 (1926): 5–69.

Rothman, Hal. *Preserving Different Pasts: The American National Monuments.* Urbana: University of Illinois Press, 1989.

Russell, James. "The Dream That Failed: The AIA's Department of Canada (1908–1915)." In *EOP,* 141–55.

Ryan, Milo S. *View of a Universe: A Love Story of Ann Arbor at Middle Age.* Ann Arbor: Ann Arbor Historic District Commission, 1985.

Sanders, Henry A. "Francis Willey Kelsey." Obituary. *Classical Philology* 22.3 (July 1927): 308–10.

Sargent, Porter. *The Handbook of Private Schools.* Boston: P. Sargent, 1916.

Schramm, Jack E., William H. Henning, and Richard R. Andrews. *When Eastern Michigan Rode the Rails.* Book 3, *Detroit to Jackson and across the State.* Glendale, CA: Interurban Press, 1988.

Schulze, Franz, Rosemary Cowler, and Arthur H. Miller. *Thirty Miles North: A History of Lake Forest College, Its Town, and Its City of Chicago.* Lake Forest, IL: Lake Forest College, 2000.

Shapiro, Susan. "Cicero and Today's Intermediate College-Level Student." *Classical Outlook* 84.4 (2007): 147–52.

Shattuck, Ralph L., ed. *100 Years of Education, 1847–1947.* Lockport, NY: Board of Education, [1948?].

Shorey, Paul. "Philology and Classical Philology." *Classical Journal* 1.6 (1906): 169–96.

Shorey, Paul. *The Roosevelt Lectures of Paul Shorey (1913–1914).* Trans. Edgar C. Reinke. Ed. Ward W. Briggs and E. Christian Kopff. Hildesheim: Georg Olms, 1994.

Silberman, Neil Asher. "Between Athens and Babylon: The AIA and the Politics of American and Near Eastern Archaeology, 1884–1997." In *EOP,* 115–22.

Sink, Charles A. "Michigan Memories and Personalities." In *Our Michigan: An Anthology Celebrating the University of Michigan's Sesquicentennial,* ed. Erich A. Walter, 26, 29. Ann Arbor: University of Michigan, 1966.

Smith, Cornelius C. *Emilio Kosterlitzky: Eagle of Sonora and the Southwest Border.* Glendale, CA: Arthur H. Clark, 1970.

Smith, Roswell Chamberlain. *Intellectual and Practical Grammar, in a Series of Inductive Questions, Connected with Exercises in Composition.* Boston: Perkins & Marvin, 1831.

Snead, James E. "The 'Western Idea': Local Societies and American Archaeology." In *EOP,* 123–40.

Stanley, Albert A. *Catalogue of the Stearns Collection of Musical Instruments.* Ann Arbor: University of Michigan, 1918.

Stevens, Horace Jared, and Walter Harvey Weed, comps. *The Copper Handbook: A Manual of the Copper Industry of the World.* Vol. 10. Houghton, MI: Horace J. Stevens, 1911.

Talalay, Lauren E., and Susan E. Alcock. *In the Field: The Archaeological Expeditions of the Kelsey Museum.* Ann Arbor: Kelsey Museum of Archaeology, 2006.

Thomas, Thelma K. *Dangerous Archaeology: Francis Willey Kelsey and Armenia (1919–1920).* Ann Arbor: Kelsey Museum of Archaeology, 1990.

"Town of Riga." Map in *Atlas of Monroe County, New York,* by F. W. Beers et al. New York: F. W. Beers, 1872.

Truett, Samuel. *Fugitive Landscapes: The Forgotten History of the U.S.-Mexico Borderlands.* New Haven: Yale University Press, 2006.

Truett, Samuel. "Transnational Warrior: Emilio Kosterlitzky and the Transformation of the U.S.-Mexico Border, 1873–1928." In *Continental Crossroads: Remapping U.S.-Mexico Borderlands History,* ed. Samuel Truett and Elliott Young, 241–70. Durham, NC: Duke University Press, 2004.

Turner, James C. *The Liberal Education of Charles Eliot Norton.* Baltimore: Johns Hopkins University Press, 1999.

van Vollenhoven, Cornelis. Review of *Hugo Grotius, "De Jure Belli ac Pacis," Libri Tres (1646),* ed. and trans. Francis W. Kelsey et al. *American Journal of International Law* 21.3 (July 1927): 628–33.

Waldstein, Charles, with the cooperation of G. H. Chase, H. F. De Cou, T. W. Heermance, J. C. Hoppin, A. M. Lythgoe, R. Norton, R. B. Richardson, E. L. Tilton, H. S. Washington, and J. R. Wheeler. *The Argive Heraeum.* 2 vols. Boston: Houghton Mifflin, 1902–5.

Wilfong, Terry G. "Fayum, Graeco-Roman Sites." In *Encyclopedia of the Archaeology of Ancient Egypt,* ed. Kathryn A. Bard and Steven Blake Shubert, 309–13. London: Routledge, 1999.

Will, Elizabeth Lyding. "Charles Eliot Norton and the Archaeological Institute of America." In *EOP,* 49–62.

Winter, John Garrett. "Francis Willey Kelsey." Obituary. *Classical Journal* 23.1 (1927): 4–6.

Winterer, Caroline. "The American School of Classical Studies at Athens: Scholarship and High Culture in the Gilded Age." In *EOP,* 93–104.

Winterer, Caroline. *The Culture of Classicism: Ancient Greece and Rome in American Intellectual Life, 1780–1910.* Baltimore: Johns Hopkins University Press, 2002.

Index

꿀